Building Financial Risk Management Applications With C++

Robert Brooks

Published by: Robert Brooks, Ph.D., CFA
                   13157 Martin Road Spur
                   Northport, AL 35473
                   U.S.A.
                   (+011) 205 799 9927

Email: rbrooks@frmhelp.com
Website: www.frmhelp.com

January 2013

Library of Congress Cataloging-in-Publication Data
Brooks, Robert, 1960–
    Building Financial Risk Management Applications with C++/Robert Brooks.
    p.   cm.
    ISBN-13: 978-1478350750 (paper)
    ISBN-10: 147835075X
    1. Financial risk management. 2. C++ (Computer programming language)

Printed in the United States of America

To my wife Ann,

as well as my children,

Joshua (and his wife Kaylee),

Stephen (and his wife Kimberlee),

Paul,

Rebekah,

Phillips,

and Rachael

Contents

Preface

This book is essentially a sequel to *Building Financial Derivatives Applications with C++* published in 2000. The focus of that book was financial derivatives valuation. There have been numerous advances in both C++ programming and financial derivatives warranting the production of a sequel. The focus in this book is on financial risk management. In Chapter 4 here, we do address several financial derivatives valuation issues.

Two driving forces that make books of this nature possible. First, developing computer programs using the C++ language is well within reach of the financial analyst. There has been some movement away from simple analytical programming. As the computer platforms propagate, the computer programming languages have had to become more complex. Every effort is made here to keep the C++ programming elementary. We focus on expressing quantitative finance concepts in C++, not creating complex computer programs for multiple platforms. The goal is for financial analysts to quickly learn to express their ideas in a computer language. Second, financial risk management is now widely practiced in a variety of career fields. Quantitative financial analysts are now needed in a variety of different arenas. The ability for these analysts to express their own ideas in C++ is a highly valued skill.

Finance is a social science. Thus, as ideas about how certain financial products should be valued and managed evolve, the actual value and risk properties also change. Therefore, there will never be a "theory of everything" in finance. More likely, we should be surprised if there ever appears a "theory of anything" that endures for very long. Because of the dynamic nature of financial markets, financial analysts need to be able to rapidly adapt their valuation and risk management models to changing times. Rather than rely on faulty communication between analysts and professional C++ programmers, financial analysts can express their ideas in prototype C++ code. This ability dramatically reduces errors and allows financial analysts greater precision in expressing their ideas.

Building Financial Risk Management Applications with C++ is written for college graduate students and entry-level financial analysts. No prior knowledge of C++ programming is assumed. As with any language, having access to multiple sources when learning technical material is highly recommended. Therefore, it is assumed that you have access to several introductory C++ books or similar web-based materials.

In 2000, when *Building Financial Derivatives Applications with C++* was first published, the combination of financial analysis with C++ was unique. Today, there are several other books on the subject. The approach taken here is distinctly different. Rather than present state-of-the-art C++ programming techniques, we use only elementary C++. The idea is that financial analysts really do not want to be professional C++ programmers. They want to rapidly learn how to express their unique analytical ideas in a form that the computer can run. Therefore, we focus on the minimal set of C++ tools necessary to perform this task.

This book contains the following features:

1) Elementary C++ programming techniques and modern financial risk management methodologies are brought together.
2) We use the modular approach starting in chapter 3 to make learning specific content easier. The modular approach allows for the independent study of that particular implementation instead of each subsequent concept requiring a thorough knowledge of the preceeding concepts. Many modules, however, incorporate prior material.
3) Extensive use of appendices for interface code allows those using other development platforms to make use of the material provided here.

4) Clear development of a repository allows for efficient code reuse.
5) Source code, numerous supplements, and other materials are provided at www.frmhelp.com.

All of the source code illustrated in this book, as well as many more materials on this subject, can be found at www.frmhelp.com.

Any book of this length addressing a technical topic of this nature will contain errors. I would be deeply grateful if you could help me locate them. Please email your feedback to rbrooks@frmhelp.com. An errata sheet will also be available at www.frmhelp.com.

At the time of this writing, my two oldest children are married and the youngest of the remaining four children is a teenager. This environment provides many opportunities to practice risk management in so many different dimensions. My family is a constant source of encouragement and they are all very supportive of my professional activities.

Robert Brooks

Tuscaloosa, Alabama
January 2013

Acknowledgements

Professor Haim Levy, an outstanding professor of finance, introduced me to the rigorous study of finance. I remain deeply influenced by his dedication to our profession and the clarity by which he expressed complex financial topics.

This work is based on more than twenty years of teaching graduate students at The University of Alabama in the Master of Science in Finance program. The diligent work of Kate Upton, my assistant at The University of Alabama, is particularly appreciated. She provided numerous insights and ideas on how to better communicate programming ideas to graduate students in finance.

Over these decades, I have learned the most from this experience. The style of presentation here has been heavily influenced by many attempts to explain the intersection between quantitative finance and C++. The work has also been impacted by numerous consulting engagements related to financial derivatives, financial risk management, and financial litigation.

My oldest two sons, Joshua and Stephen, are both finance professionals. Kimberlee, Stephen's wife, is a professional editor. They all provided an enormous amount of technical and editorial help for which I am grateful.

Chapter 1. Introduction

"Price is what you pay. Value is what you get." Ben Graham[1]

"The most important single aspect of software development is to be clear about what you are trying to build." Bjarne Stroustrup[2]

Learning objectives

- Understand several compelling reasons why aspiring financial analysts should learn a computer language
- Enumerate multiple arguments for selecting C++ as the language of choice for financial analysts
- Introduce the C++ language
- Defend the unique approach to learning C++ provided in this material

Introduction

In his outstanding book on the Psalms, C. S. Lewis opens with an interesting statement:

"This is not a work of scholarship. I am no Hebraist, no higher critic, no ancient historian, no archaeologist. I write for the unlearned about things in which I am unlearned myself. If an excuse is needed (and perhaps it is) for writing such a book, my excuse would be something like this. It often happens that two schoolboys can solve difficulties in their work for one another better than the master can. When you took the problem to a master, as we all remember, he was very likely to explain what you understood already, to add a great deal of information which you didn't want, and say nothing at all about the thing that was puzzling you. ... The fellow-pupil can help more than the master because he knows less. The difficulty we want him to explain is one he has recently met. The expert met it so long ago that he has forgotten. He sees the whole subject, by now, in such a different light that he cannot conceive what is really troubling the pupil; he sees a dozen other difficulties which ought to be troubling him but aren't."[3]

---

[1] Warren Buffett in his 2008 letter to Berkshire Hathaway shareholders attributes this quote to Ben Graham.

[2] Quoted in Herb Sutter and Andrei Alexandrescu, *C++ Coding Standards 101 Rules, Guidelines, and Best Practices* (2005), p. 55.

[3] *Reflections on the Psalms* (Orlando, FL: Harcourt, Inc., 1958), pages 1-2.

The purpose of this book is *not* to provide state-of-the-art C++ programming techniques. The purpose of this book is also *not* to provide state-of-the-art financial risk management techniques. Financial quantitative analysts (quants) often lack the foundational understanding of financial risk management, as well as basic C++ programming. Many quants have studied the graduate level financial derivatives textbooks and passed various financial risk management-type examinations. They have not, however, seen how to actually deploy these ideas in practice. Thus, I seek to fill this void by providing a launching pad where quantitative finance professionals can connect the dots between abstract theoretical finance concepts and prototype code that could be used to implement various financial risk management ideas.

The purpose here is to provide as simple an approach as possible to enable financial analysts to develop prototype implementation C++ code of their financial risk management ideas. Remember the premise here is that two novices in C++ can solve difficulties in their work for one another better than the C++ master can. Dynamic memory allocation, abstract data types, container classes, and so forth are left to the computer programming professionals. The objective of this book is to provide assistance for quantitative finance professionals who wish to implement their emerging financial risk management ideas with C++. We focus on introducing financial risk management with C++ because many of the modern financial risk management concepts require some form of computer program to successfully implement.

Computer programming is a unique, disciplined implementation of ideas. In this chapter, several reasons why financial analysts should learn a computer language are reviewed. In particular, the case will be made for C++ and it will be briefly introduced. Finally, the autonomous (compiler independent) and heteronomous (compiler dependent) approaches to teaching C++ are explored. This material takes the atypical heteronomous approach while remaining sympathetic to those learners who prefer the more popular autonomous approach.

All the C++ code illustrated in this book, as well as much more, is available at www.frmhelp.com.

Why a financial quantitative analyst should learn a computer language

There are several reasons for a financial quantitative analyst to learn a computer language such as C++. These reasons include: being better able to avoid conformity to popular 'black box' solutions, developing a precise understanding of posited models, improving the buy versus build decision-making process, providing better solutions than are possible with spreadsheets or symbolic languages, improving model debugging, and learning to decompose complex problems into manageable components. These reasons are explored in more detail later in this chapter.

Conformist versus non-conformist

There are many influences in the financial quantitative analyst profession that result in entering professionals conforming to industry standards. There is a unique language and the methods of expressing yourself are somewhat standardized (for example, client presentations, accepted valuation methodologies, expected historical statistics gathered, and standardized analysis tools, such as Bloomberg®). Every analyst, however, is unique and brings to the profession a distinct perspective that may prove very valuable to his or her long run success.

One way to preserve an analyst's unique perspective is by developing non-standardized valuation and management tools via a computer language. Knowledge of a computer language dramatically expands the analyst's means of expression. With improved compilers and more flexible software systems, the analysts' innovative tools can be easily and rapidly incorporated into the software platform.

An important contribution of analysts providing independent perspectives is the reduced likelihood of systemic events. If every analyst is performing their tasks in the same way, then the likelihood of systemic events actually increases. By equiping analyst with the power to implement independent perspectives, the global financial system becomes more robust.

Clear and crisp understanding of model

For most applications related to quantitative finance, a computer program that is 99% correct is 100% wrong. That is, an error in implementation is likely to show itself at the very time the program is most needed to be correct. Many financial quantitative analysts do not have a clear and crisp understanding of the quantitative models and techniques they use. It is analogous to observing land contours from 30,000 feet in a plane. Although everything may look fine and smooth from a high altitude, descend to 500 feet and the land contours change dramatically. Programming leads to a more precise understanding of the ground contours of quantitative models and techniques and provides a very detailed level of understanding.

For example, one way to value an interest rate swap is as a portfolio of forward rate agreements. At the highest level, an interest rate swap is simply the present value of forward rates. Plain vanilla interest rate swaps, however, reported in the H.15 file of the Federal Reserve Statistical Release is a semi-annual, 30/360 day count fixed rate and a quarterly, Actual/360 day count floating rate. The differences in payment frequency and the day counting have a significant impact on equilibrium swap rates. Thus, by learning to write a computer program, the analyst will have a much better understanding of the intricate details of actual interest rate swaps.

Build versus buy

The decision to express quantitative finance ideas in a computer language has several advantages and disadvantages. The disadvantages include the time and energy that is required to complete the tasks. One alternative is to simply purchase computer software that provides quantitative solutions ready to be deployed. In the short run, this solution is often very attractive in that one simply pays an immodest fee and within a very short period of time, the quantitative finance models are up and running. In many cases, this is a reasonable solution.

Unfortunately, one side effect of buying software solutions is that no one internal to the entity fully understands the nuances of the particular deployment. Many decisions that are made when developing software are not expressed in public documentation. Hence, purchased quantitative finance software always has an element of being a 'black box.' The best that the financial analyst can do using this purchased software is understand the required inputs and strive to accurately interpret the reported outputs.

On the other hand, the decision to build software internally has the advantage of potentially being fully understood by the financial analysts within the firm. The software can be modified as market conditions change and improvements are made. Model maintenance becomes more of a process rather than a single static decision. Because finance is a social science[4], maintaining flexibility to modify model design is very useful.

Admittedly, the decision to build software internally has unique disadvantages, such as implementation errors. Thus, one significant advantage of purchasing, as opposed to constructing software, is that implementation problems are the responsibility of someone else.

---

[4] This assertion stems from the argument that given that individuals' conception of the world has the capacity to affect real change in the marketplace (a phenomenon identified as 'performativity'), and given that there naturally exists a degree of ebb and flow in societal value systems, finance should be studied as a social science rather than a physical science.

Computer language or spreadsheets

Many financial firms rely heavily on spreadsheets for their required analytical work. Unfortunately, a common repercussion is that the only solutions posited for quantitative problems are those that can be implemented within spreadsheets. When seeking the best solution for difficult problems, one would rather have a more extensive set of solutions. The spreadsheet paradigm can limit one to the finite number of feasible solutions that are available to solve quantitative finance problems. Indeed, for large and complex problems, spreadsheet solutions can become very cumbersome and difficult to manage. With a computer language, one can easily decompose complex problems into component parts and build software solutions that are manageable. Many computer languages, such as C++, are highly optimized for numerical calculations and as a result are extremely fast.

Finally, modules can be developed in C++ and other computer languages that run within spreadsheets, thus providing the best of both worlds. These modules are typically user-defined functions facilitated by dynamic-linked libraries.

Computer language or symbolic languages

Symbolic languages provide a useful solution to many mathematical problems. Unfortunately, modules developed through symbolic languages are not portable to computer hardware that does not have the symbolic language software installed. Most computer language compilers produce solutions that are portable to any computer that contains the appropriate operating system.

In other words, if a quant writes a solution to a financial risk management problem in a symbolic language and then wishes to provide it to her superiors, they would be unable to run the program on their machines unless the machine contains the symbolic language. Given that these symbolic language programs can be costly and take up a lot of memory, it can be cumbersome to have them housed on each machine within an entity.

Improved communication

Software developers within finance organizations often have no formal training in finance. Although they may be very efficient and effective in rapid application development, often they do not understand and fully appreciate the nuances of advanced quantitative finance applications. Hence, one valuable service provided by financial analysts with a familiarity to computer programming, is the ability to enhance the information flow between the finance professional and the software developer. This skill is extremely valuable as it further refines the subsequent flow of information from finance professional to senior management. As overall communication between these disparate groups of professionals improves, the likelihood that the project gets deployed on time with minimal problems improves as well.

More efficient debugging

Quantitative finance applications are complex for many reasons, including the need for speed, real time data management, and multidimensional and advanced mathematical solutions. The finance professional often does not fully appreciate the importance of validating the accuracy of newly-implemented software. Many errors in programming, referred to as 'bugs,' do not appear until a crisis occurs. For example, during the financial crisis that started in 2007, many flaws in model implementations came to light. Unfortunately, fixing flaws is difficult when your firm is in crisis mode.

By investing in your capacity to understand computer program code like C++, you will enhance the likelihood of identifying problems before it is too late. Understanding the computer programming process improves one's ability to know where errors are likely to occur.

On September 9, 1947, Harvard University operators of a crude calculator were experiencing technical problems with their calculator. They found a moth at Relay #70, Panel F on the Mark II Aiken Relay

Calculator. In their journal entry they indicated that they had 'debugged' the machine. Hence, correcting problems with computer code is often referred to as debugging.

 We will use the symbol to your left to indicate that a particular snippet of code illustrated is not correct. The picture is a photograph of the actual moth recovered from the relay calculator. (See http://www.history.navy.mil/photos/pers-us/uspers-h/g-hoppr.htm. The bug information is at the very bottom.)

Decomposition

The process of learning a computer programming language enhances the financial analyst's ability to decompose complex problems into manageable components. Often this process is referred to as decomposition. Decomposition is the exercise of breaking a problem down into smaller, manageable pieces. Computer languages, such as C++, aid in developing skills to achieve the optimal level of decomposition. Often insurmountable problems become easily manageable when the problem is decomposed appropriately.

Why learn the C++ language?

Job postings

Many jobs available for quantitative financial analysts require some knowledge of computer programming and particularly C++. For example, job postings viewed on a Bloomberg® terminal from August 20, 2007 to August 29, 2007 were analyzed to determine whether they mentioned a computer language in the description. In this informal survey, 119 job postings, out of a total of 230, identified a need for competency in at least one computer language. Additionally, a computer language was listed a total of 232 times. Obviously, some job postings mentioned more than one computer language. C or C++ was mentioned 82 times, or in about 35 percent of all postings. The second most frequent mention was Visual Basic or VBA at 28 times. Thus, C or C++ was identified almost three times as frequent as the nearest alternative (82/28). Also identified frequently were SQL (26), Microsoft Office® (26), C# (19), Java (18), MatLab® (12), PERL (11), and SAS (10).[5]

Within the finance industry, the dominant computer language is now C++. Also, knowledge of C++ makes learning other languages easier. Although the computer language of choice changes over time, C++ is an excellent language to learn initially.

History of computer programming languages

In the mid-1950s John Backus of IBM led a group of computer programmers to create the FORTRAN (formula translation) programming language. FORTRAN was the first high-level computer programming language. A programming language is said to be high level if it hides complex details of the software's interactions with the computer. Low-level programming languages, such as machine code and assembly languages, explicitly manage the complex details of the software's interactions with the computer.

C++ combines both 'high level' (easy to use) and 'low level' (powerful) features. C++ supports the object-oriented approach to programming; this approach permits the combination of data with methods allowing for higher levels of abstraction. Historically, early languages followed the procedural approach, designed as a collection of functions that manage and manipulate data. For example, the cumulative distribution function, N(d), can be viewed as an object that contains data (d) and methods (solving for N()). Viewed as an object containing both the data input and the methods, N(d) can be incorporated into many different option valuation and risk management solutions.

---

[5] Research conducted by Randy Beavers, computer-based honors student, University of Alabama.

Bjarne Stroustrup developed C++ in the late 1970s as a highly optimized, object-oriented language. Hence it is very fast, a feature attractive to the finance industry. Financial risk management problems are suitable for object-oriented programming[6] as contrasted with sequential programming.

Rapid application development

One goal of quantitative analysts is to be able to implement their solutions within an organization rapidly. Hence, it is necessary to be able to both build applications fast, as well as implement them with ease. The object-oriented approach combined with C++ permits rapid application development (RAD). With many well developed objects prebuilt and rigorously tested, it is relatively simple to complete the implementation of a quantitative model in a very short period of time.

File types

Software languages, such as C++, are implemented with a compiler. Modern compilers provide a wide variety of useful features, including easy graphical user interfaces, forms and features with built-in code generation, optimizations, and multiple targets (executable code, dynamic linked libraries, and so forth).

The programmer writes source code. The source code is compiled into object code, and finally the object code is linked to executable code. Source code is recognized by the extensions *.cpp, *.c, *.hpp, and *.h. The files with *.cpp denote C++ code, *.c denote C code, *.hpp and *.h denote header files. When the program is compiled, the various source code files are translated into object code and have the extension *.obj. The various object code files are then linked, creating executable code with the extension *.exe. We provide more details on the structure of code in Chapter 2.

When creating software, each compiler also creates a variety of other files including project management, debugging, backups, and so forth. Hence, your program will contain a variety of files. Managing these files simultaneously with multiple projects that use the same underlying methods requires careful planning. You may consider sketching out your necessary files as they arc generated and produce notes about what is housed in each file would be very helpful.

Why learn C++ this way?

Autonomous versus heteronomous

The majority of C++ books and other training materials choose to allow the learner to be autonomous when it comes to the C++ compiler choice. These materials have the advantage of being applicable to any compiler, so long as it complies with the existing standards established for C++.

For our objectives, allowing the learning to be autonomous (having freedom to act independently) versus heteronomous (subject to external standard) was a difficult choice. We chose to limit this material to a particular compiler, rather than make the learning experience generic and applicable for any compiler.

The primary motive is to allow the financial analyst to be equipped to demonstrate his or her work in a visually appealing way. Within a very short period of time, you will be able to create stand-alone executable code that is user friendly and easily distributable. Our primary objective, however, is not to make you a professional programmer. To this end we seek the delicate balance between keeping the concepts as simple as possible while at the same time permitting the user to develop professional-looking interfaces.

---

[6] Object-oriented programming (OOP) with C++ is typically identified with four characteristics. encapsulation, inheritance, polymorphism, and abstraction. Object-oriented programming is addressed further in chapter 2.

For the autonomous among us, care is taken to separate the interface code (code focused on interactions with the end-user) and the implementation code (code focused on computing the solution). Because of this separation, it is easy to export the implementation code to other compilers and there develop different GUI's (Graphical User Interface).

Current platform

The current platform is Embarcadero® C++Builder® 2010 Version 14.0 for Windows®.

Alternate platforms

Embarcadero Turbo C++ 2006 Explorer in English (or Borland C++Builder 10.0).

This is a generation or two behind the 2010 version used here and at one time was freely available on the web. For the applications developed in this book, the uses of the compiler are very similar.

Xcode (ANSI C++ should work, need Xcode interface)

   http://developer.apple.com/technology/Xcode.html

Microsoft® Visual C++ (ANSI C++ should work, need Visual C++ interface)

   http://msdn.microsoft.com/en-us/visualc/default.aspx

Others:

   GNU C++: http://gcc.gnu.org/

   Code Blocks: http://www.codeblocks.org/

Deliverables

The main deliverables illustrated in this material are simple prototype programs. If the goal is to produce fully implementable programs in real time, then the computer source code should be refined by professional software programmers. For example, no effort is made to exhaustively error trap inputs (e.g., real numbers as opposed to alphabetic characters) and test for inputs that are out of range (e.g., volatility equal to zero causing a division by zero).

The primary solution will be executable programs. Some attention, however, will be given to developing dynamic linked libraries (DLLs) as they are easily incorporated into other software packages. Implementing DLLs will be illustrated with Microsoft Excel®.[7]

Sample programs: Program layout

In the remainder of this book there will be references to sample programs. To illustrate the process, we provide a simple program that runs a console application that does not do anything. The source code will be set in Courier type as follows.

```
#include <conio.h>
int main()
{
   getch();
   return 0;
}
```

The first line includes a file, known as a header file, that defines the function `getch()` that will receive a character from the user. This program just produces a blank, black screen as follows.

---

[7] The particular implementation of DLLs in a spreadsheet varies depending on the particular spreadsheet you are using. Therefore, how you actually implement DLLs may vary from the materials provided.

Within the text, we will direct you to the location of the functioning programs provided at www.frmhelp.com such as the statement below.

C++ Code: 1.1 Program Layout.

Summary

We began this chapter by exploring several compelling reasons why aspiring financial analysts should learn a computer language. These reasons include: to enhance one's ability to express unique analytical ideas, to improve one's understanding of financial models, to provide the opportunity to build rather than buy software, to enhance spreadsheet or symbolic language development, to improve communication with internal software developers, to provide more efficient debugging within a firm, and to enhance one's ability to decompose complex financial problems into manageable parts.

The C++ language choice was defended based on job postings, computer language historical development, and the capacity for rapid application development. We briefly reviewed key C++ file types, including source, object and executable code. Finally, we defended the unique pedagogical approach of imposing a single development platform. We seek the best blend of keeping the financial analyst autonomous while at the same time actually equipping the analyst with C++ capabilities to begin making a contribution.

For more information on C++, see Prata (2012) and for more information on financial risk management, see Chance and Brooks (2013).

For more information on one set of coding preferences, see **Appendix 1A: Coding preferences**.

For more information on building your own repository, see **Appendix 1B: Building your own repository**.

References

Chance, Don M. and Robert Brooks, *An Introduction to Derivatives and Risk Management*, 9th Edition (Mason, OH: South-Western Cengage Learning, 2013).

Lewis, C. S., *Reflections on the Psalms* (Orlando, FL: Harcourt, Inc., 1958).

Prata, Stephen, *C++ Primer Plus Developer's Library*, 6th Edition (Upper Saddle River, NJ: Addison-Wesley, 2012).

Sutter, Herb and Andrei Alexandrescu, *C++ Coding Standards 101 Rules, Guidelines, and Best Practices* (2005).

Appendix 1.A: Coding Preferences

Learning objectives

- Determine preferences related to expressing and formatting source code
- Provide guidance for naming variables, methods, classes, and files
- Prepare executable code for use without the compiler

Introduction

Writing computer code is part mundane implementation of mathematical ideas and part free-spirited, written expressions of abstract art. The goal here is not to squelch your artistic side, but to provide a consistent framework for you to begin to express your quantitative solutions using C++.

Coding preferences

Accuracy and readability are vital for any successful C++ implementation of a quantitative finance problem. Highly readable source code that is inaccurate is nonetheless fatally flawed. It is not, however, difficult to fix readable code. It is highly recommended that you comment your code extensively so that you are able to retrace your steps as well as document what you have done in each piece of code for both debugging and reuse of code. Although accurate but illegible code will work, it cannot be easily maintained.

Source code presentation

The first decision when expressing source code relates to spacing. It is important to keep track of how many brackets are open. It is also important to keep the number of pages printed when debugging to a minimum. Hence we recommend the following rule illustrated with the following snippet of code:

1)   *Indent two spaces (even for wrapped lines) after each curly bracket ({), place method and class curly brackets on a separate line, all others open ({) on the same line and close (}) on a new line*

```
void __fastcall TNOptionPricingModel::SetLocalData(void)
{
  switch (rgPriceOrVolatility->ItemIndex){
    case 0:    // Compute option values
      COD.StockPrice = POD.StockPrice
        = 0.0;
...
```

Setting aside what this code does, the two-space indention makes the code compact and readable.

Although tempting, you should use blank lines very rarely, even though you may find occasional lapses in the code presented. Hence the second rule is illustrated with the following snippet of code:

2)   *Use blank lines very rarely. If you need a space, include a comment line*

```
}
//-----------------------------------------------------------------------
void __fastcall TNOptionPricingModel::btnCancelClick(TObject *Sender)
{
```

As your programs increase in complexity, you will find it valuable to sort your variable declarations. It makes reading header files much easier and aids in spotting conflicts in naming conventions.

3)   *Sort header file information. Note that in the code below all of the TLabels are listed sequentially, then the Tbuttons, TEdits, and so forth.*

```
  TLabel *lblStockPrice;
  TLabel *lblStrikePrice;
...
  TLabel *lblbps2;
  TButton *btnOk;
  TButton *btnCancel;
  TEdit *editStockPrice;
...
  TEdit *editTimeToMaturity;
  TEdit *outputCallPrice;
...
  TEdit *outputPutVega;
```

```
TRadioGroup *rgPriceOrVolatility;
```

It is helpful to place your name within your source code both to show pride in your work, as well as give contact information in case things go wrong. Hence, the fourth rule of illustration:

4)   *Your name should be on the first line of each file's code (*.cpp, *.h, code within this book does not always do this) as well as a brief description of what is contained in the file*

```
//***********************Robert Brooks*******************************
#include <math.h>
#include <vcl.h>
```

Remember, your ultimate goal is to produce a large repository of quantitative methods that will improve your vocational abilities. Writing a brief description after the code is finished will be time consuming initially. If you have a long run perspective, however, it will save you countless hours in the future as you will not have to reinvent modules and you will quickly recall the code's purpose.

Methodological preferences

The goal is to create source code that is easily reused. For example, the particular module that computes N(d), may be used in a wide variety of C++ programs as well as implemented in a dynamic-linked library that can be used in a separate statistical package (for example, SAS) or a spreadsheet. Thus, the implementation code should be completely separated from the user interface code. Hence, the fifth rule of illustration:

5)   *Implementation code should be separated completely from interface code, linked solely by one function, named "Execute()"*

Here is where the function is called in the interface code.

```
void __fastcall TCDFForm::btnOKClick(TObject *Sender)
{
  FRMExecute();
}
//-------------------------------------------------------------------
```

Here is where the function is defined and developed in the interface code.

```
void __fastcall TCDFForm::FRMExecute(void)
{
...
  Nd = C.FRMND(inputd); // Compute N(d) when given d
...
}
```

The names attached to variables, functions, classes, and so forth are very important. Consistent naming will lead to much greater efficiency when maintaining a large repository of source code. The following naming conventions are adopted and illustrated below:

6)   *Naming conventions adopted here*
   a.   Names of variables: lower case or both upper and lower case, err on longer name
   b.   Names of functions: begin with upper case for each word
   c.   Names of constants and classes: all upper case

```
long double FRMBSMOVM::FRMBSMPutPrice()
{
  PutPrice = StrikePrice * exp(-(InterestRate/100.0) * TimeToMaturity)
    * FRMND(-(FRMd2()))
    - StockPrice * exp(-(DividendYield/100.0)* TimeToMaturity)
    * FRMND(-(FRMd1())));
  FRMPutLowerBound();
  return PutPrice;
}
```

In the code above, `PutPrice` is a floating point variable declared as a long double (very precise). One of the functions in the code above is `FRMPutLowerBound()`. The FRM lead distinguishes this code as part of a suite of classes and methods used within the FRMRepository. One approach to identifying your source code is to use the initials of your name. The benefit is ease of identifying who developed various classes and methods. The class name `FRMBSMOVM` is all capitals.

Although often precision is not an issue, it is safer just to declare all floating-point variables at least double in the header file.

> 7)   *Floating-point variables are at least double*

```
double CallPrice;
double InterestRate;
```

> 8)   *Local variable declarations should be at the top of the method*

Here the variables being declared is PutDelta and it is being declared as a double.

```
long double FRMBSMOVM::FRMBSMPutDelta()
{
  double PutDelta;
  PutDelta = ...
```

File management becomes increasingly complex as the project at hand grows. Once you have multiple projects interacting with various files within the repository, it is important to carefully manage the file names. Hence, the following naming conventions are adopted (you should substitute your initials for FRM):

> 9)   *File naming conventions*
>> a.   Interface naming conventions:
>>> i.   Program: FRMProgramNameTest.bdsproj, *.bdsproj.local, *.cpp, *.res
>>> ii.   Executable program: FRMProgramNameTest.exe
>>> iii. Interface unit: FRMUnitProgramName.cpp, *.h, *.dfm
>>> iv.   Interface via function: FRMExecute() within FRMUnitProgramName.cpp
>>> v.   Interface stored in subdirectory of the central repository (e.g., c:\FRMRepository\ProgramName)
>> b.   Implementation naming conventions:
>>> i.   Source code: FRMFileName.cpp, *.h
>>> ii.   Top of *.h contains description of methods
>>> iii. Bottom of *.h contains relevant sources for algorithms and source code
>>> iv.   Classes: FRMCLASSNAME
>>> v.   Structures: FRMStructureName
>>> vi.   Methods: FRMMethodName()
>>> vii. Implementation files stored in root directory of central repository (e.g., c:\FRMRepository)

Code shipping

> 10)   *All source code files shipped via email should not be in a repository; they should all be in the same folder so the program compiles on any machine*

Files to ship include the following extensions: *.*proj (varies based on compiler), *.cpp, *.res, *.h, *.dfm

Program appearance issues

The following are suggestions related to managing the appearance of your interface code.

Attach FRM.ico to unit left top and Program/Options/Application/FRM.ico load

For program and trash management: Compiler and linker options / Output settings / FRMRepository

Background of units: clWhite (makes printing less costly)

Interface naming conventions:

  Labels: lblInputFileName.dat, lblOutputFileName.prn

  Edit Boxes: editInputFileName

Output labels and edit boxes should be invisible until the OK button is pressed and output values are computed.

User's guide

Every test program that is built to support the implementation source code should have an accompanying user's guide. It is very helpful, within the user's guide, to have both the mathematical justification for various functions (complete with numerical examples for testing), as well as instructions for users. As an aid, screen shots are very helpful.

11) *Use screen prints to illustrate your software*
   a. Press <PrtSc> to take a copy of your desktop
   b. Press "<Ctrl> <Alt> <PrtSc> to take a copy of file in focus. This is the preferred method.

Preparing code for use without the compiler

1. Under Project→Options→Packages→Build with Runtime packages should be *unchecked*
2. To make you applications fully standalone, you must use static RTL, not dynamic. Under Project→Options→C++Linker→set the "Dynamic RTL" property to "False"

Appendix 1.B: Building Your Own Repository

Learning objectives

* Understand one approach to managing implementation code
* Explain detailed steps for managing source code
* Emphasize the importance of organizing your quantitative ideas when coding

Introduction

The goal of this appendix is to specify one approach to managing source code. The primary goal is to maximize code reuse; ideally, you will build a module that will be used over and over again. The secondary goal is to build detailed organization in your development of quantitative ideas. Often the exercise of implementing a new idea in C++ will result in numerous improvements to the idea itself. Coding is also much easier if you are detail oriented and very organized.

Repository

We will make use of a central repository for implementation code. Thus, multiple programs can access the same implementation code. For example, consider the estimation function of the cumulative normal distribution (N(d)) used in many option valuation routines, as well as risk management calculations. The approximation method deployed here is accurate to about the ninth decimal place. Suppose this routine is used in 15 different programs that you have to support. If you discover a more accurate estimation method or a bug in the existing N(d) calculation without a repository, you will have to fix 15 different programs. With a repository, you fix one implementation file and then simply recompile the 15 different programs.

Managing subdirectories for source code (recommended when first starting)

The method illustrated here is not the only one, but it is very simple. In the root directory of the operating system (or wherever you wish), create a new subdirectory. The one illustrated for this material is FRMRepository.[8] Hence, you create the subdirectory

```
C:\FRMRepository
```

All implementation source code (*.cpp, *.h) is placed in the FRMRepository (and not in a subdirectory within FRMRepository).

For efficient interface code management, all the interface source code for various programs is contained in subdirectories within FRMRepository. For example, all the interface source code covered in this material is placed in the following subdirectory.

```
C:\FRMRepository\BFRMAwCPP
```

All of the implementation source code for dynamic linked libraries covered in this material is placed in the following subdirectory.

```
C:\FRMRepository\DLLCode
```

Managing other related files

The process that generates the executable code creates many intermediate files; some of these files are rather large and need to be cleaned off your computer from time to time. The repository is an efficient means for garbage disposal. Within the compiler is a place to designate the path for these intermediate files and final executable programs. The following screen shots illustrate where these paths can be set. First, select Project and then Options.

Next, expand C++ Compiler (click the + sign in front of C++ Compiler, then select Directories and Conditionals settings (first figure below). Select the Object file output, then click the ellipses (...). Finally, select the root directory to FRMRepository.

Repeat this same process for the Directories and Conditionals at the top of the base configuration. Be sure to select the FRMRepository for both the Final output directory and the Intermediate output.

The results of setting these project options in this way are that the intermediate object files (*.obj), the debugging files (*.tds), and the final executable programs (*.exe) will all be contained in the repository. Over time, the object and debugging files can be deleted without impacting the executable programs or the source code.

The repository is also used to manage input data files (arbitrarily denoted in this material as *.dat), output data files (arbitrarily denotes in this material as *.prn), as well as other miscellaneous files such as icons (*.png or *.ico).

---

[8] Note that the source code provided for this book assumes the repository is located at C:\FRMRepository. If it is located anywhere else, the paths must be change.

Chapter 2. C++ Preliminaries

"Programs must be written for people to read, and only incidentally for machines to execute."[9]

"It is far, far easier to make a correct program fast than it is to make a fast program correct."[10]

Learning objectives

- Illustrate how learning C++ dramatically expands financial analysts' feasible quantitative solutions
- Briefly review basic C++ concepts

Introduction

The purpose here is to provide a brief review of basic C++. The '++' of C++ refers to the increment operator. The increment operator essentially adds one to a variable. Hence if k is an integer with a value of 0, then after the statement 'k++,' the value of k is 1 or k = k + 1. Thus, C++ is an increment above its base language C.

This review is not intended to be thorough or complete. Rather, the objective is to provide basic information to get you successfully up and running with C++. The goal is to get you quickly expressing your ideas with C++. Often, we will opt for the easier path to mastering the rudiments of C++ instead of professional programming methodologies, which have much steeper learning curves.

A vast number of resources are available on the subject and these resources are updated rapidly. At the moment, the best resources are available online. One particularly good set of materials can be found at Stanford University's CS106X web site, which was available in January 2013 (http://www.stanford.edu/class/cs106x/).

Expanding your quantitative solutions toolbox

The ability to deliver solutions in C++ expands the set of solutions you can bring to any given financial analyst problem. C++ is an accessible computer language that is portable. Thus, your C++ solutions can be delivered to a computer that does not have C++ installed and it will run. C++ can be implemented in a variety of styles, such as procedural programming or object-oriented programming. There is a lot of freedom with C++; hence, you can get yourself in trouble in a hurry. You can, however, also develop a wide array of solutions for one specific problem.

The first program illustrating a particular programming language is usually some form of 'Hello World.' Running the program produces the following screen.

---

[9] Herb Sutter and Andrei Alexandrescu, page 13.
[10] Herb Sutter and Andrei Alexandrescu, page 16.

A console application is distinguished with a main function. This source code is found in
FRMUnitHelloCA.cpp. FRM denotes Financial Risk Management, LLC. Unit in the name of the file
distinguishes this file as interface code as opposed to implementation code (developed later).

```
/*********************************************************
**   Hello
*********************************************************/
#include <conio.h>      // defines getch() function
#include <iostream.h>   // defines cout that permits input and output operations
int main()
{
  cout << "Hello!";   // Hello! is written to the screen
  getch();            // Waits until user enters a single character
  return 0;           // main() is expecting an integer to be returned
}
```

The first three lines are comments and the next two include header files that define various functions.
The term `cout` puts the characters Hello! on the screen. As previously noted, `getch()` will get a
character from the keyboard. Finally, `return 0;` will return the value of zero, which is not used here.
Each time you see // what follows is a comment describing what that piece of code is doing.

C++ Code: 2.1 Hello Console Application[11][12]

Alternatively, a Windows-based hello world program allows for a more elegant interface with the user.
Typically, we will illustrate implementation code through this type of interface. The program, when
run, produces the following screen once the run button is clicked (the button changes to Disappear!
once clicked and when clicked again the screen returns to blank).

---

[11] In this chapter, we illustrate the interface code based on the specific complier used here. In the
remaining chapters, we place all interface code in the appendix to help focus on the implementation
code as you are likely to be using a different compiler.
[12] The purpose of this header is to alert you that source code is available in the repository provide with
this book. See www.frmhelp.com.

Windows-based programs are distinguished by WinMain() and this program has a separate unit that we named UnitHelloWorld. The main program file is FRMHelloTest.cpp, excerpts of which we provide here. For the compiler used here, this entire file is generated automatically. You should not alter it in any way. Your alterations occur in the Unit file.

```
#include <vcl.h>
...
USEFORM("FRMUnitHello.cpp", FormHelloWorld);
//---------------------------------------------------------------------
WINAPI _tWinMain(HINSTANCE, HINSTANCE, LPTSTR, int)
{
...
}
```

The compiler we use has a visual components library (vcl.h) that provides numerous useful items that greatly simplify the programming interface with users. This program contains only one form, FRMUnitHello.cpp. Excerpts from the corresponding header file follow.

```
#ifndef FRMUnitHelloH
#define FRMUnitHelloH
...
class TFormHelloWorld : public TForm
{
__published:  // IDE-managed Components
  TButton *btnRun;
  TButton *btnExit;
  TLabel *lblHelloWorld;
  void __fastcall btnExitClick(TObject *Sender);
  void __fastcall btnRunClick(TObject *Sender);
private:  // User declarations
public:    // User declarations
    __fastcall TFormHelloWorld(TComponent* Owner);
};
//---------------------------------------------------------------------
extern PACKAGE TFormHelloWorld *FormHelloWorld;
//---------------------------------------------------------------------
#endif
```

The first two lines and the last line are known as preprocessor directives. Because header files cannot be included twice, this if statement is run. If FRMUnitHelloH has not previously been defined (ifndef), then it is defined and the subsequent lines are run until endif is encountered. The next time this header file is run, its entire contents will be skipped. Notice that the form has two buttons (Disappear! and Exit) and the header file has two TButton declarations. The compiler used here automatically generated this header file. The corresponding FRMUnitHello.cpp excerpts are below.

```
...
#include "FRMUnitHello.h"
...
void __fastcall TFormHelloWorld::btnExitClick(TObject *Sender)
{
  Close();   //this calls a function to close the current application
}
//---------------------------------------------------------------------
void __fastcall TFormHelloWorld::btnRunClick(TObject *Sender)
{
  if(lblHelloWorld->Visible == false){ //If the screen does not already say "Hello World"
    lblHelloWorld->Visible = true;     //make the statement visible
    btnRun->Caption = "Disappear!";    //and change the caption of the button to ...
  } else {                             //If the screen already says "Hello World"
    lblHelloWorld->Visible = false;    //make it disappear
    btnRun->Caption = "Run";           //and change the caption of the button to ...
  }
}
```

Because function must be declared first, the header file is included (first line above). The two functions are btnExitClick and btnRunClick. Notice that the names are self-explanatory. They are both based on the buttons, one runs the program and the other closes the program.

C++ Code: 2.2 Hello

The written C++ code is known as source code. Recall that source code has the file extension *.cpp or *.h (or possibly *.c and *.hpp). The *.cpp (or *.c in original C code) is the C++ code and the *.h (or *.hpp) is the header file containing definitions. Source code is said to be compiled into machine language by creating object code, which has the extension *.obj. Figure 2.1 illustrates the three levels of various programming files. First, you create the source code (level 1 in the figure). Numerous illustrations of source code will be presented in this material. When compiled, object code is created and can be thought of as a complex set of zeros and ones (machine language). Object code is illustrated as level 2 in the figure. Multiple object files are said to be linked to create executable code with the extension *.exe (level 3 in the figure). Users of your programs will only need the executable code.

Figure 2.1. Various Programming Files

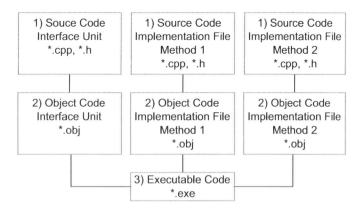

One major advantage for financial analysts who implement their solutions in C++ is portability. If one writes in standard C++, then it is very easy to develop executable code for a variety of operating systems.

User interface

Some restrictions are imposed on how the program user is allowed to interact with our software solutions. In the training materials, input is received from the user either through a graphical user interface (GUI) form or contained in a text file. A screen shot of a GUI follows this paragraph. The file extension *.dat is arbitrarily used to indicate a program inputs, and the file extension *.prn is arbitrarily used to indicate a program outputs.

Stock Price	100
Strike Price	100
Volatility (%)	30
Interest Rate (%)	5
Time To Maturity	1
Dividend Yield (%)	0
Number of Time Steps (Even Number, 3650 max)	360
Type (European=0, American=1)	1

OK   Cancel

	BSM OPM		Binomial OPM		
	Call	Put	Call	Put	
Price	14.23125478	9.35419723	14.22293528	9.86633528	
Delta	0.62425173	-0.37574827	0.62416414	-0.40621828	
Gamma	0.01264776	0.01264776	0.03996798	0.03313841	
Vega	0.00379433	0.00379433	0.00379162	0.00379477	(reported in basis points)
Theta	-8.10118990	-3.34504277	-8.09701346	-3.95209952	
Rho	0.00481939	-0.00469290	0.00481900	-0.00347983	(reported in basis points)

For now, the program user will interact with the software through a windows-based GUI. Later on, the tools necessary to build dynamic linked libraries will be covered so you can use other GUIs, such as Microsoft Excel®, SAS®, and so forth.

Within C++ code presented in this book, there will be a separation between interface code (managing interactions with the user) and implementation code (managing solving the particular quantitative task at hand). Every effort is made to write the implementation code in ANSI C++ (American National Standards Institute). ANSI C++ should compile with any C++ compiler. This separation is an effort to be sensitive to the autonomous analysts who desire to build their GUI using some other compiler, such as Microsoft's Visual C++® or Apple's Xcode®.

Managing data

Software solutions applicable to quantitative financial analysts typically involve some set of input data, a set of solution methods, and a set of outputs. One advantage of C++ is that it performs numerical calculations very fast. In chapter 3, a random number generator will be illustrated that computes statistics on 100,000,000 draws from a Monte Carlo simulator in less than 5 seconds. This high speed is achieved because the computer uses random-access memory (RAM), which is fast internal memory. Accessing the large quantities of data stored on the hard drive, however, is much slower.

Variables

All variables in C++ must be declared before they are used, they can be declared at the beginning of a method if they are only needed for that method or the can be declared in the header. Declaring variables in the header is preferred if you will use the variable in multiple methods. In the long run, it is better to give your variables longer names so your source code is easy to interpret. For example, consider the following snippet of code:

```
double w, x, y, z
...
w = x*exp(-y*z);
```

The first line of code has an error, hence the computer 'bug' icon. Every statement in C++ must end with a semi-colon; thus the statement should be `double w, x, y, z;`. The word 'double' declares w, x, y and z to be a floating point variable with a high level of precision. You can imagine, that once you have hundreds of lines of code and many declared variables that this code may be difficult to interpret. Consider the alternative snippet of code:

```
double BondPrice, ParValue, InterestRate, TimeToMaturity;
...
BondPrice = ParValue*exp(-InterestRate*TimeToMaturity);
```

Clearly, this snippet is much easier to read. Remember, the goal is to reuse C++ code. With a well-defined object-oriented approach and clearly written code, solutions can be implemented rapidly. Because of this capability, the phrase "rapid application development" or RAD came into existence. Thus, your variable should be long enough to ease interpretation when you must reuse this code after years of not seeing it.

There are four aspects to keep in mind related to variables. They obviously have a name, such as `ParValue`. Variables also have a type, such as `double`. We will review selected variable types shortly. The C++ language has a specific protocol governing the variable's lifetime and scope. Lifetime refers to how long the declared variable exists, whereas scope determines when the variable is accessible.

Names of variables must start with either a letter or underscore (_) and all other characters must be letters, numbers or the underscore without spaces. Names also cannot be a reserved keyword. There are many sources for the exhaustive list of C++ keywords. We identify the significant keywords for financial analyst applications below.

Table 2.1. Significant C++ Reserved Keywords

bool	break	case	catch	char
const	default	delete	do	double
else	extern	float	for	if
int	long	new	private	protected
public	return	static	struct	switch
throw	true	try	void	while

Variables can be either local or global. The classification is based on where in the code the variables are declared. A local variable has a lifetime of when the function is active and a scope to the end of the block where it was declared. A global variable has a lifetime as long as the program is executing and a scope to the end of the file in which it was declared.

Data types have a set of possible values and a set of allowable operations. Key data types are sketched here:

- `int (or short int)` – integer, range system dependent, older 16-bit systems -2^{16} to $2^{15}-1$ or $-32,768$ to $32,767$, newer 32-bit systems same as `long int`
- `long int` – integer, $-(2^{31})$ to $2^{31}-1$ or $-2,147,483,648$ to $2,147,483,647$
- `float` – real number, approximately seven decimals of accuracy, 3.4E +/– 38
- `double` – real number, approximately fifteen decimals of accuracy, 1.7E +/– 308
- `long double` – real number, same as double
- `char` – text, one ASCII character (American Standard Code for Information Interchange), anything that can be typed on a computer keyboard, –128 to 127
- `bool` – holds either true or false, typically zero is false and any other value is deemed true
- `unsigned short` – integer, zero to 65,535
- `unsigned long` – integer, zero to 4,294,967,295

Input, output, and basic operators

The two primary ways that inputs and outputs (I/O) will be managed in this book are with a graphical user interface (GUI) in a windows environment, or with files. In the old DOS-based environment you could send messages out to the screen or read data in from the user with `cin` and `cout`. Although we do not use DOS-based programs in this book, several basic operators are illustrated in the following simple program:

```cpp
#include <iostream.h>   // cout, cin
#include <conio.h>      // getch()
void main()             // Console application
{
  double n;          // declare n to be of type double, a floating point number
  cout << "Input real number: ";  // Send message to console
  cin >> n;          // Input number from screen, no error trapping
  cout << "\nNumber inputted was: " << n; // Send message and number to screen
  getch();           // Pause screen, get character from user
// Illustration of assignment operator
  int a, b, c, d; // a : ?, b : ?, c : ?, and d : ?
  a = 2010;    // a : 2010, b : ?, c : ?, and d : ?
  b = a;       // a : 2010, b : 2010, c : ?, and d : ?
  d = a - (c = 2000); // a : 2010, b : 2010, c : 2000, and d : 10
  a = b = c = d = 0; // a : 0, b : 0, c : 0, and d : 0
  a++;
  b += 1;
  c = c + 1;   // a : 1, b : 1, c : 1, and d : 0
  a *= 10;
  b = b*23;
  c = b / a;   // integer division, truncates (no rounds)
  d = b % a;   // modulo, return the remainder, a : 10, b : 23, c : 2, and d : 3
  a = 0;
  b--;
  c *= d*10 + 20;
  d = c;
  d /= 25;   // a : 0, b : 22, c : 100, d = 4
  getch();
  return;
}
```

C++ Code: 2.3 Input Real Number

In this book, we will rely on the more user-friendly windows environment and the easy drag-and-drop code generating capabilities of the compiler.

An alternative way to manage I/O is with input and output files. File I/O will be illustrated in chapter 3 when we address managing regression data.

Statements

Simple statements end with a semi-colon (;). Indeed, the most common syntax error is failing to end each statement with a semi-colon. Blocks of statements are created with curly brackets, {}. The simple program illustrated above opens with { in the fourth line and terminates with } in the final line. This block of statements is treated as a single compound statement.

There are a variety of ways of controlling the program flow. Several of these statements are introduced by illustrating snippets of code.

if

```cpp
if(fabs(D) > 7){  // Test for extreme values
  if(D > 0) return(1); // Positive extreme equals 1.0
  else return(0);      // Negative extreme equals 0.0
}
```

The first line in the code above tests whether the absolute value of D exceeds 7. If affirmative, then the second line tests whether D is positive. If so, then 1 is returned and if not, 0 is returned.

switch (use a default)

```
switch (FunctionIndex) {
  case 1:          // Call option
    f = DF * (x - StrikePrice)
      * (1.0 / (pow(2.0*PI, 0.5) * SD * x))
      * exp(- pow(log(x) - Mean, 2.0) / (2.0 * pow(SD, 2.0)) );
    break;
  case 2:            // Put option
    f = DF * (StrikePrice - x)
      * (1.0 / (pow(2.0*PI, 0.5) * SD * x))
      * exp(- pow(log(x) - Mean, 2.0) / (2.0 * pow(SD, 2.0)) );
    break;
  default :
    f = 0.0;
}
```

The first line of this code evaluates FunctionIndex. If it equals 1 then the case 1 statement is run. If it equals 2 then the case 2 statement is run; otherwise the default case is run. This snippet of code is the probability density function of the lognormal distribution. Later, we will go into more details on integrating the lognormal distribution (Module 4.8).

while

```
do {
  v1 = 2.0 * FRMUniformRandom01() - 1.0;     // Pick two uniform numbers
  v2 = 2.0 * FRMUniformRandom01() - 1.0;
  rsq = v1 * v1 + v2 * v2;              // Check if unit circle
} while (rsq >= 1.0 || rsq == 0.0);  // if not, try again
```

The three lines inside {} are run as long as rsq is either greater than or equal to 1.0 or rsq is zero. In this case, the test condition is evaluated after the statements within {} are run. An alternative version of the while loop can be expressed as:

```
while (rsq >= 1.0 || rsq == 0.0) { // if not, try again
  v1 = 2.0 * FRMUniformRandom01() - 1.0;     // Pick two uniform numbers
  v2 = 2.0 * FRMUniformRandom01() - 1.0;
  rsq = v1 * v1 + v2 * v2;              // Check if unit circle
}
```

In this version, the test condition is evaluated before the statements {} are run.

for

```
for (long int i = 0; i <= SampleSize-1; i++) {
  Draw = FRMUniformRandom01();     // Random uniform 0, 1
  Draw = Draw * (UpperBound - LowerBound) + Lower Bound;
  SumDraw += Draw;
  SumDrawSquared += pow(Draw, 2.0);
}
```

The mistake in this code is in the third line; Lower Bound should be one word: LowerBound.

The for loop has four major parts: first, the initial condition (`long int i = 0;`); second, the test condition (`i <= SampleSize-1;`); third, the incrementor (`i++`); and finally, the statements (lines 2 through 5). Line 2 calls the method FRMUniformRandom01() and returns a uniformly distributed random variable between 0 and 1 placing this value in the variable Draw. In the third line, Draw is modified be a value between LowerBound and UpperBound. The fourth and fifth lines contain the sum of Draw and Draw squared. These values are subsequently used to compute basic statistics.

Functions

Functions are very useful mechanisms for organizing statements. Functions can receive and return data. Financial analysts write their own functions in order to deliver solutions. The following is an illustration of a function:

```
double FRMBSMOVM::FRMd1()
{
  d1 = log(StockPrice/StrikePrice) + (InterestRate/100.0  - DividendYield/100.0
    + pow(Volatility/100.0, 2)/2.0) * TimeToMaturity;
```

```
d1 /= (Volatility/100.0) * pow(TimeToMaturity, 0.5);
return d1;
}
```

The first line of code identifies the type, class and name of the method. This function FRMd1(), is of type double (meaning it returns a double variable), and is contained within the class FRMBSMOVM (more about classes shortly); the class name is always located after the type and before the ::. This function computes the value of d_1 in the Black, Scholes, Merton option valuation model. The last line of code prior to the } shows that it returns d1 (a double variable that is defined in the header file).

Many functions perform some procedure without returning data. The following is an example of a procedure function:

```
void __fastcall TCalendarForm::btnOKClick(TObject *Sender)
{
    FRMExecute();
}
```

This function of type void __fastcall calls the FRMExecute() function when the OK button is clicked, it is a member of the TCalendarForm class. Note that __fastcall is a technical reference that is suppose to speed up functions of this nature and is specific to this compiler.

Expressions

Expressions here refer to math terms that may contain numbers, symbols or both. For example, consider the following expression:

$$d_1 = \frac{\ln\left(\frac{S}{X}\right) + \left(r + \frac{\sigma^2}{2}\right)T}{\sigma\sqrt{T}}$$

In C++, we have terms or variables and operators (+, -, *, /, and so forth). To avoid overuse of parentheses, it is important to understand precedence and associativity. Precedence addresses in what order the calculations are performed. The higher precedence operators are computed first. Many operators, however, have the same precedence. Hence, associativity addresses operators at the same precedence level. Left-associative means operators to the left are computed first. Right-associative means operators to the right are computed first. Table 2.2 provides selected C++ operators, precedence and associativity. The higher blocks in the table have higher precedence and operators in the same block have the same precedence (e.g., + and –). Under 'Associativity' in the table, left means left-associative and operators with the same precedence are computed starting from your left and moving to your right (e.g., a + b – c is the same as ((a + b) – c)).

Table 2.2. Selected Operator Precedence and Associativity for C++

Operator	Brief definition	Associativity
: :	scope resolution	left
++ -- () [] . ->	post increment and decrement, use value first and then change function call array element direct member selection indirect member selection	left
++ -- ! (type) * &	pre increment and decrement, change value first and then use (++X, --X) logical not cast to type indirection, contents of or dereference address of	right
* /	multiply divide	left

%	modulus, remainder	
+ −	plus minus	left
< <= > >=	arithmetic less than, less than or equal to arithmetic greater than, greater than or equal to	left
== !=	assessment equal or relational equal to assessment not equal or relational not equal to	left
&&	logical and	left
||	logical or	left
? :	conditional expression, a?b:c, if a is true then b else c	right
= += −= *= /= %=	assignment assignment by sum assignment by difference assignment by product assignment by division assignment by remainder	right
,	sequential expression	left

It is important to remember our goal of easily reusable code. A few extra parentheses that facilitate understanding of an expression is fine. Too many parentheses, however, make expressions in C++ difficult to follow and often have unintended consequences (for example, parentheses placed in the wrong location). We recommend that you check your mathematical coding in C++ when you are first starting. It is important to know what the answer is to a mathematical expression when given a set of inputs, send those inputs to your mathematical statement and ensure that you receive the correct answer from your code. You can also try different levels of parentheses and operators to try to see if you are coding in the most efficient manner.

Mathematical calculations in C++ are data type specific. For example, you have different results for the following snippet of code depending on the data type of x, y and z.

```
x = 13;
y = 4;
z = x / y;
```

If the data types are integer, then z = 3. If the data types are any floating point type, then z = 3.25. This type of simple coding without specifying types is a classic mistake by those just starting with C++. Now suppose x and y are integer and z is double. If you want to compute the floating-point value of x/y, you can explicitly convert x or y or both to double. The following three expressions will produce the same output:

```
z = double (x) / y;
z = x / double (y);
z = double (x) / double (y);
```

For each of these expressions, the value would be 3.25.

Another useful operator is %, the remainder operator (modulus). In our illustration here, x%y is equal to 1. If x = 12 and y = 4, then x%y is equal to zero.

There are a variety of ways to use the assignment operator, =. The following snippets of code illustrate several of them as well as the increment and decrement operators.

```
int x, y, z;
double a;
x = 0;       // Variable x is assigned the integer value 0
y = z = 0;   // Variables y and z are assigned the integer value 0
a = 10.1;    // Variable a is assigned the floating point value 10.1
x++;         // 1 is added to x, hence x is now equal to 1
x += 1;      // 1 is added to x, hence x is now equal to 2
```

```
x = x + 1; // 1 is added to x, hence x is now equal to 3
x--;       // 1 is subtracted from x, hence x is now equal to 2
x -= 1;    // 1 is subtracted from x, hence x is now equal to 1
x = x - 1; // 1 is subtracted from x, hence x is now equal to 0
y = a;     // y is equal to 10 because a is first converted to integer
```

Finally, several Boolean operators are useful in C++. The following snippet of code highlights several Boolean operators. The output from running a program with this code is presented below. To best understand this program, run it and then compare the output to the statements. Do not be concerned if several lines of code do not make sense to you yet, it will take a while to fully understand Boolean operators.

```
...
  bool w, x, y, z; // boolean, 0 is false, all else true
  w = false;
  x = true;
  y = false;
  z = (x == y);    // Note x==y not assignment x=y
  cout << "Relational equals:\n";
  cout << " If x = true and y = false, then z = (x == y) is equal to false.\n";
  cout << " x=" << x << " y=" << y << " z=" << z << " (zero denotes false).\n";
  z = (x != y);
  cout << "Relational not equals:\n";
  cout << " If x = true and y = false, then z = (x != y) is equal to true.\n";
  cout << " x=" << x << " y=" << y << " z=" << z << " (zero denotes false).\n";
  z = (y = x);     // Note x = y is assignment not x==y
  cout << "Oops, assignment:\n";
  cout << " If z = (y = x) then x, y, z, respectively, are all true.\n";
  cout << " x=" << x << " y=" << y << " z=" << z << " (zero denotes false).\n";
// Logical operators
  z = !(x == y);   // Logical not, x==y is true, hence z is false
  cout << "Logical not:\n";
  cout << " If z = !(x == y) then:\n";
  cout << " x=" << x << " y=" << y << " z=" << z << " (zero denotes false).\n";
// Logical and (&&): every statement must be true to evaluate to true
// Logical not (!): converts true to false or false to true
  z = (!(x == y)&&(w == !y)); // !(x -- y) : false, (w ==! y) : true, hence false
  cout << "Logical and:\n";
  cout << " If z = (!(x == y)&&(w==!y)) then:\n";
  cout << " w=" << w << " x=" << x << " y=" << y << " z=" << z << " (zero denotes false).\n";
// Logical or: any statement can be true to evaluate to true
  z = (!(x == y)||(w == y));   // !(x == y): false, (w == y) : false, hence false
  cout << "Logical or:\n";
  cout << " If z = (!(x == y)||(x==y)) then:\n";
  cout << " w=" << w << " x=" << x << " y=" << y << " z=" << z << " (zero denotes false).\n";
// Conditional operator: condition ? outcome1 : outcome2;
  z = (x ==! y) ? w : !y;   // ?:, if () evaluates to true, then w, else not y
  cout << "? : \n";
  cout << " If z = (x != y) ? w : !y; then:\n";
  cout << " w=" << w << " x=" << x << " y=" << y << " z=" << z << " (zero denotes false).\n";
  getch();              // Pause screen, get character from user
  return 0;
}
```

The output from running this program follows. Carefully review this code and its output.

```
Relational equals:
  If x = true and y = false, then z = (x == y) is equal to false.
  x=1 y=0 z=0 (zero denotes false).
Relational not equals:
  If x = true and y = false, then z = (x != y) is equal to true.
  x=1 y=0 z=1 (zero denotes false).
Oops, assignment:
  If z = (y = x) then x, y, z, respectively, are all true.
  x=1 y=1 z=1 (zero denotes false).
Logical not:
  If z = !(x == y) then:
  x=1 y=1 z=0 (zero denotes false).
Logical and:
  If z = (!(x == y)&&(w==!y)) then:
  w=0 x=1 y=1 z=0 (zero denotes false).
Logical or:
  If z = (!(x == y)||(x==y)) then:
  w=0 x=1 y=1 z=0 (zero denotes false).
? :
  If z = (x != y) ? w : !y; then:
  w=0 x=1 y=1 z=0 (zero denotes false).
```

C++ Code: 2.4 Boolean Operators

It is easy to get tripped up with Boolean operations. The following table, often referred to as a truth table, provides the results for the logical operators.

Table 2.3. Boolean Logical Truth Table

x	y	x&&y (and)	x||y (or)	!x (not)
true	true	true	true	false
true	false	false	true	false
false	true	false	true	true
false	false	false	false	true

Suppose x = true and y = false (the second line in this table). In this case, z = x&&y will evaluate to false because "true and false" will evaluate to false. z = x||y will evaluate to true because "true or false" will evaluate to true. Finally, z = !x will evaluate to false because not "true" will evaluate to false.

Pointers

Although difficult to grasp initially, pointers are widely used in C++. The value of a pointer is the address in memory for a data item, not the data item itself. Pointers offer the following advantages:

- allows reference to a large set of data via a single address
- enables grouping of data
- permits dynamic allocation of memory

The following complete console application illustrates many features of pointers that will be used later in financial applications. The screen capture after this code illustrates the results of running this code. Classes, such as USER here, and their uses are discussed later. For now, User1 in the main program is similar to other data types like int, but its data type is USER.

```cpp
// Pointers and String Manipulation
#include <conio.h>     // getch() - get character from user
#include <iostream.h>  // cin, cout
class USER
{
public:
  int func1(int V){ return (V + 10); };
}

void main()
{  // PART 1: Manipulate classes with direct and indirect selectors
   USER User1;       // Instantiate object User1
   int A;            // A could equal any integer, random at this point
   A = 0;            // A is now 0
   A = User1.func1(A);    // Direct member selector, A = 10
   cout << "\n After direct member selector A = " << A; // Send to screen
```

```
   cout << "  Press any key ... \n";   // \n moves cursor to new line
   getch();   // Waiting for user to input a character
   USER *User2;      // Declare pointer to type USER
   User2 = &User1;  // Assign to object User1
   A = User2->func1(A);  // Indirect member selector, A = 20
   cout << "\n After indirect member selector A = " << A;
   cout << "  Press any key ... \n";
   getch();
// PART 2: Manipulating pointers
   int *ptr1;         // Pointer to an integer, *ptr1 equal unknown integer value
   ptr1 = new(int); // Allocate memory for the integer pointed to by the pointer
                     // ptr1 holds the address of integer *ptr1
   *ptr1 = 10;        // Assign 10 to the memory location at the address ptr1
   cout << "\n *ptr1 = " << *ptr1 << " and ptr1 = " << ptr1;
   cout << "  Press any key ... \n";
   getch();
   int *ptr2;
   ptr2 = new(int);
   *ptr2 = *ptr1;    // Value stored at ptr1 is copied to ptr2 storage location
   cout << "\n *ptr2 = " << *ptr2 << " and ptr2 = " << ptr2;
   cout << "  Press any key ... \n";
   getch();
   ptr2 = ptr1;      // Address of ptr2 assigned to same location as ptr1
   cout << "\n *ptr2 = " << *ptr2 << " and ptr2 = " << ptr2;
   cout << "  Press any key ... \n";
   getch();
   int x;
   x = 20;
   ptr2 = &x;         // ptr2 assigned the address of x
   cout << "\n ptr2 = " << ptr2 << " and &x = " << &x;
   cout << "\n *ptr2 = " << *ptr2 << " and x = " << x;
   cout << "\n &(*ptr2) = " << &(*ptr2); // Address of value stored at address ptr2
   cout << "  Press any key ... \n";
   getch();
// PART 3: Manipulating strings and vectors
   int input[] = {5, 10, 15};  // Vector of size 3 with specified values
   int *ptr, *ptr_input;       // Two pointers to integers
   cout << "\n Input vector " << input << "\n";
   cout << "\n Input[0] = " << input[0];
   cout << "\n Input[1] = " << input[1];
   cout << "\n Input[2] = " << input[2];
   cout << "\n Input[3] = " << input[3];
   cout << "\n Input[-1] = " << input[-1];
   cout << "\n Pointer ptr after definition = " << ptr;
   cout << "  Press any key ... \n";
   getch();
   ptr = &input[0];
   ptr_input = &input[0];
   if(ptr == ptr_input)
     cout << "\n ptr is the same as ptr_input, which is " << ptr << "\n";
   cout << "  Press any key ... \n";
   getch();
   char cinput[] = "Stuff";
   cout << "\n Character input vector " << cinput << "\n";
   cout << "\n cinput[0] = " << cinput[0];
   cout << "\n cinput[1] = " << cinput[1];
   cout << "\n cinput[2] = " << cinput[2];
   cout << "\n cinput[3] = " << cinput[3];
   cout << "\n cinput[4] = " << cinput[4];
   cout << "\n cinput[5] = " << cinput[5] << "\n";
   cout << "  Press any key ... \n";
   getch();
   char *cptr_input;
   char *cptr = "More Stuff";
   cout << "\n cptr = " << cptr << "\n";
   cptr_input = &cinput[0];
   cout << "\n cptr_input = " << cptr_input << "\n";
   cout << "  End of Program. Press any key ... \n";
   getch();
   return; // main is void so it returns nothing
 }
```

The bug in the program above is in the eighth line. The class declaration must end with a semi-colon. Hence the eighth line should be };.

```
After direct member selector A = 10  Press any key ...

After indirect member selector A = 20  Press any key ...

*ptr1 = 10 and ptr1 = 913234  Press any key ...

*ptr2 = 10 and ptr2 = 913244  Press any key ...

*ptr2 = 10 and ptr2 = 913234  Press any key ...

ptr2 = 12ff70 and &x = 12ff70
*ptr2 = 20 and x = 20
&(*ptr2) = 12ff70  Press any key ...

Input vector 12ff64

Input[0] = 5
Input[1] = 10
Input[2] = 15
Input[3] = 20
Input[-1] = 1245072
Pointer ptr after definition = 12ff90  Press any key ...

ptr is the same as ptr_input, which is 12ff64
 Press any key ...

Character input vector Stuff

cinput[0] = S
cinput[1] = t
cinput[2] = u
cinput[3] = f
cinput[4] = f
cinput[5] =
 Press any key ...

cptr = More Stuff

cptr_input = Stuff
 End of Program. Press any key ...
```

C++ Code: 2.5 Pointers

Arrays

Arrays have an ordered set of elements and are very useful for financial applications. Arrays typically have a specified array size and each element has the same data type. The following snippets of code illustrate how to declare and use arrays in various ways. The following line declares an integer vector of size three and defines input[0] = 5, input[1] = 10, and input[2] = 15.

```
int input[] = {5, 10, 15};  // Vector of size 3 with specified values
```

Note that the number inside the brackets, [], is the indicator of location in the vector.

The following line is a method FRMCalculateX() that passes the address of a matrix LU, an integer NColumns, the address of a vector Index, and a vector of doubles B. Clearly, passing the single address of a potentially large matrix is much more efficient than creating a copy of the matrix when passing it. Although pointers are widely used here, we do not rely as heavily on pointers as professional programmers.

```
void FRMCalculateX(double **LU, int NColumns, int *Index, double B[]);
```

Note in the line above **LU denotes a pointer to a matrix (technically a pointer to a vector of pointers) and *Index denotes a pointer to a vector.

The following line declares a pointer to a vector of type integer. At this point, all we really know is that Index is a pointer of type integer.

```
int *Index;              // Pointer to vector that is an Index
```

The following line allocates NP elements of memory of type integer. At this point, we now know that Index is a vector of size NP.

```
Index = new int [NP];          // Allocate memory for Index
```

The following line declares a pointer to a pointer of type double (a matrix).

```
double **A;               // Pointer to matrix A
```

The following two lines allocate memory for the matrix A. The first line creates a vector of pointers and the second line allocates memory for each vector of pointers.

```
A = new double*[NP];          // Set up rows
for(j=0; j<NP; j++) A[j] = new double [NP]; // Set up columns
```

Classes and structures

At this point, it is important to remember that this presentation is not exhaustive. Classes involve a lot more than what is covered here, but our objective is to help you implement your quantitative solutions in C++ as rapidly as possible.

Classes are very useful mechanisms for organizing data and methods. Classes also make it easy to separate the user interface from the analysts' implementation. Additionally, classes permit some data and methods to be public or private. While public means the data or methods are accessible from other places outside of the class, private means the data or methods are accessible only from within the class. The process of combining data and methods is known as encapsulation. Encapsulation permits data hiding where the implementation is hidden from the user of the class.

Structures are classes where all data and methods are public. An example of declaring a structure with just data follows:

```
struct FRMDateMDY
{
  int Month;
  int Day;
  int Year;
};
```

The structure FRMDateMDY holds three integers: Month, Day and Year. FRMDateMDY can be treated as its own data type. See the following snippet of code that declares and uses FRMDateMDY:

```
FRMDateMDY Date;
Date = FRMFromJulian(j);
return(Date.Month);   // Returns only month of Julian number
```

The first line of code is where the variable Date is declared to be of type FRMDateMDY. Note the structure must have previously been declared. The method FRMFromJulian() is also previously declared to return a FRMDateMDY. One can access individual data elements within a structure using the direct member selector (recall the discussion about pointers). Here the code is using the month direct member selector to only return month in line 3 of the code.

A class can have data and methods, as well as public or private members. Classes can be used as building blocks where one class inherits all the features of another class. Consider the following excerpts from an implementation of the Black, Scholes, Merton option valuation model:

```
class FRMBSMOVM : public FRMCDF, FRMCALENDAR
{
public:              // Interaction with other classes
  void FRMBSMOVMSetData(double StockPrice, double StrikePrice, double InterestRate,
    double DividendYield, double Volatility, int SM, int SD, int SY, int  MM,
    int MD, int MY);
  double FRMBSMCallPrice();
  double FRMBSMPutPrice();
private:
  double CallPrice;
```

```
...
   double LowerBound;
// Private Methods
   double FRMCallLowerBound();
   double FRMPutLowerBound();
   double FRMd1();
   double FRMd2();
};
```

From line one, we see that the class FRMBSMOVM is derived from two base classes: FRMCDF and FRMCALENDAR. The first three methods are public, whereas the rest of the data and methods are private. Hence, a user of the FRMBSMOVM class can access the class through the set data (see line 4) and option valuation methods (see functions FRMBSMCallPrice and FRMBSMPutPrice on lines 6 and 7). The remaining data and methods are used internally within the class. The FRMBSMOVM class has access to all the data and methods of FRMCDF and FRMCALENDAR, even if they are declared private, because these classes are inherited on line 1.

Functions, functors, function templates, and class templates

Functions are illustrated based on the following finance equation:

$$\text{Future Value} = \frac{\text{Present Value}}{\left(1 + \dfrac{\text{Rate}}{\text{Periods Per Year}}\right)^{\text{Number of Periods} * \text{Periods Per Year}}}$$

Four separate functions are built below that solve for one of the parameters above, assuming the other four are given (we do not solve for periods per year).

There are several ways to reference a function in C++. First, the simplest way is with a function, as illustrated here with a future value calculator. The declaration in the header file is:

```
double FutureValueCalculator (const double PV, const double IR, const int PPY, const int NOP){
   return PV*pow((1.0+(IR/PPY)), (NOP*PPY));
};
```

This code declares a function FutureValueCalculator of type double (meaning it returns a double variable) and takes four inputs PV, IR, PPY, NOP; the type of inputs it requires are listed before the input name, here either const double or const int. Inside the {} lists what the function returns.

The function call, which could be called in several different implementation files which have this class, is:

```
FutureValue = FutureValueCalculator(PresentValue, ..., NumberOfPeriods);
```

The second way to reference a function in C++ is with a function object or functor, as illustrated here with a present value calculator. The declaration in the header file is:

```
struct PresentValueCalculator {
   double operator()(const double FV, const double IR, const int PPY, const int NOP){
      return FV/(pow(1.0+(IR/PPY), NOP*PPY));
   }
};
```

Note that order matters, so the future value must be the first variable past to this function.

The function call is:

```
PresentValueCalculator PV;
PresentValue = PV(FutureValue, InterestRate, PeriodsPerYear, NumberOfPeriods);
```

In this case PV is declared as type PresentValueCalculator. Once it is defined it can be used directly as shown above.

The third method is with a function template, as illustrated here with an interest rate calculator. The declaration in the header file is:

```
template <class T> T InterestRateCalculator(T FV, T PV, T PPY, T NOP){
  return PPY*((pow(FV/PV, (1.0/(NOP*PPY)))-1.0));
};
```

The function call is:

```
  InterestRate = InterestRateCalculator(FutureValue, ..., NumberOfPeriods);
```

The final way to reference a function in C++ is with a templated class, as illustrated here with a number of periods calculator. The declaration in the header file is:[13]

```
template <class T> T NOPC<T>::NumberOfPeriodsCalculator(T FV, T PV, T PPY, T IR){
    return (log(FV/PV))/(log(pow(1.0+(IR/PPY), PPY)));
};
```

The function call is:

```
  NOPC <double> N;
  NumberOfPeriods = N.NumberOfPeriodsCalculator(FutureValue, ..., InterestRate);
```

Below is the complete program, which illustrates the four primary methods. The following code is the header file:

FRMUnitTVM.h

```
#ifndef FRMUnitTVMH
#define FRMUnitTVMH
//-------------------------------------------------------------------------
#include <math.h>
#include <Classes.hpp>
#include <Controls.hpp>
#include <ExtCtrls.hpp>
#include <StdCtrls.hpp>
// Illustration of a function
double FutureValueCalculator (const double PV, const double IR, const int PPY, const int NOP){
  return PV*pow((1.0+(IR/PPY)), (NOP*PPY));
};
// Illustration of function object or functor
struct PresentValueCalculator {
  double operator()(const double FV, const double IR, const int PPY, const int NOP){
    return FV/(pow(1.0+(IR/PPY), NOP*PPY));
  }
};
// Illustration of a function template
template <class T> T InterestRateCalculator(T FV, T PV, T PPY, T NOP){
  return PPY*((pow(FV/PV, (1.0/(NOP*PPY)))-1.0));
};
// Illustration of a class template
template <class T> class NOPC{
  public:
    T NumberOfPeriodsCalculator(T FV, T PV, T PPY, T IR);
};
// Method of templated class
template <class T> T NOPC<T>::NumberOfPeriodsCalculator(T FV, T PV, T PPY, T IR){
    return (log(FV/PV))/(log(pow(1.0+(IR/PPY), PPY)));
};
//-------------------------------------------------------------------------
class TTVMsingleForm : public TForm
{
__published:  // IDE-managed Components
  TButton *btnCompute;
  TButton *btnClose;
```

---

[13] We just alert you to these capabilities. Remember our objective is to use rather elementary C++.

```
    TEdit *editPresentValue;
    TEdit *editFutureValue;
    TEdit *editInterestRate;
    TEdit *cditNumberOfPeriods;
    TComboBox *editCompounding;
    TLabel *lblPresentValue;
    TLabel *lblFutureValue;
    TLabel *lblInterestRate;
    TLabel *lblNumberOfPeriods;
    TLabel *lblCompounding;
    TRadioGroup *rbFunctionGroup;
    void __fastcall btnCloseClick(TObject *Sender);
    void __fastcall btnComputeClick(TObject *Sender);
private:    // User declarations
public:     // User declarations
    __fastcall TTVMsingleForm(TComponent* Owner);
// User functions
    void __fastcall ExecutePV(void);
    void __fastcall ExecuteFV(void);
    void __fastcall ExecuteIR(void);
    void __fastcall ExecuteN(void);
// Data Declarations
    double FutureValue;
    double InterestRate;
    double NumberOfPeriods;
    double PeriodsPerYear;
    double PresentValue;
};
//---------------------------------------------------------------------
extern TTVMsingleForm *TVMsingleForm;
//---------------------------------------------------------------------
#endif
```

The source code that illustrates the four methods is copied below:

FRMUnitTVM.cpp

```
//---------------------------------------------------------------------
#include <vcl\vcl.h>
#pragma hdrstop
#include "FRMUnitTVM.h"
//---------------------------------------------------------------------
#pragma resource "*.dfm"
TTVMsingleForm *TVMsingleForm;
//---------------------------------------------------------------------
__fastcall TTVMsingleForm::TTVMsingleForm(TComponent* Owner)
    : TForm(Owner)
{
}
//---------------------------------------------------------------------
void __fastcall TTVMsingleForm::btnCloseClick(TObject *Sender)
{
    Close();
}
//---------------------------------------------------------------------
void __fastcall TTVMsingleForm::btnComputeClick(TObject *Sender)
{
    if(rbFunctionGroup->ItemIndex==0){
        ExecutePV();
    }
    if(rbFunctionGroup->ItemIndex==1){
        ExecuteFV();
    }
    if(rbFunctionGroup->ItemIndex==2){
        ExecuteIR();
    }
    if(rbFunctionGroup->ItemIndex==3){
        ExecuteN();
    }
}
//---------------------------------------------------------------------
```

```cpp
void __fastcall TTVMsingleForm::ExecuteFV(void)
{
  PresentValue = StrToFloat(editPresentValue->Text);
  NumberOfPeriods = StrToFloat(editNumberOfPeriods->Text);
  InterestRate = StrToFloat(editInterestRate->Text);
  PeriodsPerYear = StrToFloat(editCompounding->Text);
// Illustration of function (see header file)
  FutureValue = FutureValueCalculator(PresentValue, InterestRate, PeriodsPerYear,
NumberOfPeriods);
  editFutureValue->Text = FloatToStrF(FutureValue, ffFixed, 10, 4);
}
//-------------------------------------------------------------------
void __fastcall TTVMsingleForm::ExecutePV(void)
{
  FutureValue = StrToFloat(editFutureValue->Text);
  NumberOfPeriods = StrToFloat(editNumberOfPeriods->Text);
  InterestRate = StrToFloat(editInterestRate->Text);
  PeriodsPerYear = StrToFloat(editCompounding->Text);
// Illustration of function object or functor (see header file)
  PresentValueCalculator PV;
  PresentValue = PV(FutureValue, InterestRate, PeriodsPerYear, NumberOfPeriods);
  editPresentValue->Text = FloatToStrF(PresentValue, ffFixed, 10, 4);
}
//-------------------------------------------------------------------
void __fastcall TTVMsingleForm::ExecuteIR(void)
{
  PresentValue = StrToFloat(editPresentValue->Text);
  FutureValue = StrToFloat(editFutureValue->Text);
  NumberOfPeriods = StrToFloat(editNumberOfPeriods->Text);
  PeriodsPerYear = StrToFloat(editCompounding->Text);
// Illustration of function template
  InterestRate = InterestRateCalculator(FutureValue, PresentValue, PeriodsPerYear,
NumberOfPeriods);
  editInterestRate->Text = FloatToStrF(InterestRate, ffFixed, 10, 4);
}
//-------------------------------------------------------------------
void __fastcall TTVMsingleForm::ExecuteN(void)
{
  PresentValue = StrToFloat(editPresentValue->Text);
  FutureValue = StrToFloat(editFutureValue->Text);
  InterestRate = StrToFloat(editInterestRate->Text);
  PeriodsPerYear = StrToFloat(editCompounding->Text);
// Illustration of function template class
  NOPC <double> N;
  NumberOfPeriods = N.NumberOfPeriodsCalculator(FutureValue, PresentValue, PeriodsPerYear,
InterestRate);
  editNumberOfPeriods->Text = FloatToStrF(NumberOfPeriods, ffFixed, 10, 4);
}
```

C++ Program: 2.6 Functions

Error trapping

Error trapping is a vital component of quality model development. In this section, we illustrate the use of interface-based error trapping. That is, the coder ensures that the user inputs are of the appropriate type and value. This concept is illustrated with a simple bond-pricing program illustrated below.

Although typically not a major concern for the quantitative analyst, some attention should be given to make sure the user does not input a character value, such as "A," where a numerical value is required. The FRMBondPriceETTest program contains extensive error trapping, as well as the first illustration of separating the interface code from the implementation code. If this program is run and the user inputs "A" for the Coupon Rate (%), he or she will get the following result:

The following excerpts from the FRMUnitBondPrice.h file (header file) highlight a few important issues.

```
#ifndef FRMUnitBondPriceH
#define FRMUnitBondPriceH
...
#include "c:\FRMRepository\FRMSimpleBondPrice.cpp"
//------------------------------------------------------------------------
class TBondPriceForm : public TForm
{
...
  void __fastcall btnCancelClick(TObject *Sender);
  void __fastcall btnOkClick(TObject *Sender);
  void __fastcall FormKeyPress(TObject *Sender, char &Key);
  void __fastcall editCouponRateEnter(TObject *Sender);
  void __fastcall editCouponRateExit(TObject *Sender);
  void __fastcall editYearsToMaturityEnter(TObject *Sender);
  void __fastcall editYearsToMaturityExit(TObject *Sender);
  void __fastcall editParEnter(TObject *Sender);
  void __fastcall editParExit(TObject *Sender);
  void __fastcall editYieldToMaturityEnter(TObject *Sender);
  void __fastcall editYieldToMaturityExit(TObject *Sender);
private:  // User declarations
  FRMSIMPLEBONDPRICE BondPrice;
```

```
  int inputYearsToMaturity;
  double inputCouponRate;
  double inputPar;
  double inputYieldToMaturity;
  double ModelBondPrice;
  double ModelModifiedDuration;
  void __fastcall Execute(void);
  void __fastcall Reset(void);
...
#endif
```

First, always remember to include the preprocessor conditional statements (lines 1, 2, and last). Second, the implementation code is warehoused separately in the repository. Therefore, we can have multiple programs drawing on the bond pricing implementation code. If changes are necessary to the implementation code then you only have to make changes in a single location (assuming the interface does not change). Third, the `void ... Enter()` and `void ... Exit()` functions (that is, editCouponRateEnter()) are used in error trapping. Fourth, FRMSIMPLEBONDPRICE is a class (we always capitalize it, although it is not necessary) and BondPrice is of this type. Fifth, the variables are declared private, so they cannot be easily manipulated elsewhere.

The following excerpts from the FRMUnitBondPrice.cpp file highlight several other important issues.

```
...
#include "FRMUnitBondPrice.h"
...
void __fastcall TBondPriceForm::Execute(void)
{
  BondPrice.FRMSetData(inputCouponRate, inputPar, inputYieldToMaturity,
    inputYearsToMaturity);
  ModelBondPrice = BondPrice.FRMCalculateBondPrice();
}
...
void __fastcall TBondPriceForm::btnOkClick(TObject *Sender)
{
  Execute();
  outputBondPrice->Text = FloatToStrF(ModelBondPrice, ffFixed, 15, 2);
  outputBondPrice->Visible = true;
  lblBondPrice->Visible = true;
}
...
void __fastcall TBondPriceForm::editCouponRateEnter(TObject *Sender)
{
// FloatToStrF converts floating point variable to an AnsiString
  editCouponRate->Text = FloatToStrF(inputCouponRate, ffFixed, 15, 6);
  editCouponRate->SelectAll();  // Highlight input so easy to type over
}
//-----------------------------------------------------------------------
void __fastcall TBondPriceForm::editCouponRateExit(TObject *Sender)
{
  if(editCouponRate->Text == "")editCouponRate->Text = "0.0";
  try {    // Just in case text is not a floating point number
    inputCouponRate = StrToFloat(editCouponRate->Text);
  }
  catch (Exception &exception){  // Catch the bad error
    editCouponRate->Text = "";
    Application->MessageBox(L"Input Only Positive Numbers", L"Input Error 2", MB_OK);
    ActiveControl = editCouponRate;
    return;
  }
  if(inputCouponRate < 0.0){   // Catch negative coupon error
    editCouponRate->Text = "";
    Application->MessageBox(L"Negative Number: Input Only Positive Numbers",
      L"Input Error 3", MB_OK);
    ActiveControl = editCouponRate;
  };
  editCouponRate->Text = FloatToStrF(inputCouponRate, ffFixed, 15, 2);
}
...
```

```
editYearsToMaturity->Text = IntToStr(inputYearsToMaturity);
...
```

First, source code should include its corresponding header file. Second, order of functions does not matter (e.g., `TBondPriceForm::Execute` is before `TBondPriceForm::btnOkClick()`). Our preference is to have one single method that interacts with the implementation code, if possible, typically we define it as the Execute() function. This will avoid accidental corruption of the implementation code. Third, the methods that end in Enter() will run when the edit box is selected. Fourth, the methods that end in Exit() will run when the user exits the corresponding edit box. Fifth, notice that the conversions from string to floating point and string to integer are different (e.g., `StrToFloat(editCouponRate->Text)` and `IntToStr(inputYearsToMaturity)`). Finally, the leading "L" in front of the text within the message boxes is required for some compilers and not others (e.g., `Application->MessageBox(L"Input Only Positive Numbers", L"Input Error 2", MB_OK)`).

The implementation header code follows.

```
#ifndef FRMSimpleBondPriceH
#define FRMSimpleBondPriceH
#include <math.h>  // Needed for math functions like pow(,)
//-----------------------------------------------------------------------
class FRMSIMPLEBONDPRICE
{
public:
  void FRMSetData(double ICR, double IPV, double IYLDTM, int IYRSTM);
  double FRMCalculateBondPrice();
private:
  double CouponRate;
  double ParValue;
  double YieldToMaturity;
  int YearsToMaturity;
};
#endif
```

The math.h file is included whenever built-in math functions are used. The method FRMSetData() is used to move the user data into the private implementation class. You must send the data in this exact order from the interface file, also the data sent must be of the same corresponding type as the implementation class is expecting to receive (for example, input coupon rate, ICR, must be sent as type double). These conditions for a program to run effectively are a reason error trapping can be particularly important. FRMCalculateBondPrice() actually computes the price and returns its value. The implementation source code follows.

```
#include "FRMSimpleBondPrice.h"
//-----------------------------------------------------------------------
void FRMSIMPLEBONDPRICE::FRMSetData(double ICR, double IPV, double IYLDTM, int IYRSTM)
{
  CouponRate = ICR; // Passed input coupon rate ICR to the private CouponRate
  ParValue = IPV;
  YieldToMaturity = IYLDTM;
  YearsToMaturity = IYRSTM;
};
//-----------------------------------------------------------------------
double FRMSIMPLEBONDPRICE::FRMCalculateBondPrice()
{
  int i;  // Counter used in for loop
  double PV; // Temporary variable holding sum of coupons
  PV = 0.0; // Initialize PV to zero
  for(i=1; i<=YearsToMaturity; i++){  // Loop from 1 to YearsToMaturity by 1
    PV += ((CouponRate/100.0)*ParValue) / pow((1.0 + (YieldToMaturity/100.0)), i);
  };
  return (PV + ParValue / pow((1.0 + (YieldToMaturity/100.0)), YearsToMaturity));
};
```

Note that pow(a,b) denotes a^b. Recall the first line includes the implementation file's corresponding header file. The next portion of code defines the FRMSetData method which is of type void and a member of the FRMSIMPLEBONDPRICE class. This method receives ICR, IPV, IYLDTM (all of type double) and IYRSTM (type int). Inside the {} sets each of these variables received to a new variable of the same type with a different name. The final portion of code defines the method FRMCalculateBondPrice() which returns a double and is a member of the FRMSIMPLEBONDPRICE class. This method uses the input names that are set in the previous step (CouponRate, ParValue, and so forth). These are the values that were passed as ICR, IPV, and so forth in the FRMSetData function.

C++ Program: 2.7 Error Trapping

Templated class

Although most of our applications will involve managing integers and real numbers, for completeness, we introduce templated classes. To motivate this discussion, we illustrate five simple math functions that can be performed with either integers or real numbers. Remember, for some calculations, the results will differ depending on data type (for example, divide truncates with integer – see the illustration below).

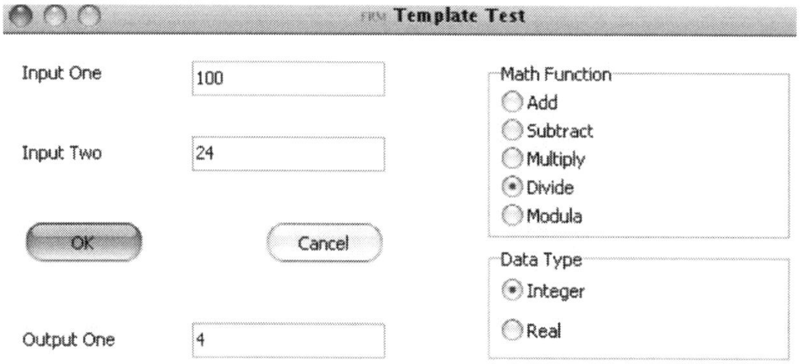

The header code excerpts follow.

```
#ifndef FRMUnitTemplateH
#define FRMUnitTemplateH
...
class TFRMUnitTemplateTest : public TForm
{
...
  TRadioGroup *rgMathFunctions;
  TRadioGroup *rgDataType;
  void __fastcall btnCancelClick(TObject *Sender);
  void __fastcall btnOkClick(TObject *Sender);
private:  // User declarations
  int inputIntOne;
  int inputIntTwo;
  int outputIntOne;
  double inputRealOne;
  double inputRealTwo;
  double outputRealOne;
  template <class T> T AddTwo(T A, T B);
  template <class T> T SubtractTwo(T A, T B);
  template <class T> T MultiplyTwo(T A, T B);
  template <class T> T DivideTwo(T A, T B);
  template <class T> T ModulaTwo(T A, T B);
  void __fastcall FRMExecute();
...
#endif
```

The template classes illustrated here leave the data type generic until it is actually called. The source code excerpts follow.

```
...
void __fastcall TFRMUnitTemplateTest::btnOkClick(TObject *Sender)
{
```

```
    FRMExecute();
}
//-------------------------------------------------------------------------
void __fastcall TFRMUnitTemplateTest::FRMExecute(void)
{
  if (rgDataType->ItemIndex == 0){
    inputIntOne = StrToInt(editInputOne->Text);
    inputIntTwo = StrToInt(editInputTwo->Text);
  } else {
    inputRealOne = StrToInt(editInputOne->Text);
    inputRealTwo = StrToInt(editInputTwo->Text);
  }
  if (rgMathFunctions->ItemIndex == 0) {
    if (rgDataType->ItemIndex == 0) outputIntOne = AddTwo(inputIntOne, inputIntTwo);
    if (rgDataType->ItemIndex == 1) outputRealOne = AddTwo(inputRealOne, inputRealTwo);
  } else if (rgMathFunctions->ItemIndex == 1) {
    if (rgDataType->ItemIndex == 0) outputIntOne = SubtractTwo(inputIntOne, inputIntTwo);
    if (rgDataType->ItemIndex == 1) outputRealOne = SubtractTwo(inputRealOne, inputRealTwo);
  } else if (rgMathFunctions->ItemIndex == 2) {
    if (rgDataType->ItemIndex == 0) outputIntOne = MultiplyTwo(inputIntOne, inputIntTwo);
    if (rgDataType->ItemIndex == 1) outputRealOne = MultiplyTwo(inputRealOne, inputRealTwo);
  } else if (rgMathFunctions->ItemIndex == 3) {
    if (rgDataType->ItemIndex == 0) outputIntOne = DivideTwo(inputIntOne, inputIntTwo);
    if (rgDataType->ItemIndex == 1) outputRealOne = DivideTwo(inputRealOne, inputRealTwo);
  } else {
    if (rgDataType->ItemIndex == 0) outputIntOne = ModulaTwo(inputIntOne, inputIntTwo);
    if (rgDataType->ItemIndex == 1) outputRealOne = ModulaTwo(inputRealOne, inputRealTwo);
  }
    if (rgDataType->ItemIndex == 0)  editOutputOne->Text = IntToStr(outputIntOne);
    if (rgDataType->ItemIndex == 1)
      editOutputOne->Text = FloatToStrF(outputRealOne, ffFixed, 10, 4);
  return;
}
//-------------------------------------------------------------------------
template <class T> T TFRMUnitTemplateTest::AddTwo(T A, T B) {
  return A + B;
}
//-------------------------------------------------------------------------
template <class T> T TFRMUnitTemplateTest::SubtractTwo(T A, T B) {
  return A - B;
}
//-------------------------------------------------------------------------
template <class T> T TFRMUnitTemplateTest::MultiplyTwo(T A, T B) {
  return A * B;
}
//-------------------------------------------------------------------------
template <class T> T TFRMUnitTemplateTest::DivideTwo(T A, T B) {
  return A / B;
}
//-------------------------------------------------------------------------
template <class T> T TFRMUnitTemplateTest::ModulaTwo(T A, T B) {
  return (int) A % (int) B;
}
```

Notice that the same method can be called with different data types.

C++ Code: 2.8 Templated Class

Function passing

For many quantitative problems, it is essential to be able to pass a function that is a member of one class into another function that is a member of a different class. See, for example, Module 3.7 *Embedded Parameters* where the yield to maturity is computed. In this program, we illustrate several ways to pass a function. The GUI is illustrated below.

To illustrate function passing, we highlight the following three types: global to global, global to class member, and class member to class member. We will deploy the latter type, class member to class member. In the header file, the first key insight is that the function's address is passed. The second key insight is that class member functions can be easily passed when they are declared static (see, `static double Multiply(double A, double B);` in the header file excerpts below). Please pay particular attention to the commented portions of the code (following the //) as it decribes exactly which type is being illustrated.

```
#ifndef FRMUnitFunctionPassingH
#define FRMUnitFunctionPassingH
...
// Type 1 function passing declarations (two global functions)
double MathTwo1(double A, double B, double (*funct)(double, double));
double Add(double A, double B);
// Type 2 function passing declarations (global function to class member)
class MATH
{
public:
  double MathTwo(double A, double B, double (*funct)(double, double));
};
double Subtract(double A, double B);
// Type 3 function passing declarations (class member to class member)
class OPERATORS
{
public:
  static double Multiply(double A, double B);
  static double Divide(double A, double B);
  static double Modula(double A, double B);
};
//-----------------------------------------------------------------------
class TFRMUnitTemplateTest : public TForm
{
...
private:  // User declarations
  MATH M;
  OPERATORS O;
  double inputOne;
  double inputTwo;
  double outputOne;
...
#endif
```

Excerpts from the FRMUnitFunctionPassing.cpp file are given below. Note the three types of ways to pass functions. It is preferable to have all functions contained within classes; consequently, type 3 will be our method of choice.

```
...
// Type 1 function passing declarations (two global functions)
double MathTwo1(double A, double B, double (*funct)(double, double)) {
  return funct(A, B);
```

```
}
double Add(double A, double B) {
  return A + B;
}
// Type 2 function passing declarations (global function to class memeber)
double MATH::MathTwo(double A, double B, double (*funct)(double, double)) {
  return funct(A, B);
}
double Subtract(double A, double B) {
  return A - B;
}
// Type 3 function passing declarations (class member to class member)
double OPERATORS::Multiply(double A, double B) {
  return A * B;
}
double OPERATORS::Divide(double A, double B)
{
  return A / B;
}
double OPERATORS::Modula(double A, double B) {
  return (int) A % (int) B;
}
...
void __fastcall TFRMUnitTemplateTest::FRMExecute(void)
{
  double (*mathop)(double, double) = NULL; // Pointer to generic function
  inputOne = StrToFloat(editInputOne->Text); // Convert input text to double
  inputTwo = StrToFloat(editInputTwo->Text);
// Global function to global function
  if (rgMathFunctions->ItemIndex == 0) {
    outputOne = MathTwo1(inputOne,inputTwo, &Add);
// Global function to class member
  } else if (rgMathFunctions->ItemIndex == 1) {
    mathop = &Subtract;
    outputOne = M.MathTwo(inputOne,inputTwo, mathop);
// Class member to class member (note member is declared static
  } else if (rgMathFunctions->ItemIndex == 2) {
    mathop = &OPERATORS::Multiply;
    outputOne = M.MathTwo(inputOne,inputTwo, mathop);
  } else if (rgMathFunctions->ItemIndex == 3) {
    mathop = &OPERATORS::Divide;
    outputOne = M.MathTwo(inputOne,inputTwo, mathop);
  } else {
    mathop = &OPERATORS::Modula;
    outputOne = M.MathTwo(inputOne,inputTwo, mathop);
  }
  editOutputOne->Text = FloatToStrF(outputOne, ffFixed, 10, 4);
  return;
}
```

The ability to pass functions will greatly enhance the flexibility of module development. For example, the method used to compute a bond's yield to maturity is the same as the method used to compute an option's implied volatility although they are obviously different functions (computing the bond price and computing the option price). Therefore, we highlight several different ways to pass functions.

C++ Code: 2.9 Function Passing

Function passing with structures

In this program, we illustrate using a structure to pass a function. The GUI, identical to the previous one, is illustrated below (title is changed only).

We can create one structure that can accommodate the five math functions required for this program. Let us consider a structure called MATHTWO. The way this structure approach works is to pass the two inputs when the structure is called.

```
struct MATHTWO {
   double X;
   double Y;
   MATHTWO(double XX, double YY) : X(XX), Y(YY) {};
   double Add() { return X + Y; }
   double Subtract() { return X - Y; }
   double Multiply() { return X * Y; }
   double Divide() { return X / Y; }
   double Modula() { return (int) X % (int) Y; }
};
```

Consider the following snippet of code. When M is created (termed instantiated), both inputOne and inputTwo are passed into the structure M.

```
inputOne = StrToFloat(editInputOne->Text);
inputTwo = StrToFloat(editInputTwo->Text);
MATHTWO M(inputOne, inputTwo);    // Instantiate M, pass two double
```

Once M contains X (inputOne) and Y (inputTwo), then we can reference the functions within the structure.

```
if (rgMathFunctions->ItemIndex == 0) {
   outputOne = M.Add();
} else if (rgMathFunctions->ItemIndex == 1) {
   outputOne = M.Subtract();
} else if (rgMathFunctions->ItemIndex == 2) {
   outputOne = M.Multiply();
} else if (rgMathFunctions->ItemIndex == 3) {
   outputOne = M.Divide();
} else {
   outputOne = M.Modula();
}
editOutputOne->Text = FloatToStrF(outputOne, ffFixed, 10, 4);
return;
}
```

It is helpful to have many different ways to pass and manipulate functions.

C++ Code: 2.10 Function Passing with Structures

Managing files

One very important capability is the ability to manage data files. This program presents a very simple illustration of reading in data from a text file and outputting the data to another text file. Throughout this material, we will arbitrarily use *.dat to denote an input file and *.prn to denote an output file. Often, within one single program a data file will be both input and output. In those cases, we use the *.prn extension (again, the extension labels are up to the user).

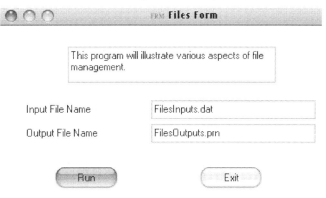

The computer program needs some facility to handle the location of the file, as well as numerous other issues. The inputs for this program are contained in FilesInputs.dat. The data in this file could be the inputs for a Monte Carlo simulation where 1,000 draws from a four dimensional, correlated, normal multivariate random number generator are desired.

```
FRMUnitFiles.cpp    FilesInputs.dat
1  | Input Parameters
·    Draws       Dimensions
·     1000            4
·       Mean        Standard Deviation
–      5.000000        10.000000
·     12.000000        20.000000
·     14.000000        30.000000
·     16.000000        40.000000
·    Correlations
10     1.000000
·     -0.200000     1.000000
·      0.100000     0.300000     1.000000
·      0.200000     0.400000     0.500000     1.000000
```

All this program does, however, is dump these inputs into an output file named FilesOutputs.prn. We inserted the additional text of " but in the output file!" so as to be able to distinguish between the two files.

```
FRMUnitFiles.cpp    FilesOutputs.prn
1  | Input Parameters but in the output file!
·    Draws       Dimensions
·     1000            4
·       Mean        Standard Deviation
···    5.000000        10.000000
·     12.000000        20.000000
·     14.000000        30.000000
·     16.000000        40.000000
·    Correlations
10     1.000000
·     -0.200000     1.000000
·      0.100000     0.300000     1.000000
·      0.200000     0.400000     0.500000     1.000000
```

In the header file, FRMUnitFiles.h, there are just a few items to emphasize. First, as noted at the top of the file, the *.dat file must be in the same subfolder as the *.exe. For simplicity, we manage all the implementation files in our repository, C:\FRMRepository, as well as data files that may have multiple programs that reference them. If you are building each program separately, independent of the repository, then you can place the *.dat file in the root directory as the code comment suggests.[14]

```
/**********************************************************************
**
** NOTE: The location of the executable file, *.exe, matters for this program
** to locate the *.dat files. You can manage the project location at:
**
** >   Project
** >      Options
** >         Directories and Conditionals
** >            Final output directory
** >               ..\2.11 Managing Files\
**
** The ..\ means go back one level and 2.11 Managing Files\ places the *.exe in the
** source root directory. Otherwise it will be in either Debug or Debug_Build and the
** *.dat file must be placed there.
**
**********************************************************************/
```

Every file that is referenced from within the program must be declared. In C++, it is easiest to use the keyword AnsiString.

```
AnsiString sinf, soutf, soutf1;
```

An AnsiString is a dynamically allocated string; hence its size can change. In this context, the AnsiString will hold the input and output file names.

In the source code file, FRMUnitFiles.cpp, there are a few items to highlight. First, notice that the AnsiString sinf is assigned the input file name from the GUI and the AnsiString soutf is assigned the output file name from the GUI. The comments below these lines remind the analyst that the input file must reside in the same subfolder as this program's executable file.

```
sinf = editInputsFileName->Text;
soutf = editOutputsFileName->Text;
// Default: sinf - FilesInputs.dat
//          soutf - FilesOutputs.prn - General outputs
// NOTE: *.exe must reside in same folder as *.dat and
// *.prn output will be in same folder
// > Project > Options > Directories set to C:\FRMRepository
```

Second, a two dimensional matrix of memory can be allocated with the try {...} function that is known as an exception inspection. The catch {...} function is the exception handler that keeps the program from crashing, should an exception be thrown. This type of code is a form of error trapping.

```
double **Correlation;
try {                                   // Allocating memory for A
   Correlation = new double*[10];                  // Set up rows
   for(int j=0; j<10; j++)Correlation[j] = new double [10]; // Set up columns
}
catch (std::bad_alloc) {
   Application->MessageBox(L"Could not allocate memory for matrix Correlation.  Bye ...",
      L"Allocation Error for Matrix Corr[][]", MB_OK);
   exit(-1);
}
```

Third, the input and output file streams are declared, facilitating the management of file data.

---

[14] Managing data files is tricky when you export your executable program to destinations unknown. Recall our focus is prototype code.

```
ifstream inf;    // Define input file stream
ofstream outf;   // Define output file stream
```

Fourth, some care should be taken to insure that the file is not already open (it cannot be in this code).

```
int Error = 20;
char name[256];
Error = inf.is_open();        // Error = 0 if false
```

Fifth, open the input file. Once open, the file pointer is at the start of the file. The next four lines of code just read in the entire file line by line. Once the end of file is reached, the while loop ceases. Just because the file pointer is at the end of the file does not mean the file is closed. It is still open.

```
inf.open(sinf.c_str(), ios::in);  // Open input file stream
while (!inf.eof()) {
   Error = inf.is_open();      // Error = 1 if true (non-zero)
   inf.getline (name,256);
}
Error = inf.is_open();      // File still open even though at end
```

Sixth, usually we are interested in either writing data at the beginning of the file or appending an existing file at the very end. The last line of this code snippet shows how to close a file.

```
inf.seekg(0, ios::end);   // Reset to end of file
inf.seekg(0, ios::beg);   // Reset to beginning of file (needs both for some reason
while (!inf.eof()) {
   Error = inf.is_open();      // File reset and do again
   inf.getline (name,256);
}
Error = inf.is_open();   // File still open
inf.close();
```

Seventh, data is read from files and written to files in a similar manner, as illustrated in the following code. Output file data must be carefully formatted if you want it to be visibly appealing.

```
inf >> NumberofDraws >> NumberofVariables;              // Line 3
```

The next two lines fix the width to be of size 6 and it is right justified. Because NumberofDraws is an integer, the precision is commented out as well as the showing the decimal point. Finally, the floatfield is set to fixed.

```
outf.width(6);  outf.setf(ios::right); //outfFC.precision(6);
outf.setf(ios::fixed, ios::floatfield); //outf.setf(ios::showpoint);
outf << NumberofDraws;
outf.width(10);  outf.setf(ios::right); //outfFC.precision(6);
outf.setf(ios::fixed, ios::floatfield); //outf.setf(ios::showpoint);
outf << NumberofVariables << "\n";
inf >> word[0] >> word[1] >> word[2];          // Line 4
outf << "     " << word[0] << "        " << word[1] << " " << word[2] << "\n";
// Loop reads through the mean an std. dev. in the input file
   for(i=0; i<NumberofVariables; i++){
//Means and standard deviations
     inf >> Mean[i] >> StdDev[i];
```

The next two lines fix the width to be of size 12 and it is right justified. Because Mean[i] is a floating-point variable, the precision is set to 6 decimals on the right hand side and the decimal point is shown. Finally, the floatfield is set to fixed.

```
     outf.width(12);  outf.setf(ios::right); outf.precision(6);
     outf.setf(ios::fixed, ios::floatfield); outf.setf(ios::showpoint);
     outf << Mean[i];
     outf.width(16);  outf.setf(ios::right); outf.precision(6);
     outf.setf(ios::fixed, ios::floatfield); outf.setf(ios::showpoint);
     outf << StdDev[i] << "\n";
   };
   inf >> word[0];                        // Correlation Label
   outf << " " << word[0] << "\n";
//the following loop reads the correlation matrix
   for(i=0; i<NumberofVariables; i++){
```

```
    for(j=0; j<=i; j++){
        inf >> Correlation [i] [j];
//the following line completes the top half of the correlation matrix
        Correlation [j] [i] = Correlation [i][j];
        outf.width(12);  outf.setf(ios::right); outf.precision(6);
        outf.setf(ios::fixed, ios::floatfield); outf.setf(ios::showpoint);
        outf << Correlation[i] [j];
    };
    outf << "\n";
};
inf.close();
outf.close();
}
```

C++ Code: 2.11 Managing Files

Object-oriented programming

Object-oriented programming (OOP) with C++ is typically identified with four characteristics: encapsulation, inheritance, polymorphism, and abstraction. We briefly review each below with emphasis on how they are applied in this book.

Encapsulation

Classes enable C++ to combine data and methods into a single point of reference. This process is known as encapsulation. Clearly, large-scale quantitative projects can be broken down into small parts; classes enable separate objects to perform specific tasks.

Inheritance

One class may inherit the data and methods of another class. This property enables large projects to be built from many smaller component parts, much like modern assembly plants. The following line of code illustrates inheritance:

```
class BONDPRICE : public BRENT
```

In this example, all of the functionality and data contained in BRENT will be fully available in BONDPRICE.

Polymorphism

Poly is derived from an ancient Greek term meaning many. Morph is derived from a Greek term meaning changing shape or form. Thus, polymorphism, in our context with C++, means the ability of the same function (actually any operator) to have many different uses. The following snippet of code illustrates polymorphism:

```
long int FRMToJulian(int Month, int Day, int Year);
long int FRMToJulian(FRMDateMDY DT);
```

These two calendar functions have the same name but receive a different type (and number) of data. The first function receives three integers and returns one long integer, whereas the second function receives one FRMDateMDY and returns one long integer. Thus, the user can pass Month, Day, and Year, or the user can pass a structure containing Month, Day, and Year to the same function.

Abstraction

Abstraction with C++ allows the analyst to hide complex details of a particular implementation from the user. Abstraction is efficiently conducted with classes. Data and methods can be hidden from the user. Thus, the user can focus on what they want to do, whereas the implementer (this is you) can focus on how to do it.

Quality source code

For our purposes, one of the key items to emphasize is efficient code reuse. You want to build objects that can easily be reused in many different applications. For example, the cumulative distribution function of a standard normal distribution, N(d), is widely used in numerous applications in quantitative finance. A quality implementation will build a class that provides a method to compute N(d), and that single class will be used over and over again.

Source code needs to have a unified structure and be well commented so you can return to it five years later and remember what was done. Although tedious, you will appreciate heavy commenting of your code, particularly when you dust it off after many years.

Writing implementation classes with sufficient abstraction is very helpful because you are able to completely redo it without changing the interface. The main reason for this is that, over time, a particular class and its methods may be used in many different applications. Thus, if you change the method, then you have to locate and change every implementation. Polymorphism and quality abstraction can go a long way to avoid having to rewrite multiple applications when the implementation code is upgraded.

A well-written interface will protect the implementation from unanticipated alteration by the user. In this project, we take great effort to make clear the separation between the interface code and the implementation code through the use of a single Execute() function.

Although a bit time consuming, we recommend using longer names for variables as an aid to making them understandable, providing them with some consistency in syntax, and improving their overall organization. It is also helpful to make a list of your variables and to be consistent in the way you name variables because you do not want to have to reference your code constantly.

Summary

One reason for pursuing a working knowledge of C++ is to expand your capacity to express financial quantitative ideas. The approach taken here is to separate the interface code from the implementation code. The financial analyst will be primarily focused on the implementation code. Professional software developers within finance organizations will easily be able to provide quality user interfaces for implementation code.

Variables in C++ must first be declared. We suggest using longer names, primarily for ease of understanding the program, particularly years later when it needs to be modified. In this chapter, we briefly reviewed significant reserved key words as well as important data types. We also briefly reviewed key statements, including if, while, and for. Functions were illustrated as a useful means for organizing statements. Coding complex mathematical expressions requires you to understand operator precedence and associativity, which allows the coder to limit extensive use of parentheses.

Pointers allow reference to a large set of data with a reference to a single address. They also allow easy grouping of data and permit dynamic allocation of memory. Next, we introduced arrays and important introductory issues related to managing data. Classes and structures were contrasted. We will rely heavily on classes in this material as a mechanism for organizing information.

We concluded this chapter with some introductory comments on object-oriented programming and producing quality source code.

Eleven complete programs accompany this chapter, including 2.1 Hello Console Application, 2.2 Hello (Windows), 2.3 Input Real Number, 2.4 Boolean Operators, 2.5 Pointers, 2.6 Functions, 2.7 Error Trapping, 2.8 Templated Class, 2.9 Function Passing, 2.10 Function Passing with Structures, and 2.11 Managing Files.

References

Sutter, Herb and Andrei Alexandrescu, *C++ Coding Standards 101 Rules, Guidelines, and Best Practices* (Upper Saddle River, NJ: Pearson Education, Inc., 2005).

Chapter 3. Financial Risk Management Tools

"Ideas have both antecedents and consequences." Author unknown

Each of the modules in this chapter has its own set of learning objectives, here we just identify those objectives for the introduction, which may be a bit challenging for those unfamiliar with philosophy.

Learning objectives

- Emphasize the importance of understanding finance as a social science
- Realize that quantitative finance rests upon important philosophical foundations
- Understand that important philosophical foundations can be categorized as logic, epistemology, metaphysics, and ethics
- Introduce the notion of warrant and the explain the difference between positivism and particularism

Introduction

In this chapter we review several fundamental methods that are widely used in financial risk management. The objective here is to introduce these methods within the C++ framework as well as help get you comfortable with the way this material will be communicated through the rest of the book. Seven programs are reviewed that address the following issues and topics: managing the calendar, calculating the cumulative distribution function from the standard normal distribution and its inverse, uniform random number generators, ordinary least squares regression, a curve-fitting procedure, numerical data sorting, and solving for embedded functions.

Each of these programs is presented as a separate module. The remainder of the book is presented in this fashion. The advantage of this approach is your ability to skip around and focus solely on those modules most important to you. Clearly, as we move through the material, more advanced materials will be covered. There will be some effort, however, to make each module stand alone. After providing some introductory comments on each module, we work our way through the modules highlighting new C++ features and /or quantitative finance concepts. Another advantage of this modular approach is your ability to find the source code within the materials you downloaded from the website.

Prior to diving into the technical material, we introduce some philosophical foundations of quantitative finance. Warning: The material that follows in this introduction is rather dense and tough to follow for someone with minimal prior exposure. After decades of industry consulting, however, I view this content as vital to a financial analyst's ultimate success.

Quantitative finance and social sciences

Quantitative finance falls within the realm of social science and not physical science.

For example, to provide quantitative support for a large, complex option trading firm, a clear understanding of the social science nature of this activity is vital. Physical science quantitative work can focus on "stock" solutions: once well tested in the lab, they will always hold. Social science quantitative work is distinctly different in that human behavior and human understanding can change rapidly; hence, the very structure of the quantitative problem changes. Security and derivative prices are inherently influenced by market participants' views. These views incorporate beliefs about future trends, beliefs about future opportunities and disasters, and even beliefs about potential future valuation models.

Because of the social science nature of the options business, a quants focus is expected to be on developing trading infrastructure that can adapt quickly to paradigm shifts in human understanding of pricing and human preferences for products. Hence, a quant should always place high value on scalability and interchangeability. A firm needs to be able to manage rapid expansions and contractions in business, as well as be able to manage rapid changes in solution technologies that work.

For example, as option markets consist of people, option models need to reflect the present driving forces motivating the trading behavior of people. Because this activity falls more in the realm of social science than physical science, an option model's usefulness will depend upon a particular market and a particular season of time, often short, in which the model will be deployed.

Thus, the value of a financial organization depends upon an infrastructure that results in a continuous flow of innovations to models, as well as numerous other complex infrastructure issues, such as computational speed and sophisticated data management, as opposed to a singular quantitative model.

The development of financial innovations typically requires the interplay between theoretical models and empirical data. It is difficult to develop useful models without access to high quality market data. The mere existence of high quality market data does not result in the development of useful models. To have a chance of developing useful models in financial markets, there must to be the interplay of researchers with high quantitative skills and practitioners with a deep understanding of markets. Both are usually required.

Philosophical foundations of quantitative finance

Thesis: Financial risk management will be improved when finance professionals better understand the basic philosophical foundations upon which this profession rests.

From doing expert testimony work to deciding which quantitative model to deploy on a trading floor, philosophical decisions are constantly present. For example, it is vital for an expert witness to provide independent analysis, which often leads to challenging moral issues. Also, how does one decide when a firm's transaction fails to qualify as a "bona fide hedge" according to the Dodd-Frank Act? We return to this question later in this introduction.

A philosophical worldview is a set of key propositions, usually foundational, that one believes. In the context here, philosophical worldview means a perspective based on an ordered set of key propositions that govern all aspects of life. The word "worldview" is derived from a German word, Weltanschauung meaning wide world perspective; specifically, from Welt (world) and anschauung (perspective).

These key propositions tend to be presuppositions and core assumptions, as opposed to the particular decision-making process taken for a particular task. Presuppositions are implicit assumptions about the world in order for it to make sense.

The decision-making process means any method of assessing the 'correctness' of a particular 'idea' within a particular worldview. Ideas, or more precisely, propositions are essentially truth claims. For example, one proposition is "Option prices reflect all publicly available information." Whether or not this proposition is deemed 'valid' will depend on both the particular decision-making process deployed as well as the philosophical worldview.

The philosophical worldview always precedes the decision-making process. The biggest influence on how decisions are made is often not the decision-making process, rather the philosophical worldview. This is particularly true in financial risk management.

Little 'Ideas'

One way to clarify the approach taken here is to consider how an individual assesses an 'idea.' Specific 'ideas' arrive from many sources: data services (Bloomberg), visual media (TV), audio media (Radio), newspapers, books, conferences, podcasts, friends, and so forth. With limited time and resources, how does one decide which 'ideas' warrant further consideration and which 'ideas' get trashed right away? The ability to quickly toss out time consuming 'ideas' before expending resources on them is a legitimate way to save precious resources.

The philosophical worldview *always* precedes the decision-making process. The biggest influence on how decisions are made is often not the decision-making process, but rather the philosophical worldview.

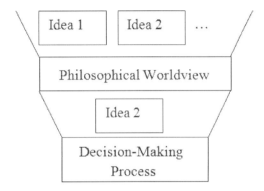

There are two key questions every 'idea' must answer for the financial analyst to be warranted in incorporating the new 'idea' into one's intellectual arsenal.

For the philosophical worldview screen, one should ask, "Is the 'idea' *coherent* within the worldview?"

For the decision-making process screen, one should ask, "Does the 'idea' *correspond* to reality?"

Philosophical foundations are based on logic, epistemology, metaphysics, and ethics.

Logic

Logic is the study of the rules of reasoning. The goal of logic is to reach a conclusion, specifically to improve one's ability to form good arguments as well as critically evaluate others' arguments. For example, the law of noncontradiction is widely held by financial analysts. Specifically, some "idea" P cannot be both true and false in the same sense at the same time.

Epistemology

Epistemology addresses how we know reality. Epistemology represents philosophical positions related to the nature of knowledge, specifically the branch of philosophy that studies knowledge. For many financial issues, it is just as important to know how we know what we know as what we know.

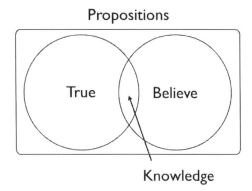

Propositions

Knowledge

Consider the figure nearby: Propositions contain the complete feasible set of 'ideas.' Assume True is a subset of propositional knowledge where the proposition is in fact true. Assume Believe is also a subset of propositional knowledge where a particular analyst in fact believes the proposition. Therefore, one definition of knowledge is the subset containing the intersection of True and Believe where there is warrant or justification. Unfortunately, as with most philosophical issues, it is not quite that simple.

Correspondence theory of truth

Consider two concepts, the truth-bearer and the truth-maker.

Truth-bearer denotes propositions that are either true or false. For example, as of today the S&P 500 index is up this calendar year.

Truth-maker is the reality or the states of affairs, that is, the facts. For example, as of today the S&P 500 index is 50 points higher since the beginning of the year.

When the truth-maker corresponds with the truth-bearer, we say truth obtains. Correspondence refers to a notion that there is a relation between a proposition (truth-bearer) and the state of affairs (truth maker) that is its intentional object. Truth is grounded in intentionality. While evidence is truth-conducive, it is not the same thing as truth itself.

Metaphysics

Metaphysics is the study of what we know about reality. That is, the philosophical study of the nature of being and the ultimate categories or kinds of things that are real. Quantitative finance relies heavily on metaphysics as finance involves 'ideas' and not physical objects. For example, consider the following quotes:

In his 1938 path-breaking work, Frederick R. Macaulay notes, "The concept of 'pure' or 'riskless' interest is metaphysical. The practical contrast is not between 'pure' and 'impure' but between 'promised' or 'expected' and 'actual' or 'realized.'" (See *Some theoretical problems suggested by the movements of interest rates, bond yields and stock prices in the United States since 1856*, NBER, p. 38.)

Jeffery M. Lipshaw concludes, "So, economics is a *science* in the logical positivist tradition. It ought not try to speculate why things are happening in a metaphysical sense, but simply to explain or predict regularities." (See "The Epistemology of the Financial Crisis: Complexity, Causation, Law, and Judgment," *Southern California Interdisciplinary Law Journal*, Vol. 19, 2009, p. 31.)

For many, the realm of metaphysics is denied. Therefore, before proceeding we introduce one important philosophical question.

Do abstract entities exist?

One metaphysical debate is whether abstract entities even exist. Milton Friedman in the 1950s and 1960s successfully advocated for taking the logical positivist approach to economics: "Positive economics is in principle independent of any particular ethical position or normative judgments. As

Keynes says, it deals with 'what is,' not with 'what ought to be.' Its task is to provide a system of generalizations that can be used to make correct predictions about the consequences of any change in circumstances." (See "The Methodology of Positive Economics," *Essays in Positive Economics*, 1966.) Thus, Friedman was one of the pioneers in migrating the economics profession away from the normative (what ought to be) to the positive (what is). Normative propositions fall within the category of abstract entities. Thus, as a practicing financial analysts one must decide whether abstract entities, such as integrity, actually exist.

Consider the following logical approach to this question.

EITHER {P: "Abstract entities exist"} OR ¬P: {"Abstract entities do not exist"}

Based on the law of noncontradiction, either P or ¬P is true, P and ¬P cannot both be true.

Consider a more detailed illustration with the following definitions:

(U) Universe – "total spatiotemporal system of matter and (impersonal) energy, that is, as the sum total of material objects, in some way accessible to the senses and to scientific investigation."

(A) Abstract objects – "immaterial (i.e., nonphysical) entities that do not exist inside space and time; instead they are timeless and spaceless." (Moreland and Craig, 2003)

Consider the following two symbolic expressions:

$x \in U$ (x is an element of U)

$x \notin U \Rightarrow x \in A$ (x is not an element of U implies x is an element of A)

If $x \in U$, then one can address where x is in space and when x is in time.

If $x \notin U \Rightarrow x \in A$, then one addressing where x is in space and when x is in time is incoherent.

x = {atoms, mountains, planes, stock certificate, mortgage document, plastic credit card}, $x \in U$

y = {properties (e.g., color, goodness), relations (e.g., greater than, father of), sets (e.g., {1, 2, 3, 4, 5}), numbers (e.g., 1, 2, 3), and propositions (e.g., grass is green)}, $y \in A$

(W) World – "sum total of everything whatever that exists including nonspatiotemporal abstract entities as well as the spatiotemporal universe of physical entities." (Moreland and Craig, 2003)

Based on logic, we can represent this issue with the following symbols (recall {P: "Abstract entities exist"}):

P v ¬P <=> W v U <=> (U & A) v U

where v denotes "or," <=> denotes "if and only if," and "&" denotes "and."

Ethics

"(T)he study of what is right and what is wrong. Epistemology is concerned with the *true*, and ontology is with the *real*, but ethics with the *good*."[15] "Ethics can be understood as the philosophical study of morality, which is concerned with our beliefs and judgments regarding right and wrong motives, attitudes, character and conduct."[16] For example, in finance, not everything that has value is priced and not everything that has a price is valuable. Integrity has value, but is not priced. Crime, such as insider trading, often has a price, but is not valuable.

---

[15] Geisler and Feinberg, page 353.
[16] Moreland and Craig, page 393.

Warrant

Before leaving the philosophical foundations discussion, we introduce the notion of warrant using a rather analytical approach. Consider the following definition:

$$\exists W_{i,t} \equiv \left\{ \forall p_j \ni \left(p_j \in W_{i,t} \right) \Leftrightarrow Ind_{i,t} \ni w_{i,t} \succ Warranted \right\} \subset K_{i,t}$$

This definition can be read as follows: There exists ($\exists$) a very small subset ($\subset$) of knowledge $K_{i,t}$, denoted $W_{i,t}$, of propositions individual i has warrant at time t. For all ($\forall$) propositions p_j such that ($\ni$) p_j is an element ($\in$) of the set $W_{i,t}$ if and only if ($\Leftrightarrow$) for a particular individual at a particular point in time ($Ind_{i,t}$) a particular proposition ($w_{i,t}$) is contained in ($\succ$) the set of propositions that are warranted.

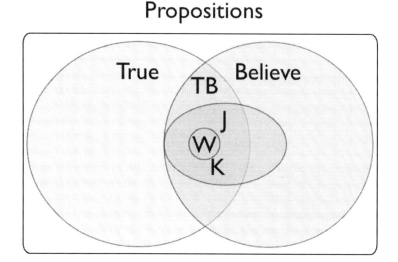

Propositions

Knowledge is a subset of propositions that are both true and believed where there is also justification. Justification implies "one has sufficient evidence for the belief, one formed and maintained the belief in a reliable way ... or one's intellectual and sensory faculties were functioning properly in a good intellectual environment when he formed the belief in question." (Moreland and Craig, 74) In this setup, we allow for the possibility that a justified belief is in fact false, whereas knowledge represents a justified belief that is also true.

The warrant property could be time variant and individual variant. The warrant property is also binary, hence, either $p_j\left(k_{i,t,j} \succ True \wedge w_j \succ True \right) \equiv p_j\left(w_{i,t,j} \right)$ or

$$p_j\left(\left\{ k_{i,t,j} \succ True \wedge w_j \succ \neg True \right\} \vee \left\{ k_{i,t,j} \succ \neg True \wedge w_j \succ \neg True \right\} \vee \left\{ k_{i,t,j} \succ \neg True \wedge w_j \succ True \right\} \right) \equiv p_j\left(\neg w_{i,t,j} \right)$$

where "$\wedge$" denotes "and" and "$\vee$" denotes "or."

Warrant can be identified as "the belief was formed by cognitive faculties that are functioning properly and in accordance with a good design plan in a cognitive environment appropriate for the way those faculties were designed and when the design plan for our faculties is aimed at obtaining truth." (Moreland and Craig, p. 103) As used here, warranted knowledge is often "properly basic," such as the law of noncontradiction that does not have direct justification. Other examples of warranted knowledge include propositions such as, "other people have minds," "abstract objects exist," "integrity exists," and so forth.

One way to categorize various philosophical worldviews is either to be along the line of a particularist epistemology or along the line of a positivist epistemology. Without going into great detail, these two categories of worldviews can analytically be expressed as follows:

$$\exists W_{i,t} \equiv \left\{ \forall p_j \ni \left(p_j \in W_{i,t} \right) \Leftrightarrow Ind_{i,t} \ni w_{i,t} \succ Warranted \right\} = \left\{ \neg \varnothing \right\} \text{ Particularist epistemology}$$

$$\exists W_{i,t} \equiv \left\{ \forall p_j \ni \left(p_j \in W_{i,t} \right) \Leftrightarrow Ind_{i,t} \ni w_{i,t} \succ Warranted \right\} = \left\{ \varnothing \right\} \text{ Positivism}$$

In this framework, warrant is a very small subset of knowledge. We now provide one illustrate of why understanding the philosophical foundations of quantitative finance is important.

Philosophy and finance illustration

When the risk management mission of a corporation is poorly defined, the corporation's stakeholders ultimately suffer. Without at least some minimal ethics viewpoint combined with financial performance benchmarks clearly defined in advance, the notion of hedging will remain meaningless.

Like many regulations related to hedging, consider the 2010 Dodd-Frank Act. "Risk-mitigating hedging activities in connection with and related to individual or aggregated positions, contracts, or other holdings of a banking entity that are designed to reduce the specific risks to the banking entity in connection with and related to such positions, contracts, or other holdings" are permitted and hence referred to as a bona fide hedge in the Act. Bona fide (Latin – with good faith) in this Act appears to imply a lack of deceit.

Based on the prevailing philosophical worldview held by financial market participants today, almost any transaction will qualify as a bona fide hedge within existing regulations because of nebulous definitions, such as the one found in the Dodd-Frank Act. Thus, it should come as no surprise that J.P. Morgan's multi-billion dollar speculative transactions gone awry in 2012 were made in the risk management group and would likely be classified as a bona fide hedge under the Act.

Although finance, like many other social sciences, is ultimately metaphysical (that is, transcending the physical), most academic finance professors have now taken the logical positivist approach together with many practitioners in our profession. One unfortunate consequence of the logical positivist worldview is that ethics, and for that matter metaphysics, is meaningless because it is non-physical in flavor.

Until we restore the metaphysical foundations at the core of our profession, concepts like "risk," "volatility," "interest rates," and even "hedging" will be ill defined. And clearly what is ill defined will remain poorly managed. In this context, the metaphysical foundations provide the rational basis for a particular ethical viewpoint.

As an illustration of the gravity of this lack of any metaphysical foundation within modern finance, just consider applications of hedging concepts. From the logical positivist perspective, most derivatives transactions cannot really be justified as either a "bona fide hedge" or not. Recall that the logical positivist's worldview renders ethical concepts like "deceit" and "good faith" meaningless.

Most firms have hundreds of positions with exposures to numerous market risks. These same firms have multiple stakeholders with different goals and objectives. There is no requirement in the Act, or for that matter in any other related regulations, for a financial performance benchmark to be clearly defined in advance. Therefore, almost any financial derivatives transaction can be deemed a "bona fide hedge" in the logical positivist tradition. All one must do is identify some existing exposure in the firm with the appropriate empirical correlation and voila, a derivatives transaction is a "bona fide hedge." But from almost any normative framework, such as the CFA Institute's Code of Ethics and Standards of Practice, many financial derivatives transactions today do not pass as a "bona fide hedge;" they would be deemed deceitful and in bad faith.

For students of the human condition, it would come as no surprise that corporate executives today assert that the activities of their traders are "bona fide hedges" in the Dodd-Frank Act sense. If these traders, however, were asked to justify their hedging transactions to their aging parents, they would struggle to do so without blushing (of course, assuming blushing was still a possibility for the traders).

Without the merest normative ethical framework justifying the corporation's existence, hedging will remain a vacuous concept. It is impossible to determine whether the corporation is on course or not without any preconceived and clearly stated risk management benchmarks.

We now turn to important financial risk management tools developed in C++. Note that these financial risk management tools are always first metaphysical in nature – just an idea. For example, the cumulative distribution function is merely an abstraction that has been implemented mathematically. We provide the C++ code to take the mathematical representations into machine language. Whether anything in finance actually adheres to this probability distribution is unlikely, but approximations of this nature assist in improving the decisions made by financial managers.

References

Friedman, Milton, "The Methodology of Positive Economics," *Essays in Positive Economics*, 1966.

Geisler, Norman L. and Paul D Feinberg, *Introduction to Philosophy A Christian Perspective* (Grand Rapids, MI: Baker Academic, 1980).

Lipshaw, Jeffery M., "The Epistemology of the Financial Crisis: Complexity, Causation, Law, and Judgment," *Southern California Interdisciplinary Law Journal*, Vol. 19, 2009.

Moreland, J. P. and William Lane Craig, *Philosophical Foundations for a Christian Worldview* (Downers Grove, IL: InterVarsity Press, 2003).

Macaulay, Frederick R., *Some theoretical problems suggested by the movements of interest rates, bond yields and stock prices in the United States since 1856*, NBER.

Module 3.1: Managing the Calendar

Learning objectives

- Explain how to manage calendar dates in C++
- Contrast the 30/360 day count method with the ACT/365 day count method
- Explain day counting with each date having separate, sequential integer value
- Use struct to manage data
- Illustrate passing structures within functions
- Introduce function overloading
- Review implementation code FRMCalendar.cpp (.h)

See program FRMCalendarTest in *3.1 Managing the Calendar*.

Module overview

The interface code is found in FRMUnitCalendar.cpp (*.h), and the implementation code is found in the repository named FRMCalendar.cpp (*.h). Recall throughout this material, we separate the interface code from the implementation code for a variety of reasons, including ease of code reuse, portability to other C++ compilers and platforms, and multiple implementations of a particular quantitative method. The naming convention will be FRMUnit*.* for interface code and FRM*.* for implementation code. The interface code (FRMUnit*.*) will be in the book subdirectory whereas the implementation code (FRM*.*) will be in the repository.

Investments can be defined as the reallocation of consumption through time. Time is easy to describe in quantitative finance books, but there are several complexities that arise. The philosophical issues related to time are set aside here: the focus is on calculating the number of days between two dates by two methods.

Central to most finance calculations is the movement of money through time. For example, to compute the present value or future value, you need to know the length of the period for the computation. There are numerous different approaches for calculating the number of days between two dates and there are numerous different approaches for calculating the total number of days in a single year. Often, one wants to compute the fraction of the year.

For bonds, this day count is used to compute the number of days in accrued interest and the number of days in a coupon period. For financial derivatives, the method of counting days has an important influence on some derivative instrument's valuation.

Meticulously accounting for day count and payment frequency is very important. For example, consider a 5 percent rate environment and quarterly pay interest rate swap with $100,000,000 notional amount and 10 year term. If the fixed leg of the swap is actual days divided by 360 day year and the floating leg of the swap is 30 day months divided by 365 day year, then over $1,500,000 of swap value is attributable to just day counting differences (see Module 5.8).

Two popular day types are referred to as "ACT/365" and "30/360". Understanding these two basic types will be foundational in understanding all of the other types.

Day type ACT/365

Intuitively, this method is fairly easy to grasp. You compute the literal number of days between two dates. To arrive at the fraction of a year, you divide by 365 (that is, ignore leap year).

Counting days is rather tedious and most software packages contain modules to take care of day counting computation for you. These modules typically use the 'Julian' date method. The Julian method converts each day to an integer and the difference between these integers gives you the correct day count.

Day type 30/360

This day counting convention is much less intuitive. The general assumption is that each month has 30 days and hence a year has 360. Obviously, this is not the case and so some adjustments are incorporated. We adopt the following notation:

M1 -- month of first date   M2 -- month of second date

D1 -- day of first date   D2 -- day of second date

Y1 -- year of first date   Y2 -- year of second date

The following adjustments are required:

1. If D1 and D2 are the last day of February (leap year - 29, non-leap year - 28), then change D2 to 30.
2. If D1 is the last day of February, then change D1 to 30.
3. If D1 is 30 or 31 and D2 is 31, then change D2 to 30.
4. If D1 is 31, then change D1 to 30.

After these adjustments, the number of days between two dates is

Day Count $= (Y2 - Y1) * 360 + (M2 - M1) * 30 + (D2 - D1)$

For example, assume the first date is September 11, 2015 and the second date is December 15, 2015. No adjustments are required and the number of days is

Day Count $= (2015 - 2015) * 360 + (12 - 9) * 30 + (15 - 11) = 94$

Several additional points must be remembered. First, the number of days in the year is always 360 regardless of whether it is a leap year or not. Second, the number of days in a period is always 360 divided by the number of periods in a year. For example, if a bond pays quarterly, then the number of days in a quarter is $360/4 = 90$. Third, the day count procedure is used to compute accrued interest within a period. Hence, the remaining days in a period is just the number of days in the period minus the number of days that have accrued. This point will be covered in more detail when we discuss interest calculations.

Other day types

A vast number of other day types and day counting conventions exist. Here are just a few:

ACT/ACT

This day type requires the actual number of days be computed for the period as well as the accrual days. Hence, a leap year would make a difference.

ACT/360

This day type requires the actual number of days be computed for the accrual period but assumes a 360 day year. Eurodollar futures contracts use this method.

30/ACT

This day type requires the actual number of days be computed for the entire period, but the accrual period is computed using the 30/360 method.

30/365

This day type requires the 30/360 method for the accrual period but assumes a 365 day year.

End-of-month rule

Almost all debt securities maturing at the end of the month followed what is called the end-of-month rule. For example, if a U.S. Treasury security matures on June 30th and is semi-annual coupon paying, then the other coupon date is December *31st*. Some securities issued by the Federal Home Loan Bank do not follow the end-of-month rule. For these securities, if they are semi-annual coupon paying and they mature on June 30th, then the other coupon date is December 30th.

Implementation code comments

FRMCalendar.h

```
/*********************************************************************
** LOCATION
**   c:\FRMRepository\FRMCalendar.cpp
** DESCRIPTION
**   Number of days between two dates under 30/360 day count method
**   int FRMCALENDAR::FRMDayCount30360(int Month1, int Day1, int Year1,
**      int Month2, int Day2, int Year2)
**   int FRMCALENDAR::FRMDayCount30360(DateMDY Date1, DateMDY Date2)
**   Convert calendar date to Julian
**   long int FRMToJulian(int Month, int Day, int Year);
**   long int FRMToJulian(FRMDateMDY DT);        // Example of function over-riding
**   Convert Julian number to calendar date
**   struct FRMDateMDY FRMFromJulian(long int j);
**   Identify day of the week where Sunday = 0
**   int FRMWeekDay(long int j);
**   int FRMFromJulianMonth(long int j);
**   int FRMFromJulianDay(long int j);
**   int FRMFromJulianYear(long int j);
**********************************************************************/
```

The implementation code's header file should contain an extensive description of the methods contained within the class. This will prove very helpful when reviewing code you have not considered for quite some time.

```
...
struct FRMDateMDY
{
  int Month;
  int Day;
  int Year;
};
```

Structures are very useful mechanisms for gathering data and methods in one location.

```
class FRMCALENDAR
{
public:
  int FRMDayCount30360(int Month1, int Day1, int Year1,
                       int Month2, int Day2, int Year2);
  int FRMDayCount30360(FRMDateMDY Date1, FRMDateMDY Date2);
```

The method FRMDayCount30360() illustrates polymorphism; that is, the same method name respresents two separate functions. The compiler can distinguish between the two based on the number and order of data types. The first method computes the number of days based on a 30/360 count when the user passes two months (Month1 and Month2), two days (Day1 and Day2), and two years (Year1 and Year2). The second method computes the the number of days based on a 30/360 count when the user passes two dates (Date1 and Date2).

```
  long int FRMToJulian(int Month, int Day, int Year);
  long int FRMToJulian(FRMDateMDY DT);        // Example of function over-riding
  struct FRMDateMDY FRMFromJulian(long int j);
```

Notice that functions can return a structure.

```
  int FRMWeekDay(long int j);
  int FRMFromJulianMonth(long int j);
```

```
   int FRMFromJulianDay(long int j);
   int FRMFromJulianYear(long int j);
};
#endif
```

Notice that Julian numbers are declared long int because the number is very large.

```
/******************************************************************
** REFERENCES
**   Jan Mayle, _Standard Securities Calculation Methods Fixed Income
**   Securities Formulas for Price, Yield, and Accrued Interest_ Volume I
**   Third Edition (New York: Securities Industry Association, 1993).
**   Source for Julian method lost.
******************************************************************/
```

It is important to document your sources somewhere. For example, the Julian date counter used here cannot now be found because we failed to document it. If you happen to know to whom to attribute this approach, please let us know and we will change it.

FRMCalendar.cpp

```
...
#include "FRMCalendar.h"
int FRMCALENDAR::FRMDayCount30360(FRMDateMDY Date1, FRMDateMDY Date2)
{
  int M1, D1, Y1, M2, D2, Y2;
  M1 = Date1.Month;
  D1 = Date1.Day;
  Y1 = Date1.Year;
  M2 = Date2.Month;
  D2 = Date2.Day;
  Y2 = Date2.Year;
  return(FRMDayCount30360(M1, D1, Y1, M2, D2, Y2));
};
```

The above method just brings in two structures containing three data elements each and then passes these six data elements to the 30/360 day counter method.

```
int FRMCALENDAR::FRMDayCount30360(int Month1, int Day1, int Year1,
  int Month2, int Day2, int Year2)
{
  int RY14, RY1400, RY24, RY2400;
  RY14 = Year1 % 4;        // Remainder of Year 1 for every 4 years
  RY1400 = Year1 % 400;    // Remainder of Year 1 for every 400 years
  RY24 = Year2 % 4;        // Remainder of Year 2 for every 4 years
  RY2400 = Year2 % 400;    // Remainder of Year 2 for every 400 years
  if(Month1 == 2 && Month2 == 2){  // Both months are February
    if(RY14 == 0 && RY1400 != 0){  // Year 1 is a leap year
      if(RY24 == 0 && RY2400 != 0){  // Year 2 is a leap year
        if(Day1 == 29 && Day2 == 29)Day2 = 30;
      } else {                  // Year 2 is not a leap year
        if(Day1 == 29 && Day2 == 28)Day2 = 30;
      }
    } else {                     // Year 1 is not a leap year
      if(RY24 == 0 && RY2400 != 0){  // Year 2 is a leap year
        if(Day1 == 28 && Day2 == 29)Day2 = 30;
      } else {                  // Year 2 is not a leap year
        if(Day1 == 28 && Day2 == 28)Day2 = 30;
      }
    }
  }
  if(Month1 == 2){
    if(RY14 == 0 && RY1400 != 0){
      if(Day1 == 29)Day1 = 30;
    } else {
      if(Day1 == 28)Day1 = 30;
    }
  } else {
    if((Day1 == 30 || Day1 == 31) && (Day2 == 31))Day2 = 30;
    if(Day1 == 31) Day1 = 30;
```

```
  }
  return((Year2 - Year1)*360 + (Month2 - Month1)*30 + (Day2 - Day1));
};
```

The algorithm above is based on Mayle's book. Since this implementation code is in the FRM Repository, you can utilize it or the other day counting methods when you need to count days for financial valuation problems.

```
long int FRMCALENDAR::FRMToJulian(FRMDateMDY DT)
{
  int M, D, Y;
  M = DT.Month;
  D = DT.Day;
  Y = DT.Year;
// Pass data to FRMToJulian(int,int,int) and returns its Julian value
  return(FRMToJulian(M, D, Y));
};


long int FRMCALENDAR::FRMToJulian(int mon, int day, int year)
{
  int a, b;
  if(year < 50) year += 2000;
  if(year < 100) year += 1900;
  if(mon > 2){
    mon -= 3;
  } else {
    mon += 9;
    year -= 1;
  }
  a = year/100;
  b = year - (100*a);
  return( (146097*(long int)a)/4 + (long int)day +
     (1461*(long int)b)/4 + 1721119 + (153*(long int)mon+2)/5);
};
```

Notice the crude year adjustment, a classic source of potential error. Although mon, day, and year are integers, Julian's size requires it to be long int.

```
struct FRMDateMDY FRMCALENDAR::FRMFromJulian(long int j)
{
  FRMDateMDY Date;
  long int m;
  long int d;
  long int y;
  long int c;
  long int tmpm;
  tmpm = j - 1721119;
  y = (4*tmpm-1) / 146097;
  tmpm = 4*tmpm - 1 - 146097*y;
  d = tmpm / 4;
  tmpm = (4 * d + 3) / 1461;
  d = 4*d + 3 - 1461*tmpm;
  d = (d + 4)/4;
  m = (5*d-3)/153;
  d = 5*d - 3 - 153*m;
  d = (d+5)/5;
  y = 100*y + tmpm;
  if(m < 10){
    m += 3;
  } else {
    m -= 9;
    y += 1;
  }
  c = y/100;
  y = y - (c*100);
  y = c*100 + y;
  Date.Month = (int) m;
  Date.Day = (int) d;
  Date.Year = (int) y;
  return(Date);
```

```
};
```

Notice that the return for this function is a structure, hence, at the end we fill in all the appropriate data elements.

```
int FRMCALENDAR::FRMWeekDay(long int j)
{
  return((j+1) % 7);  // % returns the remainder of integer division, 0-6
};
```

Modula (the remainder) is a convenient way to establish the day of the week.

```
int FRMCALENDAR::FRMFromJulianMonth(long int j)
{
  FRMDateMDY Date;
  Date = FRMFromJulian(j);
  return(Date.Month);  // Returns only month of Julian number
};
...
```

Several other calendar functions could be developed.

References

Mayle, Jan, *Standard Securities Calculation Methods Fixed Income Securities Formulas for Price, Yield, and Accrued Interest* Volume I, Third Edition (New York: Securities Industry Association, 1993).

Appendix 3.1: Interface code comments

The FRMCalendarTest program interface is illustrated below. We see that over the 20-year period from 1/1/2000 to 1/1/2020 there are 7,305 calendar days. There are typically 365 days per year except leap year where there are 366. The leap years during this 20-year period are 2000, 2004, 2008, 2012, and 2016. Typically, century years are not leap years, except when divisible by 4. Using a 360-day counting methodology, we have 7,200 days. This program divides by 365, hence the number of years is slightly greater than 20 because of the effect of leap years.

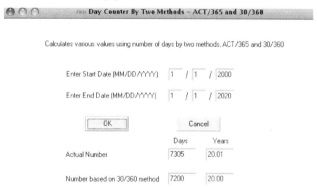

The following are excerpts from the interface header code with selected comments added. When you are looking at and using code in the repository remember to pay particular attention to the comment lines as they should be able to help you discern exactly what is goin on.

FRMUnitCalendar.h

```
#ifndef FRMUnitCalendarH
#define FRMUnitCalendarH
```

Remember that header files should contain the preprocessor conditional statement to avoid multiple definitions.

...

```
#include "c:\FRMRepository\FRMCalendar.cpp"
```

All implementation code is warehoused in the repository. Thus, the calendar implementation code can be used in a wide array of programs and we only have to maintain one copy.

```
...
private:  // User declarations
  FRMCALENDAR Calendar;
  long int JulianStartDate, JulianEndDate;
  int InputStartDay, InputStartMonth, InputStartYear;
  int InputEndDay, InputEndMonth, InputEndYear;
  int Days;
...
```

User-defined classes will be in all-caps, such as FRMCALENDAR. An instance of this class, called Calendar, will be referenced in the interface code. This line of code is what is known as the instantiation of the class. Once a class is instantiated correctly, you can type Calendar. in the interface code and call any of the methods in the class.

The following are excerpts from the interface code with selected comments added.

FRMUnitCalendar.cpp

```
...
#include <time.h>
```

The compiler's header file, time.h, provides the function for pulling the current date from the computer's operating system.

```
...
#include "FRMUnitCalendar.h"
```

Remember to always include the corresponding header file.

```
...
__fastcall TCalendarForm::TCalendarForm(TComponent* Owner)
    : TForm(Owner)
{
  Reset();
}
```

The method above is known as the constructor and is run when the class is first instantiated. Reset() is a user-defined method that places the appropriate data in the form.

```
...
void __fastcall TCalendarForm::btnOKClick(TObject *Sender)
{
  FRMExecute();
}
```

For the purpose of separating the interface code from the implementation code, we arbitrarily use the FRMExecute() function as the sole place where the interface code interacts with the implementation code.

```
//-------------------------------------------------------------------
void __fastcall TCalendarForm::Reset(void)
{
  char tmpbuf[128];        // Copy current date to tmpbuf
  _strdate(tmpbuf);
  int CurrentMonth, CurrentDay, CurrentYear;
  CurrentMonth = atoi(&tmpbuf[0]);
  CurrentDay = atoi(&tmpbuf[3]);
  CurrentYear = atoi(&tmpbuf[6]);
  CurrentYear += 2000;
```

The Reset() method is the user-defined method reset which will set default data into the form. These data are what the user will see when the form is opened prior to changing any of the inputs.

The current date is extracted from the temporary buffer.

```
...
}
//-----------------------------------------------------------------
void __fastcall TCalendarForm::SetLocalData(void)
{
  InputStartDay = StrToInt(editStartDay->Text);
  InputStartMonth = StrToInt(editStartMonth->Text);
  InputStartYear = StrToInt(editStartYear->Text);
  InputEndDay = StrToInt(editEndDay->Text);
  InputEndMonth = StrToInt(editEndMonth->Text);
  InputEndYear = StrToInt(editEndYear->Text);
}
```

The method SetLocalData() is a useful mechanism to collect all the user inputs in one location. If extensive error trapping is required, this would be a good place to do it.

```
//-----------------------------------------------------------------
void __fastcall TCalendarForm::FRMExecute(void)
{
  SetLocalData(); // Make sure to grab latest user inputs
  JulianStartDate = Calendar.FRMToJulian(InputStartMonth, InputStartDay, InputStartYear);
  JulianEndDate = Calendar.FRMToJulian(InputEndMonth, InputEndDay, InputEndYear);
```

The first line of the FRMExecute() method should always call the SetLocalData() method which insures that the latest user inputs are obtained from the form and appropriately passed by the methods in the execute function or passed to the implementation file in more complex programs. The next lines of code pass the month, day and year to the FRMToJulian() method within the FRMCALENDAR class and return the Julian number. Note that when you want to use one of the methods in the FRMCALENDAR class, you type the instance of the class (Calendar.) and then the particular method you wish to use.

```
  Days = abs(JulianEndDate - JulianStartDate); // Number of actual days
...
// 30/360 day counter
  Days = abs(Calendar.FRMDayCount30360(InputStartMonth, InputStartDay, InputStartYear,
    InputEndMonth, InputEndDay, InputEndYear)); // Number of 30/360 days
...
```

Compute the absolute value of the difference between two dates using the 30/360 day counting convention.

```
  int M, D, Y, W; // Month, Day, Year, Weekday illustrated but not used here
```

Other miscellaneous methods that could be useful in various projects.

```
  M = Calendar.FRMFromJulianMonth(JulianEndDate);
  D = Calendar.FRMFromJulianDay(JulianEndDate);
  Y = Calendar.FRMFromJulianYear(JulianEndDate);
  W = Calendar.FRMWeekDay(JulianEndDate);
}
```

Module 3.2. Cumulative Normal Distribution Function and its Inverse

Learning objectives

- Explain how to compute the cumulative distribution function of the normal distribution as well as its inverse in C++
- Understand one solution approximation for N(d) and N^{-1}(d)
- Explore new uses of preprocessor directives
- Illustrate the deployment of several math functions contained in <math.h>
- Introduce an iterative test routine for functions and their inverses
- Review implementation code FRMCDF.cpp (.h)

See program FRMCDFTest in *3.2 CDF and Inverse CDF*.

Module overview

The interface code is found in FRMUnitCDF.cpp (*.h) and the implementation code is found in the repository named FRMCDF.cpp (*.h).

Many option valuation models rely on the ability to solve for the value of the cumulative normal distribution (CDF, denoted N(d)) when given the upper limit or percentage point (d). For example, the standard Black, Scholes, Merton option valuation model (BSMOVM) had two calculations usually denoted $N(d_1)$ and $N(d_2)$.

Many risk management calculations rely on the ability to perform the inverse calculation, $N^{-1}(d_1)$. That is, estimate the percentage point d, when given the prescribed CDF probability N().

Computing N(d)

The solution to the CDF value (N()), given a known value of the percentage point (d), can be expressed as:

$$N(d) = \int_{-\infty}^{d} \frac{\exp\left\{-\frac{x^2}{2}\right\}}{\sqrt{2\pi}} dx$$

Often, option models such as the BSMOVM were labeled 'closed-form' equations. "In mathematics, an expression is said to be a closed-form expression if, and only if, it can be expressed analytically in terms of a bounded number of certain 'well-known' functions. Typically, these well-known functions are defined to be elementary functions; so infinite series, limits, and continued fractions are not permitted." (Closed-form expression, www.wikipedia.com, June 9, 2009) It is generally assumed that the solution for the expression above for N(d) is 'well-known.' Thus, we need to know it. Unfortunately, there does not exist an exact analytic expression solving this open integral. With a computer, however, it can easily be solved.

Note that the range of the percentage point d is $-\infty < d < \infty$ and the range of the CDF probability is $0 \le N(d) \le 1$. The probability density function (PDF) and the cumulative distribution function (CDF) are illustrated in the next figure. The purpose of the implementation code illustrated here is to estimate N(d), given d (using the method ND(d)) or to estimate d given N(d) (using the method D(n)). In the example below, d = −1.644853 and N(d) = 0.05.

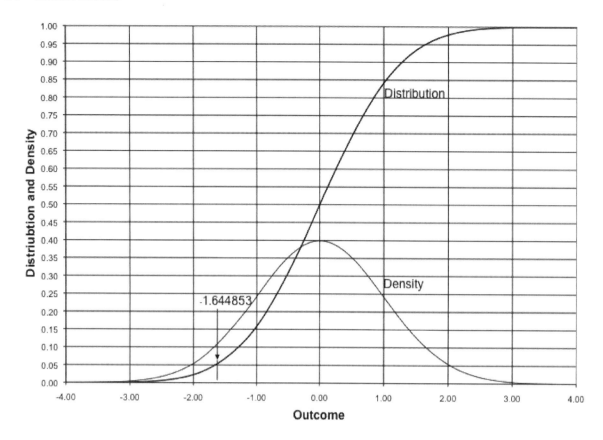

This CDF can be approximated by: (d>0)

$$N(d) = 0.5 + \frac{1}{\pi} \sum_{r=0}^{12} \frac{\exp\left\{-\frac{\left(r+\frac{1}{2}\right)^2}{9}\right\} \sin\left\{\frac{d\left(r+\frac{1}{2}\right)\sqrt{2}}{3}\right\}}{\left(r+\frac{1}{2}\right)}$$

According to Stuart and Ord, this particular approximation is accurate to nine decimal places. The method, ND(d), is based on this approximation. See Alan Stuart and J. Keith Orr, *Kendall's Advanced Theory of Statistics*, 5th Edition, Volume 1 Distribution Theory, page 185.

Computing $N^{-1}(d)$

Wichura (1988) provides a FORTRAN version of an approximation for the inverse normal CDF computation that he claims is accurate to the 16th decimal place. The method, D(n), is based on this approximation converted from FORTRAN.

Wichura (1988) breaks the CDF into two regions below N(d) < 0.5. Within these two regions, seven polynomials are estimated. The goal is to provide an accurate algorithm for estimating d, given N(d). The interface code discussed below provides a test of the accuracy of the D(n) and ND(d) programs.

Implementation code comments

Methods can be defined in preprocessor directives. For example, a maximum of two variables can be written as

```
#define max(a, b)  (((a) > (b)) ? (a) : (b))
```

and used within the program

```
    AbsError = max(tempAbsError, AbsError);
```

Also, constant numbers can be defined

```
 #define PI  3.14159265358979324
```

and subsequently used in the program

```
    CN = 0.5 + (1 / PI) * CN;
```

Because integers hold relatively small numbers, the test method loops using a long int

```
    for (long int i=1; i<10001; i++){
```

primarily because in the testing phase one could use much smaller increments and thus loop over a very large number of iterations.

The approximation equation for estimating N(d) can be computed by relying on several built in math methods, including exp(), pow(,), sin(), fabs(), and sqrt(). For example, the following is a line of code

```
    CN+=exp(-(pow((i+0.5),2))/9)*sin(fabs(D)*(i+0.5)*sqrt(2)/3)*pow((i+0.5),-1);
```

pow(a,b) calculates the value of a^b. fabs() calculates the absolute value of a floating point number. exp(), sin(), and sqrt() calculate the exponential, sin, and square root, respectively.

FRMCDF.h

```
/******************************************************************
** LOCATION
**   c:\FRMRepository\FRMCDF.h
** DESCRIPTION
**   This function is used in closed-form option valuation
**   models to compute the area under the standard normal
**   distribution.
**   double FRMND(double D)
**   D  value to accumulate area up to D from negative infinity
**   double FRMD(double N)
**   N  value of the cumulative normal distribution
** MACROS
**   PI  value of PI
******************************************************************/
```

Extensive comments at the top of the header code, though initially time consuming, will eventually be a real time saver.

```
#ifndef FRMCDFH
#define FRMCDFH
#include <math.h>
#define PI  3.14159265358979324
```

Preprocessor definitions are a convenient way to define variables in a very transparent way.

```
class FRMCDF
{
public:
  long double FRMCalculateTest();
  double FRMND(double D);
  double FRMD(double ND);
};
#endif
/******************************************************************
** REFERENCES
**   Method FRMND()
**   Alan Stuart and J. Keith Orr _Kendall's Advanced Theory of
**   Statistics_, 5th Edition, Volume 1 Distribution Theory,
**   page 185. Provides equation to program normal CDF estimation.
**   Method FRMD()
```

```
**   ALGORITHM AS241   APPL. STATIST. (1988) VOL. 37, NO. 3, 477-
**   484. Provides FORTRAN code for inverse normal CDF estimation.
*******************************************************************/
```

This header file defines the class FRMCDF, it contains three functions FRMCalculateTest(), FRMND(double D), and FRMD(double ND) all of which are public so they can be used in other implementation code. The variable inside the function's parentheses defines what type of variable they receive. For instance FRMND() requires a double variable D, and returns a double variable. Clearly documenting your references saves time when upgrading or re-evaluating your code.

FRMCDF.cpp

```
/*******************************************************************
** LOCATION
**   c:\FRMRepository\FRMCDF.cpp
** DESCRIPTION
**   These functions estimate the normal CDF and inverse normal CDF
**   double FRMND(double D)
**   D  value to accumulate area up to D from negative infinity
**   double FRMD(double N)
**   N  value of the cumulative normal distribution
** MACROS
**   PI   value of PI
*******************************************************************/
#define max(a, b)  (((a) > (b)) ? (a) : (b))
#include "FRMCDF.h"

long double FRMCDF::FRMCalculateTest()
{ // TEST CODE FOR INVERSE NORMAL
  long double AbsError, tempAbsError, tempD, tempDFN, tempN, tempN1;
  long double ErrorD, ErrorN, ErrorDFN;
  AbsError = 0.0;
  for (long int i=1; i<10001; i++){
    tempD = -5.0 + ((double)i)*0.001;
    tempN = FRMND(tempD);
    tempDFN = FRMD(tempN);
    tempAbsError = fabs(tempD - tempDFN);
    if (tempAbsError > AbsError) {
      AbsError = tempAbsError;
      ErrorD = tempD;  // Facilitates further study of error source
      ErrorN = tempN;
      ErrorDFN = tempDFN;
    }
    AbsError = max(tempAbsError, AbsError);
  }
  return AbsError;
}
```

This test of the methods in the FRMCDF class is useful for establishing the accuracy of the implementations, particularly since the inverse normal is a translation from Fortran.

```
double FRMCDF::FRMND(double D)
{
  double CN;       // Temporary variables
  int i;           // Counter
  if(fabs(D) > 7){  // Test for extreme values
    if(D > 0) return(1); // Positive extreme equals 1.0
    else return(0);      // Negative extreme equals 0.0
  }
  CN = 0;
  for(i = 0; i <= 12; i ++)
    CN+=exp(-(pow((i+0.5),2))/9)*sin(fabs(D)*(i+0.5)*sqrt(2)/3)*pow((i+0.5),-1);
  CN = 0.5 + (1 / PI) * CN;
  if(D > 0) return(CN);  // Test for positive value due to symmetry
  else return(1 - CN);   // Negative values are subtracted from 1.0
}
```

We assume below –7 or above +7 is sufficiently close to zero or one as to not require computation. In between these two extremes, the algorithm is based on an approximation provided by Stuart and Orr (1987) reference in the code.

```
double FRMCDF::FRMD(double P)
{
//      ALGORITHM AS241  APPL. STATIST. (1988) VOL. 37, NO. 3, 477-484.
//      Produces the normal deviate Z corresponding to a given lower
//      tail area of P; Z is accurate to about 1 part in 10**7.
//      The hash sums below are the sums of the mantissas of the
//      coefficients.   They are included for use in checking transcription.
  double SPLIT1, SPLIT2, CONST1, CONST2, A0, A1, A2, A3, B1, B2, B3,
    C0, C1, C2, C3, D1, D2, E0, E1, E2, E3, F1, F2, Q, R;
  double PPND7;
  SPLIT1 = 0.425;
  SPLIT2 = 5.0;
  CONST1 = 0.180625;
  CONST2 = 1.6;
//      Coefficients for P close to 0.5
  A0 = 3.3871327179E+00; A1 = 5.0434271938E+01; A2 = 1.5929113202E+02;
  A3 = 5.9109374720E+01; B1 = 1.7895169469E+01; B2 = 7.8757757664E+01;
  B3 = 6.7187563600E+01;
// HASH SUM AB    32.31845 77772 : Coefficients for P not close to 0, 0.5 or 1.
  C0 = 1.4234372777E+00; C1 = 2.7568153900E+00; C2 = 1.3067284816E+00;
  C3 = 1.7023821103E-01; D1 = 7.3700164250E-01; D2 = 1.2021132975E-01;
// HASH SUM CD    15.76149 29821 : Coefficients for P near 0 or 1.
  E0 = 6.6579051150E+00; E1 = 3.0812263860E+00; E2 = 4.2868294337E-01;
  E3 = 1.7337203997E-02; F1 = 2.4197894225E-01; F2 = 1.2258202635E-02;
//      HASH SUM EF    19.40529 10204
  if(P <= 0.000000001)P = 0.000000001;
  if(P >= 0.999999999)P = 0.999999999;
  Q = P - 0.5;
  if (fabs(Q) <= SPLIT1){
    R = CONST1 - Q * Q;
    return (Q * (((A3 * R + A2) * R + A1) * R + A0) /
      (((B3 * R + B2) * R + B1) * R + 1.0));
  } else {
    if (Q <= 0.0){
      R = P;
    } else {
      R = 1.0 - P;
    }
    if (R <= 0.0) return 0.0;
    R = sqrt(-log(R));
    if (R <= SPLIT2){
      R = R - CONST2;
      PPND7 = ((((C3 * R + C2) * R + C1) * R + C0) /
        ((D2 * R + D1) * R + 1.0);
    } else {
      R = R - SPLIT2;
      PPND7 = (((E3 * R + E2) * R + E1) * R + E0) /
        ((F2 * R + F1) * R + 1.0);
    }
    if (Q <= 0.0) PPND7 = - PPND7;
    return PPND7;
  }
};
```

The inverse normal is a translation from Fortran. Every effort was made to preserve the algorithm in its original form. Modules are developed later from *Numerical Recipes in C++*. An effort is made to modify the code so as to be readable to a finance professional. *Numerical Recipes in C++* is one of the most valuable resources for the quantitative finance professional seeking to implement modules in C++.

References

Stuart, Alan and J. Keith Orr, *Kendall's Advanced Theory of Statistics*, 5th Edition, Volume 1 Distribution Theory (1987).

Wichura, Michael J., "Algorithm AS 241: The Percentage Points of the Normal Distribution," *Applied Statistics* 37(3), 1988, 477-484.

Appendix 3.2: Interface code comments

The FRMCDF program interface is illustrated below. We see that when the value of d is 1.0, then the value N(d) is 0.841345 and when the value of N(d) is 0.1586552 (= 1.0 – 0.841345, approximately), then the value of d is –1.0. This result is due to the symmetry of the normal distribution. The maximum error iterating from –5 to 5 by 0.001 is 0.00001014. The error occurs when d is high due to slight inaccuracies with the inverse normal approximation.

The following are excerpts from the interface header code with selected comments added.

FRMUnitCDF.h

```
...
#include "c:\FRMRepository\FRMCDF.cpp"
...
private:  // User declarations
  FRMCDF C;
  double d, Nd;
  double inputd, inputNd;
...
```

Remember to include the implementation code and instantiate an object of type FRMCDF, this object will allow you to use the functions in FRMCDF in the interface code of this program. The following are selected excerpts from the interface code with selected comments added.

FRMUnitCDF.cpp:

```
...
void __fastcall TCDFForm::Reset(void)
{
  d = 0.0;
  Nd = 0.5;
  editd->Text = FloatToStrF(d, ffNumber, 8, 6);
  editNd->Text = FloatToStrF(Nd, ffNumber, 8, 6);
  rgCDFTest->ItemIndex = 0;
}
...
```

The reset method is useful for setting defaults in a manner that is apparent to someone reviewing the code.

```
void __fastcall TCDFForm::FRMExecute(void)
{
  SetLocalData(); // Make sure to grab latest user inputs
```

```
  d = C.FRMD(inputNd); // Compute inverse N(d) when given N(d)
  Nd = C.FRMND(inputd); // Compute N(d) when given d
...
```

Recall that Execute() is where the interface code interacts with the implementation code. It should contain your SetLocalData() function, followed by any outputs you wish to produce using functions from the implementation files.

```
// If extensive test run
  if(rgCDFTest->ItemIndex == 1){
    long double TestError;
    TestError = C.FRMCalculateTest(); // Separate class to run test
...
```

Often it is helpful to build in methods that provide extensive tests of the core functions. These test methods do not have to be visible to the user of the interface code.

Module 3.3. Univariate Random Number Generator

Learning objectives

- Explain how to generate univariate random numbers in C++, specifically uniform and normally distributed random variables
- Develop the capacity to generate random numbers indicating likelihood
- Learn how to initiate random number generators with either the internal clock or the built in `rand()` function, often referred to as the seed
- Emphasize the use of `long int` compared with `int`
- Illustrate how to generate random numbers for simulating rare events
- Show how to use structures as a data type for returning information from a function as well as using function overloading
- Review implementation code FRMURNG.cpp (.h)

See program FRMURNGTest in *3.3 Univariate Random Number Generator*.

Module overview

The ability to generate random numbers is very important in financial analysis. We use random number generating in Modules 6.1, 6.2, and 6.5, all related to dynamic risk managment.

Of course, generating random numbers with a deterministic computer poses some technical problems. Hence, the purist will refer to generating "pseudo" random numbers. For ease of exposition, the pseudo disclaimer is dropped. The main objective here is to introduce the ability to generate random numbers using C++. Four different random number generating tasks are presented here: uniform integer, uniform real, likelihood, and normal. Each random number generator has to be initialized with a seed value.

Seed

Because computers are deterministic machines, it is technically impossible to generate a random number. For finance applications, we can get close enough so as not to be concerned. Each random number generating method must be initialized. This initial value is called a seed. Thus, the method FRMSeed() provides two different ways to compute a seed. The most common recommended method is to pull a numerical value from the internal clock. Unfortunately, the internal clock is measured only in 1/100ths of a second. For some applications, for example dynamic linked libraries incorporated into a spreadsheet, this seed may not change fast enough.

The standard C++ library contains a uniform integer random number generator that stores a static duration seed that is updated each time it is called. Thus, the subsequent random number generator function calls will each have a different seed.

Computing Uniform Integer Random Numbers

Whenever interacting with integers, it is important to remember the numerical limitations of the data type `int` when compared to `long int`. Values of `int` typically range from $-32,768$ to $32,767$ whereas `long int` typically range from $-2,147,438,648$ to $2,147,438,647$. Due to the wide availability of memory, the computer program should use `long int` if there is any possibility that the integer will fall outside of the typical `int` range.

The discrete uniform distribution has a finite set of possible outcomes and each outcome is equally likely. The parameters of the discrete uniform distribution in this application are the lower bound (L) and upper bound (U). Each integer within and including the bounds is assumed to be equally likely. The population mean is $(L + U)/2$ and the variance is $((U - L + 1)^2 - 1)/12$.

Therefore, the method FRMUniformInteger() receives two long integer values, the upper and lower bounds, and returns one long integer value. The actual implementation of this method relies on the continuous uniform distribution implementation and the way integer values are truncated. The following snippet of code illustrates how to compute uniform discrete random numbers.

```
Draw = FRMUniformRandom01();    // Random uniform 0, 1
IDraw = long((Draw * double(UpperBound - LowerBound + 1))) + LowerBound;
```

Note because integer conversions truncate, we need to add one to the range. The long in the second equation defines the long int that is returned as IDraw. FRMUniformRandom01() is based on code provided in *Numerical Recipes in C*.

Computing Uniform Real Random Numbers

The method to generate values from a continuous uniform distribution is very straightforward. The continuous uniform distribution has an infinite set of possible outcomes. The parameters of the continuous uniform distribution in this application are the lower bound (L) and upper bound (U). The population mean is $(L + U)/2$ and the variance is $(U - L)^2/12$.

Therefore, the method FRMUniformReal() receives two double values and returns one double value. The following snippet of code illustrates how to compute uniform discrete random numbers.

```
Draw = FRMUniformRandom01();    // Random uniform 0, 1
Draw = Draw * (UpperBound - LowerBound) + LowerBound;
```

Because the boundaries are real and not integer, no adjustments outside of scaling are required. FRMUniformRandom01() is based on code provided in *Numerical Recipes in C*.

See FRMUniformRNG.cpp and FRMUniformRNG.h.

Computing Normal Random Numbers

The method to generate values from a normal distribution is based here on a procedure described in *Numerical Recipes in C*. The inputs to this method are the mean and standard deviation.

Therefore, the method FRMNormal() receives two double values and returns one double value. The following snippet of code illustrates how to compute uniform discrete random numbers.

```
Draw = FRMNormal01();    // Random uniform 0, 1
Draw = Draw * PStandardDeviation + PMean;
```

See FRMUniformRNG.cpp and FRMUniformRNG.h.

Computing Likelihood

The method to generate likelihood values is based on a uniform distribution with zero lower bound and one upper bound. The output from a call to the likelihood method is either zero or one depending on whether the uniform draw was below the desired likelihood (DL) value. The mean is just the desired likelihood, DL, and the variance is $(DL - DL^2)$

Therefore, the method FRMLikelihood() receives one double value and returns one double value. The following snippet of code illustrates how to compute likelihood.

```
Draw = FRMUniformRandom01();    // Random uniform 0, 1
if(Draw <= DesiredLikelihood) Draw = 1.0;
    else Draw = 0.0;
```

FRMUniformRandom01() is based on code provided in *Numerical Recipes in C++*.

Implementation code comments

This implementation code illustrates the use of structures and function overloading. A structure named FRMDSTATS is used, containing the population and sample mean and standard deviation, as well as a measure of time elapsed during the simulation. Function overloading is illustrated by either returning a single value or the sample statistics from a complete simulation. For example, compare the following lines of code.

```
long int FRMUniformInteger(long int LowerBound, long int UpperBound);
...
struct FRMDSTATS FRMUniformInteger(long int SampleSize, long int LowerBound,
    long int UpperBound);
```

The second method returns a structure containing five data items, whereas the first returns just one long integer.

We provide the complete implementation code here for this module. Soon we will only be providing snippets of code where we introduce something new or the code warrants further explanation.

FRMUniformRNG.h

Clearly, detailed comments at the top of the file aid in understanding what is being done. We do not provide such extensive details for future modules.

```
/*******************************************************************
** LOCATION
**   c:\FRMRepository\FRMUniformRNG.h
** DESCRIPTION
**  Generates a variety of random numbers and related support statistics
**   void FRMSeed();
**    Pulls data from internal clock to set seed
**   double FRMUniformRandom01();
**    Random uniform real, lower bound 0, upper bound 1
**   long int FRMUniformInteger(long int LowerBound, long int UpperBound);
**   double FRMUniformReal(double LowerBound, double UpperBound);
**
**   double FRMNormal01();
**    Random normal, mean 0, standard deviation 1
**   double FRMNormal(double PMean, double PStandardDeviation);
**  The following returns either 0 or 1 with frequence DesiredLikelihood
**   double FRMLikelihood(double DesiredLikelihood);
**
**  The following generates a sample of random numbers and returns both
**  the population and sample means and standard deviations as well as
**  a measure of the time taken to run the simulation (in 100ths of second)
**   struct FRMDSTATS FRMUniformReal(long int SampleSize, double LowerBound,
**       double UpperBound);
**   struct FRMDSTATS FRMUniformInteger(long int SampleSize, long int LowerBound,
**       long int UpperBound);
**   struct FRMDSTATS FRMNormal(long int SampleSize, double PMean,
**       double PStandardDeviation);
**   struct FRMDSTATS FRMLikelihood(long int SampleSize,
**       double DesiredLikelihood);
*******************************************************************/
#ifndef FRMUniformRNGH
#define FRMUniformRNGH
#define IA 16807
#define IM 2147483647
#define AM (1.0/IM)
#define IQ 127773
#define IR 2836
#define NTAB 32
#define NDIV (1+(IM-1)/NTAB)
#define RNMX (1.0-1.2e-7)
//----------------------------------------------------------------
#ifndef SFRMDSTATS
#define SFRMDSTATS
struct FRMDSTATS
{
  double SampleMean;
  double SampleStandardDeviation;
  double PopulationMean;
  double PopulationStandardDeviation;
  double SimulationTimeInSeconds;
```

```
};
#endif
class FRMURNG
{
public:
  long int NumberOfIterations;
  long int seed;
  void FRMSeed();

  double FRMUniformRandom01();
  long int FRMUniformInteger(long int LowerBound, long int UpperBound);
  double FRMUniformReal(double LowerBound, double UpperBound);
  struct FRMDSTATS FRMUniformInteger(long int SampleSize, long int LowerBound,
    long int UpperBound);
  struct FRMDSTATS FRMUniformReal(long int SampleSize, double LowerBound,
    double UpperBound);

  double FRMNormal01();
  double FRMNormal(double PMean, double PStandardDeviation);
  struct FRMDSTATS FRMNormal(long int SampleSize, double PMean,
    double PStandardDeviation);

  double FRMLikelihood(double DesiredLikelihood);
  struct FRMDSTATS FRMLikelihood(long int SampleSize,
    double DesiredLikelihood);
};
#endif
/***********************************************************************
** REFERENCES
**   William H. Press, Brian P. Flannery, Saul A. Teukolsky,
**   and William T. Vetterling, _Numerical Recipes in C  The
**   Art of Scientific Computing_, (Cambridge, England:  Cambridge
**   University Press, 1989).  (2nd Edition)
***********************************************************************/
```

FRMUniformRNG.cpp

Again, the complete source code is provided here to get a feel for how the source code files are laid out.

```
/***********************************************************************
** LOCATION
**   c:\FRMRepository\FRMUniformRNG.cpp
**     void FRMSeed();
**     double FRMUniformRandom01();
**     long int FRMUniformInteger(long int LowerBound, long int UpperBound);
**     double FRMUniformReal(double LowerBound, double UpperBound);
**     double FRMNormal01();
**     double FRMNormal(double PMean, double PStandardDeviation);
**     double FRMLikelihood(double DesiredLikelihood);
**     struct FRMDSTATS FRMUniformReal(long int SampleSize, double LowerBound,
**        double UpperBound);
**     struct FRMDSTATS FRMUniformInteger(long int SampleSize, long int LowerBound,
**        long int UpperBound);
**     struct FRMDSTATS FRMNormal(long int SampleSize, double PMean,
**        double PStandardDeviation);
**     struct FRMDSTATS FRMLikelihood(long int SampleSize,
**        double DesiredLikelihood);
***********************************************************************/
#include <math.h>
#include <dos.h>            // Defines structure "time"
#include "FRMUniformRNG.h"
```

There are two ways of initiating the random number generator: the clock (commented out now) and a built in random number generator (rand()). Note to use the clock for random number generator must include <dos.h>.

```
void FRMURNG::FRMSeed() // Must be defined prior to using RNGs
{
//   struct time t;        // For pulling the clock in C++ <dos.h>
//   getTime(&t); //fills in the time structure, t, with the system's current time
//   seed = - t.ti_sec - t.ti_min - t.ti_hund;  // Select large negative number
```

```
//   seed = -1000;    // Use for debugging purposes
  seed = - rand();   // Works with DLLs and Excel, clock does not reset fast
}
```

Notice how methods often call other methods within a given class (FRMSeed()).

```
double FRMURNG::FRMLikelihood(double DesiredLikelihood)
{
  double Draw;
  FRMSeed();
  Draw = FRMUniformRandom01();    // Random uniform 0, 1
  if(Draw <= DesiredLikelihood) Draw = 1.0;
     else Draw = 0.0;
  return(Draw);
}
```

By providing lengthy names, this source code is easy to read and comprehend. Remember, you are building your library and will likely use source code for decades to come. These methods each return a double variable.

```
double FRMURNG::FRMNormal(double PMean, double PStandardDeviation)
{
  double Draw;
  FRMSeed();
  Draw = FRMNormal01();    // Random uniform 0, 1
  Draw = Draw * PStandardDeviation + PMean;
  return(Draw);
}


long int FRMURNG::FRMUniformInteger(long int LowerBound, long int UpperBound)
{
  double Draw;
  long int IDraw;
  FRMSeed();
  Draw = FRMUniformRandom01();    // Random uniform 0, 1
  IDraw = long((Draw * double(UpperBound - LowerBound + 1))) + LowerBound;
  return(IDraw);
}


double FRMURNG::FRMUniformReal(double LowerBound, double UpperBound)
{
  double Draw;
  FRMSeed();
  Draw = FRMUniformRandom01();    // Random uniform 0, 1
  Draw = Draw * (UpperBound - LowerBound) + LowerBound;
  return(Draw);
}
```

These methods return structures.

```
struct FRMDSTATS FRMURNG::FRMLikelihood
  (long int SampleSize, double DesiredLikelihood)
{
  double Draw, SumDraw, SumDrawSquared, Mean, StandardDeviation;
  double StartTime, EndTime;
  int HH, MM, SS, HS;
  struct time s;          // For pulling the clock in C++ <dos.h>
  FRMDSTATS S;
  SumDraw = SumDrawSquared = 0.0;
  FRMSeed();
  gettime(&s);
  HH = s.ti_hour; MM = s.ti_min; SS = s.ti_sec; HS = s.ti_hund;
  StartTime = ((double)HH)*1200.0 + ((double)MM)*60.0 + (double)SS
    + ((double)HS) / 100.0;
  for (long int i = 0; i <= SampleSize-1; i++) {
    Draw = FRMUniformRandom01();    // Random uniform 0, 1
    if(Draw <= DesiredLikelihood) Draw = 1.0;
       else Draw = 0.0;
    SumDraw += Draw;
    SumDrawSquared += pow(Draw, 2.0);
  }
  Mean = SumDraw / (double) SampleSize;
  StandardDeviation = pow((1.0/((double) SampleSize - 1.0))
```

```
        * (SumDrawSquared - (double) SampleSize * pow(Mean, 2.0)), 0.5);
  gettime(&s);
  HH = s.ti_hour;   MM = s.ti_min; SS = s.ti_sec; HS = s.ti_hund;
  EndTime = ((double)HH)*1200.0 + ((double)MM)*60.0 + (double)SS
        + ((double)HS) / 100.0;
  S.PopulationMean = DesiredLikelihood;
  S.PopulationStandardDeviation
    = pow(DesiredLikelihood-pow(DesiredLikelihood,2.0),0.5);
  S.SampleMean = Mean;
  S.SampleStandardDeviation = StandardDeviation;
  S.SimulationTimeInSeconds = EndTime - StartTime;
  return(S);
}

struct FRMDSTATS FRMURNG::FRMNormal(long int SampleSize,
  double PMean, double PStandardDeviation)
{
  double Draw, SumDraw, SumDrawSquared, Mean, StandardDeviation;
  double StartTime, EndTime;
  int HH, MM, SS, HS;
  struct time s;        // For pulling the clock in C++ <dos.h>
  FRMDSTATS S;
  SumDraw = SumDrawSquared = 0.0;
  FRMSeed();
  gettime(&s);
  HH = s.ti_hour; MM = s.ti_min; SS = s.ti_sec; HS = s.ti_hund;
  StartTime = ((double)HH)*1200.0 + ((double)MM)*60.0 + (double)SS
        + ((double)HS) / 100.0;
  for (long int i = 0; i <= SampleSize-1; i++) {
      Draw = FRMNormal01();     // Random uniform 0, 1
      Draw = Draw * PStandardDeviation + PMean;
      SumDraw += Draw;
      SumDrawSquared += pow(Draw, 2.0);
  }
  Mean = SumDraw / (double) SampleSize;
  StandardDeviation = pow((1.0/((double) SampleSize - 1.0))
      * (SumDrawSquared - (double) SampleSize * pow(Mean, 2.0)), 0.5);
  gettime(&s);
  HH = s.ti_hour;   MM = s.ti_min; SS = s.ti_sec; HS = s.ti_hund;
  EndTime = ((double)HH)*1200.0 + ((double)MM)*60.0 + (double)SS
        + ((double)HS) / 100.0;
  S.PopulationMean = PMean;
  S.PopulationStandardDeviation = PStandardDeviation;
  S.SampleMean = Mean;
  S.SampleStandardDeviation = StandardDeviation;
  S.SimulationTimeInSeconds = EndTime - StartTime;
  return(S);
}

struct FRMDSTATS FRMURNG::FRMUniformInteger(long int SampleSize,
  long int LowerBound, long int UpperBound)
{
  double Draw, SumDraw, SumDrawSquared, Mean, StandardDeviation;
  double StartTime, EndTime;
  int HH, MM, SS, HS;
  struct time s;        // For pulling the clock in C++ <dos.h>
  FRMDSTATS S;
  SumDraw = SumDrawSquared = 0.0;
  FRMSeed();
  gettime(&s);
  HH = s.ti_hour; MM = s.ti_min; SS = s.ti_sec; HS = s.ti_hund;
  StartTime = ((double)HH)*1200.0 + ((double)MM)*60.0 + (double)SS
        + ((double)HS) / 100.0;
  for (long int i = 0; i <= SampleSize-1; i++) {
      Draw = FRMUniformRandom01();     // Random uniform 0, 1
      Draw = int(Draw * double(UpperBound - LowerBound + 1)) + LowerBound;
      SumDraw += Draw;
      SumDrawSquared += pow(Draw, 2.0);
  }
  Mean = SumDraw / (double) SampleSize;
  StandardDeviation = pow((1.0/((double) SampleSize - 1.0))
```

```
      * (SumDrawSquared - (double) SampleSize * pow(Mean, 2.0)), 0.5);
   gettime(&s);
   HH = s.ti_hour;    MM = s.ti_min; SS = s.ti_sec; HS = s.ti_hund;
   EndTime = ((double)HH)*1200.0 + ((double)MM)*60.0 + (double)SS
      + ((double)HS) / 100.0;
   S.PopulationMean = (LowerBound + UpperBound)/2.0;
   S.PopulationStandardDeviation
      = pow((pow((UpperBound - LowerBound + 1), 2.0)-1.0)/12.0, 0.5);
   S.SampleMean = Mean;
   S.SampleStandardDeviation = StandardDeviation;
   S.SimulationTimeInSeconds = EndTime - StartTime;
   return(S);
}

struct FRMDSTATS FRMURNG::FRMUniformReal(long int SampleSize,
   double LowerBound, double UpperBound)
{
   double Draw, SumDraw, SumDrawSquared, Mean, StandardDeviation;
   double StartTime, EndTime;
   int HH, MM, SS, HS;
   struct time s;        // For pulling the clock in C++ <dos.h>
   FRMDSTATS S;
   SumDraw = SumDrawSquared = 0.0;
   FRMSeed();
   gettime(&s);
   HH = s.ti_hour; MM = s.ti_min; SS = s.ti_sec; HS = s.ti_hund;
   StartTime = ((double)HH)*1200.0 + ((double)MM)*60.0 + (double)SS
      + ((double)HS) / 100.0;
   for (long int i = 0; i <= SampleSize-1; i++) {
      Draw = FRMUniformRandom01();    // Random uniform 0, 1
      Draw = Draw * (UpperBound - LowerBound) + LowerBound;
      SumDraw += Draw;
      SumDrawSquared += pow(Draw, 2.0);
   }
   Mean = SumDraw / (double) SampleSize;
   StandardDeviation = pow((1.0/((double) SampleSize - 1.0))
      * (SumDrawSquared - (double) SampleSize * pow(Mean, 2.0)), 0.5);
   gettime(&s);
   HH = s.ti_hour;    MM = s.ti_min; SS = s.ti_sec; HS = s.ti_hund;
   EndTime = ((double)HH)*1200.0 + ((double)MM)*60.0 + (double)SS
      + ((double)HS) / 100.0;
   S.PopulationMean = (LowerBound + UpperBound)/2.0;
   S.PopulationStandardDeviation = pow(pow((UpperBound - LowerBound), 2.0)/12.0,
      0.5);
   S.SampleMean = Mean;
   S.SampleStandardDeviation = StandardDeviation;
   S.SimulationTimeInSeconds = EndTime - StartTime;
   return(S);
}
```

These methods each return a double variable.

```
double FRMURNG::FRMNormal01()
{
// Returns a normally distributed deviate with zero mean and unit variance
// using UniformRandom01() as the source of uniform deviates
// SOURCE:  Numerical Recipes in C, 2nd edition, pages 289-290.
   static int iset=0;
   static float gset;
   float fac, rsq, v1, v2;
   if (iset == 0) {                         // No extra deviate available
      do {
         v1 = 2.0 * FRMUniformRandom01() - 1.0;    // Pick two uniform numbers
         v2 = 2.0 * FRMUniformRandom01() - 1.0;
         rsq = v1 * v1 + v2 * v2;          // Check if unit circle
      } while (rsq >= 1.0 || rsq == 0.0);  // if not, try again
      fac = sqrt(-2.0 * log(rsq) / rsq);
// Now make the Box-Muller transformation to get two normal deviates.
// Return one and save the other for next time.
      gset = v1 * fac;
      iset = 1;                  // Set flag
```

```
      return v2*fac;
  } else {
    iset = 0;                       // Unset flag
    return gset;                    // Use extra deviate
  }
}

double FRMURNG::FRMUniformRandom01()
{
// Returns a uniform random deviate between 0.0 and 1.0  Call with idum a negative
// RNMX should approximate the largest floating value that is less than 1.
  int j;
  long k;
  static long iy = 0;
  static long iv[NTAB];
  double temp;
  if (seed <= 0 || !iy) {          // Initialize
    if (-(seed) < 1) {
      seed = 1;                     // Be sure to prevent seed = 0.
    } else {
      seed = -(seed);
    }
    for (j = NTAB + 7; j >= 0; j--) {  // Load the shuffle table after 8 warm-ups
      k = (seed) / IQ;
      seed = IA * (seed - k * IQ) - IR * k;
      if (seed < 0) seed += IM;
      if (j < NTAB) iv[j] = seed;
    }
    iy = iv[0];
  }
  k = (seed) / IQ;                            // Start here when not initializing
  seed = IA * (seed - k * IQ) - IR * k;   // Compute seed = (IA*seed) % IM
  if (seed < 0) seed += IM;         // witout overflows by Schrage's method.
  j = iy / NDIV;                                // Will be in the range 0..NTAB-1.
  iy = iv[j];                                   // Output previously stored value and
  iv[j] = seed;                                 // and refill shuffle table.
  if ((temp = AM * iy) > RNMX) return RNMX; // Because users don't expect endpoint values.
  else return temp;
}
```

References

Press, William H., Brian P. Flannery, Saul A. Teukolsky, and William T. Vetterling, *Numerical Recipes in C The Art of Scientific Computing* Second Edition, (Cambridge, England: Cambridge University Press, 1989).

Appendix 3.3: Interface code comments

The FRMURNG program interface is illustrated below. This program computes the both the population and sample mean and standard deviation. It also displays the simulation time in seconds. In the normal distribution case the population mean and standard deviation are also inputs. Notice that in this particular illustration 100,000,000 draws from a normal distribution are analyzed in under 14 seconds.

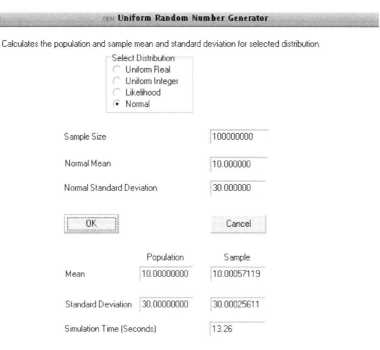

The following is the interface header code with selected comments added.

FRMUnitURNG.h

```
//----------------------------------------------------------------------
#ifndef FRMUnitURNGH
#define FRMUnitURNGH
//----------------------------------------------------------------------
#include <Classes.hpp>
#include <Controls.hpp>
#include <StdCtrls.hpp>
#include <Forms.hpp>
#include <Menus.hpp>
#include <ExtCtrls.hpp>
#include "c:\FRMRepository\FRMUniformRNG.cpp"
//----------------------------------------------------------------------
```

We use a structure here to collect several data elements. The advantage is the ability to pass or return one structure and have several data elements simultaneously. The #ifndef ... #endif is used to avoid declaring this function more than once. It is also defined in the implementation code so it could be multiply defined.

```
#ifndef SFRMDSTATS
#define SFRMDSTATS
struct FRMDSTATS
{
  double SampleMean;
  double SampleStandardDeviation;
  double PopulationMean;
  double PopulationStandardDeviation;
  double SimulationTimeInSeconds;
};
#endif

class TURNGForm : public TForm
...
```

We rely on one class and one structure and they are both instantiated below. The first line under private instatiates the class, the second instantiates the structure. Note that `long int` is used because these integer numbers may be large.

```
private:   // User declarations
```

```
    FRMURNG U;
    FRMDSTATS USS;
    long int inputSampleSize;
    long int inputIntegerUpperBound;
    long int inputIntegerLowerBound;
...
```

The following are selected parts of the interface code with some comments added.

FRMUnitURNG.cpp

The reset function is useful to set up the form in a preferred manner with default inputs. Often, when debugging, you will want to explore very specific inputs. These inputs can be entered once in the `Reset()` function and the inputs do not have to be re-entered every time you run the program.

```
...
 __fastcall TURNGForm::TURNGForm(TComponent* Owner)
       : TForm(Owner)
 {
   Reset();
 }
...
 void __fastcall TURNGForm::Reset(void)
 {
```

The following lines set the default values for the variables.

```
    inputSampleSize = 1000;
    inputRealUpperBound = 100.0;
    inputRealLowerBound = 0.0;
    inputIntegerUpperBound = 100;
    inputIntegerLowerBound = 0;
    inputDesiredLikelihood = 0.5;
    inputNormalMean = 0.0;
    inputNormalStandardDeviation = 1.0;
```

The following lines set the default values into the Text member variables of the edit boxes.

```
    editSampleSize->Text = IntToStr(inputSampleSize);
    editRealUpperBound->Text = FloatToStrF(inputRealUpperBound, ffNumber, 12, 6);
    editRealLowerBound->Text = FloatToStrF(inputRealLowerBound, ffNumber, 12, 6);
    editIntegerUpperBound->Text = IntToStr(inputIntegerUpperBound);
    editIntegerLowerBound->Text = IntToStr(inputIntegerLowerBound);
    editDesiredLikelihood->Text
       = FloatToStrF(inputDesiredLikelihood, ffNumber, 12, 6);
    editNormalMean->Text = FloatToStrF(inputNormalMean, ffNumber, 12, 6);
    editNormalStandardDeviation->Text
       = FloatToStrF(inputNormalStandardDeviation, ffNumber, 12, 6);
```

The following line set the default values to the first item in the radio group rgDistribution.

```
    rgDistribution->ItemIndex = 0; // Default uniform real
    InputsInvisible(); // Hide all inputs
```

The following lines set the edit boxes to be visible, hence they appear on the screen.

```
    lblRealUpperBound->Visible = true; // Make uniform real inputs visible
    editRealUpperBound->Visible = true;
    lblRealLowerBound->Visible = true;
    editRealLowerBound->Visible = true;
 }
```

When the user clicks the run button, the `FRMExecute()` function is run and the first line is to call the `SetLocalData()` function. Recall the Set Local data function is going to pull the most recent inputs entered on the form by the user and set the input variables equal to the text entered on the form.

```
 //-----------------------------------------------------------------------
 void __fastcall TURNGForm::SetLocalData(void)
 {
   inputSampleSize = StrToInt(editSampleSize->Text);
   inputRealUpperBound = StrToFloat(editRealUpperBound->Text);
   inputRealLowerBound = StrToFloat(editRealLowerBound->Text);
   inputIntegerUpperBound = StrToInt(editIntegerUpperBound->Text);
```

```
    inputIntegerLowerBound = StrToInt(editIntegerLowerBound->Text);
    inputDesiredLikelihood = StrToFloat(editDesiredLikelihood->Text);
    inputNormalMean = StrToFloat(editNormalMean->Text);
    inputNormalStandardDeviation = StrToFloat(editNormalStandardDeviation->Text);
}
//-----------------------------------------------------------------------
void __fastcall TURNGForm::FRMExecute(void)
{
    SetLocalData(); // Make sure to grab latest user inputs
```

Note the two different uses of pointers, -> and ., in the following two lines of code below. The interface code we use relies on the indirect member selector, ->, whereas the implementation code designed here relies on the direct member selector, '.'. Also note that USS is a structure and therefore contains several results that are referenced below. The method FRMUniformReal() receives three inputs, computes population and sample statistics based on the particular distribution and returns those values to a structure.

```
    if(rgDistribution->ItemIndex == 0){   // Uniform Real
        USS = U.FRMUniformReal(inputSampleSize, inputRealLowerBound, inputRealUpperBound);
```

The following line places the population mean value contained in the structure into the interface class population mean. This value will eventually be displayed on the screen.

```
        PopulationMean = USS.PopulationMean;
        PopulationStandardDeviation = USS.PopulationStandardDeviation;
        SampleMean = USS.SampleMean;
        SampleStandardDeviation = USS.SampleStandardDeviation;
```

ItemIndex below is based on the particular item in the radio group selected.

```
    }else if(rgDistribution->ItemIndex == 1){   // Uniform Integer
        USS = U.FRMUniformInteger(inputSampleSize, inputIntegerLowerBound, inputIntegerUpperBound);
        PopulationMean = USS.PopulationMean;
        PopulationStandardDeviation = USS.PopulationStandardDeviation;
        SampleMean = USS.SampleMean;
        SampleStandardDeviation = USS.SampleStandardDeviation;
    }else if(rgDistribution->ItemIndex == 2){   // Likelihood
        USS = U.FRMLikelihood(inputSampleSize, inputDesiredLikelihood);
        PopulationMean = USS.PopulationMean;
        PopulationStandardDeviation = USS.PopulationStandardDeviation;
        SampleMean = USS.SampleMean;
        SampleStandardDeviation = USS.SampleStandardDeviation;
    }else {   // Normal Distribution
        USS = U.FRMNormal(inputSampleSize, inputNormalMean, inputNormalStandardDeviation);
        PopulationMean = USS.PopulationMean;
        PopulationStandardDeviation = USS.PopulationStandardDeviation;
        SampleMean = USS.SampleMean;
        SampleStandardDeviation = USS.SampleStandardDeviation;
    }
```

Once the random sample has been evaluated, the appropriate information is reported back to elements on the form.

```
    outputPopulationMean->Text = FloatToStrF(PopulationMean, ffFixed, 15, 8);
    outputPopulationStandardDeviation->Text
        = FloatToStrF(PopulationStandardDeviation, ffFixed, 15, 8);
    outputSampleMean->Text = FloatToStrF(SampleMean, ffFixed, 15, 8);
    outputSampleStandardDeviation->Text
        = FloatToStrF(SampleStandardDeviation, ffFixed, 15, 8);
    outputSimulationTime->Text
        = FloatToStrF(USS.SimulationTimeInSeconds, ffFixed, 15, 2);
```

Recall lbl... denotes the labels that appear on the form.

```
    lblPopulation->Visible = true;
    lblSample->Visible = true;
    lblMean->Visible = true;
    lblStandardDeviation->Visible = true;
    lblSimulationTime->Visible = true;
    outputPopulationMean->Visible = true;
    outputPopulationStandardDeviation->Visible = true;
    outputSampleMean->Visible = true;
```

```
    outputSampleStandardDeviation->Visible = true;
    outputSimulationTime->Visible = true;
}
//------------------------------------------------------------------------
```

The method CheckType() which is defined below is performed anytime the user clicks on the radio group selecting the distribution. This method will allow you to change the inputs visible and the outputs generated, if needed, when the user selects a certain type of distribution (see below).

```
void __fastcall TURNGForm::rgDistributionClick(TObject *Sender)
{
    CheckType();
}
//------------------------------------------------------------------------
void __fastcall TURNGForm::InputsInvisible (void)
{
    lblRealUpperBound->Visible = false;
    editRealUpperBound->Visible = false;
    lblRealLowerBound->Visible = false;
    editRealLowerBound->Visible = false;
    lblIntegerUpperBound->Visible = false;
    editIntegerUpperBound->Visible = false;
    lblIntegerLowerBound->Visible = false;
    editIntegerLowerBound->Visible = false;
    lblDesiredLikelihood->Visible = false;
    editDesiredLikelihood->Visible = false;
    lblNormalMean->Visible = false;
    editNormalMean->Visible = false;
    lblNormalStandardDeviation->Visible = false;
    editNormalStandardDeviation->Visible = false;

    lblPopulation->Visible = false;
    lblSample->Visible = false;
    lblMean->Visible = false;
    lblStandardDeviation->Visible = false;
    lblSimulationTime->Visible = false;
    outputPopulationMean->Visible = false;
    outputPopulationStandardDeviation->Visible = false;
    outputSampleMean->Visible = false;
    outputSampleStandardDeviation->Visible = false;
    outputSimulationTime->Visible = false;
}
//------------------------------------------------------------------------
void __fastcall TURNGForm::CheckType (void)
{
    if(rgDistribution->ItemIndex == 0){  // Uniform Real
        InputsInvisible();
        lblRealUpperBound->Visible = true;
        editRealUpperBound->Visible = true;
        lblRealLowerBound->Visible = true;
        editRealLowerBound->Visible = true;
    }else if(rgDistribution->ItemIndex == 1){  // Uniform Integer
        InputsInvisible();
        lblIntegerUpperBound->Visible = true;
        editIntegerUpperBound->Visible = true;
        lblIntegerLowerBound->Visible = true;
        editIntegerLowerBound->Visible = true;
    }else if(rgDistribution->ItemIndex == 2){  // Likelihood
...
    }else {  // Normal Distribution
...
    }
}
```

The first step in the CheckType() method is to make all inputs invisibile, then the method has different inputs displayed depending on which distribution the user has selected.

Module 3.4. Regression

Learning objectives

- Develop a module to estimate the coefficients of an ordinary least squares regression
- Illustrate the benefits of object-oriented module development (Module 3.5 will be based on Module 3.4)
- Learn how to manipulate files, reading input and writing properly formatted output
- Emphasize the value of *Numerical Recipes in C (or C++)* and how to properly encapsulate those routines into your own source code
- Illustrate how to use the "LU" decomposition to solve a set of linear equations
- Review implementation code for regression

See program FRMRegressionTest in *3.3 Regression*.

Module overview

We introduce one method for solving for the ordinary least squares regression, based on an efficient approach of Press, et. al. (1992). We briefly review this approach and then illustrate the C++ code. This module will be used in the Module 3.5.

Ordinary least squares regression

A standard statistical problem is to find the best solution to a set of linear equations of the form

$$x_{11}\beta_1 + x_{12}\beta_2 + x_{13}\beta_3 + \cdots + x_{1n}\beta_n = y_1$$
$$x_{21}\beta_1 + x_{22}\beta_2 + x_{23}\beta_3 + \cdots + x_{2n}\beta_n = y_2$$
$$\vdots$$
$$x_{m1}\beta_1 + x_{m2}\beta_2 + x_{m3}\beta_3 + \cdots + x_{mn}\beta_n = y_m$$

or in matrix notation

$$\underset{m \times n}{\mathbf{X}} \; \underset{n \times 1}{\mathbf{b}} = \underset{m \times 1}{\mathbf{Y}},$$

where

$$\underset{m \times n}{\mathbf{X}} = \begin{bmatrix} x_{11} & x_{12} & \cdots & x_{1n} \\ x_{21} & x_{22} & \cdots & x_{2n} \\ \vdots & \vdots & \ddots & \vdots \\ x_{m1} & x_{m2} & \cdots & x_{mn} \end{bmatrix}, \; \underset{n \times 1}{\mathbf{b}} = \begin{bmatrix} \beta_1 \\ \beta_2 \\ \vdots \\ \beta_n \end{bmatrix}, \text{ and } \underset{m \times 1}{\mathbf{Y}} = \begin{bmatrix} y_1 \\ y_2 \\ \vdots \\ y_m \end{bmatrix}.$$

The **X** matrix is known as the independent variables and the **Y** vector is known as the dependent variables. The **b** vector of unknowns parameters can be found using ordinary least squares regression.

We assume here that m > n and the set of linear equations is said to be over-determined. Thus, we seek the best fit by solving for the **b** vector.

The normal equations can be written in matrix form as

$$\underset{n \times m}{\mathbf{X}^{\mathrm{T}}} \; \underset{m \times n}{\mathbf{X}} \; \underset{n \times 1}{\mathbf{b}} = \underset{n \times m}{\mathbf{X}^{\mathrm{T}}} \; \underset{m \times 1}{\mathbf{Y}}$$

$$\underset{n \times n}{\mathbf{NX}} \; \underset{n \times 1}{\mathbf{b}} = \underset{n \times 1}{\mathbf{NY}}$$

and the OLS solution to this set of linear equations can be express as

$$\hat{\mathbf{b}}_{nx1} = \left(\mathbf{X}^{T}_{nxm}\ \mathbf{X}_{mxn}\right)^{-1} \mathbf{X}^{T}_{nxm}\ \mathbf{Y}_{mx1}$$

$$\hat{\mathbf{b}}_{nx1} = \left(\mathbf{NX}_{nxn}\right)^{-1} \mathbf{NY}_{nx1}$$

where $\underset{nxn}{\mathbf{NX}}$ denotes the normalized X matrix and $\underset{nx1}{\mathbf{NY}}$ denotes the normalized Y matrix.

LU decomposition

According to Press, et. al. (1992), the LU decomposition approach is very efficient for finding the solution to this set of linear equations. The idea is to decompose the **NX** matrix into lower and upper triangular matrices, where the lower triangular matrix has elements only on the diagonal and below and the upper triangular matrix has elements only on the diagonal and above.

$$\underset{nxn}{\mathbf{NX}} = \begin{bmatrix} nx_{11} & nx_{12} & \cdots & nx_{1n} \\ nx_{21} & nx_{22} & \cdots & nx_{2n} \\ \vdots & \vdots & \ddots & \vdots \\ nx_{n1} & nx_{n2} & \cdots & nx_{nn} \end{bmatrix}$$

$$= \underset{nxn\ nxn}{\mathbf{L}\ \mathbf{U}} = \begin{bmatrix} \lambda_{11} & 0 & \cdots & 0 \\ \lambda_{21} & \lambda_{22} & \cdots & 0 \\ \vdots & \vdots & \ddots & \vdots \\ \lambda_{n1} & \lambda_{n2} & \cdots & \lambda_{nn} \end{bmatrix} \begin{bmatrix} \upsilon_{11} & \upsilon_{12} & \cdots & \upsilon_{1n} \\ 0 & \upsilon_{22} & \cdots & \upsilon_{2n} \\ \vdots & \vdots & \ddots & \vdots \\ 0 & 0 & \cdots & \upsilon_{nn} \end{bmatrix}$$

The basic idea is to solve sequentially for the unknown parameters.

$$\underset{nxn\ nx1}{\mathbf{NX}\ \mathbf{b}} = \underset{nx1}{\mathbf{NY}}$$

$$\underset{nxn\ nxn\ nx1}{\mathbf{L}\ \mathbf{U}\ \mathbf{b}} = \underset{nx1}{\mathbf{NY}}$$

That is, we first solve for the vector **Z** such that

$$\underset{nxn\ nx1}{\mathbf{L}\ \mathbf{Z}} = \underset{nx1}{\mathbf{NY}}$$

Because **L** is a lower triangular matrix, the solution is straightforward based on forward substitution. Based on this result, we can find

$$\underset{nxn\ nx1}{\mathbf{U}\ \mathbf{b}} = \underset{nx1}{\mathbf{Z}}$$

Because **U** is an upper triangular matrix, the solution is straightforward based on backward substitution. Thus, we solved for the unknown parameters without having to compute the matrix inverse or relying on numerous pivoting routines. Again, for more extensive discussion of this procedure, see Press, et. al. (1992).

Implementation code comments

The regression program is designed similar to 2.11 Managing Files. It may be helpful to review that section of chapter 2 should the material here get confusing.

FRMRegression.h

The header file references two modified programs from *Numerical Recipes in C* (FRMLUDecomposition() and FRMSolveRegression()). Selected portions of the header file with comments follow.

/***

```
** LOCATION
**   ...\FRMRegression.cpp
** DESCRIPTION
**   Solves AX = B
**   Note: A(NRows, NColumns)X(NRows, 1) = B(NRows, 1)
**   Memory is allocated by the constructor
** void FRMCalculateX(double **LU, int NColumns, int *Index, double B[])
**   Based on the LU decomposition method
** void FRMLUDecomposition(double **LU, int NColumns, int *Index, float *d); // LU Decomp
**   Data is warehoused in FRMRegressionInput.dat and managed by
** void FRMSolveRegression();  // Engine to fit curve
**   Converts A to APA (A prime A) so it is symmetric
**   Thus B is converted to APB
**   APA is converted to L*U = APA (lower and upper triangular matrices) and
**   stored in the A matrix.
**   Input data format:
**   NColumns NRows (Columns in A matrix, AX = B)
**   B[0] A[0][0] A[0][1] ... A[0][NRows-1]
**      ...
**   B[NColumns-1] A[NColumns-1][0] ...A[NColumns-1][NRows-1]
** ***********************************************************/
#ifndef FRMRegressionH
#define FRMRegressionH
```

Because we are referencing data files, we need to include several standard C++ libraries.

```
#include <iostream.h>
#include <iomanip.h>      // Used for manipulating I/O, setprecision
#include <fstream.h>
#include <math.h>
#define NP 120            //maximum number of rows used for input
#define TINY 1.0e-20;

class FRMREGRESSION
{
public:
```

The following two lines of code define the constructor and destructor. The constructor is always run whenever an instance of the class is created and the destructor is always run whenever an instance of the class is destroyed.

```
    FRMREGRESSION::FRMREGRESSION();  // Constructor, allocate memory, outf
    FRMREGRESSION::~FRMREGRESSION(); // Destructor, delete allocated memory
    void FRMSolveRegression(AnsiString sinf, AnsiString soutf,
      AnsiString soutf1);  // Engine to fit regression, one input and two output files
    void FRMCalculateX(double **LU, int NColumns, int *Index, double B[]);  // Solves AX = B
    void FRMLUDecomposition(double **LU, int NColumns, int *Index, double *d); // LU Decomp
```

Vectors and matrices are referenced with pointers, easing the ability to pass them in functions.

```
    int *Index;          // Pointer to vector that is an Index
    double **A;          // Pointer to matrix A
    double *B;           // Pointer to vector B
    double *APB;         // Pointer to vector A'B
    double **APA;        // Pointer to matrix A'A
```

FRMRegression.cpp

Selected portions of the C++ code file with comments follow.

```
...
FRMREGRESSION::FRMREGRESSION()      // Allocates memory for various matrices
{
    int j;
```

Because memory is allocated, we perform this task in the constructor. The use of try{} and catch{} assure that if memory is not available, the program will close somewhat gracefully.

```
    try { APB = new double [NP]; }      // Allocating memory for APB
    catch (std::bad_alloc) {
```

```
        Application->MessageBox(L"Could not allocate memory for vector APB.  Bye ...",
           L"Allocation Error for Vector APB[]", MB_OK);
        exit(-1);
   }
   try { B = new double [NP]; }          // Allocating memory for B
   catch (std::bad_alloc) {
        Application->MessageBox(L"Could not allocate memory for vector B.  Bye ...",
           L"Allocation Error for Vector B[]", MB_OK);
        exit(-1);
   }
   try { Index = new int [NP]; }         // Allocate memory for Index
   catch (std::bad_alloc) {
        Application->MessageBox(L"Could not allocate memory for vector Index.  Bye ...",
           L"Allocation Error for Vector Index[]", MB_OK);
        exit(-1);
   }
```

Allocating memory for a matrix is a bit more involved. We first allocate a vector of pointers and then allocate the memory for each vector.

```
   try {                                 // Allocating memory for A
      A = new double*[NP];                      // Set up rows
      for(j=0; j<NP; j++)A[j] = new double [NP]; // Set up columns
   }
   catch (std::bad_alloc) {
        Application->MessageBox(L"Could not allocate memory for matrix A.  Bye ...",
           L"Allocation Error for Matrix A[][]", MB_OK);
        exit(-1);
   }
   try {                                 // Allocating memory for APA
      APA = new double*[NP];                     // Set up rows
      for(j=0;j<NP;j++)APA[j] = new double [NP];   // Set up columns
   }
   catch (std::bad_alloc) {
        Application->MessageBox(L"Could not allocate memory for matrix APA.  Bye ...",
           L"Allocation Error for Matrix APA[][]", MB_OK);
        exit(-1);
   }
}
```

Whenever memory is allocated, it is important to deallocate it when the class is no longer needed. Note that deallocating matrices requires a for() loop to deallocate each vector.

```
FRMREGRESSION::~FRMREGRESSION()                // Destructor
{
   int j;
   delete [] Index;                          // Delete Index vector
   delete [] APB;                            // Delete APB vector
   for(j=0; j<NP; j++) delete [] A[j];       // Delete columns of A
   delete [] A;                              // Delete rows of A
   for(j=0; j<NP; j++) delete [] APA[j];     // Delete columns of A
   delete [] APA;                            // Delete rows of A
}

void FRMREGRESSION::FRMSolveRegression(AnsiString inputsinf,
   AnsiString inputsoutf, AnsiString inputsoutf1)
{
```

All three files must have the appropriate associated variable type definition (inf, outf, and outf1) and these files must be opened. See the appendix below for an illustration of the content of these files.

```
   ifstream inf;   // Input file
   ofstream outf;  // Output details file
   ofstream outf1; // Output file
   inf.open(inputsinf.c_str(), ios::in);  // Open input file
   outf.open(inputsoutf.c_str());  // Open output details file
   outf1.open(inputsoutf1.c_str());  // Open output file (just X's)
```

Input variables arc read in from the input file and written to the output files.

```
int NRows, NColumns;
inf >> NColumns; // Number of x variables
inf >> NRows; // Number of observations AX = B
for(int i=0; i < NRows; i++){
    inf >> B[i];
    for (int j=0; j < NColumns; j++) {
        inf >> A[i][j];
    }
}
inf.close();  // Closes input file
// NRows - number of rows, NColumns - number of colums
// A - NRows by NColumns matrix of A in AX = B, B - NRows by 1 of B in AX = B
int i, j, k, l;   // counters
double d;
outf << "\nOriginal A matrix:\n";
for (k=0; k<NRows; k++) {
    for (l=0; l<NColumns; l++) {
```

Note that the symbol to push data to an output file, <<, goes in a different direction than the symbol to pull data in from an input file, >>.

```
        outf << setiosflags(ios::showpoint | ios::fixed) << setprecision(6)
            << setfill(' ') << setiosflags(ios::right) << setw(12) << A[k][l];
    }
    outf << "\n";
}
outf << "\nOriginal B matrix:\n";
for (k=0; k<NRows; k++) {
    outf << setiosflags(ios::showpoint | ios::fixed) << setprecision(5)
        << setiosflags(ios::right) << setw(8) << B[k] << " ";
}
outf << "\n";
// Compute APA and APB (the normal equations of the linear least squares problem)
for(i=0; i<NColumns; i++){
    for(j=0; j<NColumns; j++){
        APA[i][j] = 0.0;
        for(k=0; k<NRows; k++) APA[i][j] += A[k][j] * A[k][i];
    }
    APB[i] = 0.0;
    for(k=0; k<NRows; k++) APB[i] += A[k][i] * B[k];
}
outf << "\nAPA matrix:\n";
for (k=0; k<NColumns; k++) {
    for (l=0; l<NColumns; l++)
        outf << setiosflags(ios::showpoint | ios::fixed) << setprecision(6)
            << setfill(' ') << setiosflags(ios::right) << setw(12) << APA[k][l];
    outf << "\n";
}
outf << "\nAPB matrix:\n";
for(k=0; k<NColumns; k++)
    outf << setiosflags(ios::showpoint | ios::fixed) << setprecision(6)
        << setfill(' ') << setiosflags(ios::right) << setw(12) << APB[k];
outf << "\n";
```

The LU decomposed matrices are stored in APA for memory efficiency.

```
// Perform the LU decomposition
FRMLUDecomposition(APA, NColumns, Index, &d);  // Decompose the matrix just once
outf << "\nAPA matrix: (LU Decomposed)\n";
for (k=0; k<NColumns; k++) {
    for (l=0; l<NColumns; l++)
        outf << setiosflags(ios::showpoint | ios::fixed) << setprecision(6)
            << setfill(' ') << setiosflags(ios::right) << setw(12) << APA[k][l];
    outf << "\n";
}
outf << "\nIndex vector:\n"; // Row permutations
for(k=0; k<NColumns; k++)
    outf << setiosflags(ios::showpoint | ios::fixed) << setprecision(6)
        << setfill(' ') << setiosflags(ios::right) << setw(12) << Index[k];
outf << "\n\nd = " << d << "\n";
```

```
outf << "\nSolution to set of linear equations \n";
```

The unknown parameters are stored in APB. Thus, after calling FRMLUDecomposition(), APA becomes the LU matrix and after calling FRMCalculateX(), APB becomes the solution to the unknown parameters (betas in the discussion above or X here).

```
//Solve linear regression based on LU decomposition in APA, solution returned in APB
    FRMCalculateX(APA, NColumns, Index, APB);
    outf1 <<  NColumns; // FRMRegression.prn (number of X parameters)
    for (k=0; k<NColumns; k++){
        outf << setiosflags(ios::showpoint | ios::fixed) << setprecision(6)
            << setfill(' ') << setiosflags(ios::right) << setw(12) << APB[k];
        outf1 << setiosflags(ios::showpoint | ios::fixed) << setprecision(6)
            << setfill(' ') << setiosflags(ios::right) << setw(12) << APB[k];
    }
    outf << "\n";
    outf.close();  // Close output details file
    outf1.close();  // Close output file (just X's)
}

void FRMREGRESSION::FRMLUDecomposition(double **LU, int NColumns, int *Index, double *d)
...
void FRMREGRESSION::FRMCalculateX(double **LU, int NColumns, int *Index, double B[])
```

The two functions above follow Press, et. al. very closely.

References

Press, William H., Brian P. Flannery, Saul A. Teukolsky, and William T. Vetterling, *Numerical Recipes in C The Art of Scientific Computing* Second Edition, (Cambridge, England: Cambridge University Press, 1989).

Appendix 3.4: Interface code comments

The interface is virtually identical with Module 2.11, modified slightly for the needs here. The GUI is illustrated below.

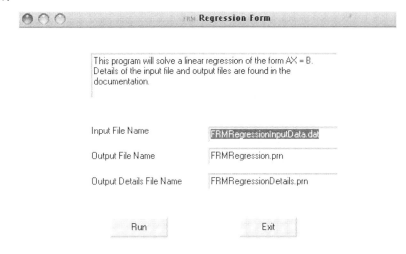

The input data file structure is illustrated in the following picture of the first portion of the FRMRegressionInputData.dat file.

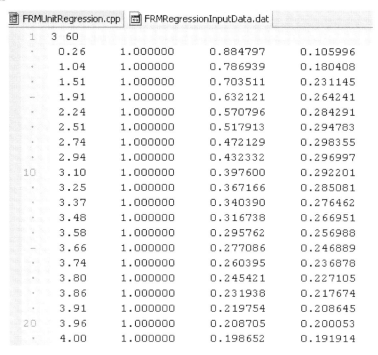

The first line indicates the ordinary least squares regression has three parameters and sixty input observations that follow in this file. The output file, FRMRegression.prn, contains the number of parameters and the parameter estimates based on the input data set.

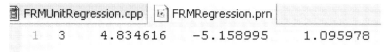

For many programs, the analyst will want to produce a detailed file. If something goes wrong with a particular program, these detailed files may contain helpful information for diagnosing problems. The picture below picks up on line 61 (the last two lines of the input data or the A matrix in the code).

FRMUnitRegression.cpp   FRMRegressionDetails.prn

```
        1.000000      0.067797      0.067796
        1.000000      0.066667      0.066666


     Original B matrix:
      0.26000   1.04000   1.51000   1.91000   2.240


     APA matrix:
        60.000000     12.684718      9.163908
        12.684718      4.801522      2.497764
         9.163908      2.497764      1.735501


     APB matrix:
       234.680000     39.292205     33.320093


     APA matrix:  (LU Decomposed)
         9.163908      2.497764      1.735501
         1.384204      1.344107      0.095477
         6.547425     -2.729847     -1.938518


     Index vector:
                   2               1               2


     d = -1.000000


     Solution to set of linear equations
         4.834616     -5.158995      1.095978
```

The notation in the source code assumes the independent variables are in the B vector, the dependent variables are in the A matrix, and we are solving for the parameter vector X.

The following are snippets of the interface header code with selected comments added. As we move forward in this material, there will be less emphasis on interface code.

FRMUnitRegression.h

```
//------------------------------------------------------------------------
#ifndef FRMUnitRegressionH
#define FRMUnitRegressionH
...
```

Depending on how your repository is set up, you may need to modify the next line of code to accommodate your system. The importance of a repository will manifest itself as we move through Module 3.5, which is built upon this module.

```
#include "c:\FRMRepository\FRMRegression.cpp"
//------------------------------------------------------------------------
class TRegressionForm : public TForm
{
...
```

An object of type FRMREGRESSION is instantiated. Note that the only point of contact between the interface code and the implementation code will be in FRMExecute() and it will be a member function in FRMREGRESSION referenced with "R. ...".

```
private: // User declarations
    FRMREGRESSION R;
```

. . .

The following are snippets of the interface code with selected comments added.

FRMUnitRegression.cpp

The execute function takes the file names and places them in the AnsiString variables.

```
...
void __fastcall TRegressionForm::btnRunClick(TObject *Sender)
{
    FRMExecute();
    lblFinished->Visible = true;
}
//-----------------------------------------------------------------------
void __fastcall TRegressionForm::FRMExecute()
{
    AnsiString sinf, soutf, soutf1;
    sinf = editInputFileName->Text;
    soutf = editOutputDetailsFileName->Text;
    soutf1 = editOutputFileName->Text;
```

Recall AnsiString holds the file names and the regression routine receives these AnsiStrings. The inputs as well as outputs are held in files; hence this function does not need to return anything. In practice, it is a good idea to return an integer that could contain various different values depending on potential errors, such as file not found. We do not address these types of issues to avoid getting too bogged down in coding minutia. The final step of FRMExecute() references the FRMSolveRegression() method in the FRMREGRESSION class through the object R and passes the AnsiStrings.

```
    R.FRMSolveRegression(sinf, soutf, soutf1);
}
```

Module 3.5. Curve Fitting Using Regression

Learning objectives

- Develop a module to estimate the parameters for a fitted curve of term structure of interest rate data
- Illustrate the benefits of object-oriented module development (this module is based on Module 3.4)
- Review how to manipulate files, read input, and write properly formatted output
- Review implementation code for fitting a curve based on ordinary least squares regression

See program FRMLSCTest in *3.5 LSC Curve Fitting Model.*

Module overview

Fitted term structure models can be viewed from two perspectives: calendar time and maturity time. The calendar time perspective is focused on the behavior of the term structure over time. For example, explaining the cross-sectional differences in bond returns is measured in calendar time, such as the past month. The maturity time perspective is focused on the shape of the term structure at a particular point in calendar time. For example, explaining the shape of U. S. Treasury notes and bonds yields with different time to maturity. The calendar time perspective addresses the stochastic nature of the term structure of interest rates whereas the maturity time perspective is solely focused on the current observed relationship of observed yields and maturity. Although our focus is maturity time, we review the literature on both perspectives, as they are important for our purposes. Once the term structure can be reasonably estimated from a maturity time perspective, only then can the stochastic nature of the time series perspective be reasonably understood.

Fitted calendar time term structure models

Prior empirical studies of the term structure of interest rates have documented several well-known observations. Crack and Nawalkha (2000) summarize that "(u)p to 95 percent of the returns to U. S. Treasury security portfolios are explained by term-structure level shifts, slope shifts, and curvature shifts (Litterman and Scheinkman 1991; Jones 1991; Willner 1996; Jamshidian and Zhu 1997)." (p. 34)

Jamshidian and Zhu (1997) apply principal components analysis to the yield curve in three countries: Germany, Japan and the United States. They find that about 94 percent of the variation in "yield curve movements" is explained by only three components. Because this analysis was based on Riskmetrics, it is unclear how these results were influenced by various smoothing techniques. It is important to note that yield curve movements are not the same as bond returns, although they are related.

Litterman and Scheinkman (1991) examine weekly excess returns to U. S. Treasury bonds from February 22, 1984 through August 17, 1988 and find that a three-factor model explains on average 97% of the cross-sectional variation of excess bond returns. The factor model employed unobservable factors where "each factor has a mean of zero and a unit variance, and that the covariance between any two distinct factors is zero." (p. 57)

Jones (1991) reports that of the variation in U. S. Treasury bond portfolio returns, "86.6% of the return has been attributable to parallel shifts in the yield curve, 9.8% to twists, and 3.6% to butterfly changes." (p. 43) Jones' results are based on annual observations of six maturity ranges provided by the Merrill Lynch Treasury bond Indexes from 1979 through 1990.

Knez, Litterman and Scheinkman (1994) examine money market security (U. S. Treasury bills, commercial paper, certificates of deposit, Eurodollar certificates of deposit, and bankers' acceptances) returns from January 1985 to August 1988 and "find that three factors explain, on average, 86 percent of the total variation in returns and four factors explain 90 percent." (p. 1880)

Fitted maturity time term structure models

The goal of this strand of research is to represent the term structure by some mathematical function that has desirable properties. As quoted in Nelson and Siegel (1987), Milton Friedman recognized the benefits of a parsimonious term structure model when he states, "Students of statistical demand functions might find it more productive to examine how the whole term structure of yields can be described more compactly by a few parameters."[17] There is a large literature on fitting the term structure dating at least back to Durand (1942) and includes piecewise polynomial splines (McCulloch (1971, 1975)), various parametric models (Fisher (1966), Echols and Elliott (1976), Cooper (1977), Dobson (1978), and Chambers, Carleton and Waldman (1984)), and exponential splines (Vasicek and Fong (1982)). Several authors offer subjectively drawn curves, including Woods (1983), Malkiel (1966), and Durand (1942).

Willner (1996) posits that the desirable properties of a curve fitting routine must address the bond "portfolio manager's need for *intuitive*, *descriptive*, and *comprehensive* risk exposure information" (p. 49, italics in original). Nelson and Siegel (1987) provide one such model and appeared to be motivated by the mathematical relationship between spot rates and forward rates. They put forward a parsimonious model that was "solved from differential equations describing rational interest rate behavior" (p. 50, Willner (1996)). Specifically, based on our notation

$$r\left(\tau_i : t_k\right) = \sum_{n=0}^{2} C_{i,n}\left(\tau_i; s\right) b_{n,t_k}$$

where

$$C_{i,0}\left(\tau_i; s\right) = 1, \quad C_{i,1}\left(\tau_i; s\right) = \frac{s}{\tau_i}\left[1 - e^{-\tau_i/s}\right], \text{ and } C_{i,2}\left(\tau_i; s\right) = \frac{s}{\tau_i}\left[1 - e^{-\tau_i/s}\right] - e^{-\tau_i/s}$$

where s denotes a scalar that applies various weights to different locations on the term structure (termed the time constant by Nelson and Siegel (1987) and the hump position parameter by Willner (1996) and "determines the rate at which the regressor variable decay to zero"[18]); $C_{i,n}\left(\tau_i; s\right)$ denotes maturity coefficients, a parameter that depends solely on maturity time and the selected scalar; and $b_{n,t}$ denotes the spot rate factor, a parameter that is typically found using ordinary least squares regression applied to maturity time spot rates.

This model has several desirable properties:

- As maturity approaches infinity, the spot rate approaches b_{0,t_k}, the 'level' of the term structure
- As maturity approaches zero, the spot rate approaches $b_{0,t_k} + b_{1,t_k}$, where $-b_{1,t_k}$ is the 'slope' of the term structure
- b_{2,t_k} measures the 'curvature' that appears in the intermediate maturities

Barret, Gosnell and Heuson (1995) and Willner (1996) both report that fitted yield curve functions are not that sensitive to the choice of the scalar.[19]

Steeley (2008) used daily UK government bond coupon STRIPS from December 8, 1997 to May 15, 2002 and thoroughly examines a variety of curve fitting methodologies. Spot yield curve fitting methodologies include cubic spline, polynomial, Vasicek and the LSC model below (referred by Steeley as the extended Svensson model). Based on a three-factor model as used below, Steeley documents that the LSC model has the lowest "average (across the sample) mean (across the curve)

---

[17] Quoted in Nelson and Siegel (1987), page 474.
[18] See Nelson and Siegel (1987), page 478.
[19] See Willner (1996), p. 51.

absolute yield error". (p. 1502) With six factors, Steeley reports that the cubic spline has the best fit, but the LSC model is a close second.

We now focus on the LSC model due to our interest in robust bond portfolio risk measures.

LSC model

Svensson (1995) developed an accurate methodology based on the work of Nelson and Siegel (1987). We call this approach the LSC model for level, slope, and curvature. We use a general form that can be expressed as

$$r(\tau_i : t_k) = \sum_{n=0}^{N_F} C_{i,n}(\tau_i; s_{n-1}) b_{n,t_k}$$

where

$$C_{i,0}(\tau_i; s_{-1}) = 1, \; C_{i,1}(\tau_i; s_0) = \frac{s_0}{\tau_i}\left[1 - e^{-\tau_i/s_0}\right], \text{ and } C_{i,n}(\tau_i; s_{n-1}) = \frac{s_{n-1}}{\tau_i}\left[1 - e^{-\tau_i/s_{n-1}}\right] - e^{-\tau_i/s_{n-1}}; n > 1$$

where s_n again denotes scalars that apply various weights to different locations on the term structure, $C_{i,n}(\tau_i; s_{n-1})$ denotes LSC maturity coefficients, a parameter that depends solely on maturity time and selected scalars; and $b_{n,t}$ denotes the LSC spot rate factor, a parameter that is typically found using ordinary least squares regression applied to maturity time spot rates. (See Appendix A for mathematical details related to the LSC model.) Again, note that as maturity goes to infinity, $\tau_i \rightarrow +\infty$, then $r(\tau_i : t_k) \rightarrow b_{0,t_k}$. Thus, b_{0,t_k} is interpreted as the 'level' of interest rates. As maturity goes to zero, $\tau_i \rightarrow 0$, then $r(\tau_i : t_k) \rightarrow b_{0,t_k} + b_{1,t_k}$. Thus, $-b_{1,t_k}$ is interpreted as the 'slope' of interest rates. Note that if the interest rate term structure is upward sloping then b_{1,t_k} is negative.

To illustrate this empirical approach, consider the market information available on October 31, 2008. Figure 1 illustrates the nine CMT yields (6 month, 1, 2, 3, 5, 7, 10, 20, and 30 year), as well as 6 month spaced, linearly interpolated yields on a yearly basis between provided CMT yields. The goal is to provide a smooth set of observations from only nine CMT yields. Thus, we first compute the linearly interpolated values and then fit the LSC model.

Figure 1. Linear interpolation

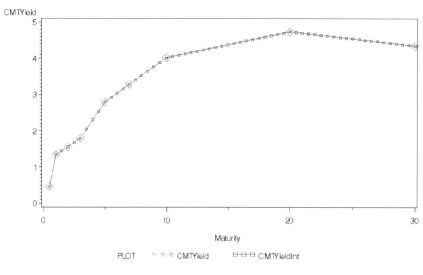

To achieve the maximum fit, we chose to use a nine-factor LSC model at this point. The eight scalars used are 0.5, 1.5, 2, 5, 7, 10, 15, and 20.[20] Figure 2 illustrates this result. It is not surprising that this model fits the data very well.

Figure 2. LSC Model with Nine Factors

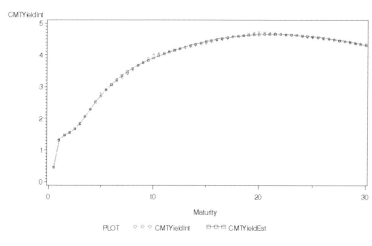

With this complete set of approximated CMT yields, we compute the implied discount factors as well as the implied, continuously compounded, spot rates. Figure 3 illustrates these implied spot rates. With this complete set of spot rates, we are now ready to estimate the three-factor LSC model developed here.

---

[20] The results are not sensitive to the choice of scalars, due to the large number of factors.

Figure 3. Implied Spot Rates

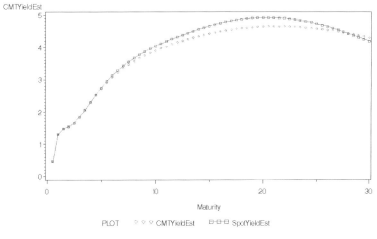

The three-factor LSC model with a single scalar set to 3.0 is applied to the spot rates. Figure 4 presents the original CMT data (all 11 observations, including 1- and 3-month CMT). Note that the fit is far from precise. By design, a three-factor model will not fit a complex interest rate data perfectly. One potential objective is bond risk measurement; hence, it should be clear that the LSC model is capturing more than just parallel shifts in spot rates.

Figure 4. Original CMT Compared with Fitted CMT

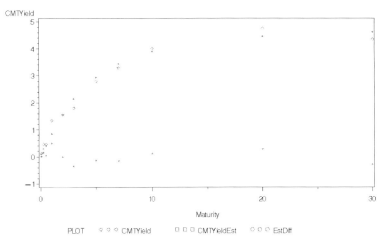

We now examine a similar problem based on interest rate swap data. The LSC model is illustrated below with interest rate swap data for January 29, 2009. Note that swap rates are not annualized, continuously compounded spot rates. The general curve fitting approach of the LSC model works well for most shapes of the term structure.

		Regression Variables		
Level	3.50618%			
Slope	-2.95534%			
Curvature	-0.35538%			
Scalar	2.00			
		Regression Variables		
Maturity	y	x1	x2	
0.00001	na	1.00000	0.00000	
1	1.16%	0.78694	0.18041	
2	1.48%	0.63212	0.26424	
3	1.84%	0.51791	0.29478	
4	2.14%	0.43233	0.29700	
5	2.33%	0.36717	0.28508	
7	2.62%	0.27709	0.24689	
10	2.89%	0.19865	0.19191	
30	3.25%	0.06667	0.06667	

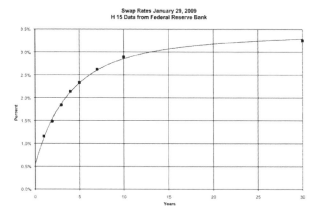

In the LSC-related data above, Maturity provides the τ_i, y denotes the observed swap rates ($r(\tau_i : t_k = 01/29/2009)$), x0 (not shown) is the intercept term ($C_{i,0}(\tau_i; s_{-1}) = 1$), x1 denotes $C_{i,1}(\tau_i; s_0)$, and x2 denotes $C_{i,2}(\tau_i; s_1)$. The resulting LSC parameters are $b_{0,01/29/2009} = 3.50618\%$ (Level), $b_{1,01/29/2009} = -2.95534\%$ (Slope), and $b_{2,01/29/2009} = -0.35538\%$ (Curvature).

Thus, the LSC curve-fitting module is very flexible and can be solved using ordinary least squares regression.

Implementation code comments

We now turn to examining the code.

FRMLSCCurveFitting.h

Selected portions of the header file with comments follow. The header file includes the regression class discussed in the previous module. Notice that the class FRMLSC inherits all the functionality of FRMREGRESSION by declaring it public in this class.

```
...
#include "c:\FRMRepository\FRMRegression.cpp"

class FRMLSC : public FRMREGRESSION
```

The FRMAnalyzeCurve() function also references AnsiString variables that hold the relevant file names.

```
...
// Solve for level, slope and curvature
   void FRMAnalyzeCurve(AnsiString inputsinf, AnsiString inputsoutf);
...
```

FRMLSCCurveFitting.cpp

Selected portions of the C++ code file with comments follow. First, recall that memory is best allocated in the constructor and it is important to use the try{} and catch{} routines.

```
#include "c:\FRMRepository\FRMLSCCurveFitting.h"

FRMLSC::FRMLSC()                    // Constructor
{   // Allocating memory for Factor
    try {
        Factor = new double*[CFARRAYSIZE];                          // Set up rows
        for(j=0;j<CFARRAYSIZE;j++)Factor[j] = new double [RFARRAYSIZE];       // Set up columns
    }
    catch (std::bad_alloc) {
        Application->MessageBox(L"Could not allocate memory for matrix Factor. Bye ...",
            L"Allocation Error for Matrix Factor[][]", MB_OK);
```

```
        exit(-1);
    }
...
```

The FRMAnalyzeCurve routine receives information from the input data file, manipulates it in a form that can be used in the FRMRegression routine that is now public in FRMLSC, and finally outputs the results to a file. The program is set up to be able to repeat these calculations if more than one set of data is contained in the input file.

```
void FRMLSC::FRMAnalyzeCurve(AnsiString inputsinf, AnsiString inputsoutf)
{
    int NColumns, NRows, Counter, NVars;
    double x;
    ifstream inf;                   // Input file
    ofstream outf1;                 // Output file
    inf.open(inputsinf.c_str(), ios::in);  // Open input file
    outf1.open(inputsoutf.c_str());  // Open output
    ...
```

In the next line, the while loop is conditioned on the input file not being at the end of the file.

```
    while(inf)
    {
        if(Counter==0)inf >> CurveDate >> ws;    // Handle date
        for(j=0; j<NRows; j++) inf >> Rate[j];
```

Manipulate the maturity data in a form consistent with the LSC model.

```
        if(Maturity[0] <= 1.0/365.0)Maturity[0] = 1.0/365.0;
        for(i=0; i<NRows; i++){
            for(j=0; j<NColumns; j++){
                if(j==0)Factor[i][j] = 1.0;
                if(j==1)Factor[i][j] = (1.0 - exp(-Maturity[i]/Tau[0]))/(Maturity[i]/Tau[0]);
                if(j>1)Factor[i][j] =
                    (1.0 - exp(-Maturity[i]/Tau[j-2]))/(Maturity[i]/Tau[j-2])
                    - exp(-Maturity[i]/Tau[j-2]);
            }
        }
```

Create an output file to be used by the regression routine. The user of the LSC module is not required to know about this file.

```
// Create FRMRegressionInputData
        ofstream outf;                  // Output file FRMRegressionInputData.dat
        outf.open("FRMRegressionInputData.dat");  // Open output details file
        outf << NColumns << ' ';
        outf << NRows << '\n';
        for(j=0; j<NRows; j++){
            outf << setiosflags(ios::showpoint | ios::fixed) << setprecision(2)
                << setfill(' ') << setiosflags(ios::right) << setw(5) << Rate[j];
            for(i=0; i<NColumns; i++){
                outf << setiosflags(ios::showpoint | ios::fixed) << setprecision(6)
                    << setfill(' ') << setiosflags(ios::right) << setw(13) << Factor[j][i];
            }
            outf << '\n';
        }
        outf.close();
        AnsiString sinf, soutf, soutf1;
```

Create the required data files that the regression program is expecting and then run the regression routine.

```
        sinf = "FRMRegressionInputData.dat";
        soutf = "FRMRegressionDetails.prn";
        soutf1 = "FRMRegression.prn";
        FRMSolveRegression(sinf, soutf, soutf1);
...
```

Now attempt to read in the next line of data. If no additional lines exist, then the next line will make inf evaluate to false and the while loop above will terminate.

```
    inf >> CurveDate >> ws;    // Handle date and check for end of file
    Counter++; // increment
  };
  inf.close();  // Closes input file
  outf1.close();
}
...
```

There are several additional functions in this module that are not referenced here.

References

Dobson, S., 1978. Estimating term structure equations with individual bond data. Journal of Finance 33, 75-92.

Durand, D., 1942. Basic yields of corporate bonds, 1900-1942. National Bureau of Economic Research, Technical Paper no. 3, Cambridge, MA.

Echols, M. and Elliott, J., 1976. A quantitative yield curve model for estimating the term structure of interest rates. Journal of Finance and Quantitative Analysis 11, 87-114..

Litterman, R. and Scheinkman, J., 1991. Common factors affecting bond returns. Journal of Fixed Income, 1 (June 1991), 54-61.

Macaulay, F., 1938. Some theoretical problems suggested by the movement of interest rates, bonds, yields, and stock prices in the United States since 1856. Columbia University Press, New York, NY.

Malkiel, B., 1966. The term structure of interest rates. Princeton University Press, Princeton, N.J.

McCulloch, J., 1971. Measuring the term structure of interest rates. Journal of Business 34, 19-31.

Nelson, C., and Siegel, A., 1987. Parsimonious modeling of yield curves. Journal of Business 60, 473-489.

Steeley, J., 2008. Testing term structure estimation methods: Evidence from the UK STRIPS Market. Journal of Money, Credit and Banking 40, 1489-1512.

Svensson, L., 1995. Estimating futures interest rates with the extended Nelson and Siegel method. Institute for International Economic Studies, Stockholm University, Reprint Series, No. 543 from Quarterly Review (Swedish Central Bank) No. 3.

Vasicek, O. and Fong, G., 1982. Term structure modeling using exponential splines. Journal of Finance 37, 339-48.

Willner, R., 1996. A new tool for portfolio managers: level, slope, and curvature durations. Journal of Fixed Income 6, 48-59.

Appendix 3.5: Interface code comments

The LSC program interface is virtually identical with Module 2.11 and 3.4 so we do not replicate it here. The graphical user interface is illustrated below.

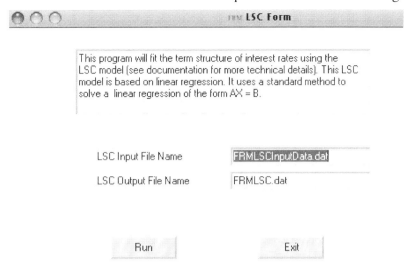

The input data file structure is illustrated in the following picture of the FRMLSCInputData.dat file.

The first line indicates that the desired fit of the LSC model has three parameters and seven input observations that follow in this file. The scalar variable used for this LSC fit is 2.0. The output file, FRMLSC.dat, contains only the parameter estimates based on the input data set. In the example below, the Level is 3.73%, the Slope is –3.15%, and the Curvature is –5.79%.

```
  FRMUnitLSC.h  |  FRMLSC.dat
      3  2.00
            2/22/2012    3.727110   -3.149825   -5.786772
```

FRMUnitRegression.h

```
//------------------------------------------------------------------------
#ifndef FRMUnitRegressionH
#define FRMUnitRegressionH
...
```

Depending on how your repository is set up, you may need to modify the next line of code to accommodate your system.

```
#include "c:\FRMRepository\FRMRegression.cpp"
//------------------------------------------------------------------------
class TRegressionForm : public TForm
{
...
```

An object of type FRMREGRESSION is instantiated. Note that the only point of contact between the interface code and the implementation code will be in FRMExecute() and it will be a member function in FRMREGRESSION referenced with "R. ...".

```
private: // User declarations
   FRMREGRESSION R;
...
```

The following are snippets of the interface code with selected comments added.

FRMUnitRegression.cpp

The execute function takes the file names and places them in the AnsiString variables.

```
...
void __fastcall TRegressionForm::btnRunClick(TObject *Sender)
{
   FRMExecute();
   lblFinished->Visible = true;
}
//-----------------------------------------------------------------
void __fastcall TRegressionForm::FRMExecute()
{
   AnsiString sinf, soutf, soutf1;
   sinf = editInputFileName->Text;
   soutf = editOutputDetailsFileName->Text;
   soutf1 = editOutputFileName->Text;
```

Recall AnsiString holds the file names and the regression routine receives these AnsiStrings. The inputs as well as outputs are held in files, hence this function does not need to return anything. In practice, it is a good idea to return an integer that could contain various different value depending on potential errors, such as file not found. We do not address these types of issues to avoid getting too bogged down in coding minutia.

```
   R.FRMSolveRegression(sinf, soutf, soutf1);
}
```

Module 3.6. Sorting Data

Learning objectives

- Explain how to sort data very efficiently using the recommended *Numerical Recipes in C* heapsort routine
- Review the manner in which data files can be manipulated
- Learn the variety of financial uses of sorting routines
- Review implementation code

See program FRMSortingDataTest in *3.6 Sorting Data*.

Module overview

The ability to sort data is very important for a wide array of financial tasks. We first review some of the financial applications and then introduce the heapsort methodology. Heapsort denotes the two-step process of first creating a "heap" and then the data is "sorted." Although the technical aspects are not that important, heapsort is a very efficient algorithm for sorting data that does not require any additional memory.

Financial applications of sorting

There are several financial tools that require numerical data to be sorted. For example, when computing value-at-risk using Monte Carlo simulation or historical simulation, the numerical data is sorted and then the value-at-risk measure is computed.

Investment managers often will produce histograms of a portfolio's historical rates of return. To produce these histograms, the data must first be sorted. When exploring the use of leverage, a variety of portfolios are constructed and various distributions can be examined. Each of these distributions would first be sorted.

Module 6.4 Stock Portfolio Historical Simulation of Value-at-Risk and Module 6.5 Futures Portfolio Monte Carlo Simulation both require returns data to be sorted.

Heapsort

The sorting routine known as heapsort is a preferred sorting routine of Press, et. al. (1992). One of the main advantages is that heapsort does not require any additional storage. If we are trying to sort results from a Monte Carlo simulation of 30,000 draws, it is very useful not to have to allocate any more memory than the vector holding the simulation results.

Other sorting routines computational time varies widely depending on the initial data. Heapsort is not that sensitive and is fairly computationally efficient.

Implementation code comments

FRMSortingData.h

We provide portions of this header file below with some comments. The input data is assumed to be less than 30,000 observations. You can easily change this maximum level on line 2 #define SORTNP. Because we read data in from a file, we need to include fstream.h.

```
...
#include <fstream.h>      // File I/O
#define SORTNP 30000

class FRMSORT
{
public:
...
```

The vector A holds both the original input data, as well as the final output data.

```
   double *A;
   ifstream inf;                    // Input file
   ofstream outf;                   // Output file
   FRMSORT::FRMSORT();
   FRMSORT::~FRMSORT();
   void FRMSetUp(AnsiString inputsinf, AnsiString inputsoutf);
   void FRMHPSort(long int, double*);
...
```

This module relies heavily on Press, et. al. for implementation of heapsort. Leaving notes for yourself can greatly lower the need to "reinvent the wheel" each time you have to revisit a particular module. Recall lines 4 and 5 above reference the constructor and destuctor used in file management.

```
/******************************************************************
** REFERENCES
** Press, William H., Saul A. Teukolsky, William T. Vetterling,
** and Brian P. Flannery, _Numerical Recipes in C_ (Cambridge: Cambridge
** University Press, 1992.
******************************************************************/
```

FRMSortingData.cpp

We provide only portions of the source code with comments here. We allocate and deallocate memory in the constructor and destructor.

```
...
FRMSORT::FRMSORT()
{
   try { A = new double [SORTNP]; }              // Allocating memory for A
   catch (std::bad_alloc) {
      Application->MessageBox(L"Could not allocate memory for vector 'A'.  Bye ...",
         L"Allocation Error for Vector A[]", MB_OK);
      exit(-1);
   }
}

FRMSORT::~FRMSORT()
{
   delete [] A;  // Delete "A" vector
}
```

We use FRMSetUp to read the input data from the appropriate file, call the FRMHPSort() function to sort the A vector and then write the sorted vector out to an output file. Read the comments after the // to find more detail of what each line of code is doing.

```
void FRMSORT::FRMSetUp(AnsiString inputsinf, AnsiString inputsoutf)
{
   ifstream inf;                 // Input file
   ofstream outf;                // Output file
   inf.open(inputsinf.c_str(), ios::in);  // Open input file
   outf.open(inputsoutf.c_str());          // Open output file
   inf >> NumberOfDraws;                    // Number of data points
   for (i = 0; i < NumberOfDraws; i++) inf >> A[i];  // Input data read in
   FRMHPSort(NumberOfDraws, A);                        // Kernel sorting routine
   outf.width(5);   outf.setf(ios::right);
   outf << NumberOfDraws << "\n";
   for (i = 0; i < NumberOfDraws; i++){
      outf.width(11);   outf.precision(6);
      outf.setf(ios::right); outf.setf(ios::fixed, ios::floatfield);
      outf << A[i];                          // Output sorted vector
      if(!((i+1)%10))outf << "\n";           // New line every 10 data points
   }
   inf.close();  // Close input file
   outf.flush();
   outf.close(); // Close output file
}
```

This method is an adaptation of Press, et. al.

```
void FRMSORT::FRMHPSort(long int n, double B[])
{
...
}
```

References

Press, William H., Brian P. Flannery, Saul A. Teukolsky, and William T. Vetterling, *Numerical Recipes in C The Art of Scientific Computing* Second Edition, (Cambridge, England: Cambridge University Press, 1989).

Appendix 3.6: Interface code comments

The interface code for the sorting data program is virtually identical to several previous modules and will not be repeated here but can be found in the following files.

FRMUnitSortingData.cpp, .h

See Modules 2.11, 3.4, and 3.5. The graphical user interface is illustrated below.

The data set used here for illustration purposes contains 100 observations, 10 observations per line.

```
FRMUnitSortingData.h    FRMSortingData.dat
1      100
       29.82  71.51   3.30  87.44  53.42  63.16  89.10  25.75  93.16  27.72
       71.58  48.34  53.11  18.34  27.13  60.31  83.34  22.81  66.84  52.91
       53.42  15.22   8.01  53.39  76.12  79.09  67.61  38.39  24.81  73.21
       13.42  52.10  34.86  99.83  38.46  81.59  61.75  79.62  93.39   3.21
       99.34  92.22  94.29   7.03   6.67  89.35  83.14   9.01  12.68  62.22
        2.95  85.02  95.82  73.96  49.29  77.72  36.65   3.48  48.98  71.83
        1.41   9.48  32.37  89.95  28.39  79.36  54.05  46.08  11.67  37.78
       77.17  74.33  10.13   4.62  49.95  68.40  19.40  34.06   4.11  98.40
10     42.44  64.14  89.41  52.99  71.79   3.94  19.73  44.91  71.44  59.10
       27.54  15.67  67.95  55.61  26.05  25.01  82.09  89.67  57.08  38.27
```

The sorted data set also contains 100 observations, 10 observations per line, but the number of significant digits is raised to six just to illustrate different file output formatting.

```
FRMUnitSortingData.h    FRMSortingData.prn
1     100
       1.410000   2.950000   3.210000   3.300000   3.480000   3.940000   4.110000   4.620000   6.670000
       8.010000   9.010000   9.480000  10.130000  11.670000  12.680000  13.420000  15.220000  15.670000
      19.400000  19.730000  22.810000  24.810000  25.010000  25.750000  26.050000  27.130000  27.540000
      28.390000  29.820000  32.370000  34.060000  34.860000  36.650000  37.780000  38.270000  38.390000
      42.440000  44.910000  46.080000  48.340000  48.980000  49.290000  49.950000  52.100000  52.910000
      53.110000  53.390000  53.420000  53.420000  54.050000  55.610000  57.080000  59.100000  60.310000
      62.220000  63.160000  64.140000  66.840000  67.610000  67.950000  68.400000  71.440000  71.510000
      71.790000  71.830000  73.210000  73.960000  74.330000  76.120000  77.170000  77.720000  79.090000
10    79.620000  81.590000  82.090000  83.140000  83.340000  85.020000  87.440000  89.100000  89.350000
      89.670000  89.950000  92.220000  93.160000  93.390000  94.290000  95.820000  98.400000  99.340000
```

Module 3.7. Embedded Parameters

Learning objectives

- Explain how to solve for embedded parameters using the Brent method
- Develop the capacity to solve for any embedded parameters using a global function
- Learn how to compute the implied yield to maturity for a simple, fixed rate bond
- Illustrate how to pass a function from one class to another
- Review implementation code to find the yield to maturity for a simple bond valuation equation

See program FRMEmbeddedParametersTest in *3.7 Embedded Parameters*.

Module overview

The ability to solve embedded parameters is introduced here, illustrated with the problem of solving for the appropriate yield to maturity given the current market price of a bond.

Bond pricing and yield to maturity

The simplest way to express the current price (P) of a bond given a fixed coupon (C) with a given face value (Par) and a stated time to maturity (t_N), as well as assumed yield to maturity (ytm) is

$$P = \sum_{i=1}^{N} \frac{C}{(1+ytm)^{t_i}} + \frac{Par}{(1+ytm)^{t_N}}$$

Our focus here is on solving for the yield to maturity, an embedded parameter. This task is accomplished by expressing a function of yield to maturity, such that when the correct embedded parameter is used, then this function returns zero. That is,

$$f(ytm) = \sum_{i=1}^{N} \frac{C}{(1+ytm)^{t_i}} + \frac{Par}{(1+ytm)^{t_N}} - MP$$

The goal of programs like the one presented here is to solve one-dimensional problems like this one numerically. The yield to maturity that makes f(ytm) = 0 is known as the root of this function.

Recall as yield goes up, bond price goes down; as yield goes down, bond price goes up. The price-yield curve can be described as convex. It means that the curve bows away from the origin of the graph illustrated below. (Bowed toward the origin would be called concave.) The idea is when we are given a bond price, we can compute the implied yield to maturity. That is, what yield to maturity will return a bond price equal (within some allowable error) to the observed market price of the bond.

Price

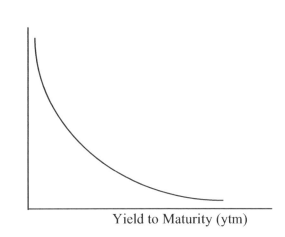

Yield to Maturity (ytm)

Numerical methods

There are no known methods to derive an exact equation for the yield to maturity problem above, as well as numerous other embedded functions in finance, such as option model implied volatility. Almost all functions in finance, however, are continuous, thus making root finding easier. There are innumerable methods, however, to solve for embedded parameters. Methods include bisection, false position, secant, Ridders, Brent, and Newton-Rhapson. Source code is available for each of these methods in *Numerical Recipes in C++*.

Because the Brent method, the one illustrated in this program, is built on concepts from other methods, we briefly introduce some root-finding concepts and methods.

First, at least one solution to an embedded parameter problem is said to be bracketed if in the interval (a, b), the function f(a) and f(b) return opposite signs. Remember that the function is configured such that f(x) = 0 when x is the correct solution to the implied parameter problem.

Second, the method of bisection is very simple and is fail proof. The idea is to take the extremes of the bracket, find the midpoint, and then determine which portion has opposite signs. That is, consider f(a) and f(m) compared to f(m) and f(b), where m = (a + b)/2. If f(a) has an opposite sign as f(m), then set b = m and proceed. Otherwise, set a = m and proceed. Repeat this process until the difference between the brackets is within the allowable error amount.

Third, the secant method assumes that the slope of the function is approximately linear and, based on this slope information, often converges faster than the method of bisection. The secant method requires an initial guess between the two extremes, thus requiring an additional input.

Fourth, Newton-Rhapson is the best choice when the first derivative of the given function is known. Rather than numerically computing the slope of the line, the information contained in the first derivatives is used for the slope. We have found, however, that Brent is extremely reliable and very fast. Therefore, we use it even when computing the first derivative is possible.

Fifth, the concept of inverse quadratic interpolation is exploited in the Brent method. Inverse quadratic interpolation relies on three points to fit an approximation function, thus it is not linear. This approach assumes the implied parameter (x) is roughly a quadratic function of the known parameter (y). Therefore, the inverse quadratic interpolation is more efficient than simple linear interpolation used in the secant and Newton-Rhapson methods.

According to Press, et. al. (1992), "Brent's method combines root bracketing, bisection, and *inverse quadratic interpolation* to converge from the neighborhood of a zero crossing. ... Brent's method combines the sureness of bisection with the speed of a higher-order method when appropriate. We recommend it as the method of choice for general one-dimensional root finding, where a function's values only (and not its derivative or functional form) are available." (p. 360-361)

The Brent method requires the user to bracket the root(s) prior to starting the analysis. Thus, we select a very high and a very low yield to maturity to assure that f(ytm=500%) < 0 and f(ytm=0.001%) > 0. The programmer, rather than the end user, determines these bounds. The programmer must also decide the numerical accuracy where the search will cease. We code an epsilon of 0.000001, thus as long as the absolute value of f(ytm) is less than 0.000001, then the Brent method will stop searching.

Implementation code comments

For this application, there are four files related to the implementation code: FRMBasicBondPrice.h, FRMBasicBondPrice.cpp, FRMBrent.h, and FRMBrent.cpp. We review snippets from each file.

FRMBasicBondPrice.h

We incorporate the functionality of the BRENT class into the BONDPRICE class. Specifically, BONDPRICE inherits from BRENT all of its functionality and data.

```
...
class BONDPRICE : public BRENT
```

Because we are seeking the yield to maturity iteratively, we need to be able to place this data into the class. Note also the use of polymorphism. The function name SetData() is used twice with different number of parameters depending on the particular analysis required.

```
void YieldSetData(double IYLDTM);
void SetData(double ICR, double IPV, int IYRSTM);
void SetData(double ICR, double IPV, double IYLDTM, int IYRSTM);
double CalculateBondPrice();
double CalculateYTM(double AP);
```

FRMBasicBondPrice.cpp

The first issue in this source code is the order of material. Because the global function references the bond price class (BONDPRICE), it must be placed after the class is defined. It does not matter where it is placed otherwise. Second, notice that function is declared and defined outside of a class; it is a global function.

```
...
#include "c:\FRMRepository\FRMBrent.cpp"
#include "FRMBasicBondPrice.h"
// Global function for using Brent method of embedded parameter
BONDPRICE BP;   // Global class instantiation of specific class function in Brent function
double function(double tempX); // function is declared
double function(double tempX)  // function is defined
{
   BP.YieldSetData(tempX);            // Unique to each Brent deployment
   return(BP.CalculateBondPrice()); // Unique to each Brent deployment
};
```

Because this simple bond price class is used in a variety of different contexts, we use polymorphism to place data in the class. The next two methods have the same name, but they have different number of inputs.

```
//-----------------------------------------------------------------------
void BONDPRICE::SetData(double ICR, double IPV, int IYRSTM)   // No YTM
{
   CouponRate = ICR; // Passed input coupon rate ICR to the private CouponRate
   ParValue = IPV;
   YearsToMaturity = IYRSTM;
};
//-----------------------------------------------------------------------
```

```
void BONDPRICE::SetData(double ICR, double IPV, double IYLDTM, int IYRSTM)
{
   CouponRate = ICR; // Passed input coupon rate ICR to the private CouponRate
   ParValue = IPV;
   YieldToMaturity = IYLDTM;
   YearsToMaturity = IYRSTM;
};
```

This is a very simplified bond pricing routine so we can focus on how embedded parameters are found.

```
double BONDPRICE::CalculateBondPrice()
{
   int i;   // Counter used in for loop
   double PV; // Temporary variable holding sum of coupons
   PV = 0.0; // Initialize PV to zero
   for(i=1; i<=YearsToMaturity; i++){   // Loop from 1 to YearsToMaturity by 1
      PV += ((CouponRate/100.0)*ParValue) / pow((1.0 + (YieldToMaturity/100.0)), i);
   };
   return (PV + ParValue / pow((1.0 + (YieldToMaturity/100.0)), YearsToMaturity));
};
```

We first pass the basic data into the bond price class (BP) and then set the data in the Brent class that has been inherited by the bond price class. Finally, the embedded parameter is found with the Brent method located in the function CalculateX(). Notice that the function is passed by address (&function).

```
double BONDPRICE::CalculateYTM(double ActualPrice)
{
   BP.SetData(CouponRate, ParValue, YearsToMaturity);   // Global BONDPRICE object
   BRENTSetData(ActualPrice, 500, 0.001);               // BRENT is public in this class
   return CalculateX(&function);                        // BRENT is public in this class
};
```

FRMBrent.h

The Brent class (BRENT) is written for reuse in a wide variety of applications. Therefore, an effort was made to be as generic as possible. We do not go to an extreme, however. We assume the programmer sets the error rate, maximum number of iterations, and the machine floating-point precision.

```
...
#define EPSILON 0.000001 // Brent error rate
#define SIGN(a,b) ((b) >= 0.0 ? fabs(a) : -fabs(a)) // Brent method
#define ITMAX 100    // Brent method maximum iterations
#define EPS 3.0e-16   // Brent machine floating-point precision, NR=8

class BRENT
{
public:
   double InitialGuess;
   void BRENTSetData(double tempObservedY, double tempMaxX, double tempMinX);
```

The function to solve for the implied parameter receives the address of the function and returns the implied parameter, assumed here to be double.

```
   double CalculateX(double (*function)(double tempX));
...
```

FRMBrent.cpp

An effort is made to preserve the integrity of the *Numerical Recipes in C* original code. Thus, there are only a few minor modifications: the way inputs are handled in the set data function (just like other applications here), how the function is received in the CalculateX() method, and how the function is slightly modified.

```
...
double BRENT::CalculateX(double (*function)(double))  // NR in C modified for C++
{
...
```

We convert the function to subtract the observed f(x) value within CalculateX() as opposed to within the function, to keep from having to pass another variable.

```
fa = function(a) - ObservedFX;
fb = function(b) - ObservedFX;
...
    fb = function(b) - ObservedFX;
...
```

References

Press, William H., Brian P. Flannery, Saul A. Teukolsky, and William T. Vetterling, *Numerical Recipes in C The Art of Scientific Computing* Second Edition, (Cambridge, England: Cambridge University Press, 1989).

Appendix 3.7: Interface code comments

We make just a few coding observations in the interface code. The interface is illustrated below.

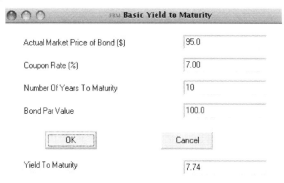

The following are selected snippets of the interface header code with selected comments added.

FRMUnitYTMBasicBrent.h

Note that in the interface code, there is no reference to the Brent method. Brent functions are completely hidden from the interface code. The only reference is to the bond price class.

```
#include "c:\FRMRepository\FRMBasicBondPrice.cpp"
//-------------------------------------------------------------------
class TYTMBrentForm : public TForm
{
...
   BONDPRICE B;
```

The following is the interface code with selected comments added.

FRMUnitYTMBasicBrent.cpp

Again, note that the Brent-related functions are not visible in the interface code.

```
...
   B.SetData(Coupon, Par, NumberOfYearsToMaturity);
   YieldToMaturity = B.CalculateYTM(ActualPrice);
```

Module 3.8: Numerical Integration and the Lognormal Distribution

Learning objectives

- Explain how to use a numerical integration routine
- Compute the probability of an option being in-the-money based on the lognormal distribution
- Contrast the normal and lognormal distribution
- Understand when it is inappropriate to assume an underlying lognormal distribution
- Use a global function to create a generic integration routine

See program FRMNumericalIntegrationTest in *3.8 Numerical Integration.*

Module overview

This module can be used to estimate the probability of a call and put option being in-the-money assuming the underlying instrument's terminal value is lognormally distributed. We also provide several summary statistics for both the lognormal and normal distribution. The parameters of this distribution are based on option-related information and we assume the underlying instrument is expected to grow at the dividend-adjusted risk-free interest rate.[21]

We review the basic properties of the lognormal distribution with a focus on the behavior of the lognormal distribution with very high dispersion. It is fairly common for option prices to imply unreasonable volatilities when we assume a lognormal distribution. One objective here is to identify when the lognormal distribution will likely need to be replaced with an alternative probability distribution.

The lognormal distribution holds a central role in finance. For example, the underlying instrument of financial derivatives is often assumed to follow a lognormal distribution. This distribution is attractive because the underlying instrument cannot be negative due to limited liability, and the lognormal distribution limits are zero (not inclusive) and positive infinity (not inclusive).

The following sections explore in great detail the properties of the lognormal distribution. After reviewing these properties and the applications to finance, we review implementing an integration routine based on C code provided in *Numerical Recipes in C.* By now it should be clear that *Numerical Recipes in C* or its latest variation is a must-have book on the financial analyst's bookshelf.

Because the lognormal distribution is widely used in finance, it is vital to understand its properties.

Properties of the Lognormal Distribution

The lognormal distribution is directly related to the normal distribution. The lognormal distribution has two parameters: the mean, μ, and the standard deviation, σ. At this point, we are using the symbols for mean and standard deviation generically. Later, we will use these same symbols for very specific finance applications.

The mean must be finite, $-\infty < \mu < +\infty$, and the standard deviation must be positive, $\sigma > 0$. The range of the lognormal distribution is the positive real number line or $0 < x < +\infty$.[22] For many finance applications, x would be the underlying instrument's market price, such as a particular stock price. Interestingly, the lognormal distribution does not admit the possibility of x = 0. Thus, one weakness of

---

[21] This assumption is not required; it just makes the transition to the Black, Scholes, Merton option valuation model easier. See modules 4.1, 4.3, and 5.4.

[22] It is unclear to me whether the range of the lognormal is actually $0 < x \leq +\infty$. That is, is positive infinity included or not? I believe not.

the lognormal distribution being used to model a stock price is that the company can never go bankrupt in such a way that the existing stock price is worthless. The financial marketplace is littered with a vast number of worthless common stock. Recall that no mathematical model of reality is correct, but many models are useful. The skilled financial analyst knows the model's limitations. Remember the purpose of analytical tools, such as the lognormal distribution, is to roughly approximate reality. The quantitative professional is always keen to know when these tools will fail to be useful.

If $y = \ln[x]$ is distributed normal, then x is said to have a lognormal distribution.

Lognormal probability density function: $f(x) = \dfrac{1}{x\sigma\sqrt{2\pi}} \exp\left\{ -\dfrac{[\ln(x)-\mu]^2}{2\sigma^2} \right\}$

Normal probability density function: $f(x) = \dfrac{1}{\sigma\sqrt{2\pi}} \exp\left\{ -\dfrac{[x-\mu]^2}{2\sigma^2} \right\}$

Recall the definition of median is $\hat{x}$ such that $\int_0^{\hat{x}} f(x)dx = \int_{\hat{x}}^{+\infty} f(x)dx = \dfrac{1}{2}$. For the lognormal distribution, the median is $\text{Median} = \exp\{\mu\}$ whereas the median of the normal distribution is its mean, μ. Notice that the lognormal distribution median is invariant to the variance of the normal distribution.

Recall the probability distribution mode satisfies $f'(x) = 0$ and $f''(x) < 0$. For the lognormal distribution, the mode is $\text{Mode} = \exp\{\mu - \sigma^2\}$ whereas the mode of the normal distribution is its mean, μ. The lognormal distribution mode is an exponentially decreasing function of the normal distribution variance. This is an important property of the lognormal distribution as it applies to financial applications. A higher normal variance causes the peak of the distribution to be lower.

The first four moments of the lognormal distribution are:

First moment about zero or mean: $\text{Mean} = \exp\left\{\mu + \dfrac{\sigma^2}{2}\right\}$. Thus, the mean is an exponentially increasing function of the normal distribution variance. By definition, the mean of the normal distribution is μ.

The mean of the lognormal distribution is an exponentially increasing function of the normal distribution variance. Recall the lognormal distribution can be viewed as an exponential transformation of a normally distributed variable, say X. Thus, X is symmetric and exp(X) is asymmetric with positive skewness because higher values of X imply values of exp(X) are further from the mean than X. Thus, the lognormal mean is higher for higher normal standard deviations.

The next three moments are presented about the mean (and not zero).

Second moment about the mean (variance): $\text{Variance} = \exp\{2\mu + \sigma^2\}\left(\exp\{\sigma^2\} - 1\right)$. The variance is an exponentially increasing function of the normal distribution variance. By definition, the standard deviation of the normal distribution is σ.

Third moment about the mean: $\mu_3 = \exp\left\{3\mu + \dfrac{3\sigma^2}{2}\right\}\left(\exp\{\sigma^2\} - 1\right)^2\left(\exp\{\sigma^2\} + 2\right)$. The third moment is an exponentially increasing function of the normal distribution variance. The third moment of the normal distribution is zero.

Fourth moment about the mean:

$\mu_4 = \exp\left\{3\mu + \dfrac{3\sigma^2}{2}\right\}\left(\exp\{\sigma^2\}-1\right)^2\left(\exp\{4\sigma^2\}+2\exp\{3\sigma^2\}+3\exp\{2\sigma^2\}-3\right)$. The fourth moment is an exponentially increasing function of the normal distribution variance. The fourth moment of the normal distribution is zero.

Measure of skewness (the third standardized moment): $\gamma_S = \dfrac{\mu_3}{\mu_2^{3/2}} = \left(e^{\sigma^2}-1\right)\sqrt{\left(e^{\sigma^2}+2\right)}$. The skewness is an exponentially increasing function of the normal distribution variance. Symmetrical distributions, such as the normal distribution, will have $\gamma_S = 0$. If $\gamma_S > 0$, then we have the following relationship: mean > median > mode. If $\gamma_S < 0$, then we have the opposite relationship: mean < median < mode. There are, however, some exceptions. See Stuart and Ord [1987], p. 107.

Measure of excess kurtosis (fourth standardized moment minus 3): $\gamma_K = \dfrac{\mu_4}{\mu_2^2} - 3 = e^{4\sigma^2} + 2e^{3\sigma^2} + 3e^{2\sigma^2} - 6$

This measure is termed "excess" because we subtract 3, the value of kurtosis for the normal distribution. The excess kurtosis is an exponentially increasing function of the normal distribution variance. Note that $\gamma_K = 0$ is called mesokurtic. The normal distribution and binomial distributions are mesokurtic. $\gamma_K > 0$ is called leptokurtic, having excess positive excess kurtosis. Leptokurtic distributions have sharper peaks and fatter tails. The lognormal distribution is leptokurtic, as are the Laplace distribution and the logistic distribution. $\gamma_K < 0$ is called platykurtic, having negative excess kurtosis. Platykurtic distributions have flatter peaks and thinner tails. The uniform distribution and Bernoulli distribution (p=1/2) are platykurtic.

Finally, we introduce differential entropy or continuous entropy. Differential entropy developed out of information theory and is supposed to measure the average surprisal, where surprisal denotes the surprise of seeing a particular outcome. (For more on differential entropy, see the information theory literature starting with Wikipedia.)

Entropy of the lognormal distribution: $h_l = \dfrac{1}{2}\left[1 + \ln\left(2\pi\sigma^2\right)\right] + \mu$

Entropy of the normal distribution: $h_n = \dfrac{1}{2}\left[1 + \ln\left(2\pi\sigma^2\right)\right]$

For clarity, consider the following example related to some asset price distribution

Asset price distribution example

Recall if $\tilde{x} \sim N\left(\mu_g, \sigma_g\right)$ (normal distribution, subscript g denote the generic mean and standard deviation – not finance specific) and $\tilde{y} = \exp\{\tilde{x}\}$, then $\tilde{y} \sim \Lambda\left(\mu_g, \sigma_g\right)$ (lognormal distribution). In the context of rates of return, suppose $\tilde{S}_T = S_t \exp\{\tilde{R}(T-t)\}$. In the material to follow, the mean and standard deviation notation uses the traditional finance form.

If a stock's continuously compounded rate of return is distributed normal $\tilde{R} \sim N\left(\mu(T-t), \sigma\sqrt{T-t}\right)$, then the terminal stock price is distributed lognormal $\tilde{S}_T \sim \Lambda\left(\ln(S_0) + \mu(T-t), \sigma\sqrt{T-t}\right)$. Thus, the terminal stock price can be expressed as $E\left[\tilde{S}_T\right] = S_0\exp\left\{\left(\mu + \dfrac{\sigma^2}{2}\right)(T-t)\right\}$ and the variance of the terminal stock price can be expressed as $\mathrm{Var}\left[\tilde{S}_T\right] = S_0^2\left[\exp\{2(\mu+\sigma^2)(T-t)\} - \exp\{(2\mu+\sigma^2)(T-t)\}\right]$. Alternatively, the normal distribution parameters can be expressed as a function of the lognormal distribution parameters,

$$\mu = \ln\left[\frac{E\left[\tilde{S}_t\right]}{S_0}\right]\Bigg/(T-t) \text{ and } \sigma^2 = \ln\left[\frac{\text{var}\left[\tilde{S}_t\right]}{\left\{E\left[\tilde{S}_t\right]\right\}^2} + 1\right]\Bigg/(T-t).$$

We now consider the application to stock returns. Suppose a stock is trading for \$100 and we have a one-year horizon. If we say the annualized, continuously compounded expected rate of return on a stock is 12 percent, what do we mean? Typically, we intend for the following equality to hold:

$$E\left[\tilde{S}_T\right] = S_0 e^{\hat{\mu}(T-t)} = 100 e^{0.12(1)} = 112.749685$$

Note the two different expressions for the terminal expected value of the stock:

$$E\left[\tilde{S}_T\right] = S_0 e^{\hat{\mu}(T-t)}$$

$$E\left[\tilde{S}_T\right] = S_0 \exp\left\{\left(\mu + \frac{\sigma^2}{2}\right)(T-t)\right\}$$

These two expressions are a source of much confusion. These two expressions are easily reconciled by setting

$$\mu = \hat{\mu} - \frac{\sigma^2}{2}$$

Suppose we have $S_0 = \$100$, $T - t = 1$ year, $\hat{\mu} = 12\%$, and $\sigma = 30\%$. Therefore,

$$E\left[\tilde{S}_T\right] = S_0 \exp\left\{\left(\mu + \frac{\sigma^2}{2}\right)(T-t)\right\} = S_0 e^{\hat{\mu}(T-t)} = 100 e^{0.12(1)} = 112.749685$$

and $\mu = \hat{\mu} - \dfrac{\sigma^2}{2} = 0.12 - \dfrac{0.3^2}{2} = 0.075$. Based on the notation above, we have

$$\tilde{S}_T \sim \Lambda\left(\ln(S_0) + \left(\hat{\mu} - \frac{\sigma^2}{2}\right)(T-t), \sigma\sqrt{T-t}\right) = \Lambda\left(\ln(S_0) + \mu(T-t), \sigma\sqrt{T-t}\right)$$

$$= \Lambda\left(\ln(100) + 0.075(1), 0.30\sqrt{1}\right) = \Lambda\left(4.680170, 0.30\right)$$

In this example, we can also compute several other statistics for this lognormal distribution:[23]

Median: $\text{Median} = e^{\ln(S_0) + \left(\hat{\mu} - \frac{\sigma^2}{2}\right)(T-t)} = e^{4.680170} = 107.788415$

Mode: $\text{Mode} = e^{\ln(S_0) + \left(\hat{\mu} - \frac{\sigma^2}{2}\right)(T-t) - \sigma^2(T-t)} = e^{4.680170 - 0.09(1)}$

$= e^{4.680170 - 0.09(1)} = 98.511194$

Variance: $\text{Variance} = e^{2[4.680170] + 0.09^2(1)}\left(e^{0.09^2(1)} - 1\right) = 1{,}197.189781$

---

[23] Note that these statistics are reported without rounding error. If you verify these results, which we recommend as a learning exercise, you will have results slightly different.

and thus the standard deviation is 34.600430. We illustrate the remaining statistics graphically below.

Asset price distributions with various standard deviations

On the following pages (Exhibits 1-4), we have the probability density functions and the cumulative distribution functions with standard deviations of increasing magnitudes. We fix the scale of the axes to ease comparison across the exhibits.

Several important observations can be made from the following exhibits. With increasing volatility, we have an increasing mean, the median remains unchanged, and the mode declines. With increasing volatility, the skewness increases. With increasing volatility, the likelihood of observing a very low value increases at an increasing rate.

Exhibit 1A. Stock Price = $100, Horizon = 1 year Expected Return = 12%, Standard Deviation = 30%

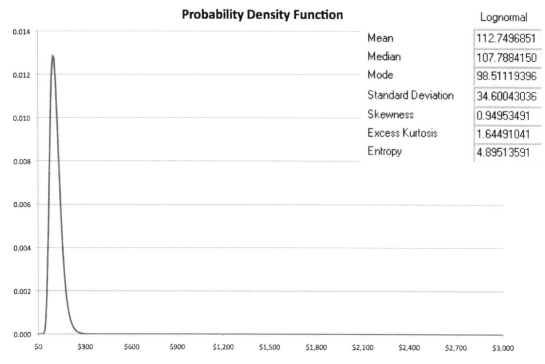

Exhibit 1B. Stock Price = $100, Horizon = 1 year Expected Return = 12%, Standard Deviation = 30%

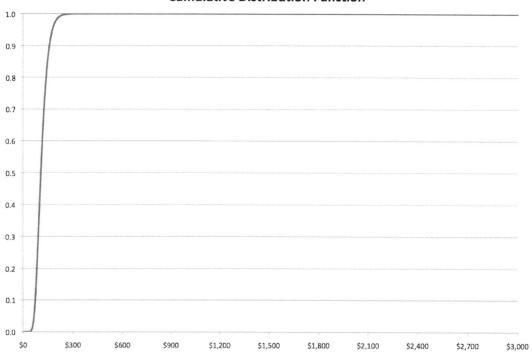

Exhibit 2A. Stock Price = $100, Horizon = 1 year Expected Return = 12%, Standard Deviation = 80%

Probability Density Function

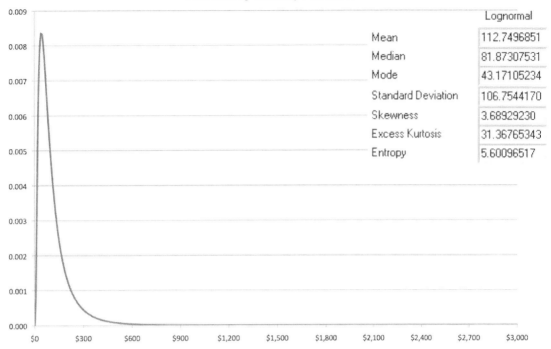

	Lognormal
Mean	112.7496851
Median	81.87307531
Mode	43.17105234
Standard Deviation	106.7544170
Skewness	3.68929230
Excess Kurtosis	31.36765343
Entropy	5.60096517

Exhibit 2B. Stock Price = $100, Horizon = 1 year Expected Return = 12%, Standard Deviation = 80%

Cumulative Distribution Function

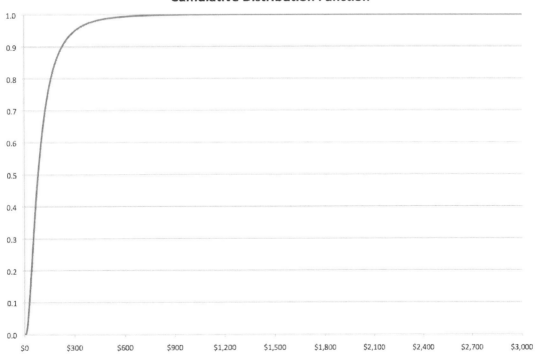

Exhibit 3A. Stock Price = \$100, Horizon = 1 year Expected Return = 12%, Standard Deviation = 130%

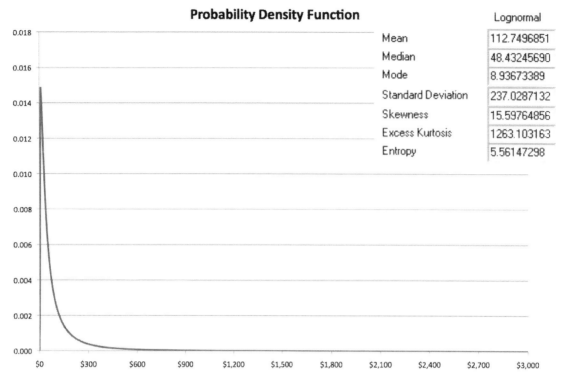

Exhibit 3B. Stock Price = \$100, Horizon = 1 year Expected Return = 12%, Standard Deviation = 130%

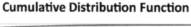

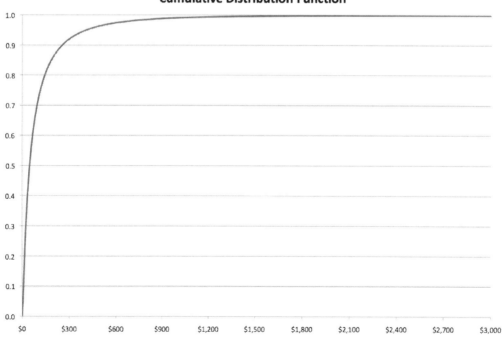

Exhibit 4A. Stock Price = $100, Horizon = 1 year Expected Return = 12%, Standard Deviation = 180%

Probability Density Function

	Lognormal
Mean	112.7496851
Median	22.31301601
Mode	0.87386462
Standard Deviation	558.4664083
Skewness	136.3787284
Excess Kurtosis	460310.5170
Entropy	5.11189538

Exhibit 4B. Stock Price = $100, Horizon = 1 year Expected Return = 12%, Standard Deviation = 180%

Cumulative Distribution Function

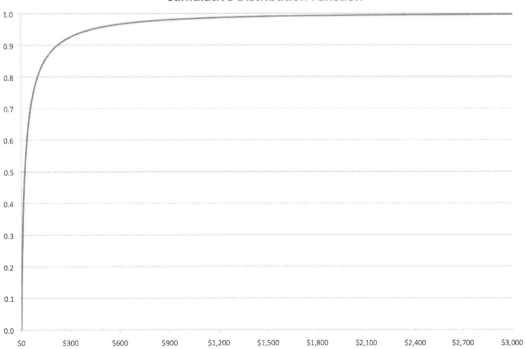

Implementation code comments

There are four files related to this implementation: the source and header files for the generic integration routine, and the source and header files related to setting up the calculation of the probability of being in-the-money (as well as all the other statistics).

FRMInTheMoneyProbability.h

Note the two different ways to incorporate one class into another. FRMCALENDAR is inherited through the class statement (at the beginning of the header code) and an instance of FRMNUMINT is created within the class definition (at the end of the header code).

```
...
#ifndef FRMCALENDARCPP  // Multiple declarations, DLLs
#define FRMCALENDARCPP
#include "c:\FRMRepository\FRMCalendar.cpp"
#endif

#ifndef FRMNUMERICALINTEGRATIONCPP
#define FRMNUMERICALINTEGRATIONCPP
#include "c:\FRMRepository\FRMNumericalIntegration.cpp"
#endif

#define PI   3.14159265358979324

class FRMITMPROB : public FRMCALENDAR
{
public:
   double FRMNumericalIntegrationSetUp(void);
   void FRMNumIntSetData(double tempStockPrice,double tempStrikePrice,
      double tempInterestRate, double tempDividendYield, double tempVolatility,
      int SM, int SD, int SY, int   MM, int MD, int MY, int FI);
   double Mean;    // Mean of normal distribution
   double SD;      // Standard deviation of normal distribution
   double DF;      // Discount factor
```

The notation "void" just reminds us that the methods below receive no inputs, it is not necessary.

```
   double FRMNormalMean(void);
   double FRMNormalSD(void);
...
   double TimeToMaturity;
  FRMNUMINT INT;
};
#endif
```

FRMInTheMoneyProbability.cpp

The source code defines the function to be integrated and passes it.

```
...
#include "FRMInTheMoneyProbability.h"
// Global function for using Brent method of embedded parameter
FRMITMPROB NI;   // Global class instantiation of specific class function in Brent function
double function(double x);
double function(double x)
{
   double f;
   switch (NI.FunctionIndex) {
      case 1:          // Call probability
         f = (1.0 / (pow(2.0*PI, 0.5) * NI.SD * x))
            * exp(- pow(log(x) - NI.Mean, 2.0) / (2.0 * pow(NI.SD, 2.0)) );
         break;
      case 2:          // Put probability
         f = (1.0 / (pow(2.0*PI, 0.5) * NI.SD * x))
            * exp(- pow(log(x) - NI.Mean, 2.0) / (2.0 * pow(NI.SD, 2.0)) );
         break;
      default :
         f = 0.0;
```

```
   }
   return f;
};
```

Integration routines can be unstable with erratic functions. Unfortunately, the lognormal distribution is just such a function. We recommend an enormous amount of care be taken when using numerical integration. The switch statement above allows for one function to compute values for either the call or the put.

```
double FRMITMPROB::FRMNumericalIntegrationSetUp()
{
   double Scalar;       // Number of standard deviations from mean
   double LowerBound;   // Integration lower bound
   double UpperBound;   // Integration upper bound
   double Result;       // Initial result
   NI.FunctionIndex = FunctionIndex;
   NI.DF = exp(-(InterestRate/100.0)*TimeToMaturity);
   NI.Mean = FRMNormalMean();
   NI.SD = FRMNormalSD();
   NI.StrikePrice = StrikePrice;
   NI.FunctionIndex = FunctionIndex;
   Scalar = 7.0;           // Used to set upper bound on integration
   if(FunctionIndex == 1){
      LowerBound = StrikePrice + 0.00000001;
      UpperBound = exp(FRMNormalMean() + Scalar*FRMNormalSD());
   } else {
      LowerBound = 0.00000001;
      UpperBound = StrikePrice;
      if (StrikePrice < exp(FRMNormalMean() - Scalar*FRMNormalSD())) {
         return -98;
      }
   }
   if (UpperBound < LowerBound + 0.00000001) return -99;
   Result = INT.FRMNumericalIntegration(LowerBound, UpperBound, &function);
// Check if integration results are reasonable, many functions result in
// very unstable numerical integration results
   if (Result < 0.0000001) Result = 0.0;
   if (Result > 1.0)Result = -97;
   return Result;
}
...
```

This class provides the capabilities to estimate a variety of parameters related to the lognormal distribution.

```
double FRMITMPROB::FRMNormalMean(void)
{
   double NormalMean;
   NormalMean = log(StockPrice)
      + ((  (InterestRate - DividendYield)/100.0) - pow( (Volatility/100.0),2.0 )/2.0)
      * TimeToMaturity;
   return NormalMean;
}
...
```

FRMNumericalIntegration.cpp, .h

The numerical integration class follows the Press, et. al. procedure very closely and is not reproduced here.

References

Aitchison, J. and J. A. C. Brown, *The Lognormal Distribution with special reference to its uses in economics*, (Cambridge University Press, 1957).

Crow, E. L. and K. Shimizu, Eds., *Lognormal Distributions: Theory and Applications*, (New York: Dekker, 1988).

Galton, F., *Natural Inheritance* (London: Macmillan, 1889).

Limpert, E., M. Abbt, and W. A. Stahel, *Lognormal Distributions across the sciences – keys and clues* (2000, submitted) www.inf.ethz.ch/~gut/lognormal/.

McAlister, D., *Proceeding of the Royal Society* 29 (1879), p. 367.

Stuart, Alan and J. Keith Ord, *Kendall's Advanced Theory of Statistics Volume 1 Distribution Theory*, Fifth Edition (New York: Oxford University Press, 1987).

Appendix 3.8: Interface code comments

The graphical user interface is illustrated for this module below.

The following is one excerpt from the interface source code with selected comments added.

FRMUnitNumericalIntegration.cpp, .h

We use an index of 1 to denote a call option and 2 to denote a put option (the last value passed in `I.FRMNumIntSetData(..., 1);`). The remaining variables are also passed to the implementation class.

```
I.FRMNumIntSetData(inputStockPrice, inputStrikePrice,
   inputInterestRate, inputDividendYield, inputVolatility,
   SettlementDateMonth, SettlementDateDay, SettlementDateYear,
   MaturityDateMonth, MaturityDateDay, MaturityDateYear, 1);
IntCallProbability = I.FRMNumericalIntegrationSetUp()*100.0;
I.FRMNumIntSetData(inputStockPrice, inputStrikePrice,
   inputInterestRate, inputDividendYield, inputVolatility,
   SettlementDateMonth, SettlementDateDay, SettlementDateYear,
   MaturityDateMonth, MaturityDateDay, MaturityDateYear, 2);
IntPutProbability = I.FRMNumericalIntegrationSetUp()*100.0;
```

Each statistic has a separate method, thus, they are called separately.

```
// Normal distribution parameters
   NMean = I.FRMNormalMean();
```

```
       NSD = I.FRMNormalSD();
       NMedian = I.FRMNormalMedian();
       NMode = I.FRMNormalMode();
       NSkewness = I.FRMNormalSkewness();
       NExcessKurtosis = I.FRMNormalExcessKurtosis();
       NEntropy = I.FRMNormalEntropy();
// Lognormal distribution parameters
       LNMean = I.FRMLognormalMean();
       LNSD = I.FRMLognormalSD();
       LNMedian = I.FRMLognormalMedian();
       LNMode = I.FRMLognormalMode();
       LNSkewness = I.FRMLognormalSkewness();
       LNExcessKurtosis = I.FRMLognormalExcessKurtosis();
       LNEntropy = I.FRMLognormalEntropy();
...
```

Chapter 4. Financial Derivatives Valuation Preliminaries

"Underlying all practical problems in connection with the financial aspects of the corporation, there is the problem of value." Arthur Stone Dewing [1941]

Learning objectives

- Introduce important presuppositions for financial markets to function; introduce clear rule of law, clean property rights and a culture of trust
- Review the typical assumptions related to quantitative finance
- Discuss three categories of approaches to financial valuation: the market comparables approach, the cash flow adjusted approach, and the discount factor adjusted approach

Introduction

In this chapter, we present different ways to compute a variety of financial derivatives valuations. The objective here is to introduce these methods within the C++ framework. Eight programs are reviewed that address various valuation issues: Black, Scholes, Merton option valuation model; Cox, Ross, Rubinstein binomial option valuation model (European-style and American-style); implied option parameters (such as implied volatility); interest rate swaps; caps and floors based on the Black, Derman and Toy model; simple mortgage-backed security; and option valuation based on numerical integration.

Each of these programs is presented as a separate module. In the remainder of the book, we focus almost exclusively on implementation code. Again, the advantage of this approach is your ability to skip around and focus solely on those modules most important to you. It also allows you to develop on whatever C++ platform you desire. This chapter is still somewhat introductory and many risk management modules require valuation calculations. As before, there will be some effort to make each module standalone. Another advantage of this modular approach is your ability to find the source code within the materials you downloaded from the website.

Prior to launching into specific financial derivatives valuation modules, we review here three categories of approaches to valuation. In our experience, there is a significant amount of confusion exists regarding how different valuation models interrelate and when various models should be reasonable to use.

We cannot fail to mention, however, important presuppositions required for financial markets to function at all.

Presuppositions for functioning financial markets

We suggest that there are at least four presuppositions for financial markets to reasonably function. A presupposition is a requirement that is antecedent in logic or fact; that is, it is what is assumed beforehand.

First, there needs to be clear rule of law. Ambiguity in law leads to tyranny in enforcement. For example, if the speed limit is set to be "reasonable," then any law enforcement officer can arrest anyone for speeding. The law enforcement officer can arbitrarily determine that your speed was unreasonable.

Second, in order to execute a transaction, there must be clean property rights. If property ownership is uncertain, then buying or selling that property will result in disputes.

Case (2003) notes, "(T)he degree to which the society is bound by law, is committed to processes that allow property rights to be secure under legal rules that will be applied predictably and not subject to the whims of particular individuals, matters." (p. 2)

Third, financial markets are much more efficient if built on a foundation of trust. Trust implies that you rely on someone with something that is valuable. If you trust, then you make yourself vulnerable in confidence. You are assuming the trusted will not exploit and will be concerned. For example, medical surgery would be impossible if doctors were not at least somewhat trustworthy. Clearly, trust makes cooperative activities, such as financial markets, possible.

Finally, we assume that the uncertainties related to future activities can reasonably be mapped to a subjective probability distribution of some form.

Typical assumptions for financial valuation models

Standard set up for financial models (see, for example, Harrison and Kreps (1979) and Harrison and Pliska (1981)):

1. $\left[0,\hat{T}\right]$, for fixed $0 \le t \le \hat{T}$, finite time horizon.

2. $(\Omega,\Im,P)$, uncertainty is characterized by a complete probability space, where the state space Ω is the set of all possible realizations of the stochastic economy between time 0 and time $\hat{T}$ and has a typical element ω representing a sample path, $\Im$ is the sigma field of distinguishable events at time $\hat{T}$, and P is a probability measure defined on the elements of $\Im$. (See explanation below.)

3. $F = \left\{\Im(t) : t \in \left[0,\hat{T}\right]\right\}$ the augmented, right continuous, complete filtration generated by the appropriate stochastic processes in the economy, and assume that $\Im\left(\hat{T}\right) = \Im$. The augmented filtration, $\Im(t)$, is generated by Z. $\Im(0)$ contains only Ω and the null sets of P.

4. F is generated by a K-dimensional Brownian motion, $Z(t) = \left[Z_1(t),\cdots,Z_K(t)\right], t \in \left[0,\hat{T}\right]$ is defined on $\{\Omega,\Im,P\}$, where $\left\{\Im(t)\right\}, t \in \left[0,\hat{T}\right]$ is the augmentation of the filtration $\left\{\Im^Z(t)\right\}, t \in \left[0,\hat{T}\right]$ generated by $Z(t)$, and satisfies the usual conditions.

5. $E_P(\cdot)$ denotes the expectation with respect to the probability measure P.

6. All stated equalities or inequalities involving random variables hold P-almost surely.

7. P is common for all agents implying uniqueness of the nature of the stochastic processes.

8.   Horizon portfolio value can be expressed by a normal distribution.

Conventional perfect market conditions are **not** assumed, such as no transaction costs, no taxes, unrestricted short selling, and no regulatory or institutional constraints. We provide more details on a few of these assumptions.

- $(\Omega,\Im,P)$ characterizes the uncertainty using a complete probability space, where the state space Ω denotes the set of all possible realizations between time 0 and time $\hat{T}$, ω represents one sample path, $\Im$ denotes the sigma field of events known at time $\hat{T}$, and P is a probability measure defined on the sigma field, $\Im$. $(\Omega,\Im,P)$ is a mathematical representation of our perceptions of unpredictable movements in underlying instrument prices
- Uncertainty means unpredictable change (both likelihood and outcome are unknown)
- Complete probability space – uncertainty is reduced to risk (both likelihood and outcome are known)
- Ω – state space, all possible sample paths representing a model of uncertainty
- 0 – time is measureable, our analysis is limited to a finite time length
- $\hat{T}$ – terminal point in time
- ω – a unique, particular event (for example, one sample path), known only at time $\hat{T}$
- $\Im$ – sigma field, a collection of sets illustrated below
- P – a probability measure defined on $\Im$

Consider a three period binomial illustration where each period is 1 year and the likelihood of up is 3/5ths:

- Ω – {φ, {d}, {u}, {d,d}, {d,u}, {u,d}, {u,u}, {d,d,d}, {d,d,u}, {d,u,d}, {d,u,u}, {u,d,d}, {u,d,u}, {u,u,d}, {u,u,u}}
- 0 – initial period in binomial illustration, $\hat{T}$ – 3
- ω – {u,d,u}, $\Im$ – keeps track of information (complete past sample path)
- t=0   {φ, {d}, {u}, {d,d}, {d,u}, {u,d}, {u,u}, {d,d,d}, {d,d,u}, {d,u,d}, {d,u,u}, {u,d,d}, {u,d,u}, {u,u,d}, {u,u,u}} (100%)
- t=1: {{d}, {d,d}, {d,u}, {d,d,d}, {d,d,u}, {d,u,d}, {d,u,u}} (40%)
  {{u}, {u,d}, {u,u}, {u,d,d}, {u,d,u}, {u,u,d}, {u,u,u}} (60%)
- t=2: {{d,d}, {d,d,d}, {d,d,u}} (16%)
  {{d,u}, {d,u,d}, {d,u,u}} (24%)
  {{u,d}, {u,d,d}, {u,d,u}} (24%)
  {{u,u}, {u,u,d}, {u,u,u}} (36%)
- t=3: {{d,d,d}} (6.4%)
  {{d,d,u}} (9.6%)
  {{d,u,d}} (9.6%)
  {{d,u,u}} (14.4%)
  {{u,d,d}} (9.6%)
  {{u,d,u}} (14.4%)
  {{u,u,d}} (14.4%)
  {{u,u,u}} (21.6%)

Approaches to financial valuation

Overview

There are a wide variety of approaches to financial valuation. A general review of various approaches to financial valuation is provided here for the purpose of appropriately characterizing various models discussed in this material. We focus on option valuation in this discussion, but most concepts are equally appropriate for other finance issues.

There are a variety of objectives for option models, including relative valuation and risk management. Relative valuation or partial equilibrium, where it is assumed that the underlying instrument is in equilibrium, seeks to identify mispriced options within an overall set asset prices. For example, one may attempt to identify mispriced options within all the options trading on a single security or several securities. Option models can also be useful for risk management purposes. The option model can provide various statistics related to estimates of different types of risk exposures.

The general framework presented here is based on Brooks [1998, 2002] where the focus was on interest rate swaps and energy options. Option valuation models can be classified into one of three categories of valuation: market comparables approach, cash flow adjusted approach and discount factor adjusted approach. Each of these categories is based on some form of rational approach. Each category is briefly reviewed here.

One approach to valuation is based on the notion of comparability or substitution. If two option-related investments will result in exactly the same future cash flows (same amount and timing) no matter what happens, then the appropriate values for these two investments should be the same. The two investments are assumed to produce exactly the same future cash flows regardless of the assumed underlying return distribution (presently known or unknown). We assign the label market comparables approach (MCA) to these types of methods. This approach is based on the law of one price and does not require any intermediate trading activities.

A second approach to valuation is also founded on the notion of comparability but requires active trading based on the principles of self-financing and dynamic replication. The seminal works of Black and Scholes [1973] and Merton [1973] are based on the idea of synthetically creating the cash flows of a risk-free bond from dynamically trading a stock and a call option on that stock. Although there have been a multitude of research papers written using this type of procedure, there is one common thread. The future cash flows can be discounted at the risk-free rate once either the cash flows or the probability distribution has been adjusted. These valuation methods are often referred to as risk-neutral valuation because the discount rate is the risk-free rate. I refer to these adjusted probabilities as equivalent martingale measures because the probabilities have been adjusted so that the stochastic process follows a martingale, after adjusting for the time value of money. Also the probability space of the original probabilities is equivalent to probability space after the adjustment. We assign the label cash flow adjusted approach (CFAA) to emphasize that these types of methods require some adjustment to the numerator of the valuation equation. It is interesting to point out that this category of approach is only viable if the related securities have a high level of marketability. The CFAA approach is the category most dependent on marketability to be viable.

The traditional approach to valuation is to forecast some future expected cash flows and then to take the present value of this future expected cash flow stream. Many stock valuation models take this approach where the appropriate discount rate increases with the degree of uncertainty related to the future. I assign the label discount factor adjusted approach to these types of methods. The identifying criterion for a valuation method to fall in the DFAA category is that the adjustment for risk is made in the denominator of the valuation equation. The higher the risk (however defined), the higher the interest rate will be for discounting.

The beauty of CFAA to valuation is that the discount rate does not have to be estimated. The appropriate discount rate is particularly difficult to estimate as it would be expected to be a function of both calendar time due to option expiration and the underlying asset price due to the degree of implied leverage in the firm (i.e., the higher the equity price, the lower the debt-to-asset ratio, hence the lower the financial risk of equity). The appropriate discount rate can also be highly subjective. Most option valuation models used today fall within the category of CFAA.

Mathematical details

The three general categories of approaches to valuation can mathematically be expressed as:

Market comparables approach: $P_i = \sum_{\substack{k=1 \\ k \neq i}}^{s} \alpha_k P_k$

Discount factor adjusted approach: $P_i = \sum_{t=1}^{T} \sum_{j=1}^{m} \frac{1}{\left(1 + r_t + RP_{i,t,j}\right)^t} p_{t,j} CF_{i,t,j}$

Cash flow adjusted approach: $P_i = \sum_{t=1}^{T} PV(\$1,t) \sum_{j=1}^{m} q_{t,j} CF_{i,t,j} = \sum_{t=1}^{T} PV(\$1,t) E_q\left[CF_{i,t}\right]$

where P_i denotes the price of some instrument i; α_k denotes number of units of instrument k held; r_t denotes the per-period risk-free interest rate; $RP_{i,t,j}$ denotes the risk premium on instrument i, at time t, when outcome j occurs; $CF_{i,t,j}$ denotes the cash flow on instrument i, at time t, when outcome j occurs; $PV(\$1,t)$ denotes the present value of $1 from 0 to t; $q_{t,j}$ denotes the equivalent martingale measure probability of outcome j occuring at time t; and $E_q[]$ denotes taking the expectation under the equivalent martingale measure.

Approaches to option valuation[24]

We now review these three approaches to valuation within the context of options.

We cover various approaches to option valuation, and provide a framework for determining the correct approach for a particular option valuation problem. The focus here is on financial "value in exchange" as opposed to "value in use." The objective is to offer three categories of approaches to valuation with a particular focus on establishing criteria for selecting the appropriate category to use for any given energy option valuation problem. We use a forward natural gas option contract to illustrate the issues. Williams (1938) and Gordon (1959) were among the pioneers in applying valuation techniques to financial assets. The capital asset pricing model (CAPM), introduced by Sharpe (1964), Lintner (1965), and others, was an early attempt to quantify the equilibrium adjustment for risk. Within the CAPM, risk was measured by the asset's beta, and future expected cash flows were discounted at a risk-adjusted rate. We classify valuation models that discount at a risk-adjusted rate within the category, the discount factor adjusted approach.

With the pioneering work of Arrow (1964), Black and Scholes (1973), Harrison and Kreps (1979), Cox and Ross (1976), and Hansen and Richard (1987), another approach to valuation has emerged that has been given a variety of names. These include state-claims valuation, equivalent-martingale valuation, stochastic discount factor valuation, or risk-neutral valuation. Within these methods of valuation, the adjustment for risk is taken in some way in the numerator of the valuation equation. For example, the typical way risk is adjusted in these methods is to adjust the probability measure. We will classify valuation models that adjust risk in this manner within the category called the cash flow adjusted approach. Cochrane (2000) demonstrates that these two general approaches to valuation can be reconciled with each other within the state-claims framework. Before reviewing cash flow adjusted approaches and discount factor approaches, we review a much simpler approach.

---

[24] See Peter C. Fusaro, "New Techniques in Energy Options," *Energy Convergence The Beginning of the Multi-Commodity Market* (New York, NY: John Wiley & Sons, Inc., 2002).

Market comparables approach (MCA)

One approach to valuation is based on the notion of comparability or substitution. Dewing [1941] expressed this approach as follows: "When several services or commodities satisfy a human want equally well, the value of each one of them is determined not by the sacrifice necessary to obtain each, but rather by the sacrifice necessary to obtain the one most easily available, which may be substituted for any one of the others."[25] If two investments will result in exactly the same future cash flows (same amount and timing) no matter what happens, then the appropriate values for these two investments should be the same. The two investments are assumed to produce exactly the same future cash flows, regardless of the assumed underlying return distribution (presently known or unknown). We assign the label market comparables approach (MCA) to these types of methods. This approach is based on the law of one price and does not require any intermediate trading activities.

The least imposing mathematical framework would involve a situation where the set of possible outcomes is not explicitly defined; that is, the circumstances for whatever reason involve future events that defy an easy mapping into a state-space. We cannot assign probabilities to future events nor even express what these future events might entail.

Suppose the state-space is not well-defined, but there is a set of actively traded securities such that

$$CF_{i,t,j} = \sum_{\substack{k=1 \\ k \neq i}}^{s} \alpha_k CF_{k,t,j} \qquad \text{for all t and j}$$

where s is the number of actively traded securities involved in replicating the cash flows (CF) for the ith security at time t for state j. Let α_k denote number of units of security k, where positive implies long and negative implies short. That is, it is possible to replicate the cash flows for the ith security with a set of other actively traded securities. If there are no trading costs, no other market frictions, and short-selling is allowed, arbitrage activities will cause

$$P_i = \sum_{\substack{k=1 \\ k \neq i}}^{s} \alpha_k P_k$$

where P_i is the market price of security i. Clearly, security i is comparable in cash flow to a portfolio of other securities. Thus, we call approaches to valuation based on employing other securities, the market comparables approach.

We emphasize the key assumptions when it is suitable to use market comparable approaches:

- There exists a set of securities that produces future cash flows in each state identical to the security being valued (even states that are currently unimaginable).
- Trading costs and other market frictions are minimal.
- Short selling is allowed.

The degree of confidence with the market comparables method will be directly related to the degree that these three key assumptions are reasonable. There are numerous examples of applications of the market comparables method. The value of a portfolio is merely the sum of the value of each security. Most finance and accounting theories hinge critically on this view.

One can value options on natural gas forward contracts using the well-known put-call parity for European-style forward options (no early exercise). Stoll (1994) established the relationship between puts and calls; however, this relationship was well understood as far back as Russell Sage in 1869. (See

---

[25] See Dewing [1941].

Sarnoff (1965).) Put-call parity with forward contracts states that the current price of a call option (c_t) is equal to the difference between the current price of the forward contract ($F_{t,T}$) (observed at t and matures at T) and the strike price (X) discounted at the risk free rate (r-annual compounding assumed or r_c – continuous compounding) plus the current price of the put (p_t). Let PV($1,T-t) denote the present value at t of a dollar at time T. Therefore, we assume

$$PV(\$1, T-t) = \frac{\$1}{(1+r)^{T-t}} = \$1 e^{-r_c(T-t)}$$

Both options are assumed to have the same expiration, T (where T-t is expressed in terms of fraction of a year). The forward put-call parity is

$$c_t = PV(\$1, T-t)(F_{t,T} - X) + p_t = \frac{F_{t,T} - X}{(1+r)^{T-t}} + p_t \quad \textbf{(forward put-call parity equation)}$$

For put-call parity to hold, the previous three conditions must be reasonably true. If the put market is not liquid or if short selling is not permissible, then we should not expect the forward put-call parity equation above to be consistently accurate in estimating the call price.

One way to validate put-call parity is with a cash flow table. This is the way most arbitrageurs view this potential opportunity. Suppose you rearranged put-call parity such that no investment was required at all:

$$c_t - \frac{F_{t,T} - X}{(1+r)^{T-t}} - p_t = 0$$

From this equation we construct a set of trades that exactly replicate these values. Specifically, $+c_t$ implies sell calls (positive cash flow means contract is sold), borrow ($F_{t,T} < X$) or lend ($F_{t,T} > X$) the discounted difference between the forward price and the strike price, and buy puts. Due to the net cash flows from these three trades, we also enter a long position in a forward contract. The following cash flow table illustrates the cash flows both today and at expiration.

Exhibit 1. Forward Put-Call Parity Cash Flow Table

Strategy	Today (t)	At Expiration (T) $F_{T,T} < X$	At Expiration (T) $F_{T,T} > X$
Sell call	$+c_t$	$0	$-(F_{T,T} - X)$
Lend or Borrow	$-PV(\$1, T-t)(F_{t,T} - X)$	$(F_{t,T} - X)$	$(F_{t,T} - X)$
Buy put	$-p_t$	$(X - F_{T,T})$	$0
Net		$(F_{t,T} - F_{T,T})$	$(F_{t,T} - F_{T,T})$
Long Forward	$0	$(F_{T,T} - F_{t,T})$	$(F_{T,T} - F_{t,T})$
NET	???	$0	$0

How much should a portfolio that pays $0 for sure be worth today? No matter what discount rate you use, the present value is zero. If ??? is positive, you have a money machine or arbitrage profits. If ??? is negative in the table above, then enter the opposite trades and you have a money machine. The following table illustrates this case, where we assume ??? is positive.

Exhibit 2. Alternative Forward Put-Call Parity Cash Flow Table

Strategy	Today (t)	At Expiration (T) $F_{T,T} < X$	At Expiration (T) $F_{T,T} > X$
Buy call	$-c_t$	$0	$+(F_{T,T} - X)$
Borrow or Lend	$+PV(\$1, T{-}t)(F_{t,T} - X)$	$-(F_{t,T} - X)$	$-(F_{t,T} - X)$
Sell put	$+p_t$	$-(X - F_{T,T})$	$0
Net		$-(F_{t,T} - F_{T,T})$	$-(F_{t,T} - F_{T,T})$
Short Forward	$0	$-(F_{T,T} - F_{t,T})$	$-(F_{T,T} - F_{t,T})$
NET	+ by assumption	$0	$0

Consider the following numerical example: Suppose the forward price for a one-year natural gas contract is $3.5 per MMBtu (million British thermal units), the strike price is $3.5 per MMBtu, the call option premium is $0.53 per MMBtu, the put option premium is $0.52 per MMBtu, the time to expiration is one year, and the continuously compounded interest rate is 5%. Because the forward price equals the strike price, in equilibrium, the call price should equal the put price. Therefore, put-call parity does not hold. Because the put price is less than the call price, we will sell the call, buy the put, and enter a long forward position. Consider the following cash flow table:

Exhibit 3. Arbitrage Example With Forward Put-Call Parity Cash Flow Table

Strategy	Today (t)	At Expiration (T) $F_{T,T} < X$	At Expiration (T) $F_{T,T} > X$
Sell call	$+c_t = \$0.53$	$0	$-(F_{T,T} - X)$ $= -(F_{T,T} - \$3.5)$
Lend or Borrow	$-PV(\$1, T{-}t)(F_{t,T} - X)$ $-0.95238(\$3.5 - \$3.5)$ $= \$0$	$(F_{t,T} - X)$ $(\$3.5 - \$3.5) = \$0$	$(F_{t,T} - X)$ $(\$3.5 - \$3.5) = \$0$
Buy put	$-p_t = \$0.52$	$(X - F_{T,T})$ $= (\$3.5 - F_{T,T})$	$0
Net		$(F_{t,T} - F_{T,T})$ $= (\$3.5 - F_{T,T})$	$(F_{t,T} - F_{T,T})$ $= (\$3.5 - F_{T,T})$
Long Forward	$0	$(F_{T,T} - F_{t,T})$ $= (F_{T,T} - \$3.5)$	$(F_{T,T} - F_{t,T})$ $= (F_{T,T} - \$3.5)$
NET	+$0.01	$0	$0

Thus we pocket $0.01 per MMBtu with no risk in the future. Notice that the arbitrage produces exactly the monetary difference based on the forward put-call parity equation.

What makes the valuation category of market comparables approach so potent is the lack of any distributional assumptions regarding future uncertainty and how this uncertainty is priced. One security is created from trading others. We now review the cash flow adjusted approach in the context of energy options.

Cash flow adjusted approach (CFAA)

A second approach to valuation is also founded on the notion of comparability but requires active trading based on the principle of self-financing and dynamic replication. The seminal works of Black and Scholes (1973) and Merton (1973) are based on the idea of synthetically creating the cash flows of a risk-free bond from dynamically trading a stock and a call option on that stock.

Although there have been a multitude of research papers written using this type of procedure, there is one common thread. The future cash flows can be discounted at the risk-free rate once either the cash flows or the probability distribution has been adjusted. These valuation methods are often referred to as risk-neutral valuation, because the discount rate is the risk-free rate. We refer to these adjusted probabilities as equivalent martingale measures because the probabilities have been adjusted so that the stochastic process follows a martingale, after adjusting for the time value of money. Also the probability space of the original probabilities is equivalent to probability space after the adjustment. We assign the label cash flow adjusted approach (CFAA) to emphasize that these types of methods require some adjustment to the numerator (the cash flow) of the valuation equation. It is interesting to point out that this approach is only viable if the related securities have a high level of marketability. The CFAA approach is the category most dependent on marketability to be viable.

When it is not possible to synthetically create the cash flows from existing securities without any assumptions about the state space, it may be possible to synthetically create a particular security's cash flows when there is sufficient structure assumed about the state space. As we will observe, either the cash flow for state j or the probability of observing state j will be adjusted to account for risk. This structure has taken many different forms depending on the valuation needs.

Underlying each of the valuation techniques classified under the CFAA is the ability to derive state-claims for all possible states in the sample space. A state-claim is the current price of receiving one unit ($1) at time t only if a particular outcome in the state-space occurs (state j) and zero units ($0) otherwise.

Assuming the state-space is well defined and enough structure exists to obtain state-claims, then the price of the ith security can be expressed as

$$P_i = \sum_{t=1}^{T}\sum_{j=1}^{m} SC_{t,j} CF_{i,t,j}$$

where SC denotes state claims and CF denotes cash flow. It can be demonstrated (see Cochrane (2000) for example) that the state-claim is equal to the discounted equivalent martingale measure or

$$SC_{t,j} = PV(\$1,t) q_{t,j} \qquad \text{for all t and j}$$

where r is assumed to be the appropriate continuously compounded risk-free rate and q denotes the equivalent martingale measure. Substituting for this definition of a state-claim and factoring out the discount function yields

$$P_i = \sum_{t=1}^{T} PV(\$1,t)\sum_{j=1}^{m} q_{t,j} CF_{i,t,j} = \sum_{t=1}^{T} PV(\$1,t)E_q[CF_{i,t}]$$

The current market price of security i is the discounted future expected cash flow based on equivalent martingale measures and the discounting is at the risk-free interest rate.

The key assumptions to reasonably use the CFAA are:

- There exists a stochastic process (or processes) that accurately depicts the future potential outcomes; that is, the state space is well defined.
- There exists a trading strategy that produces future cash flows in each state identical to the security being valued.
- Trading costs and other market frictions are minimal.
- Short selling is allowed.

Cash flow adjusted approach to valuation is built on the ability to construct reliable dynamic hedges. The famous Black-Scholes (1973) option valuation model is based on the assumption that a dynamic strategy can be designed using call options and the underlying stock to simulate a risk-free payoff in the future. Many derivative valuation models are built on the CFAA. The essence of this approach is to alter the probability distribution of future cash flows as to achieve a risk-free rate of return. As such, this approach is often referred to as an adjusted probability measure.

The CFAA is illustrated using options on natural gas forward contracts. A single period binomial framework is assumed with no market frictions of any kind and when a riskless asset exists. The binomial model assumes either an up state (u) or a down state (d).

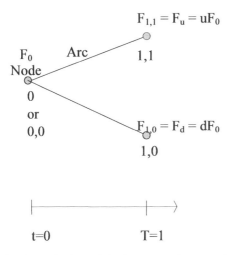

$$F_{1,1} = F_u = uF_0$$

F_0 Arc 1,1

Node

0

or

0,0

$$F_{1,0} = F_d = dF_0$$

1,0

t=0   T=1

In this single period model, there are three nodes (states) and two arcs (paths). The following market data is assumed:

S_0 = \$3 1/3 per MMBtu (spot price of natural gas observed at t)

$F_{t,T}$ = \$3.50 per MMBtu (forward price of natural gas, observed at t, expiring at T)

X = \$3.50 per MMBtu (strike price)

r = 5% (annual compounded riskless rate)

T – t = 1 year (time to expiration of forward contract)

σ = 40% (standard deviation of continuously compounded, annualized percentage price changes of forward contract)

Now several intermediate parameters are calculated. Remember the objective is to value the call option. The price relative of the forward contract when the up and down states occur (consistent with the standard option valuation assumptions) as well as the equivalent martingale probabilities (q), is calculated.

$$u = \frac{F_u}{F_t} = \exp\left\{\sigma\sqrt{T-t}\right\} = \exp\left\{0.40\sqrt{1}\right\} = 1.491825 \text{ (forward price relative - up event)}$$

$$d = \frac{F_d}{F_t} = \frac{1}{u} = \frac{1}{1.491825} = 0.670320 \text{ (forward price relative - down event)}$$

$$q_u = \frac{1-d}{u-d} = \frac{1-0.670320}{1.491825-0.670320} = 40.13123\% \text{ (equivalent martingale probability - up event)}$$

$$q_d = \frac{u-1}{u-d} = 1-q_u = 1-0.4013123 = 59.86877\% \text{ (equivalent martingale probability-down event)}$$

Note that the expected value of the forward price relatives is one.

$$E_q\left[\frac{F_T}{F_t}\right] = q_u u + q_d d = 0.4013123(1.491825) + 0.5986877(0.670320) = 1.0$$

hence q is an equivalent martingale measure. Based on these parameters, the binomial tree is:

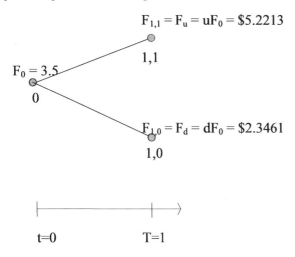

$$F_{1,1} = F_u = uF_0 = \$5.2213$$

1,1

$$F_0 = 3.5$$

0

$$F_{1,0} = F_d = dF_0 = \$2.3461$$

1,0

t=0   T=1

Therefore the binomial tree for the call option is

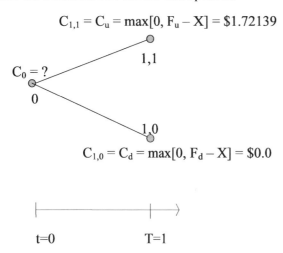

$$C_{1,1} = C_u = max[0, F_u - X] = \$1.72139$$

1,1

$$C_0 = ?$$

0

1,0

$$C_{1,0} = C_d = max[0, F_d - X] = \$0.0$$

t=0   T=1

To find the value of the call option, an additional parameter is needed. The call option delta (Δ_C) measures the sensitivity of option prices to changes in the underlying forward price.

$$\Delta_C = \frac{C_u - C_d}{F_u - F_d} = \frac{\$1.72139 - \$0}{\$5.22139 - \$2.34612} = 0.598688$$

Consider the unusual trading strategy of buying $1/\Delta_C$ call options, going short one forward contract, and borrowing the following amount (B*)

$$B^* = \frac{F_t - dF_t}{1+r} = \frac{\$3.5 - (0.670320)\$3.5}{1+0.05} = \$0.657918$$

Hence the portfolio (Π_t) is valued at time t as (remember the cost of entering a forward contract is zero)

$$\Pi_t = \frac{1}{\Delta_C} C_t - B^* = \frac{1}{\Delta_C} C_t - \frac{F_t - dF_t}{1+r} = \frac{1}{\Delta_C} C_t - \$0.657918$$

The values of this portfolio for the up and the down states are

$$\Pi_{T,u} = \frac{1}{\Delta_C} C_{T,u} + \left(F_t - uF_t\right) - B * \left(1 + r\right)$$

(up state)

$$= \frac{1}{0.598688} \$1.72139 + \left(\$3.50 - \$5.22139\right) - \$0.657918\left(1 + 0.05\right) = \$0$$

$$\Pi_{T,d} = \frac{1}{\Delta_C} C_{T,d} + \left(F_t - dF_t\right) - B * \left(1 + r\right)$$

(down state)

$$= \frac{1}{0.598688} \$0.0 + \left(\$3.50 - \$2.34612\right) - \$0.657918\left(1 + 0.05\right) = \$0$$

Due to the zero future portfolio value, the value of the portfolio at t should also be zero. Therefore the option price is

$$\Pi_t = \frac{1}{\Delta_C} C_t - B* = \frac{1}{\Delta_C} C_t - \frac{F_t - dF_t}{1 + r} = \$0$$

$$C_t = \Delta_C \frac{F_t - dF_t}{1 + r} = \$0.657918$$

This equation is referred to as the no arbitrage method of valuing the option. There are two other perspectives that yield the same result. The equivalent martingale method takes the expected future call value and discounts it at the riskless rate.

$$C_t = \frac{1}{1 + r} E_q\left[C_T\right] = \frac{1}{1 + r}\left[q_u C_u + q_d C_d\right]$$

$$= \frac{1}{1 + 0.05}\left[0.4013123\left(\$1.72139\right) + 0.5986877\left(\$0\right)\right] = \$0.657918$$

Alternatively, the state-claim method above can be deployed. Here the state-claim values for up and down states are

$$SC_{T,u} = \frac{1}{1 + r} q_u = \frac{1}{1 + 0.05} 0.4013123 = \$0.382202 \text{ (up state)}$$

$$SC_{T,d} = \frac{1}{1 + r} q_d = \frac{1}{1 + 0.05} 0.5986877 = \$0.570179 \text{ (down state)}$$

Therefore, the value of this call option is

$$C_t = SC_{T,u} C_{T,u} + SC_{T,d} C_{T,d} = 0.382202\left(\$1.72139\right) + 0.570179\left(\$0\right) = \$0.657918$$

It is possible to demonstrate that these valuation procedures can be generalized to a multi-period setting. In the multi-period setting, however, intermediate trading is required to dynamically replicate the option payoffs (called a self-financing, dynamic replicating strategy). Clearly, in order for these valuation methods to yield reasonable results, the ability to actively trade the underlying asset (forward contract in this example) is required. We now cover the final category of valuation approaches, generically called the discount factor adjusted approach, is now covered.

Discount factor adjusted approach (DFAA)

The traditional approach to valuation is to forecast some future expected cash flows and then to take the present value of this future expected cash flow stream. John Burr Williams (1938) is usually credited with first articulating this procedure for common stocks. Williams states, "The investment value of a stock [is] the present worth of all the dividends to be paid upon it adjusted for expected changes in the purchasing power of money." Interestingly, Williams goes on to argue, "That neither marketability nor stability should be permitted to enter into the meaning of the term investment value." (See Ellis [1989], p. 153 and 156.)

In 1959, Gordon, when introducing the now famous dividend discount model bearing his name, argued that the appropriate discount rate increases with the degree of uncertainty related to the future dividend stream. Hence the "stability" of Williams does influence market value. From this foundational paper, a vast literature has developed extending and testing various aspects of this approach to valuation. We assign the label discount factor adjusted approach to these types of methods. The identifying criterion for a valuation method to fall in the DFAA category is that the adjustment for risk is made in the denominator of the valuation equation. The higher the risk (however defined), the higher the interest rate will be for discounting.

When the nature of existing securities and/or the structure of the state space do not afford the ability to derive state-claims, then the valuation method typically adjusts for risk in the denominator by assuming a specific risk premium. This approach is the least favored due to the difficulty in accurately estimating required inputs and the resulting prices' sensitivity to these estimated inputs.

The discount factor adjusted method does not alter the cash flow probability distribution; rather the risk adjustment is taken in the interest rate at which the cash flows are discounted through time. There must be sufficient structure imposed upon the state-space to compute at least the expected future cash flows and the appropriate risk premium.

$$P_i = \sum_{t=1}^{T} \sum_{j=1}^{m} \frac{1}{\left(1 + r_t + RP_{i,t,j}\right)^t} p_{t,j} CF_{i,t,j}$$

where $p_{t,j}$ denotes the subjective probability based on a particular individual's perspective on future cash flows. Also, the size of the risk premium is a function of compounding method.

When sufficient structure exists to use the CFAA to valuation, using the DFAA requires a direct mapping between the risk premium and the assigned probabilities for future states; otherwise, multiple values for the same security are obtained. In some sense, such one-to-one mapping does not always hold due to the vast amount of trading that occurs daily. Obviously, when a trader's probability beliefs and risk premium result in valuations sufficiently different from market prices, trading will occur.

A simple example of the DFAA is the standard Gordon growth model for valuing common stocks, $P_0 = D_1/(k - g)$, where k is the cost of equity capital or the investor's required rate of return. The typical way the investor's required return is estimated is by using the risk-free rate plus a risk premium (for example, CAPM $k = r + \beta_i(E(r_m) - r)$). Other examples of this approach are valuing mortgage-backed securities with the option adjusted spread. These methods are extremely sensitive to parameter estimation error and are hard to externally verify. Because the DFAAs are used widely in practice, one would conclude that there is currently insufficient structure in some markets to apply either the MCA or CFAA.

The DFAA is placed within the binomial framework developed above for illustrating CFAA. Consider again the simple one period binomial framework in the previous section. The difference here is that each investor will impose there own subjective beliefs about the probability of the up and down state. For example, suppose an investor believed that the probability of an up event was 43% (as opposed to the equivalent martingale probability of 40.13123% identified earlier). Now we have two issues to address. First, what is the appropriate risk premium? Second, what is the appropriate value for the call option? Consider a constant risk premium of 7.5061%.

$$C_t = \frac{1}{1+r+RP} E_p[C_T] = \frac{1}{1+r+RP}[p_u C_u + p_d C_d]$$

$$= \frac{1}{1+0.05+0.075061}[0.43(\$1.72139)+0.57(\$0)] = \$0.657918$$

which is the same result as CFAA methods. Clearly, they are the same by selecting the appropriate risk premium. Alternatively, we can solve for the implied risk premium.

$$RP = \left[\frac{E_p[C_T]}{C_t}\right]^{1/T-t} - (1+r) = \left[\frac{0.740198}{0.657918}\right]^{1/1} - (1+0.05) = 0.075061$$

By combining the CFAA and DFAA approaches, interesting information can be gleaned from derivatives market values. The CFAA approach can be used to establish the appropriate volatility (or binomial tree) and the DFAA approach can be used with an investor's view to determine the implied risk premium. The implied risk premium is a useful measure for assessing hedging and speculative trading activities.

Selecting the best approach to valuation

Three categories of valuation methodologies encompass virtually all methods of valuation; market comparable approach (MCA), cash flow adjusted approach (CFAA), and discount factor adjusted approach (DFAA). From a confidence perspective, market comparables is the best, followed by the cash flow adjusted method. Only as a last resort does one wish to use a discount factor adjusted method. Within energy markets, however, considering the DFAA is reasonable due to lack of liquidity or other trading problems.

The next exhibit summarizes the major assumptions and their importance within the various approaches to valuation. For MCA, the existence of a set of securities that exactly replicate the future payoffs of a particular security and short selling is the critical assumptions. Is a public utility willing to short power in July? For CFAA, there are several assumptions that are critical; however, we no longer need the existence of a replicating set of securities. Finally, the critical assumption of DFAA is the ability to explicitly adjust for risk when discounting the future expected cash flows.

Exhibit 4. Major Assumptions of the Three Approaches to Valuation

Assumptions	MCA	CFAA	DFAA
Short Selling Allowed With Full Use of Proceeds	Strong	Strong	NR*
Trading Cost Minimal	Weak	Strong	NR
Set of Securities Exist to Replicate Payoffs	Strong	NR	NR
Stochastic Process to Model Risk Variable	NR	Strong	Weak
Trading Strategy Exist to Replicate Payoffs	NR	Strong	NR
Explicit Risk Adjustment	NR	NR	Strong

* Not Relevant

References

Arrow, K. J. "The Role of Securities in the Optimal Allocation of Risk-Bearing." Review of Economic Studies 31 (1964), 91-96.

Black, Fischer, and Myron Scholes. "The Pricing of Options and Corporate Liabilities." Journal of Political Economy (May 1973), 637-659.

Brooks, Robert. "Approaches to Valuation Illustrated with Interest Rate Swaps." Derivatives Quarterly 4(3), (Spring 1998), 51-62

Brooks, Robert. *Building Financial Derivatives Applications with C++*. (Westport, CT: Quorum Books, 2000).

Brooks, Robert. Interest Rate Modeling and the Risk Premiums in Interest Rate Swaps (Charlottesville, VA: The Research Foundation of The Institute of Chartered Financial Analysts, 1997).

Brooks, Robert. "New Techniques in Energy Options," in Fusaro, Peter C., *Energy Convergence The Beginning of the Multi-Commodity Market* (New York, NY: John Wiley & Sons, Inc., 2002).

Case, Ronald A., "Property Rights Systems and the Rule of Law," Boston University School of Law Working Paper Series, Public Law & Legal Theory Working Paper No. 03-06, http://ssrn.com/abstract_id=392783.

Cochrane, John H. *Asset Pricing* (Princeton University Press, 2000).

Cox, J. C., and S. A. Ross. "The Valuation of Options for Alternative Stochastic Processes." Journal of Financial Economics 3 (1976), 145-166.

Dewing, Arthur Stone, The Financial Policy of Corporations (New York: John Wiley and Sons, Inc., 1941), 275-277. Reprinted in Charles D. Ellis, Classics: An Investor's Anthology (Charlottesville, VA: Institute of Chartered Financial Analysts, 1989).

Ellis, Charles D. Classics: An Investor's Anthology (Charlottesville, VA: Institute of Chartered Financial Analysts, 1989).

Gordon, M. J. "Dividends, Earnings and Stock Prices." Review of Economics and Statistics 41 (May 1959), 99-105.

Hansen, Lars Peter, and Scott F. Richard. "The Role of Conditioning Information in Deducing Testable Restrictions Implied by Dynamic Asset Pricing Models." Econometrica 55(3) (May 1987), 587-613.

Harrison, J., and D. Kreps. "Martingales and Arbitrage in Multiperiod Securities Markets." Journal of Economic Theory 20 (1979), 381-408.

Harrison, J. M., and S. R. Pliska, "Martingales and Stochastic Integrals in the Theory of Continuous Trading," *Stochastic Process and their Applications*, 11 (1981), 215-260.

Lintner, J. "Security Prices, Risk and Maximal Gains from Diversification." The Journal of Finance (December 1965), 587-615.

Merton, Robert C. "Theory of Rational Option Prices." Bell Journal of Economics and Management Science 4 (Spring 1973), 141-183.

Sarnoff, Paul, *Russel Sage: The Money King* (New York: Ivan Obolensky, Inc., 1965).

Sharpe, William F. "Capital Asset Prices: A Theory of Market Equilibrium Under Conditions of Risk." The Journal of Finance (September 1964), 425-442.

Stoll, Hans R. "The Relationship Between Put And Call Option Prices," *The Journal of Finance* (December 1969), 801-824.

Williams, John Burr. The Theory of Investment Value (Cambridge, MA: Harvard University Press, 1938). Reprinted in Charles D. Ellis, Classics: An Investor's Anthology (Charlottesville, VA: Institute of Chartered Financial Analysts, 1989).

Module 4.1: Black, Scholes, Merton Option Valuation Model

Learning objectives

- Explain how to value options based on the Black, Scholes, Merton model in C++
- Review the standard assumptions and boundary conditions; sketch a derivation of the model
- Illustrate incorporating methods and data from one class into another class

See program FRMBSMOVMTest in *4.1 BSMOVM.*

Module overview

We review the assumptions underlying the standard option valuation model proposed by Black, Scholes and Merton.

Black, Scholes and Merton option valuation model assumptions[26]

As with any model, the Black, Scholes and Merton option valuation model is based on a set of assumptions, including:

- Standard finance presuppositions and assumptions apply (see introduction to chapter 4)
- Underlying instrument behaves randomly and follows a lognormal distribution (or follows geometric Brownian motion, denoted S)
- There exists a risk-free instrument; the risk-free rate is constant; and borrowing and lending is allowed (denoted r, continuously compounded, annualized)
- Volatility of the underlying instrument's continuously compounded rate of return is known, positive and constant
- No market frictions, including no taxes, no transaction costs, unconstrained short selling allowed, and continuous trading can occur
- Investors prefer more to less
- Options are European-style (exercise available only at maturity, C denotes call price, P denotes put price, X denotes the strike price)
- Underlying instrument pays a constant continuous cash flow yield (e.g., dividend yield, δ)

Black, Scholes and Merton option boundary conditions

Most valuation models are limited to hold within some upper and lower boundaries. For stock options, the boundaries are as follows:

Call options:

Upper bound:

$$C \leq Se^{-\delta T}$$

Lower bound:

$$C \geq \max\left[0, Se^{-\delta T} - Xe^{-rT}\right]$$

Put options:

Upper bound:

$$P \leq Xe^{-rT}$$

Lower bound:

---

[26] For more details, see Chance and Brooks (2013).

$$P \geq \max\left[0, Xe^{-rT} - Se^{-\delta T}\right]$$

Proofs for these boundary conditions can be found in most introductory financial derivatives textbooks, such as Chance and Brooks (2013).

Black, Scholes and Merton option valuation model

Fischer Black and Myron Scholes (1973) along with Robert Merton (1973) developed a mathematical model for valuing financial options that are European-style. European-style options can only be exercised at the expiration of the option. Based on a set of restrictive assumptions, they derive the following valuation model (the continuously compounded dividend yield version):

$$C = Se^{-\delta T}N(d_1) - Xe^{-rT}N(d_2)$$

$$P = Xe^{-rT}N(-d_2) - Se^{-\delta T}N(-d_1)$$

where N(d) is the area under the standard cumulative normal distribution up to d (see Module 3.2), or

$$N(d) = \int_{-\infty}^{d} \frac{e^{-x^2/2}}{\sqrt{2\pi}} dx$$

$$d_1 = \frac{\ln\left(\frac{S}{X}\right) + \left(r - \delta + \frac{\sigma^2}{2}\right)T}{\sigma\sqrt{T}}$$

$$d_2 = d_1 - \sigma\sqrt{T}$$

The N(d) function was covered in detail in Module 3.2. In this module, we will see the advantage of developing code in a manner that facilitates code reuse. This model and its components such as N(d) will be widely used in many of the models in the remainder of this material.

Derivation of the Black-Scholes-Merton Option Valuation Model

We briefly sketch the proof of their model. We assume constant costs or benefits from owning the underlying instrument in this section (e.g., continuously compounded dividend yield).

Consider the following three steps:

Step 1: Assume a specific distribution of underlying instrument and infer the call distribution

Step 2: Create arbitrage cash flow table and compute hedge ratio

Step 3: Calculate option value

Step 1: Distribution of stock and call

Assume the stock price follows geometric Brownian motion,

$$dS = \mu Sdt + \sigma Sdw$$

and we know that C = C(S,t). Therefore, by Itô's lemma, we know the call price follows and Ito process of the form,

$$dC = \left\{\mu S \frac{\partial C}{\partial S} + \frac{\partial C}{\partial t} + \frac{1}{2}\sigma^2 S^2 \frac{\partial^2 C}{\partial S^2}\right\}dt + \frac{\partial C}{\partial S}\sigma Sdw$$

Step 2: Create arbitrage cash flow table and compute hedge ratio

Consider selling 1 call and entering $\dfrac{\partial C}{\partial S}$ stock (positive number indicates purchase). Denote the portfolio as Π, the value of the portfolio is

$$\Pi = -C + \frac{\partial C}{\partial S} S$$

A small change in time results in a change in the portfolio value,

$$d\Pi = -dC + \frac{\partial C}{\partial S} dS + \delta \frac{\partial C}{\partial S} S dt$$

Note that δ denotes the dividend yield. Substituting from step 1 for dC and dS, we have

$$d\Pi = -\left\{ \mu S \frac{\partial C}{\partial S} + \frac{\partial C}{\partial t} + \frac{1}{2}\sigma^2 S^2 \frac{\partial^2 C}{\partial S^2} \right\} dt - \frac{\partial C}{\partial S}\sigma S dw + \frac{\partial C}{\partial S}\left\{ \mu S dt + \sigma S dw \right\} + \delta \frac{\partial C}{\partial S} S dt$$

$$d\Pi = -\left\{ \frac{\partial C}{\partial t} + \frac{1}{2}\sigma^2 S^2 \frac{\partial^2 C}{\partial S^2} - \delta \frac{\partial C}{\partial S} S \right\} dt$$

Note that for small changes in the portfolio, the portfolio is risk-free (there is no dw term). Therefore the portfolio should earn the risk-free rate, r. That is,

$$d\Pi = r\Pi dt = r\left\{ -C + \frac{\partial C}{\partial S} S \right\} dt$$

Step 3: Calculate option value

Combining the results of the last two equations above, we have

$$-\left\{ \frac{\partial C}{\partial t} + \frac{1}{2}\sigma^2 S^2 \frac{\partial^2 C}{\partial S^2} - \delta \frac{\partial C}{\partial S} S \right\} dt = r\left\{ -C + \frac{\partial C}{\partial S} S \right\} dt$$

Cancelling dt and rearranging,

$$rC = \frac{\partial C}{\partial t} + (r - \delta)\frac{\partial C}{\partial S} S + \frac{1}{2}\sigma^2 S^2 \frac{\partial^2 C}{\partial S^2} \quad \text{(BSM PDE)}$$

This equation is a second order, partial differential equation which when combined with the boundary condition,

$$C(S, t{=}T) = \max[0,\ S_T - X] \quad \text{(Boundary condition)}$$

is the Black-Scholes-Merton partial differential equation. This equation was originally solved by transforming it into a representation that is isomorphic to the well-known heat transfer equation in a half space. The solution to problems of this nature are unique. Therefore once you have a proposed solution all you have to do is check to be sure the BSM PDE and boundary condition equations are satisfied and you are finished. The Black-Scholes-Merton option valuation model can be represented as

$$C = Se^{-\delta T}N(d_1) - Xe^{-rT}N(d_2)$$

where N(d) is the area under the standard cumulative normal distribution up to d (see the table nearby), or

$$N(d) = \int_{-\infty}^{d} \frac{e^{-x^2/2}}{\sqrt{2\pi}}$$

$$d_1 = \frac{\ln\left(\frac{S}{X}\right) + \left(r - \delta + \frac{\sigma^2}{2}\right)T}{\sigma\sqrt{T}}$$

$$d_2 = d_1 - \sigma\sqrt{T}$$

It can be shown, based on the Black-Scholes-Merton solution, that

$$C_S = e^{-\delta T} N(d_1) \text{ (delta)}$$

$$C_{SS} = \frac{e^{-\delta T} n(d_1)}{S\sigma\sqrt{T}} \text{ (gamma)}$$

$$C_t = -\frac{e^{-\delta T} S n(d_1)\sigma}{2\sqrt{T}} - rXe^{-rT} N(d_2) + qSe^{-\delta T} N(d_1) \text{ (theta)}$$

$$n(d) = \frac{e^{-d^2/2}}{\sqrt{2\pi}}$$

Substituting these results into the BSM PDE is sufficient to prove that it is the unique solution.

Implementation code comments

The implementation of the Black, Scholes, Merton option valuation model will rely on previously built modules of FRMCalendar and FRMCDF. The following are excerpts from the header file.

FRMBSMOVM.h

Because we need calendar and CDF functionality, we will include these source code files. We use the `#ifndef ... #endif` to avoid accidentally including files more than once in larger and more complex projects.

```
#ifndef FRMBSMOVMH
#define FRMBSMOVMH
#ifndef FRMCALENDARCPP   // Multiple includes in DLLs
#define FRMCALENDARCPP
#include "c:\FRMRepository\FRMCalendar.cpp"
#endif
#ifndef FRMCDFCPP        // Multiple includes in DLLs
#define FRMCDFCPP
#include "c:\FRMRepository\FRMCDF.cpp"
#endif
```

The class FRMBSMOVM inherits all of the functions and data contained in both the FRMCDF class and the FRMCALENDAR class.

```
class FRMBSMOVM : public FRMCDF, FRMCALENDAR
{
```

We built the call and put price functions to return `long double` just for illustration purposes; `double` is sufficiently precise for most finance applications.

```
    long double FRMBSMCallValue();
    long double FRMBSMPutValue();
...
```

The following are excerpts from the source code file.

FRMBSMOVM.cpp

Note that because FRMBSMOVM inherits calendar function from FRMCALENDAR, we can use FRMToJulian() as if it were a member of FRMBSMOVM.

```
...
   JSettlementDate = FRMToJulian(SM, SD, SY);
   JMaturityDate = FRMToJulian(MM, MD, MY);
...
```

It is helpful to write code in a form that is easily read by others as well as yourself several years later, long after you have forgotten why you coded the lines the way you did. It should be easy to look at the Black, Scholes, Merton option valuation model equations for calls and puts and see how they are written in C++ in the following lines of code. The lower bounds are checked as the option price will equal the lower bound if the model price falls below it.

```
long double FRMBSMOVM::FRMBSMCallValue()
{
   CallValue = StockPrice * exp(-(DividendYield/100.0) * TimeToMaturity) * FRMND(FRMd1())
      - StrikePrice * exp(-(InterestRate/100.0)* TimeToMaturity) * FRMND(FRMd2());
   FRMCallLowerBound();
   return CallValue;
}
//-----------------------------------------------------------------------
long double FRMBSMOVM::FRMBSMPutValue()
{
   PutValue = StrikePrice * exp(-(InterestRate/100.0) * TimeToMaturity)
      * FRMND(-(FRMd2()))
      - StockPrice * exp(-(DividendYield/100.0)* TimeToMaturity)
      * FRMND(-(FRMd1()));
   FRMPutLowerBound();
   return PutValue;
}
```

Recall the option boundary conditions are

$$C_{LB} = max\left[0, Se^{-\delta T} - e^{-rT}X\right]$$

$$P_{LB} = max\left[0, e^{-rT}X - Se^{-\delta T}\right]$$

and the corresponding code follows.

```
//-----------------------------------------------------------------------
double FRMBSMOVM::FRMCallLowerBound()
{
   LowerBound = StockPrice * exp(-(DividendYield/100.0) * TimeToMaturity)
      - StrikePrice * exp(-(InterestRate/100.0)
      * TimeToMaturity);
   if (LowerBound > 0.0 && CallValue < LowerBound) CallValue = LowerBound;
   return CallValue;
}
//-----------------------------------------------------------------------
double FRMBSMOVM::FRMPutLowerBound()
{
   LowerBound = StrikePrice * exp(-(InterestRate/100.0) * TimeToMaturity)
      - StockPrice * exp(-(DividendYield/100.0) * TimeToMaturity);
   if (LowerBound > 0.0 && PutValue < LowerBound) PutValue = LowerBound;
   return PutValue;
}
```

Again, notice the effort to make the code easy to interpret for computing d_1 and d_2.

```
//-----------------------------------------------------------------------
double FRMBSMOVM::FRMd1()
{
   d1 = log(StockPrice/StrikePrice) + (InterestRate/100.0  - DividendYield/100.0
      + pow(Volatility/100.0, 2)/2.0) * TimeToMaturity;
```

```
    d1 /= (Volatility/100.0) * pow(TimeToMaturity, 0.5);
    return d1;
}
//----------------------------------------------------------------------
double FRMBSMOVM::FRMd2()
{
    return FRMd1() - (Volatility/100.0) * pow(TimeToMaturity, 0.5);
}
```

References

Black, F., and M. Scholes. "The Pricing of Options and Corporate Liabilities." *Journal of Political Economy* 81, (1973), 637-659.

Chance, Don M., and Robert Brooks. *An Introduction to Derivatives and Risk Management* 9th Edition (Mason, OH: Thomson South-Western, 2013).

Merton, Robert C. "Theory of Rational Option Prices." *Bell Journal of Economics and Management Science* 4, (Spring 1973), 141-183.

Appendix 4.1: Interface code comments

This module's graphical user interface is illustrated below.

This particular program will grab the current date for the settlement date and the maturity date is assumed to be one year later.

The interface header code contains nothing that is different than modules presented previously.

FRMUnitBSMOVM.cpp, .h

The following are excerpts from the interface code with selected comments added. This module relies on the date value stored on the computer; hence, some mechanism is needed to extract the date. The facility used is found in the standard header file time.h.

```
...
#include <time.h> // Pull current date
```

The date information will be stored in the character variable vector tmpbuf[] (a temporary buffer of size 128 as required in time.h. The function, _strdate(tmpbuf), is found in time.h and atoi() extracts information from this temporary buffer and places it in integer form as month, day, and year.

```
    char tmpbuf[128];         // Copy current date to tmpbuf
    _strdate(tmpbuf);
    SettlementDateMonth = atoi(&tmpbuf[0]);
    SettlementDateDay = atoi(&tmpbuf[3]);
    SettlementDateYear = atoi(&tmpbuf[6]);
```

```
    SettlementDateYear += 2000;
    MaturityDateMonth = SettlementDateMonth;
    MaturityDateDay = SettlementDateDay;
    MaturityDateYear = SettlementDateYear + 1;
```

...

Module 4.2: European-Style Binomial Option Valuation Model

Learning objectives

- Explain how to compute European-style call and put values using one binomial option valuation approach
- Contrast the value of plain vanilla call and put option values with cash-or-nothing digital option values
- Use the log transformation to compute binomial probabilities
- Introduce the idea of self-financing, dynamic replication of option values

See program FRMBinomialOVMTest in *4.2 Binomial OVM*.

Module overview

The module presented here is the first of several modules that will illustrate a lattice approach to valuation. For most people, lattice means strips of material in a crisscross pattern. In finance, a lattice refers to how some underlying instrument's value may change discretely over the next time step. We present a binomial lattice approach here and illustrate valuing plain vanilla, European-style calls and puts as well as cash-or-nothing, European-style, calls and puts.

Notation

0, T	initial trade date, time 0; expiration or maturity date, time T
B_0, B_T	bond, value of risk-free investment at time 0 and at time T
Π_0, Π_T	portfolio, value of some financial instrument portfolio at time 0 and at time T
S_0, S_T	value of underlying instrument, e.g., stock, at time 0 and at time T
O	option, value of options, either call or put, at time 0
O_u, O_d	option, value of option at time T if up occurs and if down occurs
u, d	up, total return of S, if up occurs and if down occurs
Δ	delta, hedge ratio, units of the financial instrument to enter to hedge option position
FV()	future value based on risk-free interest rate
PV()	present value based on risk-free interest rate
π	equivalent martingale probability of up move
r	continuously compounded, annualized, "risk-free" interest rate
$E_\pi(\ )$	expectation under equivalent martingale probability

Binomial lattice framework

Consider a single period binomial framework:

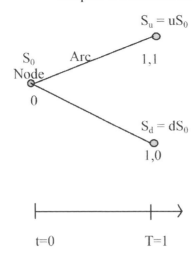

At each point in time, the underlying instrument will have a specific value (node). During each period of time, the specific value will change to one of two values (arcs). Binomial option valuation models are derived from this framework and are usually based on the following coherent set of assumptions:[27]

$0 < d < FV(1) < u$ (no boundary arbitrage condition)

$0 << \pi << 1$ (probability condition, distribution independent)

$\pi = \dfrac{e^{r\Delta t} - d}{u - d}$ (no arbitrage condition, distribution independent)

$Var_\pi\left(\ln\left(\dfrac{S_T}{S_0}\right)\right) = \left[\ln\left(\dfrac{u}{d}\right)\right]^2 \pi(1 - \pi)$ (variance condition of log of price relative, distribution independent so long as $S_0 > 0$ and $S_T > 0$)

Within this framework, we can illustrate the binomial option valuation model with the following simple one-period model. We use a theorem and proof approach.

Single period binomial option valuation theorem

The current value of an option is equal to the present value of the expected terminal payout.

$$O_0 = PV\left[E_\pi\left(O_T\right)\right]$$

Two natural questions arise: What is the appropriate probability distribution to compute the expected value? What is the appropriate discount rate? The following proof answers both of these questions.

Proof: Consider a portfolio of long Δ stock and borrowing B_0 (or short a risk-free bond)

$$\Pi_0 = \Delta S_0 - B_0$$

at expiration

$$\Pi_u = \Delta u S_0 - B_T = O_u$$

$$\Pi_d = \Delta d S_0 - B_T = O_d$$

Making the value of the portfolio risk-free at T implies

---

[27] Based, in part, on Don Chance, "A Synthesis of Binomial Option Pricing Models for Lognormally Distributed Assets," *Journal of Applied Finance* (Spring/Summer 2008).

$$B_T = \Delta u S_0 - O_u = \Delta d S_0 - O_d$$

Solving for Δ,

$$\Delta = \frac{O_u - O_d}{S(u-d)}$$

Note that for call options, $\Delta \geq 0$ and for put options, $\Delta \leq 0$. Entering Δ shares of stock and writing one option results in the payoff of the risk-free portfolio worth B_T. Note that $\Delta \geq 0$ for calls implies purchasing stock and $\Delta \leq 0$ for puts implies short selling stock.

$$FV(\Delta S_0 - O_0) = B_T = \Delta u S_0 - O_u = \Delta d S_0 - O_d$$

or

$$FV(O_0 - \Delta S_0) = O_u - \Delta u S_0$$

isolating the initial call option value

$$O_0 = \Delta S_0 - PV(\Delta u S_0 - O_u) \text{ (no arbitrage model)}$$

$$O_0 = \Delta S_0 - PV(\Delta u S_0 - O_u)$$

Lemma: $= PV\left\{ \frac{FV(1)-d}{u-d} O_u + \frac{u-FV(1)}{u-d} O_d \right\}$ (equilibrium martingale measure model)

$$= PV\{\pi O_u + (1-\pi)O_d\} = PV[E_\pi(O_T)]$$

Thus, the binomial probability distribution results in the probability of an up arc occurring being expressed in the following manner:

$$\pi = \frac{FV(1)-d}{u-d} = \frac{e^{rT}-d}{u-d}$$

and the appropriate discount rate is the "risk-free" interest rate because the hedged portfolio is without risk.

Before turning to the general model, we examine several exhibits highlighting the nature of the binomial framework.

Two-period call option illustration

A two-period call option is illustrated in detail for the purpose of highlighting various aspects of option valuation. Exhibit 1 presents a stock trading at $100 and $u = 1.25$ and $d = 0.80$. The single-period risk-free rate is assumed to be 5%. Note that because $u*d = 1$ that the stock tree recombines at time 2 at the initial stock price of $100. The call option is only in-the-money if up occurs during both time steps. Note that the hedge ratio rises when the underlying instrument rises and the hedge ratio falls when the underlying instrument falls. By examining the change in the position in stocks and bonds, we realize that this portfolio exactly replicates the option position. Therefore, the net position in the portfolio should exactly equal the value of the option.

Exhibit 1. Two-Period Call Valuation via Binomial Option Valuation Model

Two Period Binomial Option Pricing Model					
Valuation of a Standard Call Option					
R=	1.05	S(0)=	$100.00		
u=	1.25	X=	$100.00		
d=	0.8	n=	2		
p=	55.55556%				
	EMM	Stock	Terminal		
# of ups	Probability	Price	Payout	Prob*Payout	
0	0.197530864	$64.00000	$0.00000	$0.00000	
1	0.49382716	$100.00000	$0.00000	$0.00000	
2	0.308641975	$156.25000	$56.25000	$17.36111	
Sum(E)=	$17.36111				
DiscFact=	$0.90703				
C(0)=	*$15.74704*				

Stock Tree					
# of ups	0	1	2	# of ups	1
0	100.00000	80.00000	64.00000	0	=$B$20*$B5
1		125.00000	100.00000	1	=$B$20*$B4
2			156.25000		

Call Option Tree					
# of ups	0	1	2	# of ups	1
0	15.74704	0.00000	0.00000	0	=(1/$B$3)*($B$6*$D26+(1-$B$6)*$D25)
1		29.76190	0.00000	1	=(1/$B$3)*($B$6*$D27+(1-$B$6)*$D26)
2			56.25000		

Call Hedge Ratio					
# of ups	0	1		# of ups	1
0	0.66138	0.00000		0	=(D26-D25)/(D21-D20)
1		1.00000		1	=(D27-D26)/(D22-D21)

Change in Position in Stocks (Cash Flow-Negative implies Buy)				SFDR	
# of ups	0	1	2	# of ups	1	1
0	-66.13757	52.91005	0.00000	0	52.91005 =-(C30-B30)*C20
1		-42.32804	100.00000	1	-42.32804 =-(C31-B30)*C21
2			156.25000		Note: (1,2) or D35 measured from (1,1) to (2,1)

Change in Position in Bonds (Cash Flow-Negative Implies Lend)				SFDR	
# of ups	0	1	2	# of ups	1	1
0	50.39053	-52.91005	0.00000	0	-52.91005 =-C34
1		42.32804	100.00000	1	42.32804 =-C35
2			100.00000		Note: (1,2) or D35 measured from (1,1) to (2,1)

Change in Net Position in Portfolio (Cash Flow-Negative Implies Outflow)					
# of ups	0	1	2	# of ups	1
0	-15.74704	0.00000	0.00000	0	=C34+C39
1		0.00000	0.00000	1	=C35+C40
2			56.25000		

Exhibit 2 provides similar results for a two-period binomial put option.

Two-period put option illustration

The following exhibit highlights the two-period put option valuation.

Exhibit 2. Two-Period Put Valuation via Binomial Option valuation Model

Two Period Binomial Option Pricing Model						
Valuation of a Standard Put Option						
R=	1.05	S(0)=	$100.00			
u=	1.25	X=	$100.00			
d=	0.8	n=	2			
p=	55.55556%					
	EMM	**Stock**	**Terminal**			
# of ups	**Probability**	**Price**	**Payout**	**Prob*Payout**		
0	0.197530864	$64.00000	$36.00000	$7.11111		
1	0.49382716	$100.00000	$0.00000	$0.00000		
2	0.308641975	$156.25000	$0.00000	$0.00000		
Sum(E)=	$7.11111					
DiscFact=	$0.90703					
P(0)=	**$6.44999**					

Stock Tree						
# of ups	0	1	2	# of ups	1	
0	100.00000	80.00000	64.00000	0	=$B$20*$B5	
1		125.00000	100.00000	1	=$B$20*$B4	
2			156.25000			
Put Option Tree						
# of ups	0	1	2	# of ups	1	
0	6.44999	15.23810	36.00000	0	=(1/$B$3)*($B$6*$D26+(1-$B$6)*$D25)	
1		0.00000	0.00000	1	=(1/$B$3)*($B$6*$D27+(1-$B$6)*$D26)	
2			0.00000			
Put Hedge Ratio						
# of ups	0	1		# of ups	1	
1	-0.33862	-1.00000		0	=(D26-D25)/(D21-D20)	
0		0.00000		1	=(D27-D26)/(D22-D21)	
Change in Position in Stocks (Cash Flow-Negative implies Buy)				**SFDR**		
# of ups	0	1	2	# of ups	1	1
0	33.86243	52.91005	-64.00000	0	52.91005	=-(C30-B30)*C20
1		-42.32804	0.00000	1	-42.32804	=-(C31-B30)*C21
2			0.00000		Note: (1,2) or D35 measured from (1,1) to (2,1)	
Change in Position in Bonds (Cash Flow-Negative Implies Lend)				**SFDR**		
# of ups	0	1	2	# of ups	1	1
0	-40.31242	-52.91005	-100.00000	0	-52.91005	=-C34
1		42.32804	0.00000	1	42.32804	=-C35
2			0.00000		Note: (1,2) or D35 measured from (1,1) to (2,1)	
Change in Net Position in Portfolio						
# of ups	0	1	2	# of ups	1	
0	-6.44999	0.00000	36.00000	0	=C34+C39	
1		0.00000	0.00000	1	=C35+C40	
2			0.00000			

Multi-period binomial option valuation model

The multi-period binomial option valuation model is simply the present value of the expected terminal payout. For plain vanilla call and put options, we have

$$C = e^{-rT} \sum_{j=0}^{n} \left(\frac{n!}{j!(n-j)!} \right) \pi^{j}(1-\pi)^{n-j} \max\left(0, u^{j}d^{n-j}S_0 - X\right)$$

$$P = e^{-rT} \sum_{j=0}^{n} \left(\frac{n!}{j!(n-j)!} \right) \pi^{j}(1-\pi)^{n-j} \max\left(0, X - u^{j}d^{n-j}S_0\right)$$

For cash-or-nothing digital call and put options, we have

$$C = e^{-rT} D \sum_{j=0}^{n} \left(\frac{n!}{j!(n-j)!} \right) \pi^j (1-\pi)^{n-j} I_{u^j d^{n-j} S_0 > X}$$

$$P = e^{-rT} D \sum_{j=0}^{n} \left(\frac{n!}{j!(n-j)!} \right) \pi^j (1-\pi)^{n-j} I_{u^j d^{n-j} S_0 < X}$$

where D denotes the digital cash payout if the option expires in-the-money. The indicator function, I, is equal to 1 if the condition is true and 0 otherwise. Recall n! (n factorial) is equivalent to n*(n − 1)*(n − 2)* ... * 1.

Log transformation of binomial probabilities

One of the implementation difficulties when computing binomial values is the explosive nature of j! and implosive nature of π^j. For example, $60! = 8.32 \times 10^{81}$ and $0.5^{60} = 8.67 \times 10^{-19}$. Thus, machine error will become a significant problem. There is, however, an elegant solution to this problem. Note that the combination of an exploding number and an imploding number may remain reasonable. Note the probability of observing the jth node can be expressed as

$$Pr(j) = \left(\frac{n!}{j!(n-j)!} \right) \pi^j (1-\pi)^{n-j}$$

If we take the natural log, we have

$$\ln\{Pr(j)\} = \ln\left\{ \left(\frac{n!}{j!(n-j)!} \right) \pi^j (1-\pi)^{n-j} \right\}$$

$$= \ln\{n!\} - \ln\{j!\} - \ln\{(n-j)!\} + j\ln\{\pi\} + (n-j)\ln\{(1-\pi)\}$$

$$= \sum_{k=1}^{n} \ln\{k\} - \sum_{k=1}^{j} \ln\{k\} - \sum_{k=1}^{n-j} \ln\{k\} + j\ln\{\pi\} + (n-j)\ln\{(1-\pi)\}$$

because $\ln(a/b) = \ln(a) - \ln(b)$, $\ln(a^b) = b\ln(a)$, and $\ln(ab) = \ln(a) + \ln(b)$. Finally, we take advantage of the partial cancellation of the sums depending on the value of j, thus

$$\ln\{Pr(j)\} = \sum_{k=j+1}^{n} \ln\{k\} - \sum_{k=1}^{n-j} \ln\{k\} + j\ln\{\pi\} + (n-j)\ln\{(1-\pi)\}$$

This relationship is much easier to code without machine error issues.

Implementation code comments

FRMBinomialOVM.h

Recall this program just illustrates the simplest problem related to the binomial framework, the European-style option. Thus, the header file is straightforward. Just for completeness we show the method of recursion, although it should not be used in practice, as it is slow.

```
...
class FRMBINOPM
{
public:
    void FRMSetData(double tempStockPrice, double tempStrikePrice,
        double tempInterestRate, double tempVolatility, double tempTimeToMaturity,
        int tempNumberOfSteps, double tempDigitalPayout);
    void FRMSetType(int tempType);
    double FRMCalculateBinomial();
private:
```

```
...
   long double FRMBinomialProbability(int N, int J, double prob);
   long double FRMNChooseJ(int N, int J);
   long double FRMFactorial(int N);
   double FRMMax(double X, double Y);
...
```

FRMBinomialOVM.cpp

The binomial probability is computed based on a log transformation, as shown in the material above.

```
...
long double FRMBINOPM::FRMBinomialProbability(int N, int J, double prob)
{
   int i;
   double sum1, sum2;
   sum1 = sum2 = 0.0;
   if(J > N-J){
      for(i=J+1; i<=N; i++) sum1 += log(i);
      for(i=1; i<=N-J; i++) sum2 += log(i);
   } else {
      for(i=N-J+1; i<=N; i++) sum1 += log(i);
      for(i=1; i<=J; i++) sum2 += log(i);
   }
   return (exp(sum1 - sum2 + ((double)J) * log(prob)
      + ((double)(N - J)) * log(1.0 - prob)));
}
```

Note that FRMNChooseJ() and FRMFactorial() are not used in this program, but are present in the code just to illustrate the concept. The log transformation above is faster and does not suffer from floating point numbers becoming too large or too small.

```
//-------------------------------------------------------------------------
long double FRMBINOPM::FRMNChooseJ(int N, int J)
{
   return (FRMFactorial(N) / (FRMFactorial(J) * FRMFactorial(N-J)));
}
//-------------------------------------------------------------------------
long double FRMBINOPM::FRMFactorial(int N) // Illustration of method of recursion
{
   if (N == 0)
      return 1;
   else
      return (N * FRMFactorial (N-1));
}
...
double FRMBINOPM::FRMCalculateBinomial()
{
   long int TimeStep;
   double Moneyness;
   double Value;
   double Sum;
   Sum = 0.0;   // Test for sum == 1.0 for probabilities
   Moneyness = 0.0;
   Value = 0.0;
//  Preliminary Calculations (i.e. units, periods consistent and so forth.)
   AnnualRate = exp(AnnualRate/100.0);
   Sigma = Sigma / 100.0;
   Delta = Period / Steps;
   PeriodicRate = pow(AnnualRate,Delta);
```

In this module, we use the Cox, Ross, Rubinstein (1979) method of estimating the up and down arc. The `switch () {}` method is used to determine which option to value.

```
   Up = exp(Sigma*sqrt(Delta));
   Down = 1.0 / Up ;  //test that d<PeriodicRate<u otherwise quit
   Prob = (PeriodicRate - Down) / (Up - Down);
   for (TimeStep = 0; TimeStep <= Steps; TimeStep++){
      switch (Type){
      case 1:                  // Standard Call
         Moneyness = pow(Up,TimeStep)*pow(Down,Steps-TimeStep)*StockPrice
            - StrikePrice;
```

```
            break;
      case 2:                  // Standard Put
         Moneyness = StrikePrice
            - (pow(Up,TimeStep)*pow(Down,Steps-TimeStep) * StockPrice);
         break;
      case 3:                  // Digital Call
         Moneyness = pow(Up,TimeStep)*pow(Down,Steps-TimeStep)*StockPrice
            - StrikePrice;
         if(Moneyness > 0.0) Moneyness = DigitalPayout;
         break;
      case 4:                  // Digital Put
         Moneyness  = StrikePrice
            - (pow(Up,TimeStep)*pow(Down,Steps-TimeStep) * StockPrice);
         if(Moneyness > 0.0) Moneyness = DigitalPayout;
         break;
      default:
         Moneyness = -999999.0;
         break;
   };
   if (Moneyness < -999998.999 && Moneyness > -999999.001){
      Value = -999999.0;
   } else {
```

Each node at expiration is added to the option value. The variable sum is there for debugging purposes and to verify the sum of the probabilities equals one.

```
      Value = Value + FRMBinomialProbability(Steps,TimeStep, Prob)
         * FRMMax(0.0, Moneyness);
      Sum += FRMBinomialProbability(Steps,TimeStep, Prob);
   };
}
```

The present value of the expected terminal payout is returned.

```
  Price = Value / pow(PeriodicRate,Steps);
  return(Price);
}
```

References

Cox, J. C., S. A. Ross, and M. Rubinstein. "Option Pricing: A Simplified Approach." *Journal of Financial Economics* 7 (1979), 229-263.

Trigeorgis, Lenos, "A Log-Transformed Binomial Numerical Analysis Method for Valuing Complex Multi-Option Investments," *Journal of Financial and Quantitative Analysis* 26(3), (September 1991), 309-326.

Appendix 4.2: Interface code comments

The graphical user interface for this module appears as follows:

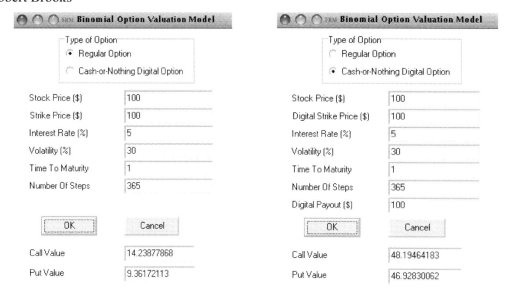

The following are excerpts from the interface code with selected comments added.

FRMUnitBinomialOVM.h

The only innovation is the radio group allowing the user to select either a regular option or a cash-or-nothing digital option.

```
...
    void __fastcall rgroupTypeOptionClick(TObject *Sender);
private: // User declarations
    FRMBINOPM Binomial;
    int Type;
...
```

FRMUnitBinomialOVM.cpp

The radio group provides the ability to have the form present different inputs.

```
...
__fastcall TBinOPMForm::TBinOPMForm(TComponent* Owner)
    : TForm(Owner)
{
  CheckType();
}
...
void __fastcall TBinOPMForm::rgroupTypeOptionClick(TObject *Sender)
{
    CheckType();
}
//---------------------------------------------------------------------------
void __fastcall TBinOPMForm::CheckType (void)
{
    if (rgroupTypeOption->ItemIndex == 1){
     lblStrikePrice->Caption = "Digital Strike Price ($)";
     lblDigitalPayout->Visible = true;
     editDigitalPayout->Visible = true;
   }
   if (rgroupTypeOption->ItemIndex == 0){
     lblStrikePrice->Caption = "Strike Price ($)";
     lblDigitalPayout->Visible = false;
     editDigitalPayout->Visible = false;
   }
}
```

Based on the radio group button selected, different inputs are transferred into the implementation code. The if statement allows for the computation and outputs of two different types of options (plain vanilla and digital), for each option there are two outputs, the call value and the put value.

```
...
   if (rgroupTypeOption->ItemIndex == 1){
    DigitalPayout = StrToFloat (editDigitalPayout->Text);
      Binomial.FRMSetData(StockPrice, StrikePrice, InterestRate,
      Volatility, TimeToMaturity, NumberOfSteps, DigitalPayout);
    Type = 3;
      Binomial.FRMSetType(Type);
      CallValue = Binomial.FRMCalculateBinomial();
      Binomial.FRMSetData(StockPrice, StrikePrice, InterestRate,
      Volatility, TimeToMaturity, NumberOfSteps, DigitalPayout);
    Type = 4;
      Binomial.FRMSetType(Type);
      PutValue = Binomial.FRMCalculateBinomial();
   } else {
      Binomial.FRMSetData(StockPrice, StrikePrice, InterestRate,
         Volatility, TimeToMaturity, NumberOfSteps, 0.0);
      Type = 1;
      Binomial.FRMSetType(Type);
      CallValue = Binomial.FRMCalculateBinomial();
      Binomial.FRMSetData(StockPrice, StrikePrice, InterestRate,
         Volatility, TimeToMaturity, NumberOfSteps, 0.0);
      Type = 2;
      Binomial.FRMSetType(Type);
      PutValue = Binomial.FRMCalculateBinomial();
   }
...
```

Module 4.3: American-Style Binomial Option Valuation Model

Learning objectives

- Explain how to build an American-style binomial option valuation model
- Contrast the Black, Scholes, Merton approach with Trigeorgis binomial approach
- Use input classes to manage sets of option parameters
- Introduce `static` as a means to manage large data vectors

See program FRMBSMBinomialDYOVMTest in *4.3 OVMs BSM European Bin American Bin.*

Module overview[28]

The module presented here computes the Black, Scholes, Merton option valuation model and the Trigeorgis (1991) method for calculating the binomial option valuation model (American-style and European-style). We provide the context for the Trigeorgis method in the discussion to follow. Clearly, with the tools gained here, you can build whatever binomial model you prefer.

The purpose now is to provide binomial lattices that converge either to geometric Brownian motion or arithmetic Brownian motion. In 1835, Scottish physicist Robert Brown allegedly observes movement of particles suspended in water. This observed motion became known as Brownian motion and was later used to model movements of stock prices. It also led to the development of option valuation theory.[29]

Binomial lattices are useful methods for computing option values, particularly for American-style options. Recall American-style options can be exercised early. Technically, early exercise should only occur when the market option price falls below the option's moneyness (that is, the dollar amount the option is in-the-money). We present various methods that converge to the Black-Scholes-Merton option valuation model for European-style options. First we consider geometric Brownian motion and then arithmetic Brownian motion.

Convergence based on geometric Brownian motion

Suppose variable S follows geometric Brownian motion in continuous time, that is

$$dS = \mu S dt + \sigma S dz$$

Hence, S is lognormally distributed. Assuming $y = \ln(S)$, then by Ito's lemma it is well known that y follows arithmetic Brownian motion in continuous time; that is

$$dy = \left(\mu - \frac{\sigma^2}{2}\right) dt + \sigma dz$$

and y is normally distributed with mean $\left(\mu - \frac{\sigma^2}{2}\right)$ and standard deviation σ. Assuming the probability of an up jump, p, must be positive and less than one, if

$$u = e^{\hat{m}\Delta t + \sigma\sqrt{\Delta t}}$$

$$d = e^{\hat{m}\Delta t - \sigma\sqrt{\Delta t}}$$

---

[28] As with most material presented here, more details can be found in a variety of sources, including Don M. Chance and Robert Brooks, *An Introduction to Derivatives and Risk Management* 9th Edition (Mason, OH, Thomson South-Western, 2013).

[29] Based, in part, on Don Chance, "Chronology of Derivatives," <u>Derivatives Quarterly</u> (Winter 1995), 53-60.

$$p = \frac{1}{2}\left[1 + \frac{\left(\mu - \frac{\sigma^2}{2}\right) - \hat{m}}{\sigma}\sqrt{\Delta t}\right]$$

where Δt denotes a discrete change in time, $\hat{m}$ is free parameter sometimes referred to as the revealed preference parameter, u and d are the multiplicative parameters used to compute future values of S ($S_{n,j} = u^j d^{n-j} S_0$), where n denotes periods in the future and j denotes the number of times up occurs. Then as $\Delta t \to dt$, the binomial process will converge to geometric Brownian motion.[30]

Convergence based on arithmetic Brownian motion

Suppose a variable y follows arithmetic Brownian motion in continuous time, that is

$$dy = \left(\mu - \frac{\sigma^2}{2}\right)dt + \sigma dz$$

Hence, y is normally distributed with mean $\left(\mu - \frac{\sigma^2}{2}\right)$ and standard deviation σ. Assuming the probability of an up jump, p, must be positive and less than one, if

$$\Delta y_u = \hat{m}\Delta t + \sqrt{\sigma^2 \Delta t + \left(\mu - \frac{\sigma^2}{2}\right)^2 \Delta t^2 - \hat{m}^2 \Delta t^2}$$

$$\Delta y_d = \hat{m}\Delta t - \sqrt{\sigma^2 \Delta t + \left(\mu - \frac{\sigma^2}{2}\right)^2 \Delta t^2 - \hat{m}^2 \Delta t^2}$$

$$p = \frac{1}{2}\left[1 + \frac{\left\{\left(\mu - \frac{\sigma^2}{2}\right) - \hat{m}\right\}\Delta t}{\Delta y_u}\right]$$

where Δt denotes a discrete change in time, $\hat{m}$ is free parameter sometimes referred to as the revealed preference parameter, Δy_u and Δy_d are the additive parameters used to compute future values of y $\left(y_{n,j} = y_0 + j\Delta y_u + (n-j)\Delta y_d\right)$, where n denotes periods in the future and j denotes the number of times up occurs. Then as $\Delta t \to dt$ the binomial process will converge to arithmetic Brownian motion, specifically $dy = \left(\mu - \frac{\sigma^2}{2}\right)dt + \sigma dz$.

In the Black-Scholes-Merton option valuation model, we assume that the stock price grows at the risk-free interest rate, r, (that is, $\mu = r$). Jarrow and Rudd (1983) selected the following parameters $\left(\hat{m} = \left(\mu - \frac{\sigma^2}{2}\right)\right)$:

---

[30] See Nawalkha and Chambers (1995).

$$u = e^{\left(\mu - \frac{\sigma^2}{2}\right)\Delta t + \sigma\sqrt{\Delta t}}$$

$$d = e^{\left(\mu - \frac{\sigma^2}{2}\right)\Delta t - \sigma\sqrt{\Delta t}}$$

$$p = \frac{1}{2}$$

Cox, Ross, and Rubinstein (1979) selected the following parameters ($\hat{m} = 0$):

$$u = e^{+\sigma\sqrt{\Delta t}}$$

$$d = e^{-\sigma\sqrt{\Delta t}}$$

$$p = \frac{1}{2}\left[1 + \frac{\left(\mu - \frac{\sigma^2}{2}\right)}{\sigma}\sqrt{\Delta t}\right]$$

The up, down, and probabilities can also be computed for arithmetic Brownian motion. Two versions, based on converging to $dy = \left(\mu - \frac{\sigma^2}{2}\right)dt + \sigma dz$ are equal probabilities of up and down movements and equal jump sizes.

Equal probabilities $p = \frac{1}{2}$ (where $y_u = y_0 + \Delta y_u$ and $\hat{m} = \left(\mu - \frac{\sigma^2}{2}\right)$)

$$\Delta y_u = \left(\mu - \frac{\sigma^2}{2}\right)\Delta t + \sigma\sqrt{\Delta t}$$

$$\Delta y_d = \left(\mu - \frac{\sigma^2}{2}\right)\Delta t - \sigma\sqrt{\Delta t}$$

$$p = \frac{1}{2}$$

Trigeorgis (1991) method with equal jump sizes $\Delta y_u = -\Delta y_d$ and $\hat{m} = 0$ has slightly better performance on average

$$\Delta y_u = \sqrt{\sigma^2 \Delta t + \left(\mu - \frac{\sigma^2}{2}\right)^2 \Delta t^2}$$

$$\Delta y_d = -\Delta y_u$$

$$p = \frac{1}{2} + \frac{1}{2}\frac{\left(\mu - \frac{\sigma^2}{2}\right)\Delta t}{\Delta y_u}$$

The Trigeorgis method is used in the deployment below with the log transformation $y = \ln(S)$; hence, this approach converges to geometric Brownian motion.

Implementation code comments

FRMAmerBinOVMNoGreeks.h

This implementation code of the binomial valuation model incorporates the early exercise feature of American-style options. Because it is a lattice, we need to keep track of the option values as we work backward through it. Hence, we need an array to hold the option values and need to limit the size (36,500 in this case). The binomial input class is also contained in this class as it may be called from any number of other programs.

```
. . .
#define OVARRAYSIZE 36500

#ifndef CBOPTIONDATA
#define CBOPTIONDATA
class BOPTIONDATA
{
public:
    double StockPrice;
    double StrikePrice;
    double InterestRate;
    double TimeToMaturity;
    double Volatility;
    double DividendYield;
    int NumberOfSteps;
    int Type;
};
. . .
```

The input class can be instantiated within the function declaration.

```
    void BinDYOVMSetData(class BOPTIONDATA B);
. . .
```

The vector OptionValue[] is rather large so we declare it static so only one vector will exist no matter how many binomial class objects are instantiated.

```
    static double OptionValue[OVARRAYSIZE];
. . .
}
double FRMBinDYOVM::OptionValue[OVARRAYSIZE];
. . .
```

FRMAmerBinOVMNoGreeks.cpp

Input data can be received with one reference to a class and not a lengthy series of input data items. In this case, B contains a whole set of variables.

```
. . .
void FRMBinDYOVM::BinDYOVMSetData(class BOPTIONDATA B)
{
  StockPrice = B.StockPrice;
  StrikePrice = B.StrikePrice;
  TimeToMaturity = B.TimeToMaturity;
  Volatility = B.Volatility;
  InterestRate = B.InterestRate;
  DividendYield = B.DividendYield;
  NumberOfSteps = B.NumberOfSteps;
  Type = B.Type;
  DividendYield /= 100.0;
  InterestRate /= 100.0;
  Volatility = Volatility / 100.0;
}
. . .
// American-style based on Trigeorgis [1992] method
double FRMBinDYOVM::FRMAmerDivBinCall()
{
//  Preliminary Calculations (i.e. units, periods consistent and so forth.)
    AnnualRateDC = exp(InterestRate);
    Deltat = TimeToMaturity / NumberOfSteps;
```

Recall $\Delta y_u = \sqrt{\sigma^2 \Delta t + \left(\mu - \dfrac{\sigma^2}{2}\right)^2 \Delta t^2}$ and $p = \dfrac{1}{2} + \dfrac{1}{2}\dfrac{\left(\mu - \dfrac{\sigma^2}{2}\right)\Delta t}{\Delta y_u}$. In this dividend-adjusted application

$\mu = r - \delta$.

```
   Deltay = pow( (pow(Volatility, 2.0) * Deltat +
      pow( (InterestRate - DividendYield - (pow(Volatility, 2.0) / 2.0)) , 2.0)
      * pow(Deltat, 2.0)), 0.5);
   PeriodicRate = pow(AnnualRateDC, Deltat);
   Prob = 0.5 + (0.5 * (InterestRate - DividendYield - (pow(Volatility, 2.0) / 2.0))
      * Deltat) / Deltay;
// Work on option value array
   for (j = NumberOfSteps; j >= 0; j--){     // Time steps (working backward through time)
      for (i = 0; i <= j; i++){       // Node steps (from lowest value to highest)
         if(j==NumberOfSteps){
```

Due to the additive nature of arithmetic Brownian motion, only Δy_u is needed and for each node in the tree, Δy_u is incremented by 2.

```
         OptionValue[i] = FRMMax(0.0,
            StockPrice * exp(-(double(NumberOfSteps - 2*i)) * Deltay) - StrikePrice);
      } else {
         OptionValue[i] = (1.0/PeriodicRate)
            * (Prob * OptionValue[i+1] + (1.0 - Prob) * OptionValue[i]);
// Test whether exercise is optimal
```

If American-style, then test whether early exercise results in more value than the model value and assume it is not exercised.

```
         if (Type == 1) OptionValue[i] = FRMMax(OptionValue[i],
            StockPrice * exp(-(double(j - 2*i)) * Deltay) - StrikePrice);
      };
   };
   };
   OptionValue[0] = FRMMax(StockPrice -
      StrikePrice*exp(-(InterestRate/100.0)*TimeToMaturity), OptionValue[0]);
   return OptionValue[0];
}

double FRMBinDYOVM::FRMAmerDivBinPut()
{
//   Preliminary Calculations (i.e. units, periods consistent and so forth.)
   AnnualRateDC = exp(InterestRate);
   Deltat = TimeToMaturity / NumberOfSteps;
   Deltay = pow( (pow(Volatility, 2.0) * Deltat +
      pow( (InterestRate - DividendYield - (pow(Volatility, 2.0) / 2.0)) , 2.0)
      * pow(Deltat, 2.0)), 0.5);
   PeriodicRate = pow(AnnualRateDC,Deltat);
   Prob = 0.5 + (0.5 * (InterestRate - DividendYield - (pow(Volatility, 2.0) / 2.0))
      * Deltat) / Deltay;
// Work on option value array
   for (j = NumberOfSteps; j >= 0; j--){     // Time steps (working backward through time)
      for (i = 0; i <= j; i++){       // Node steps (from lowest value to highest)
         if(j==NumberOfSteps){
```

Note for the put, value is determined by $X - S$ and not $S - X$.

```
         OptionValue[i] = FRMMax(0.0,
            StrikePrice - StockPrice * exp(-(double(NumberOfSteps - 2*i)) * Deltay));
      } else {
         OptionValue[i] = (1.0/PeriodicRate)
            * (Prob * OptionValue[i+1] + (1.0 - Prob) * OptionValue[i]);
// Test whether exercise is optimal
         if (Type == 1) OptionValue[i] = FRMMax(OptionValue[i],
            StrikePrice - StockPrice * exp(-(double(j - 2*i)) * Deltay));
      };
   };
   };
```

```
    if (Type == 0) OptionValue[0] = FRMMax(StrikePrice*exp((InterestRate/100.0)
      *TimeToMaturity)
      - StockPrice, OptionValue[0]);
    return OptionValue[0];
}
```

References

Black, Fischer, and Myron Scholes. "The Pricing of Options and Corporate Liabilities." *Journal of Political Economy* (May 1973), 637-659.

Chance, Don M. and Robert Brooks, *An Introduction to Derivatives and Risk Management* 9th Edition (Mason, OH, Thomson South-Western, 2013).

Chance, Don, "A Chronology of Derivatives," Derivatives Quarterly (Winter 1995), 53-60.

Cox, J. C., S. A. Ross, and M. Rubinstein. "Option Pricing: A Simplified Approach." *Journal of Financial Economics* 7 (1979), 229-263.

Jarrow, R., and A. Rudd. *Option Pricing* (Homewood, IL: Dow Jones-Irwin, 1983 and 1991).

Merton, Robert C. "Theory of Rational Option Prices." *Bell Journal of Economics and Management Science* 4, (Spring 1973), 141-183.

Nawalkha, Sanjay K. and Donald R. Chambers, "The Binomial Model and Risk Neutrality: Some Important Details," *The Financial Review*, 30(3), (August 1995), 605-615.

Trigeorgis, Lenos, "A Log-Transformed Binomial Numerical Analysis Method for Valuing Complex Multi-Option Investments," *Journal of Financial and Quantitative Analysis* 26(3), (September 1991), 309-326.

Appendix 4.3: Interface code comments

The graphical user interface for this module is presented below.

FRM BSM and Binomial Dividend Yield Option Valuation Model

Stock Price ($)	100
Strike Price ($)	100
Volatility (%)	30
Interest Rate (%)	5
Time To Maturity	1
Dividend Yield (%)	0
Number of Time Steps (Even Number, 36500 max)	360
Type (European=0, American=1)	1

OK   Cancel

	BSM OVM		Binomial OVM	
	Call	Put	Call	Put
Value	14.23125478	9.35419723	14.22293599	9.86633580

The following are excerpts from the interface header code with selected comments added.

FRMUnitBSMDYOVMNoGreeks.h

This module relies on both the Black, Scholes, Merton option valuation model and the binomial option valuation model. Therefore, we include both implementation files.

```
...
#include "c:\FRMRepository\FRMBSMDYOVMNoGreeks.cpp"
#include "c:\FRMRepository\FRMAmerBinOVMNoGreeks.cpp"
```

We pass input with a class for convenience. In the future, if we need to modify the number or types of inputs, we can just modify the input class and everything else remains the same. Classes cannot be included more than once; therefore, we use the preprocessor directive `#ifndef .... #endif`.

```
#ifndef COPTIONDATA
#define COPTIONDATA
class OPTIONDATA
{
public:
    double StockPrice;
    double StrikePrice;
    double InterestRate;
    double TimeToMaturity;
    double Volatility;
    double DividendYield;
};
#endif

#ifndef CBOPTIONDATA
#define CBOPTIONDATA
class BOPTIONDATA
{
public:
    double StockPrice;
    double StrikePrice;
    double InterestRate;
    double TimeToMaturity;
    double Volatility;
    double DividendYield;
    int NumberOfSteps;
    int Type;
};
#endif
...
```

Because we now have two valuation models and two input classes, we need to declare four different class objects.

```
    OPTIONDATA OD;          // BSM input structure
    BOPTIONDATA BOD;        // Binomial input structure
    FRMBSMDYOVM BSM;        // BSM class
    FRMBinDYOVM BIN;        // Binomial class
...
```

The following are excerpts from the interface code with selected comments added.

FRMUnitBSMDYOVMNoGreeks.cpp

Data is passed with the input class objects of OD and BOD.

```
    BSM.BSMDYOVMSetData(OD);
    CallValue = BSM.BSMDYCallValue();
    PutValue = BSM.BSMDYPutValue();
...
    BIN.BinDYOVMSetData(BOD);
    BCallValue = BIN.FRMAmerDivBinCall();
    BPutValue = BIN.FRMAmerDivBinPut();
...
```

Data is received from the interface directly into data elements of the input classes. The option data class object variables, OD, receives values directly from the edit boxes.

```
void __fastcall TBSMDYOVMForm::SetLocalData(void)
{
// BSM
  OD.StockPrice = StrToFloat(editStockPrice->Text);
  OD.StrikePrice = StrToFloat(editStrikePrice->Text);
  OD.Volatility = StrToFloat(editVolatility->Text);
  OD.InterestRate = StrToFloat(editInterestRate->Text);
  OD.TimeToMaturity = StrToFloat(editTimeToMaturity->Text);
  OD.DividendYield = StrToFloat(editDividendYield->Text);
// BIN
  BOD.StockPrice = StrToFloat(editStockPrice->Text);
  BOD.StrikePrice = StrToFloat(editStrikePrice->Text);
  BOD.Volatility = StrToFloat(editVolatility->Text);
  BOD.InterestRate = StrToFloat(editInterestRate->Text);
  BOD.TimeToMaturity = StrToFloat(editTimeToMaturity->Text);
  BOD.DividendYield = StrToFloat(editDividendYield->Text);
  BOD.NumberOfSteps = StrToInt(editNumberOfSteps->Text);
  BOD.Type = StrToInt(editType->Text);
}
```

Module 4.4: Implied Option Parameters

Learning objectives

- Explain how to use the Brent method to estimate implied option parameters, based on the Black, Scholes, Merton option valuation model
- Use multiple global functions to manage the Brent embedded parameter calculations
- Review radio groups and code reuse

See program FRMBSMOVMIVTest in *4.4 Implied Option Parameters*.

Module overview

This module brings together two modules previously covered, 3.7 Embedded Parameters and 4.1 Black Scholes Merton Option Valuation Model. The value of the modular approach is illustrated here by the flexibility to compute any implied parameter, even those not typically needing estimation. In finance, however, we often encounter unusual quantitative needs and it is helpful to have the capacity to compute any embedded parameter.

Implementation code comments

The implementation code here is rather long due to repetition. Once you understand the basic approach, you just copy code and repeat the process. The approach taken here is a bit cumbersome, but very easy to read and understand.

FRMBSMDYOVM.h

This class relies on two other classes, FRMCDF and BRENT. We again want to avoid multiple inclusions of this header file, as well as multiple inclusions of source code.

```
#ifndef FRMBSMDYOVMH
#define FRMBSMDYOVMH
//-------------------------------------------------------------------
#include <math.h>  //log

#ifndef FRMCDFFILE
#define FRMCDFFILE
#include "c:\FRMRepository\FRMCDF.cpp"
#endif

#ifndef FRMBRENTFILE
#define FRMBRENTFILE
#include "c:\FRMRepository\FRMBrent.cpp"
#endif
```

The option data class is modified to include the user-defined maximum and minimum of the implied parameter to be estimated.

```
#ifndef COPTIONDATA
#define COPTIONDATA
class OPTIONDATA
{
public:
    double StockPrice;
    double StrikePrice;
    double InterestRate;
    double TimeToMaturity;
    double Volatility;
    double DividendYield;
    double MaxX;
    double MinX;
};
#endif;
```

A class can inherit data and methods from several other classes.

```
class FRMBSMDYOVM : public FRMCDF, BRENT
{
```

The following is rather tedious, but the intent is very easy to follow due to the use of long names.

```
...
   void StockPriceSetData(double tempStockPrice);
   void StrikePriceSetData(double tempStrikePrice);
   void InterestRateSetData(double tempInterestRate);
   void TimeToMaturitySetData(double tempTimeToMaturity);
   void VolatilitySetData(double tempVolatility);
   void DividendYieldSetData(double tempDividendYield);
   void BSMDYOVMSetData(class OPTIONDATA O);
   void BSMDYOVMSetDataSP(double tempStrikePrice, double tempTimeToMaturity,
      double tempInterestRate,double tempVolatility, double tempDividendYield);
   void BSMDYOVMSetDataXP(double tempStockPrice, double tempTimeToMaturity,
      double tempInterestRate,double tempVolatility, double tempDividendYield);
   void BSMDYOVMSetDataTTM(double tempStockPrice, double tempStrikePrice,
      double tempInterestRate,double tempVolatility, double tempDividendYield);
   void BSMDYOVMSetDataIR(double tempStockPrice, double tempStrikePrice,
      double tempTimeToMaturity, double tempVolatility, double tempDividendYield);
   void BSMDYOVMSetDataIV(double tempStockPrice, double tempStrikePrice,
      double tempTimeToMaturity, double tempInterestRate, double tempDividendYield);
   void BSMDYOVMSetDataDY(double tempStockPrice, double tempStrikePrice,
      double tempTimeToMaturity, double tempInterestRate,double tempVolatility);
...
   long double BSMDYCallISP(double inputCallValue);
   long double BSMDYPutISP(double inputPutValue);
   long double BSMDYCallIXP(double inputCallValue);
   long double BSMDYPutIXP(double inputPutValue);
   long double BSMDYCallIIR(double inputCallValue);
   long double BSMDYPutIIR(double inputPutValue);
   long double BSMDYCallITTM(double inputCallValue);
   long double BSMDYPutITTM(double inputPutValue);
   long double BSMDYCallIV(double inputCallValue);
   long double BSMDYPutIV(double inputPutValue);
   long double BSMDYCallIDY(double inputCallValue);
   long double BSMDYPutIDY(double inputPutValue);
...
```

FRMBSMDYOVM.cpp

Recall the BRENT class makes use of a global function. The value of a generic class that handles any function is illustrated here. We do not need to write multiple Brent-based functions for each embedded parameter evaluated in finance. We just need one (Module 3.7) and we can wear it out with numerous applications. We create twelve different functions – six input parameters and two types of options (calls and puts). We reference, however, only one method in the BRENT class (CalculateX(&function...)). Recall we pass the function (f(x)) and the results (y) and the method returns the value of x. For example, we pass the function functionStockPriceCP(double tempX) and the inputted call price. The CalculateX() method returns the implied stock price.

```
...
// Global function for using Brent method of embedded parameter
FRMBSMDYOVM BSM;                    // Global class instantiation
double functionStockPriceCP(double tempX);
double functionStockPricePP(double tempX);
double functionStrikePriceCP(double tempX);
double functionStrikePricePP(double tempX);
double functionInterestRateCP(double tempX);
double functionInterestRatePP(double tempX);
double functionTimeToMaturityCP(double tempX);
double functionTimeToMaturityPP(double tempX);
double functionVolatilityCP(double tempX);
double functionVolatilityPP(double tempX);
double functionDividendYieldCP(double tempX);
double functionDividendYieldPP(double tempX);

double functionStockPriceCP(double tempX)
{
```

```
      BSM.StockPriceSetData(tempX);  // Unique to each Brent deployment
      return(BSM.BSMDYCallValue());  // Unique to each Brent deployment
};
double functionStockPricePP(double tempX)
{
   BSM.StockPriceSetData(tempX);
   return(BSM.BSMDYPutValue());
};
double functionStrikePriceCP(double tempX)
{
   BSM.StrikePriceSetData(tempX);
   return(BSM.BSMDYCallValue());
};
double functionStrikePricePP(double tempX)
{
   BSM.StrikePriceSetData(tempX);
   return(BSM.BSMDYPutValue());
};
double functionInterestRateCP(double tempX)
{
   BSM.InterestRateSetData(tempX);
   return(BSM.BSMDYCallValue());
};
double functionInterestRatePP(double tempX)
{
   BSM.InterestRateSetData(tempX);
   return(BSM.BSMDYPutValue());
};
double functionTimeToMaturityCP(double tempX)
{
   BSM.TimeToMaturitySetData(tempX);
   return(BSM.BSMDYCallValue());
};
double functionTimeToMaturityPP(double tempX)
{
   BSM.TimeToMaturitySetData(tempX);
   return(BSM.BSMDYPutValue());
};
double functionVolatilityCP(double tempX)
{
   BSM.VolatilitySetData(tempX);
   return(BSM.BSMDYCallValue());
};
double functionVolatilityPP(double tempX)
{
   BSM.VolatilitySetData(tempX);
   return(BSM.BSMDYPutValue());
};
double functionDividendYieldCP(double tempX)
{
   BSM.DividendYieldSetData(tempX);
   return(BSM.BSMDYCallValue());
};
double functionDividendYieldPP(double tempX)
{
   BSM.DividendYieldSetData(tempX);
   return(BSM.BSMDYPutValue());
};
```

The global function above (`double functionStockPriceCP(double tempX)`) updates the estimated implied parameter through the method defined below. This new value must be introduced into the class.

```
//-------------------------------------------------------------------------
void FRMBSMDYOVM::StockPriceSetData(double tempStockPrice)
{
   StockPrice = tempStockPrice;
}
...
```

Each embedded parameter calculation will by definition be missing its initial value. Although not necessary, by providing different function to bring data in, this code is easy to read.

```
//---------------------------------------------------------------------------
void FRMBSMDYOVM::BSMDYOVMSetDataSP(double tempStrikePrice, double tempTimeToMaturity,
   double tempInterestRate, double tempVolatility, double tempDividendYield)
{    // Used for implied volatility calculations
    StrikePrice = tempStrikePrice;
    TimeToMaturity = tempTimeToMaturity;
    InterestRate = tempInterestRate;
    Volatility = tempVolatility;
    DividendYield = tempDividendYield;
}
...
```

Each implied parameter has a separate function for estimating its value.

```
//---------------------------------------------------------------------------
long double FRMBSMDYOVM::BSMDYCallISP(double inputCallPrice)
{
    BSM.BSMDYOVMSetDataSP(StrikePrice, TimeToMaturity, InterestRate, Volatility,
        DividendYield);                          // Global Implied Vol object
    BRENTSetData(inputCallValue, MaxX, MinX);  // BRENT is public in this class
    return CalculateX(&functionStockPriceCP);        // BRENT is public in this class;
}
//---------------------------------------------------------------------------
long double FRMBSMDYOVM::BSMDYPutISP(double inputPutPrice)
{
    BSM.BSMDYOVMSetDataSP(StrikePrice, TimeToMaturity, InterestRate, Volatility,
        DividendYield);                          // Global Implied Vol object
    BRENTSetData(inputPutValue, MaxX, MinX);   // BRENT is public in this class
    return CalculateX(&functionStockPricePP);        // BRENT is public in this class;
}
//---------------------------------------------------------------------------
long double FRMBSMDYOVM::BSMDYCallIXP(double inputCallPrice)
{
    BSM.BSMDYOVMSetDataXP(StockPrice, TimeToMaturity, InterestRate, Volatility,
        DividendYield);
    BRENTSetData(inputCallValue, MaxX, MinX);
    return CalculateX(&functionStrikePriceCP);
}
//---------------------------------------------------------------------------
long double FRMBSMDYOVM::BSMDYPutIXP(double inputPutPrice)
{
    BSM.BSMDYOVMSetDataSP(StockPrice, TimeToMaturity, InterestRate, Volatility,
        DividendYield);
    BRENTSetData(inputPutValue, MaxX, MinX);
    return CalculateX(&functionStrikePricePP);
}
...
```

References

See prior modules.

Appendix 4.4: Interface code comments

The graphical user interface is illustrated below.

The interface code does not present anything new and can be found in the following files.

FRMUnitBSMOVMIV.cpp, .h

This source code highlights the difference between `switch` and `if`. The switch statement allows for more than two cases, whereas the if statement has only two cases and therefore may have to be nested with else if statement.

```
...
   switch(rgImpliedParameter->ItemIndex){
   case 0:
      editStockPrice->Visible = false;
...
   break;
   case 1:
      editStockPrice->Visible = true;
...
   break;
...
   break;
   default:
      editStockPrice->Visible = true;
   ...
      lblPutValue->Visible = false;
   break;
   }
...
   if(rgImpliedParameter->ItemIndex == 0){
      O.StockPrice = -99;
...
      lblPutOutput->Caption = "Implied Put Stock Value";
   } else if(rgImpliedParameter->ItemIndex == 1){   // Calculate implied strike price
      O.StrikePrice = -99;
...
      lblPutOutput->Caption = "Implied Put Strike Price";
   } else if(rgImpliedParameter->ItemIndex == 2){   // Calculate implied rates
...
   } else {   // Calculate call and put values
      B.BSMDYOVMSetData(O);
      ImpliedCallValue = B.BSMDYCallValue();
      ImpliedPutValue = B.BSMDYPutValue();
      outputImpliedCallParameter->Text = FloatToStrF(ImpliedCallValue, ffFixed, 10, 4);
      outputImpliedPutParameter->Text = FloatToStrF(ImpliedPutValue, ffFixed, 10, 4);
      lblCallOutput->Caption = "Implied Call Value";
      lblPutOutput->Caption = "Implied Put Value";
   }
```

Module 4.5: Analysis of Interest Rate Swaps

Learning objectives

- Explain how to manipulate the information contained in published swaps rates
- Contrast the swap rate curve and spot rate curve as well as compute related discount factors
- Use the LSC model to reduce the information required to value an entire swap book

See program FRMSwapFilesTest in *4.5 IR Swap LSC Files*.

Module overview

Module 4.5 Supplement provides additional information on interest rate swaps.[31] The module presented here uses the LSC model to fit the swap curve. It should be clear that with modest C++ development abilities, the financial analyst can create any number of analytical tools for interest rate swaps.

Parsimonious swap curve

Recall in 3.5 Curve Fitting, the LSC model was expressed as

$$r\left(\tau_i : t_k\right) = \sum_{n=0}^{N_F} C_{i,n}\left(\tau_i; s_{n-1}\right) b_{n,t_k}$$

where

$$C_{i,0}\left(\tau_i; s_{-1}\right) = 1, \; C_{i,1}\left(\tau_i; s_0\right) = \frac{s_0}{\tau_i}\left[1 - e^{-\tau_i/s_0}\right], \text{ and } C_{i,n}\left(\tau_i; s_{n-1}\right) = \frac{s_{n-1}}{\tau_i}\left[1 - e^{-\tau_i/s_{n-1}}\right] - e^{-\tau_i/s_{n-1}} ; n > 1$$

where s_n denotes scalars that apply various weights to different locations on the term structure; $C_{i,n}\left(\tau_i; s_{n-1}\right)$ denotes LSC maturity coefficients, a parameter that depends solely on maturity time and selected scalars; and $b_{n,t}$ denotes the LSC spot rate factor, a parameter that is typically found using ordinary least squares regression applied to maturity time spot rates.

In this module, we apply this methodology to the plain vanilla interest rate swap data. One of the difficult issues facing firms with interest rate swaps on their books is determining the fair market value and identifying the resultant interest rate risk. Technically, every single maturity date in the future represents a different spot rate. We know, however, that only a few parameters can explain the behavior of the term structure of interest rates. An enormous amount of research on this issue has been produced.

The goal of this strand of research is to represent the term structure by some mathematical function that has desirable properties. As quoted in Nelson and Siegel (1987), Milton Friedman recognized the benefits of a parsimonious term structure model when he said, "Students of statistical demand functions might find it more productive to examine how the whole term structure of yields can be described more compactly by a few parameters."[32] There is a large literature on fitting the term structure dating at least back to Durand (1942). It includes piecewise polynomial splines (McCulloch (1971, 1975)), various parametric models (Fisher (1966), Echols and Elliott (1976), Cooper (1977), Dobson (1978), and Chambers, Carleton and Waldman (1984)), and exponential splines (Vasicek and Fong (1982)). Several authors offer subjectively drawn curves, including Woods (1983), Malkiel (1966), and Durand (1942).

Willner (1996) posits that the desirable properties of a curve fitting routine must address the bond "portfolio manager's need for *intuitive*, *descriptive*, and *comprehensive* risk exposure information" (p. 49, italics in original). Nelson and Siegel (1987) provide one such model and appeared to be motivated

---

[31] Supplements are available at www.frmhelp.com.
[32] Quoted in Nelson and Siegel (1987), page 474.

by the mathematical relationship between spot rates and forward rates. They put forward a parsimonious model that was "solved from differential equations describing rational interest rate behavior" (p. 50, Willner (1996)). Barrett, Gosnell and Heuson (1995) and Willner (1996) both report that fitted yield curve functions are not that sensitive to the choice of the scalar.[33]

Steeley (2008) used daily UK government bond coupon STRIPS from December 8, 1997 to May 15, 2002 and thoroughly examined a variety of curve fitting methodologies. Spot yield curve fitting methodologies include cubic spline, polynomial, Vasicek as well as the Level, Slope, and Curvature (LSC) model discussed below (referred by Steeley as the extended Svensson model). Based on a three-factor model as used below, Steeley documents that the LSC model has the lowest "average (across the sample) mean (across the curve) absolute yield error" (p. 1502). With six factors, Steeley reports that the cubic spline has the best fit, but the LSC model is a close second.

Thus, we focus on the LSC model due to our interest in a parsimonious model of the term structure of interest rates. In the module explained here, we manipulate a data set of swap rates in a variety of ways.

Implementation code comments

FRMSwapFiles.h

Note that we include the FRMLSC and BRENT class into FRMSWAPFILES via the class statement.

```
#ifndef FRMSwapFilesH
#define FRMSwapFilesH
...
#ifndef FRMBRENTFILE
#define FRMBRENTFILE
#include "c:\FRMRepository\FRMBrent.cpp"
#endif

#ifndef FRMLSCCURVEFITTINGFILE
#define FRMLSCCURVEFITTINGFILE
#include "c:\FRMRepository\FRMLSCCurveFitting.cpp"
#endif

class FRMSWAPFILES : public FRMLSC, BRENT
{
public:
    int NColumns;   // Number of columns in LSC model (parameters)
    int Counter;    // Generic counter
    int QuarterlyMaturity;  // Quarterly maturity counter
    double AS;      // Accrual period for semiannual period (30/360 or 1/2)
    double AQ;      // Accrual period for quarterly period (ACT/360 approx)
    double Beta[10];      // LSC model fitted parameters
    double SwapRate[120]; // Quarterly swap rates
    double D[120];        // Quarterly discount factors
    double FRateCC[120];  // Quarterly forward rates, continuously compounded
    void FRMDiscountFactors(AnsiString inputsinf, AnsiString inputsoutf,
        AnsiString inputsoutf1);
    void FRMCCRatesFromDF(AnsiString inputsinf, AnsiString inputsoutf);
    void FRMSwapRatesFromSpotRatesCC(AnsiString inputsinf, AnsiString inputsoutf);
    double FRMCalculateDF(void);
    double FRMCalculateSV(double LastDF);
};
#endif
```

FRMSwapFiles.cpp

We proceed to explain this program by stepping through the output files produced. We then highlight a few issues in the source code. The original inputs are plain vanilla swap rates provided in the publicly

---

[33] See Willner (1996), p. 51.

available H.15 file. The data set, FRMSwapInputData.dat shown below, contains only month end observations for a subset of the past.

FRMUnitSwapFiles.cpp	FRMSwapInputData.dat	FRMSwapCurve.prn	FRMSwapDF.prn	FRMSwapDetails.prn	FRMS			
1	8	8	2					
		1	2	3	4	5	7	10	30
	7/31/2000	7.06	7.12	7.14	7.16	7.18	7.22	7.26	7.21
	8/31/2000	6.91	6.93	6.94	6.95	6.96	6.99	7.03	7.03
	9/29/2000	6.75	6.69	6.7	6.72	6.75	6.81	6.89	6.97
	10/31/2000	6.69	6.64	6.67	6.7	6.73	6.78	6.83	6.87

The input file's first line indicates the three-parameter LSC model is to be used, the inputted swap curve has eight observations, and the scalar coefficient is 2.0. The July 31, 2000 input swap data indicates a long rate (30 years) of 7.21% and a slope of –0.15% (30 year – 1 year = 7.21 – 7.06).

Step 1: Reduce the swap rates to three parameters based on the LSC model. Each date's data within the input swap data file is entered into the program and the LSC model is fit and three parameters of the model are recorded in the output file FRMSwapCurve.prn provided below.

FRMUnitSwapFiles.cpp	FRMSwapInputData.dat	FRMSwapCurve.prn	FRMSwapD		
1	3	2.00			
	7/31/2000	7.238824	–0.276567	0.189512
	8/31/2000	7.059613	–0.168422	–0.101080
	9/29/2000	7.056635	–0.228418	–0.779498
	10/31/2000	6.936833	–0.242292	–0.432527

Note that the perpetual rate from the LSC model is 7.24% and the slope is –0.28% (Infinite rate minus the instantaneous rate). Thus, with these three parameters from the LSC model we can estimate the implied swap rate for any maturity. The routine FRMAnalyzeCurve() was discussed in 3.5 Curve Fitting.

Step 2: The plain vanilla swap data is based on a fixed semiannual rate with 30/360 day count and floating quarterly rate with Actual/360 day count. The goal here is to convert the LSC model results into a complete set of semiannual discount factors. The output from this step is provided below.

FRMUnitSwapFiles.cpp	FRMSwapInputData.dat	FRMSwapCurve.prn	FRMSwapDF.prn	FRMSwapDetails.prn	FRMSpotCurveC		
1	3	2.00					
		0.5	1.0	1.5	2.0	2.5	3.0
	7/31/2000	0.966117	0.932879	0.900604	0.869276	0.838942	0.809601
	8/31/2000	0.966651	0.934305	0.902969	0.872607	0.843200	0.814726
	9/29/2000	0.967249	0.936009	0.905792	0.876529	0.848099	0.820455
	10/31/2000	0.967695	0.936538	0.906331	0.877024	0.848560	0.820910

A detailed file is also produced to ease debugging. In the detailed file, the swap rates, discount factors, and forward rates are presented on a quarterly basis.

FRMUnitSwapFiles.cpp	FRMSwapInputData.dat	FRMSwapCurve.prn	FRMSwapDF.prn	FRMSwapDetails.prn	FRMSpotCurveCC		
1	3	2.00					
		0.25	0.50	0.75	1.00	1.25	1.50
	7/31/2000	6.989746	7.014206	7.035980	7.055372	7.072653	7.088061
	7/31/2000	0.982913	0.966117	0.949353	0.932879	0.916600	0.900604
	7/31/2000	6.894010	6.894010	7.001922	7.001922	7.041901	7.041901
	8/31/2000	6.895477	6.899880	6.904348	6.908840	6.913320	6.917762
	8/31/2000	0.983184	0.966651	0.950340	0.934305	0.918503	0.902969
	8/31/2000	6.783527	6.783527	6.807018	6.807018	6.822948	6.822948

We provide portions of the source code for producing these two files below with additional commentary added.

```
void FRMSWAPFILES::FRMDiscountFactors(AnsiString inputsinf,
   AnsiString inputsoutf, AnsiString inputsoutf1)
{
   double Maturity; // Quarterly and semiannual maturity, in years
   double tempDF;   // Temporary discount factor value used in calculations
   ifstream inf;    // Input file
```

Note `outf` points to the file FRMSwapDF.prn (semiannual discount factors) and `outf1` points to the file FRMSwapDetails.prn (quarterly information).

```
   ofstream outf;   // Output file, semiannual discount factors only
   ofstream outf1;  // Output file, quarterly details
   inf.open(inputsinf.c_str(), ios::in);  // Open input file
   outf.open(inputsoutf.c_str());    // Open output DF file
   outf1.open(inputsoutf1.c_str());  // Open output details file
...
   Counter = 0;
```

Note that while the input file remains open, the program continues to evaluate the additional data.

```
   while(inf)
   {
      if(Counter==0)inf >> CurveDate >> ws;   // Handle date
      outf << setiosflags(ios::right) << setw(12) << CurveDate;
      outf1 << setiosflags(ios::right) << setw(12) << CurveDate;
      for(i = 0; i < NColumns; i++)inf >> Beta[i];
      for (i = 1; i <= 120; i++) { // Maturity of swap, load swap rate vector
```

The fitted swap curve depends on the number of LSC parameters applied. Therefore, producing the fitted swap rates depends on this same number (NColumns). The Beta variable is the estimated LSC parameter for each monthly observation.

```
         if(NColumns==2)SwapRate[i-1] = FRMCalculateCurve2(((double)i)/4.0, Beta[0],
            Beta[1], Tau[0]);
          if(NColumns==3)SwapRate[i-1] = FRMCalculateCurve3(((double)i)/4.0, Beta[0],
            Beta[1], Beta[2], Tau[0]);
...
// Work on discount factors
      AS = 0.5;    // Semiannual accrual period
      AQ = (365.25/4.0)/360.0; // Approximation of Actual/360 day count method
      outf1 << '\n';
      outf1 << setiosflags(ios::right) << setw(12) << CurveDate;
      for (i = 1; i <= 60; i++) { // Maturity of discount factors (in arrears)
         QuarterlyMaturity = i*2-1;
```

The implied discount factor is estimated directly using the Brent method; this method is discussed below. The swap data can only provide semiannual discount factors. If the per period discount factor exceeds 2.0 (above 100%) or is less than 0 (below –100%), then the program quits.

```
         tempDF = FRMCalculateDF();
         if (tempDF > 2.0 || tempDF < 0.0)return; // Wacky result
         if(i==1){
            D[0] = 1.0*tempDF;
            D[1] = 1.0*tempDF*tempDF;
         } else {
            D[QuarterlyMaturity-1] = D[QuarterlyMaturity-2]*tempDF;
            D[QuarterlyMaturity] = D[QuarterlyMaturity-2]*tempDF*tempDF;
         }
```

With the discount factors, denoted D[i], we can derive the implied forward rates (annualized, continuously compounded).

```
      FRateCC[0] = log(1.0/D[0])*400.0;  // Continuously compounded spot rate
...
         FRateCC[i+1] = log(D[i]/D[i+1])*400.0; // CC forward rate from discount factors
...
```

We use the Brent method to find the final discount factor, `SF.FRMCalculateSV(tempX)`, that makes the current swap value zero.

```
FRMSWAPFILES SF;                        // Global class instantiation
double functionDF(double tempX);
double functionDF(double tempX)
{
   return(SF.FRMCalculateSV(tempX));  // Unique to each Brent deployment
};
```

The method FRMCalculateDF() uses Brent to estimate the last implied last discount factor. Because the Brent method relies on a global function, we need to transfer information from the main implementation object "L" to the global object "SF."

```
//--- Calculate the implied discount factor ----------------
double FRMSWAPFILES::FRMCalculateDF()
{
   int i;
   MaxX = 1.0;
   MinX = 0.95;
   BRENTSetData(0.0, MaxX, MinX);
// Need to set this object's data into object SF
   SF.QuarterlyMaturity = QuarterlyMaturity;
   SF.NColumns = NColumns;
   SF.AQ = AQ;
   SF.AS = AS;
   for(i=0; i<10; i++)SF.Beta[i] = Beta[i];
   for(i=0; i<120; i++)SF.Tau[i] = Tau[i];
   for(i=0; i<120; i++)SF.D[i] = D[i];
   return CalculateX(&functionDF);
}
```

The following method assumes the LSC model for the semiannual swap rates and the two quarterly forward rates are found by simple linear interpolation. The entire set of forward rates and discount factors are found by bootstrapping.

```
double FRMSWAPFILES::FRMCalculateSV(double LastDF)
{
   double SwapValue; // Dollar swap value
   double Ratefx;    // Fixed swap rate
   double SumSDF;    // Sum of semiannual discount factors
   double SumSFDF;   // Sum of forward rate and semiannual discount factors
   double LastDFM1; // Previous discount factor (minus one)
   int SemiMaturity, i, j, k;
   SemiMaturity = (QuarterlyMaturity+1)/2; // Swap maturity
   if(NColumns==2)Ratefx = FRMCalculateCurve2(((double)SemiMaturity)/2.0, Beta[0],
      Beta[1], Tau[0]);
   if(NColumns==3)Ratefx = FRMCalculateCurve3(((double)SemiMaturity)/2.0, Beta[0],
      Beta[1], Beta[2], Tau[0]);
...
   if(SemiMaturity == 1){
      FRateCC[0] = ((1.0/LastDF) - 1.0)*(100.0/AQ); // Annualized quarterly spot rate
      FRateCC[1] = FRateCC[0];                       // First quarterly forward rate
      SwapValue = Ratefx*AS*1.0*LastDF*LastDF // Assume flat curve for 1st semi period
         - AQ*(FRateCC[0]*1.0*LastDF + FRateCC[1]*1.0*LastDF*LastDF);
   }else{
      FRateCC[QuarterlyMaturity] = ((1.0/LastDF) - 1.0)*(100.0/AQ); // Last forward rate
// Linear interpolation for next to last forward rate
      FRateCC[QuarterlyMaturity-1] = (FRateCC[QuarterlyMaturity]
       + FRateCC[QuarterlyMaturity-2])/2.0;
      LastDFM1 = 1.0/(1.0 + AQ*f[QuarterlyMaturity-1]/100.0);
      SumSDF = 0.0;    // Sum semiannual discount factors
      for (j = 2; j <= 2*SemiMaturity-2; j=j+2) SumSDF += D[j-1];
      SumSFDF = 0.0;   // Sum of quarterly discount factors times forward rates
      for (j = 1; j <= 2*SemiMaturity-2; j++) SumSFDF += FRateCC[j-1]*D[j-1];
      SwapValue = Ratefx*AS*(SumSDF + D[2*SemiMaturity-3]*LastDFM1*LastDF)
         - AQ*(SumSFDF + FRateCC[2*SemiMaturity-2]*D[2*SemiMaturity-3]*LastDFM1
          + FRateCC[2*SemiMaturity-1]*D[2*SemiMaturity-3]*LastDFM1*LastDF);
   }
   return SwapValue;
};
```

Step 3: Based on the semiannual discount factors, we estimate the continuously compounded spot rates.

FRMUnitSwapFiles.cpp	FRMSwapFiles.cpp	FRMSpotCC.prn				
1	3 60 2.00					
		0.5	1.0	1.5	2.0	2.5	3.0
	7/31/2000	6.894067	6.947978	6.979309	7.004730	7.024548	7.040458
	8/31/2000	6.783552	6.795234	6.804470	6.813500	6.822044	6.830114
	9/29/2000	6.659864	6.613019	6.596372	6.589274	6.590316	6.596540
	10/31/2000	6.567665	6.556518	6.556713	6.561046	6.568579	6.578060

Aside from data management issues, this spot rate file is based on the following line of code.

```
SpotRate = (log(1.0/tempDF)/(((double)i + 1.0)*0.5))*100.0;
```

or $r = \ln\left[\dfrac{1}{DF}\right]/T$ based on $DF = e^{-rT}$. The LSC model is applied to these spot rates to produce the following file containing the level, slope and curvature output for the spot curve.

FRMUnitSwapFiles.cpp	FRMSpotCurveCC.prn	FRMSwapCC.prn	FRMSwapRate
1	3 2.00		
	7/31/2000	7.120838	-0.275233	0.204170
	8/31/2000	6.963552	-0.184072	-0.139484
	9/29/2000	7.030289	-0.294760	-0.979757
	10/31/2000	6.881564	-0.277769	-0.557670

With the parameters of the LSC model applied to spot rates, we can compute any present or future value calculation required. We used the same routine, FRMAnalyzeCurve(), and just passed different files.

Step 4: To complete this process, we use the continuously compounded spot rates to estimate the implied swap rates for plain vanilla swaps. Ideally the entire process will not result in introducing too much error. Due to the curve fitting process, some estimation error is expected.

FRMUnitSwapFiles.cpp	FRMSpotCurveCC.prn	FRMSwapCC.prn	FRMSwapRatesCC.prn					
1	3 2.00							
		1	2	3	4	5	7	10	30
	7/31/2000	7.06	7.12	7.16	7.18	7.20	7.21	7.22	7.24
	8/31/2000	6.91	6.93	6.94	6.96	6.97	6.99	7.01	7.04
	9/29/2000	6.73	6.70	6.70	6.72	6.75	6.81	6.87	6.99
	10/31/2000	6.67	6.67	6.68	6.70	6.73	6.77	6.81	6.89

If you compare this file, FRMSwapRatesCC.prn with the input data file, FRMSwapInputData.dat, the estimation error does not appear to be very significant. At the long end of the swap curve, the error for the first four observations is less than five basis points. The error declines for shorter maturities.

References

The LSC references can be found in Module 3.5 Curve Fitting.

Appendix 4.5: Interface code comments

The graphical user interface for this module is illustrated below. The original swap inputs are contained in FRMSwapInputData.dat and a variety of computations are reported in the referenced output files (*.prn).[34]

---

[34] Depending on how your repository is set up, you will need to be careful about where you place the input files and the use of any paths.

There is only one item to note in the interface source code.

FRMUnitSwapFiles.cpp, .h

This module relies heavily on input and output files. Recall that files are managed using AnsiString.

```
...
   AnsiString sinf, soutf, soutf1, soutf2, soutf3, soutf4, soutf5;
   sinf = editInputFileName->Text;
   soutf = editOutputSwapCurveFileName->Text;
// Default: sinf - FRMSwapInputData.dat
//          soutf - FRMSwapCurve.prn
//          FRMRegressionInputData.dat
//          FRMRegressionDetails.prn
//          FRMRegression.prn
   L.FRMAnalyzeCurve(sinf, soutf);  // Swap curve, LSC
   soutf1 = editOutputSwapDFFileName->Text;
   soutf2 = editOutputSwapDetailsFileName->Text;
// Default: soutf  - FRMSwapCurve.prn
//          soutf1 - FRMSwapDF.prn
//          soutf2 - FRMSwapDetails.prn
   L.FRMDiscountFactors(soutf, soutf1, soutf2); // Quarterly, semi DFs
   soutf3 = editOutputCCFileName->Text;
// Default: soutf1 - FRMSwapDF.prn
//          soutf3 - FRMSwapCC.prn
   L.FRMCCRatesFromDF(soutf1, soutf3); // Semi spot rates, cc
   soutf4 = editOutputSpotCurveCCFileName->Text;
// Default: soutf3 - FRMSwapCC.prn
//          soutf4 - FRMSpotCurveCC.prn
   L.FRMAnalyzeCurve(soutf3, soutf4); // Spot curve, cc, LSC
   soutf5 = editOutputSwapRatesCCFileName->Text;
...
   L.FRMSwapRatesFromSpotRatesCC(soutf4, soutf5); // Spot curve, cc, LSC
...
```

Module 4.6: Introduction to Interest Rate Trees

Learning objectives

- Provide a very rough sketch of how to build interest rate trees
- Contrast the various methods of valuing interest rate-related derivatives

Module overview

This module can be used to estimate the interest rate swap curve. It generates cap and floor quote sheets based on the Black, Derman and Toy (1990) interest rate tree approach (denoted BDT). The module uses Eurodollar futures contracts as its key source for a forward curve. We also assume a user-inputted volatility curve. The BDT was one of the original arbitrage-free models of the term structure of interest rates that deployed an interest rate tree. In the supplement to this module, we review several technical aspects of the term structure of interest rates and related interest rate tree concepts.[35]

Black, Derman and Toy model

The Black, Derman and Toy (BDT) single factor, no-arbitrage model of the term structure of interest rates was one of the original models that incorporated both a non-flat term structure of interest rates, as well as a non-flat term structure of interest rate local volatility. We briefly introduce the BDT model, sketch a numerical example, and then review the code. The extensive details for this and other related models can be found in the supplement references.

The no-arbitrage models require that they exactly replicate the existing term structure of interest rates; otherwise, there would be arbitrage opportunities, at least in theory. One typically assumes a set of default-free zero coupon bond prices are observable. Randomness is introduced through the current spot interest rate. In the limit, the current short rate, r, is assumed to follow the continuous time linear stochastic differential equation known as an Itô process.

$$dr = \mu(r,t)dt + \sigma(r,t)dz$$

where $\mu(r,t)$ is the drift term, $\sigma(r,t)$ is the volatility term and dz is the standard Wiener process.

The key insight of BDT was allowing the volatility term to vary over time.

$$dr = \mu(r,t)dt + \sigma(t)dz$$

Technically, every single time step in the model can have a different volatility. The BDT model assumes a binomial lattice framework. The second key insight is that the drift term can be varied across maturities, as well as across states to force the rate tree to disallow arbitrage.

If we assume an equivalent martingale measure probability of 0.5 for both the up and down jump, then the equations for the next time step from any node in the rate tree can be expressed as

$$r_{i+1}(\Delta t : t + \Delta t) = r_i(\Delta t : t)e^{\mu_i(\Delta t:t)\Delta t + \sigma(\Delta t:t)\sqrt{\Delta t}} \text{ (BDT rates move up)}$$

$$r_i(\Delta t : t + \Delta t) = r_i(\Delta t : t)e^{\mu_i(\Delta t:t)\Delta t - \sigma(\Delta t:t)\sqrt{\Delta t}} \text{ (BDT rates move down)}$$

where $r_i(\Delta t : t)$ denotes the continuously compounded spot rate, $\mu_i(\Delta t : t)$ denotes the mean change in the natural log of interest rates observed at time t assuming i previous up jumps, and $\sigma(\Delta t : t)$ denotes

---

[35] Supplements can be found at www.frmhelp.com.

the standard deviation. Notice the standard deviation does not depend on the location in the rate tree with respect to number of up jumps, but just the maturity time.

The simplest way to motivate the BDT is by a numerical example.[36] The following exhibits are snapshots from a BDT spreadsheet. First, we need to assume a set of forward rates and corresponding volatilities. Exhibit 1 illustrates the forward curve (Row 6) and the volatility curve (Row 7) inputs, and we assume each period is one year. Note that the current volatility is zero because rates are advanced set and settled in arrears like a bank certificate of deposit.

Exhibit 1. Black, Derman and Toy Inputs and Price Outputs (Inputs tab)

◇	A	B	C	D	E	F	G	H	I
1	Black, Derman and Toy Interest Rate Model								
2	Inputs								
3	Step Size:	1							
4	Maturity:	0	1	2	3	4	5	6	7
5	Expected Rates:	3.00%	3.00%	3.00%	3.00%	3.00%	3.00%	3.00%	
6	Forward Rates:	3.00%	3.20%	3.30%	3.35%	3.36%	3.36%	3.36%	
7	Volatility:	0.00%	20.00%	18.00%	17.00%	16.00%	16.00%	16.00%	
8									
9	Outputs								
10	Maturity:		1	2	3	4	5	6	7
11	Zero-Cpn Price:		$0.97044553	$0.93988289	$0.90937293	$0.87941356	$0.85035616	$0.82225888	$0.79508997
12	Forward Price:		$0.97044553	$0.96850658	$0.96753856	$0.96705491	$0.96695821	$0.96695821	$0.96695821
13									
14	Cell formula illustrations		Row	2					
15	Zero-Cpn Price:		11	=C11*EXP(-C$6*$B$3)					
16	Forward Price:		12	=EXP(-C$6*$B$3)					
17									
18	Notes:		The Black, Derman and Toy (BDT) model is based on a binomial model with multiplicative						
19			shocks following a lognormal diffusion process. Hence spot rates will always be positive.						
20			Both the mean and standard deviation are allowed to vary over time. The standard deviation						
21			is a user input whereas the means are a free variable used to force the lattice to recombine.						
22			The standard deviation is assumed to be state invariant whereas the mean is allowed to						
23			vary depending on the state in such a way as to force the lattice to recombine. The lognormal						
24			diffusion process assumes the standard deviation is proportional to level of rates (like the Black, Scholes						
25			Merton option valuation model. For simplicity, the EMM up jump probabilities are set to 1/2 and the						
26			means are taken in the up and down jump sizes. The solver routine is used to find the						
27			appropriate mu's.						
28			Interest rates are assumed to be continuously compounded for discrete periods.						
29			Output prices are reported by maturity.						

We also include in the Inputs tab a subjective estimate of the expected future interest rates over the same time (Row 5). We will return to some important implications of the difference between the objectively observed forward rates and the subjective expected future spot rates.

Outputs on this tab include zero-coupon spot prices ($P(\tau_j : t_i)$) and forward prices ($F(\tau_j, \tau_k : t_i)$) based on the following formulas.

$$P(\tau_j : t_i) = \exp\left\{ -r_a(\tau_j : t_i)\tau_j \right\} \quad \textbf{(Zero coupon bond price)}$$

$$F(\tau_j, \tau_k : t_i) = e^{f_a(\tau_j, \tau_k : t_i)(\tau_j - \tau_k)} = \frac{P(\tau_k : t_i)}{P(\tau_j : t_i)} \quad \textbf{(Term forward price)}$$

where $r_a(\tau_j : t_i)$ denotes the annualized, continuously compounded interest rate observed at time t_i, $\tau_j > \tau_k$ denotes the time to maturity expressed in fraction of a year, and $f_a(\tau_j, \tau_k : t_i)$ denotes the annualized forward rate.

Exhibit 2 illustrates the core of the BDT approach, though it is a bit opaque and difficult to understand at first. The diagonals (B9, C8, ... G4) contain a constant used by a search routine in a spreadsheet. Each cell in the matrix holds the drift term used over the next binomial time step. Because the drift term is a free variable, we solve for it such that the sum of the state claims equals the inputted zero-

---

[36] This numerical example is available in spreadsheet form at www.frmhelp.com.

coupon bond price. That is, the no arbitrage condition is such that if we purchased at time t all the state claims available at point in n time steps (there would be n+1 of them), the cost should exactly equal the $1 par zero coupon bond ($P_i(n\Delta t : t)$, where i denotes the number of previous up jumps, t is the current calendar time (or location in maturity time), and n indicates the number of time steps in the future.

$$P_i(n\Delta t : t) = \sum_{v=0}^{n} SC_{i+v}(n\Delta t : t) = SC_i(n\Delta t : t) + SC_{i+1}(n\Delta t : t) + \ldots + SC_{i+n}(n\Delta t : t) \quad \textbf{(State claims bond value)}$$

Therefore, in Exhibit 2, Row 2 contains the difference between the sum of the state claims (State Claims tab, see Exhibit 4 covered in a bit) and the appropriate zero-coupon bond price (Inputs tab covered in Exhibit 1). In goal seek, we set B2 to equal zero by changing B9. We then set C2 to equal zero by changing C8 and continue across the term structure. The remainder of the drift terms is solved simultaneously due to the restriction that the binomial tree recombines. Specifically, we note

$$r_{n+1}(\Delta t : t + \Delta t) = r_n(\Delta t : t)e^{\mu_n(\Delta t : t)\Delta t + \sigma(\Delta t : t)\sqrt{\Delta t}} \quad \textbf{(Only up jumps have occurred)}$$

$$r_i(\Delta t : t + \Delta t) = r_i(\Delta t : t)e^{\mu_i(\Delta t : t)\Delta t - \sigma(\Delta t : t)\sqrt{\Delta t}} = r_{i-1}(\Delta t : t)e^{\mu_{i-1}(\Delta t : t)\Delta t + \sigma(\Delta t : t)\sqrt{\Delta t}} \quad \textbf{(Tree recombines)}$$

Therefore, we can solve for the mean term when up has always occurred and then fill the remaining drift terms based forcing the tree to recombine. That is,

$$\mu_{i-1}(\Delta t : t) = \frac{1}{\Delta t} \ln\left[\frac{r_i(\Delta t : t)}{r_{i-1}(\Delta t : t)}\right] + \mu_i(\Delta t : t) - \frac{2\sigma(\Delta t : t)}{\sqrt{\Delta t}} \quad \textbf{(Down mu such that tree recombines)}$$

Exhibit 2. Solving for the mean in order to achieve no arbitrage (Mu tab)

◇	A	B	C	D	E	F	G
1	MUs -- Based on Bond Maturity Date, Single Period						
2	No Arb:	0.000000%	0.000000%	0.000000%	0.000000%	0.000000%	0.000000%
3	ît	0	1	2	3	4	5
4	5						-0.783047%
5	4					-0.876713%	-0.783047%
6	3				-3.198876%	-0.876713%	-0.783047%
7	2			-1.352486%	-1.198876%	-0.876713%	-0.783047%
8	1		-0.001972%	0.647514%	0.801124%	-0.876713%	-0.783047%
9	0	4.529434%	3.998028%	2.647514%	2.801124%	-0.876713%	-0.783047%
10	Cell formula illustrations						
11		Cell D2:					
12	No Arb:	='State Claims'!F2-Inputs!F11					
13		2					
14	1	=D7+(LN('Spot Rates'!D11/'Spot Rates'!D12)/Inputs!$B$3)-(2*Inputs!E$7/SQRT(Inputs!$B$3))					
15							
16	NOTES:	The solver routine is used to find the mu's at node i=t (up jumps here). The remaining					
17		mus are analytic functions of mu(i=t). Note that the mus help determine the rates					
18		observed in the next time step and those rates determine the spot prices observed					
19		in yet the next time step. Therefore, the mus influence spot prices two time steps later.					
20		Column D (t=2) determines the mus observed at time 2. The mus are used to determine					
21		the spot rates observed at time 3 for a zero coupon bond that matures at time 4.					

Based on the drift term (mu) at each node identified in Exhibit 2 (Mu tab) and the maturity time volatility identified in Exhibit 1, we can compute the spot rates shown in Exhibit 3 Rows 7-13. We illustrate the tree recombines by showing both the move down (Rows 7-13) and the move up (Rows 18-21, extreme ups and downs not shown). Rows 24-29 show that we recover the appropriate local volatility assumed in Exhibit 1. We will return to Exhibit 3 to explain Rows 2-5 once we cover the probability trees in Exhibit 6. One of the key insights in this analysis is embedded in the difference between Row 4 (expected rates based on the subjective probability measure) and Row 5 (expected rates based on the equivalent martingale measure). We will return to this difference when discussing the probability trees.

Exhibit 3. Spot rates tree (Spot Rates tab)

◇	A	B	C	D	E	F	G	H	I
1	Spot Rates								
2	RP - First Diff		0.2020%	0.1052%	0.0580%	0.0197%	0.0135%	0.0167%	
3	Risk Premium	0.0000%	0.2020%	0.3072%	0.3653%	0.3850%	0.3985%	0.4152%	
4	E(Rates,SP)	3.0000%	3.0000%	3.0000%	3.0000%	3.0000%	3.0000%	3.0000%	
5	E(Rates,EMM)	3.0000%	3.2020%	3.3072%	3.3653%	3.3850%	3.3985%	3.4152%	
6	i\t	0	1	2	3	4	5	6	
7	6							8.2629%	
8	5						7.0965%	6.0001%	
9	4					6.1005%	5.1531%	4.3570%	
10	3				5.3675%	4.4299%	3.7419%	3.1638%	
11	2			4.5900%	3.8204%	3.2168%	2.7172%	2.2974%	
12	1		3.8340%	3.2024%	2.7193%	2.3358%	1.9731%	1.6683%	
13	0	3.0000%	2.5700%	2.2342%	1.9355%	1.6962%	1.4328%	1.2114%	
14	Cell formula Illustr.	Row	i\t	2					
15		12	1	=C$12*EXP(Mu!C$8*Inputs!$B$3-Inputs!D$7*SQRT(Inputs!$B$3))					
16		21	1	=C$13*EXP(Mu!C$9*Inputs!$B$3+Inputs!D$7*SQRT(Inputs!$B$3))					
17	Test for Recombining ==>>							6.0001%	
18							5.1531%	4.3570%	
19						4.4299%	3.7419%	3.1638%	
20					3.8204%	3.2168%	2.7172%	2.2974%	
21	Volatility			3.2024%	2.7193%	2.3358%	1.9731%	1.6683%	
22	i\t	0	1	2	3	4	5	6	
23	6								
24	5							16.0000%	
25	4						16.0000%	16.0000%	
26	3					16.0000%	16.0000%	16.0000%	
27	2				17.0000%	16.0000%	16.0000%	16.0000%	
28	1			18.0000%	17.0000%	16.0000%	16.0000%	16.0000%	
29	0	0.0000%	20.0000%	18.0000%	17.0000%	16.0000%	16.0000%	16.0000%	
30				2					
31			0	=LN(D12/D13)/2					
32	Notes:	E(Rates,EMM) denotes the expected rate based on the equivalent martingale measure.							
33		E(Rates,SP) denotes the expected rates based on the subjective probability measure.							

From Exhibit 2, we know that the no-arbitrage condition was based on the sum of the state claims equaling the current zero-coupon bond price. Exhibit 4 illustrates the state claim tree where the value of a state claim is represented in the cell where it is paid. The state claim value paid in n time steps given that i up jumps occur can be expressed as

$$SC_i(n\Delta t : t) = SC_i((n-1)\Delta t : t)\left[1 - q_i(t + (n-1)\Delta t)\right]P_i(\Delta t : t + (n-1)\Delta t)$$
$$+ SC_{i-1}((n-1)\Delta t : t)q_{i-1}(t + (n-1)\Delta t)P_{i-1}(\Delta t : t + (n-1)\Delta t)$$

(State claim value)

The illustration below emphasizes that the state claim value at node (n,i) depends on the state claim values at both (n–1,i–1), as well as the corresponding bond prices and equivalent martingale probabilities.

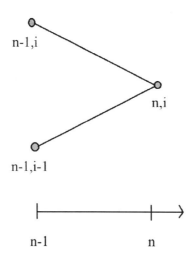

Exhibit 4. State claim tree (State Claims tab)

	A	B	C	D	E	F	G	H	I
1	State Claims								
2	Sum		$0.97044553	$0.93988289	$0.90937293	$0.87941356	$0.85035616	$0.82225888	$0.79508997
3	i\t	0	1	2	3	4	5	6	7
4	7								$0.00533
5	6							$0.01158	$0.03944
6	5						$0.02486	$0.07245	$0.12393
7	4					$0.05284	$0.12819	$0.18763	$0.21466
8	3				$0.11151	$0.21602	$0.26319	$0.25771	$0.22168
9	2			$0.23349	$0.33907	$0.33017	$0.26912	$0.19818	$0.13665
10	1		$0.48522	$0.46994	$0.34318	$0.22369	$0.13713	$0.08097	$0.04660
11	0	$1.00000	$0.48522	$0.23646	$0.11562	$0.05670	$0.02787	$0.01374	$0.00679
12	i\t	0	1	2	3	4	5	6	7
13	Im.For.Pr.	3.0000%	3.2000%	3.3000%	3.3500%	3.3600%	3.3600%	3.3600%	
14	Cell formula illustrations								
15		Row							
16		13	Im.For.Pr.	=LN(D2/E2)					
17				2					
18		10	1	=C$10*0.5*'Spot Prices'!C$9+C$11*0.5*'Spot Prices'!C$10					
19		2	Sum	=SUM(D9:D11)					
20									
21	NOTES:	The no arbitrage condition requires that we get the original spot prices back from the state-claims.							
22		Hence, using state-claims we precisely also obtain the forward rates. With state-claims and							
23		spot rates, we can value any interest rate-based contingent claim.							

Given the rate tree in Exhibit 3, it is straightforward to calculate the spot price tree illustrated in Exhibit 5. That is,

$$P(\Delta t : t_i) = \exp\{-r_a(\Delta t : t_i)\Delta t\}$$

This exhibit highlights that the expected spot price, based on the equivalent martingale measure does not correspond with the forward prices derived from the inputted observed spot rates.

Exhibit 5. Spot prices tree (Spot Prices tab)

◇	A	B	C	D	E	F	G	H
1	Spot Prices -- When Observed							
2	E(Price,EMM)	0.9704455	0.9685066	0.9675026	0.9669552	0.9667742	0.9666596	0.9665144
3	i\t	0	1	2	3	4	5	6
4	6							$0.92069
5	5						$0.93149	$0.94176
6	4					$0.94082	$0.94977	$0.95737
7	3				$0.94774	$0.95667	$0.96327	$0.96886
8	2			$0.95514	$0.96252	$0.96834	$0.97319	$0.97729
9	1		$0.96239	$0.96848	$0.97317	$0.97691	$0.98046	$0.98346
10	0	$0.97045	$0.97463	$0.97791	$0.98083	$0.98318	$0.98577	$0.98796
11	i\t	0	1	2	3	4	5	6
12	Im.For.Rate	3.0000%	3.2000%	3.3037%	3.3603%	3.3790%	3.3909%	3.4059%
13	Cell formula illustrations							
14			Im.For.Rate	=LN(1/D2)				
15	E(Price,EMM)			=Prob!D9*D8+Prob!D10*D9+Prob!D11*D10				
16				2				
17			1	=EXP(-'Spot Rates'!D12)				
18	Notes:	Notice that the expected spot price is not the forward price due to the convexity						
19		in bond prices with respect to rates. Hence the implied forward rate based on						
20		the expected future spot price is biased high.						

Exhibit 6 highlights two probability trees, one based on the no-arbitrage equivalent martingale measure and the other derived from the rate tree and the user-defined expected future spot rates (see Exhibit 1). Financial risk management, as well as investment management decision-making can be improved when you understand the implications. These management tasks depend on quality measures of market value, as well as quality measures of future outcome likelihoods.

Exhibit 6. Probability trees (Prob tab)

◇	A	B	C	D	E	F	G	H
1	Equivalent Martingale Measure (Probabilities)							
2	Up Probability:	50.000000%						
3	Total Probability	100.000000%	100.000000%	100.000000%	100.000000%	100.000000%	100.000000%	100.000000%
4	i\t	0	1	2	3	4	5	6
5	6							0.015625
6	5						0.031250	0.093750
7	4					0.062500	0.156250	0.234375
8	3				0.125000	0.250000	0.312500	0.312500
9	2			0.250000	0.375000	0.375000	0.312500	0.234375
10	1		0.500000	0.500000	0.375000	0.250000	0.156250	0.093750
11	0	1.000000	0.500000	0.250000	0.125000	0.062500	0.031250	0.015625
12	Subjective Probabilities Based on Input Expected Spot Rates							
13	E(Rates, Input)	3.000000%	3.000000%	3.000000%	3.000000%	3.000000%	3.000000%	3.000000%
14	Difference (Goal Seek)	0.000000%	0.000000%	0.000000%	0.000000%	0.000000%	0.000000%	0.000000%
15	Up Probability:	50.000000%	34.019097%	39.287901%	43.297082%	46.045000%	48.748580%	48.454688%
16	Total Probability	100.000000%	100.000000%	100.000000%	100.000000%	100.000000%	100.000000%	100.000000%
17	i\t	0	1	2	3	4	5	6
18	6							0.006294
19	5						0.012989	0.050863
20	4					0.026645	0.091153	0.169412
21	3				0.057868	0.158973	0.252663	0.297911
22	2			0.133654	0.277447	0.351163	0.346045	0.291918
23	1		0.340191	0.465762	0.437542	0.340664	0.234339	0.151226
24	0	1.000000	0.659809	0.400584	0.227143	0.122555	0.062811	0.032376
25	Cell formula illustrations			D				
26		13	E(Rates, Inputs	=Inputs!D5				
27		14	Difference (Goa	='Spot Rates'!D4-D13				
28		15	Up Prob:	39.287901%				
29		16	Total Prob	=SUM(D18:D24)				
30		22	2	=C23*D15				
31		23	1	=C23*(1-D$15)+C24*D$15				
32		24	0	=C24*(1-D$15)				
33	Notes:	The EMM probability of up is assumed to be 50% and the subjective probability of up is derived based on						
34		the inputted expected spot rates.						

We are now ready to examine Exhibit 3 and the difference in the two expected rate measures (Row 4 and 5). Based on market price and volatility information, we can estimate the expected spot rate based on the equivalent martingale measure (Row 5). Based on this same information, as well as the subjective expected spot rates, we can estimate a new probability tree. With this probability tree, we can validate the expected spot rates (all 3% in Row 4). Therefore, the subjective probability tree is internally consistent with the user-defined expected future spot rates. We now illustrate just one practical use of this information in Exhibits 7 and 8.

Exhibit 7 illustrates the value of having multiple approaches to valuation, as well as having the ability to incorporate subjective probabilities into the analysis. The top portion of Exhibit 7 just validates that both the market comparables approach to valuing swaps and the cap and floor approach yield the same equilibrium swap rate. In essence, the EMM rate tree is no arbitrage.

Exhibit 7. Two versions for swap valuation (Swap Rates tab – top)

◇	A	B	C	D	E	F	G	H
1	Swap Rates							
2								
3	FRA Version	1						
4	Maturity:	0	1	2	3	4	5	6
5	Forward Rates:	3.00%	3.20%	3.30%	3.35%	3.36%	3.36%	3.36%
6	Prices:		0.970446	0.939883	0.909373	0.879414	0.850356	0.822259
7	Forward-Discrete:	3.045453%	3.251751%	3.355054%	3.406744%	3.417086%	3.417086%	3.417086%
8	Swap Rates:	3.045453%	3.146952%	3.214066%	3.259873%	3.289258%	3.308825%	3.322783%
9			Forward Rates:	=Inputs!D6				
10			Prices:	=Inputs!D11				
11			Forward-Discrete:	=EXP(D5)-1				
12			Swap Rates:	=($B$7*$C$6+$C$7*$D$6+$D$7*$E$6)/($C$6+$D$6+$E$6)				
13	Cap-Floor Version							
14	Maturity:	0	1	2	3	4	5	6
15	Swap Rates:	3.045453%	3.146952%	3.214066%	3.259873%	3.289258%	3.308825%	3.322783%
16	Numerator:				12.059%	14.964%	2.810%	2.717%
17	Denominator:				369.911%	454.947%	82.226%	79.509%
18			=('State Claims'!$B$11*'Spot Prices'!$B$10*(EXP('Spot Rates'!$B$13)-1)					
19			+'State Claims'!$C$10*'Spot Prices'!$C$9*(EXP('Spot Rates'!$C$12)-1)					
20			+'State Claims'!$C$11*'Spot Prices'!$C$10*(EXP('Spot Rates'!$C$13)-1))					
21			/('State Claims'!$B$11*'Spot Prices'!$B$10+'State Claims'!$C$10*'Spot Prices'!$C$9					
22			+'State Claims'!$C$11*'Spot Prices'!$C$10)					
23	Diff: MCA-CFAA	0.000000%	0.000000%	0.000000%	0.000000%	0.000000%	0.000000%	0.000000%

The market comparables approach to valuing interest rate swap is based on the insight that an interest rate swap can be viewed as a portfolio of forward rate agreements (FRAs). Assuming a non-amortizing swap where both the forward rates and the discount rates are derived from the same source (default-free), we have

$$V_{Swap} = NA\left[r_{fix} \sum_{i=1}^{n_{fix}} \frac{NAD_i}{NTD_i} e^{-(r_{DC,i} t_i)} - \sum_{j=1}^{n_{flt}} r_{FC,j} \frac{NAD_j}{NTD_j} e^{-(r_{DC,j} t_j)} \right]$$

where NA denotes the notional amount, r_{fix} denotes the fixed rate, $r_{FC,j}$ denotes the appropriate forward rate, NAD_i denotes the number of accrued days over period i, NTD_i denotes the number of total days in a year for period i, $r_{DC,i}$ denotes the appropriate discount rate, and t_i denotes the fraction of the year until the payment is made. Therefore, the equilibrium swap rate can be viewed as a weighted average of the appropriate forward rates.

$$r_{fix} = \frac{\sum_{j=1}^{n_{flt}} r_{FC,j} \frac{NAD_j}{NTD_j} e^{-(r_{DC,j} t_j)}}{\sum_{i=1}^{n_{fix}} \frac{NAD_i}{NTD_i} e^{-(r_{DC,i} t_i)}} = \sum_{j=1}^{n_{flt}} w_j r_{FC,j}$$

where

$$w_j = \frac{\dfrac{NAD_j}{NTD_j} e^{-(r_{DC,j}t_j)}}{\displaystyle\sum_{i=1}^{n_{fix}} \dfrac{NAD_i}{NTD_i} e^{-(r_{DC,i}t_i)}}$$

In Exhibit 7, the accrual period (NAD/NTD) is 1 and the forward rate is assumed to be annual and discretely compounded. See Row 8.

The cash flow adjusted approach to valuing interest rate swaps requires the EMM rate tree and corresponding state claims as well as single period bond prices. Recall interest rate swaps are advanced set and settled in arrears so the observed spot rate on a floating rate reset date (say v_i,k) determines the payoff in arrears (assumed to be one period for simplicity here). Therefore,

$$V_{Swap} = NA \left[\begin{array}{l} r_{fix} \displaystyle\sum_{i=1}^{n_{fix}} \dfrac{NAD_i}{NTD_i} \displaystyle\sum_{k=0}^{m_{fix}} SC_k\left(v_i\Delta t : t\right) P_k\left(\Delta t : t + v_i\Delta t\right) \\[4mm] - \displaystyle\sum_{j=1}^{n_{flt}} \dfrac{NAD_j}{NTD_j} \displaystyle\sum_{k=0}^{m_{flt}} SC_k\left(v_i\Delta t : t\right) P_k\left(\Delta t : t + v_i\Delta t\right) r_k\left(\Delta t : t + v_i\Delta t\right) \end{array} \right]$$

Solving for the equilibrium fixed swap rate, we have

$$r_{fix} = \frac{\displaystyle\sum_{j=1}^{n_{flt}} \dfrac{NAD_j}{NTD_j} \displaystyle\sum_{k=0}^{m_{flt}} SC_k\left(v_i\Delta t : t\right) P_k\left(\Delta t : t + v_i\Delta t\right) r_k\left(\Delta t : t + v_i\Delta t\right)}{\displaystyle\sum_{i=1}^{n_{fix}} \dfrac{NAD_i}{NTD_i} \displaystyle\sum_{k=0}^{m_{fix}} SC_k\left(v_i\Delta t : t\right) P_k\left(\Delta t : t + v_i\Delta t\right)}$$

Clearly, there are more technical details to account for, but Exhibit 7 shows a simplified approach. See Row 15.

Exhibit 8 illustrates a perspective on interest rate swaps that is not well understood but is of high practical value. Even if you did not follow the technical discussion of the two approaches to valuing interest rate swaps, we have demonstrated that based on user input, we can build one rate tree and two probability trees. Exhibit 8 demonstrates the expected cash flows from entering a receive fixed swap.

182   Robert Brooks

Exhibit 8. Expected swap cash flows and an apparent paradox (Swap Rates tab – bottom)

◇	A	B	C	D	E	F
25	Swap Cash Flows: Receive Fixed, Pay Floating					
26	Notional Principal:	$1,000,000				
27	1-YEAR	0				
28	0	$0.00000				
29	E(Cash Flow)	$0.00000				
30	2-YEAR	0	1			
31	1		($7,328.44)			
32	0	$984.99	$5,298.47			
33	E(Cash Flow)	$984.99	$1,002.91			
34	3-YEAR	0	1	2		
35	2			($14,164.09)		
36	1		($6,682.54)	($388.53)		
37	0	$1,636.29	$5,952.59	$9,336.19		
38	E(Cash Flow)	$1,636.29	$1,654.23	$1,665.88		
39	4-YEAR	0	1	2	3	
40	3				($21,364.80)	
41	2			($13,726.57)	($6,106.88)	
42	1		($6,241.70)	$55.10	$4,897.96	
43	0	$2,080.82	$5,878.62	$9,784.13	$12,805.02	
44	E(Cash Flow)	$2,080.82	$1,755.39	$2,110.42	$2,120.95	
45	5-YEAR	0	1	2	3	4
46	4					($28,235.67)
47	3				($21,086.30)	($11,864.69)
48	2			($13,445.91)	($5,824.04)	$195.66
49	1		($5,958.90)	$339.69	$5,183.92	$9,045.42
50	0	$2,365.99	$6,685.42	$10,071.49	$13,093.24	$15,520.70
51	E(Cash Flow)	$2,365.99	$2,383.94	$2,395.59	$2,406.13	$2,413.77
52						*$11,965.42*
53	E(Cash Flow, EMM)	$2,365.99	$363.26	($673.76)	($1,239.18)	($1,426.13)
54						*($609.82)*
55	PV(EMM)	($295.77)				

The expected cash flows from a receive fixed swap, based on the subjective probability measure, are always negative. There are future states where the actual cash flow is negative. We now focus solely on the five-year swap. For ease of analysis, we assume advanced set and advanced settled. Therefore, the cash flows are shown at the beginning of the measurement period, so no additional discounting is needed within the period. Row 51 and 52 demonstrate positive expected cash flows each year and a total of $7,815.10 per $1,000,000 notional amount or about 78 basis point of notional amount. Based on the EMM, the expected future cash flows are both positive and negative and total –$609.82.

Clearly, if a firm has a risk exposure to falling interest rates and can hedge this exposure with a receive fixed swap, then the firm's risk is lowered and the expected cash flow is increased. Risk management becomes a profit center! If a firm has risk exposure to rising rates and can hedge this exposure with a receive floating swap, then the firm's risk is lowered but the expected cash flow is decreased. In this case, risk management is costly and the trade-offs need careful examination.

Exhibit 9 illustrates the final tab in the BDT spreadsheet documenting the ability to put rate trees, state claim trees and so forth into a single vector. You just have to be careful how you reference different cell locations. We let i denote the location in the vector of a particular node, say n time steps out (for example, i=7) and j up jumps have occurred (for example, j=4). The location in the vector for that outcome is $i(i-1)/2 + i + j$. Let iM1 denote $i-1$ time steps with the same number of up jumps, thus the location in the vector for that outcome is $(i-1)(i-2)/2 + i - 1 + j$. Finally, iM2 denote $i-2$ time steps with the same number of up jumps, thus the location in the vector for that outcome is $(i-2)(i-3)/2 + i - 2 + j$.

Exhibit 9. Counters illustration (iM1 and iM2 tab)

◇	A	B	C	D	E	F	G	H
1	Counters							
2				Current Point In Time =		7		
3	VECTOR	Time	Node	Number of Up Jumps=		4		
4	0	0	0		Vector[]			
5	1	1	0	i =		32	=$F$2*($F$2-1)/2+$F$2+$F$3	
6	2	1	1	iM1 =		25	=($F$2-1)*($F$2-2)/2+$F$2-1+$F$3	
7	3	2	0	iM2 =		19	=($F$2-2)*($F$2-3)/2+$F$2-2+$F$3	
8	4	2	1					
9	5	2	2					
10	6	3	0					
11	7	3	1					
12	8	3	2					
13	9	3	3					
14	10	4	0					
15	11	4	1					
16	12	4	2					
17	13	4	3					
18	14	4	4					
19	15	5	0					
20	16	5	1					
21	17	5	2					
22	18	5	3					
23	19	5	4					
24	20	5	5					
25	21	6	0					
26	22	6	1					
27	23	6	2					
28	24	6	3					
29	25	6	4					
30	26	6	5					
31	27	6	6					
32	28	7	0					
33	29	7	1					
34	30	7	2					
35	31	7	3					
36	32	7	4					
37	33	7	5					
38	34	7	6					
39	35	7	7					

Implementation code comments

This is a rather complex program and involves several components. We briefly review each component here.

FRMEDFutures.h

This code reads in the Eurodollar futures data and produces basic output.

```
#ifndef FRMEDFuturesH
#define FRMEDFuturesH
#include <iostream.h>
#include <iomanip.h>
#include <fstream.h>
#include <math.h>
#define EDARRAYSIZE 100
#define CHARARRAYSIZE 12
#define CHARSIZE 20

#ifndef FRMCALENDARCPP
#define FRMCALENDARCPP
#include "c:\FRMRepository\FRMCalendar.cpp"
#endif

#ifndef FRMDATEMDY
#define FRMDATEMDY
struct FRMDateMDY
{
```

```
    int Month;
    int Day;
    int Year;
};
#endif

class FRMEDFUTURES
{
public:
    int GetEDFuturesData(AnsiString inputsinf, AnsiString outputsinf);
    ofstream outf;  // Output file stream, global because used in multiple file
    int i, j;
    int BaseYear;
    int DayOfWeek;
    long int SpotRateDate;
    FRMDateMDY Current;
    FRMCALENDAR Spot;
    double SpotRate;
    double SpotRateVolatility;
    double BiasAdjustment;
    FRMDateMDY SpotRateDateMDY;
    int NumberOfEDFutures;              // Number of Futures in Input File
    void ConvertEDFuturesData(void);
    int SetEDFuturesDay(int DayOfWeek);
    void EDDiscountFactors(void);       // Compute Discount Factors
    void CurveFittingFile(void);        // Write file for Curvefitting class
    static double EDFuturesPrice[EDARRAYSIZE];         // Vector of Futures Prices
    static double EDFuturesVolatility[EDARRAYSIZE];  // Vector of Volatilities
    static double EDFuturesDF[EDARRAYSIZE+1];         // Vector of Discount Factors
    static char EDFuturesTicker[EDARRAYSIZE] [4];    // EDF Ticker Symbols
    static long int EDFuturesDates[EDARRAYSIZE+1];   // Julian dates
    static FRMDateMDY EDFuturesDatesMDY[EDARRAYSIZE+1];   // DateMDY structure
    static double ForwardRates[EDARRAYSIZE];             // Derived forward rates
    char word[CHARARRAYSIZE][CHARSIZE];//Handles miscellaneous character variables
};
```

When allocating large amounts of memory in a class, it is advisable to declare them static (see above). This prevents multiple instances of the class using up all the memory. The static declaration requires the following statements.

```
double FRMEDFUTURES::EDFuturesPrice[EDARRAYSIZE];
double FRMEDFUTURES::EDFuturesVolatility[EDARRAYSIZE];
double FRMEDFUTURES::EDFuturesDF[EDARRAYSIZE+1];
char FRMEDFUTURES::EDFuturesTicker[EDARRAYSIZE] [4];
long int FRMEDFUTURES::EDFuturesDates[EDARRAYSIZE+1];
FRMDateMDY FRMEDFUTURES::EDFuturesDatesMDY[EDARRAYSIZE+1];
double FRMEDFUTURES::ForwardRates[EDARRAYSIZE];
#endif
```

FRMEDFutures.cpp

This file contains several methods related to creating basic Eurdollar futures output, as well as forward curve output.

```
#include "FRMEDFutures.h"

int FRMEDFUTURES::GetEDFuturesData(AnsiString inputsinf, AnsiString outputsinf)
{
...
```
This method takes care of tedious file management issues.

```
}

void FRMEDFUTURES::ConvertEDFuturesData()
{
```
The information contained in the ticker symbol is enough to determine the maturity date due to expirations occurring on the Monday before the third Wednesday of the contract month.

```
    if(i == -1) {
```

```
        SpotRateDate = Spot.FRMToJulian(Current); // Current date
        SpotRateDateMDY = Spot.FRMFromJulian(SpotRateDate);
      if(SpotRateDateMDY.Year < 90){
        BaseYear = 2000;            // base year to handle ED ticker convention
      } else {
        BaseYear = 2000;
      }
  } else {
      int firstcount = 0;
      int decadecount = 0;
      if(EDFuturesTicker[i][2]=='Z' && atoi(&EDFuturesTicker[i][3])==0
        && firstcount != 0) decadecount += 10;
      if(EDFuturesTicker[i][2]=='Z' && atoi(&EDFuturesTicker[i][3]) == 0)
        firstcount = -99;
      BaseYear += decadecount;
      if(EDFuturesTicker[i][2] == 'H'){ // March Ticker
        EDFuturesDatesMDY[i].Month = 3;
        if(EDFuturesTicker[i][3] == '0')BaseYear += 10; // move to year 2000
      }
      if(EDFuturesTicker[i] [2] == 'M') EDFuturesDatesMDY[i].Month = 6; // June
      if(EDFuturesTicker[i] [2] == 'U') EDFuturesDatesMDY[i].Month = 9; // Sept
      if(EDFuturesTicker[i] [2] == 'Z') EDFuturesDatesMDY[i].Month = 12; // Dec
       EDFuturesDatesMDY[i].Year = BaseYear + atoi(&EDFuturesTicker[i][3]);
      EDFuturesDatesMDY[i].Day = 1;
      EDFuturesDates[i] = Spot.FRMToJulian(EDFuturesDatesMDY[i]);//First of month
      DayOfWeek = Spot.FRMWeekDay(EDFuturesDates[i]);
      EDFuturesDatesMDY[i].Day = SetEDFuturesDay(DayOfWeek);
      EDFuturesDates[i] = Spot.FRMToJulian(EDFuturesDatesMDY[i]); // Futures date
  }
}


int FRMEDFUTURES::SetEDFuturesDay(int DayOfWeek)
{ // Monday before third Wednesday, given DayOfWeek is the first of month
  if(DayOfWeek == 1) return 15; // Monday
  if(DayOfWeek == 2) return 14; // Tuesday
  if(DayOfWeek == 3) return 13; // Wednesday
  if(DayOfWeek == 4) return 19; // Thursday
  if(DayOfWeek == 5) return 18; // Friday
  if(DayOfWeek == 6) return 17; // Saturday
  if(DayOfWeek == 0) return 16; // Sunday
  return 0;
}


void FRMEDFUTURES::EDDiscountFactors(void)
{
...
  ForwardRates[0] = (100.0 - EDFuturesPrice[0])/100.0; //Implied futures rate
```

A variety of ad hoc adjustments could be applied, but not for the very first one as there should be no adjustment.

```
  ForwardRates[0] = ForwardRates[0] * exp(-0.0  // Adjusted forward rates
    * pow(EDFuturesVolatility[0]/100.0, 2.0)* ForwardRates[0]
    * ((float)(EDFuturesDates[0] - SpotRateDate))/360.0);
...
  for(i = 1; i < NumberOfEDFutures; i++){
    ForwardRates[i] = (100.0 - EDFuturesPrice[i])/100.0; //Implied futures rate
```

The forward rates are adjusted.

```
      ForwardRates[i]
        = ForwardRates[i] * exp(-BiasAdjustment // Adjusted forward rates
      * pow(EDFuturesVolatility[i]/100.0, 2.0)* ForwardRates[i]
      * ((float)(EDFuturesDates[i] - SpotRateDate))/360.0);
    EDFuturesDF[i] = EDFuturesDF[i-1];
      EDFuturesDF[i] *= 1.0/(1.0 + ForwardRates[i-1]
        * ((float)(EDFuturesDates[i] - EDFuturesDates[i-1]))/360.0);
...
  }
}


void FRMEDFUTURES::CurveFittingFile(void)
```

{

Creates the Forward Curve.prn file.

```
   ofstream outf2;   // Output file stream.
   outf2.open( "Forward Curve.prn", ios::out);  // Output file stream.
   outf2 << "LIBOR Forward and Volatility Data" << "\n";
   outf2 << "             0      ";
   for(i=0; i<NumberOfEDFutures; i++){
     outf2.width(8); outf2.precision(5);
     outf2.setf(ios::right); outf2.setf(ios::fixed, ios::floatfield);
// Length of tropical year is 365.24219
     outf2 << (((float)(EDFuturesDates[i] - SpotRateDate))/365.24219) << "  ";
   }
...
}
```

FRMLSCCurveFitting.h

This header file defines various methods used in deriving the current swap curve.

```
...
#ifndef FRMCALENDARCPP
#define FRMCALENDARCPP
#include "c:\FRMRepository\FRMCalendar.cpp"
#endif

#ifndef FRMREGRESSIONCPP
#define FRMREGRESSIONCPP
#include "c:\FRMRepository\FRMRegression.cpp"
#endif

#ifndef EDLSCDATA
#define EDLSCDATA
struct EDLSCOUTPUTDATA
{
public:
   double Level;
   double Slope;
   double Curvature;
   double VLevel;
   double VSlope;
   double VCurvature;
};
#endif

class FRMEDLSC : public FRMREGRESSION
{
public:
   int i, j;
   char CurveDate[CHARSIZE];
   double Level, Slope, Curvature;
   double VLevel, VSlope, VCurvature;
   double Maturity[CFARRAYSIZE];   // Maturity of swap rate inputs
   double Tau[CFARRAYSIZE]; // Hump parameter fixed
   double **Factor; // Level, slope and curvature coefficients for each maturity
   double *Rate;              // Inputted rates for each maturity
   FRMEDLSC::FRMEDLSC(); // Constructor, tau=3, open file, allocate memory
   FRMEDLSC::~FRMEDLSC();  // Destructor, delete memory for Factor and Rate
// Solve for level, slope and curvature
   void FRMAnalyzeCurve(AnsiString inputsinf, AnsiString inputsoutf);
// Use methods below to compute the rate for a given maturity
   double FRMCalculateCurve2(double Maturity, double Level, double Slope,
      double tau0);
   double FRMCalculateCurve3(double Maturity, double Level, double Slope,
      double Curvature1, double tau0);
...
   struct EDLSCOUTPUTDATA FRMAnalyzeForwardAndVolatilityCurve(void);
   EDLSCOUTPUTDATA ELD;   //Eurodollar futures LSC output results
   void PlainVanillaSwapCurve(double Level, double Slope, double Curvature);
   void SwapCurveQuaıt30360(double Level, double Slope, double Curvature);
   FRMDateMDY Current;
```

```
    FRMDateMDY SpotRateDateMDY;
    FRMCALENDAR Julian;                     // Instantiate objects
    FRMCALENDAR Spot;
};
...
```

FRMLSCCurveFitting.cpp

This file contains several methods for managing the curve-fitting task as well as estimating swap curves.

```
...
// Generic input data file
void FRMEDLSC::FRMAnalyzeCurve(AnsiString inputsinf, AnsiString inputsoutf)
{
    int NColumns, NRows, Counter, NVars;
    double x;
    ifstream inf;                   // Input file
    ofstream outf1;                 // Output file
    inf.open(inputsinf.c_str(), ios::in);  // Open input file
    outf1.open(inputsoutf.c_str());  // Open output
    inf  >> NColumns >> NRows;       // NColumns = Factors, NRows = Observations
    outf1 << NColumns << ' ';
    if(NColumns==2 || NColumns==3) {
        inf >> Tau[0];
            outf1 << setiosflags(ios::showpoint | ios::fixed) << setprecision(2)
                << setfill(' ') << setiosflags(ios::right) << setw(5) << Tau[0] << ' ';
    } else {
        for(j=0; j<NColumns-2; j++){
            inf >> Tau[j];
            outf1 << setiosflags(ios::showpoint | ios::fixed) << setprecision(2)
                << setfill(' ') << setiosflags(ios::right) << setw(5) << Tau[j] << ' ';
        }
    }
    outf1 << '\n';
    for(j=0; j<NRows; j++) inf >> Maturity[j];
    Counter = 0;
    while(inf)
    {
        if(Counter==0)inf >> CurveDate >> ws;    // Handle date
        for(j=0; j<NRows; j++) inf >> Rate[j];
        if(Maturity[0] <= 1.0/365.0)Maturity[0] = 1.0/365.0;
        for(i=0; i<NRows; i++){
            for(j=0; j<NColumns; j++){
                if(j==0)Factor[i][j] = 1.0;
                if(j==1)Factor[i][j]
                    = (1.0 - exp(-Maturity[i]/Tau[0]))/(Maturity[i]/Tau[0]);
                if(j>1)Factor[i][j] =
                    (1.0 - exp(-Maturity[i]/Tau[j-2]))/(Maturity[i]/Tau[j-2])
                    - exp(-Maturity[i]/Tau[j-2]);
            }
        }
// Create FRMRegressionInputData
        ofstream outf;                  // Output file FRMRegressionInputData.dat
        outf.open("FRMRegressionInputData.dat");  // Open output details file
        outf << NColumns << ' ';
        outf << NRows << '\n';
        for(j=0; j<NRows; j++){
            outf << setiosflags(ios::showpoint | ios::fixed) << setprecision(2)
                << setfill(' ') << setiosflags(ios::right) << setw(5) << Rate[j];
            for(i=0; i<NColumns; i++){
                outf << setiosflags(ios::showpoint | ios::fixed) << setprecision(6)
                    << setfill(' ') << setiosflags(ios::right) << setw(13)
                    << Factor[j][i];
            }
            outf << '\n';
        }
        outf.close();
        AnsiString sinf, soutf, soutf1;
        sinf = "FRMRegressionInputData.dat";
        soutf = "FRMRegressionDetails.prn";
```

```
        soutf1 = "FRMRegression.prn";
        FRMSolveRegression(sinf, soutf, soutf1);
// Manage output
        ifstream inf1;                  // Input file: FRMRegression.prn
        inf1.open("FRMRegression.prn", ios::in);  // Open input file
        inf1 >> NVars;
//      outf1  << setiosflags(ios::right) << setw(4) << NVars;
        outf1  << setiosflags(ios::right) << setw(12) << CurveDate;
        for (i = 0; i < NVars; i++) {
            inf1 >> x;
            outf1 << setiosflags(ios::showpoint | ios::fixed) << setprecision(6)
                << setfill(' ') << setiosflags(ios::right) << setw(12) << x;
        }
        inf1.close();
        outf1 << '\n';
        inf >> CurveDate >> ws;     // Handle date and check for end of file
        Counter++; // increment
    };
    inf.close();  // Closes input file
    outf1.close();
}
...
double FRMEDLSC::FRMCalculateCurve3(double M, double L, double S,
    double C1, double t0)
{
    double SlopeBeta, CurvatureBeta;
    SlopeBeta = (1-exp(-M/t0))/(M/t0);
    CurvatureBeta = SlopeBeta - exp(-M/t0);
    return L + S*SlopeBeta + C1*CurvatureBeta;
}
...
// Forward curve and volatility curve
struct EDLSCOUTPUTDATA FRMEDLSC::FRMAnalyzeForwardAndVolatilityCurve(void)
{                // inf is "Forward Curve.prn
...
}
/*********************************************************************************
**  Swap curves used with CurveFitting.cpp, level, slope and curvature
*********************************************************************************/
void FRMEDLSC::PlainVanillaSwapCurve(double Level, double Slope,
    double Curvature)
{
    double Tau = 2.0;
    int tempNAD;  // Number of accrued days in quarter
    int tempNTD;  // Number of total days in year
    int k;        // Counter for both loops - quarter counter
    double SlopeBeta, CurvatureBeta;
    double tempNumSwapCurve, tempDenSwapCurve;
    double tempDF, tempDFM1;               // Discount factor minus one quarter
    double tempDiscountRate;
    double YearsToResetDate;
    FRMDateMDY tempMaturity, tempMaturityM1;       // Maturity minus one quarter
// Retrieve Current Date, being careful not to retrieve a "/"
    Current.Month = atoi(&CurveDate[0]);
    if(Current.Month < 10){ Current.Day = atoi(&CurveDate[2]);
      if(Current.Day < 10){ Current.Year = atoi(&CurveDate[4]);
      } else { Current.Year = atoi(&CurveDate[5]); }
    } else { Current.Day = atoi(&CurveDate[3]);
      if(Current.Day < 10){ Current.Year = atoi(&CurveDate[5]);
      } else { Current.Year = atoi(&CurveDate[6]); }
    }
    ofstream curve("SwapCurve.prn", ios::out);
// FLOATING:  Quarterly, ACT/360; FIXED: Semi-annual, 30/360
// Output semi-annual swap curve header information
    curve << "SWAP CURVE (FLT: ACT/360, quart; FIX: 30/360, semi) ";
    curve << "\n\n        Maturity     Swap ";
    curve << "\nYear     Date     Curve \n";
    curve << "   0 ";
    curve.width(2); curve.setf(ios::right);
    curve.setf(ios::fixed, ios::floatfield);
    curve << Current.Month << "/" << Current.Day << "/" << Current.Year << " \n";
```

```
// Set temp maturities (reset date and reset date minus one quarter
  tempMaturityM1.Month = Current.Month;
  tempMaturityM1.Day = tempMaturity.Day = Current.Day;      // Note two = ok
  tempMaturityM1.Year = tempMaturity.Year = Current.Year;
  tempNTD = 360;    // FLT:  30/360
// Set temporary variables for loops
  k = 0;
   tempNumSwapCurve = tempDenSwapCurve = 0.0;
  tempDF = tempDFM1 = 1.0;
  for(i = 1; i <= 10*2; i++){       // semi-annual counter
    for(j = 0; j<2; j++){           // quarterly counter
      k++;
      tempMaturity.Month = tempMaturityM1.Month + 3;     // Add one quarter
      if(tempMaturity.Month > 12){
        tempMaturity.Year++;
        tempMaturity.Month = tempMaturity.Month - 12;
      }
// FLT is ACT/360
        tempNAD = Julian.FRMToJulian(tempMaturity)
            - Julian.FRMToJulian(tempMaturityM1);
// Note we assume advanced set, settled in arrears so M1 for curve
        YearsToResetDate = (float)(Julian.FRMToJulian(tempMaturityM1)
            - Julian.FRMToJulian(Current))
        / 365.25;
// Maturity cannot be zero so test if first quarter and set barely positive
      if(YearsToResetDate < 0.000001) YearsToResetDate = 0.000001;
        SlopeBeta= (1-exp(-YearsToResetDate/Tau))/(YearsToResetDate/Tau);
      CurvatureBeta= SlopeBeta - exp(-YearsToResetDate/Tau);
      tempDiscountRate = Level + (Slope*SlopeBeta) + (Curvature*CurvatureBeta);
      tempDF = tempDFM1 / (1.0 + ((float)tempNAD/(float)tempNTD)
        * (tempDiscountRate/100.0));
//NOTE:  It is actually the rare case that the appropriate discount rate for
// present value calculations is the same as the forward rate used for
// discounting.  This is true only for LIBOR.
        tempNumSwapCurve += tempDF * ((float)tempNAD / (float)tempNTD)
            * tempDiscountRate;
// Set M1 data before end quarter loop
      tempMaturityM1.Year = tempMaturity.Year;
      tempMaturityM1.Month = tempMaturity.Month;
      tempDFM1 = tempDF;
      }
    tempDenSwapCurve += tempDF * 0.5;  // Semi, 30/360
    if(k % 4 == 0){        // Test if at a year (every fourth quarter)
      curve << " "; curve.width(2); curve.setf(ios::right);
      curve.setf(ios::fixed, ios::floatfield);
      curve << k/4 << " ";
        curve.width(2); curve.setf(ios::right);
        curve.setf(ios::fixed, ios::floatfield);
      curve << tempMaturity.Month << "/" << tempMaturity.Day
          << "/" << tempMaturity.Year << " ";
      curve.width(8); curve.precision(5); curve.setf(ios::right);
      curve.setf(ios::fixed, ios::floatfield);
      curve << tempNumSwapCurve / tempDenSwapCurve << "\n";
    };
  };
};

void FRMEDLSC::SwapCurveQuart30360(double Level, double Slope, double Curvature)
{
...
};
```

BDT.h

The core header file for the Black, Derman and Toy method.

```
...
#define BDTARRAYSIZE 121
#define SWAPARRAYSIZE 10
...
```

Well, the iterative search routine can be very precise. DEBUG creates large files for detailed debugging.

```
#define EPSILON 0.00000000001
#define DEBUG 1          // 0 is false

class FRMBDT
{
public:
  ifstream inf;  // Input file stream.
   ofstream capdb;    // Cap debug file
   ofstream flrdb;    // Floor debug file
  ofstream outf;  // Output file stream.
  int CurrentPointInTime;
  int i;
  int Iteration;
  int j;
  int Node;
  int NumberOfPointsInTime;
  int NumberOfYears;
  int ResetsPerYear;
  int TimeStepsPerResetPeriod;
   double Tau;
  double BondPrice;
  double MaturityInYears;
  double TimeStep;
   double Mu;
  double Price;        // Zero Bond Price with Mu Guess
  double SwapRates30360[SWAPARRAYSIZE];
  static double Volatilities[BDTARRAYSIZE];
  static double ForwardRates[BDTARRAYSIZE];
  static double ForwardPrices[BDTARRAYSIZE];
  static double Maturity[BDTARRAYSIZE];
  static double ZeroBondPrices[BDTARRAYSIZE];
  static double Rates[BDTARRAYSIZE*(BDTARRAYSIZE-1)/2 + BDTARRAYSIZE];//t then i
  static double StateClaims[BDTARRAYSIZE*(BDTARRAYSIZE-1)/2 + BDTARRAYSIZE];
   FRMBDT::FRMBDT();
  void GetData();  // Get original data and compute initial yield curve
  void ForwardCurve(//double Tau, int NumberOfTimeSteps, double TimeStep,
  double FCLevel, double FCSlope, double FCCurvature,
  double VCLevel, double VCSlope, double VCCurvature);
   void CalculateTree();  // Calculate BDT Interest Tree and Related Data
  void CalculateTestPrice();  // Compute Test Price within Secant Method
  void ComputeCapsAndFloors();
  double DiscountFactor(int CPIT, int N);
  double CalculateCap(double StrikeRate, double CapMaturity);
  double CalculateFloor(double StrikeRate, double FloorMaturity);
   double Max(double, double);
};
double FRMBDT::Volatilities[BDTARRAYSIZE];
double FRMBDT::ForwardRates[BDTARRAYSIZE];
double FRMBDT::ForwardPrices[BDTARRAYSIZE];
double FRMBDT::Maturity[BDTARRAYSIZE];
double FRMBDT::ZeroBondPrices[BDTARRAYSIZE];
double FRMBDT::Rates[BDTARRAYSIZE*(BDTARRAYSIZE-1)/2 + BDTARRAYSIZE];        // t then i
double FRMBDT::StateClaims[BDTARRAYSIZE*(BDTARRAYSIZE-1)/2 + BDTARRAYSIZE];
#endif
```

BDT.cpp

The core source code for valuing caps and floors with Black, Derman and Toy's binomial lattice approach.

```
#include "FRMBDT.h"
FRMBDT::FRMBDT()              // Constructor
{
   capdb.open("Capsdb.prn", ios::out);
   flrdb.open("Flrodb.prn", ios::out);
}
```

```
//------------------------------------------------------------------------------
void FRMBDT::GetData() {
   double tempDate;
   inf.open("tsir.dat"); // Get Inputs
   inf >> NumberOfPointsInTime >> TimeStep;
   for(i=0; i<NumberOfPointsInTime; i++) {
      inf >> j >> tempDate >> ForwardRates[i] >> Volatilities[i];
   };
   ZeroBondPrices[0] = 1.0;        // Initial Yield Curve
   ForwardPrices[0] = 1.0;
   for(i=1; i<=NumberOfPointsInTime; i++) {
       ZeroBondPrices[i] = ZeroBondPrices[i-1]/(1.0+ForwardRates[i-1]*TimeStep);
       ForwardPrices[i] = 1.0/(1.0 + ForwardRates[i-1]*TimeStep);
   }
}
```

Illustration of the secant search method embedded in a function.

```
//------------------------------------------------------------------------------
void FRMBDT::CalculateTree()    // nodes go from highest rate to lowest
{ // Based on Secant Method: Local variable for secant method
   long double TestPrice;
  long double MaxPrice;    // Price based on MaxMu
  long double MinPrice;    // Price based on MinMu
  long double TestMu;
  long double MaxMu;
  long double MinMu;
  Rates[0] = ForwardRates[0];
  StateClaims[0] = 1.0;
  StateClaims[1] = StateClaims[2] = 0.5*ZeroBondPrices[1];
  for(CurrentPointInTime=2; CurrentPointInTime <= NumberOfPointsInTime;
     CurrentPointInTime++) {         // Building state-claims forward
     MaxMu = 1.0;
     MinMu = -1.0;
     BondPrice = ZeroBondPrices[CurrentPointInTime];   // Actual Market Price
     TestMu = 0.0;    // Initial Guess
     Mu = TestMu;
      CalculateTestPrice();  // Computes Test Price, Rates, and State Claims
      TestPrice = Price;
// Compute Maximum and Minimum Prices based on maximum and minimum yields
     Mu = MaxMu;
     CalculateTestPrice();
     MaxPrice = Price;
     Mu = MinMu;
     CalculateTestPrice();
     MinPrice = Price;
// Test to see if close enough
     Iteration = 0;
     while(fabs(TestPrice - BondPrice) > EPSILON){
        Iteration++; if(Iteration > 100)break;  // In case of infinite loop
// If difference is negative
        if(TestPrice - BondPrice < 0.0){
           MinMu = TestMu;  MinPrice = TestPrice;
           TestMu = TestMu
              + ((BondPrice - TestPrice)/(MaxPrice - TestPrice))*(MaxMu - TestMu);
        };
// If difference is positive
        if(TestPrice - BondPrice > 0.0){
           MaxMu = TestMu;  MaxPrice = TestPrice;
           TestMu = TestMu
              - ((TestPrice - BondPrice)/(TestPrice - MinPrice))*(TestMu - MinMu);
        };
// Compute Price Based on New Mu
        Mu = TestMu;
        CalculateTestPrice();
        TestPrice = Price;
     };
   };
}

void FRMBDT::CalculateTestPrice()
{ // Compute Rates, State Claims, and Price Based on Mu at a Point in Time
```

```
    long int iM1, iM2;
    iM1=(CurrentPointInTime-1)*(CurrentPointInTime-2)/2+CurrentPointInTime-1;
    iM2=(CurrentPointInTime-2)*(CurrentPointInTime-3)/2+CurrentPointInTime-2;
    for(Node=0; Node<CurrentPointInTime; Node++) {// Compute Rates
     if(Node==0)                              // Using Mus
      {
        Rates[iM1] = Rates[iM2]
          * exp(Mu*TimeStep - Volatilities[CurrentPointInTime-1]*pow(TimeStep,0.5));
      };
      if(Node==1)
      {
        Rates[iM1+Node] = Rates[iM2+Node-1]
          * exp(Mu*TimeStep + Volatilities[CurrentPointInTime-1]*pow(TimeStep,0.5));
      };
      if(Node>1)
      {
        Mu += log(Rates[iM2+Node-2]/Rates[iM2+Node-1])/TimeStep
          + 2.0*Volatilities[CurrentPointInTime-1]/pow(TimeStep,0.5);
        Rates[iM1+Node] = Rates[iM2+Node-1]
          * exp(Mu*TimeStep + Volatilities[CurrentPointInTime-1]*pow(TimeStep,0.5));
      }
    }
    Price = 0.0;
    for(Node=0; Node<=CurrentPointInTime; Node++) { // Compute State Claims
     i = CurrentPointInTime*(CurrentPointInTime-1)/2+CurrentPointInTime+Node;
     iM1=(CurrentPointInTime-1)*(CurrentPointInTime-2)/2+CurrentPointInTime-1+Node;
     if(Node==0) {
       StateClaims[i] = 0.5 * StateClaims[iM1] / (1.0 + Rates[iM1]*TimeStep);
       Price += StateClaims[i];
     } else if(Node==CurrentPointInTime) {
       StateClaims[i] = 0.5 * StateClaims[iM1-1] / (1.0 + Rates[iM1-1]*TimeStep);
       Price += StateClaims[i];
     } else {
       StateClaims[i]                                      //Previous state then down
         =0.5*StateClaims[iM1-1]/(1.0+Rates[iM1-1]*TimeStep)
         +0.5*StateClaims[iM1]/(1.0+Rates[iM1]*TimeStep); //Previous state then up
       Price += StateClaims[i];
     };
    };
};

void FRMBDT::ForwardCurve(  //double Tau, int NumberOfTimeSteps, float TimeStep,
  double FCLevel, double FCSlope, double FCCurvature,
  double VCLevel, double VCSlope, double VCCurvature)
{
    double YearsToResetDate;
    double SlopeBeta;
    double CurvatureBeta;
    double DResetsPerYear, DTimeStepsPerResetPeriod, DNumberOfYears;
    DResetsPerYear = (double)ResetsPerYear;
    DTimeStepsPerResetPeriod = (double)TimeStepsPerResetPeriod;
    DNumberOfYears = (double)NumberOfYears;
    ofstream curve("TSIR.dat", ios::out); //Final TSIR data per time step
// Compute prices and fit curve for simple interest
    int NumberOfCashFlows;
    NumberOfCashFlows = int( DNumberOfYears * DResetsPerYear + 0.000001 );
    for(j=0; j<=NumberOfCashFlows+1; j++){
        Maturity[j] = (1.0/DResetsPerYear) * ((double)j);
// Estimate 30/360, quarterly forward rate based on EDF data
// Maturity cannot be zero so test if first quarter and set barely positive
    if(Maturity[j] < 0.000001) Maturity[j] = 0.000001;
    SlopeBeta= (1-exp(-Maturity[j]/Tau))/(Maturity[j]/Tau);
    CurvatureBeta= SlopeBeta - exp(-Maturity[j]/Tau);
    ForwardRates[j]
      = ((FCLevel + (FCSlope*SlopeBeta) + (FCCurvature*CurvatureBeta))/100.0);
    if(j==0){
      ZeroBondPrices[0] = 1.0;
    } else {
        ZeroBondPrices[j] = ZeroBondPrices[j-1]
            / (1.0 + ForwardRates[j-1] / DResetsPerYear);
    };
```

```
    };
// Work on output to TSIR
   curve.width(5); curve.setf(ios::right);
    curve.setf(ios::fixed, ios::floatfield); curve.setf(ios::showpoint);
   curve << NumberOfPointsInTime << "  ";
   curve.width(15); curve.precision(12); curve.setf(ios::right);
   curve.setf(ios::fixed, ios::floatfield); curve.setf(ios::showpoint);
   curve << TimeStep << "\n";
// Set temp maturities (reset date and reset date minus one quarter
   int k;
   double tempMaturity;
   double tempRate;
   k = 0;          // Reset period counter
   for(i = 0; i <= NumberOfPointsInTime; i++){
       YearsToResetDate = ((double)i) * TimeStep;
     if(YearsToResetDate > (Maturity[k+1]-0.000001)) k++;
// Compute simple interest
       tempRate
         = (pow(1.0 + ForwardRates[k]/DResetsPerYear, 1.0/DTimeStepsPerResetPeriod)
       - 1.0)* DResetsPerYear * DTimeStepsPerResetPeriod;
     curve << i << " ";        // Time step counter
     curve.width(9); curve.precision(6); curve.setf(ios::right);
      curve.setf(ios::fixed, ios::floatfield); curve.setf(ios::showpoint);
     curve << YearsToResetDate << "  ";  // Output time to maturity
     curve.width(15); curve.precision(12); curve.setf(ios::right);
      curve.setf(ios::fixed, ios::floatfield); curve.setf(ios::showpoint);
     curve << tempRate << " ";
       tempMaturity = ((double)i) * TimeStep;
     if(tempMaturity < 0.000001)tempMaturity = 0.000001;
     SlopeBeta= (1-exp(-tempMaturity/Tau))/(tempMaturity/Tau);
     CurvatureBeta= SlopeBeta - exp(-tempMaturity/Tau);
     curve.width(15); curve.precision(12); curve.setf(ios::right);
      curve.setf(ios::fixed, ios::floatfield); curve.setf(ios::showpoint);
     curve << (double)((VCLevel + VCSlope*SlopeBeta)
       + (VCCurvature*CurvatureBeta))/100.0) << "\n";     // Volatility Curve
   };
}


double FRMBDT::DiscountFactor(int CPIT, int N)
{   // CPIT - CurrentPointInTime, N - Node
   int iTime, jNode;
   long int Cell, kSCM1, i, iM1;
   double tempStateClaims[120];
   Cell = (CPIT * (CPIT - 1))/2 + CPIT + N;
   if(TimeStepsPerResetPeriod == 1){
     return (1.0 / (1.0 + Rates[Cell] * TimeStep));
   } else {
// Build sub-tree from CPIT to TimeStepsPerResetPeriod on the time dimension
// and from node N to N + TimeStepsPerResetPeriod on the node dimension
     for(iTime=CPIT; iTime < CPIT + TimeStepsPerResetPeriod; iTime++) {
       Price = 0.0;  // Last loop holds discount factor
         for(jNode = N; jNode <= N + iTime - CPIT; jNode++) {
// Counters for sub-tree state claims
         i = ((iTime-CPIT) * (iTime-CPIT-1))/2 + (iTime-CPIT) + (jNode-N);
         iM1 =  ((iTime-CPIT-1) * (iTime-CPIT-2))/2 + (iTime-CPIT-1) + (jNode-N);
// Counters for rates in BDT tree
         kSCM1 = ((iTime-1) * (iTime-2))/2 + (iTime-1) + jNode;
         if(iTime == 1) kSCM1 = 0;
          if(iTime == CPIT) {     // At current point in time
           tempStateClaims[0] = 1.0;
               Price += 1.0;
// One time step past current point in time
             } else if (iTime == CPIT + 1 && jNode == N) {
               tempStateClaims[i] = 0.5 * tempStateClaims[0]
                   / (1.0 + Rates[kSCM1]*TimeStep);
               Price += tempStateClaims[i];
// One time step past current point in time
             } else if (iTime == CPIT + 1 && jNode == N + 1) {
           if(kSCM1 < 1) kSCM1 = 1;
               tempStateClaims[i] = 0.5 * tempStateClaims[0]
                   / (1.0 + Rates[kSCM1-1]*TimeStep);
```

```
                    Price += tempStateClaims[i];
            } else if (jNode == N + iTime - CPIT) {  // Rates always go up
                    tempStateClaims[i] = 0.5 * tempStateClaims[iM1-1]
                        / (1.0 + Rates[kSCM1-1]*TimeStep);
                Price += tempStateClaims[i];
            } else if (jNode == N) {   // Rates always go down
                    tempStateClaims[i] = 0.5 * tempStateClaims[iM1]
                        / (1.0 + Rates[kSCM1]*TimeStep);
                Price += tempStateClaims[i];
            } else {
                tempStateClaims[i] = 0.5 * StateClaims[iM1-1]
                / (1.0 + Rates[kSCM1-1]*TimeStep)    // From previous state then
                  + 0.5 * StateClaims[kSCM1]
                / (1.0 + Rates[kSCM1]*TimeStep);      // From previous state then
                Price += StateClaims[i];
            };
        };
    };
  };
  return Price;
}
// Caps and Floors.cpp
void FRMBDT::ComputeCapsAndFloors()
{
  char buf[20];
  double StrikeRate;
  double tempMaturity;                                      ,
  AnsiString scurve, scaf;
  scurve = "SCQuart30360.prn";
  scaf = "CapsAndFloors.prn";
  ifstream curve(scurve.c_str(), ios::in);    // Equilibrium Swap Rates
  for(i=0; i<15; i++) curve >> buf;
  for(i=0; i<10; i++) curve >> j >> buf >> SwapRates30360[i];
  ofstream caf(scaf.c_str(), ios::out);        // Cap and Floor Quote Sheet
  caf<<"Output: Caps and Floors from Curve Fitting Based on Swap Curve.";
  i = 0;
  caf << "\nYr  Strike    ";
  for(i=-125; i<=125; i=i+25){     // Output Strike Rates to Quote Sheet
    caf.width(4); caf.setf(ios::right); caf.setf(ios::fixed, ios::floatfield);
    caf << i << "  ";
  };
  for(j = 0; j < NumberOfYears; j++) {
    for(int ii = 0; ii < 3; ii++) {  //ii=0 - Year, ii=1 - Cap, ii=2 - Floor
      if(ii==0){
        caf << "\n    ";
        caf.width(2); caf.precision(0); caf.setf(ios::right);
        caf.setf(ios::fixed, ios::floatfield);
        caf << (j+1) << "        ";
      } else caf << "          ";
        for(i=-125; i<=125; i=i+25) {
            StrikeRate = SwapRates30360[j] + ((double)i)/100.0;
            tempMaturity = (double)(j+1);
            if(ii==0){
                caf << " ";
                caf.width(5); caf.precision(2); caf.setf(ios::right);
                caf.setf(ios::fixed, ios::floatfield); caf.setf(ios::showpoint);
                caf << StrikeRate;
            };
            if(ii==1){
                caf << " ";
                caf.width(5); caf.precision(2); caf.setf(ios::right);
                caf.setf(ios::fixed, ios::floatfield); caf.setf(ios::showpoint);
                caf << CalculateCap(StrikeRate, tempMaturity);
            };
            if(ii==2){
                caf << " ";
                caf.width(5); caf.precision(2); caf.setf(ios::right);
                caf.setf(ios::fixed, ios::floatfield); caf.setf(ios::showpoint);
                caf << CalculateFloor(StrikeRate, tempMaturity);
            };
        };      // Strike, Cap, Floor
```

```
              caf << "\n";
      };              // Strike Rates
   };              // Years
}

double FRMBDT::CalculateCap(double StrikeRate, double CapMaturity)
{
  int Counter;
  int debug;
  long int i;
  double CapValue;
   double SCSwapRate;
  double tempDeltat;
  double tempDen;
  double tempDF;
  double tempNum;
  double tempRate;
  long double sumSC;
  CapValue = 0.0;
...
  SCSwapRate = 0.0;
  tempNum = tempDen = 0.0;
  Counter = 0;
  for(CurrentPointInTime=0;
      CurrentPointInTime<=((int)CapMaturity)
        * (ResetsPerYear*TimeStepsPerResetPeriod)-1;
        CurrentPointInTime++) {
    if(CurrentPointInTime % TimeStepsPerResetPeriod == 0) {
      if(debug)capdb << "\nCurrent Point In Time = " << CurrentPointInTime;
      sumSC = 0.0;
      for(Node = 0; Node <= CurrentPointInTime; Node++) {
        i = (CurrentPointInTime * (CurrentPointInTime-1))/2
          + CurrentPointInTime + Node;
        if(Rates[i] > 200.0) Rates[i] = 200.0;   // 200% rate ceiling
        if(Rates[i] < 0.000001) Rates[i] = 0.000001;    // 0.001% floor
            tempDeltat = 1.0/(((double)ResetsPerYear)
              * ((double)TimeStepsPerResetPeriod));
        tempRate = ((double)ResetsPerYear)*(pow(1.0 + Rates[i]* tempDeltat,
            (double)TimeStepsPerResetPeriod) - 1.0);
        tempDF = DiscountFactor(CurrentPointInTime, Node);
        CapValue += 100.0 * (1.0/((double)ResetsPerYear)) *  StateClaims[i]
          * tempDF * Max(0.0, tempRate - (StrikeRate/100.0));
...
        sumSC += StateClaims[i];
// SC Swap Rate
            tempDeltat = 1.0/(((double)ResetsPerYear)
              * ((double)TimeStepsPerResetPeriod));
        tempRate = ((double)ResetsPerYear)*(pow(1.0 + Rates[i]* tempDeltat,
          (double)TimeStepsPerResetPeriod) - 1.0);
            tempNum += StateClaims[i]
              * (1.0/(1.0 + tempRate/((double)ResetsPerYear))) * tempRate;
            tempDen += StateClaims[i]
              * (1.0/(1.0 + tempRate/((double)ResetsPerYear)));
      };
      SCSwapRate = tempNum/tempDen;
      Counter = (int)(CapMaturity+0.000001) - 1;
...
    };
  };
  return(CapValue);
};

double FRMBDT::CalculateFloor(double StrikeRate, double FloorMaturity)
{
  int Counter;
  int debug;
  long int i;
  double FloorValue;
  double SCSwapRate;
  double tempDeltat;
  double tempDen;
```

```
   double tempDF;
   double tempNum;
   double tempRate;
   long double sumSC;
   FloorValue = 0.0;
...
   Counter = 0;
   SCSwapRate =0.0;
   tempNum = tempDen = 0.0;
   for(CurrentPointInTime=0;
        CurrentPointInTime<=((int)FloorMaturity)
           * (ResetsPerYear*TimeStepsPerResetPeriod)-1;
     CurrentPointInTime++) {
     if(CurrentPointInTime % TimeStepsPerResetPeriod == 0) {
        if(debug)flrdb << "\nCurrent Point In Time = " << CurrentPointInTime;
        sumSC = 0.0;
        for(Node = 0; Node <= CurrentPointInTime; Node++) {
          i = (CurrentPointInTime * (CurrentPointInTime-1))/2
             + CurrentPointInTime + Node;
          if(Rates[i] > 200.0) Rates[i] = 200.0;  // 200% rate ceiling
          if(Rates[i] < 0.000001) Rates[i] = 0.000001;    // 0.001% floor
             tempDeltat = 1.0/(((double)ResetsPerYear)
                 * ((double)TimeStepsPerResetPeriod));
          tempRate = ((double)ResetsPerYear)*(pow(1.0 + Rates[i]* tempDeltat,
             (double)TimeStepsPerResetPeriod) - 1.0);
          tempDF = DiscountFactor(CurrentPointInTime, Node);
          FloorValue += 100.0 * (1.0/((double)ResetsPerYear)) *  StateClaims[i]
             * tempDF * Max(0.0, (StrikeRate/100.0) - tempRate);
...
        sumSC += StateClaims[i];
// SC Swap Rate
             tempDeltat = 1.0/(((double)ResetsPerYear)
                 * ((double)TimeStepsPerResetPeriod));
          tempRate = ((double)ResetsPerYear)*(pow(1.0 + Rates[i]* tempDeltat,
             (double)TimeStepsPerResetPeriod) - 1.0);
             tempNum += StateClaims[i]
                 * (1.0/(1.0 + tempRate/((double)ResetsPerYear))) * tempRate;
             tempDen += StateClaims[i]
                 * (1.0/(1.0 + tempRate/((double)ResetsPerYear)));
        };
        SCSwapRate = tempNum/tempDen;
        Counter = (int)(FloorMaturity+0.000001) - 1;
...
     };
   };
   return(FloorValue);
};
...
```

References

Black, Fischer, Emanuel Derman, and William Toy, "A One-Factor Model of Interest Rates and Its Application to Treasury Bond Options," *Financial Analysts Journal* 46 (January/February 1990), pp. 33-39.

Brooks, Robert, *Interest Rate Modeling and the Risk Premiums in Interest Rate Swaps* (Charlottesville, VA: The Research Foundation of the Institute of Chartered Financial Analysts, 1997).

Appendix 4:6: Interface code comments

The interface for this module is illustrated below.

```
This program will value caps and floors using the methodology developed
  by Black, Derman and Toy. The input file:
  FRMEDfuture.dat - Eurodollar futures data for building forward rate curve
    and volatility curve
The output include:
  FRMEDFutures.prn - Eurodollar futures basic output
  ForwardCurve.prn - Forward curve based on EDF dates
  SwapCurve.prn - Plain vanilla swap curve based on EDF data
  SCQuart30360.prn - Quarterly, 30/360 swap curve based on EDF data
  TSIR.dat - Forward curve based on BDT time steps and simple interest
  CapsAndFloors.prn - Caps and floors quote sheet
DO NOT CHANGE the Eurodollar futures output file and error check test 10
indicates the program successfully passed through all 10 phases.
```

Eurodollar Futures Input File	FRMEDFutures.dat
Eurodollar Futures Output File	FRMEDFutures.prn
Error Check Test	10.00000000

Exit   Exit

Program is Finished

There are seven data files related to this program.

FRMEDFutures.dat

This file contains all of the input data as illustrated below. Specifically, it contains some preliminary information such as the date and an ad hoc adjustment factor to account for any biases in the futures data, as well as each futures contract ticker symbol, price to the third decimal (97090 means 97.090) and the volatility expressed in percent (30 means 30% annualized standard deviation of the log of the implied rate relative).

```
Input Eurodollar Futures

DATE:  2  28 2008
Bias Adjustment: 2.5
Eurodollar Futures
Contract Price     Volatility
SPOT   3.07  0
EDH8   97090 30
EDM8   97480 35
EDU8   97625 37
EDZ8   97595 48
EDH9   97490 39
EDM9   97295 38
EDU9   97065 37
EDZ9   96825 35
...
EDH7   94025 19
EDM7   94000 19
EDU7   93970 18
EDZ7   93925 18
```

FRMEDFutures.prn

This file contains basic output related to Eurodollar futures as illustrated below.

```
Input Eurodollar Futures

DATE: 2 28 2008
 Bias Adjustment: 2.5
 Eurodollar Futures             Calendar    Days to    Fraction
 Contract    Price  Volatility  Date        Maturity   of Year
  SPOT        3.07       0.00   2/28/2008         0    0.00000
  EDH8       97.09      30.00   3/17/2008        18    0.04932
  EDM8       97.48      35.00   6/16/2008       109    0.29863
  EDU8       97.62      37.00   9/15/2008       200    0.54795
  EDZ8       97.60      48.00   12/15/2008      291    0.79726
  EDH9       97.49      39.00   3/16/2009       382    1.04658
```

```
EDM9       97.30     38.00     6/15/2009    473      1.29589
EDU9       97.06     37.00     9/14/2009    564      1.54521
EDZ9       96.82     35.00    12/14/2009    655      1.79452
...
EDH7       94.02     19.00     3/13/2017   3301      9.04384
EDM7       94.00     19.00     6/19/2017   3399      9.31233
EDU7       93.97     18.00     9/18/2017   3490      9.56164
EDZ7       93.92     18.00    12/18/2017   3581      9.81096
Number of ED Futures Contracts 40
```

```
     Maturity   Discount     Futures    Forward    Financing
     Date       Factors      Rates      Rates      Bias (bps)
 1   3/17/2008  0.99847      2.91000    2.91000     0.00000
 2   6/16/2008  0.99118      2.52000    2.51412    -0.58816
 3   9/15/2008  0.98492      2.37500    2.36430    -1.07008
 4  12/15/2008  0.97907      2.40500    2.37822    -2.67802
 5   3/16/2009  0.97322      2.51000    2.48471    -2.52918
 6   6/15/2009  0.96714      2.70500    2.67052    -3.44840
 7   9/14/2009  0.96066      2.93500    2.88917    -4.58272
 8  12/14/2009  0.95369      3.17500    3.11932    -5.56758
...
37   3/13/2017  0.67322      5.97500    5.68675   -28.82526
38   6/19/2017  0.66296      6.00000    5.70095   -29.90499
39   9/18/2017  0.65354      6.03000    5.75113   -27.88695
40  12/18/2017  0.64417      6.07500    5.78480   -29.01976
```

ForwardCurve.prn

This file contains implied forward rates and implied volatility as illustrated below.

```
LIBOR Forward and Volatility Data
              0        0.04928    0.29843    0.54758    0.79673   ...    9.55530    9.80445
2/28/2008  3.07000    2.91000    2.51412    2.36430    2.37822   ...    5.75113    5.78480
2/28/2008  0.00000   30.00000   35.00000   37.00000   48.00000   ...   18.00000   18.00000
```

SwapCurve.prn

This file contains the estimated equilibrium swap rates for the first 10 years as illustrated below. These are plain vanilla swap rates with quarterly pay, actual/360 day count on the floating leg and semiannually pay, 30/360 day count on the fixed leg.

```
SWAP CURVE (FLT: ACT/360, quart; FIX: 30/360, semi)

       Maturity   Swap
Year   Date       Curve
  0   0/28/2008
  1  12/28/2008   2.67234
  2  12/28/2009   2.88690
  3  12/28/2010   3.12009
  4  12/28/2011   3.35232
  5  12/28/2012   3.57596
  6  12/28/2013   3.78119
  7  12/28/2014   3.96888
  8  12/28/2015   4.13895
  9  12/28/2016   4.29370
 10  12/28/2017   4.43138
```

SCQuart30360.prn

This file contains the estimated equilibrium swap rates for the first 10 years where both legs have quarterly pay, 30/360 day count. The high level of precision was due to some error checking during the debugging process.

```
SWAP CURVE (FLT: 30/360, quart; FIX: 30/360, quart)

       Maturity   Swap
Year   Date       Curve
  0   0/28/2008
  1  12/28/2008   2.619359993893
```

```
 2 12/28/2009  2.832848060271
 3 12/28/2010  3.062398374976
 4 12/28/2011  3.290424633742
 5 12/28/2012  3.507420054380
 6 12/28/2013  3.708790003876
 7 12/28/2014  3.892847250596
 8 12/28/2015  4.059558926306
 9 12/28/2016  4.209776899144
10 12/28/2017  4.344775401181
```

TSIR.prn

This file contains the forward rates and volatilities at 0.25-year increments as illustrated below.

```
40    0.250000000000
0   0.000000    0.024875312896    0.345215637840
1   0.250000    0.025677602526    0.353491093623
2   0.500000    0.026609550859    0.359659618406
3   0.750000    0.027642599560    0.364036240501
4   1.000000    0.028752495523    0.366894206739
5   1.250000    0.029918707814    0.368470236649
6   1.500000    0.031123921964    0.368969160770
7   1.750000    0.032353599428    0.368567984880
8   2.000000    0.033595594028    0.367419450175
...
36  9.000000    0.058450607950    0.278955634559
37  9.250000    0.058945430060    0.276585613053
38  9.500000    0.059420982717    0.274297115427
39  9.750000    0.059878121430    0.272087699879
40 10.000000    0.060317670918    0.269954858206
```

CapsAndFloors.prn

This file contains cap and floor values as illustrated below. The strike rates are based on basis points from the equilibrium swap rate. For each year the strike rate, cap value, and floor values are provided. Notice that as the strike rate rises, cap values decline and floor values rise.

```
Output: Caps and Floors from Curve Fitting Based on Swap Curve.
Yr  Strike  -125  -100   -75   -50   -25     0    25    50    75   100   125
      1     1.37  1.62  1.87  2.12  2.37  2.62  2.87  3.12  3.37  3.62  3.87
            1.23  0.99  0.75  0.53  0.35  0.22  0.15  0.08  0.06  0.03  0.02
            0.00  0.00  0.01  0.04  0.11  0.22  0.39  0.57  0.79  1.02  1.25

      2     1.58  1.83  2.08  2.33  2.58  2.83  3.08  3.33  3.58  3.83  4.08
            2.45  2.01  1.60  1.24  0.96  0.75  0.59  0.46  0.36  0.29  0.23
            0.02  0.07  0.15  0.27  0.47  0.75  1.07  1.43  1.82  2.23  2.65
...
     10     3.09  3.34  3.59  3.84  4.09  4.34  4.59  4.84  5.09  5.34  5.59
           14.31 13.29 12.36 11.51 10.73 10.02  9.37  8.77  8.21  7.71  7.23
            3.96  5.01  6.15  7.37  8.66 10.02 11.44 12.91 14.42 15.98 17.58
```

The following are excerpts from the interface header code with selected comments added.

FRMUnitBDT.h:

This interface is a bit different in the sense that three separate implementation files are included.

```
...
#include "c:\FRMRepository\FRMEDFutures.cpp"
#include "c:\FRMRepository\FRMEDLSCCurveFitting.cpp"
#include "c:\FRMRepository\FRMBDT.cpp"
```

We define a class that manages the LSC model outputs for both rates and volatility.

```
#ifndef EDLSCDATA
#define EDLSCDATA
class EDLSCOUTPUTDATA
{
public:
    double Level;
```

```
   double Slope;
   double Curvature;
   double VLevel;
   double VSlope;
   double VCurvature;
};
#endif
//--------------------------------------------------------------------------
class TBDTForm : public TForm
{
__published:    // IDE-managed Components
   TEdit *outputErrorTest;
   TEdit *editEDFuturesInputFile;
   TLabel *lblFinished;
   TLabel *lblErrorTest;
   TLabel *lblEDFuturesFile;
   TButton *btnRun;
   TButton *btnExit;
   TMemo *ProgramDescription;
   TLabel *lblEDFuturesOutputFile;
   TEdit *editEDFuturesOutputFile;
   void __fastcall btnExitClick(TObject *Sender);
  void __fastcall btnRunClick(TObject *Sender);
private: // User declarations
   AnsiString sinf;    // Input file stream
   AnsiString soutf;   // Output file stream
   double ErrorTest;
public:     // User declarations
   __fastcall TBDTForm(TComponent* Owner);
   void __fastcall Execute(void);
};
//--------------------------------------------------------------------------
extern PACKAGE TBDTForm *BDTForm;
//--------------------------------------------------------------------------
#endif
```

The following are excerpts from the interface code with selected comments added.

FRMUnitBDT.cpp:

The interface code incorporates a few crude error-checking routines. For example, if the Eurodollar futures data cannot be found or it does not contain appropriate data, an error is thrown based on FileError. ErrorTest keeps track of how far into the code the program has successfully completed. ErrorTest = 10 indicates it is finished. This was a fairly difficult program to code, so this crude error checking was helpful when debugging. If you are coding a complex program which uses input files and produces many output files, it is recommended that you utilize the error test shown here for efficient debugging.

```
   ...
   int FileError;
   FileError = 0;
   sinf = editEDFuturesInputFile->Text;
   soutf = editEDFuturesOutputFile->Text;
   FRMEDFUTURES ED;
   FileError = ED.GetEDFuturesData(sinf, soutf);
   if (FileError == -99)
      lblFinished->Caption = "File error in Eurodollar futures input file.";
   if (FileError == -98)
      lblFinished->Caption = "File error in Eurodollar futures output file.";
   ErrorTest++;       // ErrorTest = 1
   ED.EDDiscountFactors();
   ErrorTest++;       // ErrorTest = 2
   ED.CurveFittingFile();     // Create ForwardCurve.prn file
   ErrorTest++;       // ErrorTest = 3
   FRMEDLSC CF;
// Fit three-parameter curve program
   EDLSCOUTPUTDATA ELD;  //Eurodollar futures LSC output results
// Compute level, slope and curvature for LIBOR curve
   ELD = CF.FRMAnalyzeForwardAndVolatilityCurve();
```

```
    ErrorTest++;        // ErrorTest = 4
    CF.PlainVanillaSwapCurve(CF.Level, CF.Slope, CF.Curvature);
    ErrorTest++;        // ErrorTest = 5
    CF.SwapCurveQuart30360(CF.Level, CF.Slope, CF.Curvature);
    ErrorTest++;        // ErrorTest = 6
// BDT Tree Construction
    FRMBDT Bdt;
    Bdt.ResetsPerYear = 4;               // Inputs for cap and floor calculations
    Bdt.TimeStepsPerResetPeriod = 1;
    Bdt.NumberOfYears = 10;
    Bdt.NumberOfPointsInTime = Bdt.TimeStepsPerResetPeriod
       * Bdt.ResetsPerYear * Bdt.NumberOfYears;
    Bdt.TimeStep = 1.0/((float)(Bdt.ResetsPerYear*Bdt.TimeStepsPerResetPeriod));
    Bdt.Tau = 2.0;
    Bdt.ForwardCurve(CF.Level, CF.Slope, CF.Curvature,
       CF.VLevel, CF.VSlope, CF.VCurvature);
    ErrorTest++;        // ErrorTest = 7
    Bdt.GetData();
    ErrorTest++;        // ErrorTest = 8
    Bdt.CalculateTree();
    ErrorTest++;        // ErrorTest = 9
    Bdt.ComputeCapsAndFloors();
    ErrorTest++;        // ErrorTest = 10
}
```

Module 4.7: Introduction to Mortgage-Backed Securities

Learning objectives

- Explain a variety of computations related to mortgage backed securities (MBS)
- Apply the Brent method to estimating MBS spreads
- Explore one C++ application of the Brent method to solve for the static spread
- Illustrate the use of DEBUG to expand the contents of the printed file for debugging purposes
- Show how to use the `static` data type for memory management

See program FRMMBSSingleTest in *4.7 Single Mortgage Pasthrough*.

Module overview

The basic math related to mortgages is reviewed first. We then turn to mortgage-backed securities (MBS) with a particular focus on interest-only and principal-only MBS. For ease of exposition, we address the unrealistic case of a single mortgage MBS. The more realistic case of multiple mortgages with different prepayment speeds, different interest rates, and different maturities would require a much more complicated program beyond the scope of this book.

Mortgage basics

For a fixed rate mortgage, the original loan amount (OLA) is related to the original payment amount (OPA), annual yield (y), number of payments per year (n), and total number of remaining payments (m) as:

$$OPA = OLA \frac{y/n}{1 - \dfrac{1}{\left(1 + \dfrac{y}{n}\right)^m}}$$

Each monthly payment consists of three components: the required interest component (RIC), the required principal component (RPC), and the additional principal component (APC). The ability to prepay additional principal each month influences RIC and RPC over the remaining months. Hence, we need to keep track of the monthly balance (MB_i), where i denotes the month. The required interest component is based on a 30/360 day count and mortgages are usually paid on a monthly basis, thus the RIC is:

$$RIC_i = MB_{i-1}\left(\frac{y}{12}\right)$$

The OPA does not change over the life of a mortgage, thus the RPC is:

$$RPC_i = OPA - RIC_i$$

The new mortgage balance is therefore

$$MB_i = MB_{i-1} - RIC_i - APC_i$$

Note that as the mortgagor (the person who borrowed the money) pays back additional principal, the required interest component falls over the remaining shortened life of the mortgage. By prepaying the mortgage, the mortgagor will pay less interest over the life of the loan.

Mortgage-backed securities

Securitization refers to the process of converting a set of non-tradable financial instruments into financial securities that are tradable. The process typically involves acquiring a set of somewhat similar financial instruments, such as home mortgages, placing them into a separate, bankruptcy-proof legal entity such as a grantor trust, and then issuing marketable securities backed by the cash flows of the financial instruments within the legal entity.

Since the value of the mortgage to an investor is based on the interest that will be paid by the mortgagor, establishing a fair market value of MBS requires estimating prepayment activity, which affects the amount of interest paid over the life of the loan. There are a vast number of factors that influence prepayment. We provide a brief list here:

- Current mortgage rates available for refinancing
- History of refinancing mortgage rates during the life of mortgage (potential burnout)
- Housing turnover (sale of house implies 100 percent prepayment)
- Variety of mortgage products available (mortgagor changes products)
- Calendar seasonality (people move in the summer)
- General economic activity
- Changes in personal income
- Changes in home values
- Amount of unencumbered home equity (home values and loan age)
- Refinancing costs
- Labor mobility and job change frequency
- Female home occupant child-bearing age
- Interest rate expectations
- Curtailments (partial payments)
- Cultural view of debt
- Available after-tax investment alternatives
- Mortality rates
- Divorce rates
- Information availability (internet)
- Demographics
- Federal tax policy (interest tax deductible)

Forecasting prepayment is obviously difficult and the value of many MBS products are sensitive to changing prepayment. Our objective is not to provide a better model of prepayment, rather to provide the infrastructure for you to be able to build your own MBS valuation model. Any MBS valuation model must be able to address prepayment.

The prepayment of a portfolio of debt products that can be measured by the single monthly mortality for month i is denoted SMM_i. For mortgages, the SMM_i is the percentage difference between the scheduled principal balance (SPB_i) and the actual principal balance (APB_i).

$$SMM_i = \frac{SPB_i - APB_i}{SPB_i}$$

SMM can be annualized and is often called the conditional prepayment rate (CPR):

$$CPR_i = 1 - (1 - SMM_i)^{12} = 1 - \left(\frac{APB_i}{SPB_i}\right)^{12}$$

A general model for forecasting prepayment speed was originally offered by the Public Securities Association (PSA) that has subsequently become the Securities Industry and Financial Markets Association (SIFMA). The PSA prepayment model makes several assumptions related to CPR:

1) CPR starts at 0.2 in the first month of the mortgage

2) CPR increases linearly at 0.2 percent each month through month 30, reaching 6 percent

3) CPR remains constant after month 30

4) This process is assigned a 100 percent PSA

Slower or faster prepayment assumptions are given as a percentage of PSA. Thus, 200 PSA means 200 percent or 2.0 times the CPR in the PSA. The prepayment model presented here will be based on PSA.

Static spread

A simple valuation model of MBS assumes zero volatility of interest rates and prepayments over the life of the MBS. The static spread is the additional constant rate amount over the forward curve, such that the present value of future cash flows equals the current market price. That is, the analyst estimates the static spread over the given forward curve that gives the current observed market price for the MBS. Mathematically,

$$MP_i = \sum_{i=1}^{m} \frac{CF_i}{\prod_{j=0}^{i-1}\left(1+f_j+ss\right)}$$

where MP_i denotes the current observed market price, CF_i denotes the future cash flows from the MBS which are a function of PSA, f_j denotes the current forward rate of some reference index, and ss_j denotes the static spread. The program below employs the Brent method for solving for the embedded static spread in the same way as one solves for implied volatility or yield to maturity.

Total spread with Monte Carlo simulation

There are many different ways to employ Monte Carlo simulation to enhance one's understanding of MBS risks. We only illustrate one of the ways here. Assume that the simulated benchmark rate at future point i and denoted r_i, is influenced by the slope of the current forward curve representing that future point, a mean reversion adjustment, and a random number generator:

$$r_i = r_{i-1} + \left(f_i - f_{i-1}\right) + \lambda\left(f_{i-1} - r_{i-1}\right) + r_{i-1}\sigma_i\sqrt{1/12}\varepsilon$$

where ε is a normally distributed random number with mean zero and standard deviation of one. The pull parameter, λ, governs the mean reversion speed back to the current forward curve. We assume the forward curve and forward volatility curve are inputs and the application here uses linear interpolation.

A simple valuation model of MBS takes the average price over multiple simulations (ND denotes number of draws) and an assumed total spread (ts). The analyst inputs the total spread over the given forward curve and for each simulation a current value for the MBS is computed. Mathematically,

$$V_i = \frac{1}{ND}\sum_{k=1}^{ND}\sum_{i=1}^{m} \frac{CF_{k,i}}{\prod_{j=0}^{i-1}\left(1+r_{k,j}+ts\right)}$$

where MP_i denotes the current observed market price, CF_i denotes the future cash flows from the MBS which are a function of PSA, f_j denotes the current forward rate of some reference index, and ss_j denotes the static spread. The program below employs the Brent method for solving for the embedded static spread in the same way as one solves for implied volatility or yield to maturity.

Implementation code comments

This implementation contains a large number of methods addressing various statistics surrounding MBS.

FRMMBSSingle.h

```
// FRMMBSSingle.h
```

```
#ifndef FRMMBSSINGLEH
#define FRMMBSSINGLEH
#include <system.hpp>    // AnsiString
#include <iomanip.h>     // setw()
#include <fstream.h>     // ifstream, ofstream
#define MBSMAXCOUPON 360  // Maximum number of MBS payments
#define MBSLINELENGTH 100 // Length of text header input line
#define MBSMAXPERIOD 100  // Maximum number of rate periods
#define MBSEPSILON 0.01   // Error allowable for static spread analysis
#define MBSARRAYSIZE 12   // word array size (row)
#define MBSCHARSIZE 20    // word array size (column)
#define MBSEPSILON2 0.000001 // static spread
#define MBSSIGN(a,b) ((b) >= 0.0 ? fabs(a) : -fabs(a)) // Brent method
#define MBSITMAX 100      // Brent method maximum iterations
#define MBSEPS 3.0e-16    // Brent machine floating-point precision, NR=8


#ifndef FRMLINEARINTERPOLATIONCPP  // Multiple includes in DLLs
#define FRMLINEARINTERPOLATIONCPP
#include "c:\FRMRepository\FRMLinearInterpolation.cpp"  // Linear interpolation
#endif
#ifndef FRMCALENDARCPP  // Multiple includes in DLLs
#define FRMCALENDARCPP
#include "c:\FRMRepository\FRMCalendar.cpp"
#endif
#ifndef FRMUNIFORMRNGCPP  // Multiple includes in DLLs
#define FRMUNIFORMRNGCPP
#include "c:\FRMRepository\FRMUniformRNG.cpp"
#endif
```

The debug feature allows for many more details to be generated when debugging the program.

```
#define DEBUG 0           // 0 false
```

Note the use of other routines within this class.

```
class FRMMBSSINGLE : public FRMLINEARINTERPOLATION, FRMURNG
{
public:
   void FRMMBSSingleFileMgmt(AnsiString inputsinf, AnsiString inputsinf1,
      AnsiString inputsoutf);
private:   // Methods by type
   void CalculateStaticSpread(void);
   void CalculateMonthlyPayment(void);
   void CalculatePriceMBS(void);
   void CalculatePriceMBSWithTS(void);
   void CouponDiscountFactors(void);
   void CreateAmortizationTable(void);
   void GetMBSData(void);
   void GetMBSHeader(void);
   void GetUSTreasuryRates (void);
   int  CalculateTotalNumberOfPayments(void);
   int CouponCount(void);
   double CalculateXB(); // Brent method
   double function(double tempX);
...
// Structure Data Types and Class Instantiations
   FRMDateMDY CD;
   FRMDateMDY Issue;
   FRMDateMDY MD;
   FRMCALENDAR jdate;
   FRMURNG Z;       // instantiate random normal variate class in normal.h
// String Streams
   ifstream inf;  // Input file stream.
   ifstream inf1;  // Input file stream.
   ofstream outf;  // Output file stream.
// Arrays
   char Heading[MBSLINELENGTH];
   char Name[16];                   // MBS Security Name
   char word[MBSARRAYSIZE][MBSCHARSIZE];
```

Static allows for very large files and prevents multiple version being deployed.

```
   static int DaysInCouponPeriod[MBSMAXCOUPON];
   static long int CouponDates[MBSMAXCOUPON];
```

```
    static double Coupon[MBSMAXCOUPON];
    static double CouponIO[MBSMAXCOUPON];                //IO Vector
    static double CouponPO[MBSMAXCOUPON];                //PO Vector
    static double CouponDF[MBSMAXCOUPON];  // Discount to Current Date
    static double ForwardRate[MBSMAXCOUPON];
    static double ForwardVolatility[MBSMAXCOUPON];
    static double InputForwardRate[MBSMAXPERIOD];
    static double InputForwardVolatility[MBSMAXPERIOD];
    static double PeriodCount[MBSMAXPERIOD];
    static double SimulatedRate[MBSMAXCOUPON];
    static double TreasuryRate[MBSMAXPERIOD];
    static double TreasuryRateVolatility[MBSMAXPERIOD];
    static FRMDateMDY CouponDatesMDY[MBSMAXCOUPON];
};
int FRMMBSSINGLE::DaysInCouponPeriod[MBSMAXCOUPON];
long int FRMMBSSINGLE::CouponDates[MBSMAXCOUPON];
double FRMMBSSINGLE::Coupon[MBSMAXCOUPON];
...
```

FRMMBSSingle.cpp

Many of the methods in this class simply take care of tedious data management issues. We highlight just of few of them here.

This is the entry point for this program and it subsequently calls the remaining methods.

```
...
void FRMMBSSINGLE::FRMMBSSingleFileMgmt(AnsiString inputsinf,
    AnsiString inputsinf1, AnsiString inputsoutf)
{
    ii=-1;    // Counter to keep track of whether to output header information
    inf.open(inputsinf.c_str(), ios::in);
    inf1.open(inputsinf1.c_str(), ios::in);
    outf.open(inputsoutf.c_str());
    GetUSTreasuryRates();      // Read Treasury Yield Curve
    GetMBSHeader();            // Read and write header info on MBS
// Read in data for each MBS to be analyzed
    while (inf){                // inf is pointer to input file
        GetMBSData();           // Read in MBS's specific information
        Par = 1000.0;
        if(InputMonthlyPayment < 0.0){
            CalculateMonthlyPayment(); // Routine to compute monthly payment
        } else {
            MonthlyPayment = InputMonthlyPayment;
        };
        outf << "\n Monthly Payment " << MonthlyPayment;
        NCoupon = CouponCount(); // Based on inputs, remaining number of coupons
        outf << "\n Coupon Count " << NCoupon << "\n";
        CreateAmortizationTable(); // Amortization table based on number of coupons
        StaticSpread = InputStaticSpread;  // Set static spread to inputted #
        CouponDiscountFactors(); // Estimate DFs on coupon dates via linear inter
        CalculatePriceMBS();      //Compute price based on inputted discount rates
        outf << "\n Price of MBS via Treasury curve (Z-Spread) --> " << PriceMBS;
        CalculateStaticSpread(); // Estimate spread over treasury with no randomness
        clock_t Begin, End; // Measure time to compute simulation
        Begin = clock();
        CalculatePriceMBSWithTS();  // MBS value with total spread and simulation
        End = clock();
        outf << "\n Time Elapsed (in seconds) is " << ((End - Begin)/CLK_TCK);
        inf >> Name;
    }
}
// Read in U. S. Treasury rates
void FRMMBSSINGLE::GetUSTreasuryRates()
{
    int Period;
```

Getline is a useful feature for acquiring the entire line in a file.

```
    inf1.getline(Heading, MBSLINELENGTH);
    inf1 >> NumTratePeriods >> MeanReversionPull >> NumberDraws >> ws;
    inf1.getline(Heading, MBSLINELENGTH);
```

```
    inf1.getline(Heading, MBSLINELENGTH);
    inf1.getline(Heading, MBSLINELENGTH);
    Period = 0;
    for (Period = 0; Period <= NumTratePeriods-1; Period++){
        inf1 >> PeriodCount[Period] >> InputForwardRate[Period]
            >> InputForwardVolatility[Period] >> ws;
        TreasuryRate[Period] = InputForwardRate[Period]/100.0;
        TreasuryRateVolatility[Period] = InputForwardVolatility[Period]/100.0;
    }
}
...
// Calculate monthly payment, assuming no prepayment
void FRMMBSSINGLE::CalculateMonthlyPayment(void)
{
    double CouponRateDecimal;
// Compute Monthly Payment Based on Input in MBS.DAT and Par defined in main
    CouponRateDecimal = CouponRate / 100.0;
    int PaymentFrequencyPerYear = 12;     // Watch out --  integer
    TotalNumberOfPayments = CalculateTotalNumberOfPayments();
    MonthlyPayment = (Par * CouponRateDecimal / (double)PaymentFrequencyPerYear)
        / (1.0 - (1.0 / pow(1.0 + (CouponRateDecimal/(double)PaymentFrequencyPerYear),
        TotalNumberOfPayments)));
}
// Compute total number of payments-issue date to maturity date, no prepayment
int FRMMBSSINGLE::CalculateTotalNumberOfPayments(void)
{
    long int IDInJulian = jdate.FRMToJulian(Issue);
    long int TempDInJulian;
    int i = 0;
    FRMDateMDY TempD;          // Temporary Date
    TempD.Month = MD.Month;  TempD.Day = MD.Day; TempD.Year = MD.Year;
```

The infinite loop below is rather dangerous should the user provide bad data and the program never ends. One way to avoid this problem is to introduce an arbitrary counter and determine after say 1,000 cycles through the loop to break out of it.

```
    for(;;){                  // Infinite loop
        TempDInJulian = jdate.FRMToJulian(TempD);
        if(TempDInJulian <= IDInJulian)return(i);
        i++;
        TempD.Month -= 1;
        if(TempD.Month < 1){
            TempD.Month += 12;
            TempD.Year -= 1;
        }
    }
}
...
```

We use a simple linear interpolation routine as an alternative to the LSC model described elsewhere.

```
    ForwardRate[Month] = FRMLinearInterpolation(PeriodCount, TreasuryRate,
        NumTratePeriods, (double)(Month+1));            // Yearly = Monthly / 12;
    PeriodRate = ForwardRate[Month]/12.0;
    CouponDF[Month] = CouponDF[Month-1]
        * (1.0 + PeriodRate + StaticSpread/1200.0);  //1200-Monthly and decimal
...
```

Once all the tedious stuff is finished, computing the value of a MBS is easy.

```
// MBS value given coupon and discount factor vectors, no prepayment
void FRMMBSSINGLE::CalculatePriceMBS(void)
{
    PriceMBS = 0.0;
    for(int i = 0; i < NCoupon; i++){
        PriceMBS += Coupon[i] / CouponDF[i];
    }
}
```

Static spread is a bit more involved, requiring the Brent search method. We illustrate embedding the search method here, as opposed to an external call to the file FRMBrent.cpp.

```
// Solving for static spread by the Brent method
void FRMMBSSINGLE::CalculateStaticSpread(void)
```

```
{
    double EstimatedStaticSpread;
    InitialGuess = StaticSpread;
    ObservedY = MarketPrice;    // Set initial data
    MaxX = 10.0;
    MinX = -5.0;
    EstimatedStaticSpread = CalculateXB();
    outf << "\n Estimated Static Spread Based on Market Price is "
        << EstimatedStaticSpread;
}
// Solving MBS value based on total spread, crude prepayment model, simulation
void FRMMBSSINGLE::CalculatePriceMBSWithTS(void)
{
    int i, Month;
    double AverageMBSPrice;
    double AverageMBSPriceIO;
    double AverageMBSPricePO;
    double OriginalPSA;
    double PSAIncrement;        // Amount of adjustment for each 50 basis points
    double OriginalBalance;
    double MaxPrice, MinPrice;  // Extreme valuations
// Compute price of MBS using the user specified Total Spread (TS).
// Recall that TS is a discounted cash flow method based on a specified
// prepayment function. The user-specified TS will completely define the
// appropriate discount factors.
    if(DEBUG)outf << " Discount Factors with Inputted TS " << InputTS << "\n";
// Derive Interpolated Volatility Curve
    if(DEBUG) outf << "\n Month    Forward Volatility \n";
    ForwardVolatility[0] = TreasuryRateVolatility[0];
...
    for(Month = 1; Month < NCoupon; Month++){
        ForwardVolatility[Month] = FRMLinearInterpolation(PeriodCount,
            TreasuryRateVolatility, NumTratePeriods, (double)(Month+1));
...
    }
    if(DEBUG)outf << "\n";
// Need to simulate spot rates and derive cash flows for each month based
// on prepayment model. Initialize normal generator (done in class mbs)
// Simulate all 360 monthly rates based on equation found in:
// Davidson, Andrew S. and Michael D. Herskovitz, "Mortgage-Backed
// Securities, Investment Analysis & Advanced Valuation Techniques", pp. 152.
    i = 0;
    SimulatedRate[i] = ForwardRate[i] / 12.0;
...
    AverageMBSPrice = AverageMBSPriceIO = AverageMBSPricePO = 0.0;
    OriginalPSA = PSA;      // Preserve original values
// Compute cash flow for first period
    i = 1;
    Balance = Par;
    MonthlyRate = (CouponRate/100.0) / 12.0;
    Interest = Balance * MonthlyRate;
    Principal = MonthlyPayment - Interest;
    if(MonthlyPayment > Balance + Interest){
        Principal = Balance;
        AddlPrincipal = 0.0;
    } else if(i < 30) {
        AddlPrincipal = 0.01*0.2*((double)i)*(PSA/100.0)*Balance;
        if(AddlPrincipal > Balance - Principal) AddlPrincipal = Balance - Principal;
    } else {
        AddlPrincipal = 0.01*6.0*(PSA/100.0)*Balance;
        if(AddlPrincipal > Balance - Principal)AddlPrincipal = Balance - Principal;
    };
    ActualMonthlyPayment = Principal + Interest + AddlPrincipal;
    Balance = Balance - Principal - AddlPrincipal;
    if(MBSType == 1) Coupon[i-1] = ActualMonthlyPayment;
    if(MBSType == 2) Coupon[i-1] = Interest;
    if(MBSType == 3) Coupon[i-1] = Principal + AddlPrincipal;
    PSAIncrement = 25.0;       // Amount of adjustment for each 50 basis points
    OriginalBalance = Balance;  // Because Balance goes to zero for each path
    if(DEBUG)outf << "i  PSA     Rate     Balance    Coupon \n";
// Loop over all draws
```

```
         for(long int j = 1; j <= NumberDraws; j++){
             Balance = OriginalBalance;
// Loop over coupons
         for (i = 1; i < NCoupon; i++){
             SimulatedRate[i] = SimulatedRate[i-1]
                 + (ForwardRate[i] - ForwardRate[i-1])*(1.0/12.0)
                 + MeanReversionPull*(ForwardRate[i-1]/12.0 - SimulatedRate[i-1])
                 + SimulatedRate[i-1]*ForwardVolatility[i]*pow(1./12.,0.5)*Z.FRMNormal01();
// Modify PSA function here
```

The prepayment function here is very crude. More advanced models, however, can easily be incorporated.

```
             if (fabs(SimulatedRate[i]*12.0-ForwardRate[i]) < 0.005){
                 PSA = OriginalPSA;
             } else if (fabs(SimulatedRate[i]*12.0-ForwardRate[i]) < 0.01){
// Rate is within 1% but not within 0.5% of forward curve
                 if (SimulatedRate[i]*12.0 > ForwardRate[i]){
                     PSA = OriginalPSA - PSAIncrement;
                     if(PSA<0)PSA = 0.0;
                 } else {
                     PSA = OriginalPSA + PSAIncrement;
                 }
             } else if (fabs(SimulatedRate[i]*12.0-ForwardRate[i]) < 0.015){
// Rate is within 1.5% but not within 1.0% of forward curve
                 if (SimulatedRate[i]*12.0 > ForwardRate[i]){
                     PSA = OriginalPSA - 2.0*PSAIncrement;
                     if(PSA<0)PSA = 0.0;
                 } else {
                     PSA = OriginalPSA + 2.0*PSAIncrement;
                 }
             } else if (fabs(SimulatedRate[i]*12.0-ForwardRate[i]) < 0.02){
// Rate is within 2.0% but not within 1.5% of forward curve
                 if (SimulatedRate[i]*12.0 > ForwardRate[i]){
                     PSA = OriginalPSA - 3.0*PSAIncrement;
                     if(PSA<0)PSA = 0.0;
                 } else {
                     PSA = OriginalPSA + 3.0*PSAIncrement;
                 }
             } else if (fabs(SimulatedRate[i]*12.0-ForwardRate[i]) < 0.025){
// Rate is within 2.5% but not within 2.0% of forward curve
                 if (SimulatedRate[i]*12.0 > ForwardRate[i]){
                     PSA = OriginalPSA - 4.0*PSAIncrement;
                     if(PSA<0)PSA = 0.0;
                 } else {
                     PSA = OriginalPSA + 4.0*PSAIncrement;
                 }
             } else {
// Rate is greater than 2.5%
                 if (SimulatedRate[i]*12.0 > ForwardRate[i]){
                     PSA = OriginalPSA - 5.0*PSAIncrement;
                     if(PSA<0)PSA = 0.0;
                 } else {
                     PSA = OriginalPSA + 5.0*PSAIncrement;
                 }
             }
// Fill Coupon[] vector
         Interest = Balance * MonthlyRate;
         Principal = MonthlyPayment - Interest;
         if(MonthlyPayment > Balance + Interest){
             Principal = Balance;
             AddlPrincipal = 0.0;
         } else if(i+1 < 30) {
             AddlPrincipal = 0.01*0.2*((double)(i+1))*(PSA/100.0)*Balance;
             if(AddlPrincipal > Balance - Principal) AddlPrincipal = Balance - Principal;
         } else {
             AddlPrincipal = 0.01*6.0*(PSA/100.0)*Balance;
             if(AddlPrincipal > Balance - Principal) AddlPrincipal = Balance - Principal;
         }
         ActualMonthlyPayment = Principal + Interest + AddlPrincipal;
         Balance = Balance - Principal - AddlPrincipal;
         if(MBSType == 1) Coupon[i] = ActualMonthlyPayment;
```

```
            if(MBSType == 2) Coupon[i] = Interest;
            if(MBSType == 3) Coupon[i] = Principal + AddlPrincipal;
            if(DEBUG){
                if (j == 1)
                    outf << i << "    " << PSA << "    " << SimulatedRate[i]*1200.0 << "    "
                        << Balance << "    " << Coupon[i] << "\n";
            }
        }
        StaticSpread = InputTS;
        CouponDF[0] = (1.0 + SimulatedRate[0] + StaticSpread/1200.0);
        for(i = 1; i < NCoupon; i++){ // Compute appropriate discount factors
            CouponDF[i] = CouponDF[i-1]
                * (1.0 + SimulatedRate[i] + StaticSpread/1200.0);//1200-Monthly, decimal
        }
// Price MBS based on OAS and Coupon[] tied to particular path, Sum over paths
        CalculatePriceMBS();
        if(MBSType==1)AverageMBSPrice   += PriceMBS;
        if(MBSType==2)AverageMBSPriceIO += PriceMBS;
        if(MBSType==3)AverageMBSPricePO += PriceMBS;
        if(j==1){ MaxPrice = MinPrice = PriceMBS;
        } else {
            if(PriceMBS > MaxPrice)MaxPrice = PriceMBS;
            if(PriceMBS < MinPrice)MinPrice = PriceMBS;
        }
    }
...
// Function used by Brent method to solve for the static spead
double FRMMBSSINGLE::function(double tempX)
{
    StaticSpread = tempX;
    CouponDiscountFactors();
    CalculatePriceMBS();
    return(PriceMBS-ObservedY);
}
// Brent method applied to static spread within this class so all data already
// exists within the class
```

We illustrate just incorporating a method, such as Brent, into a given class, rather than bringing it in from the repository.

```
double FRMMBSSINGLE::CalculateXB() // Brent method
{
...
}
```

References

Barlett, William W. *The Valuation of Mortgage-Backed Securities* (NY: Irwin Professional Publishing, 1994).

Davidson, Andrew S. and Michael D. Herskovitz. *Mortgage-Backed Securities, Investment Analysis & Advanced Valuation Techniques* (Chicago, IL: Probus Publishing Company, 1994).

Fabozzi, Frank J., Anand K. Bhattaharya, and William S. Berliner. *Mortgage-Backed Securities: Products, Structuring, and Analytical Techniques* (Hoboken, NJ: John Wiley & Sons, Inc., 2007).

Appendix 4.7: Interface code comments

The graphical user interface for this module is illustrated below.

This module has two input files. The first file, FRMUSTRates.dat, contains forward rates and forward volatilities alone with a pull parameter for mean reversion (set to 0.0 here) and number of draws to do in the simulation.

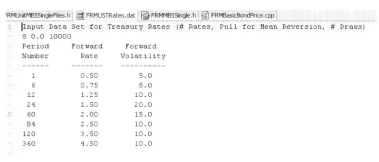

The second input file, FRMMBSSingle.dat, contains information on the particular MBSs evaluated.

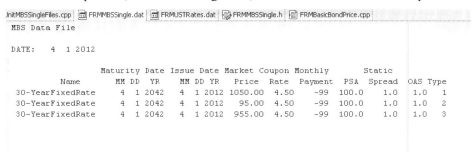

The output is placed in FRMMBSSingleOutputs.prn. A set of information is generated for each MBS.

```
itMBSSingleFiles.cpp  | FRMMBSSingleOutputs.prn  | FRMMBSSingle.dat  | FRMUSTRates.dat  | FRMMB:
MBS Data File
DATE:   4 1 2012
 *** MBS Pass Through ***
 Monthly Payment 5.06685
 Coupon Count 360

 Price of MBS via Treasury curve (Z-Spread) --> 1048.79
 Estimated Static Spread Based on Market Price is 0.944109
 Average MBS Price = 1048.73
 Difference = Market-Model = 1.26622
 Maximum Value in Simulation = 1053.7
 Minimum Value in Simulation = 1010.05
 Time Elapsed (in seconds) is 1.375

 *** MBS Interest-Only ***
 Monthly Payment 5.06685
 Coupon Count 360

 Price of MBS via Treasury curve (Z-Spread) --> 94.6355
 Estimated Static Spread Based on Market Price is 0.719645
 Average MBS IO Price = 95.2393
 Difference = Market-Model = -0.239251
 Maximum Value in Simulation = 167.289
 Minimum Value in Simulation = 88.6133
 Time Elapsed (in seconds) is 1.375

 *** MBS Principal-Only ***
 Monthly Payment 5.06685
 Coupon Count 360

 Price of MBS via Treasury curve (Z-Spread) --> 954.154
 Estimated Static Spread Based on Market Price is 0.958445
 Average MBS PO Price = 953.549
 Difference = Market-Model = 1.45104
 Maximum Value in Simulation = 963.928
 Minimum Value in Simulation = 839.527
 Time Elapsed (in seconds) is 1.39
```

The interface code was standard and therefore omitted. See the following files.

FRMUnitMBSSingleFiles.cpp, .h

Module 4.8: Black, Scholes, Merton Model via Integration

Learning objectives

- Explain the integration approach to valuing options within the Black, Scholes, Merton paradigm
- Explore one C++ application of numerical integration applied within the Black, Scholes, Merton paradigm

See program FRMBSMOVMIntegrationTest in *4.9 BSM Option Valuation via Numerical Integration.*

Module overview

Black, Scholes, Merton option valuation model

Recall the Black, Scholes, Merton option valuation model is based on the assumption that the underlying instrument follows geometric Brownian motion. The terminal distribution of the underlying instrument under geometric Brownian motion is the lognormal distribution. If the self-financing dynamic replicating portfolio of the underlying instrument and risk-free financing is feasible, then the theoretical option Value is just the present value of the expected payoff discounted at the risk-free interest rate. Specifically, let O denote either call or put option value, then

$$O_0 = PV\{E[O_T]\}$$

Thus one solution of the Black, Scholes, Merton option valuation model is (where I denotes the underlying instrument's value)

$$O_0 = e^{-rT}E[O_T] = e^{-rT}\int_0^\infty O_T f(I_T) dI_T$$

where f() denotes the appropriate lognormal distribution.

Solving for the option Value and related risk parameters will involve the single integration of a function of the lognormal distribution. The primary purpose here is to explore the unique characteristics of the lognormal distribution in an effort to improve our understanding of the limitations when using the Black, Scholes, Merton option valuation model.

Extensive details on the lognormal distribution are provided in Module 3.8. Recall the probability density function for the lognormal probability distribution can be expressed as

$$f(I_T) = \frac{1}{I_T \sigma \sqrt{2\pi}} \exp\left\{-\frac{\left[\ln(I_T) - \mu\right]^2}{2\sigma^2}\right\}$$

where

$$\mu = \ln(I_0) + \left(r - \delta - \frac{\hat{\sigma}^2}{2}\right)(T - t)$$

and

$$\sigma = \hat{\sigma}\sqrt{T - t}$$

The $\hat{\sigma}$ symbol denotes the annualized standard deviation of the continuously compounded rates of return for the underlying stock. The r denotes the annualized continuously compounded "risk-free" interest rate and δ denotes the annualized continuously compounded dividend (or any other carry cost, the minus sign indicates a negative cost).

Prior to reviewing the source code, we illustrate the relevant calculations with a numerical example.

Call option example

Suppose we have stock trading for $100 with a volatility of 30%, an interest rate of 2%, and a dividend yield also of 2%. Suppose we are interested in the fair values of an over-the-counter call and an over-the-counter put option with a strike price of $100 and assume the contemplated settlement date is 6/13/2012 and the maturity date is 5/1/2013. Based on the Black, Scholes, Merton option valuation model, estimate these options' fair value.

The number of calendar days between these two dates is 322. We assume a 365.25-day year (crude adjustment for leap years), therefore we have a time to maturity of 0.881588 years. Because the dividend yield equals the interest rate, the mean of the lognormal distribution is $100.

$$E\left[\tilde{S}_T\right] = S_0 e^{\hat{\mu}(T-t)} = S_0 e^{(r-\delta)(T-t)} = 100 e^{(0.02-0.02)0.881588} = 100$$

The mean of the underlying normal distribution can be expressed as

$$\mu = \ln(I_0) + \left(r - \delta - \frac{\hat{\sigma}^2}{2}\right)(T-t) = \ln(100) + \left(0.02 - 0.02 - \frac{0.3^2}{2}\right)0.881588 = 4.5655$$

and the standard deviation of the underlying normal distribution can be expressed as

$$\sigma = \hat{\sigma}\sqrt{T-t} = 0.3\sqrt{0.881588} = 0.281678$$

Therefore, the call option integration can be expressed as

$$C_0 = e^{-rT} \int_0^\infty C_T f(I_T) dI_T$$

$$= e^{-rT} \int_0^\infty \max[0, I_T - X] \frac{1}{I_T \sigma \sqrt{2\pi}} \exp\left\{-\frac{\left[\ln(I_T) - \mu\right]^2}{2\sigma^2}\right\} dI_T$$

$$= e^{-0.02(0.881588)} \int_X^\infty \max[0, I_T - 100] \frac{1}{I_T 0.281678\sqrt{2\pi}} \exp\left\{-\frac{\left[\ln(I_T) - 4.5655\right]^2}{2(0.281678)^2}\right\} dI_T$$

$$= \$11$$

Put option example

Similarly, the put option integration can be expressed as

$$P_0 = e^{-rT} \int_0^\infty P_T f(I_T) dI_T$$

$$= e^{-rT} \int_0^\infty \max[0, X - I_T] \frac{1}{I_T \sigma \sqrt{2\pi}} \exp\left\{-\frac{\left[\ln(I_T) - \mu\right]^2}{2\sigma^2}\right\} dI_T$$

$$= e^{-0.02(0.881588)} \int_0^X \max[0, 100 - I_T] \frac{1}{I_T 0.281678\sqrt{2\pi}} \exp\left\{-\frac{\left[\ln(I_T) - 4.5655\right]^2}{2(0.281678)^2}\right\} dI_T$$

$$= \$11$$

Implementation code comments

FRMBSMOVMIntegration.h

This implementation code primarily sets up the data and functions for a call to the FRMNUMINT class. Therefore, we need to include the appropriate file and make it public in this class.

```
...
#ifndef FRMNUMERICALINTEGRATIONCPP
#define FRMNUMERICALINTEGRATIONCPP
#include "c:\FRMRepository\FRMNumericalIntegration.cpp"
#endif

class FRMBSMOVMINT : public FRMCALENDAR, FRMNUMINT
{
...
```

FRMBSMOVMIntegration.cpp

The approach taken here is the same as the approach taken in the numerical integration Module 3.8. The only difference is the particular function passed. In this case, we are passing the lognormal distribution with the appropriate option payout. Because the integration routine is generic, we can pass any function and use this integration class in a variety of different applications.

```
...
// Global function for using Brent method of embedded parameter
FRMBSMOVMINT NI;   // Global class instantiation of specific class function in Brent function
double function(double x);
double function(double x)
{
    double f;
    switch (NI.FunctionIndex) {
        case 1:          // Call Value
            f = NI.DF * (x - NI.StrikePrice)   // Call Value
                * (1.0 / (pow(2.0*PI, 0.5) * NI.SD * x))
                * exp(- pow(log(x) - NI.Mean, 2.0) / (2.0 * pow(NI.SD, 2.0)) );
            break;
        case 2:          // Put price
            f = NI.DF * (NI.StrikeValue - x)     // Put Value
                * (1.0 / (pow(2.0*PI, 0.5) * NI.SD * x))
                * exp(- pow(log(x) - NI.Mean, 2.0) / (2.0 * pow(NI.SD, 2.0)) );
            break;
        default :
            f = 0.0;
    }
    return f;
};

double FRMBSMOVMINT::FRMNumericalIntegrationSetUp()
{
    double Scalar;       // Number of standard deviations from mean
    double LowerBound;   // Integration lower bound
    double UpperBound;   // Integration upper bound
    double Result;       // Initial result
    NI.FunctionIndex = FunctionIndex;
```

Although a bit cumbersome, long names and separate methods make it easy for others, as well as yourself years later, to understand the code. Note at times abbreviations are self-evident, such as DF denoting the discount factor and SD denoting the standard deviation.

```
    NI.DF = exp(-(InterestRate/100.0)*TimeToMaturity);
    NI.Mean = FRMNormalMean();
    NI.SD = FRMNormalSD();
    NI.StrikePrice = StrikePrice;
    NI.FunctionIndex = FunctionIndex;
    Scalar = 7.0;            // Used to set upper bound on integration
    if(FunctionIndex == 1){
        LowerBound = StrikePrice + 0.00000001;
        UpperBound = exp(FRMNormalMean() + Scalar*FRMNormalSD());
    } else {
```

```
      LowerBound = 0.00000001;
      UpperBound = StrikePrice;
      if (StrikePrice < exp(FRMNormalMean() - Scalar*FRMNormalSD())) {
          return -98;
      }
   }
   if (UpperBound < LowerBound + 0.00000001) return -99;
   Result = INTEGRATE.FRMNumericalIntegration(LowerBound, UpperBound, &function);
// Check if integration results are reasonable, many functions result in
// very unstable numerical integration results
```

We need to be sure that the integration results do not violate any option boundary conditions. Remember that integration of the lognormal will become unstable in a variety of settings, including very high standard deviation.

```
   if (Result < 0.0000001) Result = 0.0;
   if(FunctionIndex == 1){
      LowerBound = max(0.0, StockPrice -
         exp(-(InterestRate/100.0)*TimeToMaturity)*StrikePrice);
      UpperBound = StockPrice;
      if (Result < LowerBound) Result = LowerBound;
      if (Result > UpperBound) Result = UpperBound;
   } else {
      LowerBound = max(0.0,
         exp(-(InterestRate/100.0)*TimeToMaturity)*StrikePrice - StockPrice);
      UpperBound = exp(-(InterestRate/100.0)*TimeToMaturity)*StrikePrice;
      if (Result < LowerBound) Result = LowerBound;
      if (Result > UpperBound) Result = UpperBound;
   }
   return Result;
}
...
```

The remainder of this source code is nearly identical to the source code provided in the numerical integration module.

References

See lognormal references in Module 3.8.

Appendix 4.8: Interface code comments

The graphical user interface used for illustrating this module follows.

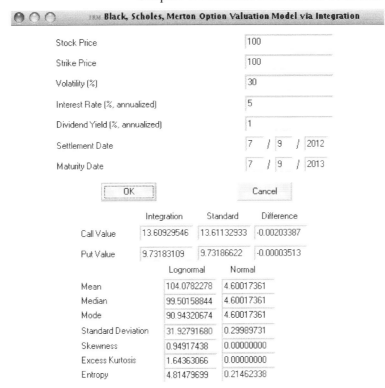

The following are excerpts from the interface header code with selected comments added.

FRMUnitBSMOVMIntegration.h:

The interface header code is typical. Notice that we include two implementation files. First, the standard Black, Scholes, Merton option valuation model, which incorporates the calendar module and the cumulative distribution function module, is included. Second, the integration approach to the Black, Scholes, Merton option valuation model, which incorporates the calendar module and the generic integration module, is included. So once the FRMBSOVM class is instantiated, methods from this class as well as FRMCALENDAR and FRMCDF can be used through the object B.

```
...
#include "c:\FRMRepository\FRMBSMOVM.cpp"
#include "c:\FRMRepository\FRMBSMOVMIntegration.cpp"

class TBSMOVMIntForm : public TForm
{
...
   FRMBSMOVM B;
   FRMBSMOVMINT I;
...
```

The following are excerpts from the interface code with selected comments added.

FRMUnitBSMOVMIntegration.cpp:

The majority of source code in this file is standard; however, notice in the code below that we call methods within two separate classes and then compare the results.

```
...
   B.FRMBSMOVMSetData(inputStockPrice, inputStrikePrice,
      inputInterestRate, inputDividendYield, inputVolatility,
      SettlementDateMonth, SettlementDateDay, SettlementDateYear,
      MaturityDateMonth, MaturityDateDay, MaturityDateYear);
   CallValue = B.FRMBSMCallValue();
   PutValue = B.FRMBSMPutValue();
// Integration approach (last variable = 1 => call, otherwise put
```

```
I.FRMBSMOVMIntSetData(inputStockPrice, inputStrikePrice,
    inputInterestRate, inputDividendYield, inputVolatility,
    SettlementDateMonth, SettlementDateDay, SettlementDateYear,
    MaturityDateMonth, MaturityDateDay, MaturityDateYear, 1);
IntCallValue = I.FRMNumericalIntegrationSetUp();
I.FRMBSMOVMIntSetData(inputStockPrice, inputStrikePrice,
    inputInterestRate, inputDividendYield, inputVolatility,
    SettlementDateMonth, SettlementDateDay, SettlementDateYear,
    MaturityDateMonth, MaturityDateDay, MaturityDateYear, 2);
IntPutValue = I.FRMNumericalIntegrationSetUp();
CallDifference = IntCallValue - CallValue;
PutDifference = IntPutValue - PutValue;
...
```

Chapter 5. Static Market Risk Management

"The only perfect hedge is in a Japanese garden." Gene Rotberg[37]

Introduction

In this chapter, we present different ways to compute a variety of static market risk management results. The objective here is to introduce these methods within the C++ framework. Seven programs are reviewed that address the following four risk management issues: bond risk, stock total risk, stock option risk, and interest rate swap risk (rate exposure only).

Each of these programs is presented as a separate module. We continue to focus almost exclusively on implementation code. The main focus of this chapter is on analytical and numerical derivatives of simple positions. As before, there will be some effort to make each module standalone. Another advantage of this modular approach is your ability to find the source code within the materials you downloaded from the website.

In this chapter, we launch immediately into specific static market risk management modules.

---

[37] See *Fortune* March 7, 1994, p. 53. This quote as well as several others can be found at Don Chance's website, specifically
http://www.bus.lsu.edu/academics/finance/faculty/dchance/MiscProf/DerivaQuote/Qt12.htm.

Module 5.1: Bond Risk Management

Learning objectives

- Review duration and convexity
- Use the Brent module to compute yield to maturity
- Review error trapping

Module overview

A detailed review of bond duration and convexity is provided in the supplement to this module.[38] We briefly sketch the mathematics here. The coupon-bearing bond's value today, V_B, depends on the number of payments per year, m; the par value, Par; the fraction of payment period elapsed already, f; the number of remaining coupon payments, N; and the yield to maturity, y.

$$V_B = \sum_{i=1}^{N} \frac{\left(\dfrac{Coupon}{m}\right)Par}{\left(1+\dfrac{y}{m}\right)^{i-f}} + \frac{Par}{\left(1+\dfrac{y}{m}\right)^{N-f}}$$

Modified duration measures the percentage change in the bond price (or portfolio) for a given change in yield to maturity

$$ModDur_B \equiv -\frac{dV_B/V_B}{dy} = \frac{1}{m}\left[\sum_{i=1}^{N} \frac{(i-f)CF_i}{\left(1+\dfrac{y}{m}\right)^{i+1-f}}\right]\frac{1}{V_B}$$

Convexity measures the curvature of the price-yield relationship

$$Convexity_B \equiv \frac{1}{V_B}\frac{d^2V_B}{dy^2} = \frac{1}{m^2}\left[\sum_{i=1}^{N} \frac{(i-f)(i+1-f)CF_i}{\left(1+\dfrac{y}{m}\right)^{i+2-f}}\right]\frac{1}{V_B}$$

With standard measures of duration, the change in the estimated price does not incorporate changes in cash flow. Effective duration is a measure of cash flow adjusted volatility. Specifically,

$$\text{Effective Duration} = \frac{\left(V_{B-}\right)-\left(V_{B+}\right)}{2V_B S}$$

where V_B denotes the current price, V_{B-} denotes the price when rates fall by some shift in the term structure denoted by S, and V_{B+} denotes the price when rates rise by S. Note that if $\Delta V_B = \left(V_{B-}\right)-\left(V_{B+}\right)$, then $\Delta y = 2S$. Assuming no changes in cash flow, then these two expressions for duration are identical. Effective duration is different when the consequences of the rate change result in a different valuation due to changes in cash flow, such as a call feature on a bond.

---

[38] Supplements for this book are provided at www.frmhelp.com.

Effective convexity corrects for this limitation of standard convexity by using a valuation model to compute bond prices that incorporates the consequences of interest rate changes on cash flows. At this point, you are not responsible for this valuation model (that is, the model that estimates V_{B-} and V_{B+}).

$$\text{Effective Convexity} = \frac{\left(V_{B-}\right) + \left(V_{B+}\right) - 2V_B}{V_B S^2}$$

The second derivative measures the change in the first derivative as we change the yield to maturity, hence $\Delta^2 V_B = \Delta V_{B-} - \Delta V_{B+} = \left(\left(V_{B-}\right) - V_B\right) - \left(V_B - \left(V_{B+}\right)\right) = \left(V_{B-}\right) + \left(V_{B+}\right) - 2V_B$. Also, $\Delta y^2 = S^2$. Hence, standard convexity and effective convexity are the same when cash flow considerations are ignored.

We now turn to reviewing the source code for this module.

Implementation code comments

FRMStaticBond.h

This class uses both the calendar and Brent classes so they are included in this header file and their classes are inherited into the FRMSTATICBOND class.

```
...
#ifndef FRMCALENDARCPP
#define FRMCALENDARCPP
#include "c:\FRMRepository\FRMCalendar.cpp"
#endif

#ifndef FRMBRENTCPP
#define FRMBRENTCPP
#include "c:\FRMRepository\FRMBrent.cpp"
#endif

//--------------------------------------------------------------------------
class FRMSTATICBOND : public FRMCALENDAR, BRENT
{
public:
...
```

Notice the multiple use of the same function name where the number of inputs varies.

```
   void FRMSetDataYTM(double ICR, double IPV, double IQBP, int IF,
      int SM, int SD, int SY, int MM, int MD, int MY);
...
   void FRMSetDataYTM(double ICR, double IPV, double IQBP, int IF,
      int SM, int SD, int SY, int MM, int MD, int MY, double ICYTM);
...
   void FRMSetDataYTM(double YTM);
...
```

FRMStaticBond.cpp

We use the Brent class so we need to pass it a function which in this case is computing the market value of the bond.

```
...
// Global function for using Brent method of embedded parameter
FRMSTATICBOND BP;   // Global class instantiation of specific class function in Brent function
double function(double tempX);
double function(double tempX)
{
   double tempFX;
   BP.FRMSetDataYTM(tempX);
   tempFX = BP.FRMCalculateBondPrice();
   return(tempFX);
};
```

The following method moves the appropriate inputs into the global class (BP) and calls the Brent CalculateX() method.

```
double FRMSTATICBOND::FRMCalculateYTM()
```

```
{
   double ActualPrice;
   BP.CouponRate = CouponRate;
   BP.ParValue = ParValue;
   BP.YieldToMaturity = -99; //YieldToMaturity;
   BP.QuotedBondPrice = QuotedBondPrice;
   BP.IFreq = IFreq; // Integer version of frequency
   BP.Frequency = Frequency;
   BP.RemainingCoupons = RemainingCoupons;
   BP.Elapsed = Elapsed;
   ActualPrice = BP.QuotedBondPrice + BP.FRMCalculateAccruedInterest();
   BRENTSetData(ActualPrice, 5000, 0.001);  // BRENT is public in this class
   return CalculateX(&function);          // BRENT is public in this class
};
```

The fraction of the coupon period that has elapsed is used to compute accrued interest and the current market value of the bond. The appropriate calculation depends on payment frequency, IFreq. A series of if statements is used to generate the appropriate calculation from annual, semiannual, quarterly, and monthly frequencies.

```
double FRMSTATICBOND::FRMElapsed(int SM, int SD, int SY, int MM, int MD, int MY)
{
// Move to separate function
   double tempE;
   long int JSettlementDate, JMaturityDate;
   JSettlementDate = FRMToJulian(SM, SD, SY);
   JMaturityDate = FRMToJulian(MM, MD, MY);
   int Counter = 0;
   if(IFreq == 1){   // Annual
      while (JMaturityDate > JSettlementDate){
         MY--;
         JMaturityDate = FRMToJulian(MM, MD, MY);
         Counter++;
      }
      MY++;
      tempE = ((double)(JSettlementDate - JMaturityDate))
         / ((double)(FRMToJulian(MM, MD, MY) - JMaturityDate));
   } else if (IFreq == 2) { // Semi-annual
      while (JMaturityDate > JSettlementDate){
         if(MM > 6){
            MM = MM - 6;
            JMaturityDate = FRMToJulian(MM, MD, MY);
         } else {
            MM = MM + 6;
            MY--;
            JMaturityDate = FRMToJulian(MM, MD, MY);
         }
         Counter++;
      }
      if(MM > 6){
         MM = MM - 6;
         MY++;
      } else {
         MM = MM + 6;
      }
      tempE = ((double)(JSettlementDate - JMaturityDate))
         / ((double)(FRMToJulian(MM, MD, MY) - JMaturityDate));
   } else if (IFreq == 4) { // Quarterly
      while (JMaturityDate > JSettlementDate){
         if(MM > 3){
            MM = MM - 3;
            JMaturityDate = FRMToJulian(MM, MD, MY);
         } else {
            MM = MM + 9;
            MY--;
            JMaturityDate = FRMToJulian(MM, MD, MY);
         }
         Counter++;
      }
      if(MM > 9){
         MM = MM - 9;
```

```
            MY++;
        } else {
            MM = MM + 3;
        }
        tempE = ((double)(JSettlementDate - JMaturityDate))
            / ((double)(FRMToJulian(MM, MD, MY) - JMaturityDate));
    } else { // Monthly
        while (JMaturityDate > JSettlementDate){
            if(MM > 1){
                MM--;
                JMaturityDate = FRMToJulian(MM, MD, MY);
            } else {
                MM = MM + 11;
                MY--;
                JMaturityDate = FRMToJulian(MM, MD, MY);
            }
            Counter++;
        }
        if(MM > 11){
            MM = MM - 11;
            MY++;
        } else {
            MM = MM + 1;
        }
        tempE = ((double)(JSettlementDate - JMaturityDate))
            / ((double)(FRMToJulian(MM, MD, MY) - JMaturityDate));
    }
    return(tempE);
}
```

The following method computes the market value of the bond. Remember the market value of the bond includes both the quoted price and accrued interest.

```
long double FRMSTATICBOND::FRMCalculateBondPrice()
{
    int i;  // Counter used in for loop
    long double fi;
    long double PV; // Temporary variable holding sum of coupons
    PV = 0.0; // Initialize PV to zero
    for(i=1; i<=RemainingCoupons; i++){  // Loop from 1 to YearsToMaturity by 1
        fi = (long double) i;
        PV += ((CouponRate/(Frequency*100.0))*ParValue)
            / pow((1.0 + ((long double)YieldToMaturity/(Frequency*100.0))), fi - Elapsed);
    };
    return (PV + ParValue
        / pow((1.0 + ((long double) YieldToMaturity/(Frequency*100.0))),
        (long double) RemainingCoupons - Elapsed));
};
//------------------------------------------------------------------------
double FRMSTATICBOND::FRMCalculateAccruedInterest()
{
    return (CouponRate/(Frequency*100.0))*ParValue*Elapsed;
};
```

The following method is used to compute modified duration.

```
double FRMSTATICBOND::FRMCalculateDuration()
{
    int i;  // Counter used in for loop
    double fi; // double version of i
    double DV; // Temporary variable holding sum of values
    DV = 0.0; // Initialize to zero
    for(i=1; i<=RemainingCoupons; i++){  // Loop from 1 to YearsToMaturity by 1
        fi = (double) i;
        DV += ((fi - Elapsed)*(CouponRate/(Frequency*100.0))*ParValue)
            / pow((1.0 + (YieldToMaturity/(Frequency*100.0))), fi + 1 - Elapsed);
    };
    DV += ((RemainingCoupons - Elapsed) * ParValue)
        / pow((1.0 + (YieldToMaturity/(Frequency*100.0))), RemainingCoupons + 1 - Elapsed);
    DV /= Frequency * FRMCalculateBondPrice();
    return DV;
};
```

The following method is used to compute standard convexity.

```
double FRMSTATICBOND::FRMCalculateConvexity()
{
    int i;  // Counter used in for loop
    double fi; // double version of i
    double Convexity; // Temporary variable holding sum of values
    Convexity = 0.0; // Initialize to zero
    for(i=1; i<=RemainingCoupons; i++){  // Loop from 1 to YearsToMaturity by 1
        fi = (double) i;
        Convexity += ((fi + 1 - Elapsed)*(fi - Elapsed)*(CouponRate/(Frequency*100.0))*ParValue)
            / pow((1.0 + (YieldToMaturity/(Frequency*100.0))), fi + 2 - Elapsed);
    };
    Convexity += ((RemainingCoupons + 1 - Elapsed) * (RemainingCoupons - Elapsed) * ParValue)
        / pow((1.0 + (YieldToMaturity/(Frequency*100.0))), RemainingCoupons + 2 - Elapsed);
    Convexity /= (pow(Frequency, 2.0) * FRMCalculateBondPrice());
    return Convexity;
};
```

The following method is used to compute effective duration.

```
double FRMSTATICBOND::FRMCalculateEffectiveDuration()
{
    double OriginalYTM, UpYTM, DownYTM, OriginalBV, UpBV, DownBV;
    double EffDur;
    OriginalYTM = YieldToMaturity;
    OriginalBV = FRMCalculateBondPrice();
    YieldToMaturity = OriginalYTM + ChangeInYTM;
    UpBV = FRMCalculateBondPrice();
    YieldToMaturity = OriginalYTM - ChangeInYTM;
    DownBV = FRMCalculateBondPrice();
    YieldToMaturity = OriginalYTM;
    EffDur = (DownBV - UpBV)/(2.0*OriginalBV*(ChangeInYTM/100.0));
    return EffDur;
};
```

The following method is used to compute effective convexity.

```
double FRMSTATICBOND::FRMCalculateEffectiveConvexity()
{
    long double OriginalYTM, UpYTM, DownYTM, OriginalBV, UpBV, DownBV;
    long double EffConv, Num, Den;
    OriginalYTM = YieldToMaturity;
    OriginalBV = FRMCalculateBondPrice();
    YieldToMaturity = OriginalYTM + ChangeInYTM;
    UpBV = FRMCalculateBondPrice();
    YieldToMaturity = OriginalYTM - ChangeInYTM;
    DownBV = FRMCalculateBondPrice();
    YieldToMaturity = OriginalYTM;
    Num = logl((DownBV - OriginalBV) - (OriginalBV - UpBV));
    Den = -logl(OriginalBV) - 2.0*logl(ChangeInYTM/100.0);
    EffConv = exp(Num + Den);
    return EffConv;
};
...
```

References

See references in the supplemental materials for this module.

Appendix 5.1: Interface code comments

The graphical user interface for this module is illustrated below.

We see this program is very flexible. Through the use of a radio group, we can compute the yield to maturity given the current quoted bond price or we can compute the bond quoted price given the current yield to maturity. This program provides the accrued interest, modified duration, standard convexity, effective duration, and effective convexity. The coupon period elapsed and number of remaining coupon payments are provided primarily for auditing the code purposes.

The following are excerpts from the interface header code with selected comments added.

FRMUnitStaticBond.h

This interface code provides some modest error trapping of faulty user inputs. Therefore, a method is provided whenever an input edit box is entered and whenever an input edit box is exited. The method definitions are identified below.

```
...
  void __fastcall editCouponRateEnter(TObject *Sender);
  void __fastcall editCouponRateExit(TObject *Sender);
  void __fastcall editParEnter(TObject *Sender);
  void __fastcall editParExit(TObject *Sender);
  void __fastcall editYieldToMaturityEnter(TObject *Sender);
  void __fastcall editYieldToMaturityExit(TObject *Sender);
  void __fastcall rgFrequencyExit(TObject *Sender);
  void __fastcall rgBVorYTMClick(TObject *Sender);
  void __fastcall editQuotedBondPriceEnter(TObject *Sender);
  void __fastcall editQuotedBondPriceExit(TObject *Sender);
  void __fastcall editChangeInYTMEnter(TObject *Sender);
  void __fastcall editChangeInYTMExit(TObject *Sender);
...
```

The following are excerpts from the interface code with selected comments added.

FRMUnitStaticBond.cpp

The reset method is an easy way to set the defaults when debugging the code. The call to this function in the constructor will place the appropriate defaults on the form.

```
...
  __fastcall TBVandYTMForm::TBVandYTMForm(TComponent* Owner)
    : TForm(Owner)
{
  Reset();
}
...
```

Recall that we use a single function FRMExecute() to link the interface code with the implementation code.

```
void __fastcall TBVandYTMForm::FRMExecute(void)
{
```

This program can compute either the quoted bond price or the yield to maturity, depending on which option is selected in the radio group. The if statement dictates which computation will be performed based on which input is selected.

```
    if (inputBVorYTM == 1){  // Bond valuation calculation
        B.FRMSetDataBV(inputCouponRate, inputPar, inputYieldToMaturity, inputFrequency,
            SettlementDateMonth, SettlementDateDay, SettlementDateYear,
            MaturityDateMonth, MaturityDateDay, MaturityDateYear, inputChangeInYTM);
        RemainingCoupons = B.FRMCouponsRemaining(
            SettlementDateMonth, SettlementDateDay, SettlementDateYear,
            MaturityDateMonth, MaturityDateDay, MaturityDateYear);
        Elapsed = B.FRMElapsed(
            SettlementDateMonth, SettlementDateDay, SettlementDateYear,
            MaturityDateMonth, MaturityDateDay, MaturityDateYear);
        AccruedInterest = B.FRMCalculateAccruedInterest();
        ModelQuotedBondPrice = B.FRMCalculateBondPrice() - AccruedInterest;
        ModelDuration = B.FRMCalculateDuration();
        ModelConvexity = B.FRMCalculateConvexity();
        ModelEffectiveDuration = B.FRMCalculateEffectiveDuration();
        ModelEffectiveConvexity = B.FRMCalculateEffectiveConvexity();
        B.FRMSetDataYTM(inputCouponRate, inputPar, ModelQuotedBondPrice, inputFrequency,
            SettlementDateMonth, SettlementDateDay, SettlementDateYear,
            MaturityDateMonth, MaturityDateDay, MaturityDateYear);
        ModelYTM = B.FRMCalculateYTM();
    } else {  // Yield to maturity calculation
        B.FRMSetDataYTM(inputCouponRate, inputPar, inputQuotedBondPrice, inputFrequency,
            SettlementDateMonth, SettlementDateDay, SettlementDateYear,
            MaturityDateMonth, MaturityDateDay, MaturityDateYear, inputChangeInYTM);
        RemainingCoupons = B.FRMCouponsRemaining(
            SettlementDateMonth, SettlementDateDay, SettlementDateYear,
            MaturityDateMonth, MaturityDateDay, MaturityDateYear);
        Elapsed = B.FRMElapsed(
            SettlementDateMonth, SettlementDateDay, SettlementDateYear,
            MaturityDateMonth, MaturityDateDay, MaturityDateYear);
        ModelYTM = B.FRMCalculateYTM();
        B.FRMSetDataBV(inputCouponRate, inputPar, ModelYTM, inputFrequency,
            SettlementDateMonth, SettlementDateDay, SettlementDateYear,
            MaturityDateMonth, MaturityDateDay, MaturityDateYear);
        AccruedInterest = B.FRMCalculateAccruedInterest();
        ModelQuotedBondPrice = B.FRMCalculateBondPrice() - AccruedInterest;
        ModelDuration = B.FRMCalculateDuration();
        ModelConvexity = B.FRMCalculateConvexity();
        ModelEffectiveDuration = B.FRMCalculateEffectiveDuration();
        ModelEffectiveConvexity = B.FRMCalculateEffectiveConvexity();
    };
}
```

The ability to alter the visible inputs depending on the desired output is handled here.

```
void __fastcall TBVandYTMForm::rgBVorYTMClick(TObject *Sender)
{
    switch (rgBVorYTM->ItemIndex){
        case 0:  // Bond valuation calculation
            inputBVorYTM = 1;
            editYieldToMaturity->Visible = true;
            lblYieldToMaturity->Visible = true;
            editQuotedBondPrice->Visible = false;
            lblQuotedBondPriceInput->Visible = false;
        break;
        case 1:  // Yield to maturity calculation
            inputBVorYTM = 2;
        editYieldToMaturity->Visible = false;
            lblYieldToMaturity->Visible = false;
            editQuotedBondPrice->Visible = true;
            lblQuotedBondPriceInput->Visible = true;
        break;
```

```
         default:
            inputBVorYTM = -99;
         break;
      };
}
```

The reset function pulls the date off the computer and performs several other tasks, namely placing default values onto the form.

```
void __fastcall TBVandYTMForm::Reset(void)
{
    char tmpbuf[128];        // Copy current date to tmpbuf
    _strdate(tmpbuf);
    SettlementDateMonth = atoi(&tmpbuf[0]);
    SettlementDateDay = atoi(&tmpbuf[3]);
    SettlementDateYear = atoi(&tmpbuf[6]);
    SettlementDateYear += 2000;
    MaturityDateMonth = SettlementDateMonth;
    MaturityDateDay = SettlementDateDay;
    MaturityDateYear = SettlementDateYear + 10;
    editSettlementMonth->Text = IntToStr(SettlementDateMonth);
    editSettlementDay->Text = IntToStr(SettlementDateDay);
    editSettlementYear->Text = IntToStr(SettlementDateYear);
    editMaturityMonth->Text = IntToStr(MaturityDateMonth);
    editMaturityDay->Text = IntToStr(MaturityDateDay);
    editMaturityYear->Text = IntToStr(MaturityDateYear);
    inputCouponRate = 6.00;
    editCouponRate->Text = FloatToStrF(inputCouponRate, ffFixed, 15, 2);
    inputPar = 1000.0;
    editPar->Text = FloatToStrF(inputPar, ffFixed, 15, 1);
    inputYieldToMaturity = 6.00;
    editYieldToMaturity->Text = FloatToStrF(inputYieldToMaturity, ffFixed, 15, 2);
    inputFrequency = 2;
    inputBVorYTM = 1;
    inputQuotedBondPrice = 1000.00;
    editQuotedBondPrice->Text = FloatToStrF(inputQuotedBondPrice, ffFixed, 15, 2);
    inputChangeInYTM = 0.01;   // One basis point
    editChangeInYTM->Text = FloatToStrF(inputChangeInYTM, ffFixed, 15, 3);
}
```

Error trapping is an important task usually left to the software professionals. We review the general idea here. When the focus is placed in an input edit box, we place the contents of inputCouponRate in the box and highlight it because the user will likely desire to change it.

```
void __fastcall TBVandYTMForm::editCouponRateEnter(TObject *Sender)
{
// FloatToStrF converts floating point variable to an AnsiString
    editCouponRate->Text = FloatToStrF(inputCouponRate, ffFixed, 15, 6);
    editCouponRate->SelectAll();   // Highlight input so easy to type over
}
```

Each input will have different values to check when the focus is moved outside of the input edit box. Here we just make sure the inputted coupon rate is non-negative and a real number.

```
void __fastcall TBVandYTMForm::editCouponRateExit(TObject *Sender)
{
    if(editCouponRate->Text == "")editCouponRate->Text = "0.0";
    try {     // Just in case text is not a floating point number
        inputCouponRate = StrToFloat(editCouponRate->Text);
    }
    catch (Exception &exception){  // Catch the bad error
        editCouponRate->Text = "";
        Application->MessageBox(L"Input Only Positive Numbers", L"Input Error 2", MB_OK);
      ActiveControl = editCouponRate;
        return;
    }
    if(inputCouponRate < 0.0){   // Catch negative coupon error
      editCouponRate->Text = "";
        Application->MessageBox(L"Negative Number: Input Only Positive Numbers",
           L"Input Error 3", MB_OK);
      ActiveControl = editCouponRate;
    };
```

```
    editCouponRate->Text = FloatToStrF(inputCouponRate, ffFixed, 15, 4);
}
...
```

There are several other error-trapping functions provided in this interface source code.

Module 5.2: Bond Risk Management With Files

Learning objectives

- Explain how to read bond input data and produce bond output data
- Contrast the form approach to the file approach

Module overview

This module is based on the same implementation source code as the previous module. The difference here is that the input data is contained in a file and the output data is also placed in a file.

Implementation code comments

The implementation code is the same file as the previous module. We just highlight a few issues in the file management method.

FRMStaticBond.cpp

Note that in this program, the user does not have control over the file names. Screen shots of the input and output files can be found ing Appendix 5.2.

```cpp
void FRMSTATICBOND::FRMAnalyzeStaticBondFiles(void)
{
   char H[8][15], Cusip[9];
   int Counter;
   int SM, SD, SY, MM, MD, MY, BorY;
   ofstream outf;  // Output file FRMStaticBond.prn
   outf.open("FRMStaticBond.prn");  // Open output file
   ifstream inf;                // Input file
   inf.open("FRMStaticBondInputData.dat", ios::in);  // Open input file
   inf >> H[0] >> H[1] >> H[2] >> H[3] >> H[4] >> H[5] >> H[6] >> H[7];// Headings
   outf << setfill(' ') << setiosflags(ios::right) << setw(9) << H[0];
   outf << setfill(' ') << setiosflags(ios::right) << setw(12) << H[1];
   outf << setfill(' ') << setiosflags(ios::right) << setw(11) << H[2];
   outf << setfill(' ') << setiosflags(ios::right) << setw(5) << H[3];
   outf << setfill(' ') << setiosflags(ios::right) << setw(4) << H[4];
   outf << setfill(' ') << setiosflags(ios::right) << setw(8) << H[5];
   outf << setfill(' ') << setiosflags(ios::right) << setw(10) << H[6];
   outf << setfill(' ') << setiosflags(ios::right) << setw(11) << H[7];
   outf << "  Quoted Price  Accrued Interest  Modified Duration  Convexity  ";
   outf << " Yield to Maturity  Period Elapsed  Remaining Coupons";
   outf << '\n';
   Counter = 0;
   while(inf)
   {
      if(Counter==0)inf >> Cusip >> ws;     // Handle date
      inf >> SM >> SD >> SY >> MM >> MD >> MY >> BorY >> IFreq >> ParValue
         >> CouponRate;
      Frequency = (double) IFreq;
      if (BorY==1) {
         inf >> YieldToMaturity >> ws;
      } else {
         inf >> QuotedBondPrice >> ws;
      }
      outf << setfill(' ') << setiosflags(ios::right) << setw(10) << Cusip;
      outf << setfill(' ') << setiosflags(ios::right) << setw(3) << SM;
      outf << setfill(' ') << setiosflags(ios::right) << setw(3) << SD;
      outf << setfill(' ') << setiosflags(ios::right) << setw(5) << SY;
      outf << setfill(' ') << setiosflags(ios::right) << setw(3) << MM;
      outf << setfill(' ') << setiosflags(ios::right) << setw(3) << MD;
      outf << setfill(' ') << setiosflags(ios::right) << setw(5) << MY;
      outf << setfill(' ') << setiosflags(ios::right) << setw(3) << BorY;
      outf << setfill(' ') << setiosflags(ios::right) << setw(5) << IFreq;
      outf << setiosflags(ios::showpoint | ios::fixed) << setprecision(2)
         << setfill(' ') << setiosflags(ios::right) << setw(9) << ParValue;
      outf << setiosflags(ios::showpoint | ios::fixed) << setprecision(5)
         << setfill(' ') << setiosflags(ios::right) << setw(9) << CouponRate;
```

```
        if (BorY==1) {
        outf << setiosflags(ios::showpoint | ios::fixed) << setprecision(5)
           << setfill(' ') << setiosflags(ios::right) << setw(12) << YieldToMaturity;
        } else {
        outf << setiosflags(ios::showpoint | ios::fixed) << setprecision(5)
           << setfill(' ') << setiosflags(ios::right) << setw(12) << QuotedBondPrice;
        }
// Produce output
        RemainingCoupons = FRMCouponsRemaining(SM, SD, SY, MM, MD, MY);
        Elapsed = FRMElapsed(SM, SD, SY, MM, MD, MY);
        double AccruedInterest, ModelQuotedBondPrice, ModelDuration, ModelConvexity,
           ModelYTM;
        if (BorY == 1){  // Bond valuation calculation
           AccruedInterest = FRMCalculateAccruedInterest();
           ModelQuotedBondPrice = FRMCalculateBondPrice() - AccruedInterest;
           ModelDuration = FRMCalculateDuration();
           ModelConvexity = FRMCalculateConvexity();
           QuotedBondPrice = ModelQuotedBondPrice;
           ModelYTM = FRMCalculateYTM();
        } else {  // Yield to maturity calculation
           ModelYTM = FRMCalculateYTM();
           AccruedInterest = FRMCalculateAccruedInterest();
           YieldToMaturity = ModelYTM;
           ModelQuotedBondPrice = FRMCalculateBondPrice() - AccruedInterest;
           ModelDuration = FRMCalculateDuration();
           ModelConvexity = FRMCalculateConvexity();
        };
        outf << setiosflags(ios::showpoint | ios::fixed) << setprecision(5)
           << setfill(' ') << setiosflags(ios::right) << setw(15) << ModelQuotedBondPrice;
        outf << setiosflags(ios::showpoint | ios::fixed) << setprecision(5)
           << setfill(' ') << setiosflags(ios::right) << setw(15) << AccruedInterest;
        outf << setiosflags(ios::showpoint | ios::fixed) << setprecision(5)
           << setfill(' ') << setiosflags(ios::right) << setw(18) << ModelDuration;
        outf << setiosflags(ios::showpoint | ios::fixed) << setprecision(5)
           << setfill(' ') << setiosflags(ios::right) << setw(15) << ModelConvexity;
        outf << setiosflags(ios::showpoint | ios::fixed) << setprecision(5)
           << setfill(' ') << setiosflags(ios::right) << setw(17) << ModelYTM;
        outf << setiosflags(ios::showpoint | ios::fixed) << setprecision(5)
           << setfill(' ') << setiosflags(ios::right) << setw(15) << Elapsed;
        outf << setfill(' ') << setiosflags(ios::right) << setw(15) << RemainingCoupons;
        outf << '\n';
        inf >> Cusip >> ws;    // Handle date and check for end of file
        Counter++; // increment
    };
    inf.close();  // Closes input file
    outf.close();
    return;
}
```

References

See references in the supplement to Module 5.1.

Interface code comments

The graphical user interface, after the program is run, follows.

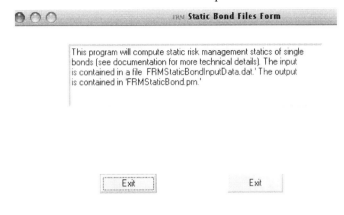

Program is Finished -- See output in FRMStaticBond.prn

Note that the button on the left of the text is reset to "Exit" from "Run." The input data was based on the U. S. Treasury bond and note market. BorY triggers either the bond calculation (1) or the yield to maturity calculation (2). Frq denotes the payment frequency per year and YTMorQBP denotes either the quoted bond price (shown here) or the provided yield to maturity (not shown here).

BondID	Settlement			Maturity			BorY	Frq	Par($)	Coupon(%)	YTMorQBP
A2009630	6	26	2009	6	30	2009	2	2	100	4.875	100.03125
A2009715	6	26	2009	7	15	2009	2	2	100	3.625	100.18750
A2009731	6	26	2009	7	31	2009	2	2	100	4.625	100.40625
A2009815	6	26	2009	8	15	2009	2	2	100	3.5	100.43750
A2009815	6	26	2009	8	15	2009	2	2	100	4.875	100.62500
A2009815	6	26	2009	8	15	2009	2	2	100	6	100.78125
A2009831	6	26	2009	8	31	2009	2	2	100	4	100.68750
A2009915	6	26	2009	9	15	2009	2	2	100	3.375	100.68750
A2009930	6	26	2009	9	30	2009	2	2	100	4	101.00000
A20091015	6	26	2009	10	15	2009	2	2	100	3.375	100.96875
A20091031	6	26	2009	10	31	2009	2	2	100	3.625	101.15625
A20091115	6	26	2009	11	15	2009	2	2	100	3.5	101.25000
A20091115	6	26	2009	11	15	2009	2	2	100	4.625	101.65625
A20091130	6	26	2009	11	30	2009	2	2	100	3.125	101.21875

The output contains the inputs, yield to maturity, and the results of several static bond risk management calculations (modified duration and convexity).

BondID	Settlement	Maturity	BorY	Frq	Par($)	Coupon(%)	YTMorQBP	Quoted Price	Accrued Interest	Modified Duration	Convexity	Yield to Ma
A2009630	6 26 2009	6 30 2009	2	2	100.00	4.87500	100.03125	100.03125	2.38393	0.01088	0.00551	1.993
A2009715	6 26 2009	7 15 2009	2	2	100.00	3.62500	100.18750	100.18750	1.62224	0.05247	0.02898	0.051
A2009731	6 26 2009	7 31 2009	2	2	100.00	4.62500	100.40625	100.40625	1.86533	0.09649	0.05745	0.414
A2009815	6 26 2009	8 15 2009	2	2	100.00	3.50000	100.43750	100.43750	1.26657	0.13790	0.08785	0.327
A2009815	6 26 2009	8 15 2009	2	2	100.00	4.87500	100.62500	100.62500	1.76416	0.13789	0.08784	0.342
A2009815	6 26 2009	8 15 2009	2	2	100.00	6.00000	100.78125	100.78125	2.17127	0.13789	0.08784	0.334
A2009831	6 26 2009	8 31 2009	2	2	100.00	4.00000	100.68750	100.68750	1.27072	0.18212	0.12412	0.224
A2009915	6 26 2009	9 15 2009	2	2	100.00	3.37500	100.68750	100.68750	0.94463	0.21984	0.15811	0.247
A2009930	6 26 2009	9 30 2009	2	2	100.00	4.00000	101.00000	101.00000	0.95652	0.26066	0.19816	0.163
A20091015	6 26 2009	10 15 2009	2	2	100.00	3.37500	100.96875	100.96875	0.66393	0.30301	0.24318	0.177
A20091031	6 26 2009	10 31 2009	2	2	100.00	3.62500	101.15625	101.15625	0.55464	0.34650	0.29306	0.287
A20091115	6 26 2009	11 15 2009	2	2	100.00	3.50000	101.25000	101.25000	0.39946	0.38538	0.34096	0.256
A20091115	6 26 2009	11 15 2009	2	2	100.00	4.62500	101.65625	101.65625	0.52785	0.38524	0.34072	0.325
A20091130	6 26 2009	11 30 2009	2	2	100.00	3.12500	101.21875	101.21875	0.22928	0.42607	0.39429	0.264
A20091215	6 26 2009	12 15 2009	2	2	100.00	3.50000	101.50000	101.50000	0.10519	0.46923	0.45444	0.303
A20091231	6 26 2009	12 31 2009	2	2	100.00	3.25000	101.50000	101.50000	1.58036	0.50503	0.51103	0.325

The outputs not shown in the figure above are the period elapsed and the number of remaining coupons.

FRMUnitStaticBondFiles.cpp

If the Visible property of the label lblFinished is false (the default is not visible), then the FRMExecute() function is run, the caption is changed, and the Visible property is set to true. This label finished (lblFinished) is mainly to let the user know the program has been run since the output is placed in a file and not returned to the GUI.

```
void __fastcall TStaticBondFilesForm::btnRunClick(TObject *Sender)
{
   if(lblFinished->Visible == false){ // Regression code designed to run only once
      FRMExecute();
      btnRun->Caption = "Exit";
      lblFinished->Visible = true;
   } else {
    Close();
   }
}
```

Module 5.3: Stock Total Risk Measures

Learning objectives

- Explain how to convert price series data into holding period rate of return statistics
- Identify ways to estimate sample means, standard deviation, skewness, and kurtosis

Module overview

The supplement to this module provides many more details on important issues related to calculating rates of returns and estimating distribution statistics.[39] In the module presented here, the input data is received in a file, e.g., FRMSingleStockRiskInputs.dat in the repository, and the outputs are reported back to the screen. Specifically, this module reports the annualized arithmetic average, annualized geometric average, the annualized harmonic average, the annualized standard deviation, skewness and excess kurtosis.

The significant mathematical details are presented here, but are explained in detail in the supplement.

Arithmetic, geometric and harmonic averages

Sample arithmetic mean is also often called the mean or average.

$$\overline{R}_A = \frac{1}{n} \sum_{i=1}^{n} R_i \text{ (Sample average)}$$

Geometric average is based on the product ex-post rates of return over the time periods and then takes the nth root to express the average on a per period basis.

$$\overline{R}_G = \left[\prod_{i=1}^{n} (1 + R_i) \right]^{\frac{1}{n}} - 1 \text{ (Geometric average)}$$

The harmonic average is often used with financial multiples like market-to-book ratio and price-to-earnings ratio. We report it here just to give you an idea of how to be creative in your analysis.

$$\overline{R}_H = n \left(\sum_{i=1}^{n} \frac{1}{(1 + R_i)} \right)^{-1} - 1 \text{ (Harmonic average)}$$

Standard deviation

The sample standard deviation can be expressed as

$$\sigma_s = \left(\frac{1}{n-1} \sum_{i=1}^{n} R_i^2 - \frac{n}{n-1} \overline{R}_A^2 \right)^{1/2} \text{ (Sample standard deviation)}$$

Skewness

Skewness is the third standardized moment and measures asymmetry in the distribution of the sample. The sample skewness can be expressed as

---

[39] Supplements can be found at www.frmhelp.com.

$$\gamma_{S,s} = \frac{\sqrt{n(n-1)}}{n-2} \frac{\frac{1}{n}\sum_{i=1}^{n}R_i^3 - \frac{3\overline{R}_A}{n}\sum_{i=1}^{n}R_i^2 - (n-3)\overline{R}_A^3}{\left[\frac{1}{n}\sum_{i=1}^{n}R_i^2 - \overline{R}_A^2\right]^{3/2}} \quad \textbf{(Sample skewness)}$$

Kurtosis

Kurtosis is the fourth standardized moment and measures the height and sharpness of the central peak of the distribution relative to the normal distribution. The sample excess kurtosis can be expressed as

$$\gamma_{K,s} = \frac{n-1}{(n-2)(n-3)}\left[(n+1)\frac{\frac{1}{n}\sum_{i=1}^{n}R_i^4 - \frac{4\overline{R}_A}{n}\sum_{i=1}^{n}R_i^3 + \frac{6\overline{R}_A^2}{n}\sum_{i=1}^{n}R_i^2 + (n-4)\overline{R}_A^4}{\left[\frac{1}{n}\sum_{i=1}^{n}R_i^2 - \overline{R}_A^2\right]^2} + 6\right] \quad \textbf{(Sample excess kurtosis)}$$

Implementation code comments

FRMSingleStockRisk.h

This header file defines the class as FRMSINGLESTOCKRISK and it inherits the sorting routine, FRMSORT. The set of outputs is contained in a simple structure, FRMSSRISKOUTPUT.

```
...
#include "c:\FRMRepository\FRMSortingData.cpp"

#ifndef FRMSSRISKOUTPUTSTRUCT
#define FRMSSRISKOUTPUTSTRUCT
struct FRMSSRISKOUTPUT
{
    double ArithmeticAverage;
    double GeometricAverage;
    double HarmonicAverage;
    double StandardDeviation;
    double Skewness;
    double ExcessKurtosis;
    double VaR;
};
#endif

class FRMSINGLESTOCKRISK : public FRMSORT
{
public:
```

Recall this next line is a constructor.

```
    FRMSINGLESTOCKRISK::FRMSINGLESTOCKRISK();
    char word[AS][CHARSIZE];
    int NumberofSecurities;
    long int m;
    double ConfidenceLevel;
    void FRMSingleStockRiskFileMgmt(AnsiString sinf, AnsiString soutf);
    struct FRMSSRISKOUTPUT
        FRMSingleStockRiskFileMgmt(AnsiString sinf, AnsiString soutf, double CL);
    FRMSSRISKOUTPUT R;
};
#endif
...
```

FRMSingleStockRisk.cpp

The implementation code results in the calculation of the sample return statistics, based on a price series. Note that this method receives a structure and passes two AnsiStrings and one double.

```
...
```

```
struct FRMSSRISKOUTPUT FRMSINGLESTOCKRISK::FRMSingleStockRiskFileMgmt(AnsiString inputsinf,
AnsiString inputsoutf, double CL)
{
    double Return;
    double ProductTotalReturn;
    double SumReturn;
    double SumReturnSquared;
    double SumReturnCubed;
    double SumReturnFourth;
    double SumHarmonicTotalReturn;
    double ArithmeticAverage;
    double GeometricAverage;
    double HarmonicAverage;
    double StandardDeviation;
    double Skewness;
    double ExcessKurtosis;
    double VaR;
    long int TotalCount;
    double TC;        // Total count as double
```

The confidence level is used for value-at-risk, a concept covered in chapter 6.

```
    ConfidenceLevel = CL;
    FRMSingleStockRiskFileMgmt(inputsinf, inputsoutf);   // Creates returns file
```

Remember when variables are defined, they can contain any number so we need to set them to zero before using them.

```
    SumReturn = SumReturnSquared = SumReturnCubed = SumReturnFourth = 0.0;
  SumHarmonicTotalReturn = 0.0;
   ProductTotalReturn = 1.0;
   ifstream inf;
   inf.open("FRMReturnData.dat", ios::in);
   inf >> TotalCount >> "\n";
   TC = (double)TotalCount; // Floating point version of total count
```

The next line is read, "while the file associated with inf is open, do the following."

```
    while (inf){
        inf >> Return >> ws;
        SumReturn += Return;
        ProductTotalReturn *= 1.0 + Return;
        SumHarmonicTotalReturn += 1.0 / (1.0 + Return);
        SumReturnSquared += pow(Return, 2.0);
        SumReturnCubed += pow(Return, 3.0);
        SumReturnFourth += pow(Return, 4.0);
    }
    ArithmeticAverage = SumReturn / TC;
    GeometricAverage = pow(ProductTotalReturn, 1.0/TC) - 1.0;
    HarmonicAverage = TC*pow(SumHarmonicTotalReturn, -1.0)-1.0;
    StandardDeviation = pow((1.0/(TC - 1.0))
       * (SumReturnSquared - TC*pow(ArithmeticAverage, 2.0)),0.5);
    Skewness = (SumReturnCubed/TC
       - (3.0*ArithmeticAverage / TC) * SumReturnSquared
       + (3.0*pow(ArithmeticAverage, 2.0) / TC) * SumReturn
       - (TC - 3.0)*pow(ArithmeticAverage, 3.0))
       / pow(StandardDeviation, 3.0);
    ExcessKurtosis = ((TC - 1.0)/((TC - 2)*(TC - 3)))
       * ( (TC + 1) * ( ( (SumReturnFourth/TC)
       - (4.0*ArithmeticAverage/TC)*SumReturnCubed
       + (6.0*pow(ArithmeticAverage,2.0)/TC)*SumReturnSquared
       + (TC - 4)*pow(ArithmeticAverage,4.0) )
       / pow( (SumReturnSquared/TC) - pow(ArithmeticAverage, 2.0), 2.0) )
       + 6.0 );
```

For simplicity, we assume a 252 trading day year when the statistics are annualized.

```
    R.ArithmeticAverage = ArithmeticAverage*252;
    R.GeometricAverage = pow(1.0 + GeometricAverage, 252.0) - 1.0;
    R.HarmonicAverage = pow(1.0 + HarmonicAverage, 252.0) - 1.0;
    R.StandardDeviation = StandardDeviation*pow(252.0,0.5);
    R.Skewness = Skewness;
    R.ExcessKurtosis = ExcessKurtosis;
    R.VaR = -A[m]*252.0;
```

```
        return R;
}
// Confidence level from standard file
void FRMSINGLESTOCKRISK::FRMSingleStockRiskFileMgmt(AnsiString inputsinf,
    AnsiString inputsoutf)
{
    int Counter, TotalCount;
    double P0, P1, R, inputCL;
    ifstream inf;
    inf.open(inputsinf.c_str(), ios::in);
    outf.open(inputsoutf.c_str());
    inf >> inputCL >> NumberofSecurities;    // Line 1
    if (ConfidenceLevel < 0.0) {    // Test if CL from GUI or file
        ConfidenceLevel = inputCL;
    }
    outf.width(6);  outf.setf(ios::right); outf.precision(2);
    outf.setf(ios::fixed, ios::floatfield); outf.setf(ios::showpoint);
    outf << ConfidenceLevel;
    outf.width(4);  outf.setf(ios::right); outf.setf(ios::fixed, ios::floatfield);
    outf << NumberofSecurities << "\n";
    inf >> word[0] >> word[1]; // Line 1
    Counter = -1;
    while (inf){
     inf >> word[0] >> P0 >> ws;
     Counter += 1;
    }
    TotalCount = Counter - 1; // Total number of returns (-1 from prices)
// Move position to top of file
    inf.clear();                // Forget reaching end of file
    inf.seekg(0, ios::beg);  // Go to beginning of file
    inf >> word[0] >> word[1];   // Line 1 - discarded here
    inf >> word[0] >> word[1];   // Line 2 - discarded here
    ofstream outs;
    outs.open("FRMReturnData.dat");
    outs.width(10);  outs.setf(ios::right); outs.setf(ios::fixed, ios::floatfield);
    outs << TotalCount << "\n";
    Counter = 0;
    while (inf){
        if(Counter==0)inf >> word[0] >> P0 >> ws;
        else {
            inf >> P1 >> ws;
```

Calculate returns from the price series.

```
            R = (P1/P0) - 1.0;
            P0=P1;
            outs.width(10);  outs.setf(ios::right); outs.precision(6);
            outs.setf(ios::fixed, ios::floatfield); outs.setf(ios::showpoint);
            outs << R;
            if(!(Counter%10))outs << "\n";
        }
        inf >> word[0] >> ws;
        Counter += 1;
    }
    outs.flush(); // Make sure all data written to file
// Used for historical value-at-risk calculation
    AnsiString infsort, outfsort;
    infsort = "FRMReturnData.dat";
    outfsort = "FRMReturnSort.prn";
```

The returns are sorted for the value-at-risk calculation covered in chapter 6.

```
    FRMSetUp(infsort, outfsort);
    m = int((double(TotalCount))*(1.0-(ConfidenceLevel/100.0)));
// Note: Because FRMSetUp() is public in FRMSPHISTORICVAR, A[m] is visible
    outf << "Historical VaR at " << ConfidenceLevel << "% for "
        << TotalCount << " returns is ";
    outf.width(10);  outf.setf(ios::right); outf.precision(6);
    outf.setf(ios::fixed, ios::floatfield); outf.setf(ios::showpoint);
    outf << -A[m]*252;
    outf << "\n (assuming daily data, annualized with 252)";
}
```

References

See references in the supplement to this module.

Appendix 5.3: Interface code comments

The graphical user interface for this module is illustrated below.

The input data for this illustration is contained in the file FRMSingleStockRiskInputs.dat.

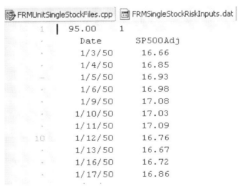

The following are excerpts from the interface header code with selected comments added.

FRMUnitSingleStockFiles.h

The output is contained in a structure for ease of implementation. Specifically, you just return the object's address and not all the variables in the object.

```
...
#include "c:\FRMRepository\FRMSingleStockRisk.cpp"
#ifndef FRMSSRISKOUTPUTSTRUCT
#define FRMSSRISKOUTPUTSTRUCT
struct FRMSSRISKOUTPUT
{
    double ArithmeticAverage;
    double GeometricAverage;
    double HarmonicAverage;
```

```
   double StandardDeviation;
   double Skewness;
   double ExcessKurtosis;
   double VaR;
};
#endif
//-----------------------------------------------------------------------
class TSingleStockRiskForm : public TForm
{
__published:   // IDE-managed Components
   TMemo *ProgramDescription;
...
   TButton *btnExit;
   void __fastcall btnExitClick(TObject *Sender);
   void __fastcall btnRunClick(TObject *Sender);
private: // User declarations
```

Both the implementation class and the output data file have to be instantiated.

```
   FRMSINGLESTOCKRISK HV;
   FRMSSRISKOUTPUT SS;
   double ConfidenceLevel;
public:      // User declarations
   __fastcall TSingleStockRiskForm(TComponent* Owner);
   void __fastcall FRMExecute(void);
};
//-----------------------------------------------------------------------
extern PACKAGE TSingleStockRiskForm *SingleStockRiskForm;
//-----------------------------------------------------------------------
#endif
```

The following are excerpts from the interface code with selected comments added.

FRMUnitSingleStockFiles.cpp

In the snippet of code below, note there is only one call to the method, FRMSingleStockRiskFileMgmt, and the return value is the structure. After this method is run, we have all the output values we need and can report them wherever desired, such as a form (in this case).

```
...
   AnsiString sinf, soutf;
   sinf = editSSRInputsFileName->Text;
   soutf = editSSROutputsFileName->Text;
   ConfidenceLevel = StrToFloat(editConfidenceLevel->Text);
   SS = HV.FRMSingleStockRiskFileMgmt(sinf, soutf, ConfidenceLevel);
   outputArithmeticAverage->Text
     = FloatToStrF(SS.ArithmeticAverage*100.0, ffFixed, 15, 6);
   outputArithmeticAverage->Visible = true;
   lblArithmeticAverage->Visible = true;
   outputGeometricAverage->Text
     = FloatToStrF(SS.GeometricAverage*100.0, ffFixed, 15, 6);
   outputGeometricAverage->Visible = true;
   lblGeometricAverage->Visible = true;
...
```

Module 5.4: Stock Option Greeks

Learning objectives

- Explain how to compute analytic Black, Scholes, Merton stock option valuation model first and second derivatives ("greeks")
- Contrast these "greeks" with the binomial option valuation model numerical "greeks"
- Use classes to manage input data

Module overview

In this module we review analytic and introduce numerical "greeks."

Option valuation models

From Module 4.1, we know Black, Scholes, Merton option valuation model can be expressed as

$$C = Se^{-\delta T} N(d_1) - Xe^{-rT} N(d_2)$$

$$P = Xe^{-rT} N(-d_2) - Se^{-\delta T} N(-d_1)$$

where $N(d)$ is the area under the standard cumulative normal distribution up to d (see Module 3.2), or

$$N(d) = \int_{-\infty}^{d} \frac{e^{-x^2/2}}{\sqrt{2\pi}} dx$$

$$d_1 = \frac{\ln\left(\dfrac{S}{X}\right) + \left(r - \delta + \dfrac{\sigma^2}{2}\right)T}{\sigma\sqrt{T}}$$

$$d_2 = d_1 - \sigma\sqrt{T}$$

The multi-period binomial option valuation model is simply the present value of the expected terminal payout. For European-style call and put options, we have

$$C = e^{-rT} \sum_{j=0}^{n} \left(\frac{n!}{j!(n-j)!}\right) \pi^j (1-\pi)^{n-j} \max\left(0, u^j d^{n-j} S_0 - X\right)$$

$$P = e^{-rT} \sum_{j=0}^{n} \left(\frac{n!}{j!(n-j)!}\right) \pi^j (1-\pi)^{n-j} \max\left(0, X - u^j d^{n-j} S_0\right)$$

where

$$u = \frac{e^{(r-q)\Delta t + \frac{\sigma\sqrt{\Delta t}}{\sqrt{\pi(1-\pi)}}}}{\pi e^{\frac{\sigma\sqrt{\Delta t}}{\sqrt{\pi(1-\pi)}}} + (1-\pi)}$$

$$d = \frac{e^{(r-q)\Delta t}}{\pi e^{\frac{\sigma\sqrt{\Delta t}}{\sqrt{\pi(1-\pi)}}} + (1-\pi)}$$

$$\Delta t = \frac{T}{n} \text{ (be sure to convert integer n to double)}$$

Black, Scholes, Merton option valuation model analytic "greeks"

We now cover what are called the "greeks." The term greeks is used for mathematical derivatives of financial derivatives, options in this case. Specifically, we focus here on understanding delta, gamma, vega, theta and rho. Delta measures an option Value's sensitivity to changes in the underlying instrument's price. Gamma measures the delta's sensitivity to changes in the underlying instrument's price. Vega (also known as kappa, lambda, and sigma) measures an option price's sensitivity to changes in the underlying asset's volatility. Theta measures an option price's sensitivity to changes in the time to maturity. Rho measures an option price's sensitivity to changes in the interest rate.

Delta: $\Delta_c \equiv \dfrac{dC}{dS} = e^{-\delta T} N(d_1), \ \Delta_p \equiv \dfrac{dP}{dS} = -e^{-\delta T} N(-d_1)$

Sketch of proof: We cover a few preliminary concepts before providing a sketch of the derivation of delta. Based on put-call parity ($C = Se^{-\delta T} - Xe^{-rT} + P$), we can infer $\Delta_c = e^{-\delta T} + \Delta_p$. Also, note from the definitions of d_1 and d_2, we can express them as

$$d_1 = \frac{\ln\left(\dfrac{S}{X}\right) + \left(r - \delta + \dfrac{\sigma^2}{2}\right)T}{\sigma\sqrt{T}} = \frac{\ln(S)}{\sigma\sqrt{T}} + \frac{-\ln(X) + \left(r - \delta + \dfrac{\sigma^2}{2}\right)T}{\sigma\sqrt{T}}$$

$$d_2 = d_1 - \sigma\sqrt{T} = \frac{\ln(S)}{\sigma\sqrt{T}} + \frac{-\ln(X) + \left(r - \delta + \dfrac{\sigma^2}{2}\right)T}{\sigma\sqrt{T}} - \sigma\sqrt{T}$$

Therefore,

$$\frac{dd_1}{dS} = \frac{dd_2}{dS} = \frac{1}{S\sigma\sqrt{T}} \ \textbf{(Derivatives of d's relation)}$$

From the definition of the standard normal cumulative distribution function ($N(d) = \int\limits_{x=-\infty}^{x=d} \dfrac{e^{-x^2/2}}{\sqrt{2\pi}} dx$), we have the first derivative of an integral is the integrand evaluated at d.

$$\frac{dN(d)}{dd} \equiv n(d) = \frac{e^{-d^2/2}}{\sqrt{2\pi}} \ \textbf{(Standard normal probability density function)}$$

Lemma: $n(d_1) = \dfrac{Xe^{-rT} n(d_2)}{Se^{-\delta T}}$ or $n(d_2) = \dfrac{Se^{-\delta T} n(d_1)}{Xe^{-rT}}$

Lemma proof: Rearranging, we have

$$\frac{Se^{-\delta T}}{Xe^{-rT}} = \frac{n(d_2)}{n(d_1)} = \frac{\dfrac{e^{-d_2^2/2}}{\sqrt{2\pi}}}{\dfrac{e^{-d_1^2/2}}{\sqrt{2\pi}}} = e^{\left(d_1^2 - d_2^2\right)/2}$$

Focusing on the exponent,

$$\frac{d_1^2 - d_2^2}{2} = \frac{1}{2}\left\{d_1^2 - \left(d_1 - \sigma\sqrt{T}\right)^2\right\} = \frac{1}{2}\left\{d_1^2 - d_1^2 + 2d_1\sigma\sqrt{T} - \sigma^2 T\right\}$$

$$= d_1\sigma\sqrt{T} - \frac{\sigma^2 T}{2}$$

$$= \left[\frac{\ln\left(\frac{S}{X}\right) + \left(r - \delta + \frac{\sigma^2}{2}\right)T}{\sigma\sqrt{T}}\right]\sigma\sqrt{T} - \frac{\sigma^2 T}{2} = \ln\left(\frac{S}{X}\right) + \left(r - \delta\right)T$$

Therefore,

$$e^{\left(d_1^2 - d_2^2\right)/2} = e^{\ln\left(\frac{S}{X}\right) + \left(r - \delta\right)T} = \frac{Se^{-\delta T}}{Xe^{-rT}} \qquad \text{Lemma QED}$$

With this background information and perhaps a review of these concepts from other sources, we are now ready to sketch the call delta proof. Based on fundamental calculus rules and the Black, Scholes, Merton call formula, we have

$$\frac{dC}{dS} = e^{-\delta T}N(d_1) + Se^{-\delta T}\frac{dN(d_1)}{dS} - Xe^{-rT}\frac{dN(d_2)}{dS}$$

$$= e^{-\delta T}N(d_1) + Se^{-\delta T}\frac{dN(d_1)}{dd_1}\frac{dd_1}{dS} - Xe^{-rT}\frac{dN(d_2)}{dd_2}\frac{dd_2}{dS}$$

From the derivatives of d's relation and the standard normal probability density function, we have

$$\frac{dC}{dS} = e^{-\delta T}N(d_1) + Se^{-\delta T}n(d_1)\frac{1}{S\sigma\sqrt{T}} - Xe^{-rT}n(d_2)\frac{1}{S\sigma\sqrt{T}}$$

Finally, based on the lemma above, we have demonstrated that

$$\frac{dC}{dS} \equiv \Delta_c = e^{-\delta T}N(d_1)$$

and based on put-call parity, we have (recall $N(-d_1) = 1 - N(d_1)$ due to the symmetry of the standard normal distribution)

$$\Delta_p = \Delta_c - e^{-\delta T} = e^{-\delta T}N(d_1) - e^{-\delta T} = e^{-\delta T}\left[N(d_1) - 1\right] = -e^{-\delta T}N(-d_1) \qquad \text{QED}$$

The value of the European call option at expiration is either \$0 if it is out-of-the-money ($S_T < X$) or the intrinsic value (the dollar amount it is in-the-money) ($S_T - X$) when the stock ends up in-the-money ($S_T > X$). Prior to expiration, the option has time value as well as intrinsic value. The time value of an option depends on the relationship between the current stock price and the strike price. Its particular functional form is illustrated below.

In the graph below, we plot the stock price on the horizontal axis and the option prices on the vertical axis. The positive sloped line is the call and the negative sloped line is the put.

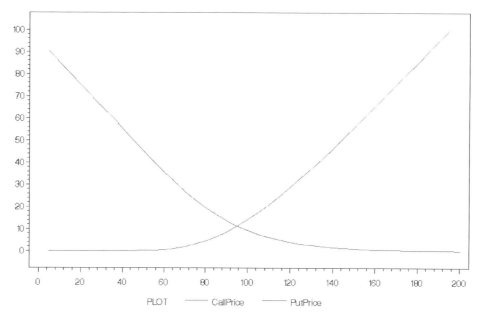

Parameters: Strike = 100, Rate = 5%, Dividend = 0%, Volatility = 30%, Maturity = 1 year

The value of the European-style put option at expiration is either $0 if it is out-of-the-money $(S_T > X)$ or the intrinsic value (the dollar amount it is in-the-money) $(X - S_T)$ when the stock ends up in-the-money $(S_T < X)$. Prior to expiration, the option has time value, as well as intrinsic value. The time value of an option depends on the relationship between the current stock price and the strike price. For puts it is theoretically possible for the put option's value to fall below its intrinsic value. The breach of the lower bound is illustrated below.

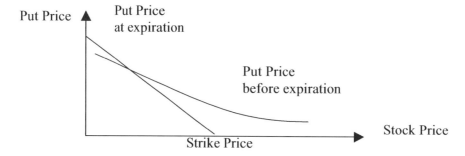

We now address the geometrical interpretation of delta. Delta is the change in the value of the option for a small change in the value of the stock or the first derivative of the option with respect to the stock. Graphically for the call option, delta is the slope of the call price with respect to the stock price. Note that the delta changes as we change the current stock price.

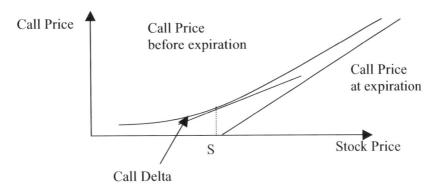

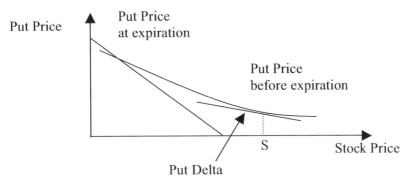

Graphically, the delta of a put option is illustrated below.

The relationship between the change in the option price, delta, and the change in the asset price can be expressed as approximately

Change in Option Value = Δ * Change in Stock Price

Example: Suppose the call option delta is 0.6 and the stock price increased by $0.5, approximately how much did the call price increase?

Change in the Call Value = 0.6 * $0.5 = $0.3

Rearranging the expression above, we have

Δ_c = Change in Option Value / Change in Stock Price

Example: Suppose an option price rises by $0.3 when the stock price increases by $0.5. What is the estimated delta?

Δ_c = $0.3 / $0.5 = 0.6 or 60%

A delta-neutral portfolio is a portfolio that has a portfolio delta of zero. A zero delta implies that the value of the portfolio does not change for infinitesimal changes in the stock price. Hence, the value of the portfolio is not affected by small changes in the stock price. Therefore, to hedge against small changes in the stock price, trades should be conducted such that the portfolio delta is zero.

Example: Suppose you had a portfolio with a delta of 24 and a particular call option has a delta of 0.6. If you desired to completely hedge this portfolio with this call option, describe the appropriate trade. You would sell 40 call options each having a delta of –0.6 (because you sold). The delta of the short 40 calls is –24 (= 40 * (–0.6)) so the new portfolio delta is zero.

Recall put-call parity can be expressed as

$$C = Se^{-\delta T} - Xe^{-rT} + P$$

Recall that delta is the first derivative of the option value with respect to the stock value. Hence, we can take the first derivative of both sides of this equation. Thus, the delta of the call is related to the delta of the put as (the discounted strike price is unaffected by changes in the stock price)

$$\Delta_c = 1 + \Delta_p$$

or

$$\Delta_p = \Delta_c - 1$$

For small changes in the stock price for a deep out-of-the-money call, the call price changes very little, hence the delta is close to zero. The same is true for deep out-of-the-money puts. For small changes in the stock for deep in-the-money calls, the call price changes almost dollar for dollar with the stock price, hence the delta is close to one. For deep in-the-money puts, the delta is close to -1 (as the stock goes up \$1, the put value falls by almost \$1). Hence, the delta of puts and calls are constrained in the following way

$$0 \le \Delta_c \le 1$$

$$-1 \le \Delta_p \le 0$$

The deltas of puts and calls can be expressed as

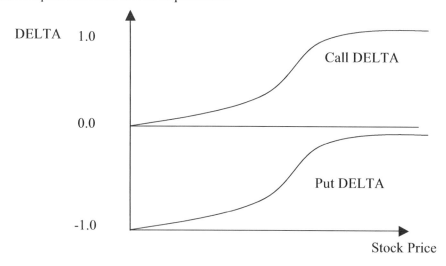

We can create a synthetic call using bonds and the underlying asset. It can be demonstrated that a portfolio of $\Pi = -C + SN(d_1)$ is riskless because $N(d_1)$ is the delta. Hence the portfolio, Π, should grow at the risk-free interest rate. Rearranging this relationship, we have $C = SN(d_1) - \Pi$ which is the Black-Scholes formula with $\Pi = Xe^{-rT}N(d_2)$. Thus, a call option can be created synthetically using the underlying asset (buying $N(d_1)$ shares) and partially financing it with borrowing of $\Pi = Xe^{-rT}N(d_2)$.

The delta-neutral portfolio and portfolio insurance: Recall that portfolio insurance can be represented as long a stock and long a put or

$$S + P = S + Xe^{-rT}N(-d_2) + S(\Delta_p) = S(1 + \Delta_p) + Xe^{-rT}N(-d_2)$$

(by substituting the Black-Scholes-Merton formula and the definition of Δ). Hence, portfolio insurance is related to the concept of a delta neutral portfolio with additional exposure in stock. Recall that $\Delta_p < 0$ and $\Delta_c = 1 + \Delta_p$.

Gamma: $\Gamma_c \equiv \dfrac{d^2C}{dS^2} = \dfrac{e^{-\delta T}n(d_1)}{S\sigma\sqrt{T}} = \dfrac{d^2P}{dS^2} \equiv \Gamma_p$

Sketch of proof: Recall based on put-call parity $\Delta_p = \Delta_c - e^{-\delta T}$ and therefore we know

$$\frac{d\Delta_p}{dS} = \frac{d\Delta_c}{dS}$$

From the definition of call delta,

$$\frac{d^2C}{dS^2} = \frac{d\Delta_c}{dS} = e^{-\delta T}\frac{dN(d_1)}{dS} = e^{-\delta T}\frac{dN(d_1)}{dd_1}\frac{dd_1}{dS} = \frac{e^{-qT}n(d_1)}{S\sigma\sqrt{T}} \qquad \text{QED}$$

Vega: $\nu_c \equiv \dfrac{dC}{d\sigma} = Se^{-\delta T}n(d_1)\sqrt{T} = Xe^{-rT}n(d_2)\sqrt{T} = \dfrac{dP}{d\sigma} \equiv \nu_p$

Sketch of proof: From put-call parity ($C = Se^{-\delta T} - Xe^{-rT} + P$), we know $\dfrac{dC}{d\sigma} = \dfrac{dP}{d\sigma}$. Note

$$\frac{dC}{d\sigma} = Se^{-\delta T}\frac{dN(d_1)}{d\sigma} - Xe^{-rT}\frac{dN(d_2)}{d\sigma}$$

$$= Se^{-\delta T}\frac{dN(d_1)}{dd_1}\frac{dd_1}{d\sigma} - Xe^{-rT}\frac{dN(d_2)}{dd_2}\frac{dd_2}{d\sigma}$$

$$= Se^{-\delta T}n(d_1)\frac{dd_1}{d\sigma} - Xe^{-rT}n(d_2)\frac{dd_2}{d\sigma}$$

From the lemma above, we know

$$n(d_2) = \frac{Se^{-\delta T}n(d_1)}{Xe^{-rT}}$$

Thus,

$$\frac{dC}{d\sigma} = Se^{-\delta T}n(d_1)\frac{dd_1}{d\sigma} - Xe^{-rT}\left[\frac{Se^{-\delta T}n(d_1)}{Xe^{-rT}}\right]\frac{dd_2}{d\sigma}$$

$$= Se^{-\delta T}n(d_1)\left[\frac{dd_1}{d\sigma} - \frac{dd_2}{d\sigma}\right] = Se^{-\delta T}n(d_1)\sqrt{T} = Xe^{-rT}n(d_2)\sqrt{T}$$

because $\dfrac{dd_2}{d\sigma} = \dfrac{dd_1}{d\sigma} - \sqrt{T}$ and by rearranging the lemma result as $n(d_1) = \dfrac{Xe^{-rT}n(d_2)}{Se^{-\delta T}}$.   QED

Vega is the first derivative of the option value with respect to volatility. Neither the stock nor the risk-free interest rate is influenced by changes in the stock's volatility. Volatility impacts both calls and puts the same. The value of puts and calls as a function of volatility can be illustrated as (we assume here that $S = X$) :

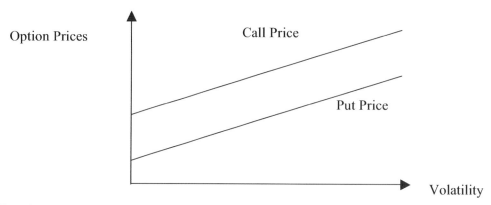

For call options that are deep out-of-the-money, the call price changes very little with a small change in volatility (it does not really change the probability of the stock reaching the strike price); hence, the vega is close to zero. The same is true for deep out-of-the-money puts. For small changes in the volatility for deep in-the-money calls, the call price does not change much because it is already in-the-money; hence, again the vega is close to zero. The relationship between the stock price and vega is illustrated in the following way.

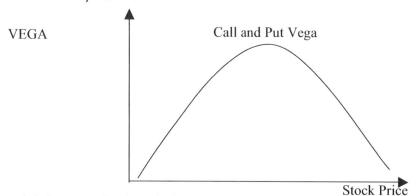

In the graph below, we plot the volatility on the horizontal axis and the option prices on the vertical axis. The higher positive sloped line is the call and the lower positive sloped line is the put. Notice that the relationship is virtually linear.

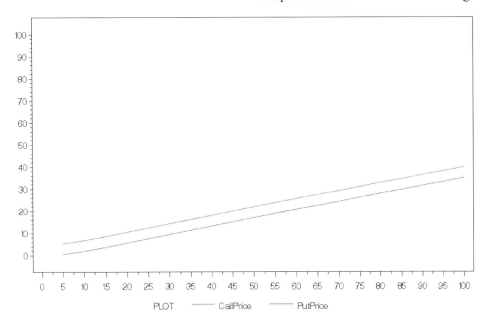

Parameters: Stock = 100, Strike = 100, Rate = 5%, Dividend = 0%, Maturity = 1 year

Theta: $\theta_c \equiv \dfrac{dC}{dt} = -\dfrac{dC}{dT} = -\dfrac{Se^{-\delta T}n(d_1)\sigma}{2\sqrt{T}} - rXe^{-rT}N(d_2) + \delta Se^{-\delta T}N(d_1)$

$\theta_p \equiv \dfrac{dP}{dt} = -\dfrac{dP}{dT} = -\dfrac{Se^{-\delta T}n(d_1)\sigma}{2\sqrt{T}} + rXe^{-rT}N(-d_2) - \delta Se^{-\delta T}N(-d_1)$

Sketch of proof: Theta is defined as the change in the option value for a given change in calendar time, measured in years. As calendar time passes, the time to maturity declines. Therefore, a negative relationship exists between calendar time and time to maturity. We derive results for time to maturity and then at the end switch the sign. Time to maturity appears in a variety of places in the option valuation formulas. Therefore, this proof is rather tedious. Consider the following preliminaries:

$$\frac{de^{-rT}}{dT} = -re^{-rT}$$

$$\frac{de^{-\delta T}}{dT} = -\delta e^{-\delta T}$$

$$\frac{dd_2}{dT} = \frac{dd_1}{dT} - \frac{\sigma T^{-1/2}}{2}$$

Therefore,

$$\frac{dC}{dT} = S\frac{de^{-\delta T}}{dT}N(d_1) + Se^{-\delta T}\frac{dN(d_1)}{dT} - X\frac{de^{-rT}}{dT}N(d_2) - Xe^{-rT}\frac{dN(d_2)}{dT}$$

$$= -\delta Se^{-\delta T}N(d_1) + Se^{-\delta T}\frac{dN(d_1)}{dd_1}\frac{dd_1}{dT} + rXe^{-rT}N(d_2) - Xe^{-rT}\frac{dN(d_2)}{dd_2}\frac{dd_2}{dT}$$

$$= -\delta Se^{-\delta T}N(d_1) + rXe^{-rT}N(d_2) + Se^{-\delta T}n(d_1)\frac{dd_1}{dT} - Xe^{-rT}n(d_2)\frac{dd_2}{dT}$$

Based on $\dfrac{dd_2}{dT} = \dfrac{dd_1}{dT} - \dfrac{\sigma T^{-1/2}}{2}$ and the lemma above ($n(d_2) = \dfrac{Se^{-\delta T} n(d_1)}{Xe^{-rT}}$), we have

$$\frac{dC}{dT} = -\delta Se^{-\delta T} N(d_1) + rXe^{-rT} N(d_2) + Se^{-\delta T} n(d_1) \frac{dd_1}{dT} - Xe^{-rT} \left[\frac{Se^{-\delta T} n(d_1)}{Xe^{-rT}} \right] \left[\frac{dd_1}{dT} - \frac{\sigma T^{-1/2}}{2} \right]$$

$$= -\delta Se^{-\delta T} N(d_1) + rXe^{-rT} N(d_2) + \frac{Se^{-\delta T} n(d_1) \sigma}{2\sqrt{T}}$$

Recall the sign change related to how time is measured, we have

$$\theta_c \equiv \frac{dC}{dt} = -\frac{dC}{dT} = -\frac{Se^{-qT} n(d_1) \sigma}{2\sqrt{T}} - rXe^{-rT} N(d_2) + qSe^{-qT} N(d_1)$$

From put-call parity, we have

$$\frac{dP}{dT} = \frac{dC}{dT} + \delta Se^{-\delta T} - rXe^{-rT}$$

Substituting for call results above,

$$\frac{dP}{dT} = -\delta Se^{-\delta T} N(d_1) + rXe^{-rT} N(d_2) + \frac{Se^{-\delta T} n(d_1) \sigma}{2\sqrt{T}} + \delta Se^{-\delta T} - rXe^{-rT}$$

$$= -\delta Se^{-\delta T} N(-d_1) + rXe^{-rT} N(-d_2) + \frac{Se^{-\delta T} n(d_1) \sigma}{2\sqrt{T}}$$

because of the normal distribution symmetry. Thus,

$$\theta_p \equiv \frac{dP}{dt} = -\frac{dP}{dT} = -\frac{Se^{-\delta T} n(d_1) \sigma}{2\sqrt{T}} + rXe^{-rT} N(-d_2) - \delta Se^{-\delta T} N(-d_1) \qquad \text{QED}$$

In the graph below, we plot the time to expiration in days on the horizontal axis and the option prices on the vertical axis. The higher positive sloped line is the call and the lower positive sloped line is the put. Notice that the value of the option declines significantly near expiration.

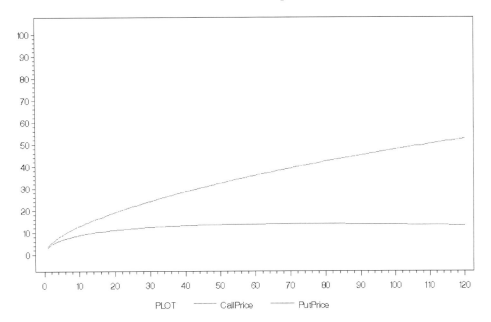

Parameters: Stock = 100, Strike = 100, Rate = 5%, Dividend = 0%, Volatility = 30%

Rho: $\rho_c = XTe^{-rT}N(d_2)$, $\rho_p = -XTe^{-rT}N(-d_2)$

Sketch of proof: From the definition of d_2, we know

$$\frac{dd_2}{dr} = \frac{dd_1}{dr}$$

and put call parity

$$\frac{dC}{dr} = rXe^{-rT} + \frac{dP}{dr}$$

From the call option formula,

$$\frac{dC}{dr} = Se^{-\delta T}\frac{dN(d_1)}{dr} - X\frac{de^{-rT}}{dr}N(d_2) - Xe^{-rT}\frac{dN(d_2)}{dr}$$

$$= Se^{-\delta T}\frac{dN(d_1)}{dd_1}\frac{dd_1}{dr} + rXe^{-rT}N(d_2) - Xe^{-rT}\frac{dN(d_2)}{dd_2}\frac{dd_2}{dr}$$

$$= rXe^{-rT}N(d_2) + Se^{-\delta T}n(d_1)\frac{dd_1}{dr} - Xe^{-rT}n(d_2)\frac{dd_2}{dr}$$

Based on $\dfrac{dd_2}{dr} = \dfrac{dd_1}{dr}$ and the lemma above ($n(d_2) = \dfrac{Se^{-\delta T}n(d_1)}{Xe^{-rT}}$), we have

$$\frac{dC}{dT} = rXe^{-rT}N(d_2) + Se^{-\delta T}n(d_1)\frac{dd_1}{dr} - Xe^{-rT}\left[\frac{Se^{-\delta T}n(d_1)}{Xe^{-rT}}\right]\frac{dd_1}{dr} = rXe^{-rT}N(d_2)$$

Substituting this result into the put-call parity expression above,

$$\frac{dP}{dr} = \frac{dC}{dr} - rXe^{-rT} = rXe^{-rT}N(d_2) - rXe^{-rT} = -rXe^{-rT}N(-d_2) \qquad \text{QED}$$

In the graph below, we plot the interest rate on the horizontal axis and the option prices on the vertical axis. The positive sloped line is the call and the negative sloped line is the put. At a zero interest rate, the value of the call equals the value of the put.

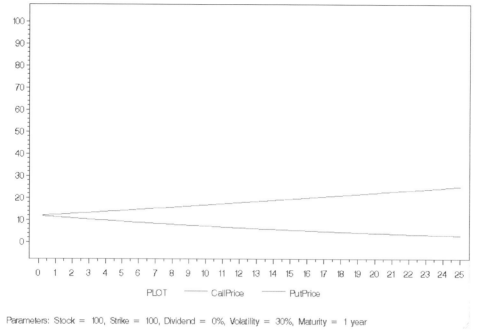

Parameters: Stock = 100, Strike = 100, Dividend = 0%, Volatility = 30%, Maturity = 1 year

In the graph below, we plot the dividend yield on the horizontal axis and the option prices on the vertical axis. The negative sloped line is the call and the positive sloped line is the put. When the interest rate equals the dividend yield, the value of the call equals the value of the put.

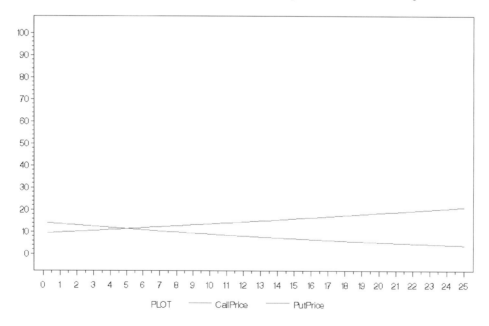

Parameters: Stock = 100, Strike = 100, Rate = 5%, Volatility = 30%, Maturity = 1 year

Binomial option valuation model numerical "greeks"

We will provide a much more extensive discussion of numerical derivatives estimation in Module 5.7. For now, recall the definition of derivative for some generic function $y = f(x)$ is the limit as h goes to zero, where the relationship can be expressed as

$$\frac{df(x)}{dx} = \lim_{h \to 0} \frac{f(x+h) - f(x)}{h}$$

As h gets "small" there are at least two sources of error: truncation error (higher order Taylor series terms are ignored) and round off error (machine floating point error). We use the centered difference approach, where

$$\frac{df(x)}{dx} = \frac{f(x+h) - f(x-h)}{2h}$$

This approach to estimating derivatives will produce inaccurate results in many circumstances. This approach, however, is easy and often very accurate. Unfortunately, you have to know the correct values in order to know when it is wrong. We can compare the binomial numerical "greeks" with the limiting Black, Scholes, Merton analytic results to spot numerical problems.

The binomial "greeks" applied here are as follows:

$$\Delta_c = \frac{C(S+0.01S) - C(S-0.01S)}{2(0.01S)}, \quad \Delta_p = \frac{P(S+0.01S) - P(S-0.01S)}{2(0.01S)}$$

$$\Gamma_c = \frac{C(S+0.01S) - 2C(S) + C(S-0.01S)}{(0.01S)^2}, \quad \Gamma_p = \frac{P(S+0.01S) - 2P(S) + P(S-0.01S)}{(0.01S)^2}$$

$$v_c = \frac{C(\sigma+0.01\sigma) - C(\sigma-0.01\sigma)}{2(0.01\sigma)}, \quad v_c = \frac{P(\sigma+0.01\sigma) - P(\sigma-0.01\sigma)}{2(0.01\sigma)}$$

$$\theta_c = \frac{C(T+0.01T) - C(T-0.01T)}{2(0.01T)}, \quad \theta_c = \frac{P(T+0.01T) - P(T-0.01T)}{2(0.01T)}$$

$$\rho_c = \frac{C(r+0.01r) - C(r-0.01r)}{2(0.01r)}, \quad \rho_c = \frac{P(r+0.01r) - P(r-0.01r)}{2(0.01r)}$$

Note: Volatility and rate expressed in decimal form.

Implementation code comments

The implementation code is separate for the binomial and Black, Scholes, Merton approach. We review first the Black, Scholes, Merton approach.

FRMBSMDYOVM.h

Several programs use this class; therefore, you have a variety of classes included. The long double type is used for testing the numerical accuracy of a variety of calculations (not done here).

```
...
#ifndef FRMCDFFILE
#define FRMCDFFILE
#include "c:\FRMRepository\FRMCDF.cpp"
#endif

#ifndef FRMBRENTFILE
```

```
#define FRMBRENTFILE
#include "c:\FRMRepository\FRMBrent.cpp"
#endif
...
class FRMBSMDYOVM : public FRMCDF, BRENT
{
...
    long double BSMDYCallValue();
    long double BSMDYPutValue();
    long double BSMDYCallDelta();
    long double BSMDYPutDelta();
...
```

FRMBSMDYOVM.cpp

With the Black, Scholes, Merton approach "greeks" are easy to compute once the input data is placed within the class and the appropriate methods, such as N(d) calculations, are available. Within the BSMDYOVMSetData method, we instantiate a class OPTIONDATA with O. We can then pass all of the inputs to the OPTIONDATA class via O. Once the data is set correctly, the methods for each greek are easy to code with the formulas from the beginning of this module.

```
...
void FRMBSMDYOVM::BSMDYOVMSetData(class OPTIONDATA O)
{
    StockPrice = O.StockPrice;
    StrikePrice = O.StrikePrice;
    TimeToMaturity = O.TimeToMaturity;
    Volatility = O.Volatility;
    InterestRate = O.InterestRate;
    DividendYield = O.DividendYield;
    MaxX = O.MaxX;
    MinX = O.MinX;
}
//-----------------------------------------------------------------------
long double FRMBSMDYOVM::BSMDYCallValue()
{
    CallValue = StockPrice*exp((-DividendYield/100.0)*TimeToMaturity) * FRMND(BSMDYd1())
        - StrikePrice * exp(-(InterestRate/100.0)* TimeToMaturity) * FRMND(BSMDYd2());
    BSMDYCallLowerBound();
    return CallValue;
}
//-----------------------------------------------------------------------
long double FRMBSMDYOVM::BSMDYPutValue()
{
    PutValue = StrikePrice*exp(-(InterestRate/100.0) * TimeToMaturity) * FRMND(-BSMDYd2())
        - StockPrice*exp((-DividendYield/100.0)*TimeToMaturity) * FRMND(-BSMDYd1());
    BSMDYPutLowerBound();
    return PutValue;
}
//-----------------------------------------------------------------------
double FRMBSMDYOVM::BSMDYCallLowerBound()
{
    LowerBound = StockPrice*exp((-DividendYield/100.0)*TimeToMaturity)
        - StrikePrice * exp(-(InterestRate/100.0) * TimeToMaturity);
    if (LowerBound > 0.0 && CallValue < LowerBound) CallValue = LowerBound;
    return CallValue;
}
//-----------------------------------------------------------------------
double FRMBSMDYOVM::BSMDYPutLowerBound()
{
    LowerBound = StrikePrice * exp(-(InterestRate/100.0) * TimeToMaturity)
        - StockPrice*exp((-DividendYield/100.0)*TimeToMaturity);
    if (LowerBound > 0.0 && PutValue < LowerBound) PutValue = LowerBound;
    return PutValue;
}
//-----------------------------------------------------------------------
double FRMBSMDYOVM::BSMDYd1()
{
    return (log((StockPrice*exp((-DividendYield/100.0)*TimeToMaturity))/StrikePrice)
        + ((InterestRate/100.0) + pow(Volatility/100.0, 2)/2.0) * TimeToMaturity)
```

```
          / ((Volatility/100.0) * pow(TimeToMaturity, 0.5));
}
//----------------------------------------------------------------------
double FRMBSMDYOVM::BSMDYd2()
{
    return BSMDYd1() - (Volatility/100.0) * pow(TimeToMaturity, 0.5);
}
//----------------------------------------------------------------------
long double FRMBSMDYOVM::BSMDYCallDelta()
{
    return exp(-(DividendYield/100.0) * TimeToMaturity)*FRMND(BSMDYd1());
}
//----------------------------------------------------------------------
long double FRMBSMDYOVM::BSMDYPutDelta()
{
    return exp(-(DividendYield/100.0) * TimeToMaturity)*(FRMND(BSMDYd1())-1.0);
}
//----------------------------------------------------------------------
long double FRMBSMDYOVM::BSMDYCallGamma()
{
    return exp(-(DividendYield/100.0) * TimeToMaturity)
        * (exp(-pow(BSMDYd1(),2)/2.0)/(pow(2.0 * PI * TimeToMaturity, 0.5)
        * StockPrice*(Volatility/100.0)));
}
//----------------------------------------------------------------------
long double FRMBSMDYOVM::BSMDYPutGamma()
{
    return BSMDYCallGamma();
}
//----------------------------------------------------------------------
long double FRMBSMDYOVM::BSMDYCallVega()
{
    return exp(-(DividendYield/100.0) * TimeToMaturity)
        * (exp(-pow(BSMDYd1(),2)/2.0)/(pow(2.0 * PI, 0.5)))
        * StockPrice * pow(TimeToMaturity, 0.5);
}
//----------------------------------------------------------------------
long double FRMBSMDYOVM::BSMDYPutVega()
{
    return BSMDYCallVega();
}
//----------------------------------------------------------------------
long double FRMBSMDYOVM::BSMDYCallTheta()
{
    return -( (StockPrice*exp((-DividendYield/100.0)*TimeToMaturity)
        * (exp(-pow(BSMDYd1(),2.0)/2.0)/pow(2.0*PI,0.5))*(Volatility/100.0))
        / (2.0 * pow(TimeToMaturity,0.5)) )
        + (DividendYield/100.0)*StockPrice*exp((-DividendYield/100.0)*TimeToMaturity)
        * FRMND(BSMDYd1())
        - (InterestRate/100.0)*StrikePrice*exp(-(InterestRate/100.0) * TimeToMaturity)
        * FRMND(BSMDYd2());
}
//----------------------------------------------------------------------
long double FRMBSMDYOVM::BSMDYPutTheta()
{
    return -( (StockPrice*exp((-DividendYield/100.0)*TimeToMaturity)
        * (exp(-pow(BSMDYd1(),2.0)/2.0)/pow(2.0*PI,0.5))*(Volatility/100.0))
        / (2.0 * pow(TimeToMaturity,0.5)))
        - (DividendYield/100.0)*StockPrice*exp((-DividendYield/100.0)*TimeToMaturity)
        * FRMND(-BSMDYd1())
        + (InterestRate/100.0)*StrikePrice*exp(-(InterestRate/100.0) * TimeToMaturity)
        * FRMND(-BSMDYd2());
}
//----------------------------------------------------------------------
long double FRMBSMDYOVM::BSMDYCallRho()
{
    return StrikePrice*TimeToMaturity*exp(-(InterestRate/100.0) * TimeToMaturity)
        *FRMND(BSMDYd2());
}
//----------------------------------------------------------------------
long double FRMBSMDYOVM::BSMDYPutRho()
```

```
{
    return -StrikePrice*TimeToMaturity*exp(-(InterestRate/100.0) * TimeToMaturity)
        *FRMND(-BSMDYd2());
}
...
```

FRMAmerBinOVM.h

The binomial approach setup is similar to the Black, Scholes, Merton approach code. The input data is set within the class and then the appropriate methods can be called. Because we need an array, we declare it static to accommodate the potential for larger sizes and avoid the array being declared multiple times.

```
...
    void BinDYOVMSetData(class BOPTIONDATA B);
    double FRMAmerDivBinCall();
    double FRMAmerDivBinPut();
    double FRMAmerDivBinCallDelta();
    double FRMAmerDivBinPutDelta();
...
    static double OptionValue[OVARRAYSIZE];
...
};
double FRMBinDYOVM::OptionValue[OVARRAYSIZE];
...
```

FRMAmerBinOVM.cpp

As before, we deploy the Trigeorgis [1992] method for solving the binomial option value.

```
#include "FRMAmerBinOVM.h"
//---------------------------------------------------------------------
void FRMBinDYOVM::BinDYOVMSetData(class BOPTIONDATA B)
{
    StockPrice = B.StockPrice;
    StrikePrice = B.StrikePrice;
    TimeToMaturity = B.TimeToMaturity;
    Volatility = B.Volatility;
    InterestRate = B.InterestRate;
    DividendYield = B.DividendYield;
    NumberOfSteps = B.NumberOfSteps;
    Type = B.Type;
    DividendYield /= 100.0;
    InterestRate /= 100.0;
    Volatility = Volatility / 100.0;
}
long double FRMBinDYOVM::FRMBinDYOVMProbability(int N, int J, double prob)
{
    int i;
    double sum1, sum2;
    sum1 = sum2 = 0.0;
    if(J > N-J){
        for(i=J+1; i<=N; i++) sum1 += log(i);
        for(i=1; i<=N-J; i++) sum2 += log(i);
    } else {
        for(i=N-J+1; i<=N; i++) sum1 += log(i);
        for(i=1; i<=J; i++) sum2 += log(i);
    }
    return (exp(sum1 - sum2 + ((float)J) * log(prob)
        + ((float)(N - J)) * log(1.0 - prob)));
}

double FRMBinDYOVM::FRMMax(double X, double Y)
{
    if (X >= Y) return X;
    else return Y;
}
// American-style based on Trigeorgis [1992] method (see p. 125, BFDAWC++)
double FRMBinDYOVM::FRMAmerDivBinCall()
{
//  Preliminary Calculations (i.e. units, periods consistent and so forth.)
```

```
      AnnualRateDC = exp(InterestRate);
      Deltat = TimeToMaturity / NumberOfSteps;
      Deltay = pow( (pow(Volatility, 2.0) * Deltat +
         pow( (InterestRate - DividendYield - (pow(Volatility, 2.0) / 2.0)) , 2.0)
         * pow(Deltat, 2.0)), 0.5);
      PeriodicRate = pow(AnnualRateDC, Deltat);
      Prob = 0.5 + (0.5 * (InterestRate - DividendYield - (pow(Volatility, 2.0) / 2.0))
         * Deltat) / Deltay;
// Work on option value array
      for (j = NumberOfSteps; j >= 0; j--){     // Time steps (working backward through time)
         for (i = 0; i <= j; i++){        // Node steps (from lowest value to highest)
            if(j==NumberOfSteps){
               OptionValue[i] = FRMMax(0.0,
                  StockPrice * exp(-(double(NumberOfSteps - 2*i)) * Deltay) - StrikePrice);
            } else {
               OptionValue[i] = (1.0/PeriodicRate)
                  * (Prob * OptionValue[i+1] + (1.0 - Prob) * OptionValue[i]);
// Test whether exercise is optimal
               if (Type == 1) OptionValue[i] = FRMMax(OptionValue[i],
                  StockPrice * exp(-(double(j - 2*i)) * Deltay) - StrikePrice);
            };
         };
      };
      OptionValue[0] = FRMMax(StockPrice -
         StrikePrice*exp(-(InterestRate/100.0)*TimeToMaturity), OptionValue[0]);
      return OptionValue[0];
}


double FRMBinDYOVM::FRMAmerDivBinPut()
{
//   Preliminary Calculations (i.e. units, periods consistent and so forth.)
      AnnualRateDC = exp(InterestRate);
      Deltat = TimeToMaturity / NumberOfSteps;
      Deltay = pow( (pow(Volatility, 2.0) * Deltat +
         pow( (InterestRate - DividendYield - (pow(Volatility, 2.0) / 2.0)) , 2.0)
         * pow(Deltat, 2.0)), 0.5);
      PeriodicRate = pow(AnnualRateDC,Deltat);
      Prob = 0.5 + (0.5 * (InterestRate - DividendYield - (pow(Volatility, 2.0) / 2.0))
         * Deltat) / Deltay;
// Work on option value array
      for (j = NumberOfSteps; j >= 0; j--){     // Time steps (working backward through time)
         for (i = 0; i <= j; i++){        // Node steps (from lowest value to highest)
            if(j==NumberOfSteps){
               OptionValue[i] = FRMMax(0.0,
                  StrikePrice - StockPrice * exp(-(double(NumberOfSteps - 2*i)) * Deltay));
            } else {
               OptionValue[i] = (1.0/PeriodicRate)
                  * (Prob * OptionValue[i+1] + (1.0 - Prob) * OptionValue[i]);
// Test whether exercise is optimal
               if (Type == 1) OptionValue[i] = FRMMax(OptionValue[i],
                  StrikePrice - StockPrice * exp(-(double(j - 2*i)) * Deltay));
            };
         };
      };
      if (Type == 0) OptionValue[0] = FRMMax(StrikePrice*exp(-(InterestRate/100.0)*TimeToMaturity)
         - StockPrice, OptionValue[0]);
      return OptionValue[0];
}
```

The binomial "greeks" are easy to code once a functioning valuation model is in place. Each "greek" follows the same general approach.

```
double FRMBinDYOVM::FRMAmerDivBinCallDelta()
{
      double Original, High, Low, Change, OHigh, OLow;
      Original = StockPrice;    // Greek dependent
      Change = 0.01*Original;
      High = Original + Change;
      StockPrice = High;        // Greek dependent
      OHigh = FRMAmerDivBinCall();
      Low = Original - Change;
      StockPrice = Low;         // Greek dependent
```

```
    OLow = FRMAmerDivBinCall();
    StockPrice = Original;    // Greek dependent
    return (OHigh - OLow)/(High - Low);
}

double FRMBinDYOVM::FRMAmerDivBinPutDelta()
{
    double Original, High, Low, Change, OHigh, OLow;
    Original = StockPrice;    // Greek dependent
    Change = 0.01*Original;
    High = Original + Change;
    StockPrice = High;        // Greek dependent
    OHigh = FRMAmerDivBinPut();
    Low = Original - Change;
    StockPrice = Low;         // Greek dependent
    OLow = FRMAmerDivBinPut();
    StockPrice = Original;    // Greek dependent
    return (OHigh - OLow)/(High - Low);
}
// Binomial Gamma (Numerical)
double FRMBinDYOVM::FRMAmerDivBinCallGamma()
{
    double Original, High, Low, Change, OHigh, OLow, OMid;
    Original = StockPrice;    // Greek dependent
    Change = 0.01*Original;
    High = Original + Change;
    StockPrice = High;        // Greek dependent
    OHigh = FRMAmerDivBinCall();
    Low = Original - Change;
    StockPrice = Low;         // Greek dependent
    OLow = FRMAmerDivBinCall();
    StockPrice = Original;    // Greek dependent
    OMid = FRMAmerDivBinCall();
    return ((OHigh - OMid) - (OMid - OLow))/pow(Change, 2.0);
}

double FRMBinDYOVM::FRMAmerDivBinPutGamma()
{
    double Original, High, Low, Change, OHigh, OLow, OMid;
    Original = StockPrice;    // Greek dependent
    Change = 0.01*Original;
    High = Original + Change;
    StockPrice = High;        // Greek dependent
    OHigh = FRMAmerDivBinPut();
    Low = Original - Change;
    StockPrice = Low;         // Greek dependent
    OLow = FRMAmerDivBinPut();
    StockPrice = Original;    // Greek dependent
    OMid = FRMAmerDivBinPut();
    return ((OHigh - OMid) - (OMid - OLow))/pow(Change, 2.0);
}
...
```

References

See previous modules.

Appendix 5.4: Interface code comments

The graphical user interface used in this module is illustrated below.

	BSM OVM		Binomial OVM		
	Call	Put	Call	Put	
Value	12.09721985	14.10128833	12.09816572	14.56005516	
Delta	0.53464478	-0.44555390	0.53485986	-0.46786047	
Gamma	0.01168429	0.01168429	0.01137656	0.01257049	
Vega	0.00369078	0.00369078	0.00368961	0.00368440	(reported in basis points)
Theta	-7.37773494	-4.48396529	-7.37587332	-5.02097200	
Rho	0.00386940	-0.00564289	0.00386645	-0.00415825	(reported in basis points)

This program provides the call and put values from both the Black, Scholes, Merton approach and the binomial approach. The basic "greeks" are also reported. The Black, Scholes, Merton approach allows for analytical "greeks." For the binomial approach, we opt to estimate the "greeks" numerically with simple first differences.

The following are excerpts from the interface header code with selected comments added.

FRMUnitBSMDYOVM.h

The prices and "greek" calculations are in two separate implementation files; Black, Scholes, Merton approach and the binomial approach, therefore we include both files. The input data is passed using a class.

```
...
#include "c:\FRMRepository\FRMBSMDYOVM.cpp"
#include "c:\FRMRepository\FRMAmerBinOVM.cpp"

#ifndef COPTIONDATA
#define COPTIONDATA
class OPTIONDATA
{
public:
   double StockPrice;
   double StrikePrice;
   double InterestRate;
   double TimeToMaturity;
   double Volatility;
   double DividendYield;
};
#endif

#ifndef CBOPTIONDATA
#define CBOPTIONDATA
class BOPTIONDATA
{
public:
   double StockPrice;
   double StrikePrice;
   double InterestRate;
```

```
      double TimeToMaturity;
      double Volatility;
      double DividendYield;
      int NumberOfSteps;
      int Type;
};
#endif
```

We have four classes: the Black, Scholes, Merton approach input data, the Black, Scholes, Merton approach calculation methods, the binomial approach input data, and the binomial approach calculation methods. Therefore, all four classes must be instantiated.

```
...
   OPTIONDATA OD;
   BOPTIONDATA BOD;
   FRMBSMDYOVM BSM;
   FRMBinDYOVM BIN;
...
```

The following are excerpts from the interface code with selected comments added.

FRMUnitBSMDYOVM.cpp

This program passes a set of input data within a class. Therefore, the input data must be placed within the appropriate class prior to running the various calculation methods. We use `SetLocalData()` method to place the most recent user input data within the input class.

```
...
void __fastcall TBSMDYOVMForm::Execute(void)
{
   SetLocalData();
   BSM.BSMDYOVMSetData(OD);
   CallValue = BSM.BSMDYCallValue();
   PutValue = BSM.BSMDYPutValue();
   CallDelta = BSM.BSMDYCallDelta();
   PutDelta = BSM.BSMDYPutDelta();
...
// Binomial
   BIN.BinDYOVMSetData(BOD);
   BCallValue = BIN.FRMAmerDivBinCall();
   BPutValue = BIN.FRMAmerDivBinPut();
   BCallDelta = BIN.FRMAmerDivBinCallDelta();
   BPutDelta = BIN.FRMAmerDivBinPutDelta();
...
}
//------------------------------------------------------------------------
void __fastcall TBSMDYOVMForm::SetLocalData(void)
{
// BSM
  OD.StockPrice = StrToFloat(editStockPrice->Text);
  OD.StrikePrice = StrToFloat(editStrikePrice->Text);
  OD.Volatility = StrToFloat(editVolatility->Text);
  OD.InterestRate = StrToFloat(editInterestRate->Text);
  OD.TimeToMaturity = StrToFloat(editTimeToMaturity->Text);
  OD.DividendYield = StrToFloat(editDividendYield->Text);
// BIN
  BOD.StockPrice = StrToFloat(editStockPrice->Text);
  BOD.StrikePrice = StrToFloat(editStrikePrice->Text);
  BOD.Volatility = StrToFloat(editVolatility->Text);
  BOD.InterestRate = StrToFloat(editInterestRate->Text);
  BOD.TimeToMaturity = StrToFloat(editTimeToMaturity->Text);
  BOD.DividendYield = StrToFloat(editDividendYield->Text);
  BOD.NumberOfSteps = StrToInt(editNumberOfSteps->Text);
  BOD.Type = StrToInt(editType->Text);
}

...
```

Module 5.5: Digital Options with Analytic Greeks

Learning objectives

- Introduce cash-or-nothing and asset-or-nothing digital call and put options
- Explain how to decompose plain-vanilla options into digital options
- Contrast the "greeks" for plain-vanilla options with digital options

Module overview

In this module, we demonstrate how to decompose plain-vanilla options into their minuscule components, digital options. We need "The Standard Model" for observed particles equivalent for financial securities. (For more information, see www.particleadventure.org.)

Can we make the analogy between the standard model for observed particles of matter and complex organizations? If so, then digital options should be in the decomposition somewhere. Common stock can be viewed as a call option on the firm with debt par value as the strike price. Firms can be viewed as having a societal call with a zero strike price. For example, the limited liability afforded companies that legally incorporate insulates them from unlimited liability from events like environmental damage and legal liability claims.

We will see here that a call option on stock (remember stock itself is a call option on firm value and firm value contains a call option on society) can itself be composed into two digital options. Through various parity relations, digital options themselves can be decomposed into other components. And the process goes on.

We provide here the standard Black, Scholes, Merton approach to valuing European-style digital options along with the "greeks." We also sketch the derivation of the "greeks" and provide some selected observations with a focus on the connections to plain vanilla options. We provide a very generic approach so as to be applicable to a wide variety of digital options on underlying instruments. The source code discussion follows.

In the supplement to this module, we provide an extensive discussion of digital options with a focus on the connection with plain vanilla options. If your interests are solely computational, you can easily skip the supplement, as it is very dense and rather technical.[40]

Digital options setup

Notation:

t,T   calendar time, expressed in fraction of calendar year from the trade date (assumed to be zero), subscripted on forward and spot prices where necessary,

Dom domestic currency (e.g., U. S. dollars ($)),

Unit units of underlying instrument (e.g., shares of stock, ounces of gold, bushels of wheat, Japanese yen (¥)),

S_t spot price expressed in traditional way, that is, expressed in domestic currency (Dom) per unit (Unit) of underlying instrument, observed at time t,

Q_{Dom}, Q_{Unit} notional amount or final exchange amount if the spot price (S_t) is above (below) the strike rate (X) for call (put), from the spot perspective or equivalently, the spot price (R_t) is above (below) the strike rate (X_{RE}) for put (call), from the reciprocal perspective,

---

[40] Supplements can be found at www.frmhelp.com.

CC_{Dom}, CC_{Unit} carry cost of the domestic currency and the carry cost of the underlying instrument

$r_{Dom} = -CC_{Dom}$ annualized, continuously compounded domestic "risk-free" interest rate

$DC_0^{AN,Unit}(Q_{Unit}, X)$ - asset-or-nothing digital call option for Q_{Unit} of the underlying if $S_T > X$

$DP_0^{AN,Unit}(Q_{Unit}, X)$ - asset-or-nothing digital put option for Q_{Unit} of the underlying if $S_T < X$

$DC_0^{CN,Dom}(Q_{Dom}, X)$ - cash-or-nothing digital call option for Q_{Dom} of the underlying if $S_T > X$

$DP_0^{CN,Dom}(Q_{Dom}, X)$ - cash-or-nothing digital put option for Q_{Dom} of the underlying if $S_T < X$

BSM option valuation model The BSM option valuation model for plain vanilla calls and puts can be expressed with this notation as

$$C_0 = e^{CC_{Dom}T}\left[E_{EMM,0}(S_T)N(d_{EMM,1}) - XN(d_{EMM,2})\right] \text{ (Plain vanilla call option)}$$

$$P_0 = e^{CC_{Dom}T}\left[XN(-d_{EMM,2}) - E_{EMM,0}(S_T)N(-d_{EMM,1})\right] \text{ (Plain vanilla put option)}$$

where

$$N(d) \equiv \frac{1}{\sqrt{2\pi}} \int_{x=-\infty}^{d} e^{-\frac{x^2}{2}} dx \text{ (Cumulative distribution function of standard normal distribution)}$$

$$d_{EMM,1} = \frac{\ln\left[\frac{E_{EMM,0}(S_T)}{X}\right] + \frac{\sigma^2 T}{2}}{\sigma\sqrt{T}}$$

$$d_{EMM,2} = \frac{\ln\left[\frac{E_{EMM,0}(S_T)}{X}\right] - \frac{\sigma^2 T}{2}}{\sigma\sqrt{T}}$$

$$E_{EMM,0}(S_T) = S_0 e^{(CC_{Unit} - CC_{Dom})T} \text{ (Expected terminal value of underlying instrument based on equivalent martingale measure)}$$

$CC_{Dom} = -r_{Dom}$ domestic currency carrying charge

The carrying charges for selected underlying instruments are

$CC_{Unit} = -r_{For}$ foreign "risk-free" interest rate

$CC_{Unit} = -\delta$ dividend yield for stock and stock indices

$CC_{Unit} = u$ storage and other costs for physical assets like gold, crude oil, and wheat

Note

$$C_0 = DC_0^{AN,Unit}(Q_{Unit} = 1, X) - DC_0^{CN,Dom}(Q_{Dom} = X, X)$$

$$P_0 = DP_0^{CN,Unit}(Q_{Dom} = X, X) - DP_0^{AN,Dom}(Q_{Unit} = 1, X)$$

Therefore, based on the BSM paradigm, we note

$$DC_0^{AN,Unit}(Q_{Unit} = 1, X) = e^{CC_{Dom}T}E_{EMM,0}(S_T)N(d_{EMM,1}) = e^{CC_{Unit}T}S_0 N(d_{EMM,1})$$

$$DP_0^{AN,Dom}\left(Q_{Unit}=1,X\right)=e^{CC_{Dom}T}E_{EMM,0}\left(S_T\right)N\left(-d_{EMM,1}\right)=e^{CC_{Unit}T}S_0N\left(-d_{EMM,1}\right)$$

$$DC_0^{CN,Dom}\left(Q_{Dom}=X,X\right)=Xe^{CC_{Dom}T}N\left(d_{EMM,2}\right)$$

$$DP_0^{CN,Unit}\left(Q_{Dom}=X,X\right)=Xe^{CC_{Dom}T}N\left(-d_{EMM,2}\right)$$

$Q_{Dom}=X$ (here, 1 with "greeks") and $Q_{Unit}=1$

Summary of digital option "greeks"

Delta: $\Delta_O\equiv\dfrac{dO}{dS}$

Plain-vanilla call delta: $\Delta_C\equiv\dfrac{dC}{dS}=e^{CC_{Unit}T}N\left(d_{EMM,1}\right)$

Plain-vanilla put delta: $\Delta_P\equiv\dfrac{dP}{dS}=-e^{CC_{Unit}T}N\left(-d_{EMM,1}\right)$

Asset-or-nothing call delta: $\Delta_{DC^{AN}}\equiv\dfrac{dDC_0^{AN,Unit}\left(X\right)}{dS}=e^{CC_{Unit}T}\left[N\left(d_{EMM,1}\right)+\dfrac{n\left(d_{EMM,1}\right)}{\sigma\sqrt{T}}\right]$

Cash-or-nothing call delta: $\Delta_{DC^{CN}}\equiv\dfrac{dDC_0^{CN,Dom}\left(Q_{Dom}=X\right)}{dS}=\dfrac{e^{CC_{Unit}T}n\left(d_{EMM,1}\right)}{\sigma\sqrt{T}}$

Asset-or-nothing put delta: $\Delta_{DP^{AN}}\equiv\dfrac{dDP_0^{AN,Unit}\left(X\right)}{dS}=e^{CC_{Unit}T}\left[N\left(-d_{EMM,1}\right)+\dfrac{n\left(d_{EMM,1}\right)}{\sigma\sqrt{T}}\right]$

Cash-or-nothing put delta: $\Delta_{DP^{CN}}\equiv\dfrac{dDP_0^{CN,Dom}\left(Q_{Dom}=X\right)}{dS}=-\Delta_{DC^{CN}}=-\dfrac{e^{CC_{Unit}T}n\left(d_{EMM,1}\right)}{\sigma\sqrt{T}}$

Gamma: $\Gamma_O\equiv\dfrac{d^2O}{dS^2}$

Plain-vanilla call gamma: $\Gamma_C\equiv\dfrac{d^2C}{dS^2}=\dfrac{e^{CC_{Unit}T}n\left(d_{EMM,1}\right)}{S\sigma\sqrt{T}}$

Plain-vanilla put gamma: $\Gamma_P\equiv\dfrac{d^2P}{dS^2}=\Gamma_C=\dfrac{e^{CC_{Unit}T}n\left(d_{EMM,1}\right)}{S\sigma\sqrt{T}}$

Asset-or-nothing call gamma: $\Gamma_{DC^{AN}}\equiv\dfrac{d^2DC_0^{AN,Unit}\left(X\right)}{dS^2}=\dfrac{e^{CC_{Unit}T}n\left(d_{EMM,1}\right)}{S\sigma\sqrt{T}}\left[1-\dfrac{d_{EMM,1}}{\sigma\sqrt{T}}\right]$

Cash-or-nothing call gamma: $\Gamma_{DC^{CN}}\equiv\dfrac{d^2DC_0^{CN,Dom}\left(Q_{Dom}=X\right)}{dS^2}=-\dfrac{e^{CC_{Unit}T}d_{EMM,1}n\left(d_{EMM,1}\right)}{S\sigma^2T}$

Asset-or-nothing put gamma: $\Gamma_{DP^{AN}}\equiv\dfrac{d^2DP_0^{AN,Unit}\left(X\right)}{dS^2}=-\dfrac{e^{CC_{Unit}T}n\left(d_{EMM,1}\right)}{S\sigma\sqrt{T}}\left[1-\dfrac{d_{EMM,1}}{\sigma\sqrt{T}}\right]$

Cash-or-nothing put gamma: $\Gamma_{DP^{CN}}\equiv\dfrac{d^2DP_0^{CN,Dom}\left(Q_{Dom}=X\right)}{dS^2}=\dfrac{e^{CC_{Unit}T}d_{EMM,1}n\left(d_{EMM,1}\right)}{S\sigma^2T}$

Vega: $\nu_O \equiv \dfrac{dO}{d\sigma}$

Plain-vanilla call vega: $\nu_C \equiv \dfrac{dC}{d\sigma} = Se^{CC_{Unit}T}n(d_{EMM,1})\sqrt{T} = Xe^{CC_{Dom}T}n(d_{EMM,2})\sqrt{T}$

Plain-vanilla put vega: $\nu_P \equiv \dfrac{dP}{d\sigma} = \nu_C = Se^{CC_{Unit}T}n(d_{EMM,1})\sqrt{T} = Xe^{CC_{Dom}T}n(d_{EMM,2})\sqrt{T}$

Asset-or-nothing call vega: $\nu_{DC^{AN}} \equiv \dfrac{dDC_0^{AN,Unit}(X)}{d\sigma} = -e^{CC_{Unit}T}S_0 n(d_{EMM,1})d_{EMM,2}$

Cash-or-nothing call vega: $\nu_{DC^{CN}} \equiv \dfrac{dDC_0^{CN,Dom}(Q_{Dom}=X)}{d\sigma} = -e^{CC_{Unit}T}S_0 n(d_{EMM,1})\left(\sqrt{T}+d_{EMM,2}\right)$

Asset-or-nothing put vega: $\nu_{DP^{AN}} \equiv \dfrac{dDP_0^{AN,Unit}(X)}{d\sigma} = -\nu_{DC^{AN}} = e^{CC_{Unit}T}S_0 n(d_{EMM,1})d_{EMM,2}$

Cash-or-nothing put vega: $\nu_{DP^{CN}} \equiv \dfrac{dDP_0^{CN,Dom}(Q_{Dom}=X)}{d\sigma} = -\nu_{DC^{CN}} = e^{CC_{Unit}T}S_0 n(d_{EMM,1})\left(\sqrt{T}+d_{EMM,2}\right)$

Theta: $\theta_O \equiv \dfrac{dO}{dt}$

Plain-vanilla call theta:

$$\theta_C \equiv \frac{dC}{dt} = -\frac{dC}{dT} = -\frac{Se^{CC_{Unit}T}n(d_{EMM,1})\sigma}{2\sqrt{T}} + CC_{Dom}Xe^{CC_{Dom}T}N(d_{EMM,2}) - CC_{Unit}Se^{CC_{Unit}T}N(d_{EMM,1})$$

Plain-vanilla put theta:

$$\theta_P \equiv \frac{dP}{dt} = -\frac{dP}{dT} = -\frac{Se^{CC_{Unit}T}n(d_{EMM,1})\sigma}{2\sqrt{T}} - CC_{Dom}Xe^{CC_{Dom}T}N(-d_{EMM,2}) + CC_{Unit}Se^{CC_{Unit}T}N(-d_{EMM,1})$$

Asset-or-nothing call theta: $\theta_{DC^{AN}} = \dfrac{dDC_0^{AN,Unit}(X)}{dt} = -e^{CC_{Unit}T}S_0\left[CC_{Unit}N(d_{EMM,1}) - \dfrac{n(d_{EMM,1})d_{EMM,2}}{2T}\right]$

Cash-or-nothing call theta:
$$\theta_{DC^{CN}} = \theta_{DC^{AN}} - \theta_C$$
$$= \frac{e^{CC_{Unit}T}Sn(d_{EMM,1})}{2\sqrt{T}}\left[\frac{d_{EMM,2}}{\sqrt{T}} + \sigma\right] + CC_{Dom}Xe^{CC_{Dom}T}N(d_{EMM,2})$$

Asset-or-nothing put theta: $\theta_{DP^{AN}} = \dfrac{dDP_0^{AN,Unit}(X)}{dt} = e^{CC_{Unit}T}S\left[CC_{Unit}\left(1+N(d_{EMM,1})\right) - \dfrac{n(d_{EMM,1})d_{EMM,2}}{2T}\right]$

Cash-or-nothing put theta:
$$\theta_{DP^{CN}} = \frac{dDP_0^{CN,Unit}(X)}{dt} = \theta_{DC^{AN}} - \theta_C$$
$$= CC_{Dom}e^{CC_{Dom}T}\left(1 - XN(d_{EMM,2})\right) - \frac{e^{CC_{Unit}T}Sn(d_{EMM,1})}{2\sqrt{T}}\left[\frac{d_{EMM,2}}{\sqrt{T}} + \sigma\right]$$

Rho: $\rho_O \equiv \dfrac{dO}{dr}$

Plain-vanilla call rho: $\rho_C \equiv \dfrac{dC}{dr} = XTe^{CC_{Dom}T} N(d_{EMM,2})$

Plain-vanilla put rho: $\rho_P \equiv \dfrac{dP}{dr} = -XTe^{CC_{Dom}T} N(-d_{EMM,2})$

Asset-or-nothing call rho:
$$\rho_{DC^{AN}} \equiv \frac{dDC_0^{AN,Unit}(X)}{dr} = -\frac{dDC_0^{AN,Unit}(X)}{dCC_{Dom}}$$
$$= -e^{CC_{Unit}T} S_0 \left[TN(d_{EMM,1}) - \frac{n(d_{EMM,1})\sqrt{T}}{\sigma} \right]$$

Cash-or-nothing call rho:
$$\rho_{DC^{CN}} \equiv \frac{dDC_0^{CN,Unit}(X)}{dr} = -\frac{dDC_0^{CN,Unit}(X)}{dCC_{Dom}} = \rho_{DC^{AN}} - \rho_C$$
$$= -\left\{ e^{CC_{Unit}T} S_0 \left[TN(d_{EMM,1}) - \frac{n(d_{EMM,1})\sqrt{T}}{\sigma} \right] + XTe^{CC_{Dom}T} N(d_{EMM,2}) \right\}$$

Asset-or-nothing put rho:
$$\rho_{DP^{AN}} \equiv \frac{dDP_0^{AN,Unit}(X)}{dr} = -\frac{dDP_0^{AN,Unit}(X)}{dCC_{Dom}}$$
$$= -\rho_{DC^{AN}} = e^{CC_{Unit}T} S_0 \left[TN(d_{EMM,1}) - \frac{n(d_{EMM,1})\sqrt{T}}{\sigma} \right]$$

Cash-or-nothing put rho:
$$\rho_{DP^{CN}} \equiv \frac{dDP_0^{CN,Unit}(X)}{dr} = -\frac{dDP_0^{CN,Unit}(X)}{dCC_{Dom}} = TS_0 Q_{Dom,Dom} e^{CC_{Dom}T} - \rho_{DC^{AN}}$$
$$= Te^{CC_{Domt}T} \left\{ 1 + SN(d_{EMM,1}) - \frac{Sn(d_{EMM,1})}{\sigma\sqrt{T}} + XN(d_{EMM,2}) \right\}$$

Details for digital option "greeks"

For more detailed information on plain-vanilla "greeks," see Module 5.4. We sketch the derivation of each asset-or-nothing "greek" followed by the cash-or-nothing "greek" with an emphasis on the relationship with the plain vanilla option "greek." We will make use of the parity relations on a per-dollar or per-unit basis ($Q_{Dom,Dom} = 1$ and $Q_{Unit,Unit} = 1$).

$$DC_0^{CN,Dom}(X) + DP_0^{CN,Dom}(X) = e^{CC_{Dom}T} \text{ (\textbf{Cash-or-nothing to bond parity})}$$

and

$$DC_0^{AN,Unit}(X) + DP_0^{AN,Unit}(X) = S_0 e^{CC_{Unit}T} \text{ (\textbf{Asset-or-nothing to asset parity})}$$

You should verify the following parities.

Parities: ($\dfrac{d}{dg}$ denotes derivative with respect to some underlying variable g – S, t, r, and σ)

$$\frac{d}{dg}C_0 = \frac{d}{dg}DC_0^{AN,Unit}(X) - \frac{d}{dg}DC_0^{CN,Dom}(Q_{Dom} = X) \;\; \textbf{(Plain-vanilla to digital call parity)}$$

$$\frac{d}{dg}P_0 = \frac{d}{dg}DP_0^{CN,Unit}(Q_{Dom} = X) - \frac{d}{dg}DP_0^{AN,Dom}(X) \;\; \textbf{(Plain-vanilla to digital put parity)}$$

$$\frac{d}{dg}DC_0^{CN,Dom}(X) + \frac{d}{dg}DP_0^{CN,Dom}(X) = \frac{d}{dg}e^{CC_{Dom}T} \;\; \textbf{(Cash-or-nothing to bond parity)}$$

$$\frac{d}{dg}DC_0^{AN,Unit}(X) + \frac{d}{dg}DP_0^{AN,Unit}(X) = \frac{d}{dg}Se^{CC_{Unit}T} \;\; \textbf{(Asset-or-nothing-asset parity)}$$

Delta:

Asset-or-nothing call delta:
$$\Delta_{DC^{AN}} \equiv \frac{dDC_0^{AN,Unit}(X)}{dS} = \Delta_C + \frac{e^{CC_{Unit}T}n(d_{EMM,1})}{\sigma\sqrt{T}}$$

$$= e^{CC_{Unit}T}\left[N(d_{EMM,1}) + \frac{n(d_{EMM,1})}{\sigma\sqrt{T}}\right]$$

With this notation:

$$\Delta_C = e^{CC_{Unit}T}N(d_{EMM,1})$$

$$d_{EMM,1} = \frac{\ln\left[\dfrac{Se^{(CC_{Unit}-CC_{Dom})T}}{X}\right] + \dfrac{\sigma^2 T}{2}}{\sigma\sqrt{T}} = \frac{\ln(S)}{\sigma\sqrt{T}} + \frac{\ln\left[\dfrac{e^{(CC_{Unit}-CC_{Dom})T}}{X}\right] + \dfrac{\sigma^2 T}{2}}{\sigma\sqrt{T}}$$

$$\frac{dd_{EMM,1}}{dS} = \frac{1}{S\sigma\sqrt{T}}$$

Therefore,

$$\frac{dDC_0^{AN,Unit}(X)}{dS} = \frac{d}{dS}e^{CC_{Unit}T}SN(d_{EMM,1})$$

$$= e^{CC_{Unit}T}N(d_{EMM,1}) + e^{CC_{Unit}T}S\frac{dN(d_{EMM,1})}{dd_{EMM,1}}\frac{dd_{EMM,1}}{dS}$$

$$= e^{CC_{Unit}T}N(d_{EMM,1}) + e^{CC_{Unit}T}Sn(d_{EMM,1})\frac{dd_{EMM,1}}{dS}$$

$$= e^{CC_{Unit}T}N(d_{EMM,1}) + \frac{e^{CC_{Unit}T}n(d_{EMM,1})}{\sigma\sqrt{T}}$$

Cash-or-nothing call delta: $\Delta_{DC^{CN}} \equiv \dfrac{dDC_0^{CN,Dom}(Q_{Dom} = X)}{dS} = \Delta_{DC^{AN}} - \Delta_C = \dfrac{e^{CC_{Unit}T}n(d_{EMM,1})}{\sigma\sqrt{T}}$

Based on the relationship between a plain vanilla call and its corresponding digital calls, $C_0 = DC_0^{AN,Unit}(X) - DC_0^{CN,Dom}(Q_{Dom} = X)$ we have $\Delta_C = \Delta_{DC^{AN}} - \Delta_{DC^{CN}}$ or $\Delta_{DC^{CN}} = \Delta_{DC^{AN}} - \Delta_C$. Because we know $\Delta_{DC^{AN}} = \Delta_C + \dfrac{e^{CC_{Unit}T}n(d_{EMM,1})}{\sigma\sqrt{T}}$ and therefore $\Delta_{DC^{CN}} = \dfrac{e^{CC_{Unit}T}n(d_{EMM,1})}{\sigma\sqrt{T}}$.

Asset-or-nothing put delta:

$$\Delta_{DP^{AN}} \equiv \frac{dDP_0^{AN,Unit}(X)}{dS} = e^{CC_{Unit}T} - \Delta_{DC^{AN}} = e^{CC_{Unit}T}\left[N(-d_{EMM,1}) + \frac{n(d_{EMM,1})}{\sigma\sqrt{T}}\right]$$

From the asset-or-nothing to asset parity, we know $\Delta_{DC^{AN}} + \Delta_{DP^{AN}} = e^{CC_{Unit}T}$ or $\Delta_{DP^{AN}} = e^{CC_{Unit}T} - \Delta_{DC^{AN}}$.

By substitution,

$$\Delta_{DP^{AN}} = e^{CC_{Unit}T} - \Delta_{DC^{AN}} = e^{CC_{Unit}T} - e^{CC_{Unit}T}\left[N(d_{EMM,1}) + \frac{n(d_{EMM,1})}{\sigma\sqrt{T}}\right]$$

$$= e^{CC_{Unit}T}\left[1 - N(d_{EMM,1}) + \frac{n(d_{EMM,1})}{\sigma\sqrt{T}}\right] = e^{CC_{Unit}T}\left[N(-d_{EMM,1}) + \frac{n(d_{EMM,1})}{\sigma\sqrt{T}}\right]$$

Cash-or-nothing put delta: $\Delta_{DP^{CN}} \equiv \frac{dDP_0^{CN,Dom}(Q_{Dom} = X)}{dS} = -\Delta_{DC^{CN}} = -\frac{e^{CC_{Unit}T}n(d_{EMM,1})}{\sigma\sqrt{T}}$

From the cash-or-nothing to bond parity, we know $\Delta_{DC^{CN}} + \Delta_{DP^{CN}} = 0$ or $\Delta_{DP^{CN}} = -\Delta_{DC^{CN}}$.

Gamma:

$$\Gamma_{DC^{AN}} \equiv \frac{d^2DC_0^{AN,Unit}(X)}{dS^2} = \Gamma_C - \frac{e^{CC_{Unit}T}d_{EMM,1}n(d_{EMM,1})}{S\sigma^2 T}$$

Asset-or-nothing call gamma:
$$= \frac{e^{CC_{Unit}T}n(d_{EMM,1})}{S\sigma\sqrt{T}}\left[1 - \frac{d_{EMM,1}}{\sigma\sqrt{T}}\right]$$

The asset-or-nothing call delta is

$$\Delta_{DC^{AN}} \equiv \frac{dDC_0^{AN,Unit}(X)}{dS} = \Delta_C + \frac{e^{CC_{Unit}T}n(d_{EMM,1})}{\sigma\sqrt{T}}$$

where

$$\Delta_C = e^{CC_{Unit}T}N(d_{EMM,1})$$

Note

$$N(d) \equiv \frac{1}{\sqrt{2\pi}}\int_{-\infty}^{d}e^{-\frac{x^2}{2}}dx \quad \text{(Cumulative distribution function)}$$

$$\frac{dN(d)}{dd} \equiv n(d) = \frac{1}{\sqrt{2\pi}}e^{-\frac{d^2}{2}} \quad \text{(Probability density function)}$$

$$\frac{dn(d)}{dd} = -dn(d) \quad \text{(First derivative of the probability density function)}$$

$$\frac{dn(d_{EMM,1})}{dS} = \frac{dn(d_{EMM,1})}{dd_{EMM,1}}\frac{dd_{EMM,1}}{dS} = -d_{EMM,1}n(d_{EMM,1})\frac{1}{S\sigma\sqrt{T}}$$

Therefore,

$$\Gamma_{DC^{AN}} \equiv \frac{d^2 DC_0^{AN,Unit}(X)}{dS^2} = \frac{d\Delta_C}{dS} + \frac{e^{CC_{Unit}T}}{\sigma\sqrt{T}} \frac{dn(d_{EMM,l})}{dS}$$

$$= \Gamma_C - \frac{e^{CC_{Unit}T} d_{EMM,l} n(d_{EMM,l})}{S\sigma^2 T} = \frac{e^{CC_{Unit}T} n(d_{EMM,l})}{S\sigma\sqrt{T}} \left[1 - \frac{d_{EMM,l}}{\sigma\sqrt{T}}\right]$$

Cash-or-nothing call gamma: $\Gamma_{DC^{CN}} \equiv \frac{d^2 DC_0^{CN,Dom}(Q_{Dom}=X)}{dS^2} = -\frac{e^{CC_{Unit}T} d_{EMM,l} n(d_{EMM,l})}{S\sigma^2 T}$

Based on the relationship between a plain vanilla call delta and its corresponding digital call deltas, $\Delta_C = \Delta_{DC^{AN}} - \Delta_{DC^{CN}}$, we have $\Gamma_C = \Gamma_{DC^{AN}} - \Gamma_{DC^{CN}}$ or $\Gamma_{DC^{CN}} = \Gamma_{DC^{AN}} - \Gamma_C$. Because we know $\Gamma_{DC^{AN}} = \Gamma_C - \frac{e^{CC_{Unit}T} d_{EMM,l} n(d_{EMM,l})}{S\sigma^2 T}$, thus $\Gamma_{DC^{CN}} = -\frac{e^{CC_{Unit}T} d_{EMM,l} n(d_{EMM,l})}{S\sigma^2 T}$.

$$\Gamma_{DP^{AN}} \equiv \frac{d^2 DP_0^{AN,Unit}(X)}{dS^2} = -\Gamma_{DC^{AN}} = -\left[\Gamma_C - \frac{e^{CC_{Unit}T} d_{EMM,l} n(d_{EMM,l})}{S\sigma^2 T}\right]$$

Asset-or-nothing put gamma:

$$= -\frac{e^{CC_{Unit}T} n(d_{EMM,l})}{S\sigma\sqrt{T}} \left[1 - \frac{d_{EMM,l}}{\sigma\sqrt{T}}\right]$$

From the asset-or-nothing to asset parity and the previous results for delta, we know $\Gamma_{DC^{AN}} + \Gamma_{DP^{AN}} = 0$ or $\Gamma_{DP^{AN}} = -\Gamma_{DC^{AN}}$.

Cash-or-nothing put gamma: $\Gamma_{DP^{CN}} \equiv \frac{d^2 DP_0^{CN,Dom}(Q_{Dom}=X)}{dS^2} = -\Gamma_{DC^{CN}} = \frac{e^{CC_{Unit}T} d_{EMM,l} n(d_{EMM,l})}{S\sigma^2 T}$

From the cash-or-nothing to bond parity, we know $\Gamma_{DC^{CN}} + \Gamma_{DP^{CN}} = 0$ or $\Gamma_{DP^{CN}} = -\Gamma_{DC^{CN}}$.

Vega:

Asset-or-nothing call vega: $\nu_{DC^{AN}} \equiv \frac{dDC_0^{AN,Unit}(X)}{d\sigma} = -e^{CC_{Unit}T} S_0 n(d_{EMM,l}) d_{EMM,2}$

Recall for the plain vanilla call and put and using the notation here, we have

$$\nu_C \equiv \frac{dC}{d\sigma} = Se^{CC_{Unit}T} n(d_{EMM,l})\sqrt{T} = \frac{dP}{d\sigma} \equiv \nu_P$$

$$DC_0^{AN,Unit}(X) = e^{CC_{Unit}T} S_0 N(d_{EMM,l})$$

$$d_{EMM,l} = \frac{\ln\left[\frac{E_{EMM,0}(S_T)}{X}\right] + \frac{\sigma^2 T}{2}}{\sigma\sqrt{T}} = \frac{\ln\left[\frac{E_{EMM,0}(S_T)}{X}\right]}{\sqrt{T}}\sigma^{-1} + \frac{\sqrt{T}}{2}\sigma$$

$$d_{EMM,2} = \frac{\ln\left[\frac{E_{EMM,0}(S_T)}{X}\right] - \frac{\sigma^2 T}{2}}{\sigma\sqrt{T}}$$

$$\frac{dd_{EMM,l}}{d\sigma} = -\frac{\ln\left[\frac{E_{EMM,0}(S_T)}{X}\right]}{\sigma^2\sqrt{T}} + \frac{\sqrt{T}}{2} = -\frac{\ln\left[\frac{E_{EMM,0}(S_T)}{X}\right] - \frac{\sigma^2 T}{2}}{\sigma\sqrt{T}} = -d_{EMM,2}$$

Thus,

$$\frac{dDC_0^{AN,Unit}(X)}{d\sigma} = e^{CC_{Unit}T}S_0\frac{dN(d_{EMM,1})}{d\sigma} = e^{CC_{Unit}T}S_0\frac{dN(d_{EMM,1})}{dd_{EMM,1}}\frac{dd_{EMM,1}}{d\sigma}$$

$$= -e^{CC_{Unit}T}S_0 n(d_{EMM,1})d_{EMM,2}$$

Cash-or-nothing call vega: $\nu_{DC^{CN}} \equiv \dfrac{dDC_0^{CN,Dom}(Q_{Dom}=X)}{d\sigma} = \nu_{DC^{AN}} - \nu_C$

$$= -e^{CC_{Unit}T}S_0 n(d_{EMM,1})\left[d_{EMM,2} + \sqrt{T}\right]$$

Based on the relationship between a plain vanilla call and its corresponding digital calls, $C_0 = DC_0^{AN,Unit}(X) - DC_0^{CN,Dom}(Q_{Dom}=X)$ we have $\nu_C = \nu_{DC^{AN}} - \nu_{DC^{CN}}$ or $\nu_{DC^{CN}} = \nu_{DC^{AN}} - \nu_C$. Because

we know $\nu_{DC^{AN}} \equiv \dfrac{dDC_0^{AN,Unit}(X)}{d\sigma} = -e^{CC_{Unit}T}S_0 n(d_{EMM,1})d_{EMM,2}$ and therefore

$$\nu_{DC^{CN}} = \nu_{DC^{AN}} - \nu_C = -e^{CC_{Unit}T}S_0 n(d_{EMM,1})d_{EMM,2} - Se^{CC_{Unit}T}n(d_{EMM,1})\sqrt{T}$$

$$= -e^{CC_{Unit}T}S_0 n(d_{EMM,1})\left[d_{EMM,2} + \sqrt{T}\right]$$

Asset-or-nothing put vega: $\nu_{DP^{AN}} \equiv \dfrac{dDP_0^{AN,Unit}(X)}{d\sigma} = -\nu_{DC^{AN}} = e^{CC_{Unit}T}S_0 n(d_{EMM,1})d_{EMM,2}$

From the asset-or-nothing to asset parity, we know $\nu_{DC^{AN}} + \nu_{DP^{AN}} = 0$ or $\nu_{DP^{AN}} = -\nu_{DC^{AN}}$.

Cash-or-nothing put vega: $\nu_{DP^{CN}} \equiv \dfrac{dDP_0^{CN,Dom}(Q_{Dom}=X)}{d\sigma} = -\nu_{DC^{CN}} = e^{CC_{Unit}T}S_0 n(d_{EMM,1})\left[d_{EMM,2} + \sqrt{T}\right]$

From the cash-or-nothing to bond parity, we know $\nu_{DC^{CN}} + \nu_{DP^{CN}} = 0$ or $\nu_{DP^{CN}} = -\nu_{DC^{CN}}$.

Theta:

Asset-or-nothing call theta: $\theta_{DC^{AN}} = \dfrac{dDC_0^{AN,Unit}(X)}{dt} = -e^{CC_{Unit}T}S_0\left[CC_{Unit}N(d_{EMM,1}) - \dfrac{n(d_{EMM,1})d_{EMM,2}}{2T}\right]$

Recall

$$DC_0^{AN,Unit}(X) = e^{CC_{Unit}T}S_0 N(d_{EMM,1})$$

$$d_{EMM,1} = \frac{\ln\left[\dfrac{E_{EMM,0}(S_T)}{X}\right] + \dfrac{\sigma^2 T}{2}}{\sigma\sqrt{T}} = \frac{\ln\left[\dfrac{E_{EMM,0}(S_T)}{X}\right]}{\sigma}T^{-1/2} + \frac{\sigma}{2}T^{1/2}$$

$$d_{EMM,2} = \frac{\ln\left[\dfrac{E_{EMM,0}(S_T)}{X}\right] - \dfrac{\sigma^2 T}{2}}{\sigma\sqrt{T}}$$

$$\frac{dd_{EMM,1}}{dT} = -\frac{1}{2}\frac{\ln\left[\dfrac{E_{EMM,0}(S_T)}{X}\right]}{\sigma}T^{-3/2} + \frac{1}{2}\frac{\sigma}{2}T^{-1/2}$$

$$= -\frac{1}{2T}\left[\frac{\ln\left[\dfrac{E_{EMM,0}(S_T)}{X}\right] - \dfrac{\sigma^2 T}{2}}{\sigma\sqrt{T}}\right] = -\frac{d_{EMM,2}}{2T}$$

Therefore,

$$\frac{dDC_0^{AN,Unit}(X)}{dt} = -\frac{dDC_0^{AN,Unit}(X)}{dT} = -\left\{CC_{Unit}e^{CC_{Unit}T}S_0 N(d_{EMM,1}) + e^{CC_{Unit}T}S_0\frac{dN(d_{EMM,1})}{dT}\right\}$$

$$= -\left\{CC_{Unit}e^{CC_{Unit}T}S_0 N(d_{EMM,1}) + e^{CC_{Unit}T}S_0 n(d_{EMM,1})\left[-\frac{d_{EMM,2}}{2T}\right]\right\}$$

$$= -e^{CC_{Unit}T}S_0\left[CC_{Unit}N(d_{EMM,1}) - \frac{n(d_{EMM,1})d_{EMM,2}}{2T}\right]$$

$$\theta_{DC^{CN}} = \theta_{DC^{AN}} - \theta_C$$

Cash-or-nothing call theta:
$$= \frac{e^{CC_{Unit}T}Sn(d_{EMM,1})}{2\sqrt{T}}\left[\frac{d_{EMM,2}}{\sqrt{T}} + \sigma\right] + CC_{Dom}Xe^{CC_{Dom}T}N(d_{EMM,2})$$

Based on the definition of theta, $\theta_C = \theta_{DC^{AN}} - \theta_{DC^{CN}}$ therefore $\theta_{DC^{CN}} = \theta_{DC^{AN}} - \theta_C$. Recall

$$\theta_C = -\frac{Se^{CC_{Unit}T}n(d_{EMM,1})\sigma}{2\sqrt{T}} - CC_{Dom}Xe^{CC_{Dom}T}N(d_{EMM,2}) - CC_{Unit}Se^{CC_{Unit}T}N(d_{EMM,1})$$

By substitution,

$$\theta_{DC^{CN}} = \theta_{DC^{AN}} - \theta_C$$

$$= -e^{CC_{Unit}T}S\left[CC_{Unit}N(d_{EMM,1}) - \frac{n(d_{EMM,1})d_{EMM,2}}{2T}\right]$$

$$-\left[-\frac{Se^{CC_{Unit}T}n(d_{EMM,1})\sigma}{2\sqrt{T}} - CC_{Dom}Xe^{CC_{Dom}T}N(d_{EMM,2}) - CC_{Unit}Se^{CC_{Unit}T}N(d_{EMM,1})\right]$$

$$= \frac{e^{CC_{Unit}T}Sn(d_{EMM,1})d_{EMM,2}}{2T} + \frac{Se^{CC_{Unit}T}n(d_{EMM,1})\sigma}{2\sqrt{T}} + CC_{Dom}Xe^{CC_{Dom}T}N(d_{EMM,2})$$

$$= \frac{e^{CC_{Unit}T}Sn(d_{EMM,1})}{2\sqrt{T}}\left[\frac{d_{EMM,2}}{\sqrt{T}} + \sigma\right] + CC_{Dom}Xe^{CC_{Dom}T}N(d_{EMM,2})$$

$$\theta_{DP^{AN}} = \frac{dDP_0^{AN,Unit}(X)}{dt}$$

Asset-or-nothing put theta:
$$= e^{CC_{Unit}T}S\left[CC_{Unit}\left(1 + N(d_{EMM,1})\right) - \frac{n(d_{EMM,1})d_{EMM,2}}{2T}\right]$$

Note that $\theta_{DC^{AN}} + \theta_{DP^{AN}} = CC_{Unit}Se^{CC_{Unit}T}$ and we know

$$\theta_{DC^{AN}} = \frac{dDC_0^{AN,Unit}(X)}{dt} = -e^{CC_{Unit}T}S_0\left[CC_{Unit}N(d_{EMM,1}) - \frac{n(d_{EMM,1})d_{EMM,2}}{2T}\right]$$

Therefore,

$$\theta_{DP^{AN}} = CC_{Unit}Se^{CC_{Unit}T} - \theta_{DC^{AN}}$$

$$= CC_{Unit}Se^{CC_{Unit}T} + e^{CC_{Unit}T}S_0\left[CC_{Unit}N(d_{EMM,1}) - \frac{n(d_{EMM,1})d_{EMM,2}}{2T}\right]$$

$$= e^{CC_{Unit}T}S\left[CC_{Unit}\left(1 + N(d_{EMM,1})\right) - \frac{n(d_{EMM,1})d_{EMM,2}}{2T}\right]$$

$$\theta_{DP^{CN}} = \frac{dDP_0^{CN,Unit}(X)}{dt} = \theta_{DC^{AN}} - \theta_C$$

Cash-or-nothing put theta:

$$= e^{CC_{Domt}T}CC_{Dom}\left[1 + XN(d_{EMM,2})\right] - \frac{e^{CC_{Unit}T}Sn(d_{EMM,1})}{2\sqrt{T}}\left[\frac{d_{EMM,2}}{\sqrt{T}} + \sigma\right]$$

Note that $\theta_{DC^{CN}} + \theta_{DP^{CN}} = CC_{Dom}e^{CC_{Domt}T}$ and we know

$$\theta_{DC^{CN}} = \frac{e^{CC_{Unit}T}Sn(d_{EMM,1})}{2\sqrt{T}}\left[\frac{d_{EMM,2}}{\sqrt{T}} + \sigma\right] + CC_{Dom}Xe^{CC_{Dom}T}N(d_{EMM,2})$$

Therefore,

$$\theta_{DP^{CN}} = CC_{Dom}e^{CC_{Domt}T} - \frac{e^{CC_{Unit}T}Sn(d_{EMM,1})}{2\sqrt{T}}\left[\frac{d_{EMM,2}}{\sqrt{T}} + \sigma\right] + CC_{Dom}Xe^{CC_{Dom}T}N(d_{EMM,2})$$

$$= e^{CC_{Domt}T}CC_{Dom}\left[1 + XN(d_{EMM,2})\right] - \frac{e^{CC_{Unit}T}Sn(d_{EMM,1})}{2\sqrt{T}}\left[\frac{d_{EMM,2}}{\sqrt{T}} + \sigma\right]$$

$$\theta_C = -\frac{Se^{CC_{Unit}T}n(d_{EMM,1})\sigma}{2\sqrt{T}} - CC_{Dom}Xe^{CC_{Dom}T}N(d_{EMM,2}) - CC_{Unit}Se^{CC_{Unit}T}N(d_{EMM,1})$$

$$\theta_p = -\frac{Se^{CC_{Unit}T}n(d_{EMM,1})\sigma}{2\sqrt{T}} + CC_{Dom}Xe^{CC_{Dom}T}N(-d_{EMM,2}) + CC_{Unit}Se^{CC_{Unit}T}N(-d_{EMM,1})$$

Rho:

$$\rho_{DC^{AN}} \equiv \frac{dDC_0^{AN,Unit}(X)}{dr} = -\frac{dDC_0^{AN,Unit}(X)}{dCC_{Dom}}$$

Asset-or-nothing call rho:

$$= -e^{CC_{Unit}T}S_0\left[TN(d_{EMM,1}) - \frac{n(d_{EMM,1})\sqrt{T}}{\sigma}\right]$$

Consider

$$DC_0^{AN,Unit}(X) = e^{CC_{Unit}T}S_0N(d_{EMM,1})$$

$$d_{EMM,1} = \frac{\ln\left[\dfrac{Se^{(CC_{Unit}-CC_{Dom})T}}{X}\right] + \dfrac{\sigma^2 T}{2}}{\sigma\sqrt{T}} = -\frac{\sqrt{T}}{\sigma}CC_{Dom} + \frac{\ln\left[\dfrac{Se^{CC_{Unit}T}}{X}\right] + \dfrac{\sigma^2 T}{2}}{\sigma\sqrt{T}}$$

$$\frac{dd_{EMM,1}}{dCC_{Dom}} = -\frac{\sqrt{T}}{\sigma}$$

Therefore,

$$\frac{dDC_0^{AN,Unit}(X)}{dCC_{Dom}} = Te^{CC_{Unit}T}S_0 N(d_{EMM,1}) + e^{CC_{Unit}T}S_0 \frac{dN(d_{EMM,1})}{dCC_{Dom}}$$

$$= Te^{CC_{Unit}T}S_0 N(d_{EMM,1}) + e^{CC_{Unit}T}S_0 n(d_{EMM,1})\left[-\frac{\sqrt{T}}{\sigma}\right]$$

$$= e^{CC_{Unit}T}S_0\left[TN(d_{EMM,1}) - \frac{n(d_{EMM,1})\sqrt{T}}{\sigma}\right]$$

$$\rho_{DC^{CN}} \equiv \frac{dDC_0^{CN,Unit}(X)}{dr} = -\frac{dDC_0^{CN,Unit}(X)}{dCC_{Dom}} = \rho_{DC^{AN}} - \rho_C$$

Cash-or-nothing call rho:
$$= -\left\{e^{CC_{Unit}T}S_0\left[TN(d_{EMM,1}) - \frac{n(d_{EMM,1})\sqrt{T}}{\sigma}\right] + XTe^{CC_{Dom}T}N(d_{EMM,2})\right\}$$

Based on the relationship between a plain vanilla call and its corresponding digital calls, $C_0 = DC_0^{AN,Unit}(X) - DC_0^{CN,Dom}(Q_{Dom}=X)$ we have $\rho_C = \rho_{DC^{AN}} - \rho_{DC^{CN}}$ or $\rho_{DC^{CN}} = \rho_{DC^{AN}} - \rho_C$. Because

we know $\rho_{DC^{AN}} = -e^{CC_{Unit}T}S_0\left[TN(d_{EMM,1}) - \dfrac{n(d_{EMM,1})\sqrt{T}}{\sigma}\right]$ and $\rho_C = XTe^{CC_{Dom}T}N(d_{EMM,2})$ therefore

$$\rho_{DC^{CN}} = \rho_{DC^{AN}} - \rho_C = -\left\{e^{CC_{Unit}T}S_0\left[TN(d_{EMM,1}) - \frac{n(d_{EMM,1})\sqrt{T}}{\sigma}\right] + XTe^{CC_{Dom}T}N(d_{EMM,2})\right\}.$$

$$\rho_{DP^{AN}} \equiv \frac{dDP_0^{AN,Unit}(X)}{dr} = -\frac{dDP_0^{AN,Unit}(X)}{dCC_{Dom}}$$

Asset-or-nothing put rho:
$$= -\rho_{DC^{AN}} = e^{CC_{Unit}T}S_0\left[TN(d_{EMM,1}) - \frac{n(d_{EMM,1})\sqrt{T}}{\sigma}\right]$$

From the asset-or-nothing to asset parity, we know $\rho_{DC^{AN}} + \rho_{DP^{AN}} = 0$ or $\rho_{DP^{AN}} = -\rho_{DC^{AN}}$.

$$\rho_{DP^{CN}} \equiv \frac{dDP_0^{CN,Unit}(X)}{dr} = -\frac{dDP_0^{CN,Unit}(X)}{dCC_{Dom}} = TS_0 Q_{Dom,Dom}e^{CC_{Dom}T} - \rho_{DC^{AN}}$$

Cash-or-nothing put rho:
$$= Te^{CC_{Domt}T}\left\{1 + SN(d_{EMM,1}) - \frac{Sn(d_{EMM,1})}{\sigma\sqrt{T}} + XN(d_{EMM,2})\right\}$$

From the cash-or-nothing to bond parity, we know $\rho_{DC^{CN}} + \rho_{DP^{CN}} = Te^{CC_{Dom}T}$ and

$$\rho_{DC^{CN}} = -\left\{ e^{CC_{Unit}T} S_0 \left[TN(d_{EMM,1}) - \frac{n(d_{EMM,1})\sqrt{T}}{\sigma} \right] + XTe^{CC_{Dom}T} N(d_{EMM,2}) \right\}$$

Therefore,

$$\rho_{DP^{CN}} = Te^{CC_{Domt}T} - \rho_{DC^{CN}}$$

$$= Te^{CC_{Domt}T} + \left\{ e^{CC_{Unit}T} S_0 \left[TN(d_{EMM,1}) - \frac{n(d_{EMM,1})\sqrt{T}}{\sigma} \right] + XTe^{CC_{Dom}T} N(d_{EMM,2}) \right\}$$

$$= Te^{CC_{Domt}T} \left\{ 1 + SN(d_{EMM,1}) - \frac{Sn(d_{EMM,1})}{\sigma\sqrt{T}} + XN(d_{EMM,2}) \right\}$$

Implementation code comments

FRMDigitalDYOVM.h

The input classes are repeated in this file because you do not know how this class will be implemented in other programs besides this one. As before we have two classes in this implementation header file, one which receives the data inputs, DIGITALOPTIONDATA and another which houses the implementation methods and inherits FRMCDF, FRMDIGITALDYOVM.

```
...
#ifndef CDIGITALOPTIONDATA
#define CDIGITALOPTIONDATA
class DIGITALOPTIONDATA
{
public:
    double StockPrice;
    double StrikePrice;
    double InterestRate;
    double TimeToMaturity;
    double Volatility;
    double DividendYield;
    double CNQuantity;
    double ANQuantity;
};
#endif
```

This class uses the cumulative distribution function estimation.

```
class FRMDIGITALDYOVM : public FRMCDF
{
...
```

FRMDigitalDYOVM.cpp

The digital option valuation and "greeks" code follow. We rely on sub-functions widely. For example, FRMND(CNDigitalDYd2()) estimates $N(d_{EMM,2})$, this code is an example of putting a method into another method as an input. The sub-functions will perform the methods inside parentheses first. You should be able to map the equations in the text with the source code provided here.

```
...
long double FRMDIGITALDYOVM::CNDigitalDYCallValue()
{
    CNCallValue = CNQuantity * exp(-(InterestRate/100.0)* TimeToMaturity)
        * FRMND(CNDigitalDYd2());
    CNDigitalDYCallLowerBound();
    return CNCallValue;
}
//----------------------------------------------------------------------
long double FRMDIGITALDYOVM::CNDigitalDYPutValue()
{
    CNPutValue = CNQuantity * exp(-(InterestRate/100.0) * TimeToMaturity)
```

```
        * FRMND(-CNDigitalDYd2());
    CNDigitalDYPutLowerBound();
    return CNPutValue;
}
...
double FRMDIGITALDYOVM::CNDigitalDYd1()
{
    return (log(StockPrice*exp((-DividendYield/100.0)*TimeToMaturity)/StrikePrice)
        + ((InterestRate/100.0) + pow(Volatility/100.0, 2)/2.0) * TimeToMaturity)
        / ((Volatility/100.0) * pow(TimeToMaturity, 0.5)));
}
//-----------------------------------------------------------------------
double FRMDIGITALDYOVM::CNDigitalDYd2()
{
    return CNDigitalDYd1() - (Volatility/100.0) * pow(TimeToMaturity, 0.5);
}
//-----------------------------------------------------------------------
long double FRMDIGITALDYOVM::CNDigitalDYCallDelta()
{
    return exp(-(DividendYield/100.0) * TimeToMaturity)
        * ( (exp(-pow(CNDigitalDYd1(), 2.0)/2.0)/(2.0*PI))
        / ((Volatility/100.0)* pow(TimeToMaturity, 0.5)) );
}
```

At times, we rely on parity conditions for specific greeks for ease of coding. We provide a separate function in case the next quant using this application does not know these parity relations.

```
long double FRMDIGITALDYOVM::CNDigitalDYPutDelta()
{
    return -CNDigitalDYCallDelta();
}
//-----------------------------------------------------------------------
long double FRMDIGITALDYOVM::CNDigitalDYCallGamma()
{
    return -exp(-(DividendYield/100.0) * TimeToMaturity)
        * CNDigitalDYd1()
        * (exp(-pow(CNDigitalDYd1(),2)/2.0)/pow(2.0 * PI, 0.5))
        / (StockPrice * pow(Volatility/100.0, 2.0) * TimeToMaturity);
}
//-----------------------------------------------------------------------
long double FRMDIGITALDYOVM::CNDigitalDYPutGamma()
{
    return -CNDigitalDYCallGamma();
}
//-----------------------------------------------------------------------
long double FRMDIGITALDYOVM::CNDigitalDYCallVega()
{
    return -exp(-(DividendYield/100.0) * TimeToMaturity) * StockPrice
        * (exp(-pow(CNDigitalDYd1(),2)/2.0)/pow(2.0 * PI, 0.5))
        * (pow(TimeToMaturity, 0.5) - CNDigitalDYd2());
}
//-----------------------------------------------------------------------
long double FRMDIGITALDYOVM::CNDigitalDYPutVega()
{
    return -CNDigitalDYCallVega();
}
```

Remember that theta is measured in calendar time, not time to maturity. Therefore, we must place a minus sign on the derivative with respect to time to maturity.

```
long double FRMDIGITALDYOVM::CNDigitalDYCallTheta()
{
    return -(InterestRate/100.0)*exp(-(InterestRate/100.0) * TimeToMaturity)
        * (1.0 - StrikePrice * FRMND(CNDigitalDYd2()))
        - ( ( StockPrice*exp((-DividendYield/100.0)*TimeToMaturity)
        * (exp(-pow(CNDigitalDYd1(),2)/2.0)/pow(2.0 * PI, 0.5)) )
        / (2.0 * pow(TimeToMaturity, 0.5)) )
        * ( (CNDigitalDYd2()/pow(TimeToMaturity, 0.5)) + (Volatility/100.0) );
}
//-----------------------------------------------------------------------
long double FRMDIGITALDYOVM::CNDigitalDYPutTheta()
{
```

```
    return ( ( StockPrice*exp((-DividendYield/100.0)*TimeToMaturity)
        * (exp(-pow(CNDigitalDYd1(),2)/2.0)/pow(2.0 * PI, 0.5)) )
        / (2.0 * pow(TimeToMaturity, 0.5)) )
        * ( (CNDigitalDYd2()/pow(TimeToMaturity, 0.5)) + (Volatility/100.0) )
        - (InterestRate/100.0)*exp(-(InterestRate/100.0) * TimeToMaturity)
        * StrikePrice * FRMND(CNDigitalDYd2());
}
//-----------------------------------------------------------------------
long double FRMDIGITALDYOVM::CNDigitalDYCallRho()
{
    return -( StockPrice*exp((-DividendYield/100.0)*TimeToMaturity)
        * ( TimeToMaturity * FRMND(CNDigitalDYd1())
        - ( ( (exp(-pow(CNDigitalDYd1(),2.0)/2.0)/pow(2.0*PI,0.5))
        * pow(TimeToMaturity, 0.5)) / (Volatility/100.0)) )
        + StrikePrice*TimeToMaturity*exp(-(InterestRate/100.0) * TimeToMaturity)
        * FRMND(CNDigitalDYd2()) );
}
//-----------------------------------------------------------------------
long double FRMDIGITALDYOVM::CNDigitalDYPutRho()
{
    return TimeToMaturity * exp(-(InterestRate/100.0) * TimeToMaturity)
        * (1.0 + StockPrice * FRMND(CNDigitalDYd1())
        - ( (StockPrice * (exp(-pow(CNDigitalDYd1(),2.0)/2.0)/pow(2.0*PI,0.5)))
        / ((Volatility/100.0) * pow(TimeToMaturity, 0.5)) )
        + StrikePrice * FRMND(CNDigitalDYd2()) );
}
```

For the asset-or-nothing methods, we create a set data function which instantiates the DIGITALOPTIONDATA class within the method and passes the inputs into this class.

```
// ****** ASSET-OR-NOTHING METHODS ******
void FRMDIGITALDYOVM::ANDigitalDYOVMSetData(class DIGITALOPTIONDATA O)
{
    StockPrice = O.StockPrice;
    StrikePrice = O.StrikePrice;
    TimeToMaturity = O.TimeToMaturity;
    Volatility = O.Volatility;
    InterestRate = O.InterestRate;
    DividendYield = O.DividendYield;
    CNQuantity = O.CNQuantity;
    ANQuantity = O.ANQuantity;
}
//-----------------------------------------------------------------------
long double FRMDIGITALDYOVM::ANDigitalDYCallValue()
{
    ANCallValue = ANQuantity * StockPrice*exp((-DividendYield/100.0)*TimeToMaturity)
        * FRMND(ANDigitalDYd1());
    ANDigitalDYCallLowerBound();
    return ANCallValue;
}
//-----------------------------------------------------------------------
long double FRMDIGITALDYOVM::ANDigitalDYPutValue()
{
    ANPutValue = ANQuantity * StockPrice*exp((-DividendYield/100.0)*TimeToMaturity)
        * FRMND(-ANDigitalDYd1());
    ANDigitalDYPutLowerBound();
    return ANPutValue;
}
//-----------------------------------------------------------------------
double FRMDIGITALDYOVM::ANDigitalDYCallLowerBound()
{
    LowerBound = 0.0;
    if (LowerBound > 0.0 && CallValue < LowerBound) CallValue = LowerBound;
    return CallValue;
}
//-----------------------------------------------------------------------
double FRMDIGITALDYOVM::ANDigitalDYPutLowerBound()
{
    LowerBound = 0.0;
    if (LowerBound > 0.0 && PutValue < LowerBound) PutValue = LowerBound;
    return PutValue;
}
```

```
//---------------------------------------------------------------------------
double FRMDIGITALDYOVM::ANDigitalDYd1()
{
    return (log(StockPrice*exp((-DividendYield/100.0)*TimeToMaturity)/StrikePrice)
        + ((InterestRate/100.0) + pow(Volatility/100.0, 2)/2.0) * TimeToMaturity)
        / ((Volatility/100.0) * pow(TimeToMaturity, 0.5));
}
//---------------------------------------------------------------------------
double FRMDIGITALDYOVM::ANDigitalDYd2()
{
    return ANDigitalDYd1() - (Volatility/100.0) * pow(TimeToMaturity, 0.5);
}
//---------------------------------------------------------------------------
long double FRMDIGITALDYOVM::ANDigitalDYCallDelta()
{
    return exp(-(DividendYield/100.0)*TimeToMaturity) * FRMND(CNDigitalDYd1())
        + exp(-(DividendYield/100.0)*TimeToMaturity)
        * (exp(-pow(CNDigitalDYd1(), 2.0)/2.0)/(2.0*PI))
        / ((Volatility/100.0)* pow(TimeToMaturity, 0.5)) ;
}
//---------------------------------------------------------------------------
long double FRMDIGITALDYOVM::ANDigitalDYPutDelta()
{
    return exp(-(DividendYield/100.0) * TimeToMaturity)
        - ANDigitalDYCallDelta();
}
//---------------------------------------------------------------------------
long double FRMDIGITALDYOVM::ANDigitalDYCallGamma()
{
    return ( (exp(-(DividendYield/100.0) * TimeToMaturity)
        * (exp(-pow(ANDigitalDYd1(),2)/2.0)/(pow(2.0 * PI, 0.5))) )
        / (pow(TimeToMaturity, 0.5) * StockPrice * (Volatility/100.0)))
        * (1.0 - (ANDigitalDYd1()/(pow(TimeToMaturity, 0.5)*(Volatility/100.0)))));
}
//---------------------------------------------------------------------------
long double FRMDIGITALDYOVM::ANDigitalDYPutGamma()
{
    return -ANDigitalDYCallGamma();
}
//---------------------------------------------------------------------------
long double FRMDIGITALDYOVM::ANDigitalDYCallVega()
{
    return -exp(-(DividendYield/100.0) * TimeToMaturity)
        * (exp(-pow(ANDigitalDYd1(),2)/2.0)/(pow(2.0 * PI, 0.5)))
        * StockPrice * ANDigitalDYd2();
}
//---------------------------------------------------------------------------
long double FRMDIGITALDYOVM::ANDigitalDYPutVega()
{
    return -ANDigitalDYCallVega();
}
//---------------------------------------------------------------------------
long double FRMDIGITALDYOVM::ANDigitalDYCallTheta()
{
    return -StockPrice * exp((-DividendYield/100.0) * TimeToMaturity)
        * ( -(DividendYield/100.0) * FRMND(ANDigitalDYd1())
        - ( ( (exp(-pow(ANDigitalDYd1(),2.0)/2.0)/pow(2.0*PI,0.5))
        * ANDigitalDYd2() ) / (2.0 * TimeToMaturity) ) );
}
//---------------------------------------------------------------------------
long double FRMDIGITALDYOVM::ANDigitalDYPutTheta()
{
    return StockPrice * exp((-DividendYield/100.0) * TimeToMaturity)
        * ( -(DividendYield/100.0) * (1.0 + FRMND(ANDigitalDYd1()))
        - ( ( (exp(-pow(ANDigitalDYd1(),2.0)/2.0)/pow(2.0*PI,0.5))
        * ANDigitalDYd2() ) / (2.0 * TimeToMaturity) ) );
}
//---------------------------------------------------------------------------
long double FRMDIGITALDYOVM::ANDigitalDYCallRho()
{
    return -exp(-(InterestRate/100.0) * TimeToMaturity) * StockPrice
```

```
        * (TimeToMaturity * FRMND(ANDigitalDYd1())
        - ( ( (exp(-pow(ANDigitalDYd1(),2.0)/2.0)/pow(2.0*PI,0.5))
        * pow(TimeToMaturity, 0.5) ) / (Volatility/100.0) ) );
}
//-----------------------------------------------------------------------
long double FRMDIGITALDYOVM::ANDigitalDYPutRho()
{
    return -ANDigitalDYCallRho();
}
```

References

See references in the supplement to this module.

Appendix 5.5: Interface code comments

An illustration of the graphical user interface for this module is given below.

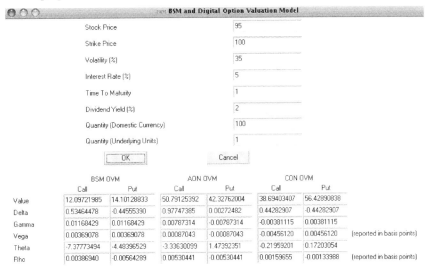

The following are excerpts from the interface header code with selected comments added.

FRMUnitDigitalOVM.h

The interface code is similar to Module 5.4. Again there are two implementation classes and both have separate input classes.

```
...
#include "c:\FRMRepository\FRMBSMDYOVM.cpp"
#include "c:\FRMRepository\FRMDigitalDYOVM.cpp"
#ifndef COPTIONDATA
#define COPTIONDATA
class OPTIONDATA
{
public:
    double StockPrice;
    double StrikePrice;
    double InterestRate;
    double TimeToMaturity;
    double Volatility;
    double DividendYield;
};
#endif
#ifndef CDIGITALOPTIONDATA
#define CDIGITALOPTIONDATA
class DIGITALOPTIONDATA
{
public:
    double StockPrice;
    double StrikePrice;
```

```
   double InterestRate;
   double TimeToMaturity;
   double Volatility;
   double DividendYield;
   double CNQuantity;
   double ANQuantity;
};
#endif
...
   OPTIONDATA OD;
   DIGITALOPTIONDATA BOD;
   FRMBSMDYOVM BSM;
   FRMDIGITALDYOVM DIGITAL;
```

The following are excerpts from the interface code with selected comments added.

FRMUnitDigitalOVM.cpp

We provide just a sample of some function calls here. All of these calls are within the FRMExecute() function.

```
   BSM.BSMDYOVMSetData(OD);
   CallValue = BSM.BSMDYCallValue();
   PutValue = BSM.BSMDYPutValue();
   CallDelta = BSM.BSMDYCallDelta();
   PutDelta = BSM.BSMDYPutDelta();
...
// Cash-or-nothing OVM
   DIGITAL.CNDigitalDYOVMSetData(BOD);
   CNCallValue = DIGITAL.CNDigitalDYCallValue();
   CNPutValue = DIGITAL.CNDigitalDYPutValue();
   CNCallDelta = DIGITAL.CNDigitalDYCallDelta();
   CNPutDelta = DIGITAL.CNDigitalDYPutDelta();
...
// Asset-or-nothing OVM
   DIGITAL.ANDigitalDYOVMSetData(BOD);
   ANCallValue = DIGITAL.ANDigitalDYCallValue();
   ANPutValue = DIGITAL.ANDigitalDYPutValue();
   ANCallDelta = DIGITAL.ANDigitalDYCallDelta();
   ANPutDelta = DIGITAL.ANDigitalDYPutDelta();
...
```

Module 5.6: Centered Differences Applied to Options

Learning objectives

- Explain how to estimate numerical derivatives using a centered difference approach that can be generalized
- Contrast the first four orders of accuracy applied to option valuation problems

Module overview

Many quantitative finance problems require the estimation of numerical derivatives. We deploy a centered difference technique that allows increasing orders of accuracy. Examples of numerical derivatives in finance include:

- Duration and convexity
- Yield volatility estimates from price volatility
- Option valuation model standard 'greeks,' delta, gamma, theta, vega, and rho
- Option valuation model advanced 'greeks,' vanna, charm, speed, zomma, color, vomma, DvegaDtime, ultima, and so forth
- Linear model and VaR (delta-VaR, delta-gamma-VaR, and so forth)
- Merton's default probabilities (delta estimate)
- Exotic option 'greeks'
- Local volatility models (volatility surface estimation)
- Marginal contribution to expected return and risk

In this module, we illustrate the centered difference technique applied to the Black, Scholes, Merton option valuation model, as well as both the American-style and European-style binomial option valuation model. The details of this approach are provided in the supplement to this module.[41]

We now present the first and second derivative approximations for up to order or accuracy 4. We assume a generic function, y = f(x) and $f^d(x)$ denotes the dth derivative of y with respect to x. Also, p denotes the $O(h^p)$ order of accuracy of the approximation from the Taylor series. That is, p is a measure of the potential error in the Taylor series estimate, the higher the p order, the lower the potential estimation error.

Numerical derivative orders of accuracy

Numerical derivative order of accuracy 1

First derivative: d = 1, p = 2

$$f^1(x) \cong \frac{f(x+h) - f(x-h)}{2h}$$

Second derivative: d = 2, p = 1

$$f^2(x) \cong \frac{f(x+h) - 2f(x) + f(x-h)}{h^2}$$

Numerical derivative order of accuracy 2

First derivative: d = 1, p = 4

$$f^1(x) \cong \frac{-f(x+2h) + 8f(x+h) - 8f(x-h) + f(x-2h)}{12h}$$

---

[41] Supplements are available at www.frmhelp.com.

Second derivative: d = 2, p = 3

$$f^2(x) \cong \frac{-f(x+2h)+16f(x+h)-30f(x)+16f(x-h)-f(x-2h)}{12h^2}$$

Numerical derivative order of accuracy 3

First derivative: d = 1, p = 6

$$f^1(x) \cong \frac{f(x+3h)-9f(x+2h)+45f(x+h)-45f(x-h)+9f(x-2h)-f(x-3h)}{60h}$$

Second derivative: d = 2, p = 5

$$f^2(x) \cong \frac{f(x+3h)-13.5f(x+2h)+135f(x+h)-245f(x)+135f(x-h)-13.5f(x-2h)+f(x-3h)}{90h^2}$$

Numerical derivative order of accuracy 4

First derivative: d = 1, p = 8

$$f^1(x) \cong \frac{1}{h}\left[\begin{array}{c} \dfrac{f(x-4h)}{280} - \dfrac{4f(x-3h)}{105} + \dfrac{f(x-2h)}{5} - \dfrac{4f(x-h)}{5} + 0f(x) \\ + \dfrac{4f(x+h)}{5} - \dfrac{f(x+2h)}{5} + \dfrac{4f(x+3h)}{105} - \dfrac{f(x+4h)}{280} \end{array}\right]$$

Second derivative: d = 2, p = 7

$$f^2(x) \cong \frac{2}{h^2}\left[\begin{array}{c} -\dfrac{f(x-4h)}{1,120} + \dfrac{4f(x-3h)}{315} - \dfrac{f(x-2h)}{10} + \dfrac{4f(x-h)}{5} - \dfrac{205f(x)}{144} \\ + \dfrac{4f(x+h)}{5} - \dfrac{f(x+2h)}{10} + \dfrac{4f(x+3h)}{315} - \dfrac{f(x+4h)}{1,120} \end{array}\right]$$

We now illustrate how this theorem and related results can be used in option risk management.

Implementation code comments

The header file presents nothing new. We highlight just the binomial model call gamma, the second derivative of the option value with respect to the stock price.

FRMBSMDYOVMCD.cpp, .h

Although much more efficient code could be written here, this code is very easy to understand and follow. The discussion above clearly lays out the ability to estimate any number of derivatives of most financial functions. We illustrate just delta for a call from this implementation code.

```
long double FRMBSMDYOVM::NGBSMDYCallDelta()
{
   if (Order==1) {
      Original = StockPrice;    // Greek dependent
      Change = Increment*Original;
      High = Original + Change;
      StockPrice = High;        // Greek dependent
      OHigh = BSMDYCallValue();
      Low = Original - Change;
      StockPrice = Low;         // Greek dependent
      OLow = BSMDYCallValue();
      StockPrice = Original;    // Greek dependent
      return (OHigh - OLow)/(High - Low);
   } else if (Order==2) {
      Original = StockPrice;    // Greek dependent
```

```
      Change = Increment*Original;
      High = Original + Change;
      StockPrice = High;          // Greek dependent
      OHigh = BSMDYCallValue();
      Low = Original - Change;
      StockPrice = Low;           // Greek dependent
      OLow = BSMDYCallValue();
      Change = 2.0*Increment*Original;
      High2 = Original + Change;
      StockPrice = High2;         // Greek dependent
      OHigh2 = BSMDYCallValue();
      Low2 = Original - Change;
      StockPrice = Low2;          // Greek dependent
      OLow2 = BSMDYCallValue();
      StockPrice = Original;     // Greek dependent
      return (-OHigh2 + 8.0*OHigh - 8.0*OLow + OLow2)/(12.0*Increment*Original);
} else if (Order==3) {
      Original = StockPrice;     // Greek dependent
      Change = Increment*Original;
      High = Original + Change;
      StockPrice = High;          // Greek dependent
      OHigh = BSMDYCallValue();
      Low = Original - Change;
      StockPrice = Low;           // Greek dependent
      OLow = BSMDYCallValue();
      Change = 2.0*Increment*Original;
      High2 = Original + Change;
      StockPrice = High2;         // Greek dependent
      OHigh2 = BSMDYCallValue();
      Low2 = Original - Change;
      StockPrice = Low2;          // Greek dependent
      OLow2 = BSMDYCallValue();
      StockPrice = Original;     // Greek dependent
      Change = 3.0*Increment*Original;
      High3 = Original + Change;
      StockPrice = High3;         // Greek dependent
      OHigh3 = BSMDYCallValue();
      Low3 = Original - Change;
      StockPrice = Low3;          // Greek dependent
      OLow3 = BSMDYCallValue();
      StockPrice = Original;     // Greek dependent
      return (OHigh3 - 9.0*OHigh2 + 45.0*OHigh - 45.0*OLow + 9.0*OLow2 - OLow3)
          /(60.0*Increment*Original);
} else if (Order==4) {
      Original = StockPrice;     // Greek dependent
      Change = Increment*Original;
      High = Original + Change;
      StockPrice = High;          // Greek dependent
      OHigh = BSMDYCallValue();
      Low = Original - Change;
      StockPrice = Low;           // Greek dependent
      OLow = BSMDYCallValue();
      Change = 2.0*Increment*Original;
      High2 = Original + Change;
      StockPrice = High2;         // Greek dependent
      OHigh2 = BSMDYCallValue();
      Low2 = Original - Change;
      StockPrice = Low2;          // Greek dependent
      OLow2 = BSMDYCallValue();
      StockPrice = Original;     // Greek dependent
      Change = 3.0*Increment*Original;
      High3 = Original + Change;
      StockPrice = High3;         // Greek dependent
      OHigh3 = BSMDYCallValue();
      Low3 = Original - Change;
      StockPrice = Low3;          // Greek dependent
      OLow3 = BSMDYCallValue();
      StockPrice = Original;     // Greek dependent
      Change = 4.0*Increment*Original;
      High4 = Original + Change;
      StockPrice = High4;         // Greek dependent
```

```
      OHigh4 = BSMDYCallValue();
      Low4 = Original - Change;
      StockPrice = Low4;        // Greek dependent
      OLow4 = BSMDYCallValue();
      StockPrice = Original;    // Greek dependent
      return ((OLow4/280.0)- (4.0*OLow3/105.0) + (OLow2/5.0) - (4.0*OLow/5.0)
          + (4.0*OHigh/5.0) - (OHigh2/5.0) + (4.0*OHigh3/105.0) - (OHigh4/280.0))
          /(Increment*Original);
   } else {
      return -99;
   }
}
```

FRMAmerBinOVMCD.cpp, .h

We illustrate just the gamma of a call in this module.

```
double FRMBinDYOVM::FRMNGAmerDivBinCallGamma()
{
   if (Order==1) {
      Original = StockPrice;   // Greek dependent
      Change = Increment*Original;
      High = Original + Change;
      StockPrice = High;       // Greek dependent
      OHigh = FRMAmerDivBinCall();
      Low = Original - Change;
      StockPrice = Low;        // Greek dependent
      OLow = FRMAmerDivBinCall();
      StockPrice = Original;   // Greek dependent
      OMid = FRMAmerDivBinCall();
      return ((OHigh - OMid) - (OMid - OLow))/pow(Change, 2.0);
   } else if (Order==2){
      Original = StockPrice;   // Greek dependent
      Change = Increment*Original;
      High = Original + Change;
      StockPrice = High;       // Greek dependent
      OHigh = FRMAmerDivBinCall();
      Low = Original - Change;
      StockPrice = Low;        // Greek dependent
      OLow = FRMAmerDivBinCall();
      Change = 2.0*Increment*Original;
      High2 = Original + Change;
      StockPrice = High2;      // Greek dependent
      OHigh2 = FRMAmerDivBinCall();
      Low2 = Original - Change;
      StockPrice = Low2;       // Greek dependent
      OLow2 = FRMAmerDivBinCall();
      StockPrice = Original;   // Greek dependent
      OMid = FRMAmerDivBinCall();
      return (-OHigh2 + 16.0*OHigh - 30.0*OMid + 16.0*OLow - OLow2)
          /(12.0*pow(Increment*Original,2.0));
   } else if (Order==3){
      Original = StockPrice;   // Greek dependent
      Change = Increment*Original;
      High = Original + Change;
      StockPrice = High;       // Greek dependent
      OHigh = FRMAmerDivBinCall();
      Low = Original - Change;
      StockPrice = Low;        // Greek dependent
      OLow = FRMAmerDivBinCall();
      Change = 2.0*Increment*Original;
      High2 = Original + Change;
      StockPrice = High2;      // Greek dependent
      OHigh2 = FRMAmerDivBinCall();
      Low2 = Original - Change;
      StockPrice = Low2;       // Greek dependent
      OLow2 = FRMAmerDivBinCall();
      Change = 3.0*Increment*Original;
      High3 = Original + Change;
      StockPrice = High3;      // Greek dependent
      OHigh3 = FRMAmerDivBinCall();
      Low3 = Original - Change;
```

```
      StockPrice = Low3;         // Greek dependent
      OLow3 = FRMAmerDivBinCall();
      StockPrice = Original;    // Greek dependent
      OMid = FRMAmerDivBinCall();
      return (OHigh3 - 13.5*OHigh2 + 135.0*OHigh - 245.0*OMid
         + 135.0*OLow - 13.5*OLow2 + OLow3)
         /(90.0*pow(Increment*Original,2.0)));
  } else if (Order==4){
      Original = StockPrice;    // Greek dependent
      Change = Increment*Original;
      High = Original + Change;
      StockPrice = High;        // Greek dependent
      OHigh = FRMAmerDivBinCall();
      Low = Original - Change;
      StockPrice = Low;         // Greek dependent
      OLow = FRMAmerDivBinCall();
      Change = 2.0*Increment*Original;
      High2 = Original + Change;
      StockPrice = High2;       // Greek dependent
      OHigh2 = FRMAmerDivBinCall();
      Low2 = Original - Change;
      StockPrice = Low2;        // Greek dependent
      OLow2 = FRMAmerDivBinCall();
      Change = 3.0*Increment*Original;
      High3 = Original + Change;
      StockPrice = High3;       // Greek dependent
      OHigh3 = FRMAmerDivBinCall();
      Low3 = Original - Change;
      StockPrice = Low3;        // Greek dependent
      OLow3 = FRMAmerDivBinCall();
      Change = 4.0*Increment*Original;
      High4 = Original + Change;
      StockPrice = High4;       // Greek dependent
      OHigh4 = FRMAmerDivBinCall();
      Low4 = Original - Change;
      StockPrice = Low4;        // Greek dependent
      OLow4 = FRMAmerDivBinCall();
      StockPrice = Original;    // Greek dependent
      OMid = FRMAmerDivBinCall();
      return 2.0*((-OLow4/1120.0) + (4.0*OLow3/315.0) - (OLow2/10.0) + (4.0*OLow/5.0)
         - (205.0*OMid/144.0)
         + (4.0*OHigh/5.0) - (OHigh2/10.0) + (4.0*OHigh3/315.0) - (OHigh4/1120.0))
         /pow(Increment*Original, 2.0);
  } else {
      return -99;
  }
}
```

References

Eberly, D. 2008. Derivative Approximation by Finite Differences. http://www.geometrictools.com/, March 2, 2008.

Appendix 5.6: Interface code comments

The following illustrates the graphical user interface for this module.

BSM and Binomial Dividend Yield Option Valuation Model With Centered Differences

Stock Price	95	Up Probability (EMM, %)	50	
Strike Price	100	Number of Time Steps (Even Number, 3650 max)	3600	
Volatility (%)	35	Type (European=0, American=1)	1	
Interest Rate (%)	5	Numerical Derivative Order of Accuracy	4	
Time To Maturity	1	Numerical Derivative Increment Percent (%)	3	
Dividend Yield (%)	2			

OK   Cancel

	BSM OVM		Binomial OVM		
	Call	Put	Call	Put	
Value	12.09721985	14.10128833	12.09688386	14.55907278	
Delta	0.53464478	-0.44555390	0.53449421	-0.46824600	
Gamma	0.01168429	0.01168429	0.01196807	0.01303187	
Vega	0.00369078	0.00369078	0.00369523	0.00368882	(reported in basis points)
Theta	-7.37773494	-4.48396529	-7.37394406	-5.01951419	
Rho	0.00386940	-0.00564289	0.00384005	-0.00418018	(reported in basis points)

Numerical Greeks

	BSM OVM		Binomial OVM		
	Call	Put	Call	Put	
Delta	0.53464478	-0.44555390	0.53482740	-0.46785481	
Gamma	0.01168429	0.01168429	0.01212041	0.01314709	
Vega	0.00369078	0.00369078	0.00369654	0.00368992	(reported in basis points)
Theta	-7.37773493	-4.48396529	-7.37316592	-5.01876072	
Rho	0.00386940	-0.00564289	0.00383044	-0.00418790	(reported in basis points)

The interface code is nearly identical to several other programs already reviewed.

FRMUnitCenteredDifferences.cpp, .h

Module 5.7: Interest Rate Swaps Risk Management

Learning objectives

- Understand one method of valuing interest rate swaps with two separate rate curves, one for discounting and one for estimating the forward rate
- Integrate the LSC curve fitting routine into a method for valuing interest rate swaps and measuring the related interest rate risk
- Illustrate both comparative statics and decomposing holding period returns
- Explain the role of cash collateral in estimating the holding period return related to interest rate swaps

Module overview

This module assumes you have previously studied several other modules. Specifically, we will estimate the first and second derivatives using numerical derivative estimation techniques introduced in Module 5.6 Centered Differences Applied to Option Valuation. We will use the LSC curve fitting model covered in Modules 3.5 Curve Fitting Using Regression (see also Module 4.5 Analysis of Interest Rate Swaps).

Interest rate swap valuation

The core valuation technique applied here is to assume that the forward rates and the discount rates have already been reasonably estimated via the LSC curve fitting model based on annualized continuously compounded interest rates. The discount curve is used to compute the present value of future cash flows and the forward curve is used to estimate the appropriate rates to use for the floating leg cash flows. Both curves are assumed to follow the LSC model based on the following:

$$r\left(\tau_i : t_k\right) = \sum_{n=0}^{N_F} C_{i,n}\left(\tau_i; s_{n-1}\right) b_{n,t_k}$$

where

$$C_{i,0}\left(\tau_i; s_{-1}\right) = 1$$

$$C_{i,1}\left(\tau_i; s_0\right) = \frac{s_0}{\tau_i}\left[1 - e^{-\tau_i/s_0}\right]$$

$$C_{i,n}\left(\tau_i; s_{n-1}\right) = \frac{s_{n-1}}{\tau_i}\left[1 - e^{-\tau_i/s_{n-1}}\right] - e^{-\tau_i/s_{n-1}}; n > 1$$

where s_n again denotes scalars that apply various weights to different locations on the term structure; $C_{i,n}\left(\tau_i; s_{n-1}\right)$ denotes LSC maturity coefficients, a parameter that depends solely on maturity time and selected scalars; and $b_{n,t}$ denotes the LSC spot rate factor, a parameter that is typically found using ordinary least squares regression applied to maturity time spot rates.

The plain vanilla interest rate swap rates reported presently in the H.15 file by the Federal Reserve assumes a semiannual pay and 30/360 day count on the fixed leg of the swap and assumes a quarterly pay and Actual/360 day count on the floating leg of the swap. The module provides limited flexibility by allowing for payment frequencies of monthly, quarterly, semiannually, and annually. The number of accrued days (NAD) can be either based on a 30 day month method or actual day month method. The number of total days (NTD) can be either 360 or 365 days per year. To keep this portion of the code manageable, we ignore issues like week-end, end-of-the-month, leap years, and so forth. The user can also select either a received fixed or receive floating swap.

With the notional amount and the fixed rate on the swap, we have enough information to value the interest rate swap based on the following formula:

$$V_{Swap} = r_{fix} \sum_{i=1}^{n_{fix}} \frac{NAD_i}{NTD_i} e^{-(r_{DC,i}t_i)} - \sum_{j=1}^{n_{flt}} r_{FC,j} \frac{NAD_j}{NTD_j} e^{-(r_{DC,j}t_j)}$$

$$= r_{fix} \sum_{i=1}^{n_{fix}} AP_i e^{-(r_{DC,i}t_i)} - \sum_{j=1}^{n_{flt}} r_{FC,j} AP_j e^{-(r_{DC,j}t_j)}$$

where r_{fix} denotes the fixed rate, $r_{FC,j}$ is the forward rate based on the LSC model for the period ending at t_j, and $r_{DC,j}$ is the discount rate based on the LSC model for the point in time t. Calendar time is managed based on the number of accrued days in a period, NAD_i, and the number of total days in a year, NTD_i. The ratio results in the accrual period, AP_i. The forward rate is imputed from the inputted spot rate based on the following relationship:

$$r_{FC,j} = \frac{r_{FC,j}t_j - r_{FC,j-1}t_{j-1}}{t_j - t_{j-1}}$$

The equilibrium swap rate is

$$\hat{r}_{fix} = \frac{\sum_{j=1}^{n_{flt}} r_{FC,j} AP_j e^{-(r_{DC,j}t_j)}}{\sum_{i=1}^{n_{fix}} AP_i e^{-(r_{DC,i}t_i)}} = \sum_{j=1}^{n_{flt}} w_j r_{FC,j}$$

where

$$w_j = \frac{AP_j e^{-(r_{DC,j}t_j)}}{\sum_{i=1}^{n_{fix}} AP_i e^{-(r_{DC,i}t_i)}}$$

Thus, the equilibrium swap rate can be viewed as a weighted average of the appropriate forward rates. Due to the possibility of different payment frequencies between the floating and fixed swap legs, the sum of the weights do not have to precisely equal one.

Interest rate swap risk measures

We estimate the first and second derivatives for each parameter of the forward curve and the discount curve using the centered difference technique at order of accuracy four. Recall the first derivative can be approximated as (see Module 5.6, Order of accuracy 4)

$$f'(x) \cong \frac{1}{h} \left[\begin{array}{c} \frac{f(x-4h)}{280} - \frac{4f(x-3h)}{105} + \frac{f(x-2h)}{5} - \frac{4f(x-h)}{5} + 0f(x) \\ + \frac{4f(x+h)}{5} - \frac{f(x+2h)}{5} + \frac{4f(x+3h)}{105} - \frac{f(x+4h)}{280} \end{array} \right]$$

and the second derivative can be approximated as

$$f^2(x) \cong \frac{2}{h^2} \left[\begin{array}{c} -\frac{f(x-4h)}{1,120} + \frac{4f(x-3h)}{315} - \frac{f(x-2h)}{10} + \frac{4f(x-h)}{5} - \frac{205f(x)}{144} \\ + \frac{4f(x+h)}{5} - \frac{f(x+2h)}{10} + \frac{4f(x+3h)}{315} - \frac{f(x+4h)}{1,120} \end{array} \right]$$

Because we are taking the derivatives of interest rates, we use h = 0.0001 for the first derivative and h = 0.01 for the second derivative. If we use more precision with h, we will then introduce significant machine error.

Interest rate swap holding period return decomposition

The first problem with estimating the holding period return for an interest rate swap is the lack of "investment." Remember, interest rate swaps are contracts and often are structured to have zero market value on the day entered. Holding period return is profit divided by investment and a zero investment is a problem. Financial derivatives, however, do require collateral and the collateral can be thought of as an "investment." Financial managers are prudent to set aside cash to support financial derivatives positions, particularly if they are risk increasing. In the case of interest rate swaps, the implied cash collateral is a measure of the degree of leverage in the position. We use continuously compounded holding period returns, as that allows for rather simple decompositions. The risk factors (F) here are the LSC parameters for both the forward curve and the discount curve (a total of M assumed here). A three factor LSC model for both curves would result in six total risk factors (M = 6). If the evaluation date's parameter does not change over the horizon period, then a certain return is earned (horizon return). If we allow only one factor to change, then that factor's return is earned. Notice in the expression below that the factor return is based on the horizon date's swap value using the evaluation date's parameters.

$$\tilde{R}_\Delta = \ln\left[\frac{\tilde{V}_\Delta\left(\tilde{F}_{1\Delta}, \tilde{F}_{2\Delta}, \dots, \tilde{F}_{M\Delta}\right)}{V\left(F_1, F_2, \dots, F_M\right)}\right]$$

$$= \ln\left[\frac{V_\Delta\left(F_1, F_2, \dots, F_M\right)}{V\left(F_1, F_2, \dots, F_M\right)}\right] + \ln\left[\frac{\tilde{V}_\Delta\left(\tilde{F}_{1\Delta}, F_2, \dots, F_M\right)}{V_\Delta\left(F_1, F_2, \dots, F_M\right)}\right] + \ln\left[\frac{\tilde{V}_\Delta\left(F_1, \tilde{F}_{2\Delta}, \dots, \tilde{F}_M\right)}{V_\Delta\left(F_1, F_2, \dots, F_M\right)}\right] + \dots + \ln\left[\frac{\tilde{V}_\Delta\left(F_1, F_2, \dots, \tilde{F}_{M\Delta}\right)}{V_\Delta\left(F_1, F_2, \dots, F_M\right)}\right] + \tilde{R}_1$$

$$= R_\Delta^h + \tilde{R}_\Delta^{F_1} + \tilde{R}_\Delta^{F_2} + \dots + \tilde{R}_\Delta^{F_M} + \tilde{I}_\Delta$$

The residual term is an interaction return that accounts for the remaining holding period return. Note that the return attributable to the horizon return is known at the beginning of the holding period, whereas the return attributable to the factors and the interaction term, are all unknown. Thus, the unknown swap return component can be expressed as the swap position's holding period return less the known horizon component.

$$\tilde{R}_\Delta^{Unknown} = \tilde{R}_\Delta - R_\Delta^h = \tilde{R}_\Delta^{F_1} + \tilde{R}_\Delta^{F_2} + \dots + \tilde{R}_\Delta^{F_M} + \tilde{I}_\Delta$$

This important insight will result in different measures of swap risk.

Implementation code comments

FRMIRSwapRiskManagement.h

This implementation code header file is rather long, but contains nothing new. We provide just a few snippets of code.

```
#ifndef FRMIRSwapRiskManagementH
#define FRMIRSwapRiskManagementH
...
#ifndef FRMCALENDARCPP
#define FRMCALENDARCPP
#include "c:\FRMRepository\FRMCalendar.cpp"
#endif
#ifndef FRMLSCCURVEFITTINGFILE
#define FRMLSCCURVEFITTINGFILE
#include "c:\FRMRepository\FRMLSCCurveFitting.cpp"
#endif
```

Because of the large number of inputs, we pass them by a single class.

```
#ifndef CIRSWAPDATA
#define CIRSWAPDATA
class IRSWAPDATA
{
public:
    int EM, ED, EY; // Evaluation Date
    int HM, HD, HY; // Horizon Date
    int MM, MD, MY; // Maturity Date
    int NumberLSCFR; // Number of LSC parameters for forward rates
    int NumberLSCDR; // Number of LSC parameters for discount rates
    int FixedPF; // Index to hold payment frequency: fixed
    int FloatingPF;//0 = Monthly, 1 = Quarterly, 2 = Semiannually, 3 = Annually
    int FixedNAD; // 0 = Actual, 1 = 30/360
    int FloatingNAD;  // 0 = Actual, 1 = 30/360
    int FixedNTD;     // 0 = 360, 1 = 365
    int FloatingNTD; // 0 = 360, 1 = 365
    int ReceivePay;  // 0 = Receive fixed, 1 = Receive floating
    double NotionalAmount;
    double FixedRate;
    double CashCollateral;
    double EDFCParameters[6]; // Evaluation date forward curve parameters
    double EDFCScalars[5];    // Evaluation date forward curve scalars
    double EDDCParameters[6]; // Evaluation date discount curve parameters
    double EDDCScalars[5];    // Evaluation date discount curve scalars
    double HDFCParameters[6]; // Horizon date information
    double HDFCScalars[5];
    double HDDCParameters[6];
    double HDDCScalars[5];
};
#endif
```

Note that the LSC model methods and calendar methods are public in this class. The input data is set into this class with a single method (FRMIRSwapRMSetData(class IRSWAPDATA IRSD)). The object IRSD stands for interest rate swap data.

```
class FRMIRSWAPRM : public FRMLSC, FRMCALENDAR
{
public:
    void __fastcall FRMIRSwapRMSetData(class IRSWAPDATA IRSD);
    int EM, ED, EY; // Evaluation Date
...
    double FRMEDFairValue();
    double FRMHDFairValue();
    double FRMEDFDLevel();
...
```

We also make use of some private variables and methods.

```
private:
    double SV, NSV;
    double OHDFCParameters[6];
    double OHDDCParameters[6];
    double Return;
    double Original, High, Low, Change, OHigh, OLow, OMid;
    double High2, Low2, OHigh2, OLow2;
    double High3, Low3, OHigh3, OLow3;
    double High4, Low4, OHigh4, OLow4;
    int i, j; // Counters
    int FRMPaymentsRemaining(int BegM, int BegD, int BegY,
        int EndM, int EndD, int EndY, int PF);
    int FRMNAD(int TM, int TD, int TY, int FixedPF);
    double FRMEDDCRate(double TTM);
    double FRMEDFCRate(double LTTM, double TTM);
    double FRMHDDCRate(double TTM);
    double FRMHDFCRate(double LTTM, double TTM);
};
#endif
```

FRMIRSwapRiskManagement.cpp

We do not reproduce the several hundred lines of code; rather, we provide a brief sample. The methods are in reverse order of development as it is easier to keep the work in progress at the top of the file. Thus, the horizon return decomposition materials come first.

```
...
double FRMIRSWAPRM::FRMHRDHorizon()
{
    SV = FRMEDFairValue();
    for (i = 0; i < 6; i++) { // Preserve original horizon date parameters
        OHDFCParameters[i] = HDFCParameters[i];
        HDFCParameters[i] = EDFCParameters[i];
        OHDDCParameters[i] = HDDCParameters[i];
        HDDCParameters[i] = EDDCParameters[i];
    }
    NSV = FRMHDFairValue();
    Return = log(1.0 + (NSV - SV)/((CashCollateral/100.0)*NotionalAmount))*100.0;
    for (i = 0; i < 6; i++) { // Replace with original horizon date parameters
        HDFCParameters[i] = OHDFCParameters[i];
        HDDCParameters[i] = OHDDCParameters[i];
    }
    return Return;
}

double FRMIRSWAPRM::FRMHRDFCLevel()
{
    for (i = 0; i < 6; i++) { // Preserve original horizon date parameters
        OHDFCParameters[i] = HDFCParameters[i];
        HDFCParameters[i] = EDFCParameters[i];
        OHDDCParameters[i] = HDDCParameters[i];
        HDDCParameters[i] = EDDCParameters[i];
    }
    SV = FRMHDFairValue();
    HDFCParameters[0] = OHDFCParameters[0];
    NSV = FRMHDFairValue();
    Return = log(1.0 + (NSV - SV)/((CashCollateral/100.0)*NotionalAmount))*100.0;
    for (i = 0; i < 6; i++) { // Replace with original horizon date parameters
        HDFCParameters[i] = OHDFCParameters[i];
        HDDCParameters[i] = OHDDCParameters[i];
    }
    return Return;
}
...
```

Next, we have the estimates of the first and second derivatives where the second derivatives are first. Note the Change = 0.01 for the second derivative and Change = 0.0001 for the first derivative.

```
double FRMIRSWAPRM::FRMEDDCSDLevel()
{
    Change = 0.01; // Absolute change because it may be zero
    Original = EDDCParameters[0];
    High = Original + Change;
    EDDCParameters[0] = High;
    OHigh = FRMEDFairValue();
    Low = Original - Change;
    EDDCParameters[0] = Low;
    OLow = FRMEDFairValue();
    High2 = Original + 2.0*Change;
    EDDCParameters[0] = High2;
    OHigh2 = FRMEDFairValue();
    Low2 = Original - 2.0*Change;
    EDDCParameters[0] = Low2;
    OLow2 = FRMEDFairValue();
    EDDCParameters[0] = Original;
    High3 = Original + 3.0*Change;
    EDDCParameters[0] = High3;
    OHigh3 = FRMEDFairValue();
    Low3 = Original - 3.0*Change;
    EDDCParameters[0] = Low3;
    OLow3 = FRMEDFairValue();
```

```
    EDDCParameters[0] = Original;
    High4 = Original + 4.0*Change;
    EDDCParameters[0] = High4;
    OHigh4 = FRMEDFairValue();
    Low4 = Original - 4.0*Change;
    EDDCParameters[0] = Low4;
    OLow4 = FRMEDFairValue();
    EDDCParameters[0] = Original;
    OMid = FRMEDFairValue();
    return 2.0*((-OLow4/1120.0) + (4.0*OLow3/315.0) - (OLow2/10.0) + (4.0*OLow/5.0)
        - (205.0*OMid/144.0)
        + (4.0*OHigh/5.0) - (OHigh2/10.0) + (4.0*OHigh3/315.0) - (OHigh4/1120.0))
        / pow(Change, 2.0);
}
...
double FRMIRSWAPRM::FRMEDDCFDLevel()
{
    Change = 0.0001; // Absolute change because it may be zero
    Original = EDDCParameters[0];
    High = Original + Change;
    EDDCParameters[0] = High;
    OHigh = FRMEDFairValue();
    Low = Original - Change;
    EDDCParameters[0] = Low;
    OLow = FRMEDFairValue();
    High2 = Original + 2.0*Change;
    EDDCParameters[0] = High2;
    OHigh2 = FRMEDFairValue();
    Low2 = Original - 2.0*Change;
    EDDCParameters[0] = Low2;
    OLow2 = FRMEDFairValue();
    EDDCParameters[0] = Original;
    High3 = Original + 3.0*Change;
    EDDCParameters[0] = High3;
    OHigh3 = FRMEDFairValue();
    Low3 = Original - 3.0*Change;
    EDDCParameters[0] = Low3;
    OLow3 = FRMEDFairValue();
    EDDCParameters[0] = Original;
    High4 = Original + 4.0*Change;
    EDDCParameters[0] = High4;
    OHigh4 = FRMEDFairValue();
    Low4 = Original - 4.0*Change;
    EDDCParameters[0] = Low4;
    OLow4 = FRMEDFairValue();
    EDDCParameters[0] = Original;
    return ((OLow4/280.0)- (4.0*OLow3/105.0) + (OLow2/5.0) - (4.0*OLow/5.0)
        + (4.0*OHigh/5.0) - (OHigh2/5.0) + (4.0*OHigh3/105.0) - (OHigh4/280.0))
        / (Change);
}
...
```

The swap's fair value at the horizon date and evaluation date come next. The equilibrium swap rate code is nearly identical.

```
double FRMIRSWAPRM::FRMHDFairValue()
{
    int NFloatingPayments;
    int NFixedPayments;
    long int JBeginningDate, JEndingDate;
    double TTM, LTTM;  // Time to maturity and lagged TTM (forward rate)
    double RateDC; // Discount curve rate (cc)
    double RateFC; // Forward curve rate (cc)
    double FairValue;
    int TM, TD, TY;   // Temporary month, day, and year
    long int TEndingDate; // Temporary ending date
    int TNAD; // Temporary number of accrued days
    int TNTD; // Temporary number of total days
    double ValueFixedLeg;
    double ValueFloatingLeg;
// Work on fixed leg
    JBeginningDate = FRMToJulian(HM, HD, HY);
```

```
    JEndingDate = FRMToJulian(MM, MD, MY);
    NFixedPayments = FRMPaymentsRemaining(HM, HD, HY, MM, MD, MY, FixedPF);
    TM = MM; TD = MD; TY = MY;
    TEndingDate = JEndingDate;
    if (FixedNTD == 0) TNTD = 360;
    if (FixedNTD == 1) TNTD = 365;
    ValueFixedLeg = 0.0;
    for (i = NFixedPayments; i > 0; i--) {
        TNAD = FRMNAD(TM, TD, TY, FixedPF);
        TTM = ((double)(TEndingDate - JBeginningDate)/365.25);
        RateDC = FRMHDDCRate(TTM);
        TEndingDate -= TNAD;      // Decrement 1 and recalculate TTM
        TM = FRMFromJulianMonth(TEndingDate);
        TD = FRMFromJulianDay(TEndingDate);
        TY = FRMFromJulianYear(TEndingDate);
        if (FixedNAD == 1) {
            if (FixedPF == 0) TNAD = 30;
            if (FixedPF == 1) TNAD = 90;
            if (FixedPF == 2) TNAD = 180;
            if (FixedPF == 3) TNAD = 360;
        }
        ValueFixedLeg += (FixedRate/100.0) * ((double)TNAD/(double)TNTD)
            * exp(-(RateDC/100.0)*TTM);
    }
// Work on floating leg
    JBeginningDate = FRMToJulian(HM, HD, HY);
    JEndingDate = FRMToJulian(MM, MD, MY);
    NFloatingPayments = FRMPaymentsRemaining(HM, HD, HY, MM, MD, MY, FloatingPF);
    TM = MM; TD = MD; TY = MY;
    TEndingDate = JEndingDate;
    if (FloatingNTD == 0) TNTD = 360;
    if (FloatingNTD == 1) TNTD = 365;
    ValueFloatingLeg = 0.0;
    for (i = NFloatingPayments; i > 0; i--) {
        TNAD = FRMNAD(TM, TD, TY, FloatingPF);
        TTM = ((double)(TEndingDate - JBeginningDate)/365.25);// End of period
        RateDC = FRMHDDCRate(TTM); // Actual fraction of year
        TEndingDate -= TNAD;    // Decrement 1 and recalculate
        TM = FRMFromJulianMonth(TEndingDate);
        TD = FRMFromJulianDay(TEndingDate);
        TY = FRMFromJulianYear(TEndingDate);
        LTTM = ((double)(TEndingDate - JBeginningDate)/365.25);// Beginning of period
        RateFC = FRMHDFCRate(LTTM, TTM); // Forward rate at beginning of period
        if (FloatingNAD == 1) {
            if (FloatingPF == 0) TNAD = 30;
            if (FloatingPF == 1) TNAD = 90;
            if (FloatingPF == 2) TNAD = 180;
            if (FloatingPF == 3) TNAD = 360;
        }
        ValueFloatingLeg += (RateFC/100.0) * ((double)TNAD/(double)TNTD)
            * exp(-(RateDC/100.0)*TTM);
    }
    FairValue = NotionalAmount*(ValueFixedLeg - ValueFloatingLeg);
    if (ReceivePay > 0) FairValue *= -1.0;
    return FairValue;
}
//----------------------------------------------------------------------------
double FRMIRSWAPRM::FRMEDFairValue()
{
    int NFloatingPayments;
    int NFixedPayments;
    long int JBeginningDate, JEndingDate;
    double TTM, LTTM;  // Time to maturity and lagged TTM (forward rate)
    double RateDC; // Discount curve rate (cc)
    double RateFC; // Forward curve rate (cc)
    double FairValue;
    int TM, TD, TY;   // Temporary month, day, and year
    long int TEndingDate; // Temporary ending date
    int TNAD; // Temporary number of accrued days
    int TNTD; // Temporary number of total days
    double ValueFixedLeg;
```

```
      double ValueFloatingLeg;
// Work on fixed leg
   JBeginningDate = FRMToJulian(EM, ED, EY);
   JEndingDate = FRMToJulian(MM, MD, MY);
   NFixedPayments = FRMPaymentsRemaining(EM, ED, EY, MM, MD, MY, FixedPF);
   TM = MM; TD = MD; TY = MY;
   TEndingDate = JEndingDate;
   if (FixedNTD == 0) TNTD = 360;
   if (FixedNTD == 1) TNTD = 365;
   ValueFixedLeg = 0.0;
   for (i = NFixedPayments; i > 0; i--) {
      TNAD = FRMNAD(TM, TD, TY, FixedPF);
      TTM = ((double)(TEndingDate - JBeginningDate)/365.25);
      RateDC = FRMEDDCRate(TTM);
      TEndingDate -= TNAD;     // Decrement 1 and recalculate TTM
      TM = FRMFromJulianMonth(TEndingDate);
      TD = FRMFromJulianDay(TEndingDate);
      TY = FRMFromJulianYear(TEndingDate);
      if (FixedNAD == 1) {
         if (FixedPF == 0) TNAD = 30;
         if (FixedPF == 1) TNAD = 90;
         if (FixedPF == 2) TNAD = 180;
         if (FixedPF == 3) TNAD = 360;
      }
      ValueFixedLeg += (FixedRate/100.0)*((double)TNAD/(double)TNTD)
       * exp(-(RateDC/100.0)*TTM);
   }
// Work on floating leg
   JBeginningDate = FRMToJulian(EM, ED, EY);
   JEndingDate = FRMToJulian(MM, MD, MY);
   NFloatingPayments = FRMPaymentsRemaining(EM, ED, EY, MM, MD, MY, FloatingPF);
   TM = MM; TD = MD; TY = MY;
   TEndingDate = JEndingDate;
   if (FloatingNTD == 0) TNTD = 360;
   if (FloatingNTD == 1) TNTD = 365;
   ValueFloatingLeg = 0.0;
   for (i = NFloatingPayments; i > 0; i--) {
      TNAD = FRMNAD(TM, TD, TY, FloatingPF);
      TTM = ((double)(TEndingDate - JBeginningDate)/365.25);// End of period
      RateDC = FRMEDDCRate(TTM); // Actual fraction of year
      TEndingDate -= TNAD;     // Decrement 1 and recalculate
      TM = FRMFromJulianMonth(TEndingDate);
      TD = FRMFromJulianDay(TEndingDate);
      TY = FRMFromJulianYear(TEndingDate);
      LTTM = ((double)(TEndingDate - JBeginningDate)/365.25);// Beginning of period
      RateFC = FRMEDFCRate(LTTM, TTM); // Forward rate at beginning of period
      if (FloatingNAD == 1) {
         if (FloatingPF == 0) TNAD = 30;
         if (FloatingPF == 1) TNAD = 90;
         if (FloatingPF == 2) TNAD = 180;
         if (FloatingPF == 3) TNAD = 360;
      }
      ValueFloatingLeg
         += (RateFC/100.0)*((double)TNAD/(double)TNTD)*exp(-(RateDC/100.0)*TTM);
   }
   FairValue = NotionalAmount*(ValueFixedLeg - ValueFloatingLeg);
   if (ReceivePay > 0) FairValue *= -1.0;
   return FairValue;
}
```

Because of the flexibility allowed in the LSC model, care must be taken to estimate the forward curve (FC) and discount curve (DC) spot rates correctly at both the horizon date (HD) and the evaluation date (ED).

```
double FRMIRSWAPRM::FRMHDFCRate(double LTTM, double TTM)
{
   double LFCRate, FCRate;
// Longer maturity
   if (TTM < 0.0001) TTM = 0.0001;
   if (NumberLSCFR == 1) {
      FCRate = HDFCParameters[0];
```

```
      } else if (NumberLSCFR == 2) {
        FCRate = FRMCalculateCurve2(TTM, HDFCParameters[0], HDFCParameters[1],
          HDFCScalars[0]);
      } else if (NumberLSCFR == 3) {
        FCRate = FRMCalculateCurve3(TTM, HDFCParameters[0], HDFCParameters[1],
          HDFCParameters[2], HDFCScalars[0]);
      } else if (NumberLSCFR == 4) {
        FCRate = FRMCalculateCurve4(TTM, HDFCParameters[0], HDFCParameters[1],
          HDFCParameters[2], HDFCParameters[3], HDFCScalars[0], HDFCScalars[1]);
      } else if (NumberLSCFR == 5) {
        FCRate = FRMCalculateCurve5(TTM, HDFCParameters[0], HDFCParameters[1],
          HDFCParameters[2], HDFCParameters[3], HDFCParameters[4],
          HDFCScalars[0], HDFCScalars[1], HDFCScalars[2]);
      } else if (NumberLSCFR == 6) {
        FCRate = FRMCalculateCurve6(TTM, HDFCParameters[0], HDFCParameters[1],
          HDFCParameters[2], HDFCParameters[3], HDFCParameters[4], HDFCParameters[5],
          HDFCScalars[0], HDFCScalars[1], HDFCScalars[2], HDFCScalars[3]);
      }
// Shorter maturity
    if (LTTM < 0.0001) LTTM = 0.0001;
    if (NumberLSCFR == 1) {
        LFCRate = HDFCParameters[0];
    } else if (NumberLSCFR == 2) {
        LFCRate = FRMCalculateCurve2(LTTM, HDFCParameters[0], HDFCParameters[1],
          HDFCScalars[0]);
    } else if (NumberLSCFR == 3) {
        LFCRate = FRMCalculateCurve3(LTTM, HDFCParameters[0], HDFCParameters[1],
          HDFCParameters[2], HDFCScalars[0]);
    } else if (NumberLSCFR == 4) {
        LFCRate = FRMCalculateCurve4(LTTM, HDFCParameters[0], HDFCParameters[1],
          HDFCParameters[2], HDFCParameters[3], HDFCScalars[0], HDFCScalars[1]);
    } else if (NumberLSCFR == 5) {
        LFCRate = FRMCalculateCurve5(LTTM, HDFCParameters[0], HDFCParameters[1],
          HDFCParameters[2], HDFCParameters[3], HDFCParameters[4],
          HDFCScalars[0], HDFCScalars[1], HDFCScalars[2]);
    } else if (NumberLSCFR == 6) {
        LFCRate = FRMCalculateCurve6(LTTM, HDFCParameters[0], HDFCParameters[1],
          HDFCParameters[2], HDFCParameters[3], HDFCParameters[4], HDFCParameters[5],
          HDFCScalars[0], HDFCScalars[1], HDFCScalars[2], HDFCScalars[3]);
    }
    double ForwardRate;
    ForwardRate = (FCRate*TTM - LFCRate*LTTM)/(TTM - LTTM);
// Adjust to annual compounding
    ForwardRate = (exp((FCRate/100.0)) - 1.0)*100.0;
    return ForwardRate;
}
...
double FRMIRSWAPRM::FRMEDDCRate(double TTM)
{
    double DCRate;
    if (TTM < 0.0001) TTM = 0.0001;
    if (NumberLSCDR == 1) {
        DCRate = EDDCParameters[0];
    } else if (NumberLSCDR == 2) {
        DCRate = FRMCalculateCurve2(TTM, EDDCParameters[0], EDDCParameters[1],
          EDDCScalars[0]);
    } else if (NumberLSCDR == 3) {
        DCRate = FRMCalculateCurve3(TTM, EDDCParameters[0], EDDCParameters[1],
          EDDCParameters[2], EDDCScalars[0]);
    } else if (NumberLSCDR == 4) {
        DCRate = FRMCalculateCurve4(TTM, EDDCParameters[0], EDDCParameters[1],
          EDDCParameters[2], EDDCParameters[3], EDDCScalars[0], EDDCScalars[1]);
    } else if (NumberLSCDR == 5) {
        DCRate = FRMCalculateCurve5(TTM, EDDCParameters[0], EDDCParameters[1],
          EDDCParameters[2], EDDCParameters[3], EDDCParameters[4],
          EDDCScalars[0], EDDCScalars[1], EDDCScalars[2]);
    } else if (NumberLSCDR == 6) {
        DCRate = FRMCalculateCurve6(TTM, EDDCParameters[0], EDDCParameters[1],
          EDDCParameters[2], EDDCParameters[3], EDDCParameters[4], EDDCParameters[5],
          EDDCScalars[0], EDDCScalars[1], EDDCScalars[2], EDDCScalars[3]);
    }
```

```
   return DCRate;
}
```

Working with interest rate swaps requires careful attention to day counting. Hence, we have separate methods for number of accrued days (NAD) within a payment period.

```
int FRMIRSWAPRM::FRMNAD(int TM, int TD, int TY, int PF)
{
   long int JBeginningDate, JEndingDate;
   JEndingDate = FRMToJulian(TM, TD, TY);
   if(PF == 0){    // Monthly
      if(TM > 1){
         TM--;
         JBeginningDate = FRMToJulian(TM, TD, TY);
      } else {
         TM = TM + 11;
         TY--;
         JBeginningDate = FRMToJulian(TM, TD, TY);
      }
   } else if (PF == 1) { // Quarterly
      if(TM > 3){
         TM = TM - 3;
         JBeginningDate = FRMToJulian(TM, TD, TY);
      } else {
         TM = TM + 9;
         TY--;
         JBeginningDate = FRMToJulian(TM, TD, TY);
      }
   } else if (PF == 2) { // Semiannually
      if(TM > 6){
         TM = TM - 6;
         JBeginningDate = FRMToJulian(TM, TD, TY);
      } else {
         TM = TM + 6;
         TY--;
         JBeginningDate = FRMToJulian(TM, TD, TY);
      }
   } else { // Annually
      TY--;
      JBeginningDate = FRMToJulian(TM, TD, TY);
   }
   return(JEndingDate-JBeginningDate);
}
```

The value of a swap is based on looping over the remaining periods for both the floating leg and the fixed leg of the swap. Thus, in each case, we need the number of remaining payments.

```
int FRMIRSWAPRM::FRMPaymentsRemaining(int BegM, int BegD, int BegY,
   int EndM, int EndD, int EndY, int PF)
{
   long int JBeginningDate, JEndingDate;
   JBeginningDate = FRMToJulian(BegM, BegD, BegY);
   JEndingDate = FRMToJulian(EndM, EndD, EndY);
   int Counter = 0;
   if(PF == 0){    // Monthly
      while (JEndingDate > JBeginningDate){
         if(EndM > 1){
            EndM--;
            JEndingDate = FRMToJulian(EndM, EndD, EndY);
         } else {
            EndM = EndM + 11;
            EndY--;
            JEndingDate = FRMToJulian(EndM, EndD, EndY);
         }
         Counter++;
      }
   } else if (PF == 1) { // Quarterly
      while (JEndingDate > JBeginningDate){
         if(EndM > 3){
            EndM = EndM - 3;
            JEndingDate = FRMToJulian(EndM, EndD, EndY);
         } else {
```

```
                EndM = EndM + 9;
                EndY--;
                JEndingDate = FRMToJulian(EndM, EndD, EndY);
            }
            Counter++;
        }
    } else if (PF == 2) { // Semiannually
        while (JEndingDate > JBeginningDate){
            if(EndM > 6){
                EndM = EndM - 6;
                JEndingDate = FRMToJulian(EndM, EndD, EndY);
            } else {
                EndM = EndM + 6;
                EndY--;
                JEndingDate = FRMToJulian(EndM, EndD, EndY);
            }
            Counter++;
        }
    } else { // Annually
        while (JEndingDate > JBeginningDate){
            EndY--;
            JEndingDate = FRMToJulian(EndM, EndD, EndY);
            Counter++;
        }
    }
    return(Counter);
}
...
```

References

See previous modules referenced in the beginning of this module.

Appendix 5.7: Interface code comments

The following illustrates the graphical user interface for this module, as you can see it is rather complex.

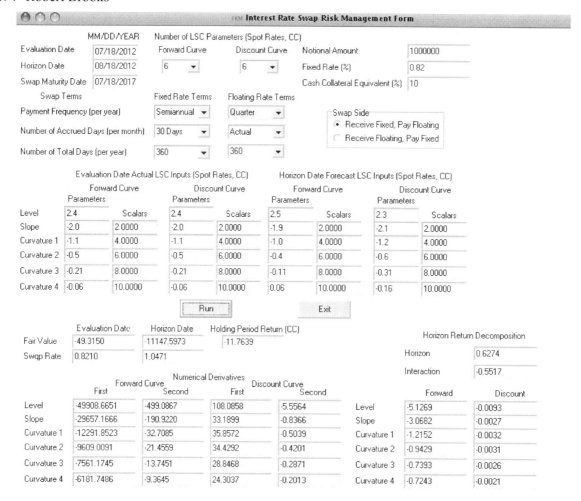

Although the interface code involves several hundreds of lines of code, there is very little that is new. The pull down boxes are provided in this compiler. The interface source code is found in:

FRMUnitIRSwapRiskManagement.cpp, .h

Chapter 6. Dynamic Market Risk Management

"I spent close to a decade and a half trying to guess volatility, the volatility of volatility, and correlations, and I sometimes shiver at the mere remembrance of my past miscalculations. Wounds from correlation matrices are still sore." Nassim Taleb[42]

Introduction

In this chapter, we present different ways to compute a variety of dynamic market risk management results. The objective here is to introduce these methods within the C++ framework. Five programs are reviewed that address the following two risk management issues: Monte Carlo simulation and a variety of value-at-risk calculations.

Each of these programs is presented as a separate module. We continue to focus almost exclusively on implementation code. The main focus of this chapter is using Monte Carlo simulation and computing a variety of parameters related to value-at-risk. As before, we will try to make each module standalone. Another advantage of this modular approach is your ability to find the source code within the materials you downloaded from the website.

In this chapter, we launch into specific dynamic market risk management modules.

---

[42] See http://www.derivativesstrategy.com/magazine/archive/1997/1296qa.asp where Nassim Taleb identifies several problems with value-at-risk.

Module 6.1: Multivariate Normal Random Number Generator

Learning objectives

- Explain how to generate multivariate random numbers in C++, specifically normally distributed random variables
- Review how to initiate random number generators with either the internal clock or the built-in `rand()` function, often referred to as the seed
- Contrast `long int` and `int`
- Illustrate inheritance of one class, FRMURNG, within another class, FRMMVNORMALRNG
- Show how to manage inputs and outputs within files
- Review source code for the program FRMMVRNGTest

Prior to studying this module, we recommend a thorough understanding of Module 3.3 Univariate Random Number Generator. The ability to generate multivariate normal random numbers is very important in financial analysis. This module assumes an understanding of univariate random number generating as described in *Univariate Random Number Generator*.

Module overview

Recall generating random numbers with a deterministic computer poses some technical problems and so the purist will refer to generating "pseudo" random numbers. The main objective here is to introduce the ability to generate vectors of *multivariate* random numbers using C++. We focus here on simulating the multivariate normal distribution.

The probability density function of a multivariate normal distribution can be expressed in matrix form as

$$f\left(\mathbf{x}|\mathbf{m},\mathbf{S}\right) = \frac{e^{\left[-\frac{\left(\mathbf{x}-\mathbf{m}\right)'\,\mathbf{S}^{-1}\left(\mathbf{x}-\mathbf{m}\right)}{2}\right]}}{\left(2\pi\right)^{N/2}\left|\mathbf{S}\right|^{1/2}}$$

where

$\mathbf{x}$ denotes the random variable vector of size N,

$\mathbf{m}$ denotes the mean of the distribution, again size N,

$\mathbf{S}$ denotes the covariance of the distribution, matrix size NxN, assumed to be symmetric and positive definite,

$\left|\;\right|$ denotes the determinant, and

$\left(\;\right)'$ denotes the transpose.

There are a variety of approaches to generating multivariate random numbers. Our approach is based on Press, et. al. (1989). The correlation matrix must be symmetric and positive definite. The correlation matrix (**C**) should be both positive definite ($\mathbf{x}^{T}\,\mathbf{C}\,\mathbf{x} > 0$ for all vectors $\mathbf{x}$) and symmetric ($z_{ij} = z_{ji}$). In this case, the Cholesky decomposition can be computed where

$$\mathbf{D}\cdot\mathbf{D}^{T} = \mathbf{C}$$

The Cholesky decomposition is analogous to taking the square root of a matrix. The multivariate normal random number vector (**M**) with mean zero and standard deviation one can be computed from a vector of univariate normal random vector (**U**) with mean zero and standard deviation one as

$$\underset{n \times 1}{\mathbf{M}} = \underset{n \times n}{\mathbf{D}} \cdot \underset{n \times 1}{\mathbf{U}}$$

Seed

Recall because computers are deterministic machines, it is technically impossible to generate a random number. Each random number generating method must be initialized. This initial value is called a seed. Thus, the method, FRMSeed() provides two different ways to compute a seed. The most common recommended method is to pull a numerical value from the internal clock. Unfortunately, the internal clock is measured only in 1/100ths of a second. For some applications, for example dynamic linked libraries incorporated into a spreadsheet, this seed may not change fast enough. The standard C++ library contains a uniform integer random number generator that stores a static duration seed that is updated each time it is called. Thus, the subsequent random number generator function calls will each have a different seed.

Computing univariate normal random numbers

The method to generate values from a univariate normal distribution is based here on a procedure described in *Numerical Recipes in C*. Recall the inputs to this method are the mean and standard deviation. Therefore, the method FRMNormal() receives two double values and returns one double value. The following snippet of code illustrates how to compute uniform discrete random numbers.

```
Draw = FRMNormal01();    // Random uniform 0, 1
Draw = Draw * PStandardDeviation + PMean;
```

FRMNormal01() is based on code provided in *Numerical Recipes in C*.

Computing multivariate normal random numbers

As discussed in the supplement to this module, the Cholesky decomposition can be used to generate a set of multivariate normal random numbers with mean zero and standard deviation. This decomposition is used with a set of univariate normal random numbers.

Implementation code comments

FRMMVNormalRNG.h

This implementation class relies on the univariate random generator, thus we need to incorporate it. The constructor and destuctor are declared under public:.

```
...
#ifndef FRMUNIFORMRNGCPP
#define FRMUNIFORMRNGCPP
#include "c:\FRMRepository\FRMUniformRNG.cpp" // FRMDLL defines multiple times
#endif
class FRMMVNORMALRNG : public FRMURNG
{
public:
   FRMMVNORMALRNG::FRMMVNORMALRNG();
   FRMMVNORMALRNG::~FRMMVNORMALRNG();
   int IENT;
```

Illustration of different ways to allocate memory:

```
double **Corr;
double B[MAXDIM];
double C[MAXDIM];
double RAND[MAXDIM];
void FRMMVNormal(int NumberofVariables, double **Corr);// Generates vector multivaritate RNs
void FRMMVNormal(void);  // Data set within class
```

```
    int NumberofVariables;
    long int NumberofDraws;
    long int j;
    double Sum[MAXDIM];
    double SumSquare[MAXDIM];
    double SumCrossProduct[MAXDIM][MAXDIM];
    double Mean[MAXDIM];
    double StdDev[MAXDIM];
// File management routines within class
    ofstream outf;
    ofstream outfFC;
    void FRMMVNormalRNGFileMgmt(AnsiString sinf, AnsiString soutf, AnsiString soutf1);
    void FRMMVRNGOutputData();
    void FRMMVRNGStatisticalData();
};
#endif
```

FRMMVNormalRNG.cpp

Memory can be allocated in the constructor and deallocated in the destructor.

```
...
// Constructor for memory management
FRMMVNORMALRNG::FRMMVNORMALRNG()      // Allocates memory for correlation matrices
{
    try {                               // Allocating memory for A
        Corr = new double*[MAXDIM];                    // Set up rows
        for(int j=0; j<MAXDIM; j++)Corr[j] = new double [MAXDIM]; // Set up columns
    }
    catch (std::bad_alloc) {
        Application->MessageBox(L"Could not allocate memory for matrix Corr.  Bye ...",
            L"Allocation Error for Matrix Corr[][]", MB_OK);
        exit(-1);
    }
}
// Destructor for memory management
FRMMVNORMALRNG::~FRMMVNORMALRNG()   // Destructor
{
    for(int j=0; j<MAXDIM; j++) delete [] Corr[j];   // Delete columns of A
    delete [] Corr;                         // Delete rows of A
}
```

This program pulls data from a file and places data into two files (the main output file and a debug file) through the use of three AnsiString variables.

```
void FRMMVNORMALRNG::FRMMVNormalRNGFileMgmt(AnsiString inputsinf,
    AnsiString inputsoutf, AnsiString inputsoutf1)
{
    char word[AS][CHARSIZE];
    int i, k;
    ifstream inf;
    inf.open(inputsinf.c_str(), ios::in);
    outf.open(inputsoutf.c_str());
    outfFC.open(inputsoutf1.c_str());
...
```

The seed method initializes the (pseudo) random number generator.

```
    FRMSeed();  // Initialize the seed to launch random number generator
    for(j=0; j<NumberofDraws; j++){//this loop uses # of Draws * Dim, random #s
// FRMMVNormal() requires IENT initially set to -1 and also requres FRMSeed() be called
    FRMMVNormal(); //Only function call to multivariate normal, returns vector of random
numbers
        for(i=0; i<NumberofVariables; i++){
```

We need to adjust our random vector for the standard deviations and means.

```
            RAND[i] = RAND[i] * StdDev[i] + Mean[i];
            Sum[i] += RAND[i];
            SumSquare[i] += pow(RAND[i], 2.0); // For standard deviation
            for(k = 0; k < i; k++) SumCrossProduct[i][k]+= RAND[i]*RAND[k];
        };
```

Two methods for handling output data:

```
    FRMMVRNGOutputData();
};
FRMMVRNGStatisticalData();
```

Remember to always flush and close the files.

```
inf.close();
outf.flush();
outfFC.flush();
outf.close();
outfFC.close();
}
...
```

Notice that the next two methods have the same name but have different number of inputs. This is known as function overloading.

```
// Function overloading allowing for internal file IO
void FRMMVNORMALRNG::FRMMVNormal(void)
{
    FRMMVNormal(NumberofVariables, Corr);
}
// Function overloading allowing for external file IO
void FRMMVNORMALRNG::FRMMVNormal(int Dimension, double **Corr)
{
    int i, j, k; // Counters
    int NB; // Correlation dimension tracker
    switch (IENT){
```

First the call to multivariate random number generator places the lower triangle of the Cholesky decomposition in the correlation matrix and the diagonals in vector C[]. The upper triangle remains the correlation matrix. IENT keeps track of whether it is the first pass.

```
        case -1:   // Estimate Cholesky decomposition on first pass through method
            double sum;   // Method based on NRC, 1992, p. 96
            for (i=0; i < Dimension; i++) {
                for (j = i; j < Dimension; j++) {
                    sum=Corr[i][j];
                    for (k = i-1; k >= 0; k--)sum -= Corr[i][k]*Corr[j][k];
                    if (i==j) {
                        if (sum <= 0.0){
                            IENT = 0;
                            return;
                        }
                        C[i] = sqrt(sum);
                    } else {
                        Corr[j][i] = sum/C[i];
                    }
                }
            }
            IENT = 1;
...
// Compute a random vector for first pass
            for(i=0;i<Dimension;i++){
                B[i] = FRMNormal01();
                RAND[i] = B[i]*C[i];
                if (i != 0){
                    NB = i - 1;
                    for(j=0;  j<=NB;  j++){
                        RAND[i] = RAND[i] + Corr[i] [j] * B[j];
                    };
                };
            };
        case 0: // Cholesky decomposition estimate failed, just return without numbers
            return;
        case 1: // Cholesky decomposition succeeded, proceed with random number generator
// Compute a random vector
            for(i=0;i<Dimension;i++){
                B[i] = FRMNormal01();
                RAND[i] = B[i]*C[i];
                if (i != 0){
```

```
            NB = i - 1;
            for(j=0; j<=NB; j++){
                RAND[i] = RAND[i] + Corr[i] [j] * B[j];
            };
        };
    };
...
    };
};
```

References

Press, William H., Brian P. Flannery, Saul A. Teukolsky, and William T. Vetterling, *Numerical Recipes in C The Art of Scientific Computing* Second Edition, (Cambridge, England: Cambridge University Press, 1992).

Appendix 6.1: Interface code comments

The graphical user interface is illustrated below. This program computes the sample means, standard deviations and correlation coefficients. The population means, standard deviations, and correlation coefficients are provided as inputs.

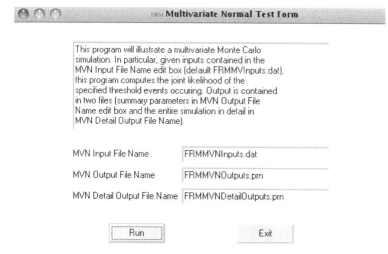

This implementation illustrates the use of data files to manage inputs and outputs. These data files enable the programmer to be completely independent of the particular implementation of the software. The end user just has to create the appropriate input files and the software application output is placed into output files.

The input data file needs to be in the following format.

FRMMVNInputs.dat

```
Input Parameters
 Draws      Dimensions
 1000000        4
   Mean        Standard Deviation
  10.000000        5.000000
  12.000000       10.000000
  14.000000       15.000000
  16.000000       20.000000
 Correlations
   1.000000
  -0.200000     1.000000
   0.100000     0.300000     1.000000
   0.200000     0.400000     0.500000     1.000000
```

Draws indicate how many vectors of multivariate normal random numbers to generate. Dimensions define how many random numbers each vector will contain. The mean and standard deviation provides the population statistics and are associated with each particular element within the random vector. Correlations provide the population correlations for the random vectors. The number of means, standard deviations, and correlations must correspond with the size of Dimensions.

Once the program has run, it produces the following two output files.

FRMMVNOutputs.prn

```
Input Parameters
 Draws      Dimensions
1000000         4
    Mean         Standard Deviation
  10.000000          5.000000
  12.000000         10.000000
  14.000000         15.000000
  16.000000         20.000000
 Correlations
   1.000000    -0.200000     0.100000     0.200000
  -0.200000     1.000000     0.300000     0.400000
   0.100000     0.300000     1.000000     0.500000
   0.200000     0.400000     0.500000     1.000000
     C        Correlations Matrix Transformed
   1.000000     1.000000    -0.200000     0.100000     0.200000
   0.979796    -0.200000     1.000000     0.300000     0.400000
   0.939858     0.100000     0.326599     1.000000     0.500000
   0.795328     0.200000     0.449073     0.354663     1.000000


Output of Simulation Statistics
    Mean         Standard Deviation
  10.002914          5.000832
  12.013210          9.990199
  13.991477         14.993405
  16.007395         19.993987
 Correlations
   1.000000
  -0.198223     1.000000
   0.101357     0.298402     1.000000
   0.200529     0.399353     0.500012     1.000000
```

The top half of this output file is just repeating the input data file with the entire correlation matrix reported. It is important for auditing purposes that the input data is in the same location as the output data. Next we provide the diagonal of the Cholesky decomposition and the transformed correlation matrix, where the bottom triangle contains the Cholesky values and the upper triangle along with the diagonals contain the original correlation matrix.

The second output data file contains details of each drawn vector of the simulation. Often the analyst will want to conduct more statistical analysis of the complete set of simulations.

FRMMVNDetailOutputs.prn

```
  Simulated Output
            0           1            2            3
    1     9.986177     9.745631     4.165310    -5.165138
    2     0.918574    32.076059    20.839947   -73.030769
    3    10.132514    23.717417     2.773865    28.285477
    4    26.601362    -1.592375    34.415333    79.913740
    5     5.811085     9.181006   -15.681307   -18.898881
...
   16    16.188099    40.617586    38.730032    21.888883
   17    14.525782    19.845557    46.498989    17.515510
   18     6.514145   -24.084575   -12.928357     6.703088
   19    15.126988    -0.814180    74.173843    89.428968
   20    -9.933032    18.688157    21.843240    26.202610
...
```

The interface code for this program is very straightforward and is not reproduced here. The interface code is found in:

FRMUnitMVRNGFiles.cpp, .h.

Module 6.2: Multivariate Normal Random Number Generator and Outcome Likelihood

Learning objectives

- Explain how to estimate complex outcome likelihoods using multivariate random numbers in C++
- Review source code for the program FRMMVRNGLikelihoodTest

Prior to studying this module, we recommend a thorough understanding of Module 6.1 Multivariate Normal Random Number Generator, as well as Module 3.3 Univariate Random Number Generator. We illustrate the use of multivariate normal random numbers to estimate the likelihood of complex outcomes.

Module overview

Recall in chapter 5, we focused on analytic and numerical derivatives as risk measures. One weakness of this approach is that the likelihood of various outcomes is not estimated. In this module, we sketch a process for computing the likelihood of complex outcomes, given a set of distribution inputs.

Here we assume a multivariate normal distribution and estimate the joint likelihood of several user-defined functions. This module is best understood by diving into the code itself.

Implementation code comments

FRMMVLikelihood.h

We use preprocessor directives to define various matrix sizes. Because we are using a simulator, some of these sizes can be very large (MAXDRAWS). Note also that the likelihood class incorporates the multivariate random number generator and the AnsiString variable type is used for file management.

```
#define MAXDIMENSION 20
#define MAXDRAWS 1000000
#include "c:\FRMRepository\FRMMVNormalRNG.cpp"

class FRMMVLIKELIHOOD
{
public:
...
   FRMMVLIKELIHOOD::FRMMVLIKELIHOOD();
   FRMMVLIKELIHOOD::~FRMMVLIKELIHOOD();
   FRMMVNORMALRNG MV;
   ifstream inf;
   ofstream outf;
   ofstream outfFC;
   void FRMMVLikelihoodSimulation(AnsiString sinf, AnsiString soutf, AnsiString soutf1);
   void FRMMVAnalyzeData();
   void FRMMVAnalyzeStatisticalData();
};
#endif
```

FRMMVLikelihood.cpp

This program is based on the multivariate random number generator, thus we skip that portion of the code. Notice how easy it is to incorporate complex likelihood calculations with a simulator.

```
...
    k = 0;
    for (i = 0; i < NumberofVariables; i++){      // this loop initializes all
       if (Condition[i][0] == 'G') {              // test for greater than
          if (MV.RAND[i] > Threshold[i]) { Variable[i] = 1;
          } else { Variable[i] = 0; };            // if GT condition false
       } else {                                   // condition is not greater than
          if (MV.RAND[i] < Threshold[i]) { Variable[i] = 1;
```

```
        } else { Variable[i] = 0; };          // assume everything else LT
      }
      TestSum[i] += Variable[i];
      if (Variable[i] == 1) k += 1;
    }
    if (k == NumberofVariables) BinSum += 1;
    FRMMVAnalyzeData();
//  Draw = j+1;
  };
  FRMMVAnalyzeStatisticalData();
}
...
```

References

Press, William H., Brian P. Flannery, Saul A. Teukolsky, and William T. Vetterling, *Numerical Recipes in C The Art of Scientific Computing* Second Edition, (Cambridge, England: Cambridge University Press, 1989).

Appendix 6.2: Interface code comments

The graphical user interface is illustrated below. This program computes the likelihood of an outcome that is contingent on several constraints. The population means, standard deviations, and correlation coefficients as well as required constraints, are provided as inputs.

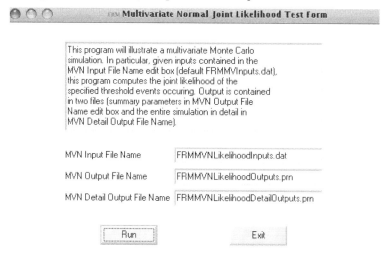

As with the previous module, this implementation relies on data files to manage inputs and outputs. These data files enable the programmer to be completely independent of the particular implementation of the software. The end-user just has to create the appropriate input files and the software application output is placed into output files.

The input data file needs to be in the following format.

FRMMVNLikelihoodInputs.dat

The difference here when compared to the last module is the introduction of the test conditions. Each variable has a threshold amount and a condition (GT denotes greater than – actually only the "G" is tested). Any letter but "G" on the first variable of the condition will be treated as less than.

```
Input Parameters
 Draws     Dimensions   Horizon
 1000000         4         1.0
 Test Condition
 Variable    Threshold    Condition
    1         5.000000        GT
```

```
   2          10.000000      LT
   3          15.000000      GT
   4          20.000000      LT
  Mean          Standard Deviation
  5.000000          10.000000
 10.000000          20.000000
 15.000000          30.000000
 20.000000          40.000000
Correlations
   1.000000
  -0.200000      1.000000
   0.100000      0.3000000      1.000000
   0.200000      0.4000000      0.500000      1.000000
```

Draws indicate how many vectors of multivariate normal random numbers to generate. Dimensions define how many random numbers each vector will contain. Horizon is the measurement period. The inputs are assumed to be annualized continuously compounded rates of return.

The annualized means and standard deviations provide the population statistics and are associated with each particular element within the random vector. Correlations provide the population correlations for the random vectors. The number of means, standard deviations, and correlations must correspond with the size of Dimensions.

Once the program has run, it produces the following two output files.

FRMMVNLikelihoodOutputs.prn

The inputs are also produced in the output file. The sample likelihood of each condition is produced, as well as the sample joint likelihood.

```
Input Parameters
 Draws       Dimensions   Horizon
1000000           4          1.000000
 Test Condition
 Variable    Threshold    Condition
    1          5.000000        GT
    2         10.000000        LT
    3         15.000000        GT
    4         20.000000        LT
   Mean         Standard Deviation
  5.000000         10.000000
 10.000000         20.000000
 15.000000         30.000000
 20.000000         40.000000
Correlations
   1.000000
  -0.200000      1.000000
   0.100000      0.300000      1.000000
   0.200000      0.400000      0.500000      1.000000


Output of Simulation Test Results
Sample Joint Likelihood is 0.049374
Sample Likelihood of test 0 is 0.501141
Sample Likelihood of test 1 is 0.499912
Sample Likelihood of test 2 is 0.500039
Sample Likelihood of test 3 is 0.499456


Output of Simulation Statistics
Mean of 0 is 5.023834
Mean of 1 is 10.003827
Mean of 2 is 15.016711
Mean of 3 is 20.035195
StdDev of 0 is 9.997986
StdDev of 1 is 19.985314
StdDev of 2 is 30.031087
```

```
StdDev of 3 is 40.016100
Correlation of 1 with 0 is -0.200141
Correlation of 2 with 0 is 0.100333
Correlation of 2 with 1 is 0.299355
Correlation of 3 with 0 is 0.198953
Correlation of 3 with 1 is 0.400654
Correlation of 3 with 2 is 0.500283
```

FRMMVNLikelihoodDetailOutputs.prn

The second output data file contains details of each drawn vector of the simulation. Often the analyst will want to conduct more statistical analysis of the complete set of simulations. Notice that observation number 20 satisfies the joint condition.

```
Simulated Output
                        Sample Output                       Binary Test Output
              0            1           2           3         0   1   2   3
     1     1.259711    30.441301   57.311173   51.011430    0   0   1   0
     2     1.133267    29.571802   -9.140763   39.651040    0   0   0   0
     3    20.409251   -18.093459    1.015464  -30.467621    1   1   0   1
     4    15.030424     7.457321   15.789449   33.251650    1   1   1   0
     5    -1.669086     9.996188   21.642122   43.485047    0   1   1   0
...
    16    20.452322   -23.637069    0.729293  -20.340010    1   1   0   1
    17     0.425435    10.790933  -43.003847    2.698943    0   0   0   1
    18    -0.562630     0.157562  -13.873860   25.683268    0   1   0   0
    19    10.814248   -21.249670   67.113348   42.733457    1   1   1   0
    20    20.730331   -13.011941   33.958734   14.572390    1   1   1   1
```

The interface code for this program is very straightforward and is not reproduced here. The interface code is found in the following files:

*FRMUnitMVRNGLikelihoodFiles.cpp, *.h.*

Module 6.3: Analytic Value-At-Risk

Learning objectives

- Explain how to compute analytic value at risk using C++
- Review analytic value at risk and related concepts
- Review implementation code FRMSPAnalyticVaR.cpp (.h)

The goal here is to illustrate the computation of the value at risk (VaR) of a portfolio based on the analytic method. Due to the large number of inputs and outputs, the inputs and outputs are stored in files rather than put back to the screen.

Extensive details are provided in the supplement that supports Modules 6.3 – 6.5.[43]

Module overview

The mathematical details for this module can be found in the supplement. The key equations are reproduced here for convenience.

Value-at-risk

VaR measures the anticipated worst loss over a stated time period (h for horizon) under normal market conditions at a pre-specified confidence level (C). Note that the parameter $\lambda_{VaR} = N^{-1}[C] = -N^{-1}[1-C]$ is a function of the confidence level and the inverse cumulative distribution function of the underlying normal distribution. Value-at-risk can be mathematically expressed in terms of the lower bound in the following integration

$$C \equiv \int_{-VaR_{\Pi}(C,h)}^{\infty} f(x)dx \quad \text{(Value-at-risk definition)}$$

where f(x) denotes the estimated probability density function. For simplicity, we assume a normal distribution, hence

$$f(x) = \frac{1}{\sqrt{2\pi\sigma^2\Pi^2}} \exp\left\{-\frac{(x-\mu\Pi)^2}{2\sigma^2\Pi^2}\right\} \quad \text{(Normal probability density function)}$$

where Π denotes the current market value of the portfolio, μ denotes the expected rate of return of the portfolio, and σ denotes the standard deviation of the portfolio. Based on this setup, we provide the following summary of VaR measures:[44]

$$VaR_{\Pi}^{MR}(C,h) = \lambda_{VaR}\sigma \quad \text{(\textbf{VaR Mean – Return})}$$

$$VaR_{\Pi}^{ZR}(C,h) = -\mu + \lambda_{VaR}\sigma \quad \text{(\textbf{VaR Zero – Return})}$$

$$VaR_{\Pi}^{MD}(C,h) = \lambda_{VaR}\sigma\Pi \quad \text{(\textbf{VaR Mean – Dollar})}$$

$$VaR_{\Pi}^{ZD}(C,h) = -\mu\Pi + \lambda_{VaR}\sigma\Pi \quad \text{(\textbf{VaR Zero – Dollar})}$$

Conditional value-at-risk

Conditional value-at-risk is the expected loss given that a value-at-risk event has occurred. The following equations summarize the main results:

---

[43] Supplements can be found at www.frmhelp.com.
[44] The supplement provides more detailed discussion of VaR.

$$CVaR_\Pi^{MR}(C,h) = \lambda_{CVaR}\sigma \text{ (CVaR Mean – Return)}$$

$$CVaR_\Pi^{ZR}(C,h) = -\mu + \lambda_{CVaR}\sigma \text{ (CVaR Zero – Return)}$$

$$CVaR_\Pi^{MD}(C,h) = \lambda_{CVaR}\sigma\Pi \text{ (CVaR Mean – Dollar)}$$

$$CVaR_\Pi^{ZD}(C,h) = -\mu\Pi + \lambda_{CVaR}\sigma\Pi \text{ (CVaR Zero – Dollar)}$$

where

$$\lambda_{CVaR} = \frac{\exp\left\{-\dfrac{N^{-1}(C)^2}{2}\right\}}{(1-C)\sqrt{2\pi}}$$

Component value-at-risk

Component value-at-risk is the portion of value-at-risk that each position contributes to the overall value-at-risk. The sum of component VaR is VaR. Component value-at-risk is the result of decomposing value-at-risk attributable to each risky exposure. The following equations summarize the main results:

$$\text{Component VaR}_i^{MR}(C,h) = w_i\left[\lambda_{VaR}\sigma\beta_i\right] \text{ (Component VaR Mean – Return)}$$

$$\text{Component VaR}_i^{ZR}(C,h) = w_i\left[-\mu_i + \lambda_{VaR}\sigma\beta_i\right] \text{ (Component VaR Zero – Return)}$$

$$\text{Component VaR}_i^{MD}(C,h) = w_i\left[\lambda_{VaR}\sigma\beta_i\right]\Pi \text{ (Component VaR Mean – Dollar)}$$

$$\text{Component VaR}_i^{ZD}(C,h) = w_i\left[-\mu_i + \lambda_{VaR}\sigma\beta_i\right]\Pi \text{ (Component VaR Zero – Dollar)}$$

Component conditional value-at-risk

Component conditional value-at-risk is the portion of conditional value-at-risk that each position contributes to the overall conditional value-at-risk. The sum of component conditional VaR is conditional VaR. The following equations summarize the main results:

$$\text{Component CVaR}_i^{MR}(C,h) = w_i\left[\lambda_{CVaR}\sigma\beta_i\right] \text{ (Component CVaR Mean – Return)}$$

$$\text{Component CVaR}_i^{ZR}(C,h) = w_i\left[-\mu_i + \lambda_{CVaR}\sigma\beta_i\right] \text{ (Component CVaR Zero – Return)}$$

$$\text{Component CVaR}_i^{MD}(C,h) = w_i\left[\lambda_{CVaR}\sigma\beta_i\right]\Pi \text{ (Component CVaR Mean – Dollar)}$$

$$\text{Component CVaR}_i^{ZD}(C,h) = w_i\left[-\mu_i + \lambda_{CVaR}\sigma\beta_i\right]\Pi \text{ (Component CVaR Zero – Dollar)}$$

Marginal value-at-risk

Marginal value-at-risk is defined as the partial derivative of value-at-risk with respect to the proportion allocated to instrument i. The following equations summarize the main results:

$$\text{Marginal VaR}_i^{MR}(C,h) = \left[\lambda_{VaR}\sigma\beta_i\right] \text{ (Marginal VaR Mean – Return)}$$

$$\text{Marginal VaR}_i^{ZR}(C,h) = \left[-\mu_i + \lambda_{VaR}\sigma\beta_i\right] \text{ (Marginal VaR Zero – Return)}$$

$$\text{Marginal VaR}_i^{MD}(C,h) = \left[\lambda_{VaR}\sigma\beta_i\right]\Pi \text{ (Marginal VaR Mean – Dollar)}$$

$$\text{Marginal VaR}_i^{ZD}(C,h) = \left[-\mu_i + \lambda_{VaR}\sigma\beta_i\right]\Pi \text{ (Marginal VaR Zero – Dollar)}$$

Marginal conditional value-at-risk

Marginal conditional value-at-risk is defined as the partial derivative of conditional value-at-risk with respect to the proportion allocated to instrument i. The following equations summarize the main results:

$$\text{Marginal CVaR}_i^{MR}(C,h) = \left[\lambda_{CVaR}\sigma\beta_i\right] \text{ (\textbf{Marginal CVaR Mean – Return})}$$

$$\text{Marginal CVaR}_i^{ZR}(C,h) = \left[-\mu_i + \lambda_{CVaR}\sigma\beta_i\right] \text{ (\textbf{Marginal CVaR Zero – Return})}$$

$$\text{Marginal CVaR}_i^{MD}(C,h) = \left[\lambda_{CVaR}\sigma\beta_i\right]\Pi \text{ (\textbf{Marginal CVaR Mean – Dollar})}$$

$$\text{Marginal CVaR}_i^{ZD}(C,h) = \left[-\mu_i + \lambda_{CVaR}\sigma\beta_i\right]\Pi \text{ (\textbf{Marginal CVaR Zero – Dollar})}$$

Incremental value-at-risk

Incremental value-at-risk is defined as the change in value-at-risk resulting from removing (or adding) a position to the portfolio. There are a wide variety of ways to conduct this analysis, each way may result in different values. For our purposes here, we assume that when the position is sold, the proceeds are reinvested in the remaining portfolio with the same weights as before the disposition. For example, if the portfolio comprised 1/3 in each of three positions, incremental VaR calculations would assume 1/2 invested in the remaining two positions. The following equations summarize the main results:

$$\text{Incremental VaR}_i^{MR}(C,h,N)$$
$$= \text{VaR}_\Pi^{MR}(C,h,N) - \text{VaR}_\Pi^{MR}(C,h,i \notin N) \quad \text{(\textbf{Incremental VaR Mean–Return})}$$

$$\text{Incremental VaR}_i^{ZR}(C,h,N)$$
$$= \text{VaR}_\Pi^{ZR}(C,h,N) - \text{VaR}_\Pi^{ZR}(C,h,i \notin N) \quad \text{(\textbf{Incremental VaR Zero–Return})}$$

$$\text{Incremental VaR}_i^{MD}(C,h,N)$$
$$= \text{VaR}_\Pi^{MD}(C,h,N) - \text{VaR}_\Pi^{MD}(C,h,i \notin N) \quad \text{(\textbf{Incremental VaR Mean–Dollar})}$$

$$\text{Incremental VaR}_\Pi^{ZD}(C,h,N)$$
$$= \text{VaR}_\Pi^{ZD}(C,h,N) - \text{VaR}_\Pi^{ZD}(C,h,i \notin N) \quad \text{(\textbf{Incremental VaR Zero–Dollar})}$$

Incremental conditional value-at-risk

Incremental conditional value-at-risk is defined as the change in conditional value-at-risk resulting from removing (or adding) a position to the portfolio. The following equations summarize the main results:

$$\text{Incremental CVaR}_i^{MR}(C,h,N)$$
$$= \text{CVaR}_\Pi^{MR}(C,h,N) - \text{CVaR}_\Pi^{MR}(C,h,i \notin N) \quad \text{(\textbf{Incremental CVaR Mean–Return})}$$

$$\text{Incremental CVaR}_i^{ZR}(C,h,N)$$
$$= \text{CVaR}_\Pi^{ZR}(C,h,N) - \text{CVaR}_\Pi^{ZR}(C,h,i \notin N) \quad \text{(\textbf{Incremental CVaR Zero–Return})}$$

$$\text{Incremental CVaR}_i^{MD}(C,h,N)$$
$$= \text{CVaR}_\Pi^{MD}(C,h,N) - \text{CVaR}_\Pi^{MD}(C,h,i \notin N) \quad \text{(\textbf{Incremental CVaR Mean–Dollar})}$$

$$\text{Incremental CVaR}_i^{ZD}(C,h,N)$$
$$= \text{CVaR}_\Pi^{ZD}(C,h,N) - \text{CVaR}_\Pi^{ZD}(C,h,i \notin N)$$
(Incremental CVaR Zero–Dollar)

Percentage marginal contribution to risk

In a similar approach, we can estimate the percentage marginal contribution to risk based on the following formula:

$$\%\text{MCTR}_j = w_j \beta_{j\Pi}$$

Percentage marginal contribution to expected excess return

Also, we can estimate the percentage marginal contribution to expected excess return based on the following formula:

$$\%\text{MCEER}_j = w_j \frac{E\{\tilde{R}_j\} - r}{E[\tilde{R}_\Pi] - r}$$

Implementation code comments

FRMSPAnalytics.h

The maximum number of positions is hard coded to 100, but can be easily changed, should there be a need for more or less. The inverse normal CDF is needed, hence we inherit the FRMCDF class.

```
...
#define SPAVARMAXDIM 100  // Maximum number of securities, 100
...
class FRMSPANALYTICVAR : public FRMCDF
{
public:
...
   double PMCTER[SPAVARMAXDIM];
   double PMCTR[SPAVARMAXDIM];
   double Mean[SPAVARMAXDIM];
   double StdDev[SPAVARMAXDIM];
   double Units[SPAVARMAXDIM];
   double Price[SPAVARMAXDIM];
   double Weight[SPAVARMAXDIM];
   double Beta[SPAVARMAXDIM];
   double CompVaR[SPAVARMAXDIM];
   double MargVaR[SPAVARMAXDIM];
   double IWeight[SPAVARMAXDIM];
   double IUnits[SPAVARMAXDIM];
   double IPrice[SPAVARMAXDIM];
   double Corr[SPAVARMAXDIM][SPAVARMAXDIM];
```

We have both input and output files.

```
   ifstream inf;
   ofstream outf;
   void FRMAnalyticVaRFileMgmt(AnsiString sinf, AnsiString soutf);
   void FRMPortfolioParameters(void);
};
#endif
```

FRMSPAnalytics.cpp

This program manages input and output data through files. Therefore, the primary method receives two files, one for input and one for output. We will exhibit code to generate each different type of VaR, remember to read the comments within the code, following the // to futher understand what the code is doing line by line.

```
#include "FRMSPAnalyticVaR.h"
// Manage data from standard file
```

```
void FRMSPANALYTICVAR::FRMAnalyticVaRFileMgmt(AnsiString inputsinf,
   AnsiString inputsoutf)
{
   inf.open(inputsinf.c_str(), ios::in);
   outf.open(inputsoutf.c_str());
...
```

We have a separate method to estimate the portfolio parameters. Because the inputs and outputs are all defined in the class, we do not have to pass or receive any variables. Outputting values to files is rather tedious due to formatting issues. We strongly recommend that you spend some time with code of this nature to better understand file management.

```
// Portfolio parameters method
   FRMPortfolioParameters();
   outf << "\nPortfolio Parameters: (Horizon Independent)\n";
   outf << "Portfolio Mean              = ";
   outf.width(12);  outf.setf(ios::right); outf.precision(6);
   outf.setf(ios::fixed, ios::floatfield); outf.setf(ios::showpoint);
   outf << PortfolioMean << "\n";
   outf << "Portfolio Standard Deviation = ";
   outf.width(12);  outf.setf(ios::right); outf.precision(6);
   outf.setf(ios::fixed, ios::floatfield); outf.setf(ios::showpoint);
   outf << PortfolioStandardDeviation << "\n";
// Value-at-risk
   InverseNormal = FRMD(ConfidenceLevel/100.0);
...
```

Value-at-risk

```
   ReturnVaRMean = PortfolioStandardDeviation*sqrt(Horizon)*InverseNormal;
   ReturnVaRZero = - PortfolioMean*Horizon + ReturnVaRMean;
   DollarVaRMean = PortfolioValue * (ReturnVaRMean/100.0);
   DollarVaRZero = PortfolioValue * (ReturnVaRZero/100.0);
...
```

Conditional value-at-risk

```
   LambdaCVaR = exp(-pow(InverseNormal,2.0)/2.0)
      / ((1.0 - (ConfidenceLevel/100.0)) * pow(2.0*PI, 0.5));
   ReturnCVaRMean = PortfolioStandardDeviation*sqrt(Horizon)*LambdaCVaR;
   ReturnCVaRZero = - PortfolioMean*Horizon + ReturnCVaRMean;
   DollarCVaRMean = PortfolioValue * (ReturnCVaRMean/100.0);
   DollarCVaRZero = PortfolioValue * (ReturnCVaRZero/100.0);
```

Component value-at-risk

```
   TotalComponentVaRReturn = 0.0;
   AverageBeta = 0.0;
   for(i=0; i<NumberofSecurities; i++){
      Beta[i] = 0;
      for(j=0; j<NumberofSecurities; j++){
         Beta[i] += Weight[j] * Corr[i][j] * StdDev[i] * StdDev[j]
            / pow(PortfolioStandardDeviation, 2.0);
      }
      AverageBeta += Weight[i] * Beta[i];
      CompVaR[i] = Weight[i] * InverseNormal * PortfolioStandardDeviation
         * sqrt(Horizon) * Beta[i];
      TotalComponentVaRReturn += CompVaR[i];
   }
...
```

Note that for some items, they are calculated in the outf stage. Therefore, component VaR zero – return is not computed as a separate variable, it is computed at the time the value is placed in the file.

```
   for(i=0; i<NumberofSecurities; i++){
      outf << "Security [" << i << "] = ";
      outf.width(18);  outf.setf(ios::right); outf.precision(6);
      outf.setf(ios::fixed, ios::floatfield); outf.setf(ios::showpoint);
      outf << -Weight[i]*Mean[i]*Horizon + CompVaR[i] << "\n";
   }
   outf << "  Total        = ";
      outf.width(18);  outf.setf(ios::right); outf.precision(6);
      outf.setf(ios::fixed, ios::floatfield); outf.setf(ios::showpoint);
      outf << - PortfolioMean*Horizon + TotalComponentVaRReturn << "\n";
```

```
    outf << "\n" << "Component VaR Mean (Dollar)" << "\n";
    for(i=0; i<NumberofSecurities; i++){
        outf << "Security [" << i << "] = ";
        outf.width(18);  outf.setf(ios::right); outf.precision(6);
        outf.setf(ios::fixed, ios::floatfield); outf.setf(ios::showpoint);
        outf << PortfolioValue * (CompVaR[i]/100.0) << "\n";
    }
    outf << "  Total      = ";
        outf.width(18);  outf.setf(ios::right); outf.precision(6);
        outf.setf(ios::fixed, ios::floatfield); outf.setf(ios::showpoint);
        outf << PortfolioValue * (TotalComponentVaRReturn/100.0) << "\n";
    outf << "\n" << "Component VaR Zero (Dollar)" << "\n";
    for(i=0; i<NumberofSecurities; i++){
        outf << "Security [" << i << "] = ";
        outf.width(18);  outf.setf(ios::right); outf.precision(6);
        outf.setf(ios::fixed, ios::floatfield); outf.setf(ios::showpoint);
        outf << PortfolioValue*(-Weight[i]*Mean[i]*Horizon+CompVaR[i])/100.0 << "\n";
    }
    outf << "  Total      = ";
        outf.width(18);  outf.setf(ios::right); outf.precision(6);
        outf.setf(ios::fixed, ios::floatfield); outf.setf(ios::showpoint);
        outf << PortfolioValue*(-PortfolioMean*Horizon
            + TotalComponentVaRReturn)/100.0 << "\n";
```

Component conditional value-at-risk

```
// Component conditional value-at-risk (return, in %)
    TotalComponentVaRReturn = 0.0;
    for(i=0; i<NumberofSecurities; i++){
// Note switch to LambdaCVaR and not InverseNormal, hence conditional VaR
        CompVaR[i] = Weight[i] * LambdaCVaR * PortfolioStandardDeviation
            * sqrt(Horizon) * Beta[i];
        TotalComponentVaRReturn += CompVaR[i];
    }
...
```

Marginal value-at-risk

```
    double TotalMarginalVaRReturn = 0.0;
    for(i=0; i<NumberofSecurities; i++){
        MargVaR[i] = InverseNormal * PortfolioStandardDeviation
            * sqrt(Horizon) * Beta[i];
        TotalMarginalVaRReturn += MargVaR[i];
    }
...
```

Marginal conditional value-at-risk

```
    TotalMarginalVaRReturn = 0.0;
    for(i=0; i<NumberofSecurities; i++){
// Note switch to LambdaCVaR and not InverseNormal, hence conditional VaR
        MargVaR[i] = LambdaCVaR * PortfolioStandardDeviation
            * sqrt(Horizon) * Beta[i];
        TotalMarginalVaRReturn += MargVaR[i];
    }
...
```

Incremental value-at-risk

```
    for(i=0; i<NumberofSecurities; i++){  // Iterate over all securities
        if (i==0) {
            outf << "\nIncremental Value-at-Risk Output\n";
        }
        outf << "\nSecurity[" << i << "]\n";
        for(j=0; j<NumberofSecurities; j++){ // New weights
            if (i==j){
                IUnits[j] = 0.0;
                IPrice[j] = 0.0;
            } else {
                IUnits[j] = Units[j];
                IPrice[j] = Price[j];
            }
        }
// New portfolio standard deviation
        IPortfolioValue = 0.0;
```

```
        for(k=0; k<NumberofSecurities; k++){      // Portfolio value
            IPortfolioValue += IUnits[k] * IPrice[k];
        }
        for(k=0; k<NumberofSecurities; k++){      // Portfolio weights
            IWeight[k] = (IUnits[k]*IPrice[k])/IPortfolioValue;
        };
        IPortfolioMean = IPortfolioStandardDeviation = 0.0;
        for(k=0; k<NumberofSecurities; k++){ // Portfolio mean and standard deviation
            IPortfolioMean += IWeight[k]*Mean[k];
            for(j=0; j<NumberofSecurities; j++){
                IPortfolioStandardDeviation
                    += IWeight[k]*IWeight[j]*StdDev[k]*StdDev[j]*Corr[k][j];
            }
        }
        IPortfolioStandardDeviation = sqrt(IPortfolioStandardDeviation);
        outf << "\nIncremental Portfolio Parameters: (Horizon Independent)\n";
        outf << "Incremental Portfolio Mean                = ";
        outf.width(12);  outf.setf(ios::right); outf.precision(6);
        outf.setf(ios::fixed, ios::floatfield); outf.setf(ios::showpoint);
        outf << IPortfolioMean << "\n";
        outf << "Incremental Portfolio Standard Deviation = ";
        outf.width(12);  outf.setf(ios::right); outf.precision(6);
        outf.setf(ios::fixed, ios::floatfield); outf.setf(ios::showpoint);
        outf << IPortfolioStandardDeviation << "\n";
        IReturnVaRMean = IPortfolioStandardDeviation*sqrt(Horizon)*InverseNormal;
        IReturnVaRZero = - IPortfolioMean*Horizon + IReturnVaRMean;
        IDollarVaRMean = PortfolioValue * (IReturnVaRMean/100.0);
        IDollarVaRZero = PortfolioValue * (IReturnVaRZero/100.0);
        outf << "Incremental VaR Mean (Return)    = ";
        outf.width(18);  outf.setf(ios::right); outf.precision(6);
        outf.setf(ios::fixed, ios::floatfield); outf.setf(ios::showpoint);
        outf << ReturnVaRMean - IReturnVaRMean << "\n";
        outf << "Incremental VaR Zero (Return)    = ";
        outf.width(18);  outf.setf(ios::right); outf.precision(6);
        outf.setf(ios::fixed, ios::floatfield); outf.setf(ios::showpoint);
        outf << ReturnVaRZero - IReturnVaRZero << "\n";
        outf << "Incremental VaR Mean (Dollar)    = ";
        outf.width(18);  outf.setf(ios::right); outf.precision(6);
        outf.setf(ios::fixed, ios::floatfield); outf.setf(ios::showpoint);
        outf << DollarVaRMean - IDollarVaRMean<< "\n";
        outf << "Incremental VaR Zero (Dollar)    = ";
        outf.width(18);  outf.setf(ios::right); outf.precision(6);
        outf.setf(ios::fixed, ios::floatfield); outf.setf(ios::showpoint);
        outf << DollarVaRZero - IDollarVaRZero << "\n";
```

Incremental conditional value-at-risk

```
// Incremental conditional value-at-risk
        IReturnCVaRMean = IPortfolioStandardDeviation*sqrt(Horizon)*LambdaCVaR;
        IReturnCVaRZero = - IPortfolioMean*Horizon + IReturnCVaRMean;
        IDollarCVaRMean = PortfolioValue * (IReturnCVaRMean/100.0);
        IDollarCVaRZero = PortfolioValue * (IReturnCVaRZero/100.0);
        outf << "\n" << "Incremental conditional value-at-risk measures" << "\n";
...
    }
```

Percentage marginal contribution to risk and percentage marginal contribution to expected excess return

```
    for(i=0; i<NumberofSecurities; i++){
        PMCTER[i] = 100.0*((Weight[i]*Mean[i])/PortfolioMean);
        PMCTR[i] = 0.0;
        for(j=0; j<NumberofSecurities; j++){
            PMCTR[i] += Weight[j]*StdDev[i]*StdDev[j]*Corr[i][j];
        }
        PMCTR[i] = 100.0 * Weight[i] * PMCTR[i]/pow(PortfolioStandardDeviation, 2.0);
    }
...
}

void FRMSPANALYTICVAR::FRMPortfolioParameters(void)
{
```

```
PortfolioValue = 0.0;
for(i=0; i<NumberofSecurities; i++){    // Portfolio value
    PortfolioValue += Units[i]*Price[i];
}
for(i=0; i<NumberofSecurities; i++){    // Portfolio weights
    Weight[i] = (Units[i]*Price[i])/PortfolioValue;
};
PortfolioMean = PortfolioStandardDeviation = 0.0;
for(i=0; i<NumberofSecurities; i++){ // Portfolio mean and standard deviation
    PortfolioMean += Weight[i]*Mean[i];
    for(j=0; j<NumberofSecurities; j++){
        PortfolioStandardDeviation
            += Weight[i]*Weight[j]*StdDev[i]*StdDev[j]*Corr[i][j];
    }
}
PortfolioStandardDeviation = sqrt(PortfolioStandardDeviation);
}
```

References

See reference in the supplement to Modules 6.3 – 6.5.

Appendix 6.3: Interface code comments

The graphical user interface is illustrated below.

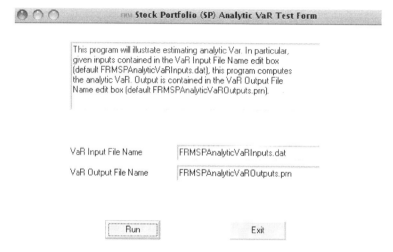

The input data file, FRMSPAnalyticVaRInputs.dat, is illustrated below.

```
Analytic VaR
   Horizon     Securities     Confidence Level
 0.01923077        5                95.0
         Name    Units    Price     Mean         Standard Deviation
          ABC    100.0    100.0    5.000000           5.000000
          EDF    100.0    100.0   10.000000          10.000000
          GHI    100.0    100.0   15.000000          15.000000
          JKL    100.0    100.0   20.000000          20.000000
          MNO    100.0    100.0   25.000000          25.000000
  Correlations
    1.000000
    0.300000      1.000000
    0.100000      0.200000     1.000000
    0.400000      0.800000     0.700000     1.000000
   -0.200000     -0.400000     0.250000    -0.700000     1.000000
```

A portion of the output data file, FRMSPAnalyticVaROutputs.prn, is illustrated below.

...
Portfolio Parameters: (Horizon Independent)

```
Portfolio Mean               =      15.000000
Portfolio Standard Deviation =       7.842194


Value-at-Risk Parameters
VaR Horizon                  =        0.019231
VaR Confidence Level         =       95.000000%
Lambda - Inverse Normal (C)  =        1.644853


Analytic Value-at-Risk Output (Plain-Vanilla VaR)
VaR Mean (Return)     =        1.788805
VaR Zero (Return)     =        1.500344
VaR Mean (Dollar)     =      894.402724
VaR Zero (Dollar)     =      750.171949


Conditional value-at-risk measures
Lambda CVaR (C)                   =        2.062713
Conditional VaR Mean (Return)     =        2.243235
Conditional VaR Zero (Return)     =        1.954773
Conditional VaR Mean (Dollar)     =     1121.617509
Conditional VaR Zero (Dollar)     =      977.386734


Component value-at-risk measures
Beta Estimates
Beta[0] =        0.203252
Beta[1] =        0.666667
Beta[2] =        1.841463
Beta[3] =        1.495935
Beta[4] =        0.792683
  Average Beta =    1.000000


Component VaR Mean (Return)
Security [0] =        0.072716
Security [1] =        0.238507
Security [2] =        0.658804
Security [3] =        0.535187
Security [4] =        0.283591
  Total      =        1.788805


Component VaR Zero (Return)
Security [0] =        0.053485
Security [1] =        0.200046
Security [2] =        0.601112
Security [3] =        0.458264
Security [4] =        0.187437
  Total      =        1.500344


Component VaR Mean (Dollar)
Security [0] =       36.357834
Security [1] =      119.253696
Security [2] =      329.401979
Security [3] =      267.593660
Security [4] =      141.795554
  Total      =      894.402724


Component VaR Zero (Dollar)
Security [0] =       26.742449
Security [1] =      100.022926
Security [2] =      300.555824
Security [3] =      229.132120
Security [4] =       93.718629
  Total      =      750.171949


Component Conditional Value-at-Risk Measures
Component Conditional VaR Mean (Return)
Security [0] =        0.091188
Security [1] =        0.299098
Security [2] =        0.826167
Security [3] =        0.671147
Security [4] =        0.355635
  Total      =        2.243235
```

```
Component Conditional VaR Zero (Return)
Security [0] =          0.071958
Security [1] =          0.260636
Security [2] =          0.768475
Security [3] =          0.594224
Security [4] =          0.259481
  Total     =          1.954773

Component Conditional VaR Mean (Dollar)
Security [0] =         45.594208
Security [1] =        149.549001
Security [2] =        413.083522
Security [3] =        335.573369
Security [4] =        177.817410
  Total     =       1121.617509

Component Conditional VaR Zero (Dollar)
Security [0] =         35.978823
...
Security [4] =        129.740485
  Total     =        977.386734

Marginal value-at-risk measures
...
Marginal VaR Zero (Dollar)
Security [0] =        133.712246
...
Security [4] =        468.593144
  Total     =       4327.782843

Marginal Conditional Value-at-Risk Measures
...
Marginal Conditional VaR Zero (Dollar)
Security [0] =        179.894113
...
Security [4] =        648.702425
  Total     =       5463.856771

Incremental Value-at-Risk Output

Security[0]

Incremental Portfolio Parameters: (Horizon Independent)
Incremental Portfolio Mean           =     17.500000
Incremental Portfolio Standard Deviation =   9.478594
Incremental VaR Mean (Return)     =      -0.373263
Incremental VaR Zero (Return)     =      -0.325186
Incremental VaR Mean (Dollar)     =    -186.631618
Incremental VaR Zero (Dollar)     =    -162.593155

Incremental conditional value-at-risk measures
Incremental conditional VaR Mean (Return)   =       -0.468087
Incremental conditional VaR Zero (Return)   =       -0.420010
Incremental conditional VaR Mean (Dollar)   =     -234.043664
Incremental conditional VaR Zero (Dollar)   =     -210.005201
...
Marginal Contribution Analysis
     Name     Weight     %MCTER     %MCTR
      ABC   20.000000    6.666667    4.065041
      EDF   20.000000   13.333333   13.333333
      GHI   20.000000   20.000000   36.829268
      JKL   20.000000   26.666667   29.918699
      MNO   20.000000   33.333333   15.853659
```

Due to the simplicity of the interface code, it is not repeated here. It can be found in the following files:

FRMUnitSPAnalytic.cpp, .h

Module 6.4: Historical Simulation Value-At-Risk

Learning objectives

- Explain how to compute historic value at risk using C++
- Illustrate file management with both inputs and outputs
- Review implementation code FRMSPHistoricVaR.cpp (.h)

The goal here is to illustrate the computation of the value at risk (VaR) of a stock portfolio based on the historical simulation method. Due to the large number of inputs, the inputs as well as outputs are stored in files rather than put back to the screen.

Module overview

The historical simulation approach, as introduced in supplement to Modules 6.3 – 6.5, assumes the historical returns are independent and identically distributed.[45] We illustrate a value-at-risk (VaR) calculation based on historical simulation here.

Implementation code comments

FRMSPHistoricVaR.h

The historical simulation approach relies on the ability to sort data, hence we inherit the FRMSORT class. The setup for this class is very straightforward.

```
...
#include "c:\FRMRepository\FRMSortingData.cpp"
class FRMSPHISTORICVAR : public FRMSORT
{
public:
    FRMSPHISTORICVAR::FRMSPHISTORICVAR();
    char word[AS][CHARSIZE];
    int NumberofSecurities;
    long int m;
    double ConfidenceLevel;
    void FRMHistoricVaRFileMgmt(AnsiString sinf, AnsiString soutf);
    double FRMHistoricVaRFileMgmt(AnsiString sinf, AnsiString soutf, double CL);
};
#endif
```

FRMSPHistoricVaR.cpp

We use the constructor to set the confidence level to a negative number.

```
...
FRMSPHISTORICVAR::FRMSPHISTORICVAR()
{
    ConfidenceLevel = -1000.0;   // Any negative number
}
```

We overload the FRMHistoricVaRFileMgmt function depending on how this class is accessed. There are two separate methods with the name `FRMHistoricVaRFileMgmt()`, one with the confidence level (CL) passed and the other without the confidence level passed. If the confidence level is not passed, then the confidence level contained in the input file is used.

```
// GUI version with confidence level
double FRMSPHISTORICVAR::FRMHistoricVaRFileMgmt(AnsiString inputsinf,
    AnsiString inputsoutf, double CL)
{
    ConfidenceLevel = CL;
    FRMHistoricVaRFileMgmt(inputsinf, inputsoutf);
    return A[m];
```

---

[45] Supplements are provided at www.frmhelp.com.

```cpp
}
// Confidence level from standard file
void FRMSPHISTORICVAR::FRMHistoricVaRFileMgmt(AnsiString inputsinf,
    AnsiString inputsoutf)
{
    int Counter, TotalCount;
    double P0, P1, R, inputCL;
    ifstream inf;
    inf.open(inputsinf.c_str(), ios::in);
    outf.open(inputsoutf.c_str());
    inf >> inputCL >> NumberofSecurities;    // Line 1
    if (ConfidenceLevel < 0.0) { // Test if CL from GUI or file
        ConfidenceLevel = inputCL;
    }
    outf.width(6);  outf.setf(ios::right); outf.precision(2);
    outf.setf(ios::fixed, ios::floatfield); outf.setf(ios::showpoint);
    outf << ConfidenceLevel;
    outf.width(4);  outf.setf(ios::right); outf.setf(ios::fixed, ios::floatfield);
    outf << NumberofSecurities << "\n";
    inf >> word[0] >> word[1]; // Line 1
    Counter = -1;
    while (inf){
     inf >> word[0] >> P0 >> ws;
     Counter += 1;
    }
    TotalCount = Counter - 1; // Total number of returns (-1 from prices)
// Move position to top of file
    inf.clear();               // Forget reaching end of file
    inf.seekg(0, ios::beg);  // Go to beginning of file
    inf >> word[0] >> word[1];   // Line 1 - discarded here
    inf >> word[0] >> word[1];   // Line 2 - discarded here
    ofstream outs;
    outs.open("FRMReturnData.dat");
    outs.width(10);  outs.setf(ios::right); outs.setf(ios::fixed, ios::floatfield);
    outs << TotalCount << "\n";
    Counter = 0;
    while (inf){
        if(Counter==0)inf >> word[0] >> P0 >> ws;
        else {
            inf >> P1 >> ws;
            R = (P1/P0) - 1.0;
            P0=P1;
            outs.width(10);  outs.setf(ios::right); outs.precision(6);
            outs.setf(ios::fixed, ios::floatfield); outs.setf(ios::showpoint);
            outs << R;
            if(!(Counter%10))outs << "\n";
        }
        inf >> word[0] >> ws;
        Counter += 1;
    }
    outs.flush(); // Make sure all data written to file
    AnsiString infsort, outfsort;
    infsort = "FRMReturnData.dat";
    outfsort = "FRMReturnSort.prn";
    FRMSetUp(infsort, outfsort);
    m = int((double(TotalCount))*(1.0-(ConfidenceLevel/100.0)));
// Note: Because FRMSetUp() is public in FRMSPHISTORICVAR, A[m] is visible
    outf << "Historical VaR at " << ConfidenceLevel << "% for "
        << TotalCount << " returns is ";
    outf.width(10);  outf.setf(ios::right); outf.precision(6);
    outf.setf(ios::fixed, ios::floatfield); outf.setf(ios::showpoint);
    outf << -A[m]*252;
    outf << "\n (assuming daily data, annualized with 252)";
}
```

References

See references in the supplement to Modules 6.3 – 6.5.

Appendix 6.4: Interface code comments

The graphical user interface for this module is illustrated below.

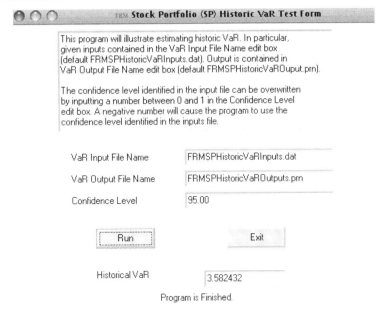

The input data contains stock index values for a very long history as illustrated below, and is contained in FRMSPHistoricVaRInputs.dat.

```
95.00     1
    Date       SP500Adj
    1/3/50      16.66
    1/4/50      16.85
    1/5/50      16.93
    1/6/50      16.98
    1/9/50      17.08
   1/10/50      17.03
   1/11/50      17.09
   1/12/50      16.76
   1/13/50      16.67
   1/16/50      16.72
   1/17/50      16.86
   1/18/50      16.85
   1/19/50      16.87
   1/20/50       16.9
...
```

The output is reported back to the screen, as well as in the output file FRMSPHistoricVaROutputs.prn.

```
95.00    1
Historical VaR at 95.00% for 14976 returns is    3.582432
 (assuming daily data, annualized with 252)
```

The source code for this interface is straightforward and not reproduced here.

FRMUnitSPHistoricVarFiles.cpp, .h

Module 6.5: Monte Carlo Simulation Value-At-Risk

Learning objectives

- Explain how to compute Monte Carlo simulation value-at-risk using C++

The goal here is to illustrate the computation of the value at risk (VaR) of a stock portfolio based on the Monte Carlo simulation method. Due to the large number of inputs and outputs, the inputs and outputs are stored in files rather than put back to the screen.

Module overview

The Monte Carlo simulation approach, as reviewed in detail in the supplement to Modules 6.3 – 6.5, is useful because it provides a large number of simulations.[46] It can also be used in VaR estimation when the portfolio contains complex, non-linear positions. A random number generator is used to provide the probability distribution, where the random number generator is calibrated based on the information contained in historical data.

Implementation code comments

FRMFPMonteCarloVaR.h

This implementation relies on three other classes and is appropriately incorporated.

```
...
#include "c:\FRMRepository\FRMCDF.cpp"  // Inverse normal
#include "c:\FRMRepository\FRMMVNormalRNG.cpp" // MVN RNG
#include "c:\FRMRepository\FRMSortingData.cpp" // MC vis Historic
class FRMFPMONTECARLOVAR : public FRMCDF, FRMMVNORMALRNG, FRMSORT
{
public:
    FRMFPMONTECARLOVAR::FRMFPMONTECARLOVAR();
    FRMFPMONTECARLOVAR::~FRMFPMONTECARLOVAR();
    char word[FPAS][FPCHARSIZE];
    char Name[FPMAXDIM][FPCHARSIZE];
    int i, j, NumberofSecurities;
    double PortfolioMean, PortfolioStandardDeviation;
    double ReturnVaRMean, ReturnVaRZero, DollarVaRMean, DollarVaRZero;
    double Horizon, ConfidenceLevel, InverseNormal;
    double PMCTER[FPMAXDIM], PMCTR[FPMAXDIM];
    double Mean[FPMAXDIM];
    double StdDev[FPMAXDIM];
    double Units[FPMAXDIM];
    double Price[FPMAXDIM];
    double **Corr;
    long int Draws;
    double Margin[20];
    double PortfolioValue;
    double Weight[FPMAXDIM];
    double ReturnMCVaR, DollarMCVaR;
    AnsiString MVNInputFile;
    AnsiString MVNOutputFile, MVNOutputDetailsFile;
    ifstream inf;
    ofstream outf;
    void FRMMonteCarloVaRFileMgmt(AnsiString sinf, AnsiString soutf);
    void FRMFPAnalyticVaR(void);
    void FRMFPMCViaAnalyticVaR(void);
    void FRMFPMCViaHistoricVaR(void);
};
#endif
```

---

[46] Supplements can be found at www.frmhelp.com.

FRMFPMonteCarloVaR.cpp

We use the constructor to allocate memory and the destructor to delete memory.

```
...
FRMFPMONTECARLOVAR::FRMFPMONTECARLOVAR()        // Allocates memory for correlation matrices
{
   try {                                   // Allocating memory for A
      Corr = new double*[MAXDIM];                         // Set up rows
      for(int j=0; j<MAXDIM; j++)Corr[j] = new double [MAXDIM]; // Set up columns
   }
   catch (std::bad_alloc) {
      Application->MessageBox(L"Could not allocate memory for matrix Corr.  Bye ...",
         L"Allocation Error for Matrix Corr[][]", MB_OK);
      exit(-1);
   }
}
// Destructor for memory management
FRMFPMONTECARLOVAR::~FRMFPMONTECARLOVAR()   // Destructor
{
   for(int j=0; j<MAXDIM; j++) delete [] Corr[j];   // Delete columns of A
   delete [] Corr;                          // Delete rows of A
}
```

We attempt to keep the main functions clear through the use of separate functions.

```
// Manage data from standard file
void FRMFPMONTECARLOVAR::FRMMonteCarloVaRFileMgmt(AnsiString inputsinf,
   AnsiString inputsoutf)
{
   inf.open(inputsinf.c_str(), ios::in);
   outf.open(inputsoutf.c_str());
   FRMFPAnalyticVaR();
   FRMFPMCViaAnalyticVaR();
   FRMFPMCViaHistoricVaR(); // Must run after FRMFPMCViaAnalyticVaR()
   outf.flush();
}
```

We compute the analytic results here for comparison purposes. For more details on this approach, see Module 6.3.

```
void FRMFPMONTECARLOVAR::FRMFPAnalyticVaR(void)
{
...
}
```

Use Monte Carlo to estimate analytic parameters.

```
void FRMFPMONTECARLOVAR::FRMFPMCViaAnalyticVaR(void)
{
// Monte Carlo VaR via Analytic Method, create input file
   MVNInputFile = "MVNInputs.dat";
   ofstream outfMVN;
   outfMVN.open(MVNInputFile.c_str());
   outfMVN << " Input Parameters\n";
   outfMVN << "  Draws          Dimensions\n";
   outfMVN.width(8);  outfMVN.setf(ios::right); outfMVN.setf(ios::fixed, ios::floatfield);
   outfMVN << Draws;
   outfMVN.width(9);  outfMVN.setf(ios::right); outfMVN.setf(ios::fixed, ios::floatfield);
   outfMVN << NumberofSecurities << "\n";
   outfMVN << "   Mean          Standard Deviation\n";
   for(i=0; i<NumberofSecurities; i++){ //Means and standard deviations
      outfMVN.width(13);  outfMVN.setf(ios::right); outfMVN.precision(6);
      outfMVN.setf(ios::fixed, ios::floatfield); outfMVN.setf(ios::showpoint);
      outfMVN << Mean[i];
      outfMVN.width(18);  outfMVN.setf(ios::right); outfMVN.precision(6);
      outfMVN.setf(ios::fixed, ios::floatfield); outf.setf(ios::showpoint);
      outfMVN << StdDev[i] << "\n";
   }
   outfMVN << " Correlations\n";
   for(i=0; i<NumberofSecurities; i++){
      for(j=0; j<=i; j++){
//the following line completes the top half of the correlation matrix
```

```
           outfMVN.width(12);  outfMVN.setf(ios::right); outfMVN.precision(6);
           outfMVN.setf(ios::fixed, ios::floatfield); outfMVN.setf(ios::showpoint);
           outfMVN << Corr[i] [j];
        }
        outfMVN << "\n";
     }
     outfMVN.close();
// delete outfMVN;
     MVNOutputFile = "MVNOutput.prn";
     MVNOutputDetailsFile = "MVNOutputDetails.prn";
     FRMMVNormalRNGFileMgmt(MVNInputFile, MVNOutputFile, MVNOutputDetailsFile);
// Read in MVN output file for sample parameters
     ifstream infMVN;
     infMVN.open(MVNOutputFile.c_str(), ios::in);
// First 4 lines of the output
     int SDimensions;
     long int SDraws;
// double SMean[MAXDIM], SStdDev[MAXDIM];
     infMVN >> word[0] >> word[1]; // Line 1
     infMVN >> word[0] >> word[1];                     // Line 2
     infMVN >> SDraws >> SDimensions;                  // Line 3
     infMVN >> word[0] >> word[1] >> word[2];      //  Means and Stdev
// Loop reads through the population mean an std dev
     for(i=0; i<SDimensions; i++){
        infMVN >> Mean[i] >> StdDev[i];     // Population
     };
     infMVN >> word[0];                        // Correlation Label
     for(i=0; i<SDimensions; i++){
        for(j=0; j<=i; j++){
           infMVN >> Corr [i] [j]; // Population correlation
        };
     };
     infMVN >> ws;
     infMVN >> word[0] >> word[1] >> word[2] >> word[3]; // Line 1 Simulation
     infMVN >> word[0] >> word[1] >> word[2];      //  Means and Stdev
// Loop reads through the mean an std. dev. in the simulation file
     for(i=0; i<SDimensions; i++){
        infMVN >> Mean[i] >> StdDev[i]; // Sample
     };
     infMVN >> word[0]; // Correlation Label
     for(i=0; i<SDimensions; i++){
        for(j=0; j<=i; j++){
           infMVN >> Corr [i] [j]; // Sample correlations
        };
     };
     PortfolioMean = PortfolioStandardDeviation = 0.0;
     for(i=0; i<NumberofSecurities; i++){
        PortfolioMean += Weight[i]*Mean[i];
        for(j=0; j<NumberofSecurities; j++){
           PortfolioStandardDeviation += Weight[i]*Weight[j]*StdDev[i]*StdDev[j]*Corr[i][j];
        }
     };
     PortfolioStandardDeviation = sqrt(PortfolioStandardDeviation);
     outf << "\nMonte Carlo via Analytic Method Selected Parameters\n";
     outf << "MC Portfolio Mean              = ";
     outf.width(12);  outf.setf(ios::right); outf.precision(6);
     outf.setf(ios::fixed, ios::floatfield); outf.setf(ios::showpoint);
     outf << PortfolioMean << "\n";
     outf << "MC Portfolio Standard Deviation = ";
     outf.width(12);  outf.setf(ios::right); outf.precision(6);
     outf.setf(ios::fixed, ios::floatfield); outf.setf(ios::showpoint);
     outf << PortfolioStandardDeviation << "\n";
// Compute VaR
...
}
```

Use Monte Carlo results as historical simulation and estimate VaR.

```
void FRMFPMONTECARLOVAR::FRMFPMCViaHistoricVaR()
{
     ifstream infSO;
     infSO.open(MVNOutputDetailsFile.c_str(), ios::in);
```

```
    ofstream outs;
    outs.open("FRMReturnData.dat");
    double PR, Return[FPMAXDIM];
    infSO >> word[0] >> word[1];
    for(i=0; i<NumberofSecurities; i++)infSO >> word[i];
    outs.width(10);  outs.setf(ios::right); outs.setf(ios::fixed, ios::floatfield);
    outs << Draws << "\n";
    int Counter;
    Counter = 1;
    while (infSO){
        if (Counter==1) {
            infSO >> word[0];
            for(i=0; i<NumberofSecurities; i++) infSO >> Return[i];
        } else {
            for(i=0; i<NumberofSecurities; i++)infSO >> Return[i];
        }
        PR = 0.0;
        for(i=0; i<NumberofSecurities; i++){
            PR += Weight[i] * (Return[i]/100.0);
        }
        outs.width(10);  outs.setf(ios::right); outs.precision(6);
        outs.setf(ios::fixed, ios::floatfield); outs.setf(ios::showpoint);
        outs << PR;
        if(!(Counter%10))outs << "\n";
        infSO >> word[0] >> ws;
        Counter++;
    }
    outs.flush(); // Make sure all data written to file
    outs.close();
    AnsiString infsort, outfsort;
    infsort = "FRMReturnData.dat";
    outfsort = "FRMReturnSort.prn";
    FRMSetUp(infsort, outfsort);
    int m;
    m = int((double(Draws))*(1.0-ConfidenceLevel) + 0.0000001);
// Note: Because FRMSetUp() is public in FRMSPHISTORICVAR, A[m] is visible
    ReturnMCVaR = - A[m-1]*100.0;
    DollarMCVaR = PortfolioValue * (ReturnMCVaR/100.0);
    outf << "\n\Monte Carlo VaR Via Historic Method Output\n";
    outf << "Monte Carlo VaR (Return)    = ";
    outf.width(18);  outf.setf(ios::right); outf.precision(6);
    outf.setf(ios::fixed, ios::floatfield); outf.setf(ios::showpoint);
    outf << ReturnMCVaR << "\n";
    outf << "Monte Carlo VaR (Dollar)    = ";
    outf.width(18);  outf.setf(ios::right); outf.precision(6);
    outf.setf(ios::fixed, ios::floatfield); outf.setf(ios::showpoint);
    outf << DollarMCVaR << "\n";


    outf.flush();
...
}
```

References

Reference can be found in the supplement to Modules 6.3 – 6.5.

Interface code comments

The graphical user interface for this module is illustrated below.

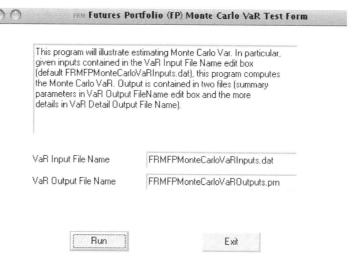

The inputs can be found in FRMFPMonteCarloVaRInputs.dat and are illustrated below.

```
Input Parameters
    Draws     Horizon     Contracts    Confidence Level
    30000      1.0000          4            95.0
        Name     Margin    Positions       Price        Mean       Standard Deviation
          AB     100.000    100.00        100.000     5.000000         10.000000
         EDF     100.000    100.00        100.000    10.000000         20.000000
         GHI     100.000    100.00        100.000    15.000000         30.000000
        JKLM     100.000    100.00        100.000    20.000000         40.000000
 Correlations
    1.000000
    0.000000      1.000000
    0.000000      0.000000     1.000000
    0.000000      0.000000     0.000000     1.000000
```

The outputs can be found in FRMFPMonteCarloVaROutputs.prn and are illustrated below.

```
Input Parameters
...

Selected Parameters
Portfolio Mean                   =      12.500000
Portfolio Standard Deviation =         13.693064
VaR Horizon                =            1.000000
VaR Confidence Level =                 95.000000%
Inverse Normal (1-C) =                 -1.644853

Analytic VaR Output
VaR Mean (Return)      =              22.523084
VaR Zero (Return)      =              10.023084
VaR Mean (Dollar)      =            9009.233463
VaR Zero (Dollar)      =            4009.233463

Analytic VaR Marginal Contribution Analysis
      Name      Weight       %MCTER        %MCTR
        AB     25.000000    10.000000      3.333333
       EDF     25.000000    20.000000     13.333333
       GHI     25.000000    30.000000     30.000000
      JKLM     25.000000    40.000000     53.333333

Monte Carlo via Analytic Method Selected Parameters
MC Portfolio Mean                   =      12.574630
MC Portfolio Standard Deviation =         13.622473
MC VaR Horizon                =            1.000000
MC VaR Confidence Level =                 95.000000%
MC Inverse Normal (1-C) =                 -1.644853
```

```
Monte Carlo VaR Output
MC VaR Mean (Return)    =         22.406971
MC VaR Zero (Return)    =          9.832342
MC VaR Mean (Dollar)    =       8962.788455
MC VaR Zero (Dollar)    =       3932.936655

Monte Carlo VaR Marginal Contribution Analysis
      Name      Weight      %MCTER       %MCTR
        AB   25.000000   10.062628    3.310179
       EDF   25.000000   19.770298   13.473099
       GHI   25.000000   29.639547   30.186716
      JKLM   25.000000   40.527526   53.030006

Monte Carlo VaR Via Historic Method Output
Monte Carlo VaR (Return)    =          9.811300
Monte Carlo VaR (Dollar)    =       3924.520000
```

The source code for this implementation is very straightforward and can be found in the following files.

FRMUnitFPMonteCarloVarFiles.cpp, .h

Chapter 7. Advanced Financial Risk Management Topics

"(T)he theory of compound options can be used to price out the capital structure of the firm." Robert Geske[47]

Introduction

In this chapter, we introduce several unique issues relevant to financial risk management. The objective here is to introduce these methods within the C++ framework. Six programs are reviewed that address the following three risk management issues: credit risk, compound options and spread options.

Each of these programs is presented as a separate module. We continue to focus almost exclusively on implementation code. The main focus of this chapter is on using credit risk, compound options and spread options. As before, we will strive to make each module standalone. Another advantage of this modular approach is your ability to find the source code within the materials you downloaded from the website.

In this chapter, we launch directly into these specific modules.

---

[47] See Robert Geske, "The valuation of compound options," *Journal of Financial Economics* (1979) 7, 63-81.

Module 7.1: Zero Coupon Bond Default Measures

Learning objectives

- Explain a variety of estimates related to default on zero coupon bonds
- Glean expectation information from zero coupon bond prices
- Discriminate between the risk premium, excess risk premium and other bond metrics

Module overview

In this module, we review some important concepts related to zero coupon bond default measures. Afterward, we illustrate a simple program that computes a variety of results.

Default risky and default-free zero coupon bonds

For a zero coupon bond, it is assumed that the value today is related to the expected cash flow at maturity. Default is assumed to only occur at maturity. Thus, using annualized continuous compounding for expressing interest rates, the value of a default risky bond is

$$P_0 = Par\left(e^{-rT}\right)$$

and the value of a default free bond is

$$_{rf}P_0 = Par\left(e^{-rT}\right)$$

Recall that under the equivalent martingale measure (EMM) there is no compensation for bearing risk: the market price of risk is zero. Assuming no compensation for bearing default risk, the dollar risk premium RP($) or present value of the expected loss from default based on the equivalent martingale measure is

$$RP(\$) = PV_{rf}\left[E_{EMM}(Loss)\right] = _{rf}P_0 - P_0$$

Assuming the recovery rate (R) is zero when there is a default, then

$$PV_{rf}\left[E_{EMM}(Loss)\right] = \left[Prob_{EMM,R=0}(Default)Par\right]e^{-r_fT}$$

Therefore,

$$Prob_{EMM,R=0}(Default) = \frac{PV_{rf}\left[E_{EMM}(Loss)\right]}{_{rf}P_0}$$

When one assumes an expected recovery rate (R) and when it is known with certainty default will occur, the present value of the expected terminal cash flow is

$$PV_{rf}\left[E_{EMM,R}(CF_T)\right] = \left[(1 - Prob_{EMM,R}(Default))Par + Prob_{EMM,R}(Default)RPar\right]e^{-r_fT}$$

Thus,

$$\frac{PV_{rf}\left[E_{EMM,R}(CF_T)\right]}{_{rf}P_0} = \left[(1 - Prob_{EMM,R}(Default)) + Prob_{EMM,R}(Default)R\right]$$

Note

$$E_{EMM,R}(CF_T) = Par - E_{EMM,R}(Loss)$$

Estimating the probability of default

Substituting for $E_{EMM,R}(CF_T)$ and rearranging we have

$$Prob_{EMM,R}(Default) = \frac{Prob_{EMM,R=0}(Default)}{1-R}$$

Thus, one interesting comparison is the difference in the projected probability of default and the implied probability of default, assuming the same recovery rate (projected and EMM)

$$Prob(Difference) = Prob_{EMM,R}(Default) - ProjectedDefault$$

The present value of the expected loss based on the projected default probability can be expressed as

$$PV_{rf}\left[E_{Proj}(Loss)\right] = Prob_{Proj,R}(Default)(1-R)_{rf}P_0$$

The dollar excess risk premium (ERP) based on the projected default probability can be expressed as

$$ERP(\$) = RP(\$) - PV_{rf}\left[E_{Proj}(Loss)\right]$$
$$=_{rf}P_0 - P_0 - PV_{rf}\left[E_{Proj}(Loss)\right]$$
$$=_{rf}P_0 - \dot{P}V_{rf}\left[E_{Proj}(Loss)\right] - P_0$$
$$=_{rf}P_0\left(1 - Prob_{Proj,R}(Default)(1-R)\right) - P_0$$
$$= e^{-r_f T}\left[Prob_{Proj,R}(Default)RPar + \left(1 - Prob_{Proj,R}(Default)\right)Par\right] - P_0$$
$$= PV_{rf}\left[E_{Proj}(CF_T)\right] - P_0$$

Expected loss

We now turn to expressions of risk premiums in annualized continuously compounded rate form. The annualized continuously compounded *percent* risk premium (RP), *percent* excess risk premium (ERP), and *percent* expected loss (ELoss) can be extracted from bond prices, the projected default probability, and the projected recovery rate. Assume the default risky bond can be expressed as

$$P_0 = Par\left(e^{-rT}\right) = Par\left(e^{-(r_f + RP)T}\right) = Par\left(e^{-(r_f + ELoss + ERP)T}\right)$$
$$=_{rf}P_0\left(e^{-(ELoss + ERP)T}\right)$$

By definition,

$$ERP = r - r_f - ELoss$$

The present value of the expected projected loss as a percentage of the current bond price is

$$\frac{PV_{rf}\left[E_{Proj}(Loss)\right]}{P_0} = \frac{Prob_{Proj,R}(Default)(1-R)_{rf}P_0}{P_0}$$

Converting this percentage to annualized continuous compounding is based on the following relationship.

$$1 + \frac{Prob_{Proj,R}(Default)(1-R)_{rf}P_0}{P_0} = e^{ELossT}$$

Therefore, ELoss is

$$\mathrm{ELoss} = \frac{1}{T}\ln\left[1 + \frac{\mathrm{Prob}_{\mathrm{Proj,R}}\left(\mathrm{Default}\right)\left(1-R\right)_{\mathrm{rf}}P_0}{P_0}\right]$$

Substituting this result and solving for the annualized percentage risk premium (ERP),

$$\mathrm{ERP} = r - r_f + \frac{1}{T}\ln\left[\frac{\mathrm{Prob}_{\mathrm{Proj,R}}\left(\mathrm{Default}\right)\left(1-R\right)_{\mathrm{rf}}P_0}{P_0}\right]$$

Implementation code comments

FRMCRMZeroCoupon.h

This class incorporates some calendar calculations, hence FRMCALENDAR has to be included in the implementation class.

```
...
#ifndef FRMCALENDARCPP
#define FRMCALENDARCPP
#include "c:\FRMRepository\FRMCalendar.cpp"
#endif

class FRMCRMZEROCOUPON : public FRMCALENDAR
{
public:               // Interaction with other classes
   void FRMCRMZeroCouponSetData(double tempParValue,double tempYieldToMaturity,
      double tempRFYieldToMaturity, double tempProjectedRecoveryRate,
      double tempProjectedDefaultProbability,
      int SM, int SD, int SY, int   MM, int MD, int MY);
   double FRMCCZeroBondPrice(void);
   double FRMCCZeroRFBondPrice(void);
   double FRMCCZeroPVExpectedLoss(void);
   double FRMCCZeroDefaultProbabilityNo(void);
   double FRMCCZeroDefaultProbability(void);
   double FRMCCZeroDefaultProbabilityDifference(void);
   double FRMCCZeroDollarPVELoss(void);
   double FRMCCZeroDollarExcessRiskPremium(void);
   double FRMCCZeroAnnualizedPercentRiskPremium(void);
   double FRMCCZeroAnnualizedPercentELoss(void);
   double FRMCCZeroAnnualizedPercentExcessRiskPremium(void);
private:
   double ParValue;
   double YieldToMaturity;
   double RFYieldToMaturity;
   double ProjectedRecoveryRate;
   double ProjectedDefaultProbability;
   double TimeToMaturity;
};
#endif
```

FRMCRMZeroCoupon.cpp

Most of the methods in this class are very simple. Once the data has been set into the class, we proceed with computing each result.

```
...
void FRMCRMZEROCOUPON::FRMCRMZeroCouponSetData(double tempParValue,
   double tempYieldToMaturity, double tempRFYieldToMaturity,
   double tempProjectedRecoveryRate, double tempProjectedDefaultProbability,
   int SM, int SD, int SY, int   MM, int MD, int MY)
{
   long int JSettlementDate, JMaturityDate;
   ParValue=tempParValue;
   YieldToMaturity=tempYieldToMaturity;
   RFYieldToMaturity=tempRFYieldToMaturity;
   ProjectedRecoveryRate=tempProjectedRecoveryRate;
   ProjectedDefaultProbability=tempProjectedDefaultProbability;
```

```
    JSettlementDate = FRMToJulian(SM, SD, SY);
    JMaturityDate = FRMToJulian(MM, MD, MY);
    TimeToMaturity=((double)(JMaturityDate - JSettlementDate))/365.;// 365.25 ???
}

double FRMCRMZEROCOUPON::FRMCCZeroBondPrice()
{
    double BondPrice;
    BondPrice = ParValue*exp(-(YieldToMaturity/100.0)*TimeToMaturity);
    return BondPrice;
}

double FRMCRMZEROCOUPON::FRMCCZeroRFBondPrice()
{
    double RFBondPrice;
    RFBondPrice = ParValue*exp(-(RFYieldToMaturity/100.0)*TimeToMaturity);
    return RFBondPrice;
}

double FRMCRMZEROCOUPON::FRMCCZeroPVExpectedLoss()
{
    double PVExectedLoss;
    PVExectedLoss = FRMCCZeroRFBondPrice() - FRMCCZeroBondPrice();
    return PVExectedLoss;
}

double FRMCRMZEROCOUPON::FRMCCZeroDefaultProbabilityNo()
{
    double DefaultProbabilityNo;
    DefaultProbabilityNo = 100*(1.0
        - (FRMCCZeroBondPrice()/FRMCCZeroRFBondPrice()));
    return DefaultProbabilityNo;
}

double FRMCRMZEROCOUPON::FRMCCZeroDefaultProbability()
{
    double DefaultProbability;
    DefaultProbability = FRMCCZeroDefaultProbabilityNo()
      / (1.0 - (ProjectedRecoveryRate/100.0));
    return DefaultProbability;
}

double FRMCRMZEROCOUPON::FRMCCZeroDefaultProbabilityDifference()
{
    double DefaultProbabilityDifference;
    DefaultProbabilityDifference = FRMCCZeroDefaultProbability()
        - ProjectedDefaultProbability;
    return DefaultProbabilityDifference;
}

double FRMCRMZEROCOUPON::FRMCCZeroDollarPVELoss()
{
    double DollarPVELoss;
    DollarPVELoss = (ProjectedDefaultProbability/100.0)
        * (1.0 - (ProjectedRecoveryRate/100.0))
        * FRMCCZeroRFBondPrice();
    return DollarPVELoss;
}

double FRMCRMZEROCOUPON::FRMCCZeroDollarExcessRiskPremium()
{
    double DollarExcessRiskPremium;
    DollarExcessRiskPremium = FRMCCZeroPVExpectedLoss() - FRMCCZeroDollarPVELoss();
    return DollarExcessRiskPremium;
}

double FRMCRMZEROCOUPON::FRMCCZeroAnnualizedPercentRiskPremium()
{
    double AnnualizedPercentRiskPremium;
    AnnualizedPercentRiskPremium = YieldToMaturity - RFYieldToMaturity;
    return AnnualizedPercentRiskPremium;
```

```
}

double FRMCRMZEROCOUPON::FRMCCZeroAnnualizedPercentELoss()
{
   double AnnualizedPercentELoss;
   AnnualizedPercentELoss = 100.0*(1.0/TimeToMaturity)
      * log( 1.0 + (FRMCCZeroDollarPVELoss()/FRMCCZeroBondPrice()) );
   return AnnualizedPercentELoss;
}

double FRMCRMZEROCOUPON::FRMCCZeroAnnualizedPercentExcessRiskPremium()
{
   double AnnualizedPercentExcessRiskPremium;
   AnnualizedPercentExcessRiskPremium = YieldToMaturity - RFYieldToMaturity
      - FRMCCZeroAnnualizedPercentELoss();
   return AnnualizedPercentExcessRiskPremium;
}
```

References

Credit Risk: Models and Management. London: Risk Books, 1999.

Derivatives Credit Risk: Further Advances in Measurement and Management, 2nd ed. London: Risk Books, 1999.

Merton, Robert, "On the Pricing of Corporate Debt: The Risk Structure of Interest Rates," *Journal of Finance* 29 (1974), 449-470.

Saunders, A., *Credit Risk Measurement: New Approaches to Value-at-Risk and Other Paradigms*. New York: Wiley, 1999.

Appendix 7.1: Interface code comments

The graphic user interface is illustrated below.

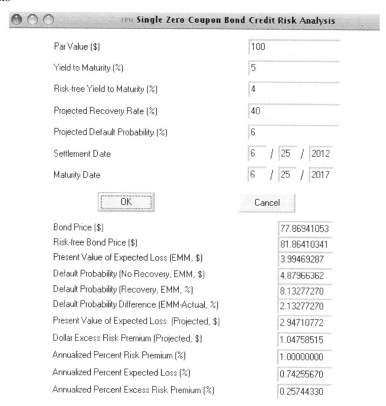

There is nothing new related to the interface code for this module.

FRMUnitCRZeroBond.cpp, .h

Module 7.2: Bivariate Normal Cumulative Distribution Function

Learning objectives

- Introduce the bivariate normal cumulative distribution function
- Contrast the univariate with the bivariate normal cumulative distribution function

Module overview

This module forms the basis upon which the compound option modules are built. Recall the Black, Scholes, Merton option valuation model relies on the univariate standard normal cumulative distribution function, N(d). The compound options valuation model, as well as other quantitative problems, relies on the bivariate standard normal cumulative distribution function, $BN(a,b;\rho)$. Note that the implementation of the bivariate standard normal cumulative distribution function relies on the univariate standard normal cumulative distribution function.

The bivariate cumulative distribution function can be expressed as

$$BCDF(a,b;\rho) = \Pr[x < a] \cap \Pr[y < b] \text{ (Bivariate cumulative distribution function)}$$

where x and y are random variables and a and b are real numbers.

The bivariate normal cumulative distribution function can be expressed as

$$BN(a,b;\rho) = \frac{1}{2\pi\sqrt{1-\rho^2}} \int_{-\infty}^{a} \int_{-\infty}^{b} e^{-\frac{x^2 - 2\rho xy + y^2}{2(1-\rho^2)}} \, dxdy \text{ (Bivariate normal cumulative distribution function)}$$

The focus of the algorithm used here is the bivariate standard normal distribution (means zero and standard deviation one).

Implementation code comments

FRMBivariateNormal.h

The numerical estimation of the bivariate normal rests upon the numerical estimation of the univariate normal.

```
...
#ifndef FRMCDFFILE
#define FRMCDFFILE
#include "c:\FRMRepository\FRMCDF.cpp"
#endif

class FRMBIVARIATE : FRMCDF
{
public:          // User declarations
   double FRMM(double, double, double);
   double FRMMNeg(double, double, double);
   double FRMMZero(double, double, double);
   double FRMsgn(double);
};
#endif
```

FRMBivariateNormal.cpp

It is important to always document your coding sources. As an example, I now cannot locate the source I relied upon to build these methods.

```
...
//----------------------------------------------------------------
double FRMBIVARIATE::FRMM(double a, double b, double rho)
```

```
{
    if(a * b * rho <= 0.0){
        if(a <= 0.0 && b <= 0.0 && rho <= 0.0) return FRMMNeg(a, b, rho);
        else if(a <= 0.0 && b >= 0.0 && rho >= 0.0)
            return  FRMND(a) - FRMMNeg(a, -b, -rho);
        else if(a >= 0.0 && b <= 0.0 && rho >= 0.0)
            return  FRMND(b) - FRMMNeg(-a, b, -rho);
        else return  FRMND(a) + FRMND(b) - 1.0 + FRMMNeg(-a, -b, rho);//a>=0,b>=0,r<=0
    } else return FRMMZero(a, b, rho); // a*b*rho > 0
};

double FRMBIVARIATE::FRMMZero(double a, double b, double rho) // a*b*rho = 0
{
    double rho1, rho2, delta;
    rho1 = ((rho*a-b)*FRMsgn(a))/sqrt(pow(a,2)-2*rho*a*b+pow(b,2));
    rho2 = ((rho*b-a)*FRMsgn(b))/sqrt(pow(a,2)-2*rho*a*b+pow(b,2));
    delta = (1.0 - FRMsgn(a)*FRMsgn(b))/4.0;
    return FRMM(a, 0, rho1) + FRMM(b, 0, rho2) - delta;
}

double FRMBIVARIATE::FRMMNeg(double a,double b,double rho)//a,b,and rho non-positive
{
    double A1, A2, A3, A4, B1, B2, B3, B4 , f11, f12, f13, f14, f21, f22, f23,
        f24, f31, f32, f33, f34, f41, f42, f43, f44, f11a, f12a, f13a, f14a, f21a,
        f22a, f23a, f24a, f31a, f32a, f33a, f34a, f41a, f42a, f43a, f44a, f11b,
        f12b, f13b, f14b, f21b, f22b, f23b, f24b, f31b, f32b, f33b, f34b, f41b,
        f42b, f43b, f44b, aprime, bprime, aneg, bneg, rho1, rho2,
        delta, aa, bb, BN, BN1, BN2;
//Coefficients
    A1 = 0.3253030; A2 = 0.4211071; A3 =0.1334425; A4 = 0.006374323;
    B1 = 0.1337764; B2 = 0.6243247; B3 = 1.3425378; B4 = 2.2626645;
//Compute the Bivariate Normal for a<=0, b<=0, rho<=0
    aprime = a/sqrt(2*(1-pow(rho,2)));
    bprime = b/sqrt(2*(1-pow(rho,2)));
    f11=exp(aprime*(2*B1-aprime)+ bprime*(2*B1-bprime)+2*rho*(B1-aprime)*(B1-bprime));
    f12=exp(aprime*(2*B1-aprime)+ bprime*(2*B2-bprime)+2*rho*(B1-aprime)*(B2-bprime));
    f13=exp(aprime*(2*B1-aprime)+ bprime*(2*B3-bprime)+2*rho*(B1-aprime)*(B3-bprime));
    f14=exp(aprime*(2*B1-aprime)+ bprime*(2*B4-bprime)+2*rho*(B1-aprime)*(B4-bprime));
    f21=exp(aprime*(2*B2-aprime)+ bprime*(2*B1-bprime)+2*rho*(B2-aprime)*(B1-bprime));
    f22=exp(aprime*(2*B2-aprime)+ bprime*(2*B2-bprime)+2*rho*(B2-aprime)*(B2-bprime));
    f23=exp(aprime*(2*B2-aprime)+ bprime*(2*B3-bprime)+2*rho*(B2-aprime)*(B3-bprime));
    f24=exp(aprime*(2*B2-aprime)+ bprime*(2*B4-bprime)+2*rho*(B2-aprime)*(B4-bprime));
    f31=exp(aprime*(2*B3-aprime)+ bprime*(2*B1-bprime)+2*rho*(B3-aprime)*(B1-bprime));
    f32=exp(aprime*(2*B3-aprime)+ bprime*(2*B2-bprime)+2*rho*(B3-aprime)*(B2-bprime));
    f33=exp(aprime*(2*B3-aprime)+ bprime*(2*B3-bprime)+2*rho*(B3-aprime)*(B3-bprime));
    f34=exp(aprime*(2*B3-aprime)+ bprime*(2*B4-bprime)+2*rho*(B3-aprime)*(B4-bprime));
    f41=exp(aprime*(2*B4-aprime)+ bprime*(2*B1-bprime)+2*rho*(B4-aprime)*(B1-bprime));
    f42=exp(aprime*(2*B4-aprime)+ bprime*(2*B2-bprime)+2*rho*(B4-aprime)*(B2-bprime));
    f43=exp(aprime*(2*B4-aprime)+ bprime*(2*B3-bprime)+2*rho*(B4-aprime)*(B3-bprime));
    f44=exp(aprime*(2*B4-aprime)+ bprime*(2*B4-bprime)+2*rho*(B4-aprime)*(B4-bprime));
//Compute M
    BN = (sqrt(1-pow(rho,2))/PI)
        * (A1*A1*f11+A1*A2*f12+A1*A3*f13+A1*A4*f14+A2*A1*f21
        + A2*A2*f22+A2*A3*f23+A2*A4*f24+A3*A1*f31+A3*A2*f32+A3*A3*f33+A3*A4*f34
        + A4*A1*f41+A4*A2*f42+A4*A3*f43+A4*A4*f44);
    return BN;
};
//-------------------------------------------------------------------------
double FRMBIVARIATE::FRMsgn(double X)
{
    if(X>=0) return(1);
    else return(-1);
};
...
```

References

Drezner, Z., "Computation of the Bivariate Normal Integral," *Mathematics of Computation* Vol. 32, No. 141 (Jan., 1978), 277-279.

Drezner, Z. and Wesolowsky, G.O., "On the computation of the bivariate normal integral," *Journal of Statistical Computation and Simulation* Vol. 35, 101-107.

Genz, Alan, "Numerical computation of rectangular bivariate and trivariate normal and t probabilities," *Statistics and Computation* Vol. 14 (2004), 251-260.

West, Graeme, "Better approximations to cumulative normal functions," *WILMOTT Magazine*, July 2009, 70-76.

Appendix 7.2: Interface code comments

The graphical user interface for this program is illustrated below.

The interface code is very straightforward so it is not reproduced here.

FRMUnitBivariateN.cpp, .h

Module 7.3: Compound Options Valuation

Learning objectives

- Introduce compound options
- Contrast call on call, call on put, put on call and put on put
- Use standard arbitrage arguments to demonstrate compound option's upper and lower boundaries
- Introduce multiple forms for inputs (two ways to input dates)

Module overview

In this module, we introduce compound options along with their boundary conditions. In the supplement to this module, we provide the derivation of the boundary conditions.[48] We introduce building a compound option valuation program in this module.

A compound option is an option on an option. Thus, for European-style compound options there are two expiration dates, $t < T_1 < T_2$, where t denotes the valuation date, T_1 denotes the compound option's expiration date and T_2 denotes the underlying option's expiration date, where dates are reported in fraction of a year. There are also two strike prices, X_1 and X_2, where X_1 is the strike price of the compound option and X_2 is the strike price of the underlying option.

We assume the strike prices are positive and $0 < X_1$ and $0 < X_2$. The following exhibit illustrates the three dates in calendar time.

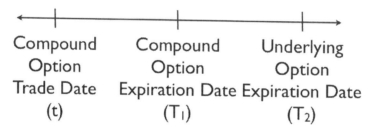

Compound Option Trade Date (t)   Compound Option Expiration Date (T_1)   Underlying Option Expiration Date (T_2)

Therefore, the payoffs on the underlying options at maturity (T_2) are:

$$C_{T_2}(S,X_2,T_2) = max(0, S_{T_2} - X_2) \text{ (Plain vanilla call option)}$$

$$P_{T_2}(S,X_2,T_2) = max(0, X_2 - S_{T_2}) \text{ (Plain vanilla put option)}$$

The plain vanilla call and put option values observed at time T_2 (subscript) for the underlying instrument S with strike price X_2 and the option matures at time T_2.

Therefore, the payoff on the compound option at maturity (T_1) is:

$$CoC_{T_1}(C(S,X_2,T_2),X_1,T_1) = max(0, C_{T_1}(S,X_2,T_2) - X_1) \text{ (Call on call compound option)}$$

$$CoP_{T_1}(P(S,X_2,T_2),X_1,T_1) = max(0, P_{T_1}(S,X_2,T_2) - X_1) \text{ (Call on put compound option)}$$

$$PoC_{T_1}(C(S,X_2,T_2),X_1,T_1) = max(0, X_1 - C_{T_1}(S,X_2,T_2)) \text{ (Put on call compound option)}$$

$$PoP_{T_1}(P(S,X_2,T_2),X_1,T_1) = max(0, X_1 - P_{T_1}(S,X_2,T_2)) \text{ (Put on put compound option)}$$

---

[48] Supplements are available at www.frmhelp.com.

The decision to exercise a compound option depends on whether the compound option is in-the-money. Specifically, whether the underlying option's value at time T_1 is greater than its strike price. The underlying option's value depends on the underlying instrument's value, S_{T_1}, and time to expiration, $T_2 - T_1$.

Compound option boundary conditions

The following boundary conditions apply to compound options:

Call on call lower bound: $CoC_t(C(S,X_2,T_2),X_1,T_1) \geq \max\left[0, C_t(S,X_2,T_2) - X_1 e^{-r(T_1-t)}\right]$

Call on call upper bound: $CoC_t(C(S,X_2,T_2),X_1,T_1) \leq C_t(S,X_2,T_2)$

Call on put lower bound: $CoP_t(P(S,X_2,T_2),X_1,T_1) \geq \max\left[0, P_t(S,X_2,T_2) - X_1 e^{-r(T_1-t)}\right]$

Call on put upper bound: $CoP_t(P(S,X_2,T_2),X_1,T_1) \leq P_t(S,X_2,T_2)$

Put on call lower bound: $PoC_t(C(S,X_2,T_2),X_1,T_1) \geq \max\left[0, X_1 e^{-r(T_1-t)} - C_t(S,X_2,T_2)\right]$

Put on call upper bound: $PoC_t(C(S,X_2,T_2),X_1,T_1) \leq X_1 e^{-r(T_1-t)}$

Put on put lower bound: $PoP_t(P(S,X_2,T_2),X_1,T_1) \geq \max\left[0, X_1 e^{-r(T_1-t)} - P_t(S,X_2,T_2)\right]$

Put on put upper bound: $PoP_t(P(S,X_2,T_2),X_1,T_1) \leq X_1 e^{-r(T_1-t)}$

Compound option valuation assumptions

As with any model, the compound option valuation model presented here is based on a set of assumptions. The initial assumptions are the same as the Black, Scholes and Merton option valuation model which are repeated here for convenience.

- Standard finance presuppositions and assumptions apply (see introduction to chapter 4)
- Underlying instrument behaves randomly and follows a lognormal distribution
- Risk-free interest rate exists and is constant
- Volatility of the underlying instrument's continuously compounded rate of return is positive and constant
- No market frictions, including no taxes and no transaction costs
- Options are European-style (exercise available only at maturity)
- Underlying instrument pays a constant cash flow yield (e.g., dividend yield)

Note that because we assume the underlying instrument's volatility is constant, by definition the underlying option's volatility upon which the compound option is based, is not constant.

Compound option valuation

Based on Geske (1979), the standard compound option valuation models are expressed as follows:

Call on call:
$$CoC_t(C(S,X_2,T_2),X_1,T_1) = S_t e^{-q(T_2-t)}BN(a_1,b_1;\rho) - X_2 e^{-r(T_2-t)}BN(a_2,b_2;\rho) - X_1 e^{-r(T_1-t)}N(a_2)$$

Put on call:
$$PoC_t(C(S,X_2,T_2),X_1,T_1) = X_2 e^{-r(T_2-t)}BN(-a_2,b_2;-\rho) - S_t e^{-q(T_2-t)}BN(-a_1,b_1;-\rho) + X_1 e^{-r(T_1-t)}N(-a_2)$$

Call on put:

$$\text{CoP}_t\big(P(S,X_2,T_2),X_1,T_1\big) = X_2 e^{-r(T_2-t)} \text{BN}(-a_2,-b_2;\rho) - S_t e^{-q(T_2-t)} \text{BN}(-a_1,-b_1;\rho) - X_1 e^{-r(T_1-t)} N(-a_2)$$

Put on put:

$$\text{PoP}_t\big(P(S,X_2,T_2),X_1,T_1\big) = S_t e^{-q(T_2-t)} \text{BN}(a_1,-b_1;-\rho) - X_2 e^{-r(T_2-t)} \text{BN}(a_2,-b_2;-\rho) + X_1 e^{-r(T_1-t)} N(a_2)$$

where

$$a_1 = \frac{\ln\left(\dfrac{S_t}{\hat{S}}\right) + \left(r-q+\dfrac{\sigma^2}{2}\right)(T_1-t)}{\sigma\sqrt{T_1-t}}$$

$$a_2 = a_1 - \sigma\sqrt{T_1-t}$$

$$b_1 = \frac{\ln\left(\dfrac{S_t}{X_2}\right) + \left(r-q+\dfrac{\sigma^2}{2}\right)(T_2-t)}{\sigma\sqrt{T_2-t}}$$

$$b_2 = b_1 - \sigma\sqrt{T_2-t}$$

$$\text{BN}(a,b;\rho) = \frac{1}{2\pi\sqrt{1-\rho^2}} \int_{-\infty}^{a}\int_{-\infty}^{b} e^{-\frac{x^2-2\rho xy + y^2}{2(1-\rho^2)}} \, dxdy \quad \text{(Cumulative bivariate normal distribution)}$$

$$\rho = \sqrt{\frac{T_1-t}{T_2-t}}$$

$\hat{S}$ denotes the critical stock price at time T_1 such that the second option has the value X_1 (at-the-money)

$$C_{T_1}\big(\hat{S},X_2,T_2\big) - X_1 = 0 \quad \text{(Underlying call option is at-the-money)}$$

$$P_{T_1}\big(\hat{S},X_2,T_2\big) - X_1 = 0 \quad \text{(Underlying put option is at-the-money)}$$

The compound option valuation model above is based on standard finance conditions and assumes the underlying stock price follows geometric Brownian motion (proofs available in Geske (1979) and Lajeri-Chaherli (2002)).

Intuition for the compound option valuation models

The underlying instrument of a compound option is an option referred to here as the underlying option. Therefore, the underlying option's volatility is not constant and the standard Black-Scholes-Merton approach is invalid. Recall a call option on stock can be viewed as a leveraged position in the stock, where the degree of leverage is a function of the stock price. The greater the implied leverage, the greater the volatility of the underlying option.

The formulas above are based on the same 'no-arbitrage' approach to valuation (within the cash flow adjusted approach to valuation). Note that the valuation formulas do not depend on the expected return on any financial instrument, nor the underlying option, nor the underlying instrument (the instrument delivered when the underlying option is exercised).

Applications of compound options

Option on firm equity Black and Scholes (1973) and Merton (1974) both consider firm equity as a call option on firm assets. If the firm is not leveraged, then the strike price is zero due to limited liability. In the unleveraged case, the equity holders can decide not to exercise their firm option if firm assets have negative value.

If the firm is leveraged, then firm debt holders have a put option on the firm assets. If the firm is leveraged, then the strike price is par due to limited liability (assuming single bond, zero coupon debt). In the leveraged case, the equity holders can decide not to exercise their firm option if firm assets value is less than the firm liability value (par).

Assuming constant volatility of annualized, continuously compounded percentage changes in firm value, then the volatility of firm debt and firm equity is not constant; it depends on the level of firm value. As firm value falls, the firm is more highly leveraged and therefore the firm equity volatility is higher. Thus, valuing firm equity as a call option on firm assets corrects for the well-known leverage effect on firm equity volatility. Also, a call option on firm equity, valued using a compound option approach, implicitly corrects for the leverage effect within the underlying option.

Executive stock options can also be viewed as a long maturity (usually ten years) compound option.

Option on firm liabilities Corporate liabilities can also be viewed as containing options on firm assets. Zero coupon debt contains two options. First, the debt holders are short the option held by equity holders should firm value fall below the debt's par value. Second, the debt holders are long the limited liability option provided by legal firm incorporation. Therefore, an option on debt, such as that contained in callable debt, can be viewed as a compound option.

Other potential applications

- Bid on project containing options (e.g., portfolio of liabilities from FDIC)
- Sequential opportunities (grad school only if undergrad performance good)
- Insurance policies with sequential premiums

Implementation code comments

FRMCompoundOptions.h

The compound options class relies upon both the standard Black, Scholes and Merton option valuation model as well as the bivariate normal distribution. We also rely on a simple max() function for the boundary conditions defined in the preprocessor directive below.

```
...
#ifndef FRMBSMDYOPMCPP
#define FRMBSMDYOPMCPP
#include "c:\FRMRepository\FRMBSMDYOPM.cpp"
#endif
#ifndef FRMBIVARIATENORMALCPP
#define FRMBIVARIATENORMALCPP
#include "c:\FRMRepository\FRMBivariateNormal.cpp"
#endif
#define max(a, b)  (((a) > (b)) ? (a) : (b))

class FRMCOMPOUNDOPTIONS
{
...
   void FRMSetData(double StockPrice, double StrikePrice1,double StrikePrice2,
      double TimeToMaturity1, double TimeToMaturity2,double Volatility,
      double InterestRate, double DividendYield);
   double FRMCallOnCallValue(void);
   double FRMCallOnPutValue(void);
   double FRMPutOnCallValue(void);
   double FRMPutOnPutValue(void);
```

```
    double FRMCallOnCallValueLB(void);
    double FRMCallOnPutValueLB(void);
    double FRMPutOnCallValueLB(void);
    double FRMPutOnPutValueLB(void);
    double FRMCallOnCallValueUB(void);
    double FRMCallOnPutValueUB(void);
    double FRMPutOnCallValueUB(void);
    double FRMPutOnPutValueUB(void);
```

Because the following two classes were not inherited in this class, we instantiate an object for use here.

```
    FRMBSMDYOPM BD;
    FRMBIVARIATE BIV;
};
...
```

FRMCompoundOptions.cpp

We illustrate just the call on call compound option as the other three are very similar. Note that the upper and lower bounds are checked in the valuation method and also calculated separately.

```
...
// Call on call option
double FRMCOMPOUNDOPTIONS::FRMCallOnCallValue(void)
{
    double x1, x2, x3, M1, M2, N2;
    BD.BSMDYOPMSetDataSP(StrikePrice2, TimeToMaturity2 - TimeToMaturity1,
        InterestRate, Volatility, DividendYield);
    BD.BSMDYOPMSetDataMM(0.00001, 10000.0);
    StockPriceD = BD.BSMDYCallISP(StrikePrice1);
    if (StockPriceD < 0.0) return -999999.99;
    M1 = BIV.FRMM(FRMCalculatea1(), FRMCalculateb1(),
        pow(TimeToMaturity1/TimeToMaturity2, 0.5));
    x1 = StockPrice*exp(-(DividendYield/100.0) * TimeToMaturity2) * M1;
    M2 = BIV.FRMM(FRMCalculatea2(), FRMCalculateb2(),
        pow(TimeToMaturity1/TimeToMaturity2,0.5));
    x2 = StrikePrice2 * exp(-(InterestRate/100.0) * TimeToMaturity2) * M2;
    N2 = BD.FRMND(FRMCalculatea2());
    x3 = exp(-(InterestRate/100.0) * TimeToMaturity1) * StrikePrice1 * N2;
// Check boundary
    BD.BSMDYOPMSetData(StockPrice, StrikePrice2, InterestRate, TimeToMaturity2,
        Volatility, DividendYield);
    CO = x1 - x2 - x3;
    UpperBound = BD.BSMDYCallPrice();
    LowerBound = max( 0.0, BD.BSMDYCallPrice() - StrikePrice1
        * exp(-(InterestRate/100.0)*TimeToMaturity1) );
    if (UpperBound < LowerBound) return -99.99;
    if (CO > UpperBound) CO = UpperBound;
    if (CO < LowerBound) CO = LowerBound;
    return CO;
}

double FRMCOMPOUNDOPTIONS::FRMCallOnCallValueLB(void)
{
    BD.BSMDYOPMSetData(StockPrice, StrikePrice2, InterestRate, TimeToMaturity2,
        Volatility, DividendYield);
    LowerBound = max( 0.0, BD.BSMDYCallPrice() - StrikePrice1
        * exp(-(InterestRate/100.0)*TimeToMaturity1) );
    return LowerBound;
}

double FRMCOMPOUNDOPTIONS::FRMCallOnCallValueUB(void)
{
    BD.BSMDYOPMSetData(StockPrice, StrikePrice2, InterestRate, TimeToMaturity2,
        Volatility, DividendYield);
    UpperBound = BD.BSMDYCallPrice();
    return UpperBound;
}
...
```

References

Black, F. and M. Scholes, 1973. The pricing of options and corporate liabilities. Journal of Political Economy, May-June.

Geske, R. (1979). The valuation of compound options. Journal of Financial Economics 7, 63-81.

Lajeri-Chaheri, F. (2002). A note on the valuation of compound options. Journal of Futures Markets 22, 1103-1115.

Merton, R., 1973. Theory of rational option pricing. Bell Journal of Economics and Management Science, Spring.

Merton, R., 1974. On the pricing of corporate debt: The risk structure of interest rates. Journal of Finance.

Appendix 7.3: Interface code comments

The graphical user interface is illustrated below.

	Compound Option Pricing Model	
Stock Price (in Dollars)	95.00	
Strike on Option Price (in Dollars)	15.00	
Time To Maturity 1 (in Years)	1	Edit
Strike on Spot Price (in Dollars)	100	
Time To Maturity 2 (in Years)	2	
Volatility (in %)	30.0	
Interest Rate (in %)	5.00	
Dividend Yield (in %)	2	

Run   Close

	Option Value ($)	Option Lower Bound ($)	Option Upper Bound ($)
Call on Call ($)	6.592725	1.397721	15.666162
Put on Call ($)	5.195004	0.000000	14.268441
Call on Put ($)	1.918363	0.606466	14.874907
Put on Put ($)	1.311897	0.000000	14.268441

If the "Edit" button on this form is selected, then another form opens and the user is allowed to input actual calendar dates that are then incorporated into the previous form.

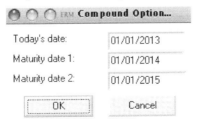

Compound Option...	
Today's date:	01/01/2013
Maturity date 1:	01/01/2014
Maturity date 2:	01/01/2015

OK   Cancel

Therefore, this interface code has two forms and two sets of *.cpp and *.h files. The following are excerpts from the main form's interface header code with selected comments added.

FRMUnitCompoundOptions.h

The time to maturity unit could be incorporated in a variety of ways, but this way is most transparent.

```
...
#include "FRMUnitTimeToMaturity.h"
```

We include the implementation code here and instantiate an object of the compound options class.

```
#include "c:\FRMRepository\FRMCompoundOptions.cpp"
//------------------------------------------------------------------------
class TCompoundOptionForm : public TForm
{
...
    FRMCOMPOUNDOPTIONS C;
...
```

The following are excerpts from the main form's interface code with selected comments added.

FRMUnitCompoundOptions.cpp

The source code here is fairly typical with the exception of the second form. We also provide some error checking, although not much.

```
//------------------------------------------------------------------------
void __fastcall TCompoundOptionForm::btnEditClick(TObject *Sender)
{
```

The command below is unique to this compiler and provides a way to send the focus to another form.

```
    TimeToMaturityForm->ShowModal();  // Open new form with calendar inputs
    if (StrToFloat(editTimeToMaturity1->Text) <= 0.0) {
    Application->MessageBoxA(L"Time to Maturity must be positive: please enter a new one",
        L"Error: Positive Number", MB_OK);
    editTimeToMaturity1->Text = "0.500";
    }
}
```

The Execute function results in the option values, as well as the option boundaries. Compound options are best understood in the context of their static boundaries.

```
void __fastcall TCompoundOptionForm::Execute(void)
{
    SetLocalData();
    C.FRMSetData(inputStockPrice, inputStrikePrice1, inputStrikePrice2,
        inputTimeToMaturity1, inputTimeToMaturity2, inputVolatility,
        inputInterestRate, inputDividendYield);
    CallOnCall = C.FRMCallOnCallValue();
    PutOnCall = C.FRMPutOnCallValue();
    CallOnPut = C.FRMCallOnPutValue();
    PutOnPut = C.FRMPutOnPutValue();
...
    CallOnCallLB = C.FRMCallOnCallValueLB();
    PutOnCallLB = C.FRMPutOnCallValueLB();
    CallOnPutLB = C.FRMCallOnPutValueLB();
    PutOnPutLB = C.FRMPutOnPutValueLB();
...
    CallOnCallUB = C.FRMCallOnCallValueUB();
    PutOnCallUB = C.FRMPutOnCallValueUB();
    CallOnPutUB = C.FRMCallOnPutValueUB();
    PutOnPutUB = C.FRMPutOnPutValueUB();
...
}
```

Limited error trapping is also provided in this module.

```
void __fastcall TCompoundOptionForm::editStockPriceExit(TObject *Sender)
{
    if (StrToFloat(editStockPrice->Text) <= 0.0) {
    Application->MessageBoxA(L"Stock price must be positive: please enter a new one",
        L"Error: Positive Number", MB_OK);
    editStockPrice->Text = "100.00";
    }
}
...
```

The following are excerpts from the calendar form's interface header code with selected comments added.

FRMUnitTimeToMaturity.h

Mask edits are compiler specific but provide a convenient way to incorporate dates and the FRMCALENDAR class provides the methods to calculate the results necessary to compute the fraction of the year.

```
...
#include <Mask.hpp>
#ifndef FRMCALENDARCPP
#define FRMCALENDARCPP
#include "c:\FRMRepository\FRMCalendar.cpp"
#endif
//--------------------------------------------------------------------------
class TTimeToMaturityForm : public TForm
{
...
   TMaskEdit *editToday;
   TMaskEdit *editMaturity1;
   TMaskEdit *editMaturity2;
...
   FRMCALENDAR Calendar;
...
```

FRMUnitTimeToMaturity.cpp

Because the fraction of the year is on the main form and the calendar dates are on the time form, the order of the header files is important. We also need to access the computer system's clock.

```
...
#include <time.h>
#include <sys\types.h>
#include <sys\timeb.h>
#include "FRMUnitTimeToMaturity.h"
#include "FRMUnitCompoundOptions.h" // References CompoundOptionForm
...
```

Mask edit objects, editToday, editMaturity1 and editMaturity2, hold the calendar date in the Text[] variable and have to be carefully extracted.

```
void __fastcall TTimeToMaturityForm::SetLocalData (void)
{
   Temp[0] = StrToInt (editToday->Text[1]);
   Temp[1] = StrToInt (editToday->Text[2]);
   BeginDateMonth = Temp[0] * 10 + Temp[1];
   Temp[0] = StrToInt (editToday->Text[4]);
   Temp[1] = StrToInt (editToday->Text[5]);
   BeginDateDay = Temp[0] * 10 + Temp[1];
   Temp[0] = StrToInt (editToday->Text[7]);
   Temp[1] = StrToInt (editToday->Text[8]);
   Temp[2] = StrToInt (editToday->Text[9]);
   Temp[3] = StrToInt (editToday->Text[10]);
   BeginDateYear = Temp[0] * 1000 + Temp[1] * 100 + Temp[2] * 10 + Temp[3];
   Temp[0] = StrToInt (editMaturity1->Text[1]);
   Temp[1] = StrToInt (editMaturity1->Text[2]);
   EndDateMonth1 = Temp[0] * 10 + Temp[1];
   Temp[0] = StrToInt (editMaturity1->Text[4]);
   Temp[1] = StrToInt (editMaturity1->Text[5]);
   EndDateDay1 = Temp[0] * 10 + Temp[1];
   Temp[0] = StrToInt (editMaturity1->Text[7]);
   Temp[1] = StrToInt (editMaturity1->Text[8]);
   Temp[2] = StrToInt (editMaturity1->Text[9]);
   Temp[3] = StrToInt (editMaturity1->Text[10]);
   EndDateYear1 = Temp[0] * 1000 + Temp[1] * 100 + Temp[2] * 10 + Temp[3];
   Temp[0] = StrToInt (editMaturity2->Text[1]);
   Temp[1] = StrToInt (editMaturity2->Text[2]);
   EndDateMonth2 = Temp[0] * 10 + Temp[1];
   Temp[0] = StrToInt (editMaturity2->Text[4]);
   Temp[1] = StrToInt (editMaturity2->Text[5]);
   EndDateDay2 = Temp[0] * 10 + Temp[1];
   Temp[0] = StrToInt (editMaturity2->Text[7]);
   Temp[1] = StrToInt (editMaturity2->Text[8]);
```

```
Temp[2] = StrToInt (editMaturity2->Text[9]);
Temp[3] = StrToInt (editMaturity2->Text[10]);
EndDateYear2 = Temp[0] * 1000 + Temp[1] * 100 + Temp[2] * 10 + Temp[3];
}
```

We return the fraction of the year and arbitrarily assume 365.0 days per year.

```
void __fastcall TTimeToMaturityForm::Execute (void)
{
    SetLocalData();
    JBeginDate = Calendar.FRMToJulian(BeginDateMonth, BeginDateDay, BeginDateYear);
    JEndDate1 = Calendar.FRMToJulian(EndDateMonth1, EndDateDay1, EndDateYear1);
    JEndDate2 = Calendar.FRMToJulian(EndDateMonth2, EndDateDay2, EndDateYear2);
```

Place the fraction of the year on the main form using the two lines of code below.

```
    CompoundOptionForm->editTimeToMaturity1->Text
        = FloatToStrF((JEndDate1 - JBeginDate)/365.0, ffFixed, 15, 6);
    CompoundOptionForm->editTimeToMaturity2->Text
        = FloatToStrF((JEndDate2 - JBeginDate)/365.0, ffFixed, 15, 6);
    Close();
}
...
```

Module 7.4: Compound Options Implied Parameters

Learning objectives

- Identify the need for computing compound options implied parameters
- Present a module to solve for the implied parameters of the compound option valuation model

Module overview

In this module, we assume you have already mastered Module 7.3 Compound Options Valuation. This module is similar to Module 4.4 Option Implied Parameters. Here we bring together two modules previously covered, Module 3.7 Embedded Parameters and Module 7.3 Compound Options Valuation. Again, the value of the modular approach is illustrated here by the flexibility to compute any implied parameter, even those not typically needing estimation. In finance, however, we often encounter unusual quantitative needs; and having the capacity to compute any embedded parameter is helpful.

Compound option valuation

Recall the standard compound option valuation models are expressed as follows:

Call on call:
$$CoC_t\big(C(S,X_2,T_2),X_1,T_1\big) = S_t e^{-q(T_2-t)}BN(a_1,b_1;\rho) - X_2 e^{-r(T_2-t)}BN(a_2,b_2;\rho) - X_1 e^{-r(T_1-t)}N(a_2)$$

Put on call:
$$PoC_t\big(C(S,X_2,T_2),X_1,T_1\big) = X_2 e^{-r(T_2-t)}BN(-a_2,b_2;-\rho) - S_t e^{-q(T_2-t)}BN(-a_1,b_1;-\rho) + X_1 e^{-r(T_1-t)}N(-a_2)$$

Call on put:
$$CoP_t\big(P(S,X_2,T_2),X_1,T_1\big) = X_2 e^{-r(T_2-t)}BN(-a_2,-b_2;\rho) - S_t e^{-q(T_2-t)}BN(-a_1,-b_1;\rho) - X_1 e^{-r(T_1-t)}N(-a_2)$$

Put on put:
$$PoP_t\big(P(S,X_2,T_2),X_1,T_1\big) = S_t e^{-q(T_2-t)}BN(a_1,-b_1;-\rho) - X_2 e^{-r(T_2-t)}BN(a_2,-b_2;-\rho) + X_1 e^{-r(T_1-t)}N(a_2)$$

where

$$a_1 = \frac{\ln\left(\dfrac{S_t}{\hat{S}}\right) + \left(r - q + \dfrac{\sigma^2}{2}\right)(T_1 - t)}{\sigma\sqrt{T_1 - t}}$$

$$a_2 = a_1 - \sigma\sqrt{T_1 - t}$$

$$b_1 = \frac{\ln\left(\dfrac{S_t}{X_2}\right) + \left(r - q + \dfrac{\sigma^2}{2}\right)(T_2 - t)}{\sigma\sqrt{T_2 - t}}$$

$$b_2 = b_1 - \sigma\sqrt{T_2 - t}$$

$$BN(a,b;\rho) = \frac{1}{2\pi\sqrt{1-\rho^2}} \int_{-\infty}^{a}\int_{-\infty}^{b} e^{-\frac{x^2 - 2\rho xy + y^2}{2(1-\rho^2)}} \, dxdy \quad \text{(Cumulative bivariate normal distribution)}$$

$$\rho = \sqrt{\frac{T_1 - t}{T_2 - t}}$$

$\hat{S}$ denotes the critical stock price at time T_1 such that the second option has the value X_1 (at-the-money)

$$C_{T_1}\left(\hat{S},X_2,T_2\right)-X_1 = 0 \quad \text{(Underlying call option is at-the-money)}$$

$$P_{T_1}\left(\hat{S},X_2,T_2\right)-X_1 = 0 \quad \text{(Underlying put option is at-the-money)}$$

Again the compound option valuation model above is based on standard finance conditions and assumes the underlying stock price follows geometric Brownian motion.

Implementation code comments

FRMCompoundOptions.h

Note this is the same implementation file as the previous module. We highlight here issues related to estimating implied parameters. The compound options implementation code is based on three other classes. Note that BRENT is inherited in this class whereas FRMBSMDYOVM and FRMBIVARIATE are instantiated within the class.

```
#ifndef FRMCompoundOptionsH
#define FRMCompoundOptionsH
#include <math.h>
#ifndef FRMBSMDYOPMCPP
#define FRMBSMDYOPMCPP
#include "c:\FRMRepository\FRMBSMDYOVM.cpp"
#endif
#ifndef FRMBIVARIATENORMALCPP
#define FRMBIVARIATENORMALCPP
#include "c:\FRMRepository\FRMBivariateNormal.cpp"
#endif
#ifndef FRMBRENTCPP
#define FRMBRENTCPP
#include "c:\FRMRepository\FRMBrent.cpp"
#endif
#define max(a, b)   (((a) > (b)) ? (a) : (b))

class FRMCOMPOUNDOPTIONS : public BRENT
{
...
public:
   void FRMSetData(double StockPrice, double StrikePrice1, double StrikePrice2,
      double TimeToMaturity1, double TimeToMaturity2, double Volatility,
      double InterestRate, double DividendYield);
   double FRMCallOnCallValue(void);
...
   double FRMPutOnPutValueUB(void);
   FRMBSMDYOVM BD;
   FRMBIVARIATE BIV;
// Compound options implied parameters file
   void FRMSetDataMM(double MinX, double MaxX);
   double MaxX, MinX;
   double OMaxX, OMinX;   // Original maximum and minumum
   void StockPriceSetData(double tempStockPrice);
...
   void COSetDataSP(double tempStrikePrice1, double tempStrikePrice2,
      double tempTimeToMaturity1, double tempTimeToMaturity2, double tempVolatility,
      double tempInterestRate, double tempDividendYield);
...
   long double COCallOnCallISP(double COCallPrice);
...
```

FRMCompoundOptions.cpp

Because of the sheer size of this program, we break the code into parts and place them in separate files. Separate files allows for easier editing and understanding how various parts fit together. The part addressed here is found in the file referenced below.

```
#include "c:\FRMRepository\FRMCompoundOptionsImpliedParameters.cpp"
```

FRMCompoundOptionsImpliedParameters.cpp

This is a very large file and we present only the methods related to call-on-call options and the implied stock price. Recall that for the Brent method, we must send the method a function in order to search for the implied parameter, we send it `functionStockPriceCoCP(double tempX)`.

```
...
// Global function for using Brent method of embedded parameter
FRMCOMPOUNDOPTIONS COM;                    // Global class instantiation
```

Declare the function for computing the call on call price based on varying the stock price.

```
double functionStockPriceCoCP(double tempX);
...
// Implied stock price
```

Define the function for computing the call on call price based on varying the stock price.

```
double functionStockPriceCoCP(double tempX) // Call on call CO
{
    COM.StockPriceSetData(tempX);          // Unique to each Brent deployment
    return(COM.FRMCallOnCallValue());      // Unique to each Brent deployment
};
...
```

Define the function within FRMCOMPOUNDOPTIONS for setting the input data into the class, except for the stock price.

```
void FRMCOMPOUNDOPTIONS::COSetDataSP(double tempStrikePrice1,
    double tempStrikePrice2, double tempTimeToMaturity1, double tempTimeToMaturity2,
    double tempVolatility, double tempInterestRate, double tempDividendYield)
{
    StrikePrice1 = tempStrikePrice1;
    StrikePrice2 = tempStrikePrice2;
    TimeToMaturity1 = tempTimeToMaturity1;
    TimeToMaturity2 = tempTimeToMaturity2;
    Volatility = tempVolatility;
    InterestRate = tempInterestRate;
    DividendYield = tempDividendYield;
}
...
```

Define the function within FRMCOMPOUNDOPTIONS for setting the just the stock price.

```
void FRMCOMPOUNDOPTIONS::StockPriceSetData(double tempStockPrice)
{
    StockPrice = tempStockPrice;
}
...
// CO implied stock price
```

Define the function within FRMCOMPOUNDOPTIONS for computing the implied stock price based on a call on call compound option.

```
long double FRMCOMPOUNDOPTIONS::COCallOnCallISP(double COCallPrice)
{
    COM.COSetDataSP(StrikePrice1, StrikePrice2, TimeToMaturity1, TimeToMaturity2,
        Volatility, DividendYield);        // Global Implied Vol object
    BRENTSetData(COCallPrice, MaxX, MinX);     // BRENT is public in this class
    return CalculateX(&functionStockPriceCoCP);    // BRENT is public in this class;
}
...
// Max and min for Brent method
void FRMCOMPOUNDOPTIONS::FRMSetDataMM(double tempMinX, double tempMaxX)
{
    MinX = tempMinX;
    MaxX = tempMaxX;
}
```

References

See references in Module 7.3 Compound Options Valuation.

Appendix 7.4: Interface code comments

The graphical user interface is illustrated below.

The following are excerpts from the interface header code with selected comments added.

FRMUnitCompoundOptionImpliedParameters.h:

As illustrated above, this interface is fairly complicated with several components.

```
#ifndef FRMUnitCompoundOptionsImpliedParametersH
#define FRMUnitCompoundOptionsImpliedParametersH
...
#include "FRMUnitTimeToMaturityImpliedParameters.h"
#include "c:\FRMRepository\FRMCompoundOptions.cpp"
//--------------------------------------------------------------------
class TCompoundOptionForm : public TForm
{
__published:    // IDE-managed Components
    TButton *btnRun;
    TButton *btnClose;
    TButton *btnEdit;
    TRadioGroup *rgCompoundOptionType;
    TRadioGroup *rgImpliedParameter;
    TLabel *lblStockPrice;
...
    TEdit *outputImpliedPutParameter;
    void __fastcall FormKeyPress(TObject *Sender, char &Key);
    void __fastcall btnCloseClick(TObject *Sender);
    void __fastcall btnRunClick(TObject *Sender);
    void __fastcall editStockPriceExit(TObject *Sender);
    void __fastcall editStrikePrice1Exit(TObject *Sender);
    void __fastcall editTimeToMaturity1Exit(TObject *Sender);
    void __fastcall editVolatilityExit(TObject *Sender);
    void __fastcall editInterestRateExit(TObject *Sender);
    void __fastcall editDividendYieldExit(TObject *Sender);
    void __fastcall editStrikePrice2Exit(TObject *Sender);
    void __fastcall editTimeToMaturity2Exit(TObject *Sender);
    void __fastcall btnEditClick(TObject *Sender);
    void __fastcall FormCreate(TObject *Sender);
    void __fastcall rgCompoundOptionTypeClick(TObject *Sender);
    void __fastcall rgImpliedParameterClick(TObject *Sender);
```

```
   void __fastcall rgImpliedParameterEnter(TObject *Sender);
   void __fastcall rgCompoundOptionTypeEnter(TObject *Sender);
private: // User declarations
   double inputStockPrice;
...
   void __fastcall Execute(void);
   void __fastcall SetLocalData(void);
   FRMCOMPOUNDOPTIONS C;
public:     // User declarations
   __fastcall TCompoundOptionForm(TComponent* Owner);
};
//---------------------------------------------------------------------
extern PACKAGE TCompoundOptionForm *CompoundOptionForm;
#endif
```

The following are excerpts from the interface code with selected comments added.

FRMUnitCompoundOptionImpliedParameters.cpp

This interface code is very long and we only provide a few snippets here. Remember it is easier to place default settings in a manner that is easy to change during the debugging process. In this case, we define the defaults when the form is created.

```
...
void __fastcall TCompoundOptionForm::FormCreate(TObject *Sender)
{
   editStockPrice->Text = 100.0;
   editStrikePrice1->Text = 22.28;
   editStrikePrice2->Text = 100.0;
   editInterestRate->Text = 5.0;
   editTimeToMaturity1->Text = 1.0;
   editTimeToMaturity2->Text = 2.0;
   editVolatility->Text = 30.0;
   editDividendYield->Text = 0.0;
   editCOCallPrice->Text = 7.302653;
   editCOPutPrice->Text = 7.302309;
   editMax->Text = 1000.00;
   editMin->Text = 0.0001;
   rgImpliedParameter->ItemIndex = 5;   // Implied volatility
   rgCompoundOptionType->ItemIndex = 0; // Compound option calls (on call and put)
   editVolatility->Visible = false;
   lblVolatility->Visible = false;
   lblCOCallPrice->Caption = "Call on Call ($)";
   lblCOPutPrice->Caption = "Put on Call ($)";
}
...
```

We move the variable maximum and minimum in separately, via their own FRMSetDataMM() function, and then condition the analysis on the selected compound option type and the selected implied parameter. Notice in the first if statement when we are computing the implied stock price, we set the implied stock price to –99 to highlight that this is not an input value.

```
   C.FRMSetDataMM(inputMinX, inputMaxX);
   if(rgCompoundOptionType->ItemIndex == 0){ // CoC and PoC
      if(rgImpliedParameter->ItemIndex == 0){ // Implied stock price
         inputStockPrice = -99;
         C.FRMSetData(inputStockPrice, inputStrikePrice1, inputStrikePrice2,
            inputTimeToMaturity1, inputTimeToMaturity2, inputVolatility,
            inputInterestRate, inputDividendYield);
         ImpliedCOCallOutput = C.COCallOnCallISP(inputCOCallPrice);
         ImpliedCOPutOutput = C.COPutOnCallISP(inputCOPutPrice);;
         outputImpliedCallParameter->Text
            = FloatToStrF(ImpliedCOCallOutput, ffFixed, 10, 4);
         outputImpliedPutParameter->Text
            = FloatToStrF(ImpliedCOPutOutput, ffFixed, 10, 4);
         lblCallOutput->Caption = "Implied Call Stock Price";
         lblPutOutput->Caption = "Implied Put Stock Price";
         lblCallOutput->Visible = true;
         outputImpliedCallParameter->Visible = true;
         lblPutOutput->Visible = true;
```

```
                outputImpliedPutParameter->Visible = true;
        } else if(rgImpliedParameter->ItemIndex == 1){ // Implied option strike price
...

        } else if (rgImpliedParameter->ItemIndex == 8){// Option prices and boundaries
            C.FRMSetData(inputStockPrice, inputStrikePrice1, inputStrikePrice2,
                inputTimeToMaturity1, inputTimeToMaturity2, inputVolatility,
                inputInterestRate, inputDividendYield);
            ImpliedCOCallOutput = C.FRMCallOnPutValue();
            ImpliedCOPutOutput = C.FRMPutOnPutValue();
            outputImpliedCallParameter->Text
                = FloatToStrF(ImpliedCOCallOutput, ffFixed, 10, 4);
            outputImpliedPutParameter->Text
                = FloatToStrF(ImpliedCOPutOutput, ffFixed, 10, 4);
            lblCallOutput->Caption = "Call on Put Option Price";
            lblPutOutput->Caption = "Put on Put Option Price";
            lblCallOutput->Visible = true;
            outputImpliedCallParameter->Visible = true;
            lblPutOutput->Visible = true;
            outputImpliedPutParameter->Visible = true;
// Boundaries
            C.FRMSetData(inputStockPrice, inputStrikePrice1, inputStrikePrice2,
                inputTimeToMaturity1, inputTimeToMaturity2, inputVolatility,
                inputInterestRate, inputDividendYield);
            CallOnPutLB = C.FRMCallOnPutValueLB();
            PutOnPutLB = C.FRMPutOnPutValueLB();
            outputCOCallLB->Text = FloatToStrF(CallOnPutLB,ffFixed, 15, 6);
            outputCOPutLB->Text = FloatToStrF(PutOnPutLB,ffFixed, 15, 6);
            CallOnPutUB = C.FRMCallOnPutValueUB();
            PutOnPutUB = C.FRMPutOnPutValueUB();
            outputCOCallUB->Text = FloatToStrF(CallOnPutUB,ffFixed, 15, 6);
            outputCOPutUB->Text = FloatToStrF(PutOnPutUB,ffFixed, 15, 6);
            lblLowerBound->Visible = true;
            lblUpperBound->Visible = true;
            outputCOCallLB->Visible = true;
            outputCOPutLB->Visible = true;
            outputCOCallUB->Visible = true;
            outputCOPutUB->Visible = true;
        }
    }
}
...
```

Quite a bit of work remains to get the form to behave the way it does. The form inputs vary, depending on which choices are selected, so we must have the labels and output boxes change depending on user selection.

```
void __fastcall TCompoundOptionForm::rgCompoundOptionTypeClick(TObject *Sender)
{
    rgImpliedParameterClick(Sender);  // Set implied parameters correctly
    lblLowerBound->Visible = false;
    lblUpperBound->Visible = false;
    outputCOCallLB->Visible = false;
    outputCOPutLB->Visible = false;
    outputCOCallUB->Visible = false;
    outputCOPutUB->Visible = false;
    lblCallOutput->Visible = false;
    lblPutOutput->Visible = false;
    outputImpliedCallParameter->Visible = false;
    outputImpliedPutParameter->Visible = false;
    switch(rgCompoundOptionType->ItemIndex){
    case 0:
        lblCOCallPrice->Caption = "Call on Call ($)";
        lblCOPutPrice->Caption = "Put on Call ($)";
    break;
    case 1:
        lblCOCallPrice->Caption = "Call on Put ($)";
        lblCOPutPrice->Caption = "Put on Put ($)";
    break;
    default:
    break;
    }
```

```
}
//---------------------------------------------------------------------------
void __fastcall TCompoundOptionForm::rgImpliedParameterClick(TObject *Sender)
{
    lblLowerBound->Visible = false;
    lblUpperBound->Visible = false;
    outputCOCallLB->Visible = false;
    outputCOPutLB->Visible = false;
    outputCOCallUB->Visible = false;
    outputCOPutUB->Visible = false;
    lblCallOutput->Visible = false;
    lblPutOutput->Visible = false;
    outputImpliedCallParameter->Visible = false;
    outputImpliedPutParameter->Visible = false;
    switch(rgImpliedParameter->ItemIndex){
    case 0:
        editStockPrice->Visible = false;
        editStrikePrice1->Visible = true;
        editTimeToMaturity1->Visible = true;
        editStrikePrice2->Visible = true;
        editTimeToMaturity2->Visible = true;
        editVolatility->Visible = true;
        editInterestRate->Visible = true;
        editDividendYield->Visible = true;
        editCOCallPrice->Visible = true;
        editCOPutPrice->Visible = true;
        lblStockPrice->Visible = false;
        lblStrikePrice1->Visible = true;
        lblTimeToMaturity1->Visible = true;
        lblStrikePrice2->Visible = true;
        lblTimeToMaturity2->Visible = true;
        lblVolatility->Visible = true;
        lblInterestRate->Visible = true;
        lblDividendYield->Visible = true;
        lblCOCallPrice->Visible = true;
        lblCOPutPrice->Visible = true;
    break;
...
    default:
    break;
    }
}
```

Module 7.5: Compound Options Greeks

Learning objectives

- Estimate numerical "greeks" for compound options

Module overview

In this module, we assume you have already mastered Module 7.3 Compound Options Valuation. A mastery of Module 7.4 Compound Options Implied Parameters is not a prerequisite for understanding this module.

Compound option valuation

Again, recall the standard compound option valuation models are expressed as follows:

Call on call:

$$CoC_t\left(C\left(S,X_2,T_2\right),X_1,T_1\right)=S_t e^{-q(T_2-t)}BN\left(a_1,b_1;\rho\right)-X_2 e^{-r(T_2-t)}BN\left(a_2,b_2;\rho\right)-X_1 e^{-r(T_1-t)}N\left(a_2\right)$$

Put on call:

$$PoC_t\left(C\left(S,X_2,T_2\right),X_1,T_1\right)=X_2 e^{-r(T_2-t)}BN\left(-a_2,b_2;-\rho\right)-S_t e^{-q(T_2-t)}BN\left(-a_1,b_1;-\rho\right)+X_1 e^{-r(T_1-t)}N\left(-a_2\right)$$

Call on put:

$$CoP_t\left(P\left(S,X_2,T_2\right),X_1,T_1\right)=X_2 e^{-r(T_2-t)}BN\left(-a_2,-b_2;\rho\right)-S_t e^{-q(T_2-t)}BN\left(-a_1,-b_1;\rho\right)-X_1 e^{-r(T_1-t)}N\left(-a_2\right)$$

Put on put:

$$PoP_t\left(P\left(S,X_2,T_2\right),X_1,T_1\right)=S_t e^{-q(T_2-t)}BN\left(a_1,-b_1;-\rho\right)-X_2 e^{-r(T_2-t)}BN\left(a_2,-b_2;-\rho\right)+X_1 e^{-r(T_1-t)}N\left(a_2\right)$$

where

$$a_1=\frac{\ln\left(\frac{S_t}{\hat{S}}\right)+\left(r-q+\frac{\sigma^2}{2}\right)\left(T_1-t\right)}{\sigma\sqrt{T_1-t}}$$

$$a_2=a_1-\sigma\sqrt{T_1-t}$$

$$b_1=\frac{\ln\left(\frac{S_t}{X_2}\right)+\left(r-q+\frac{\sigma^2}{2}\right)\left(T_2-t\right)}{\sigma\sqrt{T_2-t}}$$

$$b_2=b_1-\sigma\sqrt{T_2-t}$$

$$BN\left(a,b;\rho\right)=\frac{1}{2\pi\sqrt{1-\rho^2}}\int_{-\infty}^{a}\int_{-\infty}^{b}e^{-\frac{x^2-2\rho xy+y^2}{2\left(1-\rho^2\right)}}\,dxdy \quad \text{(Cumulative bivariate normal distribution)}$$

$$\rho=\sqrt{\frac{T_1-t}{T_2-t}}$$

$\hat{S}$ denotes the critical stock price at time T_1 such that the second option has the value X_1 (at-the-money)

$$C_{T_1}\left(\hat{S},X_2,T_2\right)-X_1=0 \quad \text{(Underlying call option is at-the-money)}$$

$$P_{T_1}\left(\hat{S},X_2,T_2\right)-X_1 =0 \quad \text{(Underlying put option is at-the-money)}$$

The compound option valuation model above is based on standard finance conditions and assumes the underlying stock price follows geometric Brownian motion. (Proofs available in Geske (1979) and Lajeri-Chaherli (2002).)

Compound options numerical derivatives

We follow the procedure introduced in Module 5.6 Centered Differencing and just present a sketch here for convenience.

In this module, we illustrate the centered difference technique applied to the compound option valuation model presented above, as well as in Modules 7.3 and 7.4.

Recall this procedure is based on the univariate Taylor series and the numerical derivatives approximation theorem (reproduced here for convenience).

Theorem 1: Numerical derivatives approximation theorem

If

$$f^d(x) = \frac{d!}{h^d} \sum_{n=0}^{d+p-1}\left(\sum_{i=i_{min}}^{i_{max}} i^n C_i\right)\frac{h^n}{n!}f^n(x_0) \quad \text{(\textbf{dth order derivative})}$$

then

$$f^d(x) = \frac{d!}{h^d}\sum_{i=i_{min}}^{i_{max}} C_i f(x+ih)+O(h^p) \quad \text{(\textbf{Approximation theorem equation})}$$

where $h = x - x_0, > 0$ (small), $p > 0$ denotes integer order of error, d denotes the integer derivative order, i_{max}, and i_{min} denote extreme indices, C_i denotes some coefficients where $C = \{C_{min}, ..., C_{max}\}$ denotes the template of approximation.

Note that the dth order derivative equation above holds if and only if

$$\sum_{i=i_{min}}^{i_{max}} i^n C_i = \begin{cases} 0 \text{ for } 0 \le n \le d+p+1 \text{ and } n \ne d \\ \quad\quad 1 \text{ for } n=d \end{cases} \quad \text{(\textbf{Template sum equation})}$$

Centered differencing implies $i_{max} = i_{min} = (d + p - 1)/2$ where $(d + p - 1)$ is assumed to be even. The template sum equation holds if and only if

$$\underline{C}_{d+px1} = \underline{A}_{d+pxd+p}^{-1}\underline{B}_{d+px1}$$

where the A matrix and B vector are defined as follows

$$\underline{A}_{d+pxd+p} = \begin{bmatrix} i_{min}^0 & i_{min+1}^0 & \cdots & i_{max-1}^0 & i_{max}^0 \\ i_{min}^1 & i_{min+1}^1 & \cdots & i_{max-1}^1 & i_{max}^1 \\ \vdots & & \ddots & & \vdots \\ i_{min}^{d+p-2} & i_{min+1}^{d+p-2} & \cdots & i_{max-1}^{d+p-2} & i_{max}^{d+p-2} \\ i_{min}^{d+p-1} & i_{min+1}^{d+p-1} & \cdots & i_{max-1}^{d+p-1} & i_{max}^{d+p-1} \end{bmatrix}, \quad \underline{B}_{d+px1} = \begin{bmatrix} 0 \\ \vdots \\ 1 \\ \vdots \\ 0 \end{bmatrix} \begin{matrix} 0 \\ \vdots \\ d \\ \vdots \\ d+p-1 \end{matrix}$$

Proof: Expand the approximation theorem equation to order $d + p - 1$, based on Taylor series.[49]

---

[49] See Eberly (2008).

We provide centered difference approximations for integer derivative order up to 4 and allow the user to set the increment size. We only present the standard "greeks," but clearly many others could be computed with this procedure.

Implementation code comments

FRMCompoundOptions.h

We supplemented the header file with new variables and methods.

```
...
// Centered differenes numerical greeks
   void FRMSetData(double StockPrice, double StrikePrice1, double StrikePrice2,
      double TimeToMaturity1, double TimeToMaturity2, double Volatility,
      double InterestRate, double DividendYield, int Order, double Increment);
   double Original, High, Low, Change, OHigh, OLow, OMid;
   double High2, Low2, OHigh2, OLow2;
   double High3, Low3, OHigh3, OLow3;
   double High4, Low4, OHigh4, OLow4;
   int Order;
   double Increment;
   long double NGCOCallOnCallDelta();
...
   long double NGCOPutOnPutRho();
...
```

FRMCompoundOptionsCenteredDifferencing.cpp

We placed this large amount of code in a separate file. Each routine is very similar to the routines presented in Module 5.6 Centered Differencing Applied to BSM and Binomial Models. An extremely small sample of code is produced below.

```
// No header file, just supplemental to FRMCompoundOptions.cpp
// Centered differencing, numerical greeks
void FRMCOMPOUNDOPTIONS::FRMSetData(double StkPr, double StrPr1, double StrPr2,
   double TTM1, double TTM2, double Vol, double IR, double DivYld, int OR,
   double INCR)
{
   StockPrice = StkPr;
   StrikePrice1 = StrPr1;
   StrikePrice2 = StrPr2;
   TimeToMaturity1 = TTM1;
   TimeToMaturity2 = TTM2;
   Volatility = Vol;
   InterestRate = IR;
   DividendYield = DivYld;
   Order = OR;
   Increment = INCR;
   Increment = Increment / 100.0;
};
//-----------------------------------------------------------------------
long double FRMCOMPOUNDOPTIONS::NGCOCallOnCallDelta()
{
   if (Order==1) {
      Original = StockPrice;   // Greek dependent
      Change = Increment*Original;
      High = Original + Change;
      StockPrice = High;       // Greek dependent
      OHigh = FRMCallOnCallValue();
      Low = Original - Change;
      StockPrice = Low;        // Greek dependent
      OLow = FRMCallOnCallValue();
      StockPrice = Original;   // Greek dependent
      return (OHigh - OLow)/(High - Low);
   } else if (Order==2) {
      Original = StockPrice;   // Greek dependent
      Change = Increment*Original;
      High = Original + Change;
      StockPrice = High;       // Greek dependent
      OHigh = FRMCallOnCallValue();
```

```
    Low = Original - Change;
    StockPrice = Low;          // Greek dependent
    OLow = FRMCallOnCallValue();
    Change = 2.0*Increment*Original;
    High2 = Original + Change;
    StockPrice = High2;        // Greek dependent
    OHigh2 = FRMCallOnCallValue();
    Low2 = Original - Change;
    StockPrice = Low2;         // Greek dependent
    OLow2 = FRMCallOnCallValue();
    StockPrice = Original;     // Greek dependent
    return (-OHigh2 + 8.0*OHigh - 8.0*OLow + OLow2)/(12.0*Increment*Original);
} else if (Order==3) {
    Original = StockPrice;     // Greek dependent
    Change = Increment*Original;
    High = Original + Change;
    StockPrice = High;         // Greek dependent
    OHigh = FRMCallOnCallValue();
    Low = Original - Change;
    StockPrice = Low;          // Greek dependent
    OLow = FRMCallOnCallValue();
    Change = 2.0*Increment*Original;
    High2 = Original + Change;
    StockPrice = High2;        // Greek dependent
    OHigh2 = FRMCallOnCallValue();
    Low2 = Original - Change;
    StockPrice = Low2;         // Greek dependent
    OLow2 = FRMCallOnCallValue();
    StockPrice = Original;     // Greek dependent
    Change = 3.0*Increment*Original;
    High3 = Original + Change;
    StockPrice = High3;        // Greek dependent
    OHigh3 = FRMCallOnCallValue();
    Low3 = Original - Change;
    StockPrice = Low3;         // Greek dependent
    OLow3 = FRMCallOnCallValue();
    StockPrice = Original;     // Greek dependent
    return (OHigh3 - 9.0*OHigh2 + 45.0*OHigh - 45.0*OLow + 9.0*OLow2 - OLow3)
       /(60.0*Increment*Original);
} else if (Order==4) {
    Original = StockPrice;     // Greek dependent
    Change = Increment*Original;
    High = Original + Change;
    StockPrice = High;         // Greek dependent
    OHigh = FRMCallOnCallValue();
    Low = Original - Change;
    StockPrice = Low;          // Greek dependent
    OLow = FRMCallOnCallValue();
    Change = 2.0*Increment*Original;
    High2 = Original + Change;
    StockPrice = High2;        // Greek dependent
    OHigh2 = FRMCallOnCallValue();
    Low2 = Original - Change;
    StockPrice = Low2;         // Greek dependent
    OLow2 = FRMCallOnCallValue();
    StockPrice = Original;     // Greek dependent
    Change = 3.0*Increment*Original;
    High3 = Original + Change;
    StockPrice = High3;        // Greek dependent
    OHigh3 = FRMCallOnCallValue();
    Low3 = Original - Change;
    StockPrice = Low3;         // Greek dependent
    OLow3 = FRMCallOnCallValue();
    StockPrice = Original;     // Greek dependent
    Change = 4.0*Increment*Original;
    High4 = Original + Change;
    StockPrice = High4;        // Greek dependent
    OHigh4 = FRMCallOnCallValue();
    Low4 = Original - Change;
    StockPrice = Low4;         // Greek dependent
    OLow4 = FRMCallOnCallValue();
```

```
        StockPrice = Original;    // Greek dependent
        return ((OLow4/280.0)- (4.0*OLow3/105.0) + (OLow2/5.0) - (4.0*OLow/5.0)
            + (4.0*OHigh/5.0) - (OHigh2/5.0) + (4.0*OHigh3/105.0) - (OHigh4/280.0))
            /(Increment*Original);
    } else {
        return -99;
    }
}
...
```

References

See references in Module 7.3 Compound Options Valuation.

Appendix 7.5: Interface code comments

The graphical user interface is illustrated below.

The following are excerpts from the interface code with selected comments added.

FRMUnitCompoundOptions.cpp, .h

Outside of rather tedious repetitions, the code here is straightforward. We needed to add the derivative order and the increment to use for the centered differencing technique. We also added some additional labels on the form

```
// Centered differences numerical greeks
    C.FRMSetData(inputStockPrice, inputStrikePrice1, inputStrikePrice2,
        inputTimeToMaturity1, inputTimeToMaturity2, inputVolatility,
        inputInterestRate, inputDividendYield, inputOrder, inputIncrement);
    lblCallOnCall2->Visible = true;
    lblPutOnCall2->Visible = true;
    lblCallOnPut2->Visible = true;
    lblPutOnPut2->Visible = true;
    lblDelta->Visible = true;
    lblGamma->Visible = true;
    lblTheta1->Visible = true;
    lblTheta2->Visible = true;
    lblVega->Visible = true;
    lblRho->Visible = true;
```

```
   CallOnCallDelta = C.NGCOCallOnCallDelta();
...
   PutOnPutRho = C.NGCOPutOnPutRho();
   outputCallOnCallDelta->Text = FloatToStrF(CallOnCallDelta,ffFixed, 15, 6);
...
   outputPutOnPutRho->Text = FloatToStrF(PutOnPutRho,ffFixed, 15, 6);
   outputCallOnCallDelta->Visible = true;
...
   outputPutOnPutRho->Visible = true;
}
```

Module 7.6: Spread Options Valuation and Greeks

Learning objectives

- Explain two approaches to valuing spread options
- Contrast the normal distribution with the lognormal distribution
- Use the numerical integration routine to estimate spread option values
- Use the Brent search routine to find implied volatility for the normal distribution approach to value spread options based on the lognormal distribution approach's option value

Module overview

Closed form solutions for valuing European-style spread options do not exist when the underlying instruments are lognormally distributed except for certain special cases such as exchange options (see Margrabe (1978)). When referring to "closed form," we use the finance definition of an expression whose numerical complexity is no greater than an "easy to compute" function of cumulative normal distribution functions. As a result, numerical techniques and approximations must be used for these types of spread option valuation models.

For options on underlying instruments other than spreads, current industry practice is to model the underlying instrument options assuming they are *lognormally* distributed. This assumption is often justified by the fact that the financial instrument prices are non-negative due to limited liability. Continuous time models based on geometric Brownian motion (GBM) imply the terminal distribution of the underlying instrument is lognormal. Current industry practice, however, is to model spread options by assuming the spread is *normally* distributed, primarily because the spread can be and often is negative. Continuous time models based on arithmetic Brownian motion (ABM) imply the terminal distribution of the underlying instrument is normal. These modeling procedures are internally inconsistent because the difference between two variables that are lognormally distributed does not follow a normal distribution.[50]

This internal inconsistency creates integrity concerns for risk systems. These integrity concerns are especially manifest for risk management of large portfolios. We present one module that estimates the spread option value from both the lognormal and normal perspectives. Therefore, we provide two spread option valuation models, one assuming both underlying instruments follow GBM, the second assuming both underlying instruments follow ABM. The general framework of Black and Scholes (1973), Merton (1973) and Black (1976) is followed.

Margrabe (1978) developed a closed-form equation for exchange options, which are zero strike spread options. Poitras (1998) developed a pricing formula for European-style spread options by extending a special case of the Bachelier (1900) option-pricing model. Schaefer (2002) demonstrates that option values from the Bachelier model are nearly identical to values found using Monte Carlo simulation assuming GBM for selected parameters. Wilcox (1990) assumes ABM to derive a closed form solution for pricing spread options.

The two option valuation models for spread options are used in this module.

Lognormal spread option valuation model

We briefly review the assumptions and our notation for spread options. The general payoff at expiration, T, of a spread option can be expressed as:

$$CSO_T = \max\left[0, \alpha_1 I_{1,T} + \alpha_2 I_{2,T} - X\right]$$

---

[50] Poitras (1998) points out that since the difference of lognormal variables is not lognormal, a simplification of the Bachelier model is not possible.

$$PSO_T = \max\left[0, X - \alpha_1 I_{1,T} - \alpha_2 I_{2,T}\right]$$

where

CSO_T denotes the call option value at time T

PSO_T denotes put option value at time T

$\alpha_1 > 0$ denotes positive constant (index 1 coefficient)

$\alpha_2 < 0$ denotes negative constant (index 2 coefficient)

$-\infty < X < \infty$ denotes strike price

$I_{1,T} > 0$ denotes the value of index 1 at time T (stochastic)

$I_{2,T} > 0$ denotes the value of index 2 at time T (stochastic)

If we assume indexes follow geometric Brownian motion with geometric drift, then

$$dI_j = \left(\hat{\mu}_j - \delta_j\right)I_j dt + \hat{\sigma}_j I_j dz_j; \, j = 1,2$$

where

$-\infty < \hat{\mu}_j < \infty$ denotes the mean growth rate of index j

$-\infty < \delta_j < \infty$ denotes the carry costs related to index j

$\hat{\sigma}_j < \infty$ denotes the standard deviation of index j

$-\infty < dz_j < \infty$ denotes the standard Wiener process associated with index j

The value of a spread option today can be expressed generically as,

$$SO_0 = PV\left[E_0\left(SO_T\right)\right]$$

where the expectation is taken with the equivalent martingale measure. The value of call and put options, using the *lognormal* distribution can be expressed as:

$$CSO_1\left(I_{1,0}, I_{2,0}, X, T, \sigma_1, \sigma_2, \rho_{1,2}, r\right) = \exp\{-rT\}\left[\int_0^\infty \int_0^\infty \max\left[0, \alpha_1 I_{1,T} + \alpha_2 I_{2,T} - X\right] f_1\left(I_1, I_2\right) dI_2 dI_1\right]$$

$$PSO_1\left(I_{1,0}, I_{2,0}, X, T, \sigma_1, \sigma_2, \rho_{1,2}, r\right) = \exp\{-rT\}\left[\int_0^\infty \int_0^\infty \max\left[0, X - \alpha_1 I_{1,T} + \alpha_2 I_{2,T}\right] f_1\left(I_1, I_2\right) dI_2 dI_1\right]$$

where

1 = (subscript) denotes the LNSOPM,

r = risk-free interest rate; annualized with continuous compounding, and

$f_1\left(I_1, I_2\right)$ = bivariate lognormal density function.

Although a closed form solution to this model does not exist, there are several single integral representations. Again, we assume the standard finance assumptions that afford using the risk-free rate as the mean for both indexes. For example, the following single integral version of this model is used with a standard numerical integration methodology.[51]

$$\mathrm{CSO}_{1,0}(I_1,I_2) = I_1 e^{-\delta_1 T} \int_{-\infty}^{\infty} N(d_{1,1}(z)) n(z) dz + \frac{\alpha_2 I_2}{\alpha_1} e^{-\delta_2 T} \int_{-\infty}^{\infty} N(d_{1,2}(z)) n(z) dz - \frac{X}{\alpha_1} e^{-rT} \int_{-\infty}^{\infty} N(d_2(z)) n(z) dz$$

$$\mathrm{PSO}_{1,0}(I_1,I_2) = \mathrm{CSO}_{1,0}(I_1,I_2) - \alpha_1 I_1 e^{-\delta_1 T} - \alpha_2 I_2 e^{-\delta_2 T} + X e^{-rT}$$

where

$$n(z) = \frac{e^{\frac{-z^2}{2}}}{\sqrt{2\pi}}$$

$$N(d_i(z)) = \int_{-\infty}^{d_i(z)} \frac{e^{\frac{-x^2}{2}}}{\sqrt{2\pi}} dx$$

$$d_{1,1}(z) = \frac{\ln\left[\frac{\alpha_1 I_1 e^{(r-\delta_1)T + \rho^2 \frac{\sigma_1^2 T}{2} + \rho\sigma_1\sqrt{T}z}}{X - \alpha_2 I_2 e^{(r-\delta_2)T - \frac{\sigma_2^2 T}{2} + \rho\sigma_1\sigma_2 T + \sigma_2\sqrt{T}z}}\right] + (1-\rho^2)\frac{\sigma_1^2 T}{2}}{\sigma_1\sqrt{T(1-\rho^2)}}$$

$$d_{1,2}(z) = \frac{\ln\left[\frac{\alpha_1 I_1 e^{(r-\delta_1)T - \rho^2 \frac{\sigma_1^2 T}{2} + \rho\sigma_1\sigma_2 T + \rho\sigma_1\sqrt{T}z}}{X - \alpha_2 I_2 e^{(r-\delta_2)T - \frac{\sigma_2^2 T}{2} + \sigma_2^2 T + \sigma_2\sqrt{T}z}}\right] - (1-\rho^2)\frac{\sigma_1^2 T}{2}}{\sigma_1\sqrt{T(1-\rho^2)}}$$

$$d_2(z) = \frac{\ln\left[\frac{\alpha_1 I_1 e^{(r-\delta_1)T - \rho^2 \frac{\sigma_1^2 T}{2} + \rho\sigma_1\sqrt{T}z}}{X - \alpha_2 I_2 e^{(r-\delta_2)T - \frac{\sigma_2^2 T}{2} + \sigma_2\sqrt{T}z}}\right] - (1-\rho^2)\frac{\sigma_1^2 T}{2}}{\sigma_1\sqrt{T(1-\rho^2)}}$$

It is important to emphasize that this solution is not an approximation like Pearson (1995), Carmona and Durrleman (2003, 2006), Li, Deng and Zhou (2008) and others, rather it is an exact result. We do not, however, claim it is closed-form in the usual finance sense. It is still technically a double integral (recall the standard N(d) function is an integral). Practically, however, it is a single integral because of the existence of very accurate numerical approximations available to compute the standard N(d) function. Even the standard Black, Scholes, Merton option valuation model requires some sort of numerical approximation to N(d).

---

[51] Integral solving routines, such as Mathcad, can be used to find reduced form results such as this one. Although complex in appearance, N(d) is easily approximated and standard univariate integration routines can be used. Because bivariate integration is often unstable and therefore unreliable, this single integral solution is very useful.

Zhang (1998) provides one solution, but it restricts the strike price to be positive. Spread options often have negative strike prices. We present the solution to the above lognormal approach, as well as Zhang's approach to check validity.

Normal spread option valuation model

If we assume that the spread follows arithmetic Brownian motion with geometric drift, then

$$dS = \mu_S S dt + \sigma_S dz_S$$

$-\infty < \mu_S < \infty$ denotes the mean growth rate of the spread

$\sigma_S < \infty$ denotes the standard deviation of the spread (same units of measure as S)

$-\infty < dz_S < \infty$ denotes the standard Wiener process associated with the spread

The value of call and put spread options, based on the *normal* distribution can be expressed as:

$$CSO_n\left(I_{1,0}, I_{2,0}, X, T, \sigma_1, \sigma_2, \rho_{1,2}, r\right) = \exp\{-rT\}\left[\int_0^\infty \int_0^\infty \max\left[0, \alpha_1 I_{1,T} + \alpha_2 I_{2,T} - X\right] f_n\left(I_1, I_2\right) dI_2 dI_1\right]$$

$$PSO_n\left(I_{1,0}, I_{2,0}, X, T, \sigma_1, \sigma_2, \rho_{1,2}, r\right) = \exp\{-rT\}\left[\int_0^\infty \int_0^\infty \max\left[0, X - \alpha_1 I_{1,T} + \alpha_2 I_{2,T}\right] f_n\left(I_1, I_2\right) dI_2 dI_1\right]$$

where

  n = denotes the NSOPM, and

  $f_n\left(I_1, I_2\right)$ = bivariate normal density function.

The advantage of the normal distribution is that the difference between normally distributed random variables is also normally distributed. Hence, there *does* exist a closed form solution to this model.

Note that the spread is normally distributed and is denoted as:

$$S_T = \alpha_1 I_{1,T} + \alpha_2 I_{2,T}$$

Where the expected terminal spread is:

$$E\left[S_T\right] = \alpha_1 I_{1,0} e^{(\hat{\mu}_1 - \delta_1)T} + \alpha_2 I_{2,0} e^{(\hat{\mu}_2 - \delta_2)T} = S e^{\mu_s T}$$

and the variance of the spread is:

$$V\left[S_T\right] = \sigma_S^2 \frac{e^{2\mu_s T} - 1}{2\mu_s}$$

and σ_S is the standard deviation of changes in the spread. We assume the usual finance conditions that afford using the risk-free rate. Therefore, we have the following version of this model:

$$CSO_{n,0}\left(I_1, I_2\right) = e^{-rT}\left[\left\{E\left[S_T\right] - X\right\}N(d_n) + V\left[S_T\right]^{1/2} n(d_n)\right]$$

$$PSO_{n,0}\left(I_1, I_2\right) = CSO_{n,0}\left(I_1, I_2\right) - \alpha_1 I_1 e^{-\delta_1 T} - \alpha_2 I_2 e^{-\delta_2 T} + Xe^{-rT}$$

where

$$n(d_n) = \frac{e^{\frac{-d_n^2}{2}}}{\sqrt{2\pi}}$$

$$N(d_n) = \int_{-\infty}^{d_n} \frac{e^{\frac{-d_n^2}{2}}}{\sqrt{2\pi}} dx$$

$$d_n = \frac{E[S_T] - X}{V[S_T]^{1/2}}$$

NOTE:

$$E[S_T] = \alpha_1 I_{1,0} e^{(\hat{\mu}_1 - \delta_1)T} + \alpha_2 I_{2,0} e^{(\hat{\mu}_2 - \delta_2)T} = S e^{\mu_s T}$$

Solving for μ_s,

$$\mu_s = \frac{1}{T} \ln\left[\frac{\alpha_1 I_{1,0} e^{(\hat{\mu}_1 - \delta_1)T} + \alpha_2 I_{2,0} e^{(\hat{\mu}_2 - \delta_2)T}}{S}\right] \text{ if } S > 0 \text{ and } E[S_T] > 0 \text{ or } S < 0 \text{ and } E[S_T] < 0$$

or

$$\mu_s = r \text{ assuming } \hat{\mu}_1 = \hat{\mu}_2 = r \text{ and if } S = 0 \text{ or } E[S_T] = 0 \ \hat{\mu}_1 = \hat{\mu}_2 = r$$

The standard deviation of the spread, based on the lognormal parameters is as follows:

$$\sigma_S = \sqrt{e^{2\mu_s T}\left\{a^2 I_1^2\left(e^{\sigma_1^2 T} - 1\right) + b^2 I_2^2\left(e^{\sigma_2^2 T} - 1\right) + 2ab I_1 I_2\left(e^{\rho\sigma_1\sigma_2 T} - 1\right)\right\}}$$

This result is based on the mean and variance of the lognormal parameters, based on the normal parameters. Recall

$$E[\tilde{S}_T] = S_0 \exp\left\{\left(\mu + \frac{\sigma^2}{2}\right)(T - t)\right\}$$

$$Var[\tilde{S}_T] = S_0^2\left[\exp\left\{2(\mu + \sigma^2)(T - t)\right\} - \exp\left\{(2\mu + \sigma^2)(T - t)\right\}\right]$$

Thus, if

$$E[\tilde{S}_T] = S_0 e^{\hat{\mu}(T - t)}$$

then

$$\mu = \hat{\mu} - \frac{\sigma^2}{2}$$

Implementation code comments

FRMSpreadOptions.h

The inputs are passed by class and we need to inherit the functionality of several other classes.

```
#ifndef FRMSpreadOptionsH
#define FRMSpreadOptionsH
//-----------------------------------------------------------------
// Zhang Approach
#include <math.h>
#ifndef SPREADOPTIONDATACLASS
#define SPREADOPTIONDATACLASS
class SPREADOPTIONDATA
{
public:
```

```
   double IndexPrice1;
   double IndexPrice2;
   double Volatility1;
   double Volatility2;
   double Payout1;
   double Payout2;
   double StrikePrice;
   double TimeToMaturity;
   double InterestRate;
   double Correlation;
   double a;
   double b;
   int w;
   int FunctionIndex;
};
#endif

#include "c:\FRMRepository\FRMBrent.cpp"

#ifndef FRMCDFCPP        // Multiple includes in DLLs
#define FRMCDFCPP
#include "c:\FRMRepository\FRMCDF.cpp"
#endif

#ifndef FRMNUMERICALINTEGRATIONCPP
#define FRMNUMERICALINTEGRATIONCPP
#include "c:\FRMRepository\FRMNumericalIntegration.cpp"
#endif

class FRMSPREADOPTIONS : public FRMCDF, FRMNUMINT, BRENT
{
public:
   double Original;
   double Change;
   double High, Low, OHigh, OLow, OMid;
   double High1, Low1, OHigh1, OLow1;
   double High2, Low2, OHigh2, OLow2;
   double High3, Low3, OHigh3, OLow3;
   double High4, Low4, OHigh4, OLow4;
   double Increment;
   void FRMSOSetData(class SPREADOPTIONDATA F);
// Normal distribution OVM approach
   double SD;
   void FRMSONDSD();
   long double FRMNDISD(double SOLICallPrice);
   long double FRMSONDCallPrice();
   long double FRMSONDPutPrice();
   double FRMSONDCallDelta();
...
   double FRMSONDPutRho();

// Lognormal integration approach
   long double FRMSOLICallPrice();
   long double FRMSOLIPutPrice();
   double FRMSOLICallDelta();
...
   double FRMSOLIPutRho();
// Zhang's Approach
   long double FRMSOCallPrice();
   long double FRMSOPutPrice();
   double FRMSOCallDelta();
...
   double FRMSOPutRho();
...
   FRMNUMINT INTEGRATE;
};
#endif
```

FRMSpreadOptions.cpp

This implementation involves a lot of code, therefore, we partition it into three files and then include the other two.

```
#pragma hdrstop
#include "FRMSpreadOptions.h"
#pragma package(smart_init)
#include "c:\FRMRepository\FRMSpreadOptionsNormalDistribution.cpp"
#include "c:\FRMRepository\FRMSpreadOptionsLognormalDistribution.cpp"
// Main set data followed by Zhang's method (function in Lognormal file
void FRMSPREADOPTIONS::FRMSOSetData(class SPREADOPTIONDATA F)
{
    IndexPrice1 = F.IndexPrice1;
    IndexPrice2 = F.IndexPrice2;
    Volatility1 = F.Volatility1;
    Volatility2 = F.Volatility2;
    Payout1 = F.Payout1;
    Payout2 = F.Payout2;
    StrikePrice = F.StrikePrice;
    TimeToMaturity = F.TimeToMaturity;
    InterestRate = F.InterestRate;
    Correlation = F.Correlation;
    w = F.w;
    a = F.a;
    b = F.b;
}

long double FRMSPREADOPTIONS::FRMSOCallPrice()
{
    double LowerBound, UpperBound;
    long double A1, A2, A3;
    long double CallPrice;
    NI.IndexPrice1 = IndexPrice1;
    NI.IndexPrice2 = IndexPrice2;
    NI.Volatility1 = Volatility1;
    NI.Volatility2 = Volatility2;
    NI.Payout1 = Payout1;
    NI.Payout2 = Payout2;
    NI.StrikePrice = StrikePrice;
    NI.TimeToMaturity = TimeToMaturity;
    NI.InterestRate = InterestRate;
    NI.Correlation = Correlation;
//  NI.w = w;   // Not used for Zhang's method
    NI.a = a;
    NI.b = b;
//  NI.w = 1.0;
    NI.FunctionIndex = 3;
    LowerBound = -10.0;
    UpperBound = 10.0;
```

Zhang's approach is based on integration.

```
    A1 = INTEGRATE.FRMNumericalIntegration(LowerBound, UpperBound, &function);
    NI.FunctionIndex = 4;
    A2 = INTEGRATE.FRMNumericalIntegration(LowerBound, UpperBound, &function);
    NI.FunctionIndex = 5;
    A3 = INTEGRATE.FRMNumericalIntegration(LowerBound, UpperBound, &function);
    CallPrice = exp( -(NI.InterestRate/100.0)*NI.TimeToMaturity )
        * (NI.a*exp(((NI.InterestRate/100.0) - (NI.Payout1/100.0))
        * NI.TimeToMaturity)*NI.IndexPrice1*A1
        + NI.b*exp(((NI.InterestRate/100.0) - (NI.Payout2/100.0))
        * NI.TimeToMaturity)*NI.IndexPrice2*A2
        - NI.StrikePrice*A3);
    return CallPrice;
}
```

We rely on put-call parity for the put price.

```
long double FRMSPREADOPTIONS::FRMSOPutPrice()
{
    long double PutPrice,
```

```
NI.IndexPrice1 = IndexPrice1;
NI.IndexPrice2 = IndexPrice2;
NI.Volatility1 = Volatility1;
NI.Volatility2 = Volatility2;
NI.Payout1 = Payout1;
NI.Payout2 = Payout2;
NI.StrikePrice = StrikePrice;
NI.TimeToMaturity = TimeToMaturity;
NI.InterestRate = InterestRate;
NI.Correlation = Correlation;
NI.a = a;
NI.b = b;
PutPrice = FRMSOCallPrice()
    - NI.a*exp(-(NI.Payout1/100.0)*NI.TimeToMaturity)*NI.IndexPrice1
    - NI.b*exp(-(NI.Payout2/100.0)*NI.TimeToMaturity)*NI.IndexPrice2
    + NI.StrikePrice*exp(-(NI.InterestRate/100.0)*NI.TimeToMaturity);
return PutPrice;
}
```

We assume a fourth order centered difference and arbitrarily set the increment size for each parameter.

```
double FRMSPREADOPTIONS::FRMSOCallDelta()
{
    Increment = 0.0001;
    Original = IndexPrice1;
    Change = Increment*Original;
    High = Original + Change;
    IndexPrice1 = High;
    OHigh = FRMSOCallPrice();
    Low = Original - Change;
    IndexPrice1 = Low;
    OLow = FRMSOCallPrice();
    Change = 2.0*Increment*Original;
    High2 = Original + Change;
    IndexPrice1 = High2;
    OHigh2 = FRMSOCallPrice();
    Low2 = Original - Change;
    IndexPrice1 = Low2;
    OLow2 = FRMSOCallPrice();
    IndexPrice1 = Original;
    Change = 3.0*Increment*Original;
    High3 = Original + Change;
    IndexPrice1 = High3;
    OHigh3 = FRMSOCallPrice();
    Low3 = Original - Change;
    IndexPrice1 = Low3;
    OLow3 = FRMSOCallPrice();
    IndexPrice1 = Original;
    Change = 4.0*Increment*Original;
    High4 = Original + Change;
    IndexPrice1 = High4;
    OHigh4 = FRMSOCallPrice();
    Low4 = Original - Change;
    IndexPrice1 = Low4;
    OLow4 = FRMSOCallPrice();
    IndexPrice1 = Original;
    return ((OLow4/280.0)- (4.0*OLow3/105.0) + (OLow2/5.0) - (4.0*OLow/5.0)
        + (4.0*OHigh/5.0) - (OHigh2/5.0) + (4.0*OHigh3/105.0) - (OHigh4/280.0))
        / (Increment*Original);
}
...
```

References

Alexander, C. and A. Scourse, 2004. Bivariate Normal Mixture Spread Option Valuation. *Quantitative Finance*, 4 (6), 637-648.

Alexander, Carol and Aanand Venkatramanan, 2007. Analytic Approximations for Spread Options, ICMA Centre Discussion Papers in Finance DP2007-11, 15th August 2007, 1-23.

Bachelier, Louis, 1900. Theory of Speculation, *Ann. Sci. Ecole Norm. Sup.* (3), No. 1018 (Paris, Gauthier-Villars) as a thesis at the Academy of Paris presented on March 29, 1900. Translated by J. Boness in Cootner, P., 1964. *The Random Character of Stock Market Prices*, (MIT Press, Cambridge, MA), 17-78.

Benth, Fred Espen and Jurate Saltyte-Benth, Analytical Approximation for the Price Dynamics of Spark Spread Options, *Studies in Nonlinear Dynamics & Econometrics*, 10(3), 2006, 1334-1355.

Black, Fischer, 1976. The Pricing of Commodity Contracts, *Journal of Financial Economics* 3, 167-79.

Black, Fischer and Myron Scholes, 1973. The Pricing of Options and Corporate Liabilities, *Journal of Political Economy* 81, 637-659.

Borovkova, Svetlana, Ferry J. Permana, and Hans V.D. Weide, 2007. A Closed Form Approach to the Valuation and Hedging of Basket and Spread Options, *The Journal of Derivatives* 14, 8-24.

Brooks, Robert, 1995. A Lattice Approach to Interest Rate Spread Options, *Journal of Financial Engineering* 4, 281-296.

Carmona, René and Valdo Durrleman, 2003. Pricing and Hedging Spread Options, *SIAM Review* 45, 627-685.

Carmona, René and Valdo Durrleman, 2006. Generalizing the Black-Scholes Formula to Multivariate Contingent Claims, *Journal of Computational Finance* 9, 43-67.

Dempster, M.A.H. and S.S.G. Hong, 2000. Spread Option Valuation and the Fast Fourier Transform, in Mathematical Finance, Bachelier Congress, H. Geman, D. Madan, S. R. Pliska, and T. Vorst, eds. Springer-Verlag, Berlin.

Harrison, J. Michael and David Kreps, 1979. Martingales and Arbitrage in Multiperiod Securities Markets, *Journal of Economic Theory* 20, 381-408.

Harrison, J. Michael and Stanley R. Pliska, 1981. Martingales and Stochastic Integrals in the Theory of Continuous Trading, *Stochastic Process and their Applications* 11, 215-260.

Heenk, B. A., A. G. Z. Kemna and A. C. F. Vorst, 1990. Asian Options on Oil Spreads, *Review of Futures Markets* 9, 510-528.

Jarrow, Robert A. and Andrew Rudd, 1982. Approximate Option Valuation for Arbitrary Stochastic Processes, *Journal of Financial Economics* 10, 347-369.

Li, Minqiang, Shijie Deng, and Jieyun Zhou, 2008. Closed-Form Approximations for Spread Option Prices and Greeks, *Journal of Derivatives* 15, 58-80.

Margrabe, William, 1978. The Value of an Option to Exchange One Asset for Another, *Journal of Finance* 33, 177-186.

Merton, Robert C., 1973. Theory of Rational Option Pricing, *Bell Journal of Economics*, The RAND Corporation 4, 141-183.

Pearson, Neil D., 1995. An Efficient Approach for Pricing Spread Options, *The Journal of Derivatives* 3, 76-91.

Poitras, Geoffrey, 1998. Spread Options, Exchange Options, and Arithmetic Brownian Motion, *Journal of Futures Markets* 5, 487-517.

Rubinstein, Mark, 1991. Somewhere Over the Rainbow, *Risk* 4, 63-66.

Schaefer, Matthew, 2002. Pricing and Hedging European Options On Futures Spreads Using the Bachelier Spread Option Model, Working Paper.

Shimko, David, 1994. Options on Futures Spreads: Hedging, Speculation, and Valuation, *Journal of Futures Markets* 14, 183-213.

Wilcox, D., 1990. Energy Futures and Options: Spread Options in Energy Markets. Goldman Sachs & Co., New York.

Zhang, Peter G., Exotic Options: A Guide to Second Generation Options. (London, UK: World Scientific Publishing Co. Pte. Ltd., 1998.)

Appendix 7.6: Interface code comments

The graphical user interface for this module is illustrated below.

The following are excerpts from the interface header code with selected comments added.

FRMUnitSpreadOptions.h

This form does not involve anything unique, it just involves a lot of components. Selected pieces of the header file are presented next.

```
#ifndef FRMUnitSpreadOptionsH
#define FRMUnitSpreadOptionsH
...
#include "c:\FRMRepository\FRMSpreadOptions.cpp"
```

At times, we manage the input data with a class.

```
#ifndef SPREADOPTIONDATACLASS
#define SPREADOPTIONDATACLASS
class SPREADOPTIONDATA
{
public:
    double IndexPrice1;
    double IndexPrice2;
    double Volatility1;
    double Volatility2;
```

```
      double Payout1;
      double Payout2;
      double StrikePrice;
      double TimeToMaturity;
      double InterestRate;
      double Correlation;
      double a;
      double b;
      int w;
      int FunctionIndex;
};
#endif

class TSOIntForm : public TForm
{
__published:   // IDE-managed Components
    TMemo *memoDescription;
   TLabel *lblIndexValue;
...
```

There are obviously numerous input labels and edit boxes on this form. This form has very few methods.

```
   TEdit *outputNBPutVega3;
   void __fastcall btnCancelClick(TObject *Sender);
   void __fastcall btnOkClick(TObject *Sender);
   void __fastcall FormCreate(TObject *Sender);
   void __fastcall FormKeyPress(TObject *Sender, char &Key);
private:
   int inputw;
...
  double NPortfolioVolatility;
  FRMSPREADOPTIONS SO;
  SPREADOPTIONDATA SOD;
  void __fastcall Execute(void);
  void __fastcall SetLocalData(void);
...
```

The following are excerpts from the interface code with selected comments added.

FRMUnitSpreadOptions.cpp

After the form inputs are set into the input variable, we move them to the input class instance, SOD, of the implementation code.

```
...
  SetLocalData();
// Option valuation based on Zhang integration approach
  double LowerBound, UpperBound;
  SOD.IndexPrice1 = inputIndexPrice1;
  SOD.IndexPrice2 = inputIndexPrice2;
  SOD.Volatility1 = inputVolatility1;
  SOD.Volatility2 = inputVolatility2;
  SOD.Payout1 = inputPayout1;
  SOD.Payout2 = inputPayout2;
  SOD.StrikePrice = inputStrikePrice;
  SOD.TimeToMaturity = inputTimeToMaturity;
  SOD.InterestRate = inputInterestRate;
  SOD.Correlation = inputCorrelation;
  SOD.w = inputw;
  SOD.a = inputa;
  SOD.b = inputb;
  SO.FRMSOSetData(SOD);
```

Recall Zhang's methodology does not allow zero or negative strike prices. Vega3 is based on changing the correlation coefficient.

```
// Zhang's Methodology
   if (SO.StrikePrice > 0.0001) {
      CallPrice = SO.FRMSOCallPrice();
      PutPrice = SO.FRMSOPutPrice();
      CallDelta = SO.FRMSOCallDelta();
      CallDelta2 = SO.FRMSOCallDelta2();
```

```
        PutDelta = SO.FRMSOPutDelta();
        PutDelta2 = SO.FRMSOPutDelta2();
        CallGamma = SO.FRMSOCallGamma();
        CallGamma2 = SO.FRMSOCallGamma2();
        PutGamma = SO.FRMSOPutGamma();
        PutGamma2 = SO.FRMSOPutGamma2();
        CallTheta = SO.FRMSOCallTheta();
        PutTheta = SO.FRMSOPutTheta();
        CallVega = SO.FRMSOCallVega();
        CallVega2 = SO.FRMSOCallVega2();
        CallVega3 = SO.FRMSOCallVega3();
        PutVega = SO.FRMSOPutVega();
        PutVega2 = SO.FRMSOPutVega2();
        PutVega3 = SO.FRMSOPutVega3();
        CallRho = SO.FRMSOCallRho();
        PutRho = SO.FRMSOPutRho();
    } else {
        CallPrice = -99;
        PutPrice = -99;
        CallDelta = -99;
        CallDelta2 = -99;
        PutDelta = -99;
        PutDelta2 = -99;
        CallGamma = -99;
        CallGamma2 = -99;
        PutGamma = -99;
        PutGamma2 = -99;
        CallTheta = -99;
        PutTheta = -99;
        CallVega = -99;
        CallVega2 = -99;
        CallVega3 = -99;
        PutVega = -99;
        PutVega2 = -99;
        PutVega3 = -99;
        CallRho = -99;
        PutRho = -99;
    };
    outputCallPrice->Text = FloatToStrF(CallPrice, ffFixed, 12, 4);
```

There is obviously a lot to output. The lognormal model and normal model below follow a similar format.

```
...
    outputPutRho->Visible = true;
// Lognormal Integration Methodology
    LCallPrice = SO.FRMSOLICallPrice();
...
    LPutRho = SO.FRMSOLIPutRho();
    outputLICallPrice->Text = FloatToStrF(LCallPrice, ffFixed, 12, 4);
...
    lblLIPutOption->Visible = true;
```

We wanted to have some flexibility, so we let NCallPrice (normal distribution call price) hold either the implied volatility that equate the normal and lognormal approaches ($w > 0$), the normal distribution call price based on inputted volatilities and correlation coefficient ($w = 0$), or the normal distribution call price based on a specific inputted volatility (in Volatility 1 editbox) ($w < 0$). *Note if $w < 0$ then only the option price for the normal distribution is valid; the remainder of the form is invalid.*

```
// Normal distribution
    SO.FRMSONDSD();
    NPortfolioVolatility = SO.SD;
    outputPortfolioVolatility->Text
        = FloatToStrF(NPortfolioVolatility, ffFixed, 12, 4);
    lblPortfolioVolatility->Visible = true;
// Computes SD in a variety of ways
    if (SO.w > 0) {      // Report implied volatility in call price edit box
        NCallPrice = SO.SD = SO.FRMNDISD(SO.FRMSOLICallPrice());
    } else if (SO.w < 0) { // Arbitrarily use Volatility1 for input SD
        SO.SD = SO.Volatility1;
        NCallPrice = SO.FRMSONDCallPrice();
```

```
   } else {
      SO.FRMSONDSD();                      // Base SD on all inputs
      NCallPrice = SO.FRMSONDCallPrice();
   };
   NPutPrice = SO.FRMSONDPutPrice();
...
   NPutRho = SO.FRMSONDPutRho();
   outputNBCallPrice->Text = FloatToStrF(NCallPrice, ffFixed, 12, 4);
...
   lblNBPutOption->Visible = true;
...
```

23130414R00210